ENCYCLOPEDIA OF
CATHOLIC LITERATURE

ENCYCLOPEDIA OF CATHOLIC LITERATURE

VOLUME II

Edited by Mary R. Reichardt

GREENWOOD PRESS
Westport, Connecticut • London

Library of Congress Cataloging-in-Publication Data

Encyclopedia of Catholic literature/edited by Mary R. Reichardt.
  p. cm.
  Includes bibliographical references.
  ISBN 0-313-32802-1 (v. 1 : alk. paper)—ISBN 0-313-32803-X (v. 2 : alk. paper)—
ISBN 0-313-32289-9 (set : alk. paper)
  1. Catholic literature—History and criticism. 2. Catholic literature—
Bio-bibliography—Dictionaries. I. Reichardt, Mary R.
PN485.E53 2004
809'.933822—dc22   2004047511

British Library Cataloguing in Publication Data is available.

Library of Congress Catalog Card Number: 2004047511
ISBN: 0-313-32289-9 (Set)
      0-313-32802-1 (Vol. I)
      0-313-32803-X (Vol. II)

First published in 2004

Greenwood Press, 88 Post Road West, Westport, CT 06881
An imprint of Greenwood Publishing Group, Inc.
www.greenwood.com

Printed in the United States of America

The paper used in this book complies with the
Permanent Paper Standard issued by the National
Information Standards Organization (Z39.48-1984).

10 9 8 7 6 5 4 3 2 1

Contents

Works Listed by Chronology

Note: Most works are listed by publication date. For some works, an approximate writing date, or both a writing date and a publication date, may be listed if the work was published long after it was written. An approximate range of writing dates is listed for an essay that covers a variety of works (for example, Flannery O'Connor's short stories).

Works Listed by Author's Gender

WORKS BY MEN

Peter Abelard, *The Letters of Abelard and Heloise*

Augustine of Hippo, *Confessions of St. Augustine*

Hilaire Belloc, *The Path to Rome*

Georges Bernanos, *The Diary of a Country Priest*

Heinrich Böll, *Group Portrait with Lady*

Orestes Brownson, *The Spirit-Rapper; An Autobiography*

Geoffrey Chaucer, *The Canterbury Tales*

G. K. Chesterton, *The Everlasting Man*

Paul Claudel, *Break of Noon*

Dante Alighieri, *The Divine Comedy*

John Dryden, *The Hind and the Panther*

Andre Dubus, *Voices from the Moon*

William Dunbar, Poems

T. S. Eliot, *Four Quartets*

Shusaku Endo, *Silence*

Desiderius Erasmus, *The Praise of Folly*

William Everson (Brother Antoninus), *The Veritable Years: Poems 1949–1966*

Graham Greene, *The Power and the Glory*

Ron Hansen, *Mariette in Ecstasy*

Jon Hassler, *North of Hope*

Gerard Manley Hopkins, Poems

John of the Cross, *The Dark Night of the Soul*

James Joyce, *A Portrait of the Artist as a Young Man*

Christopher J. Koch, *The Year of Living Dangerously*

Robert Lax, *The Circus of the Sun*

François Mauriac, *A Woman of the Pharisees*

François Mauriac, *Viper's Tangle*

Thomas Merton, *The Seven Storey Mountain*

Brian Moore, *Catholics*

Thomas More, *Utopia*

John Henry Newman, *Apologia Pro Vita Sua*

John Henry Newman, *Callista, A Sketch of the Third Century*

John Henry Newman, *Loss and Gain, The Story of a Convert*

Walker Percy, *Lancelot*

Alexander Pope, *Essay on Man*

J. F. Powers, *Morte d'Urban*

Piers Paul Read, *A Season in the West*

Henryk Sienkiewicz, *Quo Vadis?*

Jean Sulivan, *Eternity, My Beloved*

Henry Suso, *Exemplar*

J. R. R. Tolkien, *The Lord of the Rings*

Evelyn Waugh, *Brideshead Revisited*

Evelyn Waugh, *Sword of Honor*

Larry Woiwode, *Beyond the Bedroom Wall*

WORKS BY WOMEN

Angela of Foligno, *The Book of the Blessed Angela of Foligno*

Willa Cather, *Death Comes for the Archbishop*

Catherine of Siena, *Dialogue*

Sandra Cisneros, *The House on Mango Street*

Elizabeth Cullinan, *House of Gold*

Dorothy Day, *The Long Loneliness*

Annie Dillard, *Holy the Firm*

Isak Dinesen (Karen Blixen), *Babette's Feast*

Rumer Godden, *In This House of Brede*

Caroline Gordon, *The Malefactors*

Mary Gordon, *Final Payments*

Hildegard of Bingen, *Scivias*

Sor Juana Inés de la Cruz, *Response to Sor Filotea*

Julian of Norwich, *Revelations of Divine Love*

Mary Lavin, *Selected Stories*

Gertrud von le Fort, *The Song at the Scaffold*

Denise Levertov, *The Stream and the Sapphire*

Alice Meynell, Poems

Kathleen Norris, *The Cloister Walk*

Flannery O'Connor, Short Stories

Flannery O'Connor, *Wise Blood*

Katherine Anne Porter, *Ship of Fools*

Jessica Powers, Poems

Christina Rossetti, Poems

Dorothy L. Sayers, *The Man Born to Be King*

Elizabeth Ann Seton, *Letters of Mother Seton to Mrs. Julianna Scott*

Muriel Spark, *Memento Mori*

Edith Stein, *Essays on Woman*

Teresa of Avila, *The Interior Castle*

Thérèse of Lisieux, *Story of a Soul*

Sigrid Undset, *Kristin Lavransdatter*

Simone Weil, *Waiting for God*

Antonia White, *Frost in May*

Works Listed by Genre

Note: Some works cross genres and are therefore not easy to categorize. For the sake of simplicity, however, they are placed here in the category they best represent.

Autobiography

Augustine of Hippo, *Confessions of St. Augustine*
Dorothy Day, *The Long Loneliness*
Thomas Merton, *The Seven Storey Mountain*
John Henry Newman, *Apologia Pro Vita Sua*
Kathleen Norris, *The Cloister Walk*
Thérèse of Lisieux, *Story of a Soul*

Collected Letters

Peter Abelard, *The Letters of Abelard and Heloise*
Elizabeth Ann Seton, *Letters of Mother Seton to Mrs. Julianna Scott*

Drama

Paul Claudel, *Break of Noon*
Dorothy L. Sayers, *The Man Born to Be King*

Literary Nonfiction

Hilaire Belloc, *The Path to Rome*
Annie Dillard, *Holy the Firm*

Mystical Works/Spiritual Instruction

Angela of Foligno, *The Book of the Blessed Angela of Foligno*
Catherine of Siena, *Dialogue*
Hildegard of Bingen, *Scivias*
John of the Cross, *The Dark Night of the Soul*
Julian of Norwich, *Revelations of Divine Love*
Henry Suso, *Exemplar*
Teresa of Avila, *The Interior Castle*
Simone Weil, *Waiting for God*

Novels

Georges Bernanos, *The Diary of a Country Priest*
Heinrich Böll, *Group Portrait with Lady*
Orestes Brownson, *The Spirit-Rapper; An Autobiography*
Willa Cather, *Death Comes for the Archbishop*
Sandra Cisneros, *The House on Mango Street*
Elizabeth Cullinan, *House of Gold*
Shusaku Endo, *Silence*
Rumer Godden, *In This House of Brede*
Caroline Gordon, *The Malefactors*
Mary Gordon, *Final Payments*
Graham Greene, *The Power and the Glory*
Ron Hansen, *Mariette in Ecstasy*
Jon Hassler, *North of Hope*
James Joyce, *A Portrait of the Artist as a Young Man*
Christopher J. Koch, *The Year of Living Dangerously*
François Mauriac, *Viper's Tangle*
François Mauriac, *A Woman of the Pharisees*

Novellas

Poems

Short Stories

Social/Political Satires

Theological/Philosophical Writings

Mary Lavin [1912–1996]

Selected Stories

BIOGRAPHY

An only child, Mary Lavin was born to Tom Lavin and Nora Mahon in East Walpole, Massachusetts, on June 11, 1912. At age nine, Mary went with her mother to Athenry, Ireland, for a year; then they joined Tom Lavin in Dublin. In 1926, the family moved to the eighteenth-century country estate Bective House in County Meath, where Tom had been appointed manager. Mary attended Loretto Convent in Dublin and then University College, Dublin, from which she graduated with honors in 1934. She returned to school for a master's degree, writing her thesis on Jane Austen, and was accorded first-class honors in 1938. She taught French at the Loretto Convent for two years but again retuned to school to pursue a doctorate; she began a thesis on Virginia Woolf but never submitted it.

On the back of the draft of that thesis, Lavin composed her first short story, published as "Miss Holland" in the April–June 1939 issue of *Dublin Magazine* (then edited by Seamus O'Sullivan). Lord Dunsany, a neighbor who wrote tales of the supernatural, introduced her to the editor of the *Atlantic Monthly* and also wrote the introduction to her first collection of stories, *Tales from Bective Bridge* (1942), which won the James Tait Black Memorial Prize in 1943. In 1942, Lavin married lawyer William Walsh, and they divided their time between Bective House and Dublin, where Walsh had his practice. Lavin gave birth to three daughters, Valentine (1943), Elizabeth (1945), and Caroline (1952). William died in 1954, leaving Lavin to support their three children. By then, she had published five volumes of short stories and two novels, but she turned her attention to running the farm at Bective while raising the children. During this time she did very little writing. In 1958, the *New Yorker* accepted her short story "The Living"; this began a fruitful relationship with that magazine (Levenson 1998, 97). The American publication of *Selected Stories* in 1959 revived her writing career on this side of the Atlantic. It also encouraged her to apply to the Guggenheim Foundation for a fellowship, granted for 1959–60 and renewed for 1960–61. Lavin spent some of this time in Italy at a *pensione* with her children, but she wrote productively when she returned to Ireland. *The Great Wave and Other Stories* (1961) was awarded the Katherine Mansfield Prize. In 1969, Lavin married Michael Scott, a Jesuit priest who became laicized in order to marry her.

In 1975, Lavin received the Erie Society medal as well as the Gregory Medal. To honor Mary Lavin's eightieth birthday, RTE made *An Arrow in Flight* (1992), a documentary. Her work has been translated into Dutch, German, Hebrew, French, Italian, Polish, Russian, and Japanese.

Mary Lavin died in Dublin on March 25, 1996. Her gravestone bears a few lines from one of her poems that assert the beauty of the Irish midlands.

MAJOR THEMES

The 1959 publication of Mary Lavin's *Selected Stories* assured her place in literary history and confirmed her talent as one of Ireland's finest short-story writers. Moreover, it singled her out as one of the few prominent short-story writers who maintained a Roman Catholic sensibility as a component of her ironic vision. Subsequent books assured her international status as she was translated into numerous languages.

Selected Stories contains twelve stories each displaying a deep conflict between outward appearances and inward spirituality. Such emphasis upon the personal rather than the collective is often perceived by the Irish as the Protestant pilgrim-age to salvation (as in Bunyan), but Lavin locates this theme within the frame-work of Catholic belief as she explores the tendency of Catholics to indulge in spiritual hypocrisy. Another way of stating this paradox is to say that Mary Lavin writes about traditional Protestant themes within the tradition of Catholic piety and theology. Several other collections of Lavin's stories have appeared, but *Selected Stories* remains the most "Catholic" selection.

The collection begins with "The Will" and ends with a rewritten version of "A Happy Death." Both stories focus on the theme of death, but they are, of course, about life and how to live it. "The Will," a story about private con-science (Harmon 1979, 291), offers a dialectic between the worldly conception of respectability and charity toward others. Lally, the youngest daughter in the family, has been cut out of her mother's will because she married below the middle-class standard of material wealth prescribed by her mother. Out of embarrassment and a desire to make Lally conform to her dead mother's sense of propriety, her elder siblings offer her money on the condition that she give up the rooming house she runs. Lally cares nothing for the tawdry respectability of her siblings, nor their offer. After her brother demurs from driving her to the train station because he fears local gossip, she rushes on foot to the local priest amid a torrential rain. Fearing for her mother's soul at Judgment, she begs the priest to say a few Masses immediately for her mother, promising to post the fee for them. The priest, oblivious to Lally's concerns, declares that her mother has left money in her will for plenty of Masses. Lally has little time—the hoot of the evening train rends the air—but she quickly tries to explain that *she* must pay for the Masses. Ironically, the priest—like Lally's mother and siblings—remains insensitive to the spirituality Lally invokes. The ultimate irony is that Lally is the only *practicing* Catholic in the story: she lives the Christian mystery of suffering for others without a care for herself. It is clear that she runs the rooming house for the sake of helping others. Unlike the complacent priest, she has a true vocation in life that actively aids others.

What remains remarkable about this story is not that we have a model of Christian charity, nor that the reader pities Lally for the narcissism and selfishness of her family, but that the reader begins to fear that we are all closer in character to Lally's siblings or the priest than we are to Lally. At the close of the story, Lally sits in the train fervently praying that her mother be released from purgatory while the reader realizes that it is Lally who lives the purgatorial life. We join Lally in wishing for a more intense spiritual life within our own lives, because the purgatorial vision—here symbolized by the train's flecks of ash trailing in the air—is shown to be the moral source of beauty, poetry, and truth. Lavin's story is unusual in capturing Dante's aesthetic of purgatorial beauty, an idea rejected by Protestantism. Lally is by no means an unusual woman but someone who is fiercely ordinary, someone who lives a profound spiritual life within the circumscribed ordinary, the kind of person intellectuals might hold in contempt. We observe common heroism without descending into mere sentiment, although there is sentiment enough here. The story is reminiscent of the French tradition of scorning middle-class respectability while accepting such propriety as the inevitable way of the world (Ireland being no different from anywhere else). Those who long for conformity are the damned.

"Chamois Gloves" tells the story of a young girl about to take her vows as a nun along with two other postulants. But the girl has chosen to be a nun for the wrong reason: she wants to escape the emotional entanglements of her family and the world. Her family arrives for the ceremony, and Veronica is cold to both her pregnant sister Mabel and the rest of the family. She imagines that life as a nun will provide her with a respectable life devoid of self-sacrifice. We feel pity for Veronica because of her extreme narcissism and immaturity. After the public recitation of vows and the family's departure, Veronica has a Joycean epiphany: washing the chamois gloves her sister left behind, memories of family life flood her mind and, for the first time, an inkling of what she has done dawns. Two tears well in her eyes and course down her cheeks. Her guardian angel is astonished because "As far as she knew, Veronica's mind was filled only with memories of cracked sanitary ware, steamy walls, and a litter of quite unsightly broken combs and misused tubes of toothpaste" (*Selected Stories*, 30–31). Sister Veronica sleeps while heaven celebrates her first awareness of the sacrificial nature of life. The appearance of a guardian angel in the story (*deus ex machina*) is a rather bold and unusual populist decision for an author who works in the realistic tradition, but it unexpectedly succeeds because of its wit and gentle humor.

The collection's third story, "Assigh," portrays the extinction of a peasant family due to a father's momentary abuse of his seventeen-year-old daughter, whom he beats with his belt buckle in the church graveyard when he finds her talking to a local boy. The father's anger is intensified by the fact that she's not chatting with the neighbor he wants her to marry (she, too, wants to marry the neighbor, who is attracted to her). But the festering wound and gimp she acquires from the public beating discourages the neighbor, who perceives women chauvinistically in terms of beauty and breeding. Although he still lives at home on the farm, Assigh's brother Tom secretly marries, but his wife has no children. With her father dead at thirty-seven, Assigh finds herself burdened with the urge to share the beauty of love and nature with someone, but she stoically realizes that we are only "but a part" of the cosmos. (Assigh accepts her father's deathbed explanation that her lifelong infection from verdigris was just bad luck because he never meant to do her serious harm.) For Assigh, religion exists as a social institution, like the post office or farmer's market; her point of view consists of an uneducated but poignant aesthetic no different from that articulated by the Roman poet Lucretius. And therein lies the tragedy: such fatalistic acceptance of chance was the way of the world before Christianity. The story's attack on Epicureanism implies that it originates from a male need to rationalize power over women. Although the story is by no means a philosophical tract, it seems an eloquent reply to the rural atheism of Thomas Hardy, which romantically hymns the fecundity of pagan nature.

The next story, "Posy," reverses, quite drolly, the theme of sexual domination. Here a bachelor never married the girl he loved because his sisters thought that she, Posy, the servant girl they hired, was beneath them in class, a "disgrace." The story describes the visit of Posy's son, who is curious about his extraordinary mother's mysterious past. He gets the shopkeeper, Daniel, to show him the house where Posy once lived, but they must resort unsuccessfully to subterfuge from the sisters in order to see the house. Daniel, whose timidity and alert intelligence create an amusing and unforgettable amalgam, never consciously comprehends that the curious visitor is Posy's own son. Daniel (the name of an Old Testament hero who can face lions) lives out his lonely and miserable life "in the dungeon of obscurity and petty provincial existence" (72), but he finds consolation through realizing that Posy, whom he nicknamed, flew free of his sisters. In the end, the story is about charity and its importance in life. Daniel rejoices at the vague success of someone he loved who escaped the haughty hell where his sisters dominated, a "respectable" hell that has not the slightest smidgeon of charity. Like "Assigh," the story is about the extinction of love; as in "The Will," the siblings devoted to social convention live in a hell of narcissism that they wish to evangelize.

"The Cemetery in the Demesne," the structure of which closely resembles that of Gaelic fairy tales in which the hero travels to the Otherworld, presents a meditation on self-knowledge. A garrulous truck driver becomes haunted by a spiritual revelation. He delivers a load of gravel to a cemetery. The gatekeeper at the cemetery, a young woman with a sick child, acts so courteously and intimately toward him that it reveals a world of male-female possibility in relationships— a world of genuine communion and love—that he has never experienced. Here, the driver meets a Madonna-child icon rather than a dragon or goddess, but like many Gaelic heroes he brings back from this Otherworld an otherworldly gift: the nonstop talker acquires the gift of silence because he finally realizes that his chatter is opportunistic nonsense that compensates for an awareness that people do not take him seriously. He habitually harangues his wife and sister-in-law, but his monologue to the woman-with-child passes as a "blessing" that is received. His lifelong aspiration to have someone really listen to him for once is fulfilled.

Both the woman and the driver perceive religion as superstition: she recites the Gospel repeatedly over her sick child; the carter argues that he's heard—from pagan folklore—that doing so can bring bad luck. Arguing the merits of Christian and pagan superstitions—from a medical point of view—provides comedy, but the story is about the miracle of communication. The Madonna has given the truck driver a vision of divine grace; he returns home to the ordinary world, which now becomes his purgatory. He suffers the meaningless spite and gossip of his wife and her sister in silence; in their ignorant hell they ponder the transformation of the carter, the sister-in-law saying that "there's something on his mind" (97), the wife hopefully conjecturing that it might be something he ate.

In this story, the act of eating evokes communion. The carter ate in the Other-world, not in this prosaic world; in the world of metaphor, not the world of the literal. The use of pagan typologies in the service of Christian stories has been taking place in Irish literature for over a millennium. Here we have a story about how Christian communion can transform lives. Of course, the official Church ceremony of communion remains irrelevant; this is a complex, ironic story based upon Gaelic archetypes and Protestant perceptions of Christian fellowship combined with an orthodox understanding of how grace operates in Catholic theology. "The Cemetery in the Demesne" lingers in memory as one of the most sentimental, ironic, and amusing of adult fairy tales.

The collection's sixth story, "The Little Prince" examines sibling estrangement and guilt. Bedelia, an elder sister of Tom, wants to marry Daniel, whose ambition is to run the family pub; her father Mathias finds himself confined to a sickbed, but Bedelia does not want to marry until Mathias dies because she would be marrying the shop assistant. Handsome Tom, whom as a child Bedelia used to dress up as a little prince, persists in ordering drinks on the house for his sponging buddies. Bedelia wants some agreement about the coming estate with Tom, but Tom refuses and says his share of the pub is her wedding present. Bedelia takes this as an insult, since Tom has nothing but contempt for Daniel; Bedelia suggests that Tom go off to America to make his fortune, which he does, but they never hear from him again. Daniel punctiliously banks one-third of all pub profits every month. Family expenses, pub upkeep, and a decline in business leave Bedelia and Daniel pinched, but they never touch the growing sum in trust. Forty years later they hear that a person who may be Tom is dying in a hospital. They take a ship for Boston but arrive too late. Bedelia looks into the coffin and collapses in hysteria: she cannot tell if that is her brother or not, but the fact is moot: Bedelia's frustrated greed and Tom's pride has created a cancer common to many Irish families.

This somewhat prolix story is the fourth of five stories about the Grimes family, who live in Castlerampart, a fictive name for Athenry (Kelly 1980, 53ff). The cycle begins and ends with the death of the matriarch, Alicia; it examines love and tensions within familial bonds. In "The Little Prince" both Daniel and Belinda inhabit a purgatorial world, dutifully bound to Tom's inheritance. On the ship to America, Bedelia is identified by a passenger as a "conniving woman" (128), which she clearly is. The mysterious widow in black (Charon-like) who befriends Bedelia on the ship provides foreshadowing for Bedelia's demonic fit before the coffin. Having crossed the bar, Bedelia descends to hell, depicted here as clinical insanity.

The next story, "My Vocation," belongs to the genre of the Dublin prank, whose distinguishing characteristic remains an exuberant mockery of authority, whether this authority be parents, Church, or state. A thirteen-year-old girl temporarily convinces herself, her family, and an order of nuns that she wants to live the religious life. This letter-monologue captures brilliantly the insouciance, *joie de vivre*, and adolescent mischief of a girl who cannot take the adult world seriously. The home visit of the nuns receives sardonic treatment. The humiliation of the nuns that she impulsively instigates resembles a Laurel and Hardy skit: the nuns, fat and thin, the bottom of the cab having fallen out, running for their lives as the horse that the narrator frightened gallops down the street. Although one might presume that this is an anticlerical story in the vein of Rimbaud's lice (Rimbaud, it is said, allowed lice to grow in his hair so as to flick them at priests), the saving grace of this prank story remains its innocent and whimsical quality. The narrator resolves to have her children educated by the nuns—that is, if she can find the right man.

"The Small Bequest," a hilarious and extended anecdote of revenge, centers on the bigotry of family lineage. Miss Blodgett has displayed tireless devotion toward eighty-year-old Aunt Adeline Tate. Everyone agrees that Adeline's bequest will provide for Miss Blodgett, who is sixty. Miss Blodgett has but one flaw: she has addressed her superior with the familiar address of "Aunt Adeline," the family's form of address. In Adeline's will the promised bequest is addressed to "my fond niece Emma." Since Emma Blodgett is not a niece, the family lawyers go to work. Miss Blodgett gets nothing for her twenty-seven years of service because of her impertinent insult to the eleven generations of Tates. The narrator, a bemused neighbor, adeptly notices small tensions and undercurrents between Adeline and Emma, silk dress and imitation silk. Years later, Emma is still suing the estate; she cannot comprehend the revenge or the class sentiment behind it. Like the previous story, this is in the manner of a Dublin prank—here ridiculing social snobbery. While "My Vocation" exalts the humor of young, impulsive mischief, "The Small Bequest" exposes the premeditated cruelty of the elderly upper crust.

"A Woman Friend," the only story in the collection written strictly from the male point of view, concerns the pride and self-obsession of a top-level Dublin surgeon who remains oblivious to everything except his professional reputation. Dr. Lew looks down upon the marriages of the other doctors; to him, they have married from "propinquity." One day, after Dr. Lew left the hospital, the administration tried to reach him at home on an emergency call, but he had fallen asleep at the wheel of his car in front of his house. (He testifies later at the malpractice investigation—the boy died of burst appendix—that he was home and that they must have repeatedly called the wrong number). Lew finds immediate consolation at his friend Bina's hotel; he confesses to her that he is fearful of a prospective investigation going badly and having to begin life anew. On the doorstep, he proposes marriage to Bina. Of course, if she is his wife, she could not later testify about his confession to her! At the end it is clear that Bina accepted his proposal: "And now everything would be the same as ever—only for Bina. Not that he was altogether sorry. And he badly needed a holiday" (191). So the man of misogynistic pride marries impulsively merely to preserve his career.

Yet, as in the following story, "Brigid," we have a subterranean level of Gaelic myth. The god Lugh (same pronunciation as "Lew"), the most talented of Gaelic gods as well as the god of healing, marries the mortal woman Dechtiré and transports her to the Otherworld. The portrait of sleepy Bina in "A Woman Friend" parallels the mythological associations of sleep with Dechtiré. If the story receives only a realistic interpretation, it would appear to be a flatly moralistic (yet ironic) commentary on how men choose wives; but, as in "Brigid," the story is taken to the mythic level and it turns quite comic: it becomes a modern version of how the parents of Sétanta come to be married. Sétanta grows up to be Cúchulainn (the Irish Achilles), the hero of the national epic, the *Táin Bó Cuailgne,* "The Cattle-Raid of Cooley." Presenting the Irish god as a scheming rationalizer is both cutely absurd and quite amusing, as it is consonant with the trickster personality of Lugh. What appears to be a rather insignificant modern story about the origin of a doctor's marriage then becomes a feminist critique of traditional male-centered mythology, exposed for its complacent, self-serving nature. On one level the story offers a witty satire on medieval Irish literature, not a schoolmarm critique of a man who "has failed with women" (Kelly 1980, 79). While the story appears to meander in the anecdotal ordinary, it is a high critique of the male epic tradition—that is, in the Dublin of 1942. It implies that little has changed over the last millennium.

In "Brigid," Owen does not want to put his mysteriously retarded sister in a nursing home; he quarrels about this with his wife, who argues that it's best for Brigid and for their two daughters, who are approaching marriageable age. After the quarrel, Owen goes to visit Brigid's isolated cottage; he does not return. At dark, the wife goes to the cottage looking for Owen and has a seemingly inane conversation in the dark before a flickering hearth with the simple-minded Brigid, who says, "He wouldn't get up" (199). Owen had slipped before the fire, knocked his head in the fall, and partially burnt his head. The wife rebukes herself, remembering how Owen had so loved her and how she had not returned that love. The townspeople think they know the widow's mind and suggest placing Brigid in a nursing home. Stricken with guilt and love for her dead husband, the wife decides to move Brigid into her own house. A story about love's ironies, the wife is never named because this is more than a realistic story: it also operates as an allegory about Irish culture. Brigid is the pagan fertility goddess who ruled at the hearth. Owen represents the Christian dispensation; the unnamed wife, Ireland. What we have is a fable about how, through guilt and sentiment, Ireland has retained its pagan mythology. The goddess Brigid now rules over the all-female household trinity, whose project will be to marry off the daughters Rosie and Mamie. New husbands will be saddled with the responsibility for ancient Brigid, who inhabits a modern world incomprehensible to her.

"A Wet Day" recounts the moment when the narrator's aunt lost her crush on the parish priest, who has expertly exploited this crush by vigilantly harvesting vegetables grown for him. The niece does not like the priest, but the aunt chalks this up to her intellectual anticlericalism. One day when elderly Father Gogarty comes for dinner, he recounts, as he is leaving, an anecdote of his own niece's folly. This anecdote reveals his meanness, narcissism, and pride; pretending that he does not have one, he has refused his niece a thermometer for her boyfriend, who is dying of pneumonia. The narrator-niece concludes that since that visit she and her aunt get on with each other much better—her aunt has seen how selfish and shallow the priest is. An expertly droll presentation, this story captures both the banality and small wit of midlands Irish speech while mocking bourgeois self-preservation.

Selected Stories' concluding novella, "A Happy Death," charts the troubled marriage of Ellie and Robert, a man who works in a library but suffers from emphysema. Ellie is a strong-willed social conformist; Robert a daydreaming reader of poetry. Ellie takes in several boarders to make ends meet, but when Robert is demoted to janitor due to his constant coughing, Ellie's pride in her man is broken. Flashbacks of youthful love and their past tenderness splinter through the gloomy narrative like shafts of sunlight. Near death, Robert laments that all he ever wanted was to spend a quiet life in some backwater town with Ellie, yet their lives were spent in the big city cluttered with strangers. Taken to the hospital, he lapses into a coma. On the same floor of the ward, there's a man noted for his atheism and blasphemy; his wife is ever by his side urging repentance. Ellie arranges for a Franciscan priest to hear Robert's confession, but Robert does not respond. A so-called miracle occurs—the atheist has a deathbed conversion, repenting of his sins and his hatred of God. The priest rushes to give absolution; the nurse-nun acclaims this event as "an exemplary death" (276). Robert emerges from his coma; Ellie urges him to repent and repeat the scene just enacted. Robert is delirious, raving about Ellie's golden hair, their youthful romance, his dislike of Ellie's mother. This eloquent, disjointed hymn of innocent love (not unlike that of Gretta's memories in James Joyce's novella, "The Dead," in his collection *Dubliners*) contrasts with Ellie's cold and unresponsive conformity (similar to Gabriel's in "The Dead"). Robert has kept the flame of his love for Ellie alive until his last breath. The climax of the story reaches a nearly unbearable pathos. After Robert's death, Ellie becomes hysterical because she thinks that God did not hear her prayers for a happy death. Robert had displayed no interest in the priest or an act of contrition. Ellie rejects the wise words of her daughters: "Never mind, Mother . . . He led a good life. He never did anyone any harm" (281).

That Roman Catholics put more faith in the visible than the invisible is an accusation that Protestants have made for centuries. As in the first story of the collection, "The Will," the theme here is the external aspects of religion compared to the internal, the unmediated personal. In "The Will," the young protagonist opted for the more internal view, as opposed to that of her siblings and the priest. In "A Happy Death," an older protagonist finds herself rigidly connected to the external because the sentiment in her love has died. The reader has no doubt that Robert died the "happy death" and that the deathbed conversion of the sinner is dubious, a comic parody. Ironically, Ellie's belief in only the externals of religion leads her to despair and even disbelief at the end of the story—to be, like Gabriel in "The Dead," one of the living dead. Using a male protagonist, Joyce reflects the female perspective, while Lavin reflects that of the male with a female protagonist. As in Joyce's story, which ends *Dubliners*, the concluding words to "A Happy Death" also comprise the title of the story. While theologically faithful to Catholicism, Lavin acknowledges the truth of the Protestant perspective because she realizes that the externals of love and religion are but metaphors for the reality. Writing within the Catholic tradition, Lavin critiques its shortcomings even as she affirms the vision of her faith. While imitating Joyce's artistic technique (as well as Joyce's attack on the self-satisfied middle class), Lavin locates her artistic vision within Catholicism rather than atheism.

The Catholic vision locates itself in self-sacrifice and hard work as the path to the Mystical Body of Christ, yet Lavin is a moralist, not a mystic. Unconcerned with examining Church doctrine or theology, she remains centered upon character study. Her perception of suffering and selfless devotion as salvific vehicles charts the psychological struggle within an individual's character, the triumph or failure of the individual to live up to the moral and spiritual values of the Church. Lavin accepts the Catholic Church in its totality while directing her satiric gaze on the sociology of the lower middle class, which often perceives religion as merely a social convention rather than as spiritual reality. Because so many of her stories treat the behavior of nuns or clergy in a critical manner, some have questioned her orthodoxy, but Lavin replied that "I have never to my knowledge written an anti-clerical story, although I have written about priests and nuns who were weak and human" (Levenson 1998, 89). Near the end of her life, Lavin affirmed, "I am still a Catholic but one who is highly critical of a lot of things in my church" (Stevens and Stevens 1997, 45).

The failure of individuals to live up to ideals, or even to be aware of the true nature of their ideals, continued to preoccupy her dramatic aesthetic. The *agon* of a character to apprehend or embrace charity leads to a peripety that may have either a comic, or more commonly, a tragic, ending. In this sense, Lavin presents a tragic (and often ironic) vision of Catholicism, although she is quite capable of writing with astonishing flights of bemused irony or even hilarious ridicule. The salvation of the soul in the crucible of free will leads to either purification or the smug self-delusion of the unexamined life. Most stories present the testing of a character's spiritual life, and the reader (as in a play) becomes the jury. The terrain of the testing occurs in the ordinary and sometimes the banal; a great number of characters live life in a minor kind of self-imprisonment, and the presence of purgatorial motifs looms perhaps larger in her work than in the work of W. B. Yeats, James Joyce, Samuel Beckett, Patrick Kavanagh, or Seamus Heaney.

Writing since the early 1940s, Mary Lavin had a large repertoire of works from which to make a careful selection. *Selected Stories* has a meticulously binary structure, something like a rhyming lyric with the following pattern: ab cc dd ee ff ba. The first and last stories are about death and how to live life with love; the second and penultimate stories concern the religious life, presenting two narcissists (a nun and priest) who are professional religious for the wrong reason (that is, bourgeois self-preservation). The third and fourth stories center upon the dialectic of male/female domination; the fifth and sixth upon the pilgrimage of the soul, male and female, from hell to purgatory (the carter) and from purgatory to hell (Bedelia). The seventh and eighth stories are humorous Dublin-style prank stories (lower-class and upper-class, teenager and elderly); and the ninth and tenth stories employ Gaelic myth while illustrating the powerlessness of women in contemporary society. Balance, counterpoint, and varied treatments of themes mark this book as an intricately composed fugue, similar to the fourteen stories and concluding musical novella of Joyce's *Dubliners*.

CRITICAL RECEPTION

Zach Bowen's *Mary Lavin* remains a good introduction to Mary Lavin's work and contains a stimulating discussion of her two novels. The noted Joyce scholar's assessment is high: "There are few living writers in Ireland, and none among the short-story writers, who measure up to her standard" (1975, 71). Richard F. Peterson's *Mary Lavin* (1978) presents a far more detailed, comprehensive, and valuable study. Peterson treats the themes of contending sensibilities, the middle class, the Irish mother, artifice, and widowhood, as well as providing a brief consideration of Lavin in the context of world literature. Leah Levenson's biography *The Four Seasons of Mary Lavin* (1998) contains important personal information, empathetic commentary on the autobiographical angle of her stories, and delightful information on the community of writers whom Lavin knew.

Journal articles on Mary Lavin tend to be of four kinds: (1) thematic investigations of several stories; (2) elucidation of individual stories; (3) gender studies; and (4) comparisons with other short-story writers. Fashionable deconstructive analysis has bypassed Mary Lavin (even though some later stories exhibit a postmodern sensibility in narrative technique), perhaps because her stories possess such clarity, abundant humor, and irony. Also, the deep spirituality of her stories lacks sympathy with the predominant trend of philosophical nihilism: after Petrarch and Montaigne, philosophers have remained disinterested in the study of character. In the preface to *Selected Stories*, the only critical commentary that Lavin ever published, she says: "Short story writing—for me—is only looking closer than normal into the human heart. . . . Intuitive imagination can focus more directly upon the object of its interest than memory or direct observation" (vii–viii). All her life, Lavin resisted psychoanalysis in order to preserve her intuitive, creative powers.

The published body of critical work on Lavin remains small despite her accomplishment. Lavin's work attracts neither the pious nor the nonreligious, drawing those who value tragic ironies in a spiritual context. Of those examining the spiritual side of her work, A. A. Kelly and Ann Owens Weekes stand out. In her book *Mary Lavin: Quiet Rebel*, Kelly, quite rightly, puts emphasis on the Catholic Church's "saving of souls" and the theme of the good death. Kelly accurately comments on the plights and difficulties that celibacy poses in Lavin's stories: "Few are capable of sublimating all physical expression of love and expanding themselves to the full on a purely spiritual plane" (1980, 111). Lavin criticizes not the institutions of the Church but the limitations of its members. And the treatment of clergy is not any different than the treatment of the laity. As Kelly says, "The importance of love in the burgeoning of the full human being is stressed in the religious, as in the laity, throughout Mary Lavin's work" (105). In that way, Lavin is no different from Dante, whose *Purgatorio* enjoys significant clerical attendance.

In a more optimistic vein, Ann Owens Weekes, in *Irish Women Writers* (1990), comments upon the sacramental nature of exchange as communion, linking this communion to gardening, the frequency of giving gifts, and especially conversational exchange. Weekes achieves considerable success in her analysis when it centers upon character and the drama of individual salvation in the context of the community.

Mary Lavin's conservative Roman Catholicism documents a predominantly rural Catholic middle class insensitive to its own ideals; her work may lack contemporary urgency, partly because that middle class has become more urban and more liberal. Lavin's true successor in Ireland with regard to chronicling that class is John McGahern, but McGahern accepts neither the Church not the consolation of religion, presenting the atheistic vision that Mary Lavin rebuts in the story "Assigh."

Lavin's world retains an elemental and universal quality rooted in the ordinary lives of unremarkable people, yet she manages to encompass them in a world of lyric understatement. In accomplishment, variety of technique, and deft use of irony and myth, her only American peer remains Eudora Welty. Few writers of prose can display such lyricism, force, and beauty amid the quotidian; in a general way, Mary Lavin, an endless reviser of her own stories, may be indebted to Gustave Flaubert as a model, but Flaubert lacks the deep spirituality found in Lavin. Her approach to the fallible institution of the Catholic Church often proffers humor, but her spiritual perception of the moral life retains an eloquence and power to invoke both intimacy and an echoing social nuance. Although validating Protestant individualism, Lavin's overriding vision of human character in *Selected Stories* is Catholic and purgatorial.

NOTE

Mary Lavin, *Selected Stories* (New York: Macmillan, 1959). All references are to this edition.

WORKS CITED

Bowen, Zach. 1975. *Mary Lavin*. Lewisburg, PA: Bucknell University Press.

Harmon, Maurice. 1979. "From Conversations with Mary Lavin." *Irish University Review* 9, no. 2 (Autumn): 294–307.

Kelly, A. A. 1980. *Mary Lavin: Quiet Rebel*. New York: Barnes and Noble.

Levenson, Leah. 1998. *The Four Seasons of Mary Lavin*. Dublin: Marino Press.

Peterson, Richard F. 1978. *Mary Lavin*. Boston: Twayne.

Stevens, Robert L., and Sylvia Stevens. 1997. "An Interview with Mary Lavin." *Studies: An Irish Quarterly Review* 86: 43–50.

Weekes, Ann Owens. 1990. *Irish Women Writers: An Uncharted Tradition*. Lexington: University Press of Kentucky.

BIBLIOGRAPHY

Arkin, Stephen. "Mary Lavin and Chekhov: Something Autumnal in the Air." *Studies: An Irish Quarterly Review* 88 (1999): 278–83.

Caswell, Robert W. "The Human Heart's Vagaries." *Kilkenny Review* 12–13 (1965): 69–89.

Gottwald, Maria. "Narrative Strategies in the *Selected Stories* of Mary Lavin." In *Anglo-Irish Literature: Aspects of Language and Culture*, ed. Brigit Bramsback and Martin Croghan, vol. 2, 183–89. Uppsala: Uppsala University Press, 1988.

Krawschak, Ruth. *Mary Lavin: A Checklist*. Berlin: Erschienen im Selbstverlag, 1979.

Murphy, Catherine A. "The Ironic Vision of Mary Lavin." *Mosaic* 12 (1979): 69–79.

O'Brien, George, and Richard F. Peterson. Brief entries on Lavin's stories. In *Reference Guide to Short Fiction*, ed. Noelle Watson, 307–08, 710–11, 731–32. Detroit: St. James Press, 1994.

— Kevin T. McEneaney

Robert Lax [1915–2000]

The Circus of the Sun

BIOGRAPHY

Who *is* Robert Lax? Some readers may recognize the name through Thomas Merton's references in *The Seven Storey Mountain*, in which he characterizes Lax as a "potential prophet, but without rage" (1975, 180–81). Others may be familiar with Lax's humor, wit, and compassion from the published correspondence between Merton and Lax, *A Catch of Anti-Letters* ([1978] 1994), or from Arthur Biddle's *When Prophecy Still Had a Voice: The Letters of Thomas Merton & Robert Lax* (2001), which received the Book of the Year Award at the 2001 Thomas Merton convention held in Louisville, Kentucky. Only recently has Lax received some of the recognition that his accomplishments deserve: the spring 2001 issue of *The Merton Seasonal*, for example, was devoted to his life and work, and St. Bonaventure University presented its Arts Award in honor of Lax in the same year. Lax is less known as a truly gifted American minimalist poet. The Beat Generation writer Jack Kerouac once described him as "simply a Pilgrim in search of beautiful innocence, writing lovingly, finding it, simply, in his own way" (quoted in Miller and Zurbrugg 1999, 13).

Born on November 30, 1915, in the small town of Olean in upstate New York, Lax was the son of Jewish immigrants from Austria who had met and married after becoming Americans. His father, Sigmund, owned a men's clothing store, and his mother had an interest in the arts. Lax, who was the youngest of three children, was raised primarily in Olean but also partly in New York City. He attended Columbia University, where he met and formed a close friendship with Thomas Merton. He graduated with his bachelor's degree in 1938 and worked for a time on the editorial staff of *The New Yorker* and as a reviewer for *Time* magazine. Merton's entrance into the monastery in 1942 greatly affected Lax; his friend's Catholic convictions influenced his own conversion to Catholicism in 1943. Although Merton's conversion had taken place five years prior, Merton was heavily influenced by Lax's humility with respect to God and others.

Lax did not find that by becoming Catholic he had abandoned his Jewish roots; rather, he felt as if his identity was completed in the embrace of Christ

while cherishing his Old Testament roots. Just as the New Testament is a fulfillment of the Old, Lax recognized that accepting Christ brought fulfillment to
his life. His Catholicism would be lived out in a hermitage of his own finding—
writing in isolation on the Greek islands, enjoying the companionship of others
who also valued living simply, and being happily convinced of God's goodness. He
maintained a contemplative lifestyle as an alternative to the fast-paced, success-
oriented, and economically driven culture of New York City.

In 1950, Lax composed *The Circus of the Sun* while living in Olean. In 1953, he
joined writer and fellow Columbia friend Edward Rice in editing *Jubilee*, a liberal
Catholic magazine he helped found. A decade later, he chose to move to the
Greek islands, settling first on Kalymnos and then on Patmos, where he produced
more than 300 published works of poetry, journals, and essays in addition to
hundreds of pages of unpublished works and photos. These are stored at the Lax
archives at St. Bonaventure University, near Olean. Lax remained in Greece until
just weeks before his death at age eighty-four in Olean, on September 26, 2000.

Merton and Lax maintained a close friendship until Merton's death in 1968
and had a mutual respect and appreciation for each other's philosophies and art.
Throughout their lives as artists and Christian thinkers, they influenced each other
significantly. Evidence of this can be found in their poetry and artwork (drawings
and photographs) as well as in their correspondence with each other and with
other writers and thinkers. In a tribute to Merton, Lax remarked, "In all the ages
of Christianity there have been at least a few joyous hermits who have filled
the world about them with divinely inspired joy" (1988, 37). In a letter to poet
Czeslaw Milosz, Merton referred to Lax's epic poem *The Circus of the Sun*,
stating, "I wish you could see one good book, though, that is unknown, by my
friend Robert Lax. . . . Lax you would like" (1997, 74, 75).

Lax has more of a following throughout Europe than in the United States.
Merton believed that Lax was unappreciated because his verse lacks "angst," a
common criteria for poetic greatness throughout the twentieth century. In his
poetry, Lax integrates inner observations and reflections with his Catholicism.
His entire body of work reflects his Jewish roots and his conversion to Catholicism. Lax's prolific writings from the last few decades of his life acutely convey
his passion for searching for the holy in all things, including the self. He sees God
as the source of the realization of selfhood and of the call of that self to responsibility for others and for the world. Such a position opposes the claim that there is
nothing but culturally constructed frameworks in human experience. Lax's poetry
provides a reclaiming of notions of the self that understand faith, the Spirit, and
encounters with God as real-life experiences that transcend cultural and historical
circumstances while, paradoxically, remaining wholly immanent within human
experience.

Lax's poetic vision was shaped by his migratory life. He once traveled with a
circus throughout Europe and later observed the famed Cristiani family circus in
western Canada as a journal reporter, an experience that inspired his acclaimed
The Circus of the Sun, a book-length sequence of poems. Through this epic work
about a circus, Lax reinvents, as poets do, the story of creation. Yet, this story—
in its method and message—is not much more than a stone's throw or a metaphor
away from the biblical account; Lax's verse is an impressionistic, imaginative,
and contemporary reflection on what Genesis records in fact.

SUMMARY

The Circus of the Sun relates the setting up of a circus to the Christian story of the creation. Lax extends his metaphor to a consideration of how there can be a "Circus of the Lord" here on earth. He suggests that our "tabernacles" on earth—that is, our places of worship and ministry, a word evoking Lax's Jewish heritage—are only "temporary tabernacles" and that we should aim to bring the earth to its full blossom. As T. S. Eliot's "waste land" motif served as a spiritual warning for poets of modernity, Lax's poetics of the circus provide an alternative vision of the Christian story for postmodernity. Through this sequence of poems of play and devotion, contemporary readers and writers are led to recover from dualistic notions of the material and spiritual, creator and creation, and grace and nature that have so characterized the modern waste land.

By the use of a cast of charming characters in a detailed circus setting, *The Circus of the Sun* depicts a communal way of life in which there is no domination and no sense of doom that overshadows the minds of humanity. Lax's circus is all about the movements of divine grace, figured in the juggler's objects, in the finely tuned somersault of the acrobat, and in the "unfolding" generations of families. It is a hopeful, idealistic text, encouraging love and brotherhood based upon biblical commands. Lax's depiction of a creative atmosphere suggests that God does not hoard the power to create to himself; rather, he has invested human beings with the ability to create in certain situations as long as they respect his ordained boundaries. The metaphor and reality of the circus, for Lax, embodies this atmosphere of ordained praise and play.

MAJOR THEMES

The circus that Lax creates in *The Circus of the Sun* serves as a microcosm of the universe, where there is free play and a unity of people and activities, where a spiritual presence is not separate from the natural, worldly existence. The circus manifests variety and difference and yet a constant unity and community. Lax's verse maintains a fine balance of grace, both human and godly; he invokes a dynamic conceptualization of the term "grace" that includes both a sacred and a secular connotation. The circus is a "song of praise, / A song of praise unto the Lord. / The acrobats, His chosen people, / Rejoice forever in His love" (*The Circus of the Sun*, 62). What is valued in the circus is how well performers please and give to the audience as well as how they cooperate with others as they work and play. For example, the graced actions of Mogador, a member of the Cristiani circus family and a major circus performer, are poignantly described as follows:

> [he] walks the earth like a turning ball: knowing
> and rejoicing in his sense of balance:
> he delights in the fulcrums
> and levers, teeter-boards, trampolines, high-wires,
> swings, the nets, ropes and ring-curbs of the natural
> universe. (63)

This sequence of poems embodies the notion of the carnival (an idea articulated by literary theorist Mikhail Bakhtin), which allows for community as opposed to hierarchy. The metaphor of the circus challenges traditional societal structures and roles: in his poem, Lax refigures a world where grace enables human beings to relate to others without dominance and without violence. The circus, evoking the basic definition of the word, turns the real world and its conventions on its head. This opens up for Lax as well as his readers a world of possibilities to be creative and to be good to one's neighbor. The structure and tone of the text itself is one that values community: the text is dialogic and consists of many layers of voices as opposed to a monologic, authoritative tone and style. The text is also in the form of novelized epic poetry, a genre described by Bakhtin that is open-ended and accessible, as opposed to traditional epic poetry, which is closed in that it requires an accepted, universal understanding of history that distances the reader from the plot. In light of this novelized style of poetry, it is not at all surprising to learn that Lax's poem was originally intended to be a novel.

Lax's novelized epic poetry allows for a spontaneity and emphasis on process and movement, a fluid paradigm for a contemporary community of humanity and nature. It is within such a context that grace is the most free: for grace to be grace, the giver must be free to give and the receiver must be free to receive. Although there is a sense of a universal community of the circus, the characters' differences and individualities are celebrated and accented as each plays his or her part. And yet, neither differences nor individual personalities lead to isolation or alienation, for every individual is dependent upon another and the whole; community is desired and required to maintain the circus. In such a world, grace is both present and transcendent: The natural is supernatural and vice versa. The multilayered circus Lax depicts serves as a paradigm for community, difference, individuality, presence, and transcendence. This world is in process, never fixed or stationary; it is a wandering community, yet there is a definite confidence in knowing one's place, a comfort in home even though it is moving, transitory, and unfinished.

The interconnectedness of the circus Lax depicts can best be understood within the context of grace. In fact, the "postscript" to the work overtly addresses elements of grace that are interwoven throughout the entire sequence. In this section, which can be read as prose, poetry, or commentary (or a combination of the three— this blurring of genres is a feature of much postmodern literature), the poet-persona writes a letter to Mogador and reveals that Mogador had wanted a poem in *The Circus of the Sun* to be called "Unfolded Grace." He then proceeds to consider the implications of this phrase:

> Unfolded Grace: the acrobat in somersault unfolding, landing lightly on horse-back; the family in its generations unfolding, and arriving at the same moment, those same moments of unfolding grace. Why talk about the somersault, the leap, and landing as such a great thing? It is great and small. It is a high achievement for a man and no achievement at all for god or angel. It is proud and humble. It represents graceful victory over so many obstacles; the most elegant solution of so many problems. And yet like the blossoming of the smallest flower or the highest palm, it is a very little thing, and very great. Think, Mogador, of the freedom, in a world of bondage, a world expelled from Eden; the freedom of the priest, the artist, and the acrobat. In a world of men condemned to earn their bread by the sweat of their brows, the liberty of those who, like the lilies of the field, live by playing. For playing is like Wisdom before the face of the Lord. Their play is praise. Their praise is prayer. This play, like the ritual gestures

of the priest, is characterized by grace; Heavenly grace unfolding, flowering and reflected in the physical grace of the player. (95)

This passage conveys a sense of grace that unfolds in and through the world, where the divine presence is realized in the physical and material world. Moreover, this grace "at play" is also "in praise," encouraging an association of pleasure and joy with the acts of obedience and ritual in religious experience.

Continuing to address Mogador, the poet then relates his *The Circus of the Sun* to a possible realization of its form in contemporary reality:

I think there can be a "Circus of the Lord." For we are all wanderers in the earth, and pilgrims. We have no permanent habitat here. The migration of people for foraging & exploiting can become, with grace (in the latter days), a traveling circus. Our tabernacle must in its nature be a temporary tabernacle. We are wanderers in the earth, but only a few of us in each generation have discovered the life of charity, the living from day to day, receiving our gifts gratefully through grace, and rendering them, multiplied through grace, to the giver. That is the meaning of your expansive, outward arching gesture of the arm in the landing; the graceful rendering, the gratitude and giving. (96)

This depiction of human relations refutes the modern notion of self as isolated and autonomous, encouraging a selfhood that is realized in giving to others, in becoming part of grace by both experiencing and transmitting it.

Lax begins the sequence of poems that constitute *The Circus of the Sun* with an improvisation on the Gospel of John, making the reader aware of the presence of the divine within the context of a human-operated place. This divine presence is immanent throughout the circus universe. In the description of the circus grounds, an interconnectedness between human beings and the natural universe is shown to exist; while maintained by human effort, it responds simultaneously to the unfolding of the universe by God. This "unfolding grace" that the poet describes in the postscript is illustrated in the section "Penelope and Mogador," in which Penelope the tightrope walker asks Mogador the acrobat "how he was able to land so gracefully after he did a somersault on horse-back" (71). Mogador's failed previous attempts to accomplish this task demonstrate that the flaws of arrogance, pride, self-righteousness, and desire to impress, control, or make demands of others will result in failure and the graced act will not be realized. It is not until he is free of all such pretense and personal ambition that Mogador, with his mind now clear and focused, simply does the somersault and lands exactly "with two feet on the horse's back" (71). It is then that he is able to gesture with his arms held out, having completed the task, and this gesture indicates his complete generosity to God and to his fellow human beings. Unfolded grace suggests that human mental or physical effort alone cannot accomplish a task. Rather, it is the graced non-self-conscious deliverance of an action that succeeds, a moment when all things—skill, habit, mind, matter, physics—come together. Unfolded grace blurs distinctions between the supernatural and the natural.

Lax's use of the concept of grace in *The Circus of the Sun* mirrors the work of theologians such as Thomas Aquinas and Karl Rahner. Aquinas described a person who acts in grace as one who has acquired the "habit of grace." Lax's characters exhibit a habit of grace that Rahner, the primary contemporary Catholic theologian of grace, emphasizes is always the free action of divine love that is only "at the disposal" of man precisely to the extent that he is at the disposal of divine love (1975, 180).

The characters in Lax's circus are virtuosos in their performances, experiencing and revealing habitualized grace that unites the supernatural and natural and is both given and received. Inherent in the performer's acts are not only the graces that allow them to be accomplished and thereby delight the onlookers but also those of giving: the open generosity with which the gift is given by God as well as, in turn, the generosity of the receiver, who is then transformed into a giver. This is the significance, as the poet explicitly points out and the entire text implies, of the outstretched arms at the completion of the performance. Such a conceptualization of grace is contingent upon the receiver becoming the giver: otherwise grace is static, merely an impotent, deflating thing. The circus is built by, through, and for grace:

> Our dreams have tamed the lions,
> have made pathways in the jungle,
> peaceful lakes; they have built new
> Edens ever-sweet and ever-changing
> By day from town to town we carry
> Eden in our tents and bring its won-
> ders to the children who have lost
> their dream of home. (76)

Within such a context, all the performers' various acts become rituals:

> What was begun
> As a run
> through the field
> is turned
> to ritual. (89)

To view even mundane activities as rituals instills a reverence for the play and work of life. It does not marginalize or categorize experience but values the holy in the everyday. Every act becomes an act of worship. This deeply sacramental view of life is at the heart of Catholic spirituality.

Graced and ethical behavior are the moral ideals in Lax's circus. The poem highlights a character who is exemplary of a life of graced ethics: Rastelli, a circus hero, is esteemed "Not because his work was dangerous / But because he was excellent at it / And because he was excellent as a friend" (90). Rastelli, who is symbolically linked with Christ, died at age thirty-three. He is emulated for his graceful acts as well as his graceful spirit: he is described as having been

> good at juggling
> At talking
> At coffee
> Loving everyone
> He died juggling for everyone. . . . He loved the world and things he juggled,
> He loved the people he juggled for. (90–91)

Rastelli is revered as a juggler whose "clubs and flames and hoops / Moved around him like planets" (90). He did not need to manipulate objects to answer to his will; rather, "[h]e moved all things according to their natures: / They were ready when he found them / But he moved them according to their love" (90). The poem highlights the way that Rastelli recognized his place in the world, how it led him to see himself as a part of creation, and how this sense of place reflects the Creator. He discovered that grace is both reciprocal and cyclical:

> Seeing the world was willing to dance,
> Rastelli fell in love with creation,
> Through the creation with the Creator,
> And through the Creator again with creation,
> And through the creation, the Lord. (90–91)

The closing section of *The Circus of the Sun* asks the reader to consider the effects of when the circus begins and ends. The idea of what it means to be human held by those involved in the circus as well as those who witness it is not left unchallenged. Indeed, in its depiction of the circus as a fluid paradigm for living in, with, and through grace, *The Circus of the Sun* may cause the reader's notions of grace and the perceived dualities of the sacred/secular, human/divine, and natural/supernatural to be altered. This possibility reflects postmodern theologian Mark C. Taylor's claim regarding carnivalesque play:

> By upsetting traditional hierarchies, carnivalesque play inverts inherited values and established meanings. This inversion does not leave opposites unmarked. The reversal enacted in festive celebration dissolves the original identity of the exclusive opposites that have defined the poles of most Western theology and have formed the foundation of Western society and culture. (1984, 161)

The Circus of the Sun depicts a wide variety of circus characters, each using his or her various talents to give glory to God and, in turn, to give joy and fulfillment to the audience and themselves. The interplay of grace and ethical behavior is revealed through the depiction of a world that is structured around play and entertainment, skill and risk. The circus does not contain the hierarchies of a capitalist society, in which money and power determine human relations. Rather, toward the end of the sequence, the community is likened to a wedding with its implied sacramental union of grace and celebratory atmosphere. "Have you seen the noon-day banners / Of this wedding?" the poet asks readers, involving them in a direct dialogue with the text. We are left to answer the question:

> Have you known such a thing?
> That men and animals
> Light and air,
> Graceful acrobats,
> And musicians
> Could come together
> In a single place. (94)

Lax's circus suggests that it is possible to attain in modern society relationships between human beings that are based on mutual love and a community that is founded on grace and ethical behavior. Lacking a monetary or capitalist basis for human interaction, the circus thus challenges Marxist notions of an effective society. Lax's verse provides a unique defense of Christianity against the Marxist view of religion as merely a cultural institution that determines, coerces, or controls a person's behavior. Lax views the presence of God transcending and infusing human experience in a sacramental manner as that which mediates between the human and the world and which assists humans in discerning between the just and the unjust, the true and the false, the Spirit-centered and the self-centered. This reliance upon the Spirit for guidance and discernment in the world does not suggest that faith fails to confront uncertainties, ambiguities, and paradoxes, for, according to Christian belief, human life on earth can only see through a "glass darkly." Yet Lax's poetry implicitly counters the Marxist conception of religion as "the opiate of the people." It challenges the postmodern stance that an authentic self is illusory and that all human experiences or personal beliefs are merely historically or ideologically determined. Moreover, *The Circus of the Sun* provides a space to wrestle with notions of the self in ways that help dislodge from our minds the western, humanist idea of the autonomous self, allowing for the reclaiming of a selfhood that prioritizes the role of our neighbors—our fellow workers and players—in the "circus" of our lives.

CRITICAL RECEPTION

The Circus of the Sun was first published in its complete form in 1959 by Emil Antonucci of Journeyman Books. Prior to this volume, there were two publications of material that would later become part of the complete epic. The first was in *New-Story* magazine in Paris (no. 4, June 1951); the material there was described by Lax as an "excerpt for a novel-in-progress." The second was in *New World Writing* #13 (New York: New American Library, 1958). That piece was entitled "The Circus"; it contained only one-third of the full text and had extra material that was later honed down. The second complete edition of *The Circus of the Sun* was published by Bernhard Moosbrugger of Pendo Verlag in Zurich, Switzerland, in 1981. More recently, *The Circus of the Sun* has appeared in several Lax anthologies, such as *33 Poems* (1987) and *Love Had a Compass* (1996). *Mogador's Book*, a companion piece to the poem written within six months of *The Circus of the Sun* but not published until thirty years later, was released by Pendo Verlag in Zurich in 1992. Another related piece, *Voyage to Pescara*, was written in 1951 and published by Overlook Press in 2000. The collection of the entire circus epic, entitled *Circus Days & Nights* (2000), was edited by Paul Spaeth, curator of the Robert Lax Archives at St. Bonaventure University.

Although not well known, *The Circus of the Sun* has received high praise from certain critics. In a 1959 journal entry, Thomas Merton records having just read Lax's work. He found it to have

an Isaiah-like prophecy which has a quality you just don't find in poetry today, a completely unique simplicity and purity of love that is not afraid to express itself. The circus as symbol and sacrament, cosmos and church—the mystery of the primitive world, of paradise, in which men have wonderful and happy skills, which they exercise freely, as at play. But also a sacrament of the eschaton, our heavenly Jerusalem. The importance of human love in the circus—for doing things well. It is one of the few poems that has anything whatever to say. And I want to write an article about it. (1996, 360–61)

In a 1978 review published in the *New York Times Book Review*, Richard Kostelanetz wrote, "I regard Robert Lax as among America's greatest experimental poets, a true minimalist who can weave awesome poems from remarkably few words. Though a survivor, Lax remains the last unacknowledged—and alas, uncollected—major poet of his post-60 generation" (quoted in Miller and Zurbrugg 1999, 183). Moreover, R. C. Kennedy stated, "*Circus of the Sun* is, in all probability, the finest volume of poems published by an English-speaking poet of the generation which comes in the wake of T. S. Eliot" (quoted in Lax 2000, 21).

As Merton suggested, Lax provides a prophetic voice for our times. His optimistic vision, however, leaves him open to criticism that presumes that he neglects the world's atrocities, poverty, and violence. Contemporary American poet Denise Levertov praised Lax's *The Circus of the Sun* even as she acknowledged, "One might feel Lax's book too much ignores the world's anguish, if it were not full of a gentleness, a tenderness, that is not smug." Levertov insists that the significant "neglect" of Lax's work is "undeserved"; she continues, "but it is easy to ignore work of such lucidity because by its very nature it is not controversial; nor can one bracket it with any 'movement'" (quoted in Miller and Zurbrugg 1999, 181).

The 1999 collection of criticism on Lax, *The ABC's of Robert Lax*, edited by David Miller and Nicholas Zurbrugg, takes a significant step toward making reparations for the neglect of Lax's work. As this book illustrates, Lax's fans are a varied lot and include such acclaimed writers and critics as Allen Ginsberg, e. e. cummings, Sun Ra, Mark Van Doren, and Susan Howe. Other literary critics, such as myself, are drawn toward his minimalist, experimental technique; his valuing of silence, contemplation, meditation, and prayer as embodied in monastic life; and his exploration of spiritual issues. Paul J. Spaeth is an invaluable resource on Lax's work and life. In his introduction to *Circus Days & Nights*, a recent republication of *Circus of the Sun* that includes additional previously unpublished material, Spaeth describes the poet's involvement and enchantment with the circus. He gives a detailed account of the development and completion of Lax's circus epic. Spaeth also provides an insightful contextualization of the Catholic dimensions of Lax's circus writings. Such endeavors lend hope that Lax as poet, pilgrim, and prophet will be appreciated by a new generation. After all, as Lax maintained in an interview, the poets of any society "should be carriers of vision" (personal interview with me—Lax's last interview—conducted on Patmos, May 2000).

NOTE

Robert Lax, *The Circus of the Sun*. In *Love Had a Compass: Journals and Poetry*, ed. James J. Uebbing (New York: Grove/Atlantic, Inc., 1996). Used by permission. All references are to this edition.

WORKS CITED

Biddle, Arthur W., ed. 2001. *When Prophecy Still Had a Voice: The Letters of Thomas Merton and Robert Lax*. Lexington: University Press of Kentucky.

Lax, Robert. 1987. *33 Poems*, ed. Thomas Kellein. New York: New Directions.

———. 1988. "Harpo's Progress: Notes Toward an Understanding of Merton's Ways." *The Merton Annual* 1, 35–54.

———. 2000. *Circus Days & Nights*, ed. and intro. Paul J. Spaeth. New York: Overlook Press.

Lax, Robert, and Thomas Merton. [1978] 1994. *A Catch of Anti-Letters*. Foreword by Brother Patrick Hart. Reprint, Kansas City, MO: Sheed and Ward.

Merton, Thomas. 1975. *The Seven Storey Mountain*. London: Sheldon Press.

———. 1996. *A Search for Solitude: The Journals of Thomas Merton*, vol. 3, ed. Lawrence Cunningham. San Francisco: Harper.

———. 1997. *Striving Towards Being: The Letters of Thomas Merton and Czeslaw Milosz*, ed. Robert Faggen. New York: Farrar, Straus & Giroux.

The Merton Seasonal 26, no.1 (spring 2001). Special edition devoted to the life and work of Robert Lax, ed. Patrick F. O'Connell. Louisville, KY: International Thomas Merton Society and the Thomas Merton Center of Bellarmine University.

Miller, David, and Nicholas Zurbrugg, eds. 1999. *The ABC's of Robert Lax*. Devon, England: Stride.

Rahner, Karl. 1975. *A Rahner Reader*, ed. Gerald A. McCool. New York: Seabury.

Taylor, Mark C. 1984. *Erring: A Postmodern A/Theology*. Chicago: University of Chicago Press.

BIBLIOGRAPHY

Mizingou, Jeannine. "'Bringing the Earth to Flower' 1915–2000: A Tribute to Robert Lax." *The Merton Annual* 15 (2002): 23–60.

———. "Robert Lax: Poet, Pilgrim, Prophet." *Logos: A Journal of Catholic Thought and Culture* 4, no. 1 (Winter 2001): 98–113.

Thyreen-Mizingou, Jeannine. "Grace and Ethics in Contemporary American Poetry: Resituating the other/Other, the World, and the Self." *Religion and Literature* 32, no. 1 (Spring 2000): 67–97.

— Jeannine Mizingou

Gertrud von le Fort [1876–1971]

The Song at the Scaffold

BIOGRAPHY

Gertrud von le Fort's career as a writer reached its height in the decade before the Nazi takeover of Germany in 1933, when she was well into middle age. After World War II and until her death in 1971, she gracefully played the role of a respected author in the classical tradition.

Born in Germany in 1876 to a military family, von le Fort moved frequently as a child according to her father's postings. The family lived at various times in Minden, Berlin, and Koblenz. Her father, Prussian major Lothar Friedrich Franz Peter, Baron von le Fort, was a descendant of an Italian Protestant family that fled from the Savoy via Geneva to Russia and then to Germany to escape religious persecution. One of three children, Gertrud led a quiet life in a well-to-do family, publishing occasional fiction and poetry on a small scale. Summers were spent on various family estates in eastern Germany. She was very close to her father, from whom she got her love for history. Since her schooling did not include the official graduation diploma, the *Abitur*, von le Fort started auditing classes at the University of Heidelberg in 1908; she later also attended the universities of Marburg and Berlin. This was quite unusual for a woman at the time.

Among the many important academics von le Fort was to meet, the most influential was the Protestant sociologist of religion, Ernst Troeltsch (1865–1923), with whom she formed a deep friendship. She followed him to Berlin in 1914, and she edited his papers, *Glaubenslehre* (Teachings on Faith), in the late 1920s. Troeltsch, who also wrote *Der Historismus und seine Probleme* (Historicism and its Problems, 1922), profoundly influenced her in what was to become her main interest: historical fiction. His central notions of how religion had to be understood in relation to a historical context translated into her early understanding of religious tolerance and ecumenism. Theodor Haecker (1879–1945) was another of von le Fort's role models. His *Christentum und Kultur* (Christianity and Culture, 1927) expressed ideas similar to those of Troeltsch; the author was prohibited from publishing by the Nazis in 1938. Karl Jaspers (1883–1963), whose lectures on Kierkegaard von le Fort attended in 1914, gave her an introduction to what later developed as existential philosophy. Kierkegaard's concept of *angst*, or fear, as a basic precept of human existence would become the main theme of *The Song at the Scaffold*. Von le Fort's intellectual circle of friends and acquaintances later also included such eminent figures as Edith Stein (Sister Teresa Benedicta of the Cross, 1891–1942), with whom she shared her introduction to the mysticism of the Carmel, and Paul Claudel (1868–1955), who wrote an introduction to the French translation of her books *The Hymns to the Church* and *The Song at the Scaffold*.

Gertrud von le Fort was affected very directly by the chaotic time after World War I. With her sister, she had joined the Red Cross in order to take care of wounded soldiers, and she soon experienced firsthand the realities of a Germany slowly but surely sliding into a decisive defeat. After the war, her brother was actively involved in the civil turmoil as a right-wing militant: he formed his own private army, was involved in the Kapp-Putsch (a failed nationalist uprising in Berlin in 1920), and was forced into exile. As his sister, Gertrud had to become the administrator of the family estate, Boek, at Lake Müritz in Mecklenburg, until it was expropriated by the government in 1920. Later, the Nazis confiscated all her family property. In this position, von le Fort was forced into using her literary output to earn a living.

Even before her conversion to Catholicism in Rome in 1926, von le Fort was actively involved in the liturgical renewal movement with such reformers as Romano Guardini (1885–1968) in Germany—a trend that, like many other promising developments, fell victim to the brutal cultural policies of the Nazis. Today, her *Hymns to the Church* ([1924] 1938) sound like very dated para-phrases of liturgical texts. But at the time, such work brought her into contact with the very prestigious literary circle that had formed around renowned poet Stefan George (1868–1933). She also made the acquaintance of the Jesuit Erich Przywara (1889–1972), probably the most influential Catholic theologian in Germany at the time and one of the most eminent Catholic theologians of the twentieth century. He strongly promoted her work as a representative voice of religious renewal and was also influential in her conversion to Catholicism. He was the first dialogue partner of Karl Barth (1886–1968) and Paul Tillich (1886–1965), and he introduced her to the Carmelite spirit of mysticism.

Von le Fort's literary production, mostly historical narratives, made her a respected author, and she was able to undertake extended reading tours even after 1933 until, in 1938, the government expressed its disapproval of her work by omitting her name from official histories of literature. Apart from *The Song at the Scaffold* (1931), three other major works of fiction made von le Fort an estab-lished Catholic writer. Each of these is written in a kind of elegant neo-Baroque style that sometimes sounds propagandist, even pompous. *Das Schweißtuch der Veronika* (*The Veil of Veronica: The Roman Fountain* [1928] 1932) was the first volume of a planned trilogy; it follows the traditional genre of the German *Entwicklungsroman* (novel of development) and concerns an adolescent girl in Rome who develops a type of religious hysteria when her family tries to thwart her religious conversion. The very obtuse plot was carried over into *Der Kranz der Engel* (The Wreath of Angels, 1946), a work that became the focus of a bitter controversy in the postwar years in Germany because it advocated tolerance for meaningful human relations outside the strict confines of Catholic teaching and religious salvation for those involved in unions outside the traditional forms of marriage. In this novel, Veronika's dilemma is to become engaged to and remain with a man who is antireligious and tries to destroy any religious feelings in those around him. These two novels deal with von le Fort's central concern: how a renewed form of Catholicism could make sense in a modern world. But compared to *The Song at the Scaffold*, the stories and the problems appear stifled and almost contrived.

Der Papst aus dem Ghetto (1930; translated as *The Pope from the Ghetto* in 1934) is a fascinating story set in Rome in the twelfth century dealing with legendary conversions of prominent Jews in order to penetrate the ecclesiastical establishment. The plot leads to schism in the Church and eventually to the setting up of an antipope. It is obvious that the turbulent events depicted in this novel reflect the chaotic times in Germany when it was written.

Die Magdeburger Hochzeit (The Wedding in Magdeburg, 1938) is von le Fort's boldest work. Its thinly disguised criticism of the Hitler regime resulted in her name being removed from the list of writers whose works could be published in Germany. The plot is also unusual in that the protagonist, the unfaithful bride-to-be Erdmuth Plöthgen, is a decidedly negative figure. The story unfolds during the Thirty Years' War, a devastating event in German history that was comparable to the catastrophe of the advent of World War II. The narrative depicts the horrors of a war that take place in the name of religion and draws a moving portrait of the faithful bridegroom, Willigis Ahlemann, who, as a city councilor, stays loyal to the Catholic emperor before the devastation of Magdeburg and also remains true to his bride, who is raped by Croat soldiers during the storming of the town.

Von le Fort's most concise statement about the function of fiction is to be found in her foreword to a German translation of some of Graham Greene's essays entitled *Vom Paradox des Christentums* (On the Paradox of Christianity, 1952). Here, she identifies with Greene's insistence that he was not a "Catholic writer" but rather a writer who happened to be a Catholic. On the basis of her two favorite Greene novels, *The Power and the Glory* (1940) and *The Heart of the Matter* (1948), she justifies the freedom of fiction to broach moral issues that are antithetical to traditional Christian morals, such as adultery and suicide. Analyzing the fallacious equation of western bourgeois and Christian ethics, she comes to the conclusion that fiction is grace and morals are merely judgmental.

Gertrud von le Fort had the gift of friendship. Among the many fellow writers in Germany and Europe whom she befriended was Hermann Hesse, who nominated her for the Nobel Prize in literature. Von le Fort was also able to reconcile the mother of Edith Stein with her daughter, for Stein's mother had great difficulty in accepting first her daughter's conversion from Judaism to Catholicism and then her entrance as a nun into the Carmelite convent.

Of frail health, von le Fort moved to the country town of Oberstdorf in Bavaria in 1941. She remained there until her death in 1971, except for the years 1946 to 1949, which she spent in Switzerland. Occasional publications during the last period of her life did not reach a wide audience. But even though she remained very traditional and rather conservative, her nobility of outlook and generous spirit of tolerance were even more in evidence in the wake of World War II. Unlike the vast majority of religious and political figures of the establishment who went into a prolonged period of denial, her public lectures tried to get her audiences to come to grips with the terror of an evil past that was not just the work of a few demented criminals. She gracefully accepted the numerous honors bestowed on her without compromising herself. She died a venerated and respected figure.

PLOT SUMMARY

A novella or novelette, *The Song at the Scaffold* is presented in epistolary form. A French nobleman, Herr von Villeroi, is writing in the year 1794 to an aristocratic friend who is now an émigré. He recounts events that he witnessed in Paris during the closing days of the revolutionary Reign of Terror. In particular, he describes the execution of sixteen Carmelite nuns and the killing of Blanche de la Force by the mob when she joins the sisters in their song of defiance from the scaffold. Blanche is the child of a free-thinking nobleman, the Marquis de la Force, who is firmly devoted to the thoughts of Rousseau and the ideals of the Enlightenment. She is plagued by pathological fears and anxieties. Prematurely born because her mother was frightened by a mob that went out of control during the festivities surrounding the wedding of Louis XVI, the semi-orphan is brought up by a very conservative governess, Madame de Chalais, who has no understanding of the tormented life and the organic fear of her ward. Blanche decides to enter the Carmelite convent at Compiègne at the age of seventeen. Her motivation is a mixture of religious vocation and the desire to be protected from the harsh realities of a world in turmoil. She learns to accept her existential fear and, as a postulant, is given the appropriate name "de Jésus au Jardin de l'Agonie" (of Jesus' Agony in the Garden).

But the outside terror reaches the convent when the revolutionary government eventually orders the dissolution of religious houses, and the prospect of impending martyrdom becomes the dominant feature of life in the cloister. While the prioress of the convent, Madame Lidoine (Sister Teresa of Saint Augustine), cautions her sisters to remain humble and prudent, Sister Marie de l'Incarnation, an illegitimate child of aristocrats who as subprioress is in charge of the novices, strongly advocates the triumphant and jubilant embracing of martyrdom. She is opposed to admitting Blanche to the order, but "the bishop wishes it," and Blanche is accepted. Blanche enjoys the confidence of another very earthy and confident postulant, Constance of Saint Denis. But, overwhelmed by these tensions and the open questioning of whether she is capable of such a sacrifice, she flees the convent. While Blanche's father becomes a victim of the revolutionary forces, the nuns undergo a mock trial and are eventually led to their execution. Blanche, in the meantime, has become a darling of the mob during the Reign of Terror. Horrible scenes are narrated, such as that of an aristocrat drinking a cup of blood of killed aristocrats at the wish of a bloodthirsty mob in order to save her father from execution (a feat Blanche is forced to imitate by blasphemously drinking a sacrilegious chalice of blood, although without saving her father). Blanche is dragged to witness the scene of execution of her fellow nuns. But when the sisters, in defiance of their tormentors, submit to the guillotine by chanting the *Salve Regina* and then the *Veni Creator Spiritus* and are beheaded, one after the other, Blanche, at the end, takes up singing the hymn and, consequently, is killed by an enraged mob. Marie de l'Incarnation, in an ironic twist, is denied the martyrdom that she had so ardently desired.

The story of *Song at the Scaffold* evolved from a cursory note about the historical event that von le Fort came across when browsing through the archives of the Munich university library. While the historical incident is based on fact, the figure of Blanche is the author's creation. In her autobiography, *Hälfte des Lebens Erinnerungen* (Mid-Life Memoirs, 1965), von le Fort narrates her life up to 1931, when *Song at the Scaffold* was published. She was deeply affected by the chaotic years after World War I and the uncertainty of public affairs during the Weimar Republic. She reports how her family's modest fortune was lost when the Nazis came to power and concludes her short memoir with the following statement. "Of all things lost, only my little Blanche de la Force lives on as a being, whose existence rests on all my family's records that perished. The abysmal fear of existence (*abgründige Weltangst*) which she represents and transcends—was going to be my part during the Third Reich" (151). The pun on the heroine's name (von le Fort/de la Force—indicating strength) is clearly not a coincidence.

Von le Fort's fictional account is all the more impressive since we now know more about the historical events thanks to scholar William Bush, who edited the original film scenarios in manuscript of the *Dialogues of the Carmelites* (1948– 49), the last work of French writer Georges Bernanos (1965), who based his dramatization on von le Fort's novella. Bush's historical account, *To Quell the Terror: The Mystery of the Vocation of the Sixteen Carmelites of Compiègne Guillotined July 17, 1794* (1999), reports that the execution was truly extraordinary. The nuns, in defiance of the revolutionary authority's ordinances, wore their religious habits, they did indeed go to their death by singing hymns, and the mob that was usually heckling and mocking the victims remained in stunned silence when faced with their joyfully accepted martyrdom.

MAJOR THEMES

The Song at the Scaffold is a very Catholic work. As Margaret Klopfle Devinney states, the "reader understands the power of the supernatural and values the principles whereby the apparently weak are strong, the apparent losers are winners, the apparent poor are rich" (1989, 32).

Two particular German traits of this novella, or short novel, merit attention. The novella was a popular nineteenth-century literary form of fiction. Its distinguishing feature from the novel is a one-dimensional course of action that usually culminates in a dramatic conclusion. Von le Fort was an aristocrat of Protestant origin who had converted to Catholicism. As a noblewoman in the best sense of the word and as a very self-confident aristocrat, she also displayed a religious tolerance that was unusual at the time the work was written. Catholics, who had been mostly excluded from mainstream German literature, tried to reestablish themselves during the first quarter of the twentieth century. Gertrud von le Fort fitted this context perfectly. One of her mentors was Carl Muth (1867–1944), editor of *Hochland*, an Austrian journal devoted to publishing Catholic authors of a new generation. While her protofeminism and protoecumenism appear limited from today's perspective, she undoubtedly was a pioneer in both domains. *Die ewige Frau; Die Frau in der Zeit; Die zeitlose Frau (The Eternal Woman; Woman in Time; Timeless Woman*, [1934] 1954) traces the three traditional women's roles as the betrothed (*sponsa*), the virgin (*virgo*), and the mother (*mater*). But while she ascertained the important role of women in religious life, von le Fort's fiction far transcends the fairly traditional role that she assigns to women in that work. Her social background grounded her thinking in a larger European context—again, quite unusual for a nonpolitical German writer at that time.

The major Christian theme of *The Song at the Scaffold* is one of calling on God in times of fear. As such, it echoes a familiar prayer from the communion rite of the liturgy of the Mass: "protect us from all anxiety as we wait in joyful hope for the coming of our Savior, Jesus Christ." In a more positive sense, it reflects the mystery of divine grace in the face of adversity. It also echoes Psalm 4, verse 1, which is recited as part of the Sunday prayer of Compline: *in tribulatione dilatasti mihi* (thou hast enlarged me when I was in distress). This theme of overwhelming fear was the main reason why von le Fort's novella produced such a fascination in Christian existentialists, such as the German Reinhold Schneider (1903–1958) and the French writer Albert Béguin (1901–1957). In the work, Blanche moves from a spoiled adolescent terrified by unspecified fears, to a young woman torn by self-doubt, to a self-confident witness for her faith. Both a victim and a mirror of the turbulent times, she panics and betrays her vocation and her fellow nuns. The final scene is an existential moment of finding herself and choosing to be true to her vocation.

A dominant secular theme in the work is the pernicious power of mob justice. After World War I, Germany was a very violent society, even during the Weimar Republic and before the Nazi takeover. Always on the brink of social and economic chaos, the analogy to prerevolutionary and revolutionary times in France was obvious. Von le Fort's brother, a violent rightist, was ultimately responsible for involving her in a harsh learning experience about the causes and effects of civil violence. His persecution made her take over the administration of her family's estate and provided an authentic object lesson in how uncertain times make their demands on individuals who are set in charge of others, those who try to lead and protect their flock. That two of the three protagonists in *Song at the Scaffold*, Madame Lidoine and Marie de l'Incarnation, represent two very different views of how a religious superior should react to hostile worldly power demonstrates this issue. Von le Fort presents these differing attitudes in a convincing and non-judgmental way.

CRITICAL RECEPTION

Dramatist Lavery Emmet produced a two-act version of *The Song at the Scaffold* that premiered in New York in 1948. But more importantly, von le Fort's novella inspired the French writer Georges Bernanos, whose play *Dialogues des Carmélites* (1948), his only dramatic text, became a cornerstone piece of the "New Catholic Theater" in postwar France. Albert Béguin's text edition of the work appeared in 1951 in Paris (with an introduction by Paul Claudel) and was released simultaneously in a German translation, *Die begnadete Angst* (Blessed Fear), in Zurich. It is ironic that Bernanos's version far exceeded von le

Fort's original in terms of critical reception. In part, this is due to the powerfully nuanced dialogue of Bernanos's script, which is divided into five acts and some sixty gripping scenes. Every character is very distinct. As Yvonne Guers states in her introduction to Bernanos's text, "There is poetry in the Chevalier's words: Marie de l'Incarnation speaks with dignity and pride; Constance, with a simple transparency. Mère Lidoine, a peasant's daughter, draws on proverbs and popular lore. The old Mother Superior speaks in biblical metaphors, beautiful in their simplicity, whereas Blanche's father speaks the language of everyday conversation and of solid common sense" (13). Other reasons for the success of Bernanos's version are obvious. At the time he composed the play he was an accomplished writer at the height of his craft who inserted many of his major literary themes—grace, rejection, and even hatred of the self—into the story. Bernanos shifts the emphasis between Blanche and the community of Carmelite nuns. Sister Constance, with her practical spirituality of simplicity based on that of Thérèse of Lisieux, stands in sharp contrast to the heroine's insecurity. The end, when Blanche follows her fellow sisters to their death, provides a more detailed portrayal of the fear and anguish that the heroine undergoes in order to overcome her existential anxieties.

After a lifetime of advocating right-wing and monarchist causes, in his final years Bernanos realized the fallacies of these attitudes. He died a believing Catholic but an entirely disillusioned man. He must have felt an elective affinity to the work of von le Fort, his traditional German-Prussian counterpart, and *Dialogue of the Carmelites* reflects this insight. He certainly shared von le Fort's negative view of the French Revolution as an antiroyalist movement. But even more importantly, he was literally dying while working on the play and it was nearly left unfinished. Many of his own anxieties and his fear of death resonate in his version. In addition, his experience of the horrors of World War II influenced his writing. His play, therefore, is far more intense than the source text from which he worked. A film version of Bernanos's play, by Raymond Bruckberger and P. Agostini, was released in 1960.

Francis Poulenc's (1899–1963) opera, *Dialogue des Carmélites*, had its world première at La Scala in Milan in 1957. The opera is composed in the original and personal neoclassicist style that is so marked in other Poulenc works, and it contains passages of lamentation that are particularly haunting. The libretto is based on the script by Bernanos, and Gertrud von le Fort's novel is also acknowledged as a source. The opera compresses the plot into three acts and twelve scenes. The two major changes, contributing to a powerful development of the *angst* theme, are the omission of the governess and a very impressive expanded death scene of the old prioress, Mme de Croissy. Already in von le Fort's story this character had been doubting the true vocation of Blanche. But close to her death, she slips from the anguish of *peur de la mort* (fear of death) into a delirious agony, doubting the validity of her own vocation. Her final desperation thus foreshadows Blanche's fear in very negative terms. In Poulenc's version, the main emphasis is given to the four female figures. The requirements of an opera are met in that the role of the narrator and his distancing effect are practically eliminated, and the four nuns represent symmetrically four distinctive experiences of faith in the face of death and martyrdom. The opera remains in the international repertoire and was recently performed, for example, at L'Atélier d'Opéra de l'Université de Montréal, in February 2003.

NOTE

Gertrud von le Fort, *The Song at the Scaffold. A Novel of Horror and Holiness in the Reign of Terror*, trans. Olga Marx (1933; Manchester, NH: Sophia Institute Press, 2001). All references are to this edition.

WORKS CITED

Bernanos, Georges. 1965. *Dialogues des Carmélites*, ed. and intro. Yvonne Guers. New York: Macmillan.

Bernanos, Georges, and Francis Poulenc. 1957. *Dialogues des carmélites. Opera en trois actes et douze tableaux*. Choeur et Orcherstre de l'Opera de Lyon, Kent Nagano. 1992, released by Virgin Classics Ltd., London.

Bush, William. 1999. *To Quell the Terror: The Mystery of the Vocation of the Sixteen Carmelites of Compiègne Guillotined July 17, 1794*. Washington, DC: Institute of Carmelite Studies.

Klopfle Devinney, Margaret. 1989. *The Legends of Gertrud von Le Fort: Text and Audience*. New York: Peter Lang.

le Fort, Gertrud von. [1924] 1938. *Hymns to the Church*, trans. Margaret Chanler. London: Sheed and Ward.

———. [1928] 1932. *The Veil of Veronica*, trans. Conrad M. R. Bonacina. London: Sheed and Ward.

———. [1934] 1954. *The Eternal Woman; Woman in Time; Timeless Woman*, trans. Marie Cecilia Buehrle. Milwaukee, WI: Bruce Publishing Company.

———. 1934. *The Pope From the Ghetto: The Legend of the Family of Pier Leone*, trans. Conrad M. R. Bonacina. London: Sheed and Ward.

———. 1952. Foreword to *Vom Paradox des Christentums* (collected essays by Graham Greene), 9–23. Zürich: Arche.

———. 1965. *Hälfte des Lebens Erinnerungen*. Munich: Ehrenwirth.

BIBLIOGRAPHY

Bush, William. *Georges Bernanos*. New York: Twayne, 1969.

Kranz, Gisbert. *Gertrud von le Fort: Leben und Werk in Daten, Bildern und Zeugnissen*. Frankfurt am Main: Insel, 1976.

Meyerhofer, Nicolas J. *Gertrud von le Fort. Köpfe des 20. Jahrhunderts*, vol. 119. Berlin: Morgenbuch/Spiess, 1993.

O'Boyle, Ita. *Gertrud von le Fort: An Introduction to Her Prose Work*. New York: Fordham University Press, 1964.

Schmidt, Josef. "Gertrud von Le Fort." In *Dictionary of Literary Biography, German Fiction Writers, 1885–1913*, ed. James Hardin, vol. 66, no. 1, A–L, 306–10. Detroit: Bruccoli Clark Layman, 1988.

— Josef Schmidt

Denise Levertov [1923–1997]

The Stream and the Sapphire

BIOGRAPHY

Poet and essayist Denise Levertov, who died in 1997 at the age of seventy-four, has been published and widely sought for over half a century. She was born in 1923 in Ilford, Essex, England, to a father by the name of Levertoff, a Russian Jewish scholar who became an Anglican priest, and to a Welsh mother who was raised a Congregationalist. Both were active in political and humanitarian causes, including helping Jewish refugees in England during World War II. Levertov carried on this legacy of scholarship, religious belief, and social activism—she became not only a major figure within post-1960s American literature but also an activist in the civil rights, feminist, and antiwar movements. Levertov came to the United States after the war in 1948, newly married to the American writer Mitch Goodman, and she was naturalized as a citizen in 1955. Significantly influenced by the imagist poet William Carlos Williams, she thereafter began to identify herself primarily as an American poet.

Levertov's first book of poems, *The Double Image* (1946), began her long career in poetry, which culminated in more than twenty collections as well as numerous translations and essays published in her lifetime. Her last publications include *The Life Around Us: Selected Poems on Nature* and *The Stream and the Sapphire: Selected Poems on Religious Themes*, both published by New Directions in 1997, and the collection *This Great Unknowing: Last Poems*, published after her death.

Early in her career, Levertov was associated with the Black Mountain poets, a group of avant-garde writers including Charles Olson, Robert Creeley, and Robert Duncan who wrote in open-verse form that resisted mimesis in art. In its organic style, Levertov's poetry uses the technique that most fits the initiation as well as the unfolding of the poem. Nature is a frequent subject of her poetry, often interwoven with strains of political and social awareness. During the late 1960s, her work concentrated on political and social issues, such as protest against the Vietnam War. Since the 1970s, her poems have been highly regarded in feminist circles, testifying to the feminist nature of their form and content. In later decades, Levertov's work provided a Christian witness. Around 1981, she converted to the Christian faith, and she entered the Roman Catholic Church in the early 1990s. Christian poets whom she was influenced by include T. S. Eliot, George Herbert, Gerard Manley Hopkins, Henry Vaughan, Thomas Traherne, Abraham Cowley, and Richard Crashaw.

In its thirty-eight poems, *The Stream and the Sapphire* exhibits Levertov's religious doubts and affirmations. Selected from seven previous collections dating as early as 1978, these poems attest to the fact that religion was not just a concern that arose in her later works. Poems here come from *The Sands of the Well* (1996), *Evening Train* (1992), *A Door in the Hive* (1989), *Breathing the Water* (1987), *Oblique Prayers* (1984), *Candles in Babylon* (1982), and *Life in the Forest* (1978). In the author's careful assembly of these previously published poems, *The Stream and the Sapphire* reenacts her pilgrimage of faith. These poems exemplify, as does Levertov's life, that "Faith's a tide" that only recedes from our lack of use (*The Stream and the Sapphire*, 26).

SUMMARY

Arranged in thematic groupings, the poems in *The Stream and the Sapphire* chart the poet's journey from doubt to faith. As Levertov claims in her foreword, they "trace" her "own slow movement from agnosticism to Christian faith, a movement incorporating much of doubt and questioning as well as of affirmation" (vii). The combined effect of the poems is one of rich metaphor and an intimate persona. Reflective of the poet's social activism before and after her conversion to Catholicism, Levertov's faith expression is inextricable from the needs of the real world. Moreover, the faith she affirms in the poems is substantiated, testifying to the lived nature of faith while celebrating the infinite reasons to believe. Levertov's persona takes nothing at face value but only the present face of God.

The collection invites the reader to delight in the hits and misses of meditation, mystical embrace, prayer, and faith: this is the significance of the "stream" and the "sapphire" of the title. As Levertov illustrates in a poem addressed to the Lord entitled "The Flickering Mind," it is we as human beings who try and try again to focus our minds, hearts, and souls as we seek "the sapphire [we] know is there"; that is, the jewel in the midst of the "stream" of everyday life (15, 16). The poet's expressions of faith indeed arrive at the sapphire of intimacy with God the Father, Jesus the Son, and the Holy Spirit, but not before much failure, fear, questioning, resistance, and risk.

MAJOR THEMES

In her essay "Work that Enfaiths" in the collection *New and Selected Essays*, Denise Levertov shares her own personal struggle for how to account for "the suffering of the innocent and the consequent question of God's nonintervention, which troubled [her] less in relation to individual instances than in regard to the global panorama of oppression and violence." It was in the writing of poetry, Levertov reveals, "through images given me by creative imagination while pondering this matter—that I worked through to a theological explanation which satisfied me" (1992, 251). The explanation at which she arrives is effectively conveyed in her poetry, which recognizes the responsibility human beings have for one another through the grace of God.

In *The Stream and the Sapphire*, Levertov utilizes both a poetics of protest and a poetics of praise to indict humankind's failure to respond to grace through ethical action. Likewise, the twentieth century's most prominent Catholic theologian of grace theology, Karl Rahner, defines grace as the enabler and nourishment of ethical response; he asserts that grace cannot be thought of independently of one's personal love of God and one's consequent treatment of other humans (1975, 179, 180). Grace, as conveyed by Levertov, is the absolute fulfillment of one's being; it both enables and nourishes one's ethical actions.

Levertov's poetics refuses complacency with regard to the needs of the world and resists giving in to despair. In the essay "Poetry and Peace: Some Broader Dimensions," collected in *New and Selected Essays*, she articulates the necessity of both a poetics of protest, a record of struggle, and a poetics of praise for life and a vision for the future (1992, 169). The first type she defines in the essay "Poetry, Prophecy, Survival" (also in *New and Selected Essays*) as a "poetry of anguish . . . anger . . . rage . . . [that] has the obvious functions of raising consciousness and articulating emotions" (143, 144). However, she asserts, "we need also the poetry of praise, of love for the world, the vision of the potential for good even in our species" (144). Without the second type balancing the first, Levertov argues, "we lose the reason for trying to work for redemptive change" (144). Poems of protest and poems of praise help us "to know the dimension of community," to recognize "that we humans are not just walking around on this planet but that we and all things are truly, physically, biologically, part of one living organism" ("Poetry and Peace," 169).

In a poem in *The Stream and the Sapphire* entitled "Standoff," Levertov describes the lethargy of humanity: we allow oppression and violence to occur, the needy to be forgotten. Her narrator concludes in a prophetic tone, wondering when we will actually "dare to fly" (18). This sentiment is also conveyed in the sequence "Psalm Fragments." The section of this poem entitled "Tyrant God" lists the various accusations that human beings hurl at God. Yet, the speaker's resolution is clear as she implies that such accusations arise out of human rationalizations: "Scapegoat god" (21). This poem suggests that the human denial of God's existence is an escape from responsibilities and accountability.

According to Thomas Merton, peace activist, poet, Trappist monk, and friend of Levertov, acts of protest against injustice and efforts for global social activism are in accord with the unconditional love of God. Liberation theologians are oriented toward the future, hope for a better society, and are concerned with the impact of religious belief in cultural and social transformations. Grace as a liberating force informs much of Levertov's religious writing. For example, the poem "Dom Helder Camara at the Nuclear Test Site" details a peace demonstration as an imperative of religious faith. The Mass and peace gathering held at a nuclear test site is conducted by the Gandhian archbishop from northeastern Brazil, Dom Helder Camara, who was significant in the Latin American liberation movement that began in the 1960s. Following the service, the participants enter the forbidden ground, where arrest awaits them. On the site, they are placed in wire-fenced enclosures and must wait for hours to be charged with criminal activity and then released to a "freedom that's not so free" (48). United in their service to God, they begin to dance as though they are performing a ritual. The sense of community, commitment, and the interconnectedness of the gathered people is revealed in this action. The demonstrators dance together at the center of life, conveying the jubilance and praise that accompanies one's response to grace.

Levertov articulates the pain, suffering, destruction, and inequalities in the world while also providing visions of hope that create the potential for a better future. She particularly points to hope through the immanence of God's grace culminating in the living Jesus as Son of God and ethical model. As liberation theologians and activists believe, "God's liberating grace enters to change the situation" of the oppressed and the unjustly imprisoned (Duffy 1993, 69). According to Karl Rahner, grace enters daily life experience as a reality given by God; our history and God are intertwined and made one in Jesus Christ (1975, 266). Levertov's persona envisions a world that is fed and satisfied by the Incarnation of the Son of God.

In the poem "On the Mystery of the Incarnation," the poet reflects upon the potential for evil in humanity and considers how, for the sake of the salvation of humanity, grace became flesh. It is when we witness the horrors of human history unfolding and recognize our own sins that we realize that no other creature is Godlike. God became flesh, despite our failures, to provide us with salvation: it is for the sake of faulty creatures that the Word enters the world "as guest, as brother" (*The Stream and the Sapphire*, 19).

Levertov explores the myriad ways grace is particularized in personal experience. In "The Avowal," for example, she uses several simple, yet profound analogies to illustrate a human being's acceptance of grace. The poet's figurative language here provides a sense of the oneness of grace in the deep embrace of the Creator God: our relationship to God is likened to our bodies afloat in water and to hawks steadied on currents of air. As in these images, Levertov's poems also highlight the risk and courage that are involved in trusting God. Human persons are neither passive nor dominant but risk being receptive to grace. "Psalm Fragments," for example, images faith as a hammock that hangs by a single thread tied to weak twigs that do not break. "Suspended" also stresses the risk involved in trusting God: the narrator's hands cling to "God's garment in the void," yet, although she is desperately grabbing, she does not fall (24). Levertov insists that God's grace is faithful in sustaining us.

As noted, Levertov's poetry couples her gifted imagination with her genuine ethical concerns. One such concern is that of women's condition in the world. Several poems in *The Stream and the Sapphire* reclaim a feminine agency for Christianity and challenge its paternal base of authority. In two poems, Levertov aligns herself with Julian of Norwich, the fourteenth-century mystic. Both "The Showings: Lady Julian of Norwich" and "On a Theme from Julian's Chapter XX" uphold Julian as a spiritual authority. In these poems, the speaker emphasizes the spiritual aggressiveness of Julian as well as her God-given commission in life, intellectual ingenuity, boldness, and courage. In her book *Revelations of Divine Love*, also called *Showings*, Julian gives account of the "showings" or visions she received from God as she lay deathly ill. One of these visions involves the Lord putting in her hand a "little thing" the size of a hazelnut. Julian asks the Lord what this means, to which he responds: "It is everything that is made." In this little thing, "round as a ball," Julian states that she sees three properties: "God made it . . . God loves it . . . God preserves it" (1978, 131). Levertov weaves this famous story through the six parts of "The Showings: Lady Julian of Norwich." As the poem's speaker addresses Julian, she relates contemporary life to Julian's time. Astounded by Julian's revelation, she asks whether we also are expected to look at the "little thing" in her hand and accept her explanation of God's love and care for all that exists. The second part of the sequence depicts Julian, devoted to the spiritual life of an anchoress, as a woman of authority and determination, having become an anchoress of her own free will. The poem reveals that she had not married, and her empowered state as a single, contemplative individual is emphasized. Julian's one longing is to witness God. Her desire to receive "three wounds" causes the speaker to respond in shock at the boldness of this request.

Levertov focuses on the fact that Julian is a female living in a patriarchal culture who is obedient to God's will rather than to the demands of that culture. In the poem's fourth part, Levertov juxtaposes images of Julian's vibrant childhood with the adult Julian who receives the hazelnut-like object from the Lord. This juxtaposition depicts her empowerment as a young girl, as the seed that was cultivated in her fertile childhood prepared her for her later role as a spiritual guide and emissary. The speaker reveals that God has placed the entire universe into the hands of this woman, the same hands that once may have held "a newlaid egg, warm from the hen," given to her by her mother (*The Stream and the Sapphire*, 54). Using this analogy of the hazelnut-object and the newlaid egg, Levertov's verse suggests a connection between creation and the feminine. However, it is not a maternal calling that Julian receives but rather one of devotion and contemplation—a spiritual rather than a physical birthing.

Levertov relates Julian's medieval revelations to the speaker's—and the reader's—contemporary times, and she concludes that Julian is a trustworthy guide in the modern world. Her strength, courage, steadfastness, and integrity are likened to an acrobat, clinging to a delicate "high-wire" of faith (58). In retelling the life of this spiritual foremother, Levertov reminds readers, among other things, that feminist rebellion and resistance are nothing new in the history of Christianity. As Alicia Ostriker asserts, "Christianity throughout its history has produced wave after wave of anti-institutional reform." Feminist rebellion, Ostriker continues, "against fathers, husbands, and political authorities on Christian grounds" is not at all "confined to the twentieth century: it is a key theme in Christian martyrology, in the lives of the female saints, in women's conversion narratives; indeed, wherever women's spirituality has arisen as an independent force, there we are again reminded that we are to call no man father, master or Lord, and that 'whosoever humbleth himself shall be exalted' (Matthew 23: 1–12)" (1991, 13). Furthermore, contemporary women poets such as Levertov read the Bible with an eye toward discerning the feminine nature of God. Biblical scholars have begun to rediscover Sophia from Scripture, claiming that translators of the Old Testament obscured the feminine characteristics of this figure by translating her name as "Wisdom." Like other contemporary women thinkers, Levertov reclaims and revalues Sophia in her poetry.

In the poem "'I learned that her name was Proverb,'" the very title immediately refers to the "learning" of a name that is generally not spoken; that is, to a feminine conceptualization of the divine. Such "secret names" as that of Proverb, Levertov's poem asserts, in everyday life draw us nearer to the mysteries of heaven and grace. The failure to attribute the name of Proverb to God, according to feminist theologians, results from a culmination of factors, including the failure to find femininity in God; the insistence that woman is derivative from and hence secondary to man and maleness; the assumption that woman is character-ized by passivity, which is in opposition to God and creation; and the tendency to identify woman with bodiliness as opposed to transcendence (Loades 1990, 5). The learning of the name of Proverb for Levertov's speaker is one of the steps that will lead us deeper into a reality that for now we can only ponder.

The task of feminist theologians is to reread and reinterpret the biblical text in order to restore women's stories in our understanding of early Christianity and to reclaim this history as the history of women and men of the Christian faith. The central female figure Levertov revalues is Mary, the mother of Jesus. She depicts Mary as an active agent in Christian history and relates her courage to that of women and men in the contemporary world. The poem "Annunciation" highlights Mary's consent to bear the Son of God. The poem's epigraph, taken from the sixth-century Greek Agathistos Hymn, sets the stage for the poem: an affirmation and celebration of Mary's body as the "space for the uncontained God" (*The Stream and the Sapphire*, 59). The poem engages persuasive rhetoric: the speaker confronts the reader with significant points to consider in relation to Mary's consent. The speaker reminds the reader that we are familiar with church plays and sermons in which the story of the birth of Jesus is told and in which there are certain predictable props setting the scene. But the speaker dismisses such props in light of what is often neglected in the stories of The Annunciation and Nativity: Mary as an active agent. While the Church places emphasis on Mary's obedience, we seldom hear of her courage. The speaker defends this claim by insistently reminding the reader that Mary did not become pregnant without her prior acceptance of the call to carry the Son of God in her womb. She extrapolates, invoking the Judeo-Christian belief of free will. Continuing the rhetorical strategy in the next stanza, the speaker relates the act of Mary's acceptance to people of today, referring to the fact that often we do things against our natural inclinations; furthermore, there are moments when there are opportunities of grace presented to us that are *not* taken, out of fear or lack of conviction. However, when we turn away from these opportunities, they close before us just like the womb of Mary would have closed had she refused the calling. This imagery evokes Mary's act in allowing her body to receive the engendering spirit. Levertov's depiction of Mary not only celebrates courage and intuitiveness but also emphasizes the dependency the Son of God had upon Mary. The speaker tells of the time when Mary will give birth to the Son of God, who will need her affection and care. She acknowledges the baby will need Mary's milk and love; that is, that her agency will continue after the birth of the child.

"The Servant-Girl at Emmaus" also enlightens the reader on biblical women, particularly the women who saw Jesus after he arose. This poem was inspired by the Velázquez painting that depicts a young black girl ready to serve the meal to Jesus and the disciples he has met on the Emmaus road after the Resurrection. The poem captures the young girl's expression, one that Levertov describes in her notes to the volume as "acutely attentive" (88). The speaker imagines the girl eagerly listening and watching the man she suspects is Christ. The poem highlights the fact that no one but the black servant girl—one of the most marginalized of persons then and now—recognizes that the strange guest is Christ, as the disciples will soon in the breaking of the bread.

Besides their ethical dimensions and focus on biblical characters and women's issues, the poems in *The Stream and the Sapphire* also emphasize an intense engagement with mystical experiences of God. Levertov's mystical poems resonate an air of "unknowing" reflective of the Christian mystical tradition of the fifth- or sixth-century philosopher Pseudo-Dionysius as well as that of *The Cloud of Unknowing*, a treatise on centered prayer by an anonymous English monk of the late fourteenth century. For example, the momentary status of the mystical "impulse" is the focus of "Flickering Mind," in which Levertov's speaker laments her inability to remain centered on God. "To Live in the Mercy of God" and "'In Whom We Live and Move and Have Our Being'" locate the innate capacity of human beings to seek a relationship with God. In these poems, Levertov evokes images of nature to describe the mercy and love of God, and she suggests that these qualities are as unassuming, unconditional, and abundant as a waterfall, pouring down upon the rocks, "flung on resistance" (32). Moreover, the understanding of self that Levertov's poetry conveys is a thing not fully knowable until the afterlife. In "'I learned that her name was Proverb,'" humans are spiritually drawn "towards the time and the unknown place" where all will make sense (8). In "The Beginning of Wisdom," the poet praises the wisdom of a life of faith yet acknowledges the limits to what humans can know in this life. "Human Being" and "Of Being" emphasize the mystery of faith while viewing prayer and praise as stepping stones in approaching this mystery. "Human Being" conveys the fact that, despite the doubt and spiritual wanderings that we humans undergo, there are still times when we seek ritual and need to give thanks to God. Human beings experience both times of "doubt" and moments of "praise." In "Of Being," the speaker acknowledges that happiness in life is limited and is not the ultimate experience: rather, the highest experience of humanity is dancing or kneeling before the mysteries of God.

Levertov's "To Rilke," a poem in the collection *A Door in the Hive*, describes one of the twentieth century's most celebrated religious poets as "the enabling voice" that leads readers on their journey. Yet Levertov herself provides this enabling voice, guiding readers through the indeterminate and paradoxical sedimentation that the postmodern condition has stirred as she speaks Christian truths that give meaning and sustenance to humankind's journey.

At various times in history, such as in the 1960s, poetry has played a role both in the formation of political efforts and in the expression of the hopes and frustrations with these efforts. In such times, Cary Nelson finds that "poetry was not only a valid place to comment on [political] matters . . . but also one of the places where political consciousness was forged" (1989, 128). Not only can poetry motivate people toward action and instill hope and vision, but, as Nelson states, "[i]n the process, other categories of social meaning begin to change as well, for the nature of what people take to be 'political,' the issues considered necessarily part of the valid domain of politics, are also continually at issue in such renegotiations of the discursive registers of social life" (128). Levertov asserted that she sought poetry that "while it does not attempt to ignore or deny the ocean of crisis in which we swim, is itself 'on pilgrimage,' as it were, in search of significance underneath and beyond the succession of temporal events" (1992, 4). *The Stream and the Sapphire* speaks to contemporary readers who seek direct encounters with God and who refuse to isolate love and responsibility for the human other and the world from one's devotion to God. Levertov's erudite and highly crafted religious poetry is timely in an age of postmodern suspicion of absolutes and of disillusionment with the notion of selfhood, for she articulates an identity that is learned and lived in relation to God the Father, Jesus the Son, and the Holy Spirit, both at the level of abstract discourse (that is, through the medium of poetry) and at the level of human experience.

CRITICAL RECEPTION

Levertov is considered one of the twentieth century's finest writers of poetry in English. She has been widely appreciated, studied, and recognized. Having garnered a significant audience over decades of published poetry and essays, Levertov's postconversion poetry also won respect, to her surprise. Yet, due to the fact that her notoriety as a master of verse, feminist writer, and activist came about decades before her conversion to Catholicism and the writing of poetry that affirmed the Christian faith, coupled with the common bias against contemporary Christian voices in mainstream anthologies, Levertov's explicitly Christian poetry has not received the attention, recognition, and exposure that it deserves in either the mainstream canon or in literary criticism. As critic Paul A. Lacey explains,

> The most negative criticism of her recent work argues that she has lost much of the energetic, exploratory quality of her earlier poetry and that her attention to form has suffered in her preoccupation with personally relevant religious and political themes. Citing her political poetry or her religious poetry as evidence of a falling-off from her previously high achievement, critics accuse her, to borrow a phrase originally applied to Robert Browning, of selling her poetic birthright for a pot of message. (1997–98, 17)

Despite this criticism, religion and literature journals such as *Renascence*, *Christianity and Literature*, and *Religion and Literature* have recognized Levertov's religious poems as significant contributions to twentieth-century American literature as a whole and to Christian literature in particular.

More recent criticism provides a revised treatment of Levertov's religious poetics. I consider in my article "Grace and Ethics in Contemporary American Poetry: Resituating the other/Other, the World, and the Self" (2000) Levertov's distinctive use of a poetics of grace and ethics: her poetry addresses contemporary agnostic and atheistic views of God by indicting humanity's failure to respond to grace. Levertov affirms the commonality and particularity of grace in specific terms of the incarnated grace of Jesus Christ through rich metaphor and the inventive use of open form that is her trademark.

Levertov as a religious poet is the focus of a special issue of the journal *Renascence*, "Spirit in the Poetry of Denise Levertov," edited by Ed Block Jr. (1997–98). This issue, which includes an interview with Levertov, conveys that her poetic excellence is well intact as she explores religious faith in her later poetry to a degree that she never had before. Her maintaining of aesthetic as well as ethical integrity is considered in the work of several critics, including Edward Zlotkowski (whom Levertov compliments as the one critic who seemed to really "get her") in his articles "Levertov and Rilke: A Sense of Aesthetic Ethics" (1992) and "Presence and Transparency: A Reading of Levertov's *Sands of the Well*" (1997–98).

A "new perspective" indeed is being given to Levertov's religious poetry, as in the solid collection *Denise Levertov: New Perspectives*, edited by Anne Colclough Little and Susie Paul (2000) and published by Locust Hill. This volume includes several essays that articulate the spiritual themes in Levertov's poetry: tracing the patterns of the spiritual world; identifying the evolving image of "Jacob's ladder" in a number of poems; elaborating on the liturgical mode in Levertov's expression of Christianity; and exploring how the author's technique incorporates the journey of faith and the encounters of belief into her poetry.

NOTE

Denise Levertov, *The Stream and the Sapphire* (New York: New Directions, 1997). All references are to this edition.

WORKS CITED

Block, Ed, Jr., ed. 1997–98. *Renascence: Essays on Values in Literature* (special Denise Levertov issue) 50, nos. 1–2 (Fall/Winter).

Duffy, Stephen J. 1993. *The Dynamics of Grace.* Collegeville, MN: Liturgical Press.

Julian of Norwich. 1978. *Showings*, trans. Edmund Colledge, O. S. A., and James Walsh, S. J. Classics of Western Spirituality Series. New York: Paulist Press.

Lacey, Paul A. 1997–98. "'To Meditate a Saving Strategy': Denise Levertov's Religious Poetry." *Renascence* 50, nos. 1–2 (Fall/Winter): 17–33.

Levertov, Denise. 1992. *New and Selected Essays.* New York: New Directions.

Little, Anne Colclough, and Susie Paul, eds. 2000. *Denise Levertov: New Perspectives.* West Cornwall, CT: Locust Hill.

Loades, Ann, ed. 1990. *Feminist Theology: A Reader.* Louisville, KY: Westminster John Knox.

Nelson, Cary. 1989. *Repression and Recovery: Modern American Poetry and Cultural Memory.* Madison: University of Wisconsin Press.

Ostriker, Alicia. 1991. "A Word Made Flesh: The Bible and Revisionist Women's Poetry." *Religion and Literature* 23, no. 3 (Autumn): 9–26.

Rahner, Karl. 1975. *The Rahner Reader*, ed. Gerald A. McCool. New York: Seabury.

Thyreen-Mizingou, Jeannine. 2000. "Grace and Ethics in Contemporary American Poetry: Resituating the other/Other, the World, and the Self." *Religion and Literature* 32, no. 1: 67–97.

Zlotkowski, Edward. 1992. "Levertov and Rilke: A Sense of Aesthetic Ethics." *Twentieth Century Literature* 38: 324–42.

———. 1997–98. "Presence and Transparency: A Reading of Levertov's *Sands of the Well*." *Renascence* 50, nos. 1–2 (Fall/Winter): 135–52.

— Jeannine Mizingou

François Mauriac [1885–1970]

Viper's Tangle and A Woman of the Pharisees

BIOGRAPHY

Born October 11, 1885, in Bordeaux, François Mauriac was the youngest of five children. His father died when François was just under two, and his mother moved with the children to her mother's home. Raised by strong-willed, assertive women, Mauriac grew up in a devoutly Catholic atmosphere. The home was frequented by nuns and priests and was marked by all the signs of nineteenth-century piety—regular prayers, strict observance of the Church calendar, and a continual watchfulness for any sign of sinful tendencies. When he was four, Mauriac suffered an injury to his eyelid, leaving him sensitive about his appearance for the rest of his life (even as an adult, he preferred to be photographed in profile); many of the characters in his novels also suffer from a sense of inner or outer disfigurement and inferiority, reflecting Mauriac's own self-image. On the whole, though, his was a happy childhood that he remembered fondly. His mother's religious rigor only bound him more closely to her—and to Catholicism. And while we can see elements of his mother in characters like the Pharisee Brigitte Pian in *A Woman of the Pharisees*, we should also note that such characters are dramatic exaggerations rather than portraits of her.

As a young man in Bordeaux, Mauriac became involved in a Catholic progressivist political movement called Le Sillon, and he published his first short story in the group's journal. He soon became disenchanted with politics (or, rather, of mixing politics with religion, as the group did), and in 1906 he moved to Paris, ostensibly to study at the Ecole des Chartes but in fact to pursue a career in literature. His first book of poems, *Les Mains jointes* (*The Clasped Hands*), appeared in 1909 and was favorably reviewed by Maurice Barrès, at the time one of France's most eminent writers. The review boosted Mauriac's confidence and launched his career. In 1913, he married Jean Lafont, and he began publishing novels. During World War I, he was declared unfit for military service (the lingering effect of a bout of pleurisy a decade earlier); he joined the Red Cross as a stretcher-bearer, but he was sent back to Paris when he became ill.

The 1920s saw Mauriac rise to prominence in the literary world with an extraordinary sequence of novels, including *A Kiss for the Leper* (1922), *Genitrix*

(1923), *The Desert of Love* (1925), and *Thérèse Desqueyroux* (1927). All these are psychologically intense, claustrophobic, often grim stories of obsession and despair, and all are set in the Bordeaux region of his youth. They made Mauriac famous as one of the most important voices of the postwar era. But while the literary world applauded him, the Catholic press began to criticize him, arguing that these novels glorified sin and failed to inculcate any moral or religious lesson. At first Mauriac shrugged off these attacks, but toward the end of the 1920s he entered a period of spiritual crisis in which he feared he was losing his faith. The years from 1928 to 1932 were a time of serious personal examination for him, and he began to think very seriously about the relationship between his faith and his art, a topic he treated brilliantly in the essay *Dieu et Mammon* (*God and Mammon*, 1929), in which he explores the complexities of what it means to be a Catholic novelist. His next novel, *What Was Lost* (1930), attempted to put his newly formulated theories into practice, to give equal weight to the realities of both sin and grace, and to give equal attention to both his art and his faith. While the novel is not entirely successful, it was a necessary step for Mauriac on the path that led to the novel many consider his masterpiece, *Viper's Tangle* (1932).

In 1932, Mauriac noticed a hoarseness creeping into his voice. Assuming the problem was minor, he consulted a doctor but learned that he had throat cancer. He endured long, painful treatments that were, ultimately, successful. During his treatment, he was elected to the French Academy, the highest honor a French writer could achieve. As he recovered from his cancer, he felt a deep gratitude for the presence and support of his family, and his next book was something of a tribute to them, *The Frontenac Mystery* (1933), which depicts the Mauriac family as the fictional Frontenacs. It is by far his most warm-hearted, optimistic work, and it marks the happy conclusion to a period of crisis.

But if his crises in both health and spirituality were now largely resolved, his artistic life seemed to decline somewhat, for the novels he wrote during the remainder of the 1930s were not nearly as successful and are relatively little read today. Perhaps it is not simplifying too much to speculate that for Mauriac, as for many other artists, a settled life is not the best inspiration; his genius came to life most intensely in moments of turmoil and uncertainty. Another such period of turmoil, though, was rapidly approaching, with the Nazi occupation of France in 1940.

Mauriac was seen from the outset of the occupation as an enemy of the Germans and of the collaborationist Vichy government. He was decried—on the street, in print, and in public lectures—as an unhealthy, unpatriotic writer and as a "Jew-lover." *A Woman of the Pharisees* (1941) is a product of the early years of the occupation; it marks Mauriac's return to greatness as a novelist. He wrote against the Nazis under the pseudonym Forez, but his identity became known, and in 1943 he was forced to hide for several months in a friend's apartment; in 1944, he once had to hide himself alone in the countryside to evade the Gestapo. But he was never captured or imprisoned. A staunch supporter of General De Gaulle (whose biography he would later write), Mauriac's stature only increased after the war. During the postwar period, he produced a great deal of journalism, and he refused to join in the general cry for vengeance against collaborationists. He was one of the very few who called for mercy during the trial of the critic Robert Brasillach (although Brasillach had in fact vigorously attacked Mauriac in his own writings), but to no avail; Brasillach became the only writer to be executed for his pro-Nazi role during the war.

Mauriac's fame and stature had become international, and his recognition came in being awarded the Nobel Prize for Literature in 1952. His Nobel address playfully alludes to the old charges the Catholic press once made against him, admitting that his novels constitute something of a "museum of horrors." But he also asserts there that his work is in fact centered on the human person "made in the image of the Father, redeemed by the Son, illumined by the Spirit."

The last two decades of Mauriac's life remained prolific, and among his very last works are the powerful novels *Un adolescent d'autrefois* (*An Adolescent of Yesteryear*, 1969) and *Maltaverne* (1970). But his greatest achievements during these decades were in nonfiction, notably in the column he wrote for the newspaper *Le Figaro* titled *Bloc-Notes*; here, among other topics, he campaigned vigorously for an end to torture in French-held Algeria. Also of great interest are his two volumes of *Mémoires Intérieures*, which are a meditative spiritual and literary autobiography. He died in 1970 at the age of eighty-five, universally recognized as one of the twentieth century's greatest Catholic writers.

PLOT SUMMARY

Viper's Tangle (*Le Noeud de Vipères*, 1932) focuses on Louis, a wealthy but deeply bitter lawyer and landowner of seventy years who has become almost consumed by his lifelong hatred for his wife and family. An early draft of the novel used the title *The Crocodile*; the phrase settled on for the final title, "viper's tangle," is used by Louis himself in describing his heart. He has for years expressed his loathing chiefly through his greed and miserliness toward his children, but as he writes we come to understand that this greed has been his way of fighting back against the overpowering sorrow of his life.

The novel is in two major parts: part one is a long letter Louis writes to his wife, intended for her to read after his death; with part two, the letter breaks off, and Louis narrates a sequence of events leading almost to his death. Following this narration, the novel concludes with several letters exchanged among his children after his death. The long letter serves as Louis's autobiography and is intended both as a self-justification and an attack on his wife. We learn that Louis grew up as a sullen, sickly boy, attracted to Voltairean antireligious sentiments; his widowed mother doted on him, but despite the wealth and lands her husband left her, she remained essentially a peasant farmer. His own sickliness combined with his acute awareness of their social inferiority made Louis into an angry and oversensitive young man. When he was twenty-one, his mother took Louis on a vacation to Luchon, where they met the Fondaudège family, an upper-class set with some aristocratic connections; they were supercilious toward Louis and his mother, but they were also in financial trouble. Before long, they encouraged a romance between Louis and their daughter Isa. She and her family dazzled Louis, and he fell in love with her; two years later, in 1885, they were married. He recalls that for those courtship years he let himself believe that he was capable of being loved—but that self-acceptance was smashed on the night, soon after the wedding, when Isa told him she was really in love with another man whom she knew a year before she met Louis. Isa had come close to scandal in this earlier relationship, and her mother, fearing her damaged reputation would render her unmarriageable, had encouraged the match between Isa and the well-off peasant Louis. On the night she confessed all this to him, Louis's life changed; after a sleepless night of profound suffering, he rose the next morning and dedicated himself to a life of hatred and revenge.

The letter he writes now, at seventy, reflects on the forty years of their marriage. They had three children, two of whom, Hubert and Genevieve, are still living. As he writes in his bedroom, in the family home in the countryside outside Bordeaux, he can hear them and Isa talking about money and the inheritance they hope to get after his death, which enrages him further and spurs on his desire to hurt them. And he reflects on Marie, the child who died of typhus at age ten. Marie was almost Christlike in her suffering and in her ability to see into her father's heart, and Louis loved her deeply—she was, in fact, the only person he ever really loved. His grief over her loss is compounded by the memory that Isa blamed him for her death, believing he had refused to spend money on a higher-priced doctor for her; the accusation is false, but of course the memory of it continues to fuel his rage toward Isa. Louis came very close to having an affair with Isa's sister, Marinette, who had run away from her husband, but at the last moment he broke it off. She later had a child with another man, and Louis came to love the boy, Luc, much as he had loved Marie; like Marie, Luc was innocent and pure, and Louis saw him as Marie's reincarnation. But Luc died in the first months of World War I, and Louis was again bereft.

As he continues his letter, Louis overhears his wife and children discussing the possibility of having him declared incompetent to ensure they get hold of his fortune. The next morning, he leaves for Paris with a plan to disinherit them. We learn that he did have an affair with a local woman some twenty years ago, and he now seeks out her and his son, Robert, planning to leave everything to him. But Robert proves to be a fool and a coward; frightened of the legal ramifications, Robert secretly tells Louis's son Hubert about the plan. Louis's plan is undone, and he now gets a telegram telling him that Isa has died. He returns, defeated, for the funeral, and finally comes to an agreement with his children, giving up all his wealth except for the house. He is surprised that he feels no resentment about it all, and he enters into a deep process of self-examination, realizing now how little he had known himself and how little he had tried to know others. After a period of grief and contrition, he begins to experience a sense of peace. His granddaughter Janine, who had had a breakdown when her husband left her, comes to live with him. Louis begins to feel needed and loved—not just by Janine but by the God he has spent his life denying. He dies in the middle of writing about this love. The novel concludes with letters among Hubert, Genevieve, and Janine about the meaning of Louis's long letter and the sincerity of his late conversion.

A Woman of the Pharisees (*La Pharisienne*, 1941) is likewise narrated by a character named Louis, but in this case the main focus is on his stepmother, Brigitte Pian, the "Pharisee" of the title. A bitter and tangled family situation is the subject of this novel as well. The narrator, Louis Pian, like many others in the novel, is a victim of Brigitte's piety.

The story opens when Louis, then thirteen, and his fourteen-year-old sister, Michèle, are living under the domination of their stepmother, Brigitte. Their father, a decent but weak-willed man, is unable to stand up to her. Brigitte is motivated in part by the desire to be a good mother to the children, but this takes the form of an almost paranoid compulsion to erase the memory of their biological mother and soon becomes a drive to control the lives of anyone within her reach. She justifies her behavior by her religious zeal, imagining herself battling against the sin she sees everywhere around her.

In the course of the novel, two different couples have their lives ruined by Brigitte. The first couple is the Puybarauds. Monsieur Puybaraud is an assistant master at Louis's school and is a good, fatherly friend to Louis. He is in love with Octavia Tranche, and makes plans to marry her. Octavia, however, is something of a protégé of Brigitte's. Brigitte becomes outraged that Octavia wants to desert her and have a life of her own; in her jealousy, she is convinced that the love of Octavia and Puybaraud is mere animal lust. There is a subtle hint that Brigitte's feelings derive from a repressed lesbian attachment to Octavia, but Mauriac leaves this merely a suggestion; certainly, Brigitte would never have been able to admit feeling such a thing, and her inability to admit it helps account for the merciless rage she develops. Despite her best efforts to instill a sense of guilt and shame into the young Octavia, the two do get married, and now Brigitte takes her vengeance. She uses her considerable influence to get Puybaraud dismissed from his teaching post, and soon the couple is living in desperate poverty. But Brigitte is not only vindictive, she is also a master of hypocritical deceit, and she manages to keep the couple in hope, convincing them she is really on their side. Eventually, Octavia dies in childbirth; her weakened physical condition is the direct result of Brigitte's manipulations and of the poverty she has arranged for the pair. To say Brigitte is guilty of murder is not an overstatement.

The story of the second couple Brigitte destroys is the more psychologically complex of the two, and if it is less melodramatic, it is also the more disturbing. Her stepson Louis befriends a schoolmate named Jean de Mirbel. Jean, who has been separated from his mother and placed under the guardianship of his arrogant uncle, is an unhappy boy; the uncle thinks the boy should be kept away from his mother in order to strengthen him and make him more manly, and the boy suffers inwardly. Things get worse for him when the uncle decides that Jean needs further discipline and sends him for the summer to live with the Abbé Calou, whom the uncle understands is a demanding taskmaster. The Abbé is indeed effective with troubled boys, but not through the kind of discipline the uncle imagines: instead, this middle-aged priest is one of the rare characters in the story who listens to other people and strives to understand them. He is, indeed, the closest the novel has to a real hero and moral center. The Abbé's village is close to the Pian family's farm, and Louis invites his young friend to visit. Soon, though, Louis's friend begins to prefer the company of Louis's sister Michèle. As their young love blossoms, Louis develops a childish anger and jealousy at being left out; his jealousy subtly mirrors that of his stepmother, Brigitte.

The crisis comes when Jean's adored mother, the Comtesse de Mirbel, arrives finally for one of her rare visits to her son. After a blissful day spent together, she goes to a nearby village to spend the night in a hotel. Jean, determined to see her again, slips out of the Abbé's house at night and bicycles to the village, where he spends the entire night hoping for a last glimpse of his mother. After some hours, she appears at the hotel window—but accompanied by a current lover, about whom Jean had known nothing. He feels more abandoned than ever, and faints. The Abbé, meanwhile, has missed him and has been looking for him; he finds the boy by the roadside in a state of nervous breakdown and takes him back. The priest nurses him devotedly, treating him as if he were his own son. Brigitte, meanwhile, finds out—from Louis—about the attachment between Michèle and Jean, and in a rage similar to the one she showed with Octavia determines to end the relationship. She sends Michèle off to a convent school and forbids all communication between the two. The Abbé, in his innocent zeal to help Jean recover, writes to Michèle urging her to write to Jean; but one of the nuns at the school intercepts the letter and informs Brigitte. She begins a campaign to blacken his character in the eyes of his superiors; her connections and her Machiavellian talents for manipulating others win the day for her again, and eventually the innocent Abbé is stripped of his parish and all but defrocked.

But before all this plays out, Jean, driven to desperation by both his mother's abandonment of him and having Michèle forbidden to him, runs away from the Abbé. He meets up with Madame Voyod, the wife of a local pharmacist, who has long nursed a grudge against the Abbé and now sees Jean as an instrument for hurting him. Mauriac depicts the Voyod couple as nearly demonic predators, comparable to the sexual evildoers of the eighteenth-century novelist Pierre Laclos. Madame Voyod runs off with Jean, not out of any love or even attraction for the boy but simply to do as much harm as she can. The Abbé has lost everything that mattered to him; his good has proven ineffectual in the face of the Voyods' malice, and he soon suffers further harm from the machinations of Brigitte.

Brigitte herself, to this point in the novel, is one of Mauriac's most monstrous characters; it is not just that she does many people great harm, but she does it in the name of her faith and Christian morality. It is no small triumph on Mauriac's part that he now shows her beginning to experience self-doubt. Her husband drinks himself to death, driven to despair when Brigitte shows him a letter from his first wife proving she had been unfaithful to him. Soon after this, Octavia dies in childbirth. Mauriac subtly deepens our view of Brigitte, and we see that she is in fact not just a monster but a deeply flawed human being. Her conscience begins to torment her; she finally begins to experience the Christian humility she has so long pretended to feel. She humbles herself in every way she can and tries to undo what she can. She confesses the truth to the Abbé (who is now living with his parents), and she consents to an engagement between Jean and Michèle. As with the case of Louis in *Viper's Tangle*, Mauriac attempts in this segment of the novel to illustrate the operations of grace on the individual soul. Years pass, and Brigitte, to the shock of everyone, especially her stepson Louis, falls in love—with a widowed Protestant doctor. She knows human love—including the physical attraction she had so long condemned in others—for the first time. The doctor dies in an accident, but Brigitte finds a kind of happiness in feeling that she remains in communion with his soul. In the last lines, Louis tells us Brigitte has finally learned that what counts is not our merits but our love.

MAJOR THEMES

Viper's Tangle and *A Woman of the Pharisees* by any standards are among Mauriac's finest and most respected works. They were written a decade apart, in very different circumstances, but they can be seen as thematically complementary, as offering two sides of the novelist's complex vision of the human condition: the first novel depicts a man who rejects God and the Church and sinks into a life of sin and misery, while the second shows a woman whose sin comes from a too-tight embrace of the Church and a dangerously narrow perception of what the Church is and means. Thus, Louis and Brigitte present two extremes, the atheist and the Pharisee. Ironically, these apparently opposite extremes have a great deal in common. The novels, considered together, can be seen as Mauriac's vision of how religion becomes twisted in the lives and minds of desperate and unhappy people. And while both novels include deeply tragic elements, both ultimately depict the operations of grace as it overcomes the wills of the protagonists.

Viper's Tangle is a brilliantly crafted novel, especially with regard to its management of point of view and plot. Choosing Louis, the "old crocodile," as the narrator is important: Louis has spent his adult life as a lawyer, and having interrogated and examined the hidden motives and desires of so many others, he has become expert at it; he now turns those powers of analysis on himself and his own life. And although he is consumed with rage and vindictiveness, he is intelligent and sensitive enough to see, as he continues writing his long letter, how he himself has wronged his wife. What begins as an indictment of her ends up being far more nuanced, and his own guilt for things he did and failed to do over the years slowly develops. Toward the end of his letter, indeed, he is on the point of a sort of conversion, almost ready to forgive the others, accuse himself, and begin to take steps to salvage what is left of his time with his wife. But this happy ending would have felt too sudden, too easy, for the novel to be completely convincing. When he overhears his family members plotting against him, all the old resentments come back to the fore and the wisdom he had almost grasped evaporates. Mauriac then sweeps us into the second half of the book and a far different kind of narrative: we are no longer looking back on a life but instead are following events as they unfold. Suspense takes over, and the novel's second half is fast-paced and artistically powerful.

The above plot synopsis necessarily omits a great many minor characters and events, but one important additional layer in the novel involves the Oedipal theme. In 1893, when Louis was a young lawyer, he defended a Bordeaux woman, Madame Villenave, accused of murdering her husband; now, many years later, writing his letter of accusation against his wife, he is drawn back to the trial for what it suggests about his own character. The case had been quite a famous one, and his success in defending the woman could have been a stepping stone for his career; he could have moved on to practice in Paris. But held back by the avarice he had inherited from his mother, and by the pettiness of his wife, he decided to stay in Bordeaux, to take the safe and sure way and simply make as much money as he could. He succeeded in the Villenave case by proving that the wife had not shot the husband—their fifteen-year-old son had, in a fit of Oedipal rage; Louis says he wrote about the case, and it even attracted the attention of Sigmund Freud (the implication is that Louis indirectly contributed to Freud's Oedipal theories, which were not published until 1897—a curious thing for Mauriac to have written into his novel since he had an abiding distrust of Freud and the new science of psychoanalysis). This case is subtly related, Louis realizes, to his own: part of his hatred for his wife is based on the contemptuous treatment she and her family gave to his mother. While Louis does not go much further with this analysis, Mauriac invites the reader to do so and thus creates a deeper and richer character out of his narrator. Conflicted relationships between mothers and sons are featured in many of Mauriac's novels; the stepmother-stepson relationship in *A Woman of the Pharisees* is another example, and there are many others. Hovering behind all of these is the archetypal example from Greek myth of Phaedra and her stepson Hippolytus, the subject of Jean Racine's great 1677 play entitled *Phaedra*; Mauriac in fact wrote a biographical study of Racine in 1928. These tortured mother-son relationships play an important part in Mauriacian psychology and in his view of what it is to be human.

In terms of the specifically Catholic themes in *Viper's Tangle*, the role played by the innocent daughter Marie is extremely important. Her suffering and early death in subtle ways operate on Louis's consciousness and, indeed, on his soul. Many Catholic novels—Graham Greene's *The End of the Affair* is another example—employ the theme of vicarious suffering: Marie in a mysterious but very real sense takes on Louis's suffering. In so doing, she pays for his sins, and her death opens the door to his redemption. This theme is less dominant in *A Woman of the Pharisees*, but it plays out in various ways in many, perhaps all, of Mauriac's novels. It is one of the most important ways in which Mauriac's universe is one with a very real, nearly palpable spiritual element: while employing the traditional techniques of the classic realist novelists, Mauriac always depicts something beyond the "real," a spiritual dimension that transcends the world of the senses and yet shapes and guides the human person in this world.

Vicarious suffering has a role in *A Woman of the Pharisees* (the suffering of Octavia, for example, paves the way for Brigitte's redemption), but the dominant theme marking this as a truly Catholic novel has to do with the role of love. It is love that finally heals the conflict between the fleshly and the spiritual, the conflict Brigitte had devoted so much of her energy to, shaping her life around what she believed to be the highly righteous desire to stamp out the needs and pleasures of the flesh. And, viewed from a certain angle, Mauriac's theology suggests that Brigitte is correct: the flesh is and should be subordinate to the spirit. But her own repressed and twisted motives turn this doctrine of transcendence into an instrument of cruelty, wreaking much pain and suffering on the lives of everyone around her. When at last Brigitte is redeemed and comes to know love, remaining in a state of love and communion even when the doctor has died, she is at peace; flesh and spirit are reconciled and harmonized. But Brigitte's redemption, like that of Louis in *Viper's Tangle*, comes about not through her own doing: Brigitte and Louis are both positively pursued by God's grace, and ultimately that grace is victorious. And this is perhaps the most important Catholic theme in Mauriac: the power of grace seeks out even the most vicious of sinners, and it is far more powerful than them and their sins. Thus, for all the "museum of horrors" that Mauriac's fictional world seems to be, it is much more important to see that this is a world presided over by a loving God—an active, intervening God.

CRITICAL RECEPTION

While both *Viper's Tangle* and *A Woman of the Pharisees* were very successful and critically acclaimed by French readers and critics, the first important study of Mauriac as a Catholic novelist written in English was that of Conor Cruise O'Brien (1952). O'Brien's study centers on the double, contradictory role of women in the novels, seeing them as both Eve and Mary, both temptation and redemption; his book is titled after Maria Cross, the central figure in Mauriac's *The Desert of Love*, who is beloved by both a father and his son. O'Brien also emphasizes the twentieth-century Catholic novel as being reactionary, a turning away from disturbing trends in the modern world—a hallmark of much modern literature, of course, not just the Catholic. O'Brien's is a highly stimulating, informed discussion, valuable to anyone beginning to study Mauriac.

Another very useful study of the Catholic novel in general is Theodore P. Fraser's. After an excellent, brief overview of the chief themes and techniques of the genre, Fraser devotes chapters to novelists from France, England, Germany, and Scandinavia. His discussion of Mauriac touches on several early novels and emphasizes *Viper's Tangle*, seeing it as "Mauriac's greatest achievement in re-creating the way of grace in a soul" (1994, 49). Also valuable as a general study of the genre is Malcolm Scott's (1990), which examines the affinities and differences between the Catholic and the realist novel. His chapter on Mauriac centers on the novelist's period of crisis in the 1920s leading up to *Viper's Tangle*.

Among the books in English devoted entirely to Mauriac, among the very best is David O'Connell's (1995), which serves both as a biography and a careful analysis of many individual works. O'Connell's book includes a strong discussion of the theme of vicarious suffering, tying it in with Catholic doctrine on the relationship between nature and grace. His reading of *A Woman of the Pharisees* is especially illuminating on the ways in which the novel suggests a kind of allegory of the condition of France in 1940 and 1941, helping us see how the novel would have been read by a contemporary and opening up yet another dimension of this rich and complex work. O'Connell's discussion of *Viper's Tangle* is also excellent, stressing the ways in which the novel is shaped by the sacrament of Penance and pre-Vatican II spirituality.

One of the foremost English Mauriac scholars is J. E. Flower (1969), and his study is an elegant analysis of Mauriac's world, psychology, and theology. It is less historically and biographically grounded than O'Connell's, although it does not neglect those elements; its strengths, though, are in its literary analyses. Flower emphasizes Mauriac's critique of bourgeois life in the novels and argues that Catholicism as such is really important only in *Viper's Tangle* and *The Dark Angels*—a provocative view, although one with which most critics would disagree. Michael Moloney's study (1958) is also primarily a literary one, with analyses well worth the student's consideration. Among the specialized studies, that by Margaret Mein (1989) is important for its discussion of Jansenism in Mauriac. Strictly speaking, Jansenism was a seventeenth-century movement stamped out as heretical, but the spirit of Jansenism lives on, expressing itself in the Catholicism of Mauriac's childhood, with its dark emphasis on sin and damnation. Its importance in forming Mauriac's thinking, and the ways in which he either adapted it or rejected it, are essential in understanding the views of grace and divine love employed in *Viper's Tangle* and *A Woman of the Pharisees*.

NOTE

François Mauriac, *Viper's Tangle*, trans. Gerard Hopkins (New York: Carroll and Graf, 1987); *A Woman of the Pharisees*, trans. Gerard Hopkins (New York: Carroll and Graf, 1987). These editions of the texts are recommended.

WORKS CITED

Flower, J. E. 1969. *Intention and Achievement: An Essay on the Novels of François Mauriac*. Oxford: Clarendon Press.

Fraser, Theodore P. 1994. *The Modern Catholic Novel in Europe*. New York: Twayne.

Mein, Margaret. 1989. "François Mauriac and Jansenism." In *François Mauriac: Visions and Reappraisals*, ed. John E. Flower and Bernard C. Swift, 147–64. Oxford: Berg.

Moloney, Michael F. 1958. *François Mauriac: A Critical Study*. Denver, CO: Alan Swallow.

O'Brien, Conor Cruise. 1952. *Maria Cross: Imaginative Patterns in a Group of Modern Catholic Writers*. New York: Oxford University Press.

O'Connell, David. 1995. *François Mauriac Revisited*. New York: Twayne.

Scott, Malcolm. 1990. *The Struggle for the Soul of the French Novel: French Catholic and Realist Novelists, 1850–1970*. Washington, DC: Catholic University of America Press.

BIBLIOGRAPHY

Kellogg, Gene. *The Vital Tradition: The Catholic Novel in a Period of Convergence*. Chicago: Loyola University Press, 1970.

Smith, Maxwell A. *François Mauriac*. New York: Twayne, 1970.

Stratford, Philip. *Faith and Fiction: Creative Process in Greene and Mauriac*. Notre Dame, IN: University of Notre Dame Press, 1964.

— Raymond N. MacKenzie

Thomas Merton [1915–1968]

The Seven Storey Mountain

BIOGRAPHY

Thomas Merton was born in Prades in the southeastern corner of France in 1915. His parents were both artists, his father, Owen, from New Zealand and his mother, Ruth, from the United States. In 1916, Merton moved with his parents to Douglaston, Long Island, where his maternal grandparents lived. His mother died there of cancer in 1921 when he was six. In 1922, he traveled to Bermuda with his father, who went there to paint. In 1925, he accompanied his father to St. Antonin Noble Val in the middle of France. Following an initial happy year at the primary school in St. Antonin, Merton spent two stressful years at the lycée in Montauban, after which his father took him to England, where he attended Ripley Court School in Surrey and later Oakham School in the English Midlands. In 1931, when Merton was sixteen, his father died of a brain tumor.

Following a trip to Italy, Merton was admitted on a scholarship in the autumn of 1933 to Clare College, Cambridge, where he studied modern languages, French and Italian. In 1934, following a high-spirited but academically undistinguished year at Cambridge, he returned to his maternal grandparents' home on Long Island and enrolled at Columbia University, where he became editor of the 1937 yearbook and art editor of the school's *Jester* magazine. In 1938, he graduated from Columbia and began work on his master's degree, subsequently writing his thesis on "Nature and Art in William Blake." In the same year he was received into the Roman Catholic Church and prepared for life as an academic, a life that had already begun with his writing of reviews for newspapers in the New York area. In this period as well, he entered into the charitable work of Baroness Catherine de Hueck in Harlem. From 1940 to 1941 he taught English at St. Bonaventure College in upstate New York. Following an ill-fated attempt to join the Franciscans, he made a retreat at the Trappist Abbey of Gethsemani in Kentucky. Forced to a decision about his vocation by the onset of World War II and the prospect of being drafted, Merton, who had decided that he could only participate in the war in a noncombative role, resolved the issue by entering the Abbey of Gethsemani in December 1941.

Although he had burned the manuscripts of some early novels when he entered the monastery, Merton had sent some poems to his friend, Robert Giroux, who submitted them for publication. Thus began a life of paradox in which the monk devoted to silence would produce over fifty books. By far the most successful of these writings was *The Seven Storey Mountain*, which came out in 1948. In 1949, Merton was ordained to the priesthood and given the name Father Louis. From 1951 to 1955 he served as Master of Scholastics, and from 1955 to 1965 as Master of Novices. From 1965 to 1968 he moved permanently into a small house on the grounds of his monastery in order to live the life of a hermit monk. In 1968, he was given permission to travel to New Mexico, Alaska, and California. In the same year he traveled to Thailand, where, on the outskirts of Bangkok, he gave a paper on Marxism and monasticism at a meeting of Asian Benedictines and Cistercians. He died suddenly in his quarters at this conference after touching a faulty electric floor fan.

PLOT SUMMARY

The Seven Storey Mountain is an autobiographical narrative in which Thomas Merton depicted the sequence of events that led to his conversion to Roman Catholicism and subsequently to his ordination and life as a Trappist monk. The title of the book alludes to Dante's *Purgatorio* and in particular to the interval in which Dante and Virgil passed through hell to the sea at the foot of the mountain of purgatory. While the purgatorial setting reflects the narrator's awareness of guilt and the need for atonement, the book is essentially hopeful in mood. Resembling the *Confessions* of Saint Augustine in structure, *The Seven Storey Mountain* depicts Merton's geographical and spiritual wanderings and the eventual resolution of the uncertainties and conflicts embedded in these wanderings.

The first part of the narrative shows Merton as a youth caught up in a nomadic search for direction following the deaths of both parents. What he gradually becomes aware of is that his search is for a place where he can find an acceptable context of meaning in which to live out his life. A crucial incident occurs on a trip to Rome during school vacation, when Merton becomes conscious of supernatural reality through looking at mosaics in the old churches of Rome. At this time he also feels himself visited by the spirit of his dead father, who thereby provides him with a needed link between his past and his emerging future. The first section of *The Seven Storey Mountain* ends on a desultory note, however, with Merton depicted as an outwardly successful but essentially unfulfilled university student.

The second part of the book involves an intense period of restless inner reflection culminating in Merton's baptism and in his desire to become a priest. In part three, Merton continues his spiritual quest while living in Greenwich Village. He subsequently becomes involved in a mission house for the poor directed by the Baroness de Hueck in Harlem. The third section's dramatic high point occurs in a scene in which Merton visits Cuba and there becomes aware of the presence of God in a transforming experience during a Mass in Havana. Following a retreat at the monastery in Kentucky, Merton resolves at last to become a Trappist monk. The section ends with the baptism and then the death of Merton's younger brother, John Paul, the only remaining member of his immediate family. The book concludes with an epilogue that breaks the narrative thread and instead offers a short, contemplative reflection on the spiritual significance of Merton's monastic vocation.

MAJOR THEMES

One of the signs of narrative excellence in *The Seven Storey Mountain* is the presence of formal, controlling motifs that branch through the book. Of these, the most commanding is that of the journey. While the effects of this motif are many-sided, what makes it effective as narrative is the narrator's projection of an increasingly intense awareness that only when he understood where he was to live his life would he understand the nature of his identity.

While he was aware of the presence of a spiritual consciousness in his father due to his father's vocation as an artist, Merton saw that essentially he had been raised in an atmosphere that encouraged a belief in the norms of humanism and self-reliance. He became aware of a very different cultural atmosphere in the town of St. Antonin Noble Val in central France, where he went to elementary school. Architecturally, the parish church in St. Antonin, Merton recognized in hindsight, formed the centerpiece of the town's visual order in that everything else in the town pointed toward it. This impression would be lasting in its influence on him, challenging a merely humanistic view of the world with its turning of the mind toward a building and a culture that symbolized the supremacy of the transcendental. A further stage in the journey toward a consciousness of the transcendental occurred during the holiday trip to Rome prior to Merton's going to Cambridge. Having tired of the ruins of imperial Rome, Merton found himself increasingly fascinated by the sacred mosaics that he encountered in ancient Christian churches—powerful images of Christ coming in judgment, for example, that suggested a world of spiritual energy and significance far beyond anything he had yet encountered.

What makes the depiction of Merton's journey so vivid is his narrative strategy, whereby in portraying his progress at any particular stage of his journey he captured the limited view of his life that he possessed at that time. Thus, the reader is made sensitively to feel Merton's uncertainty and timidity as he entered Catholic churches in New York while he was a student at Columbia in the 1930s, afraid of the scrutiny of regular churchgoers. This yielding to the perceptions of the past alternates, however, with retrospective, interpretive comment. Merton interwove these two perspectives, the contemporary and the retrospective, with considerable skill. In this way, one can move through the minds of both the young, searching Merton, who had many of the steps of his journey before him, and the older Merton, who intervenes periodically in order to show the trajectory of the whole journey. In the sequence in Rome in part one, for example, Merton recounts the episode of the apparition of his dead father at night. The narrator conveys the episode intact and refrains from taking up the question of the authenticity of the apparition so that the depicted experience lingers in the reader's mind with the same haunting air of strangeness and of hyperreality that it originally possessed. At the same time, from a long-range, retrospective point of view, a connection is created between his father's supportive, posthumous mission and his son's awakened interest in Christianity in a city that embodied the history of the faith.

Along Merton's journey the reader is provided with some picturesque and well-told anecdotes. An example is the mad car ride in St. Antonin in which Merton found himself, along with other young members of the local rugby team, in the hands of a maniacal driver intent upon running down a terrified rabbit racing ahead of the car. As they came to a sudden fork in the road in which a stone wall stood between the two sides of the fork, the rabbit, Merton adds fatalistically, "headed straight for the wall" (*The Seven Storey Mountain*, 41). While the tone of the passage is understated and humorous, its effectiveness as narration derives from the perception that this incidental car chase might have ended Merton's life then and there, thus cutting off the possibilities that were to lie before him. The anecdotal passages in *The Seven Storey Mountain* provide not only fluctuations in atmosphere but also a sense that, while Merton focused more and more intensely on his spiritual quest, life in the ordinary sense, both others' and his own, continued apace. At a deeper level the anecdotes, especially the humorous ones, convey the impression that Merton was essentially a joyful person and that his frustration and alienation proceeded not from ingrained character traits but rather from a sense of the unfulfillment of his experience in what was, after all, an active life.

What one sees as Merton slowly recounts and reviews the events that made up his young life is that all roads eventually led to his vocation by providing him finally with a range of thought and experience that were rich enough to elicit the joy that was latent within him. The steps toward the fulfillment of Merton's experience are portrayed by the narrator as indebted to both traditional Catholicism and to non-Catholic influences. In the first instance, Merton makes it clear that he was led to his destiny by the actions of other Catholics, thereby acknowledging the communal action of grace that is a part of Catholic doctrine. In this connection, people like Dan Walsh, who taught medieval philosophy at Columbia, and Father Ford and Father Moore at Corpus Christi parish in New York, are seen as important influences in Merton's conversion and vocation, as were Catholic authors such as Etienne Gilson and Jacques Maritain, who led him toward the Church. Similarly, as a reader he felt parallels between his own searching for contact with the transcendental and that of the English Jesuit poet Gerard Manley Hopkins, who had in the preceding century approached Cardinal Newman about his attraction to and indecision about Roman Catholicism.

If his experience in St. Antonin and in Rome had given Merton a sense of contact with Christian and specifically Catholic transcendentalism, other experiences, such as his visit to Cuba in 1936, reinforced his growing respect for the communal value of Catholicism. What Merton recognized on the trip to Cuba was that in a culture that was predominantly Catholic—as the United States for the most part was not—there was present a distinct social atmosphere that derived in part from the sacramental life of the Church. He felt this sense of community in a more particular way later when he noticed on his visit to the Abbey of Gethsemani in Kentucky the conspicuousness of a newly arrived postulant wearing ordinary street clothes who had joined in the liturgy with the monks. Soon thereafter, the man was given a white habit that caused him to disappear into the monastic community. For Merton, the effect was powerful, suggestively prefiguring his own possible entry into that community. He saw the change in the young man's clothes as paradoxical because in thereby becoming less visibly individual to outside observers the man had simultaneously become, Merton believed, more fully himself. What Merton perceived was that the kind of community life offered by the Church and in particular by the monastic community helped to nourish the growth of the person by sidestepping the usual, distracting demand of the ego for recognition and status.

At the same time, what strikes one about *The Seven Storey Mountain* is how often the influences on Merton's conversion were not Catholic. An example is his interest in Aldous Huxley, whose novels he had admired and whose nonfiction book, *Ends and Means*, led Merton to a discovery of the richness of both western and eastern mysticism. The most important of the non-Catholic influences on Merton was William Blake, whose parents were Protestant dissenters and who himself was at odds with institutional Christianity. Yet it was Blake, as much as anyone else, who led Merton to the Roman Catholic Church. "As Blake worked himself into my system," Merton recalled, "I became more and more conscious of the necessity of a vital faith, and the total unreality and unsubstantiality of the dead, selfish rationalist which had been freezing my mind and will for the last seven years" (190–91). This does not mean that Merton abjured the philosophy of Saint Thomas Aquinas. Indeed, in terms of the growing inclusiveness of his point of view, he valued not only Aquinas but Scholastic philosophy as well. This can be seen in his admiration for Mark Van Doren, Merton's professor and mentor at Columbia, who seemed to Merton to think and teach in a "balanced and sensitive and clear way," fundamentally "scholastic, though not necessarily and explicitly Christian" (180). Merton's attraction to medieval Scholasticism stemmed from his valuing of the primacy of being. For this reason, during his study of medieval philosophy at Columbia in the 1930s he preferred Saint Thomas's definition of God as pure act or pure being in contrast to the Platonic view of God as idea.

Merton's penchant for inclusiveness in philosophy was strengthened by Dan Walsh, who, according to Merton, was able to show how Saint Thomas Aquinas, Duns Scotus, and Saint Bonaventure threw "diverse and individual light on the same truths from different points of view," thus avoiding the "evil of narrowing and restricting Catholic philosophy and theology" (220). Merton moved toward inclusiveness without compromising his growing commitment to Catholic philosophy and theology, since he valued Catholic thought for affirming whatever was true and was inclined to be receptive to truth from wherever it came. The Hindu contemplative Bramachari, for example, unexpectedly referred him to the *Confessions* of Saint Augustine as well as to Thomas à Kempis's *Imitation of Christ*. Most impressively, in terms of inclusiveness, Merton was struck by the weightiness of the priest's sermon on hell in James Joyce's *Portrait of the Artist as a Young Man* even while recognizing Joyce's abandonment of his faith. Nevertheless, Merton maintained, the sermon was "accurate" and true to its source, the fruit of Joyce's "loyalty to the vocation of artist" (212). Merton's journey toward inclusiveness can be seen in the way he admired Saint Thérèse of Lisieux, a saint whose bourgeois culture he found unappealing, noting however that she turned the substance of her life into sainthood all the same. The meaning of this for Merton was that God's mercy was without measure, allowing for the transformation of all, including

Merton himself with his burden of guilt involving transgressions that are rather vaguely indicated in the narrative.

Merton's journey led him not only to embrace Catholicism but to feel early on in his conversion experience the need for some stronger commitment and status—that of the priesthood. Inevitably, the consciousness of a call took the form not only of a generic attraction to the priesthood but of particular forms of the priesthood. His reflections about the matter are of interest because they illustrate not only what Merton saw in the various priestly orders that he considered joining but also his discovery in the searching process of inner springs of preference in himself that were to be definitive. In particular, he decided against the Jesuits and orders of that sort that required intense activity in the world. Thus, Merton found himself drawn to orders like the Franciscans and the Trappists, which seemed to him to foster or at least to allow for what was becoming a gathering, perceived need for solitude. In this way, he reflected, he could grow in the manner in which a "plant spreads out its leaves in the sun" under the "gaze of God" (260).

In 1941, while teaching at St. Bonaventure College in New York State, Merton determined the course of his journey by choosing the Trappists. Not unlike the earlier, extraordinary experience involving the apparition of his father in Rome, he had the experience at St. Bonaventure of thinking that he heard the bells of the Trappist Abbey in Kentucky tolling in his ear, a sign from within, if not verifiably—as he himself conceded—a sign from without. If the Abbey offered him a haven from the war, he was not severing his tie with the human community in general or America in particular but rather attempting to meet America's deepest needs by winning for it the "protection and friendship of God" (325). In Merton's view, the contemplative vocation was at least in part directed toward and involved with the good of society, as his subsequent, penetrating writings on social justice were to confirm.

As has been intimated, paralleling Merton's journey forward was the retrospective journey backward by the older Merton as he considered the meaning of the direction in which he had moved. This consideration also took into account the false starts, such as that which saw him temporarily attracted to Communism. That attraction had been stimulated by his initial impression in the 1930s that Communism, more than religion, for example, had addressed itself to the relief of suffering and the combating of injustice. This same view he later heard repeated by the Baroness de Hueck, whose Christian apostolate at Friendship House in Harlem had originated in part because of the challenge posed by Communism. Merton became a part of Friendship House in 1941 prior to making up his mind to enter the Abbey of Gethsemani. In Harlem he saw that the Communists were indeed active in attempting to gain the support of the poor. He later distanced himself from his earlier attraction to Communism by noting that Communists were inclined to support a particular morality if it provided a means to the ultimate end of securing power. This was brought home to him when he realized that, although he had been initially attracted to the pacifism of Communists he had encountered, Communists entered the Spanish Civil War without any apparent qualms. Similarly, while protesting against the injustice of capitalism, the Communists, Merton observed, discredited the idea of any absolute system of ethics independent of the goals of Communism itself. What becomes apparent in the narrative is that not only is the hindsight of the older Merton brought to bear on the searching of the, to some extent, ingenuous young man he had been in the 1930s but that even that young man was, through trial and error, beginning to appreciate that the goal which he sought was not primarily political but ontological.

Another example of the illumination provided by the retrospective framing of Merton's narrative journey was his guilt over his treatment of his younger brother, John Paul, in their youthful years. Remembering their youth, he recalled his younger brother pressing to be near him only to be rejected. The story of the brothers is strengthened by the maturity of Merton's retrospective view by which, having been seasoned by a number of years in the monastic life, he realized that his exclusion of John Paul was a quintessential sin because in rejecting the "disinterested" love proffered by his brother he had sinned in an entirely "arbitrary" way, rejecting love simply because he "did not want it" (23). Merton's juxtaposing of the curiously distanced and unemotional terms "disinterested" in connection with John Paul and "arbitrary" in connection with himself registers with judicious subtlety a distinctive theological feature of sin, the fact that it is chosen.

While there are some retrospective passages in *The Seven Storey Mountain* that in their ungraceful didacticism should probably have been excised, there are many that are apt even if this may sometimes only become clear with further reflection. An example is Merton's repeated praising of France and his expressed gratitude at having been born in France. In part he was grateful to have been born a European, and although he later became an American citizen he attempted throughout his life to think of himself as a cosmopolitan whose identity and consciousness were related to a number of different cultures. For the narrator in *The Seven Storey Mountain*, however, it was not only that part of his identity was French but, more importantly, that his boyhood days in St. Antonin had fortuitously and, as it eventually seemed, providentially formed him. Thus, in later life, in a momentous visit to Corpus Christi church near Columbia University on the upper west side of Manhattan, for example, he found that images of the churches of Italy and France that he had visited in his youth came back to him. In this case, the retrospective framing is provided not primarily by the older Merton but rather—through a structured relativity in the application of the narrative technique—by the younger Merton at Columbia, who had matured sufficiently to revisit the past in order to see how his life's journey had evolved from it.

As did Saint Augustine and William Wordsworth, both among his favorite authors, Merton valued memory as a crucial instrument in constructing his autobiographical identity. Along with these authors, he realized that through memory one could recover not only incident but the sensations of sight, hearing, touch, and smell that were part of the color and texture of the original experience. These sensations and emotions, he realized, framed the experience and in a sense froze it in quasi-permanent form as a particular impression. On a number of occasions in *The Seven Storey Mountain*, Merton lays out for the reader his consciousness of the selectivity of memory and thus implicitly cautions the reader about its limits. For example, in recalling his mother, whom he had known only in his earliest years, Merton pictures her as a "thin, sober little person" who was "worried, precise, quick" and "critical" of her son. At the same time, he concedes that his grandmother's memory of his mother was quite different, evoking an image of his mother as "gay and very light-hearted" (5). Merton's way of handling this impasse is to try to explain his mother's behavior toward himself as driven by her perfectionism. In this sense, his interpretation of her behavior follows the groove of his memory of her. At the same time, in a characteristic act of inclusiveness, he goes out of his way to record an alternative view of her, an action that leads the reader to consider other possibilities. These include the possibilities that his mother might have been more complex than he had understood at the time, that his grandmother's memory of her daughter was of an earlier time than his own years with her, that the arrival of his brother, John Paul, in 1918 drew his mother's attention away from himself, and so on. That Merton in retrospect felt that he had been wounded by his mother's behavior is evident, but so is his inclusive desire to understand—even though he recognizes that the time for certainty had long passed. Nonetheless, the depiction of Ruth Merton reflects both the impressionistic selectivity of the narrator's consciousness and the concomitant tendency of that consciousness to want to widen the circle of perception.

The most intriguing aspect of the journey motif is its conclusion with its atmosphere of suspension and ambivalence. Clearly, if the narrative had reached a point of arrival with Merton's entry into the monastery, that point led to a further journey of sorts in that two competing sides of Merton's nature needed to be reconciled to his monastic vocation. The first of these was straightforward enough—the life of a contemplative. The second was more difficult to accommodate—the life of a writer. Merton referred to this writer-self as his "shadow," the "double" who had followed him into the monastery (410). The description of this bifurcated struggle forms an important part of the ending of *The Seven Storey Mountain*, keeping open the mood of tension and suspense that had characterized many of the earlier sections of the narrative. While the contemplative/writer dilemma is a secondary stream, one that is subordinated to the concluding atmosphere of blissful arrival, it holds the note of finality in check and leads the reader to wonder how the issue will be resolved.

The dilemma presented itself to Merton in the following manner. Writing took the contemplative out of the flooding light of the attentive and yet also passive awareness of God into the craft of composition with its discipline of actively fashioning art. Such a deflection Merton regarded as a dilution of the contemplative experience, and he struggled with this issue particularly through the 1940s and well into the 1950s. The effect on *The Seven Storey Mountain* as narrative is to portray the beginnings of a drama that lay ahead for Merton beyond the closing pages, resulting in a complexity that adds unexpectedly and significantly to the book's psychological and spiritual depth. Overall, one comes to understand that much of the book's value stems from this sort of introspective, dialectical journeying of the author. That inner dialectical process was in fact a search for what Merton thought of as the true self, which he finally understood could be undertaken most effectively by himself in the contemplation of the creative intelligence that had originally fashioned that self.

There are two important secondary motifs that are interwoven with the journey motif in *The Seven Storey Mountain*. The first is that of the prison, the motif that is present at the very beginning of the book. In the first section, drawing on the image of the prisoner's base, a traditional children's game, Merton extends the image of the prison throughout his narrative, elaborating its significance as he goes. For example, although he portrayed all human beings as congenitally locked within the prison of self-centeredness, he saw the artist, including his own parents, as having been liberated to some extent by the "integrity" of the artist's vocation, which lifted the artist "above the level of the world without delivering" him or her from the world (3). The journey and prison motifs connect thematically in that the rootless wanderings of Merton's life are all seen to occur within a macro-prison of contemporary materialism that spanned the world of his travels. This is a world that the narrator insists can only be transcended on an individual or micro-level, so to speak, through an act of separation from the ego analogous to that which he had chosen in entering the Abbey of Gethsemani. At the broad social level, though, there was need for a further detachment from the blind undertow of the collective will.

The prison motif is often invested with paradox and irony. An example of this sort of complexity occurs in connection with Merton's decision to join the Trappists at the Abbey of Gethsemani. Upon passing into the monastic enclosure on a December evening, he suddenly felt a fresh sense of freedom. The incident recalls Merton's earlier, transformative visit to the Abbey to make an Easter retreat. Unexpectedly on that occasion he drew back at one point, experiencing the monastery as a "prison" containing an overwhelming "spiritual pressure" (331). Once outside of the monastery, however, he underwent a sudden change in perspective in a scene of dramatic reversal through which he felt the dead weight of the outside world as never before, feeling himself longing to be back in the monastery (332–33). From this point on, Merton's picture of the outside world as a spiritual prison is sustained even if the resolution of his journey's end remains in suspension. Intensifying the motif of imprisonment, in his brief involvement in the work of Friendship House in Harlem Merton believed that the Baroness de Hueck had found a way out of the "labyrinth" and the "cauldron" of Harlem through a charitable work that reversed the world's norms and freed the ego from its captivity (348).

Another notable unifying motif in *The Seven Storey Mountain* is that of fire. Fire is, of course, implicit in the book's title, with its allusion to purgatorial purification and its accompanying echoes of Dante and of T. S. Eliot, with whose writings Merton was thoroughly familiar. In harmony with these two writers, the connection between fire and carnality is especially emphasized in the Cambridge episodes of *The Seven Storey Mountain*, in which the imagery of purgatory ripens into that of hell, a hell that Merton portrays himself as embodying. The fire motif appears most strikingly in the epilogue and is thus one of the structural devices through which the epilogue is tied to the preceding narrative. At the very end of the epilogue, the narrator suddenly claims that he must come to know "the Christ of the burnt men" (423). The asceticism of the image of the burnt men is startling following the elegiac and yet hopeful narrative denouement with its pronounced mood of arrival. The image of the burnt men is connected to the divine admonition that everything that can be "desired will sear you, and brand you with a cautery" so that "solitude" becomes the soul's only refuge (422). If in one sense Merton saw himself as fortunate in having been set on the road to purgatory, that destination involved a disciplined resistance to the world—not a resistance to the world in itself, in its creational beauty, for example, but rather a resistance to its self-proclaimed autonomy, its enclosed, self-referential way of seeing and behaving. The connection between the state of the world and the state of the self in this respect is made evident. The ascetic flames that Merton depicts as releasing one from the prison of the world are the same flames that separate one from the prison of self-absorption. They are also the flames that can lead the self to transcendence.

Apart from these prominent structural motifs in *The Seven Storey Mountain*, the book's richness as narrative arises from the writer's limpid prose and fine descriptive strokes. In addition to the vividly drawn pictures of particular characters, such as the narrator's English uncle with his white, waterfall moustache, for example, there are other, more resonant symbolic touches that reach into the heart of the book's major themes, as in Merton's suggestive observation that the Abbey of Gethsemani constituted the real capital of America, unobtrusively providing the country with an underlying spiritual life and worth that God and presumably some other Americans would not fail to recognize. The observation is striking because it suddenly makes the reader aware of the social dimension of the contemplative life that Merton had adopted and, in a sense, prepares the reader for the extensive writings in social analysis and criticism that would come from his pen in the 1960s. The rhetorical strengths of *The Seven Storey Mountain* are manifold, contributing significantly to the book's deserved reputation as arguably the most important spiritual autobiography written by an American in the last hundred years.

CRITICAL RECEPTION

The Seven Storey Mountain was an unexpected best seller from its publisher's point of view, even though Merton himself thought that it would do well, and sales have continued strong since its publication. The book appealed to the generation that had survived World War II and that found itself in need of spiritual bearings following that conflict. Since then, *The Seven Storey Mountain* has appealed to a much more diverse audience spanning different religious and cultural traditions. The reason for the book's power and appeal was well described by Robert Inchausti, who observed that Merton had translated the "rigorous ascetic traditions" of Trappist monasticism into the "language of contemporary experience" (1998, 40).

The Seven Storey Mountain has been praised by readers representing various levels of sophistication, including some as fastidious as Evelyn Waugh, who edited an abridged version of the book entitled *Elected Silence* (1949). Moreover, Merton's autobiographical narrative has had an influence in some unexpected quarters, such as on the African-American revolutionary Eldridge Cleaver, who noted in his own well-known autobiography, *Soul On Ice*, that he found himself stirred by *The Seven Storey Mountain* while serving time in Folsom Prison in the 1960s. While Cleaver rejected Merton's theism, he found that he could not, as he put it, keep Merton "out of the room" (1968, 34). Cleaver was especially moved by Merton's descriptions of Harlem. In spite of the didactic and religiously partisan sections of the book, which some critics and Merton himself regretted, *The Seven Storey Mountain* has continued to attract discussion by critics such as David Leigh (2000), who in a recent study analyzed *The Seven Storey Mountain*'s complex narrative structure and set the book prominently within the increasingly visible scholarly field of modern spiritual autobiography.

NOTE

Thomas Merton, *The Seven Storey Mountain* (New York: Harcourt Brace, 1948). All references are to this edition.

WORKS CITED

Cleaver, Eldridge. 1968. *Soul On Ice*. New York: McGraw-Hill.
Inchausti, Robert. 1998. *Thomas Merton's American Prophecy*. Albany: State University of New York Press.
Leigh, David. 2000. *Circuitous Journeys: Modern Spiritual Autobiography*. New York: Fordham University Press.
Waugh, Evelyn. 1949. Forward to *Elected Silence*. London: Hollis and Carter. pp. v–vi.

— Ross Labrie

Alice Meynell [1847–1922]

Poems

BIOGRAPHY

Alice Meynell was born Alice Christiana Gertrude Thompson on October 11, 1847, the second daughter of unconventional, artistic, and peripatetic English parents. Much of her quite bohemian childhood was spent in Italy, and Alice and her older sister Mimi (christened Elizabeth) received much of their education from their father. In adolescence, Meynell suffered through periods of ill health and depression, read the Romantics avidly, and began tentatively exercising what she called "that rhyming faculty." In 1868 she converted to Catholicism, a decision that profoundly influenced her spiritual and creative life for as long as she lived. She always saw her faith and her poetry in similar terms, those of discipline and keen control, but she embraced this discipline willingly, even lovingly. Years afterward, she wrote of her conversion: "It was by no sudden counter-revolution, but slowly and gradually that I returned to the hard old common path of submission and self-discipline which soon brought me to the gates of the Catholic Church" (Badeni 1981, 36). Her poem "The Laws of Verse" explores the paradox of the joyful liberty to be found in discipline:

> Dear laws, come to my breast!
> Take all my frame, and make your close arms meet
> Around me; and so ruled, so warmed, so pressed,
> I breathe, aware; I feel my wild heart beat.
>
> Dear laws, be wings to me! (*The Poems of Alice Meynell*, 173)

A romantic story attaches to Meynell's conversion: she was instructed in Catholic doctrine by a young priest, Father Augustus Dignam, to whom she became closely attached. Their inevitable but wrenching parting gave rise to some of her most poignant poems, including the beautiful sonnet "Renouncement," which Dante Gabriel Rossetti called one of the best sonnets ever penned by a woman.

Meynell's life and writing were to be prodigiously productive. In adulthood, settled in England, she met and married the journalist Wilfred Meynell, and the couple embarked on years of editing and writing for periodicals, including eighteen years as editors of and frequent contributors to the Catholic magazine *The Weekly Register*. Despite physical frailty and debilitating migraines, Alice Meynell worked passionately as an essayist and poet and bore eight children (seven of whom survived). Her essays, published in periodicals ranging from *The Spectator* and *The Saturday Review* to *The National Observer*, won her a devoted reading public. These essays, which varied from occasional topics to social and literary criticism, were at intervals collected and published in volumes, including *The Rhythm of Life and Other Essays* (1896), which took its name from her best-known work. W. E. Henley, one of her editors, told her, "You would write well about a broomstick" (quoted in Viola Meynell 1929, 73).

Meynell's poetic output was more sparing, and for thirteen of her busiest years as a mother and essayist she barely wrote a single poem. She was also a ruthless critic of her own work, ultimately destroying all the verses she did not consider worthy enough for publication. After the youthful 1875 *Preludes*, she published slim volumes of poetry in 1893, 1895, and 1901, and collections in 1913 and 1921; these volumes demonstrate an ever-increasing mastery of what one critic described as a "chastened" form. Her poems, few as they were, won her considerable critical acclaim. Coventry Patmore, who loved her immoderately, suggested her for poet laureate (she was twice nominated for this honor), but his admiration for her verse was widely shared by literary figures as diverse as John Ruskin, George Meredith, and Walter de la Mare. She was a central figure in the Catholic Literary Revival of the last decade of the nineteenth and first decade of the twentieth centuries, and evenings in her Palace Court home brought together and helped make a community out of diverse artists: the old guard, consisting of Aubrey de Vere and Coventry Patmore, and the new generation, including Francis Thompson, Katharine Tynan, Agnes Tobin, Hilaire Belloc, and G. K. Chesterton. Her friendships with leading writers of her day were remarkable for the passionate devotion she inspired; Patmore's attentions became so pressing she had to break off their association, but that relationship was succeeded by one of almost equal closeness with the novelist George Meredith, who insisted she would become "one of the great Englishwomen of letters" (1896, 770).

Meynell was also profoundly politically engaged. She wrote and spoke and marched for women's suffrage, taking an active part in the demonstrations of 1910 to 1912 and serving on the executive committees of at least two suffrage societies. She believed firmly in socialist ideals. Opposed to the Boer War and deeply distressed by the First World War (in which a son-in-law was killed and a son briefly imprisoned for conscientious objection), she wrote powerfully of war's horrors. When she died in 1922, her literary reputation was carefully tended by her husband and her son Francis; in 1940, a collected edition of her poems was produced, and in 1947, a centenary collection of poems and essays appeared, selected and with an introduction by the then Sir Francis Meynell.

MAJOR THEMES

Especially in her first volume of poems, the 1875 *Preludes*, Meynell shows the strong influence of the Romantic poets she adored. A number of introspective lyrics dwell on natural beauty and its effects on the perceptive poet. "In Early Spring," for example, presents a speaker who knows nature "by heart," who is so in tune with the natural world that she can understand the secrets of the "yet leaf-folded violet" and "can foretell / The cuckoo's fitful bell" (*Poems*, 3–4). As well as contemplating nature, Meynell contemplates the self, dwelling in an often melancholy vein on love, memory, and the relationship of present (and future) to past. In her time, one of the more famous poems from her first collection was "A Letter from a Girl to her own Old Age," in which the poet imagines an unusual communication—a mature woman must confront and mourn the lost dreams and wildness of her own youth. Meynell's later themes include motherhood and war, themes she explores with emotional complexity, and throughout her slender oeuvre Meynell is concerned with the nature of poetic inspiration. Her poems are spare both in number and in form; particularly in her later volumes she wrote few poems longer than twenty lines, and she favored the highly crafted sonnet.

The common thread that connects all of Meynell's verse is the centrality of faith, but Meynell was more than a Christian poet; her work is infused with Roman Catholic doctrine and observance. Her daughter Viola Meynell wrote of her mother's conversion: "never surely was so rational a choice as hers more absolutely embraced in its farthest implications. No single act of hers in life or literature was not pledged and bound by her when she chose that law" (1929, 42). Meynell's poetry closely examines the human role in constructing and celebrating the Catholic faith, and it repeatedly explores the relationship of faith and art. Meynell's poetry is underpinned by an awareness of the mystery of the Incarnation: her poems suggest that the workings of God are to be found in all human activities, from the most elevated to the most mundane. Whether taking as a subject a communicant at the Eucharist or an atheist on a soapbox, Meynell's poems illustrate the penetration of the Divine into the everyday.

One of Meynell's most thought-provoking poems takes up words that are spoken every day but that are nonetheless holy words—the words of the Lord's Prayer. As she examines how Catholics utter ritual formulas such as those of the Mass to help them worship, she suggests in her poem "The Lord's Prayer" that these "every day" words may have a God-given power to help us comprehend the divine mystery:

> "The Lord's Prayer"
> *Audemus dicere "Pater Noster"*—Canon of the Mass
>
>   There is a bolder way,
> There is a wilder enterprise than this
> All-human iteration day by day.
> Courage, mankind! Restore Him what is His.
>
>   Out of His mouth were given
> These phrases. O replace them whence they came.
> He, only, knows our inconceivable "Heaven,"
> Our hidden "Father," and the unspoken "Name";
>
>   Our "trespasses," our "bread,"
> The "will" inexorable yet implored;
> The miracle-words that are and are not said,
> Charged with the unknown purpose of their Lord.

> "Forgive," "give," "lead us not"—
> Speak them by Him, O man the unaware,
> Speak by that dear tongue, though thou know not what,
> Shuddering through the paradox of prayer. (*Poems*, 142)

Meynell explores a subtle paradox in this poem as she suggests that the "all-human iteration" is, in fact, Christ-language. The poem reminds readers that the words of the prayer are quite literally said "day by day"; Meynell includes the Latin epigraph taken directly from the Mass to further emphasize how these words are embedded in daily practice. But the poem goes on to show that the significance of the words infinitely exceeds the sphere of daily practice. Literally, Christ gave humankind these phrases when he instructed the disciples how to pray, but Meynell also points out the metaphorical function of the Christ-given words: in repeating them, believers "speak by that dear tongue"—figuratively speaking the language of God. Even more provocatively, the poem suggests that by repeating the prayer, believers can become part of a mysterious divinity that they are not even capable of understanding; that even though mortal limitations render humans "unaware," speaking "thou know not what," the act of praying makes them participants in God's work.

Meynell presents another far more unconventional prayer in "Veni Creator." This poem suggests to Christ that he left one "path of lowliness untrod" when he was on earth: he never had to suffer another man's forgiveness. The poem directly addresses God as the all-powerful Creator, but also tenderly, even wistfully, calls him down to a human level:

> Come, then,
> Endure undreamed humility: Lord of Heaven,
> Come to our ignorant hearts and be forgiven. (76)

This poem, with its suggestion that God might have done something that requires pardon, seems radical and may be illuminated by words Meynell wrote after the death of an infant son: "It is easy to forgive; to be forgiven is not easy; shall man alone play that noble part, and so be more noble than God? Will not God, too take our pardon? We forgive Thee, our Maker, for Thy infinite inventiveness in planning the anguish of human life" (Badeni 1981, 75). The prayer of "Veni Creator" does not rail at or question God, as Job did in his suffering, but it nonetheless passionately longs for comprehension and intimacy.

Meynell finds poetic subjects in the Scriptures, too, and in "I Am the Way" she meditates on Jesus' words: "I am the way, the truth, and the life." The poem presents a kind of response to Christ. "Thou art the Way," she agrees:

> Hadst Thou been nothing but the goal,
> I cannot say
> If Thou hadst ever met my soul. (*Poems*, 80)

The speaker calls herself "a child of process," distracted by the difficulties and windings of the Christian path. The poem extends the names of Christ to show how he is himself a traveler and also the guide who makes possible the finding of himself: "Access, Approach / Art Thou, Time, Way, and Wayfarer."

While many of Meynell's poems, like "I Am the Way," adopt a direct, first-person, prayer-like address to God, several meditate in the third person on rituals or celebrations of the Church calendar. But these, too, can express a personal and immediate communion with a vividly realized God. Two lovely Advent season poems serve as examples. "Advent Meditation" concentrates on the humble miracle of the Incarnation; few poems communicate as simply the humanness of the baby Christ:

> No sudden thing of glory and fear
> Was the Lord's coming; but the dear
> Slow Nature's days followed each other
> To form the Saviour from His Mother
> —One of the children of the year. (11)

Another poem, "Unto Us a Son Is Given," compares the season of Advent to the seasons of nature and to the arrival of a child to show how mystery and joy appear even in what may seem "to be expected":

> New every year,
> New born and newly dear,
> He comes with tidings and a song,
> The ages long, the ages long;
>
> Even as the cold
> Keen winter grows not old,
> As childhood is so fresh, foreseen,
> And spring in the familiar green—
>
> Sudden as sweet
> Come the expected feet.
> All joy is young, and new all art,
> And He, too, Whom we have by heart. (95)

Christ's coming is "sudden" yet "expected"; each year our joy is new, although we know Christ, like a poem, by heart. The poem communicates the fresh-springing wonder found in a regularly observed celebration in a similar way to the poems in which Meynell examines the sacrament of the Eucharist.

Delicate and crafted as her poems are, Meynell's work is deeply doctrinally informed, and while she never sought notoriety, she spoke out (and wrote out) on many controversial issues. In her concern with the wording and celebrating of the Eucharist and with the symbolism of the bread and the wine, Meynell engages with a central point of Victorian religious debate. For many in the nineteenth century, the significance accorded the Eucharist was the crux of the difference between Catholicism and Protestantism. On the one hand, Protestants assert the metaphorical meaning of Christ's words "this is my body"; on the other hand, Catholics take a more literal interpretation. The Roman Catholic Church teaches that upon the uttering of the words of consecration the bread and the wine are transubstantiated, transformed into, as the Catholic catechism states, "the entire body, blood, soul and divinity of Jesus Christ." While the "accidental" nature of the elements is that of bread and wine, the "essential" nature is the literal flesh and blood of Christ. The transformation of sheaf and grape into flesh and blood is, therefore, dependent on *words*, the words of institution uttered by the priest. According to Saint Thomas Aquinas, while the bread and wine are the potential matter of the sacrament, the words constitute the form of the sacrament. Because the words "this is the chalice of my blood" come from Christ himself, they derive from Christ their creative power. In her concentration on the power of poetic words, Alice Meynell inherits not only the symbolic emphasis of the Catholic tradition to which she pledged herself but also the rich representational potential that Catholicism grants to the wording of ritual. The poems in which she explores the symbolism of the Eucharist and the power of poetic language are some of her most complex and rewarding.

In "The Fugitive," Meynell takes a provocative view of Christ's sacrifice, suggesting that he must be regularly hunted down, like prey, and torn apart into the elements of the Eucharist:

> Hunted, He never will escape
>   The flesh, the blood, the sheaf, the grape,
> That feed His man—the bread, the wine. (114)

The emotional tone here is complex, as is the central metaphor. This is no orthodox hunt, and the fugitive's escape is definitely not desirable. The scenes that the victim cannot escape do not appear as scenes of crucifixion but rather "the lands where ripen brown / A thousand thousand hills of wheat," and "The Southward, sunward range of vine." These vistas present literally, in wheat fields and grape-vines, the forms that symbolize Christ's death, and for humankind they are scenes of nourishment and life. The poem invites a closer examination of symbolic language, suggesting that to save humankind Christ transformed himself into earthy elements and also transformed himself into metaphor.

Other poems that examine how the Eucharist functions assert the power of poetic words to break down differences between humans and to enable identifica-tion with Christ. In "A General Communion," the "deeply separate" group of communicants is made, mystically, one by partaking of Christ's body, which is fragmented and yet "ever unparted, whole":

> I saw the throng, so deeply separate,
> Fed at one only board—
> The devout people, moved, intent, elate,
> And the devoted Lord.
>
> O struck apart! not side from human side,
> But soul from human soul,
> As each asunder absorbed the multiplied,
> The ever unparted, whole. (113)

The last two stanzas of the poem present an extended metaphor of the believers as a daisy, a single flower made up of thousands of individual flowers. In the gentle pun of the last line, Meynell points out that every one of those individuals receives the priceless gift of "the whole of the devoted sun."

In a similar fashion, "The Unknown God" meditates on how participating in the mystery of the Eucharist breaks down the differences between human beings, just as it broke down the barrier between humans and God. The first three stanzas set the scene:

> One of the crowd went up,
> And knelt before the Paten and the Cup,
> Received the Lord, returned in peace, and prayed
> Close to my side. Then in my heart I said:
>
> "O Christ, in this man's life—
> This stranger who is Thine—in all his strife,
> All his felicity, his good and ill,
> In the assaulted stronghold of his will,
>
> "I do confess Thee here,
> Alive within this life; I know Thee near
> Within this lonely conscience, closed away
> Within this brother's solitary day." (112)

The speaker comes to recognize that although individual humans are unknown to and "closed away" from each other, when they separately participate in the Lord's Supper they are bonded not just to Christ but also to each other. She recognizes the Christ within her unknown companion, and in this way connects more deeply to humanity as well as to her Lord.

"In Portugal, 1912" is not a joyful Eucharist poem, as are "A General Communion" and "The Unknown God"; it meditates on a troubled situation and an uncompleted sacrifice:

> And will they cast the altars down,
>   Scatter the chalice, crush the bread?
> In field, in village, and in town
>   He hides an unregarded head;
>
> Waits in the corn-lands far and near,
>   Bright in His sun, dark in His frost,
> Sweet in the vine, ripe in the ear—
>   Lonely unconsecrated Host.
>
> In ambush at the merry board
>   The Victim lurks unsacrificed;
> The mill conceals the harvest's Lord,
>   The wine-press holds the unbidden Christ. (115)

In Meynell's poetry every word is significant, and in this poem as in numerous others Meynell begins constructing meaning with the title. The question of what happened or who was in Portugal in 1912 is not directly answered, but Meynell was probably referring to the contemporary political situation. In 1910, Portuguese Republicans had overthrown the monarchy and disestablished the Catholic Church. Many church buildings and lands were seized by the new government, the clergy's freedoms of speech and association were curtailed, and by 1912 widespread persecution of Catholics was occurring. In the troublesome scene of the poem's first two lines, the speaker worries that the destructive "they" will lay waste to the symbols—and thus the redemptive power—of the Eucharist. If "unregarded" or uncelebrated, Christ is an "unsacrificed" victim; the bread and the wine have no higher meaning, and Christ remains hidden in the mill and the wine press that represent unsanctified and thus insignificant forms. The symbolic power of words cannot operate, and Christ cannot save.

Meynell writes several poems on religious figures, and almost always concentrates on women, examining how their (often) lesser known stories are of genuine importance. A poem such as "San Lorenzo's Mother" reveals the tender, often overlooked, feminine face of devotion. This poem speaks poignantly of a mother's loss of a son and her enduring faith in the Son. San Lorenzo himself is not the focus of the poem, but rather his absence; it has been so long since his mother has seen him that, when one of the monks of his order asks her for alms, she cannot tell if the man is her own child. But in a moment of what seems supreme loss, when the deepest of human relations seems to have given way, San Lorenzo's mother sees the true significance of the Son of Man. She recognizes that the Incarnation has made Christ one of us, but that his Godhead is also immutable:

> There is One alone who cannot change;
> Dreams are we, shadows, visions strange;
> And all I give is given to One.
> I might mistake my dearest son,
> But never the Son who cannot change. (39)

"Saint Catherine of Siena" also has an element of tragedy, but Meynell transforms the story of a death into a strong feminist assertion of the moral strength and holy power of women—and, in the last stanza, asserts the justice of women's demand for suffrage. The first four stanzas of the poem detail the plight of a terrified young man sentenced to death who falls at the feet of "the sacred, young, provincial nun" (104). By the force of her compassion and conviction, Saint Catherine claims him for Christ and sends him to die triumphant. The poem turns traditional power relations on their head: "On her courageous breast he leant, / The breast where beat the heart of Christ." Meynell's last stanza trenchantly conflates the might and mercy of Saint Catherine with the call for women's rights, demanding respect from "the man of modern years / —Stern on the Vote" for her Christlike but utterly feminine heroine, "Thou prop, thou cross, erect, in tears."

Meynell does not restrict herself to historical figures when she examines women's devotion, and she consistently and carefully shows the interweaving of religious experience with the concerns and demands of everyday life. "The Young Neophyte" was written upon Meynell's conversion to Catholicism on July 20, 1868. It is an emotionally complex sonnet in which a novice dedicates her life, yet unlived, to her order. She sees herself double, as both the inexperienced young girl she is and the faded, feeble, elderly self she is simultaneously sealing to conventual life. The poem lingers on natural images of buds, unripeness, and yet-ungathered wheat, and while there is no hint of doubt in the novice's mind, the poem conveys the solemnity of a voluntarily chosen but supreme sacrifice: "I light the tapers at my head and feet, / And lay the crucifix on this silent heart" (53).

This kind of combined power and tenderness characterizes several of Meynell's portrayals of Christ as well as of women. "Aenigma Christi" (which remained unpublished during Meynell's lifetime) imagines the uncontainable and incomprehensible contained within the flesh of the woman who bore God, suggesting the peculiarly feminine aspect of the mystery of the Incarnation:

> None can be like Him, none!
> In love? In grief? Nay, man's capacity,
> Rifled unto its depths, is reached, is done—
>   Christ's, an unfathomed sea.
>
> None, can be like Him, none;
> Not she who bore Him. Yet I saw the whole
> Eternal, infinite Christ within the one
>   Small mirror of her soul. (195)

Another poem, "To the Mother of Christ the Son of Man," explicitly compares our condition as Christians struggling to comprehend Christ with the condition of Mary. Here again Meynell chooses to emphasize not just Christ's humanity and our brotherhood with him but also the contribution of womankind to our understanding of who Christ is:

> We too (one cried), we too,
> We the unready, the perplexed, the cold,
> Must shape the Eternal in our thoughts anew,
>   Cherish, possess, enfold. (179)

All believers must be like Mary the Mother of God, argues Meynell: each of us must individually conceive Christ within ourselves. We are often bewildered, and it is a hard labor, but Mary's example has made it possible for us: "He lingers in the breast / Of our humanity."

The figure of the Madonna (which Meynell explored at length in her 1912 book, *Mary the Mother of Jesus*, a combination of art criticism, history, poems, and meditations) is one of the most clearly Roman Catholic elements in Meynell's verse. Another distinctly Catholic form is found in the provocatively titled "Veneration of Images," a highly compressed, almost mystical address to the figure of Christ on a crucifix. The Christ the speaker addresses is a new Adam: "Thou man, first-comer, whose wide arms entreat, / Gather, clasp, welcome, bind" (98). Verbs of reconciliation pile up in language that reveres Christ as God but knows him as human: "Whose warm pulses beat / With love of thine own kind." As she closes, "Thou rood of every day!," Meynell's primary position as a Catholic poet is again evident. While for Meynell the rites and observances of Catholicism are always sacred and never to be engaged without reverence, she also insists that engagement with religious mystery should be for humankind quite literally an everyday event. As at Christmas Christ is always born, always at Bethlehem, always in the familiar formulary, but always born anew, so Christ's sacrifice is always new as the communicant receives the wine and the wafer; so too every time the Lord's Prayer is uttered, the holy words consecrate the Christian afresh. And for Meynell, the courts of the Lord, the means by which we can draw near to the holiest place, is through words, especially inspired poetic words, which can achieve for humans a true epiphany. She sees beyond human utterances "ultimate poetry," the ultimate representation of Christ:

> Plain, behind oracles, it is; and past
> All symbols, simple; perfect, heavenly-wild,
> The song some loaded poets reach at last—

> The kings that found a Child. ("The Courts, A Figure of the
>   Epiphany," 121)

For Meynell, poetry is a highly regulated discipline. But it is also a holy quest, a means of comprehending the divine.

CRITICAL RECEPTION

Alice Meynell's prose and poetry have fallen from critical attention in the eighty years since her death. Her fame in her own day was primarily based on her essays, which reached a huge audience, but her poetry was also so revered by her contemporaries that she was on two occasions (in 1895 and again in 1914) nominated for poet laureate. Meynell's concise, evocative verses were admired by John Ruskin, Alfred Lord Tennyson, and Dante Gabriel Rossetti as well as by her two great Victorian champions, Coventry Patmore and George Meredith (although Patmore did reserve his highest compliment—that of "genius"—for her essays rather than her poems). Certainly, the disciplined spareness and surface simplicity of her poetry was unusual in a late Victorian period characterized by much poetic ornamentation. Her friend and admirer G. K. Chesterton stated that she "differed from most of the advanced artists of the period in the detail that she was facing the other way, and advancing in the opposite direction" (1923, 11). In fact, a number of critics compared her work to that of the seventeenth-century metaphysical poets, whom she much admired. Her poetic restraint was regularly noted, as in the *Pall Mall Gazette* review of *Later Poems* in 1901: "She has accustomed us to look for quality rather than quantity and we are not disappointed. The rarity of her verses, measured by the gross test of counting pages and lines, is paralleled by the uncommon beauty of the poetry they embody, and the distinction wherewith it is expressed" (quoted in Badeni 1981, 170). When Meynell's poetry was criticized, it was for a self-conscious "distinction" or overfastidiousness.

Meynell's reputation was not confined to the United Kingdom, and later in her life when she had more time to travel she undertook a lecture tour of the United States. The tour lasted some months and her lectures, drawn mostly from her sprightly essays, were enthusiastically received; she was even invited to the White House by Eleanor Roosevelt (but had to decline). After her death, encomiums were reverential. Chesterton wrote in the *Dublin Review*: "The point about [Meynell's] poetry, as compared with most modern poetry, was this; that she never wrote a line, or even a word, without putting brains into it; or, in the most exact sense, meaning what she said. She never wrote a line, or even a word, that does not stand like the rib of a strong intellectual structure; a thing with the bones of thought in it" (1923, 3).

Although a centenary volume of selected essays and poems appeared in 1947, critics and readers were already turning away from Meynell to newer, postwar voices. After decades of neglect, a small number of literary critics have recently revisited Meynell's condensed and witty poetry. Especially initially, these recent reevaluations sought primarily to categorize a body of work that is not easily classifiable and is profoundly unlike most Victorian and turn-of-the-century verse. Vanessa Furse Jackson (1998) echoes Chesterton in noting the seventeenth-century influence on Meynell; in "Looking 'Past Wordsworth and the Rest,'" Sharon Smulders (2000) has traced Meynell's debt to the Romantics. Maria Frawley (1997) suggests that Meynell's verse is modernist, concerned with issues of identity and thought processes.

Part of Meynell's challenge to twentieth-century readers is that she straddles traditions that to modern eyes appear incompatible: she was a staunch feminist and working mother and vocally supported women's rights, but she was also a committed Catholic and her faith is central to much of her poetry. Politically quite radical, Meynell was domestically, religiously, and stylistically traditional. Modern critics have been divided on whether Meynell was avant-garde or conservative, and Talia Schaffer sees Meynell as artistically and psychologically conflicted: "Alice Meynell managed, though at some psychological cost, to be both an Angel in the House and a suffragist" (2000, 32).

Meynell's poetic output was slender—her collected poems take up a bare 150 pages. However, the discipline with which she culled what she considered inferior works ensured that the poems that do survive are exceptionally highly crafted, evocative, and provocative, still presenting a rewarding challenge to twenty-first-century readers. Furthermore, her influence upon a very broad circle of Catholic artists contributed to the flourishing of many talents, men and women who spoke of her as inspirational: Alfred Noyes wrote "in her lifetime she was a tower of intellectual and spiritual strength, lifting through the mists one of the very few steadfast lights" (quoted in Alexander 1968, 128). Alice Meynell's poetry, condensed and thought-provoking, succeeds in evoking the richness of the Roman Catholic faith, its humanist and even feminist facets, and its recognition of Christ in everyday life.

NOTE

Alice Meynell, *The Poems of Alice Meynell* (London: Oxford University Press, 1940). All references are to this edition.

WORKS CITED

Alexander, Calvert, S. J. 1968. *The Catholic Literary Revival*. Port Washington, NY: Kennikat Press.

Badeni, June. 1981. *The Slender Tree: A Life of Alice Meynell*. Padstow, England: T. J. Press Ltd.

Chesterton, G. K. 1923. "Alice Meynell." *Dublin Review* 172, no. 1: 1–12.

Frawley, Maria. 1997. "Modernism and Maternity: Alice Meynell and the Politics of Motherhood." In *Unmanning Modernism: Gendered Re-Readings*, ed. Elizabeth Harrison and Shirley Peterson, 31–43. Knoxville: University of Tennessee Press.

Jackson, Vanessa Furse. 1998. "'Tides of the Mind': Restraint and Renunciation in the Poetry of Alice Meynell." *Victorian Poetry* 36: 443–74.

Meredith, George. 1896. "Mrs. Meynell's Two Books of Essays." *National Review* (August): 762–70.

Meynell, Alice. 1896. *The Rhythm of Life and Other Essays*. London: John Lane; Boston: Copeland and Day.

Meynell, Viola. 1929. *Alice Meynell: A Memoir*. New York: C. Scribner's Sons.

Schaffer, Talia. 2000. *The Forgotten Female Aesthetes: Literary Culture in Late-Victorian England*. Charlottesville: University Press of Virginia.

Smulders, Sharon. 2000. "Looking 'Past Wordsworth and the Rest': Pretexts for Revision in Alice Meynell's 'The Shepherdess.'" *Victorian Poetry* 38: 35–48.

BIBLIOGRAPHY

Norman, Edward. *The English Catholic Church in the Nineteenth Century*. Oxford: Clarendon Press, 1984.

Schlack, Beverly Ann. "The Poetess of Poets: Alice Meynell Rediscovered." *Women's Studies* 7 (1980): 111–26.

Smulders, Sharon. "Feminism, Pacifism and the Ethics of War: The Politics and Poetics of Alice Meynell's War Verse." *English Literature in Transition* 36, no. 2 (1993): 159–77.

Tuell, Anne Kimball. *Mrs. Meynell and Her Literary Generation*. New York: E. P. Dutton and Co., 1925.

— F. Elizabeth Gray

Brian Moore [1921–1999]

Catholics

BIOGRAPHY

Brian Moore was born on August 21, 1921, in Belfast, Northern Ireland. His father was a successful doctor and his uncle was Eoin MacNeill, an Irish language scholar and the man who famously countermanded the Easter Rising of 1916. Moore enjoyed the financial comforts of a prominent middle-class Catholic family, and he attended school at St. Malachy's College, which is regarded as one of the premier institutions for Catholic education in Northern Ireland. Such notable Northern Irish personalities as Eoin MacNeill, Michael McLaverty, Cardinal Cahal Daly, Bernard Mac Laverty, and Robert McLiam Wilson all attended St. Malachy's. Moore, however, was a relatively poor student, and he was always more interested in fiction writing than he was in the Republican and Catholic ideals that were taught at St. Malachy's. Even at a fairly young age, Moore understood that he was good at writing and that he could make money off his talent—in relation to the English essays set by his teachers, for example, Moore's classmates often paid handsomely for his ghostwriting skills.

At the beginning of World War II, Moore decided to join the Air Raid Precautions in Belfast instead of attending medical school like his illustrious father. By joining the British war effort, Moore was not actively challenging the Northern Irish state, and while this caused some friction in his Catholic family, it was soon forgotten when Belfast was bombed by the *Luftwaffe* in 1941. Moore then joined the British Ministry for War Transport, which sent him to Algeria, and after the war he volunteered for the United Nations Relief and Rehabilitation Association. He was made redundant in 1947, but rather than return to Northern Ireland, he decided to emigrate to Canada, where he began work at the *Montreal Gazette* and eventually met his first wife, Jacqueline Sirois. It was during this time that he began writing pulp fiction under the pseudonyms of Bernard Mara and Michael Bryan. Even though these potboilers offered some financial security, Moore wanted to devote his talent to literary fiction, and he began to focus his attention on a novel that would highlight the Catholic Belfast of his youth. His first literary effort, *The Lonely Passion of Judith Hearne* (1955), was written relatively quickly, and when it was published it garnered him immediate critical acclaim. It remains a masterpiece of Irish literature. Just as Joyce helped put Dublin on the literary landscape, Moore did much the same for Belfast.

With his literary reputation growing, Moore moved to New York after winning a Guggenheim Fellowship, and it was there that he met his second wife, Jean Russell. The two moved to California when Alfred Hitchcock hired Moore to write the screenplay for *Torn Curtain* (1966). After settling in Malibu, Moore was hired as a professor of creative writing at UCLA. For the last several decades of his life, he led a relatively quiet existence that was only broken by trips to his second home in Nova Scotia and his annual pilgrimages to Ireland. He died suddenly in January 1999 of pulmonary fibrosis and, due to an oeuvre that includes a total of nineteen very disparate and inventive novels, he is remembered as a writer's writer.

Moore's relationship to Catholicism remains slippery because he was simultaneously attracted to and repulsed by the religion of his youth. Even though he claimed to be an atheist at the end of his life, many of his characters undergo a crisis of faith and their spiritual anguish is sympathetically rendered. Moore has been called an Irish Dickens due in part to a narrative structure that is deceptively easy to read. A writer of realism, he dabbled in magic realism and the thriller genre, but regardless of form his fiction often highlights difficult moments of moral perplexity. Moore's female protagonists are always convincing, and the settings of his novels range from the Quebec Province of 1635, to a fictitious Caribbean island, to nineteenth-century Algeria, and to contemporary France, New York, and Montreal.

Even though Moore is an exceedingly difficult writer to categorize, his interest in Catholicism can be found throughout his novels. Some of his most celebrated works include *The Lonely Passion of Judith Hearne*, *The Emperor of Ice Cream* (1965), *I am Mary Dunne* (1966), *Cold Heaven* (1983), *Black Robe* (1985), *No Other Life* (1993), and *The Magician's Wife* (1997). One his most famous pieces, however, is a slender novel simply titled *Catholics* (1972).

PLOT SUMMARY

Although *Catholics* was written in the middle of Moore's career, it is his first novel to be set not in the urban landscape of Northern Ireland but on the rural coastline of the Republic of Ireland. It is a popular text, and in 1973 it was made into a movie that starred Trevor Howard and Martin Sheen. The text itself asks difficult questions about the nature of miracles, dogma, and faith.

At the close of the twentieth century, the Father General in Rome has enacted Vatican IV. While the rest of the world willingly adopts the tenets of a new version of Catholicism—one that is based upon a merger with Buddhism and a belief in liberation theology—the monastery on Muck Island continues to celebrate the Tridentine Mass in Latin. These rouge Irish monks also continue to hear the sacrament of Confession, believe in the outmoded concept of transubstantiation, and stand with their backs to the congregation. Crowds begin to gather near Muck Island, and the monks that uphold these traditions of the past are a threat to the authority of the Vatican. An American television crew plans to create a documentary of the events occurring at the monastery, but Rome is worried that Muck's devotion to tradition might be viewed around the world as a form of rebellion.

Father James Kinsella has been given plenipotentiary status by the Father General so that he might control these monks. Kinsella, a young Irish American who wears the standard-issue military uniform of a Catholic priest, must convince Tomás O'Malley, the abbot of Muck, that the old ways of Catholicism are obsolete and childish. The novella opens with Kinsella trying to get to Muck Island by a small Irish boat known as a *curragh*. The boatman, Padraig—who operates much like Charon on the river Styx—does not recognize that Kinsella is a priest because he is wearing green-gray denim fatigues instead of the traditional trappings of his holy office. Padraig refuses to bring Kinsella to Muck, thus suggesting that the young man is "fundamentally out of step with local time and place: not a soul he meets recognizes him as a priest" (Dahlie 1981, 59). Kinsella eventually does arrive on the island by helicopter, but his presence is clearly unwelcome. Tomás disperses his monks, and Kinsella delivers the Father General's holy edict. According to Rome, the celebration of the Latin Mass must stop immediately.

Tomás, a bookworm who no longer uses his sacristy, knows that his monks rely on tradition and that their faith is largely rooted in the sanctity of a Mass that has not changed for centuries. Telling them that their beliefs are unfashionable and wrong will be difficult, but Tomás agrees to obey the edict because he believes that he should honor the wishes of Rome. His acquiescence, however, is not necessarily based upon a belief in Church hierarchy, because we later learn that Tomás lost his faith when he went on a pilgrimage to Lourdes, the holy site where the Virgin Mary appeared to a French girl. The current Catholic Church has shut down Lourdes, presumably because it challenges the Vatican's position on the importance of miracles (*Catholics*, 80). While the holy shrine of Lourdes was in operation, however, Tomás went there with four other priests. Amid the "tawdry religious supermarkets, crammed with rosaries and statuettes," Tomás did not feel the presence of God and he came to believe that there was no afterlife (81). Rather than bolster Tomás's faith, Lourdes brought about his atheism. His role as abbot for the past decade, therefore, has been a sham. He wishes to remain on Muck because it is the only life he knows. Muck is his home and the monks trust his judgment even though he is, quite literally, a doubting Tomás (Porter 1975, 84).

The next day, after Kinsella leaves the island by helicopter, Tomás informs his monastery that they must adopt the new beliefs of Catholicism even if they feel that these new regulations are wrong. Father Matthew, who has led the charge to retain the Latin Mass with some degree of vociferousness—including a midnight vigil beneath Kinsella's window—sensibly asks in relationship to transubstantiation, "how can a thing be a miracle one day and not a miracle the next day?" (*Catholics*, 105). Tomás has no answer for this other than to lead his monks in prayer.

The novella closes with Tomás pretending to honor his role as abbot, but since he no longer believes in God his actions become otiose and he suffers a nervous breakdown. He loves the men around him and wishes to protect them, but he also understands that his atheism disallows him from ever feeling at home again. He cannot bring himself to tell the other monks that—whether it is a Latin Mass or a contemporary Mass—neither matter to him because God does not exist. He must go on with the façade because he cannot imagine a different life for either himself or for his men.

MAJOR THEMES

That this story takes place on the west coast of Ireland was a deliberate and conscious choice. While *Catholics* certainly explores the shifting theological landscape that Vatican II produced, it also registers the changes that Roman Catholicism experienced in Ireland. Being Irish, at least when Moore was growing up, meant being Catholic, and to question one of these identities necessarily meant questioning the other. Moore understood that the type of Catholicism practiced in Ireland was the most draconian in Europe and that anything other than complete obedience to the Church was a potential threat to Irish culture, as represented in his first two novels, *The Lonely Passion of Judith Hearne* and *The Feast of Lupercal*. Roman Catholicism, after all, had challenged English colonialism for several centuries, so to question the Catholic Church meant at least tacitly questioning what it meant to be Irish as well. It is little wonder, then, that in *Catholics* the small town of Cahiriciveen has joined the monastery of Muck Island in the rejection of Vatican IV. They want to retain the Latin Mass in part because it symbolizes their own Irish identity.

Moore set *Catholics* on the west coast of Ireland because it is here that the stereotypical version of the noble Irish peasant—the image promoted by Douglas Hyde, the Gaelic League, Arthur Griffith, Eamon de Valera, and, to a certain extent, William Butler Yeats—could be found. Moore crafts the text of *Catholics* to make us feel that we are traveling back in time. Indeed, the spiritual ethos of Muck not only predates Vatican II, but it also feels as if it predates that morning in 1517 when Martin Luther nailed a sheaf of paper to a church door. The fact that the helicopter that brings Kinsella to the island is described by Tomás O'Malley as the "first flying machine of any description that has ever landed on Muck" suggests that an invasion of sorts is occurring (37). Technology and ideology are encroaching upon a lifestyle and a version of Catholicism that has existed on Muck for centuries. Change is about to come to the monastery whether the monks are willing to embrace it or not.

Moore's setting is therefore rather ingenious because he is able to represent symbolically the history of Catholicism (at least the Irish narrative of it) but at the same time largely remove himself from discussions of Irish Catholicism as it existed in Ireland and Northern Ireland at that time. Since this novella was published shortly after the occurrence of Bloody Sunday, it would have been relatively easy for Moore to relate Irish Catholicism with Irish nationalism. Moore, however, forces his story outside a precise historical matrix, and although we get the sense that we are going back in Irish history, we are outside any particular version of that history. In other words, this small monastery resides outside Irish history because it has miraculously survived the purges of Henry VIII, the genocidal pogroms of Oliver Cromwell, and the British penal laws of the early nineteenth century (56). The monastery on Muck is, at the end of the twentieth century, under attack from the very institution that gives it purpose in the first place: the Roman Catholic Church. This is what makes *Catholics* more than merely an Irish story, because Moore forces us to consider the ramifications of the Church challenging its own history and tradition. If the mysteries and the miracles of the Latin Mass helped to support individual understandings of faith, what happens to that faith when the Mass is changed?

Before we progress to other Catholic themes evident in this text, a few words should be said about what Catholicism meant to Brian Moore, both before and after the implementation of Vatican II. First, by attending St. Malachy's College in Belfast, Moore learned at a young age that Catholicism was closely linked to Irish nationalism. This is due in large part to the Christian Brothers who took over the curriculum of St. Malachy's in 1866. The version of Catholicism that the Brothers taught was grounded in the Gaelic cultural revival, and, in fact, many of the men responsible for the Easter Rising of 1916 in Dublin were taught under the Brothers' openly nationalist stance. Although the Irish Christian Brothers challenged English colonialism, they demanded unwavering obedience to Catholicism, and it was this, more than any other facet of his education, that Brian Moore found unconscionable. If rejecting Catholicism meant also rejecting Irish identity, Moore rebelled against both modes of thought and chose emigration to Canada.

After Vatican II, which challenged the Catholic Church around the world regardless of national identification, Moore was forced to reconsider the religious institution that had shaped his youth. In a sense, the Catholic identity he understood as a boy in Northern Ireland had been undermined. Growing up as he did in Belfast, Catholicism and nationalism were bound together, but due to Vatican II, Moore was given a view of a Church that physically no longer resembled that of his youth. This both intrigued and worried him. Gone were the trappings of a Latin Mass and, perhaps more importantly, the Church was beginning to dabble in liberation theology. Since liberation theology is predicated upon Marxist concerns, it has been adopted by various political communities around the globe: in Europe (as explored by J. B. Metz and Jürgen Moltmann); in Latin America (Paulo Freire and Gustavo Gutiérrez); in feminist considerations (Judith Plaskow and Elisabeth Schüssler-Fiorenza); as well as in black political discourse (Cornel West and Gayraud Wilmore). In his youth, Moore became interested in socialism in part because it allowed him to rebel against Irish Catholicism. As an adult, the shift in Catholicism toward issues of social justice for poor countries meant that Catholicism, for Moore, was no longer a repressive force.[1]

While Brian Moore never embraced liberation theology, James Kinsella—the young priest in *Catholics* who must bring the monastery of Muck into line with the rest of the Church—does embrace this vision for Catholicism. A devotee of Gustav Hartmann, we learn that Kinsella became a priest because he wanted to be a revolutionary leader and that "the Church, Hartmann taught, despite its history and its dependence on myth and miracle, exists today as the quintessential structure through which social revolution can be brought to certain areas of the globe" (25). One reason that Kinsella initially cares so little about the traditions of Muck is that, as a peripatetic priest who has traveled extensively, he is accustomed to change. This is a man who has lived in Rome, Amsterdam, Cambridge, Brazil, and Thailand. For Kinsella, Catholicism is merely a tool that can bring social justice to various corners of the globe. Even though Moore ultimately portrays Kinsella's idealism as naïve, he is still drawn as a relatively sympathetic character. This is something of a turning point for an author who, in all of his novels previous to

Catholics, depicted priests as vicious and dangerously parochial in their thinking. Here, suddenly, we have a priest with a global perspective, but—and this is a tribute to Moore's sensitivity in relationship to plot and aesthetics—this character is not the hero of *Catholics*. While Kinsella's version of Catholicism appears initially more open and accepting than Tomás's dogmatic understanding of the Church, Moore shows Kinsella to be equally intolerant.

The genius behind *Catholics* is that we, as readers, are not allowed to side with either Tomás or Kinsella. We are cast adrift at the end of the narrative because Kinsella, for all his idealism, has achieved a pyrrhic victory on Muck Island. Moore draws these two priests as he does because of the division between an older version of Catholicism and a newer one rooted in the changes of Vatican II. This novella, in other words, cannot be understood without first recognizing that Moore was exploring the collision between two differing versions of Catholicism, old and new. *Catholics* bridges the gap between the draconian Church that Moore understood as a young man in Belfast and the type of Roman Catholicism that came into existence when he was an adult. This is not to suggest that Vatican II softened Moore's overall displeasure with Catholicism, but he was concerned that if the Church continued to change it might no longer exist (Dahlie 1981, 106).

This collision between tradition and liberalization explains why duality is such a major theme in *Catholics*. Divisions are delineated between such categories as young and old, belief and atheism, and rebellion and conformity. Kinsella is young, at peace with his faith, and, due to his background as an American, relatively free from a damaging colonial history. Tomás, on the other hand, is in the twilight of his life, increasingly more convinced of his atheism, and, due to his background as an Irishman, caught within a historical and national matrix that has relied upon Catholicism for an identity outside that of Englishness. While these two characters deliver moral weight and ultimately drive the plot of *Catholics*, the qualities that they represent are not as important as the dichotomy established between rebellion and conformity.[2] The entire story hinges upon a younger man's attempts to silence the rebellion of older men. This is a clever form of spiritual colonialism because although Vatican IV outwardly appears more welcoming and tolerant (a merger with Buddhism is about to occur), Moore offers the subtle suggestion that little has changed if challenges to orthodoxy must be met with swift and immediate condemnation. The older ways that Tomás and his monks represent may have once represented the status quo, but such devotion to the past is now radically dangerous, as becomes evident when Tomás acutely states, "yesterday's orthodoxy is today's heresy" (*Catholics*, 63). In spite of the high-minded ideals set forth by Vatican IV, the juxtaposition that Moore establishes between Muck and Rome, old and new, and tradition and innovation exposes Kinsella's understanding of the new Catholicism to be just as intolerant as Tomás's older version when it comes to acts of rebellion. Conformity to Rome, as Moore learned at a young age in Belfast, still supersedes individual desire.

The duality that Moore constructs between young and old, faithful and faithless, and conformity and rebellion in *Catholics* helped set a new precedent in Moore's fiction, because after this novella his subsequent examinations of Roman Catholicism were generally less harsh than the critiques that appeared in his earlier work. After writing *Catholics*, Moore began to place other belief systems into dialogue with Catholicism, as is evident in such novels as *Cold*

Heaven, which depicts an atheist who experiences a miracle near a convent, *Black Robe*, which portrays Jesuits converting Native Americans to Catholicism, and *The Magician's Wife*, which pits a French Catholic against Arab Muslims. Such dialogue between differing belief systems in Moore's later work was encouraged by a shift within Catholicism itself. Thus, ironically, one of the most Catholic themes in this particular novella is grounded in a moment of history when the very nature of what it meant to be Catholic was itself called into question. If Vatican II challenged the orthodoxy and primacy of the Latin Mass, it also opened up the possibility that the Church could be wrong—that it could be scrutinized—and it is this specific dialogue between the old and the new that powers the plot of *Catholics*.

One of the most noticeable themes of this narrative is not necessarily the clash between pre- and post-Vatican II ideology but the more disturbing questions regarding what role the Church has in sustaining the faith of its parishioners. If, as Moore suggests, faith depends upon mystery and ritual, what right does the Church have to strip away centuries of tradition? What does this do to individual identity? While Vatican IV appears to be inclusive, Moore suggests that a loss of faith equals a loss of identity, which is a theme that manifested itself early on in his career in the ending of *Judith Hearne*. For good or bad, Catholics are Catholics precisely because they are not like other religious believers elsewhere in the world. If the Church changes to suit the secular world, how can it maintain a stable identity? This is why Moore does not have his monks rebel against the changes brought about by Vatican II. Rather, he sets his story in the future and creates a Church that is in the grip of Vatican IV. This means, of course, that the monastery on Muck Island has endured the changes of Vatican II and III. These monks are searching for stability in a religion that is unstable. Given that they have witnessed three radical changes in Catholicism, it is little wonder that they return to the traditional understandings of their theology, which is a Catholicism that is more conservative but at least it has existed for centuries.

Although the novella is called *Catholics*, we finish the text with the understanding that Catholicism, as it exists in the narrative, can no longer offer a concrete sense of identity. The Mass, as it is celebrated, is devoid of transubstantiation, the prayers are no longer conducted in Latin, and all of the sacraments have been abandoned. The only thing that rests at the heart of Vatican IV is liberation theology and a secular commitment to social justice. Understanding that mystery and miracle are no longer a part of Catholicism, Tomás informs his scared and angry monks that "prayer is the only miracle" (107). Although he has avoided prayer since he lost his faith at Lourdes, he can no longer deny his responsibilities as a priest (Porter 1975, 87). In the small church that has existed for centuries, he leads the monks in the Our Father because he loves his flock and wants to protect them. Tomás enters "null"—as Moore describes his psychological breakdown—so that his monks might be spared. Love and endurance, at the end of *Catholics*, become more important than faith, or dogma, or even tradition.

CRITICAL RECEPTION

Graham Greene once famously mentioned that Brian Moore was his favorite living novelist, and in a blurb of support for the back cover of the first edition of *Catholics* he wrote that it "is probably the best book of a writer whom I very much admire." Since its publication, critics have routinely ranked *Catholics* alongside such masterpieces as *Judith Hearne*, *I am Mary Dunne*, and, later, *Cold Heaven*.

Moore is a difficult writer to categorize because, although he was born in Northern Ireland, he emigrated to Montreal and retained his Canadian citizenship for the rest of his life. However, he then spent his last thirty years living in California. Does this make him Irish, Canadian, or American? Then there is the further conundrum of his relationship to Catholicism. Born and raised a Catholic, he largely shunned the religion of his youth but nevertheless wrote many novels that are sympathetic to characters who struggle with their faith. It is this loss of faith that has intrigued most of Moore's critics, and this is most especially true with regard to *Catholics*.

Hallvard Dahlie was Moore's first critic and he remains one of his best. In his critical analysis, *Brian Moore*, he praises *Catholics* as well as Moore's ability to create "a metaphysical drama which is paradoxically both an urgent invocation to 'the beauty of belief' and a spare chronicle of existential despair" (1981, 106). While applauding the literary craftsmanship of *Catholics*, Dahlie also focuses his attention upon how the plot turns on a moment of lost faith. He reminds us that although Tomás turns to atheism after his experience at Lourdes, Kinsella is also an unbeliever in miracles of the Church. In this sense, the two priests share a common lack of faith (110). Dahlie finds that the brilliance behind *Catholics* rests in a clash between two differing belief systems and yet, when we examine Tomás and Kinsella, they have more in common with each other than may first appear.

The next major work to address *Catholics* can be found in Jeanne Flood's monograph, also titled *Brian Moore*. While her examinations are competently argued, there is a critical overreliance on Freudianism. The larger theological issues that drive *Catholics* are presented as subordinate to what Flood sees as the father/son nexus that manifests itself between Tomás and Kinsella (1974, 94). She further postulates that *Catholics* is an apocalyptic novel and that Tomás's "fear of God's nonexistence is unfounded, for the world is preparing for its destruction just as orthodox Catholicism taught that it would" (95). Although Flood praises *Catholics*, this is largely because the text slots nicely into her psychoanalytical reading of Moore's various novels.

Jo O'Donoghue, in *Brian Moore: A Critical Study*, also concerns herself with issues of belief and faith. Coming later, her analysis is necessarily more encompassing than either Dahlie's or Flood's. Although she does not spend much time analyzing *Catholics* in comparison to Moore's other works, O'Donoghue observes that "*Catholics* seems to envisage the ordinary Catholic, lay or clerical, merely exchanging a conservative hegemony for a liberal one. Both, ultimately, are equally tyrannical" (1991, 143). O'Donoghue is also the first critic to place *Catholics* into dialogue with *Cold Heaven*, *Black Robe*, and *The Color of Blood*. She also registers Moore's attitude about Vatican II and how this influenced his later work (142–43).

The most recent critical assessment is Robert Sullivan's *A Matter of Faith: The Fiction of Brian Moore*. Like previous critics, Sullivan also lauds *Catholics* and applies a poststructuralist reading to the text. He concentrates upon absence, semiology, and how the deconstruction of the Mass equates to a loss of identity (1996, 94–95). He further observes that *Catholics* is the first of three novels that features a priest who sacrifices himself in the name of love for the greater good of his community, as can also be seen in *Black Robe* and *The Color of Blood* (90). In this sense, Sullivan persuasively argues that *Catholics* established a pattern for Moore's subsequent priests.

Critical analysis of Moore's work is still ongoing, but *Catholics* is almost universally regarded as one of his literary triumphs. As a matter of further interest, two biographies have recently been published that explain the intersections between Moore's personal life and his art. The first is Denis Sampson's unauthorized biography, *Brian Moore: The Chameleon Novelist* (1998), and the second, Patricia Craig's *Brian Moore: A Biography* (2002), will undoubtedly be regarded as a seminal text for future critics.

NOTES

Brian Moore, *Catholics* (New York: Holt, Rinehart and Winston, 1972). All references are to this edition.

1. Liberation theology makes a stronger appearance in Moore's later work. Cardinal Bem of *The Color of Blood* rejects liberation theology so that Catholicism might thrive under Soviet colonialism, and Jeannot Cantave of *No Other Life* embraces liberation theology in order to bring democracy to his destitute Caribbean island.

2. Aside from Moore's abiding interest in faith, many of his novels grapple with individual acts of rebellion against Catholicism, as is evident in *Judith Hearne*, *The Feast of Lupercal*, *An Answer from Limbo*, *The Emperor of Ice Cream*, *Fergus*, *Cold Heaven*, and *No Other Life*.

WORKS CITED

Craig, Patricia. 2002. *Brian Moore: A Biography*. London: Bloomsbury.

Dahlie, Hallvard. 1981. *Brian Moore*. Boston: Twayne.

Flood, Jeanne. 1974. *Brian Moore*. Lewisburg, PA: Bucknell University Press.

O'Donoghue, Jo. 1991. *Brian Moore: A Critical Study*. Montreal: McGill-Queen's University Press.

Porter, Raymond J. 1975. "Mystery, Miracle, and Faith in Brian Moore's *Catholics*." *Eire-Ireland: A Journal of Irish Studies* 10 (Autumn): 79–88.

Sampson, Denis. 1998. *Brian Moore: The Chameleon Novelist*. Dublin: Marino.

Sullivan, Robert. 1996. *A Matter of Faith: Brian Moore*. World Literature Series, vol. 69. Westport, CT: Greenwood Press.

— Patrick Hicks

Thomas More [1477 or 1478–1535]

Utopia

BIOGRAPHY

Thomas More was born in 1477 or 1478, the son of John More, a London lawyer. In 1494, after attending Oxford University for two years, More took up legal study at the Inns of Court in London, where he joined a circle of mostly ecclesiastical, reform-minded humanist scholars. In 1499, More met and befriended Desiderius Erasmus. At about this time, More was considering a priestly or a monastic vocation, but he soon gave up this idea and married Jane Colte. Together they produced three daughters and a son: Margaret, Elizabeth, Cecilia, and John. When Jane More died in 1511, More married Alice Middleton, a widow eight years older than himself.

In 1510, More became undersheriff of London, a post with considerable judicial duties. In 1515, Cardinal Wolsey sent More to Flanders as part of a delegation negotiating trade issues with representatives of the king of Spain (the future emperor Charles V). More began to write *Utopia* while he was on this mission. In 1516, he completed the manuscript of *Utopia* and sent it to be published in Louvain. That year, More also became a royal counselor formally, as a member of the Council of the Star Chamber. In October 1529, the arc of More's career reached its apex when he succeeded Wolsey as chancellor of England, the first lay person to hold the position. His tenure as chancellor lasted less than three years and was dominated by judicial business and combating the spread of Protestant heresy in England through pen and ink—and through fire. About thirty-five heretics were burned in 1531 and 1532 while More was chancellor.

Henry VIII's attempts to pressure the Church for a divorce and remarriage to Ann Boleyn became too much for More in 1532. He resigned the chancellorship and retired to private life. In April 1534, More refused to take the oath recognizing the legitimacy of Henry's marriage to Ann and was imprisoned in the Tower of London for the next fifteen months. On July 1, 1535, he was finally brought to trial for treason at Westminster Hall. On the evidence of Richard Rich's testimony, More was convicted and sentenced to death. He was beheaded on July 6 of that year. In 1886, Thomas More was beatified by Pope Leo XIII along with fifty-three other martyrs, including his friend, Bishop John Fisher. He was canonized by Pope Pius XI in 1935. In 2000, Pope John Paul II named Thomas More the patron saint of statesmen and politicians.

PLOT SUMMARY

Although it appeared in several editions during More's life, *Utopia* did not become widely popular until it was translated into English by Ralph Robinson in 1551. The Latin text is somewhat more than 27,000 words in length, divided into two books, the second about twice as long as the first. The work is a dialogue between three men: Morus, Peter Gillis, and the imaginary Raphael Hythlodaeus, a Portuguese sailor learned especially in Greek and recently returned from a journey around the world.

In book one, the three men meet; Hythlodaeus recounts his journey and begins to describe some of the lands he has visited. On account of his learning and experience, Peter Gillis suggests that Hythlodaeus become a royal counselor, but the man refuses. Gillis briefly, and then Morus and Hythlodaeus, go back and forth on this topic. Hythlodaeus asserts that a philosopher does not belong in politics because his ideas would not be welcome and he would have to compromise on the truth too often. Morus responds that the philosopher has a duty to offer counsel and that such counsel must be sober and realistic. In the course of this dialogue, Hythlodaeus brings up a series of problems plaguing European states and England specifically: endemic violence and war, some persons living in luxury while others starving, the idle rich destroying rural life by enclosure, and cruel, disproportionate enforcement of laws. Hythlodaeus then argues that European society is so corrupted by the institution of private property that good counsel cannot improve it. Morus expresses doubt that a society without private property is possible, and this leads to Hythlodaeus's description of Utopia in book two.

Book two begins by describing the geography of Utopia and its fifty-four nearly identical cities, each dominating an autonomous district, with the island's capital, Amaurot, near the center. The Utopians are rotated in and out of rural farming cadres every year. In Utopia, each of the fifty-four cities has an identical form of government, a republic based on family units. Groups of thirty families each elect a magistrate over themselves called a Syphogrant. There are 200 Syphogrants in Amaurot (making 6,000 families), and for every ten of these there is a higher magistrate called a Tranibor. The twenty Tranibors and a rotating pair of Syphogrants make up the Utopian Senate. The town leader, called the Barzanes, is elected by the citizens through a secret ballot. Utopia's leaders come from a privileged aristocracy of scholars chosen by the Syphogrants who are freed from the obligation to work at a trade. Membership in this class may be revoked for unproductivity.

Everyone in Utopia works. The day is carefully regulated with a strict schedule of work, dining, recreation, and rest. Because everyone works, six hours of labor each day suffices to produce a great bounty of food and material goods. The Utopians' clothes are made of plain undyed linen and wool rather than dyed wool and fur.

The Utopians have a thoroughly regimented society. Everyone learns to farm and has the obligation to learn another practical trade. Families serve as both political and economic units under the benevolent rule of fathers. Children must follow in the trades of their parents; those who wish to follow some other trade are adopted out to a family that practices it. Strict limits restrict family and city size. If a family has more than sixteen children, some must leave or be adopted out. If the city were to have more than 6,000 families, then a portion would have to be sent to establish a new city. For this reason only do the Utopians make aggressive war: the need for land and for it to be used properly.

In each quarter of the city there is a center where food is made available to all. The Syphogrants oversee dining halls where all of the families under their authority take their meals every day. Regulations give precedence according to age and gender. Men are seated during meals. Women prepare all of the meals and join their men to dine. Older children serve the food or stand silently waiting to be handed food by their parents. Slaves do all of the cleaning.

Preventing the concentration of wealth in private hands together with the social pressure to work and to live without excess results in the communal creation of great wealth. The Utopians have plenty to eat, comfortable living conditions, and need to work only six hours a day. The Utopians do mine and refine gold and silver, but only for foreign trade. So as not to waste the effort, they create chamber pots and fetters out of the metals. The Utopians are utilitarian and hold excess and ostentation contemptible.

The Utopians were fascinated by the numerous texts of Greek philosophy and literature the Europeans had brought along with them. When Hythlodaeus left them, they were enthusiastically assimilating the Greek language and learning into their own culture.

The Utopians accept slavery as an individual, not a heritable, condition. They enslave prisoners taken in their own wars and use slavery as a punishment for serious crimes. The Utopians also accept as slaves people condemned to death in other states, and they permit people from other states to become slaves in Utopia because the life of a Utopian slave is a relatively good one.

The Utopians encourage those who are gravely sick and in great pain to end their lies through starvation or assisted suicide, but one is never compelled to do this. Those who commit suicide for any other reason are publicly dishonored. The Utopians have monogamous marriage. Divorce is rare but possible for cause or even due to very serious incompatibility, with the permission of the Senate. Adultery is cause for divorce, and an adulterer is punished by enslavement. A second adultery is punished by death.

Utopia has few laws and no lawyers. Quotidian regulation of society and chastisement in Utopia are left to the strongly patriarchal family. Children are disciplined by their parents and women by their husbands or fathers, but apparently men are disciplined only by other men. For serious offenses, enslavement is the normal punishment; the death penalty is used where enslavement has failed or been refused.

The Utopians loathe war, but they wage it with great aplomb. Beyond the acquisition of territory needed for surplus population, the Utopians make war in defense of themselves and of their "friends," even to the extent of retribution for raids launched by enemies or in response to threats against their own or their allies' merchants abroad. The Utopians prefer assassinating enemy rulers. In war, they rely upon their friends' troops and employ vicious Zapolete mercenaries. But when they do fight, the Utopians fight together, husbands and wives side by side accompanied even by their children. Naturally, they are terrifyingly successful.

Utopia is in a period of religious ferment. Its founder, Utopus, established a policy of toleration in religious matters that permits Utopians to worship one of a number of deities. Some of these are named, such as Mythras and Saturn, but more and more Utopians worship a single, unnamed, transcendent god. The Utopians have a common religious system. They have priests elected by the community, including even a few women. The Utopians' churches and their religious ceremonies are sufficiently ambiguous that all, or at least the overwhelming majority, may participate without sensing any infringement upon their individual beliefs. Some Utopians undertake "regular" religious vocations, giving up the pleasures of the world, and some of them choose lives of persisting service and devotion. Although the Utopians have a form of religious toleration, they protect as a social norm the core element of religion most important to good social order: the belief in the reward or punishment of the individual after physical death. Those who do not believe this are not allowed to discuss their views in public, but only with priests. They may not hold public offices, and they are "looked down on as . . . lazy and spineless" (*Utopia*, 119).

Hythlodaeus sums up his description by noting that the Utopians have a system oriented to the public good. Private property, he argues, creates inequities that lead to starvation, for it forces everyone to pursue their own private interests at the expense of the common good. But in Utopia, "where everything belongs to everyone," people are able to pursue the common good. Morus, however, concludes the book by expressing very serious doubts about some of the Utopians' practices, especially about property held in common: that one fact, he maintains, undermines all nobility, magnificence, splendor, and majesty, which are (in the popular view) the true adornments and ornaments of a commonwealth (134). Upon this, the author reports, the three men went to dinner. He concludes by observing that he believed he would not see many of the desirable features of Utopia implemented.

MAJOR THEMES

Utopia is a work of deep irony and of many meanings and levels of meaning. The two books that constitute *Utopia* are quite different in both structure and content. Book one creates the outer structure for the dialogues that follow, moves on to the "dialogue of counsel," and establishes the context for the description of Utopia in book two. Even though Hythlodaeus does most of the talking, book one is a balanced dialogue with a good deal of give and take between himself and Morus. Book two contains Hythlodaeus's description of Utopia. It is a monologue right up to the very end, when Morus concludes the work with reservations that call the whole thing into question. Numerous major and lesser themes run through *Utopia*, but three seem to rise above the rest: the relationship between the philosopher and public life, the satiric presentation of various ills of Christian European societies, and the work's standing in humanism. The "Catholicity" of *Utopia* is also an important question. Although it is difficult to call *Utopia* an *essentially* Catholic work, it certainly does explore a variety of Catholic themes.

The Philosopher and the World of Politics

Book one of *Utopia* is taken up largely with the so-called dialogue of counsel, the discussion between the three men over Gillis's question to Hythlodaeus: "[w]hy do you not enter the service of some king[?]" (15). The first thing the reader needs to understand about this dialogue is its timeliness; when More wrote it he was being recruited for the court of King Henry VIII. Less than a year after he started writing *Utopia*, More joined the Council of the Star Chamber and moved into the close orbit of his king. So he too was facing Gillis's question. Book one of *Utopia* thus reflects More's thoughts on advancing into Henry VIII's court. The risks in becoming a royal counselor were not inconsiderable. Henry VIII began his reign by arranging the quick conviction and execution of two of his father's counselors, Richard Empson and Edmund Dudley, for treason. Thomas More himself witnessed their executions in 1510. The two men were trained lawyers like More who were charged with using judicial power to increase royal revenues; their executions were intended to signal the repudiation of Henry VII's misuses of judicial power. Although the two men were generally despised and were reputed to have lined their own pockets as well as the king's, their conviction and execution were arbitrary and politically motivated acts. This sort of risk attached to royal service is never mentioned explicitly in *Utopia*, but it would have been familiar to any contemporary. It is an important subtext of Hythlodaeus's arguments.

The second thing the reader needs to understand is *Utopia*'s humanist context. One can liken the purpose of books one and two of *Utopia* to Erasmus's *Education of a Christian Prince* and his *Praise of Folly*. The latter blasts many foolish things in society, and the former outlines a sort of humanist prescription to ameliorate them. The description of the Utopian commonwealth in book two presents a social critique in an ironic way, while in book one, More presents the possible remedy: experienced, well-educated counselors giving the king prudent advice. Although Gillis opens the dialogue, his exchange with Hythlodaeus only serves to raise and then put aside self-serving motives for becoming a king's counselor. It is Morus who takes up the question from the standpoint of principles and ideals. Hythlodaeus gives three basic reasons for not seeking to become a royal counselor: that kings value above all military expertise, of which he has none; that there is a basic incompatibility between being a philosopher and being a counselor because the counsel he would offer as a philosopher would not be well received in court; and finally, that European states are so sick with the corruption that derives from having private property that good counsel will not be sufficient to improve them. The first reason is not at issue in the dialogue; More himself lacked military experience and likely took this as an uncontestable platitude. The second issue, the compatibility of philosophy and political life, is the subject of the dialogue. It was not a new issue, nor a dead one. The Greeks and Romans from Plato on had argued whether the philosopher should prefer a *vita contemplativa*, a life of contemplation and study at arm's length from the public arena, or a *vita activa*, an active life in the world of politics. The legend is that Plato attempted unsuccessfully to reform Dionysus, the tyrant of Syracuse; otherwise, he counseled philosophers to avoid politics "until philosophers become kings or kings become philosophers." Hythlodaeus repeatedly cites Plato to support his position. Morus and Hythlodaeus put the matter precisely in these terms:

> *Morus*: "But it seems obvious to me that you would be acting in a fashion worthy of yourself and of your noble and truly philosophical nature if you could bring yourself to apply your intelligence and industry to public affairs, even at the cost of some private convenience."
> *Hythlodaeus*: "I would sacrifice my contemplative leisure to active endeavor without contributing anything to the common good." (16)

To support this contention, Hythlodaeus recounts the dialogue with Cardinal Morton and gives two contrived examples of the sort of unacceptable counsel he might offer. The recollected dialogue between Hythlodaeus, Morton, and the "laymen learned in the laws" is interesting because it does not quite prove the point Hythlodaeus says it does. Certainly it demonstrates the hypocrisy and the unprincipled maneuverings of courtiers. But since Morton accepts in the end Hythlodaeus's suggestion to suspend the execution of thieves, the anecdote also appears to show that good counsel can succeed. Hythlodaeus's two other examples of the unacceptable counsel he might offer, advising the French king to give up his Italian campaigns as wasteful and advising any prince to promote the people's welfare and uphold the laws justly rather than seeking to maximize royal revenues at any cost (was this an allusion to the fate of Empson and Dudley?), seem clear, and Morus agrees that such advice would likely not succeed. Hythlodaeus concludes from this that "[a]mong princes there is no room for philosophy" (43). But Morus has a strong reply: he adopts a Ciceronian position, arguing essentially that the philosopher has a duty not only to offer counsel but also to offer good counsel moderated by clear-eyed realism: "That's how it is in the commonwealth; that's how it is in the councils of princes. If you cannot thoroughly eradicate corrupt opinions or cure long-standing evils to your own satisfaction, that is still no reason to abandon the commonwealth, deserting the ship in a storm because you cannot control the winds" (44).

Hythlodaeus's third and final reason for not seeking to become a royal counselor is his claim that politics and social order in European states are so corrupted by private property that good counsel cannot effect any meaningful improvement. The description of Utopia in book two is presented as proof that a society without private property is possible. Scholars have long noted the balanced ambiguity of this dialogue. Each side has good arguments based on classical sources and on a realistic view of political life. Given that More wrote this dialogue after completing the description of Utopia and then placed it first, it seems that it was intended to create a context in which the description should be understood. The purpose of the dialogue of counsel is to raise the question of the relationship between the philosopher and political life in a nuanced way. Hythlodaeus's description of Utopia in book two is the final example of the dialogue of counsel in book one. It is a society devised by a philosopher seriously in conflict with the real world. The work as a whole depicts the triumph of Cicero over Plato; that is the basis of its unity. Ultimately, Thomas More's decision to do in his own life what Hythlodaeus refuses to do can be said to have affirmed this resolution more clearly than words. The philosopher should indeed take up the active life, but with a sober appreciation for the complexity and compromise the political arena requires.

The Meaning of the Satire

In the course of book one, More describes, in the voices of his various players, a range of problems afflicting European states: shocking inequities in the material conditions of people's lives, endemic violence, cruel justice, vainglorious war, and a political culture opposed to meaningful reform. The description in book two of the island state of Utopia as representing the "best form of a commonwealth" is an implicit criticism of European society as it stood.

Utopia is subtler than Erasmus's *Praise of Folly* in that its criticism is mouthed by Hythlodaeus (or "Nonsenso" in Paul Turner's [1965] fine translation), and, particularly in book two, this fact is implied rather than baldly stated for comic effect. Some aspects of the Utopians' society are so strange, outrageous, and contrary to European traditions that they also seem to cover the text with the mantle of foolishness. Could a society without private property be taken seriously by a sixteenth-century European Christian? What about a society that accepts divorce with remarriage, suicide and assisted suicide, and husbands, wives, and children going to war and into combat all together? Numerous commentators have interrogated the text of *Utopia* in an attempt to determine whether More intended the implied criticisms and remedies to be taken seriously or as jokes. Was he mocking forms of social and religious corruption, or was he mocking those who were in the business of mocking social and religious corruption? The context suggests the former over the latter.

Given the debate that *Praise of Folly* set off, More was wise not to present another boldly transparent satire. In 1516, a straightforward attack on aspects of royal policy and social and religious convention would have stirred up trouble that would have threatened his career prospects. More was almost certainly interested in winning a measure of acclaim among his humanist colleagues. To this effect, he created a dialogue far more nuanced and complex than Erasmus's, a dialogue demonstrating a facile command of classical literature that attacked various forms of corruption in society, traced them to their roots, and proposed remedies based on ethical principles. And all this was done in a way that would not taint More as a radical or a heretic.

Utopia is one of the most sophisticated examples of humanist parody ever written. Its debts to Plato's *Republic*, Plutarch's *Moralia* and *Lives* of Lycurgus and Agis, and the works of Cicero are clear; but its heavy irony and uncertain truthfulness trace back to more obscure works by the satirist Lucianus and to Plato's *Parmenides* (as Peter Ackroyd [1998] has noted). Lucianus used names to mean things contrary to what they designated, as More used *Ademus*, or "without people," for the ruler; *Anydrus*, or "without water," for a river; and *Utopia*, or "no place," for the ideal state. And one of Lucianus's dialogues, *The True Story (I)*, dealt with a journey to the moon and a description of life there. More translated several of Lucianus's works from Greek into Latin. The *Parmenides* was a complex dialogue centered on responses to various logical and rhetorical attacks on the theory of forms. These connections affirm *Utopia*'s humanist pedigree. It was not fundamentally an attack on humanism based on Scholastic thought or on ideas outside of the classical tradition; it was a fully humanist work.

The contours of More's critique reflect fundamentally Catholic values. Consider the problem of vainglorious war. In the Europe of book one, we have the French king going to war to conquer parts of Italy. The short-term consequences of war waged so frequently for so little justification are clearly stated as the wasting of national resources and the surety of more war in the future. In the longer term, there is the problem of wounded veterans whose lives are destroyed and the creation of a violent class of former soldiers who easily turn to prey on their own society. Of course, the Utopians avoid all of these problems. They do not go to war merely for the glory of conquest but in defense of themselves and their friends and when population growth absolutely requires expansion. The Utopians adopt tactics that supposedly minimize the destructive effects of war on the populous. They fight through proxies whenever possible. And when they go to war, they go as a whole society of men, women, and children. And finally, because their system has eliminated poverty through goods being held in common, they have all but eliminated the long-term ruination of the lives of wounded veterans.

It need not be imagined that England or any European state could adopt the Utopians' war-fighting methods. The comparison is intentionally provocative; it seems absurd but it reflects reality in several ways. Regarding justification for war, the Utopians' approach seems far closer to Saint Augustine's "just war" theory than was the French king's. Regarding the seemingly absurd idea of families going off to war together, it should be considered that this is exactly what the French and English had inflicted on each other in the *chevauchee*, or raids of destruction, of the Hundred Years' War. But the most interesting and possibly useful aspect of the Utopians' approach was the preference for the assassination of leaders.

Throughout *Utopia*, More argues for a particular set of social values within the humanist reform community, values that corresponded to the traditions of medieval Christianity and that may be labeled "Catholic." One must be cautious about this term, however, because so much of what is Catholic was defined in contrast to the complaints and the interpretations articulated against the Catholic Church by the Protestants. Of course, Utopia is not a Christian commonwealth, but this fact only heightens the contrast between its well-ordered society and Christian Europe's disorderly one. The Utopians' communism can be traced back to its ancient roots in Plato's *Republic* and to the common holding of goods among Jesus' disciples. But the most direct source for More seems to have been the Catholic monastic tradition.

The holding of goods in common in Utopia serves several functions. It permits the formation of an unchallenged hierarchy based on family, scholarly achievement, and public reputation. In More's day, the growing preeminence of commercial wealth created more and more visible examples of the elevation of corruption and tawdriness than might have been apparent in earlier times. It also resulted in all sorts of objective inequities: some laboring long and hard for little return, others rich and idle. The medieval Schoolmen had long explored the immorality of material inequality in glosses and treatises on the just price and the just wage. The notion of excessive individual wealth remains a part of the Catholic liberal tradition. In More's *Utopia*, the point of attack is not so much wealth per se as it is idleness. The elimination of private property and social pressure to serve the common good through the established institutions makes idleness impossible:

> So you see that nowhere is there any chance to be idle; there is no excuse for laziness, no wine taverns, no alehouses, no brothels, no occasion to be corrupted, no hideouts, no hangouts. With the eyes of everyone upon them, they have no choice but to do their customary work or to enjoy pastimes which are not dishonorable. (73)

As Lisa Jardine beautifully traces in *Worldly Goods: A New History of the Renaissance* (1996), a spirit of acquisitiveness and opulence had taken hold of the early sixteenth-century cultural mainstream. Wealth and material excess seemed to have reached a new level of respectability. Even Erasmus chose to sit for his portrait by Quentin Massys wearing merchant's clothes with a fat purse around his neck. The Utopians' communism was not a realistic solution to corruption and inequity, but it presented a high level of contrast with European society that points the reader toward the essential moral problems at the root: greed, sloth, and above all pride—three of the seven deadly sins.

The monastic idea manifests itself in other aspects of the Utopians' society. Like monks, the Utopians break up the day into discrete segments for work, prayer, and recreation. They prefer simple dress and loathe ostentatious display. They use election to determine their administrators. The Utopians place a premium on learning and are obsessed with combating idleness. In many ways, the Utopians' society seems like a monastery writ large. Moreover, the Utopian clergy, while not Christian, mirrors the system of the Roman Catholic Church, with a formal secular component and an informal regular component, people who choose to give their whole lives to service in the manner of friars rather than monks. Although celibacy is not required of the clerics (except the small number of women priests, who must be older widows!), for those who follow the "regular" path celibacy is considered a more virtuous condition. And here we find one general criticism by contrast to the Christian clergy, for the priests of Utopia are regarded as uniformly morally excellent.

Utopia and Humanism

It is clear that *Utopia* must be understood within the context of the humanist movement. The decades before 1516 were the decisive period for the development of Christian humanism. In the fourteenth century, humanism was an artistic and literary movement. In the fifteenth century, it became an aspect of secular political discourse in Italy. From the late fifteenth century on, humanists were adapting their methods and attitudes to politics generally, to the literature of Christian faith, and to the Christian Church itself. This was a matter of controversy in 1516.

Humanists such as More's close friend Erasmus were optimists who believed in the power of good ideas (drawn from Europe's classical past) and of education (of princes and their officials) to improve the condition of Europe, the Church, and the world. Humanists and nonhumanists alike acknowledged that the Church was plagued by serious corruption; the controversy was over modes of reform and what might follow from them. Many of the entrenched Scholastics in the universities were hostile to the humanists, and with good reason. Since Petrarch, those proponents of going back to the sources and to classical literature had little good to say about Scholasticism. Christian humanist culture was also a paradox, for that classical past was also largely a pagan past, forcing a Christian to embrace it with a measure of ambivalence. The Catholic Church relied upon tradition as a vital force in establishing matters of faith and institutions. But in pursuit of the true and original text, humanists looked upon alterations and accretions with great suspicion. It was not much of a leap to imagine the humanists' method applied to the Church as a whole, something that could put many settled issues (for example, conciliarism) again into question. More aligned himself clearly with Erasmus and the optimists.

Utopia had a very specific humanist context as well as a general one. As Lisa Jardine has discussed in her book, *Erasmus: Man of Letters*, *The Praise of Folly* triggered a debate at Louvain in 1515 over the appropriate subjects of humorous satire in pursuit of humanist reform (1995, 110–22). More joined this debate in 1516 with the very long *Letter to Martinus Dorp* (*Complete Works*, 1965, vol. 15), defending Erasmus's satire and his work on a Greek New Testament. Dorp was a theologian at the University of Louvain who objected to Erasmus's satirizing of the Church and of religious matters. More's decision to have *Utopia* printed at Louvain, where Erasmus held a post by late 1516, also appears to have been intended specifically to support his efforts. It also appears that the use of numerous Greek neologisms in *Utopia* (More had originally intended to use the Latin title *Nusquama*, meaning "Nowhere") and the Utopians' quick embrace of Greek learning were part of an ongoing debate among humanists whether to put more emphasis on Greek study or not.

CRITICAL RECEPTION

Given the renown of *Utopia* and of its author, it should be no surprise that the work has been subjected to numerous attempts at analysis and criticism. Since More's canonization in 1935, and especially since the publication of the Yale *Complete Works of St. Thomas More* began in the early 1960s, there has been a torrent of serious and original work on More and his writings, particularly his *Utopia*. Interpretations of *Utopia* may be mapped on a continuum. At one end are those who believe that More intended *Utopia* to be taken literally, as the subtitle says, "[t]he Best Form of a Commonwealth." At the other end are those who believe that this claim is intentionally and manifestly false. At the one extreme may be placed those who have understood *Utopia* as a literal prescription. Proponents of socialism, such as Karl Marx and Karl Kautsky, identified More as a socialist before his time. Also close to this end of the continuum can be placed J. H. Hexter (1973), who believed that More anticipated many aspects of the modern state in his system, and the discussion of *Utopia* in

Quentin Skinner's *The Foundations of Modern Political Thought*. There, Skinner made the intriguing argument that More was satirizing not only problems in European society but also the humanist approach to the problems in European society; it was a "humanist critique of humanism" (1978, 255–62). At the other end of the continuum, scholars such as R. W. Chambers (1935) have seen *Utopia* as a manifestly untenable ideal the essential purpose of which was to embarrass Christian Europeans. Focusing on Lucianus's influence on More, T. S. Dorsch (1966–67) argued that *Utopia* is detestable and that the work is purely satirical.

In the vast middle of this continuum may be placed a very long list of interpretations. Here I will mention only a few. As stated above, I take it that *Utopia* was a humanist work in sync with Erasmus's *Praise of Folly*, although more ironic and less whimsical. G. M. Logan's book *The Meaning of More's Utopia* (1983) makes this argument at great length. Perhaps the best recent humanist explication of *Utopia* was Quentin Skinner's article "Sir Thomas More's *Utopia* and the Language of Renaissance Humanism" (1987). Three recent biographers, Alistair Fox (1982), Richard Marius (1984), and Peter Ackroyd (1998), each give attention to *Utopia* in the context of More's life, providing extensive citations to the literature on *Utopia*.

Finally, a very extensive bibliography of works on *Utopia* can be found on the World Wide Web by searching under "More Utopia Bibliography."

NOTE

Thomas More, *Utopia*, trans. Clarence H. Miller (New Haven, CT: Yale University Press, 2001). All references are to this edition.

WORKS CITED

Ackroyd, Peter. 1998. *The Life of Thomas More*. London: Nan A. Talese.

Chambers, R. W. 1935. *Thomas More*. New York: Harcourt Brace.

Dorsch, T. S. 1966–1967. "Sir Thomas More and Lucian: An Interpretation of *Utopia*." *Anchiv fur das Studium der NeuerenSprachen und Literaturen* 203: 345–63.

Fox, Alistair. 1982. *Thomas More, History and Providence*. New Haven, CT: Yale University Press.

Hexter, J. H. 1973. *The Vision of Politics on the Eve of the Reformation: More, Machiavelli, de Seyssel*. New York: Basic Books.

Jardine, Lisa. 1995. *Erasmus: Man of Letters*. Princeton, NJ: Princeton University Press.

———. 1996. *Worldly Goods: A New History of the Renaissance*. London: Nan A. Talese.

Logan, G. M. 1983. *The Meaning of More's Utopia*. Princeton, NJ: Princeton University Press.

Marius, Richard. 1984. *Thomas More: A Biography*. New York: Knopf.

More, Thomas. 1965. *Utopia*. In *The Complete Works of St. Thomas More*, vol. 4, ed. Edward Surtz, S. J., and J. H. Hexter. New Haven, CT: Yale University Press.

———. 1965. *Utopia*, trans. Paul Turner. Baltimore, MD: Penguin.

Skinner, Quentin. 1978. *The Renaissance*. Vol. 1 of *The Foundations of Modern Political Thought*. Cambridge, MA: Harvard University Press.

———. 1987. "Sir Thomas More's *Utopia* and the Language of Renaissance Humanism." In *The Language of Political Theory in Early Modern Europe*, ed. Anthony Pagden, 123–57. Cambridge, MA: Harvard University Press.

— Brendan McManus

John Henry Newman [1801–1890]

Apologia Pro Vita Sua

BIOGRAPHY

John Henry Newman was born on February 21, 1801, in London. Brought up in a conventional middle-class Church of England home, he underwent a conversion to Evangelicalism in 1816 and fell under Calvinist influences, including the belief that the pope was the Antichrist. Entering Oxford in 1817, he was elected a fellow of Oriel College in 1822, where he came under liberal influences, a tendency that was checked by his beginning to read systematically the Church Fathers in 1822, when he was also appointed vicar of St. Mary's, the university church, having taken holy orders in 1824.

A Mediterranean tour in 1832 and 1833 left Newman uneasily impressed by the Catholic Church. On his return, he began *Tracts for the Times* as part of the so-called Oxford Movement, which arose in protest against a Whig government that threatened liberal reforms of the Church of England. He attempted to construct a *via media* between Rome and Geneva for Anglican theology, but the condemnation by the bishops of *Tract 90* (1841) and other events weakened his belief that the Church of England was Catholic. Finally convinced by the claims of Rome, he left unfinished his classic *An Essay on the Development of Christian Doctrine*, which was published in 1845 when he was received into the Church.

Ordained a Catholic priest in Rome in 1847, he founded the Oratory of St. Philip Neri in Birmingham in 1848. That year, he published the novel *Loss and Gain, The Story of a Convert* and later a second novel, *Callista, A Sketch of the Third Century* (1855). Appointed rector of the new Catholic University of Ireland (he resigned in frustration in 1858), his inaugural lectures (1852) became the first half of *The Idea of a University* (1873). Dismay at clericalism led him to write his first theological essay as a Catholic, *On Consulting the Faithful in Matters of Doctrine* (1859), which he followed with other ecclesiological writings, especially *A Letter to the Duke of Norfolk* (1875) on papal infallibility. His account of his conversion, *Apologia Pro Vita Sua* (1864), was published in response to an attack on his integrity by Charles Kingsley. His poem about purgatory, *The Dream of Gerontius* (1865), became a best-seller and was made into an oratorio by Edward

Elgar (1900). In 1870, he finally completed his philosophical masterpiece, *An Essay in Aid of a Grammar of Assent*, in which he examined the nature of religious assent.

In 1879, Newman was made a cardinal by Pope Leo XIII, an honor that vindicated his orthodoxy against the dominant extreme papal Ultramontane party that had long harassed him. He died at the Birmingham Oratory on August 11, 1890; on his memorial were inscribed the words he had chosen: "*Ex umbris et imaginibus in veritatem*" (Out of shadows and images into the truth). In 1991, Pope John Paul II declared him "Venerable," the first stage toward canonization.

SUMMARY

Apologia Pro Vita Sua, excepting the preface, which explains the circumstances in which the book was written, consists of five chapters. The first takes us up to 1833 and the beginning of the Oxford or Tractarian Movement (which sought to establish the Catholic identity of the Church of England); here, Newman recounts the early religious influences on him and his theological development at Oxford. The second chapter covers the years up to 1839, when Newman emerged as the dominant personality in the movement and the principal architect of the *via media*. But it anticipates the publication in 1841 of *Tract 90* and the effective end of Newman's leading role in the movement. However, he had experienced his own first doubts in 1839 about the theory of the Anglo-Catholic *via media*, which he describes vividly in chapter three, culminating in the "three blows which broke" him in 1841 (*Apologia Pro Vita Sua*, 133). Chapter four explains why he did not immediately become a Roman Catholic: he was on his "death-bed" as an Anglican, but not until all his objections to Rome had been resolved and he had worked out the theory of development was he ready to become a Roman Catholic. Having attempted to prove his own integrity in the preceding chapters, in the final chapter Newman proceeds to argue in defense of the Catholic Church that "its system is in no sense dishonest" (216).

MAJOR THEMES

Newman made it clear that the *Apologia* was not intended to be a history of the Oxford Movement. And yet it obviously is, to some extent at least, a historical account, and one seen from the point of view of the man who effectively inspired and led the movement until he began to have serious doubts. But it is this very fact that may easily be disguised by Newman's modest narrative, in which he does not make clear how crucial was his own role and influence. So closely documented is his account by means of letters and quotations from published writings that there is little room for any serious factual errors, while the author's comments on and interpretation of the facts tend to be carefully expressed as simply his own personal opinions, thus disarming any complaints about their lack of objectivity. After all, the point of the *Apologia* was to try to describe as far as possible the development of the narrator's theological views leading to his conversion to Rome. As such, it is fully supported by the wealth of autobiographical materials, nor has the book ever been seriously challenged,[1] although the actual ideas and their evolution have been subjected to plenty of critical scrutiny.

The truth is that the *Apologia* is essentially an autobiography. But unlike that other Victorian classic, John Ruskin's *Praeterita*, the *Apologia* is an austerely intellectual work, purporting to be merely what its subtitle, "A History of his Religious Opinions," indicates. Certainly, it is often called a "spiritual" autobiography, but in the strict sense of the word it is very far from being a spiritual work like Saint Augustine's *Confessions*, with which it is often compared. If it is at all confessional, it is only in its theological revelations, and such disclosures as there are of the author's soul are almost incidental to the account of his theological development. Thus, for example, Newman tells us nothing of his prayer life, there is no mention of his Anglican confirmation and First communion, nor is his ordination ever referred to, or the parochial work he did as a curate in the Oxford parish of St. Clement's, or his strongly held convictions about the pastoral responsibilities of a college tutor. Central autobiographical themes like these, of great importance for understanding Newman's spiritual life, are simply ignored.

In at least two cases, the silence may be misleading, as there were important effects on his theological development. In the first place, there is the question of Newman's gradual deconversion from Evangelicalism. In his "Autobiographical Memoir," which he wrote in the 1870s, he records that after receiving Anglican orders he discovered from "personal experience" that the kind of Christianity he had imbibed from reading books by Evangelicals "would not work in a parish; that it was unreal; that this he had actually found as a fact.... that Calvinism was not a key to the phenomena of human nature, as they occur in the world." In other words, it was not only through the kind of theological discussion and study that he records in the *Apologia* that he became disenchanted with Evangelicalism but also as a result of the actual pastoral work he did in the working-class parish of St. Clement's. But to this practical experience—"the teaching of facts"—he makes no reference at all in the *Apologia* (*Autobiographical Writings*, 1956, 79).

That the silence was quite deliberately self-imposed can be shown by the even more glaring omission of any real description of the effect on his religious imagination of his Mediterranean tour of 1832 and 1833, immediately prior to the beginning of the Oxford Movement. Newman's visits to Italy, Malta, and the Greek islands are dismissed in six paragraphs in the first chapter, and yet the letters and verses he wrote on his travels, as well as the extraordinarily vivid account he later wrote of his near-fatal illness in Sicily, show how crucial this intense period was for his subsequent religious development. Here too, then, the *Apologia* is quite misleading autobiographically.

Actually, in a later passage in the second chapter, Newman does let drop a hint that his earlier brief account of his foreign travels was less than complete. In the course of discussing his theological position in 1833, he alludes to his ingrained prejudice that the pope was the Antichrist predicted in Scripture, which he had acquired through his adolescent Evangelical reading. When he noted in the first chapter, "My imagination was stained by the effects of this doctrine up to the year 1843," he qualified this by adding, "it had been obliterated from my reason and judgment at an earlier date" (*Apologia*, 27). This contrast reappears in the second chapter, when he traces the gradual diminution of his antipathy to the papacy. But this time it is his imagination that becomes less antipapal than his reason. When he went abroad for the first time to Catholic countries, "the sight of so many great places, venerable shrines, and noble churches, much impressed my imagination" (65). His "heart was touched also," he recalled, by Catholic devotions and worship, and although his "reason was not affected at all," for his "judgment was against her, when viewed as an institution, as truly as it has ever been," nevertheless "he learned to have tender feelings towards her" (65).

The contradiction between these two passages seems obvious, but the discrepancy is more apparent than real. Keenly sensitive as he always was to the complex interaction of the imaginative and the rational, Newman was well aware that just as the imagination may anticipate ideas only later embraced by the reason, so too the imagination may refuse to keep pace with the reason's progress. Thus, while a view of the pope as the Antichrist may leave a "stain" on the imagination that the reason finds itself unable to expunge, so too the imagination may embrace ideas that are not yet entertained by the reason.

As Newman's philosophical masterpiece, the *Grammar of Assent* (1870), shows so profoundly, the reason and the imagination are integrally connected; nevertheless, the *Apologia*, in its scrupulous concentration on the intellectual development of its author's religious beliefs, downplays the impressions he received during those eventful months abroad. It is of course true that Newman's two traumatic experiences in the summer of 1839 could be called as much imaginative as intellectual, as they are described in the *Apologia*. But such is the force of those celebrated pages that a reader would conclude that Newman's deconversion from Anglicanism only really began in that fateful long vacation. In fact, what the travel letters of 1832 and 1833 reveal so graphically is that the imaginative seeds of Newman's eventual conversion were sown during his time in southern Europe, where he experienced at first hand for the first time the two forms of Christianity that had never been "reformed" by the events of the sixteenth century and that could trace back their origins directly to the primitive Church of the apostles and martyrs. There was a sense in which Eastern Orthodoxy may have interested him more than Roman Catholicism, as after all it was the Greek rather than the Latin Fathers who were his real theological mentors, especially his hero Saint Athanasius. Witnessing Orthodox devotion to the Virgin Mary, which is more prominent in its liturgy than in the Latin Mass, and to the saints clearly disconcerted Newman, as such alleged idolatry and superstition were supposed to be the peculiar mark of the Church of Rome. Most perplexing of all were his very mixed emotions on reaching Rome—the supposed city of the Antichrist but also the city where Peter and Paul were martyred; the city to which England owed its Christian faith but also the city where the most famous church in Christendom, St. Peter's, had been built partly by the sale of indulgences; the city doubtless full of superstition but also full of churches and shrines conspicuous for their devotion. It was all very confusing given that he had been taught to believe that Rome was one of the four beasts of the Apocalypse. He was impressed by the devoutness of the seminarians he saw, and yet he had to believe that the Roman Catholic priesthood was deeply corrupt—but then again he found himself wondering if the pompous Anglican chaplain in Rome was really closer to Christian truth than were the Italian priests he saw. In the end, he came to the somewhat contradictory conclusion that while Roman Catholicism itself was hopelessly corrupt, individual Roman Catholics could be very impressive indeed. But what, he dared wonder, if this was an example of the principle that the corruption of the best is the worst? He was beginning to glimpse that the argument from corruption was a two-edged weapon. As he waited in Palermo for a ship to take him home, he put into verse his new attitude to Roman Catholicism, full of ambivalence and of significance for a decision that was still twelve years away:

> Oh that thy creed were sound!
> For thou dost soothe the heart, Thou Church of Rome,
>   By thy unwearied watch and varied round
> Of service, in thy Saviour's holy home. (*Verses on Various Occasions*,
>   1888, 153)

In both Newman's deconversion from Evangelicalism and his conversion to Rome, personal experience of a very concrete nature was an important factor, reinforcing the more theological aspects to which the *Apologia* very largely confines itself. It is time now to look at what kind of autobiography the *Apologia* is, rather than what it is not.

First of all, the *Apologia* clearly belongs to a recognizable genre, as its author indicates when he acknowledges his enormous debt to the Evangelical Thomas Scott (1747–1821), who recounted his own religious pilgrimage in his best-selling little autobiography *The Force of Truth* (1779), a work that Newman says deeply impressed him because it showed how Scott "followed truth wherever it led him, beginning with Unitarianism, and ending in a . . . faith in the Holy Trinity" (*Apologia*, 26). Scott's book, of course, belonged to the English Protestant autobiographical tradition that originated with John Bunyan's *Grace Abounding to the Chief of Sinners* (1666). The autobiography of conversion was especially congenial to Evangelicals, whose spirituality and theology were so overwhelmingly centered on personal conversion to Christ. The typical Evangelical pattern of conversion was to be found, for example, in the extremely popular *Rise and Progress of Religion in the Soul* (1745) by Philip Doddridge (1702–1751), which Newman lent to his parishioners at St. Clement's. It was a book that his own Evangelical schoolmaster mentor, Walter Mayers, had recommended to him after Newman's conversion in 1816 in a letter that accompanied the gift of a copy of *Private Thoughts upon Religion and Private Thoughts upon a Christian Life* (1709) by William Beveridge (1637–1708). It is significant that nearly sixty years later Newman himself testified to the intellectual nature of his own autobiography when he noted that he had not mentioned Beveridge's *Private Thoughts* in the *Apologia* because he was "speaking there of the formation of my doctrinal opinions, and I do not think they were influenced by it. I had fully and eagerly taken up Calvinism into my religion before it came into my hands. . . . But no book was more dear to me, or exercised a more powerful influence over my devotion and my habitual thoughts. In my private memoranda I even wrote in its style" (*Letters and Diaries*, 1978, 196, 30 n.1).

Unlike the autobiographies of Bunyan, Cowper, Newton, and Whitefield, Scott's *The Force of Truth* was, like the *Apologia*, devoid of emotional introspection, being wholly concerned with giving a strictly theological account of the author's religious development. Scott also avoided the personal details of his life—although in this reticence he was only following Bunyan and Newton. Again, as if to prove that his conversion was based on intellectual rather than emotional grounds, Scott emphasized that the Trinitarian Christianity he eventually embraced was derived ultimately from his reading of orthodox Anglican divines. Similarly, as if to show that he was not influenced by subjective considerations, Newman stressed that his conversion had little or nothing to do with reading or meeting Roman Catholics. Whereas the Protestant autobiographical tradition naturally depended upon biblical motifs, particularly that of the exodus of the Israelites, Newman was influenced by the analogies he found in his study of the primitive Church and the early heresies.

The *Apologia* was not only in the English Protestant tradition but, as noted above, also bears marked resemblances to the most famous of all spiritual autobiographies, the *Confessions* of Saint Augustine. Indeed, it was, Newman tells us, a sentence from another of Augustine's writings that was one of the causes of his crisis of doubt in 1839, just as, he reminds us, Augustine himself had been converted to Catholic Christianity from Manichaeism by hearing some chance words of a child—an event that is the dramatic turning point of the *Confessions*. Rather, as with Augustine's depiction of his conversion in terms of a transition from death to life, Newman finds himself on what he called his Anglican "deathbed," an image that in effect replaces the traditional Protestant idea of the religious seeker wandering in the desert like the Israelites in search of the promised land. Like Augustine, too, Newman has to recant his misconceptions of Catholicism. And again, rather like Augustine, who commends his mother Saint Monica to the prayers of his readers at the end of book nine, so Newman prays at the end of chapter five for his old Oxford friends, a finale that contrasts with the traditional Protestant closure that concerns the salvation of the individual Christian. Finally, just as, with the achievement of conversion, the last four books (X–XIII) of the *Confessions* abandon narrative for reflective exposition, so too the last chapter of the *Apologia* turns to a different kind of "apologia" in which Newman defends Catholicism against the traditional Protestant charges in the same way that Augustine ends by defending the Catholic doctrine of creation against the Manichaean heresy he himself had previously held.[2]

But if it is true that in the *Apologia* Newman has drawn, however unconsciously, from a Catholic model, thus modifying the Protestant or Evangelical tradition from within which he is clearly and more or less self-consciously writing, it is also the case that the *Apologia* is much more dryly theological, like Scott's *The Force of Truth*, than the introspective, spiritual *Confessions*. So, it may be asked, how is it that the *Apologia* has continued to grip readers very far removed from the events of nineteenth-century Oxford?

First, the austere, largely documentary form that Newman employs paradoxically serves to highlight the few personal details that are divulged. In the first chapter, for instance, a large number of people appear whom Newman acknowledges as formative influences, but because he wishes for his own apologetic reasons to confine himself to their theological significance, such description of them as his uncompromising narrative concedes is tantalizingly fleeting and elusive. For example, in his generously detailed account of the influence of the Provost of Oriel, Edward Hawkins, he alludes with extreme politeness to the fact that "he provoked me very much from time to time, though I am perfectly certain that I have provoked him a great deal more" (*Apologia*, 28). That is all that he says about the row over the college office of tutor, which was not only germane to future developments of the Oxford tutorial system but also highly relevant to the formation of Newman's own views on education, which would achieve their classic expression in *The Idea of a University*. The sparsity of the text gives a certain resonance to the narrative as the reader picks up the vibrations of the carefully controlled voice of the narrator. Similarly, there is no attempt to convey the actual atmosphere of the famous Oriel common room, but small details are allowed to escape: for example, it was on a walk through Christ Church meadow that the Reverend William James taught Newman the doctrine of apostolic succession, while, on another, this time solitary walk as a new, shy fellow of Oriel, he encountered the then provost, Edward Copleston, who "turned round, and with the kind courteousness which sat so well on him, made me a bow and said 'one was never less alone than when alone'" (34). It is the small and apparently incidental touches like these that give the narrative a personal immediacy that is the more strongly felt precisely because of the sense of suppressed emotion. Moreover, the reader is affected by the sense that it is only the author's overriding desire to present as frankly and squarely as possible his developing doctrinal views that restrains him from more personal revelations. And it is this very impression of severe self-restraint that enhances the dramatic tension of the theological story, as our attention is focused relentlessly on the pressure of ideas on a mind both alertly responsive to new problems and questions and keenly aware of its own moral responsibility to follow the truth wherever it might lead.

It was, as we have seen, this single-minded pursuit of the truth that had so impressed Newman in Scott's *The Force of Truth*. And the great triumph of the *Apologia* is the way in which Newman not only holds our attention by the detached documentary report of his theological pilgrimage but also draws us into the dim historical events of the early Church, against the background of which he resolves his own religious identity. We find ourselves as surprised at our own interest in the Monophysites ("I saw my face in that mirror, and I was a Monophysite" [114]) as Newman himself was astonished that a particularly unsavory episode in the history of the early Church should have caused his first really serious doubt about the Anglican position. The dramatic passage that he then quotes from a later controversial writing in which he revisited this moment of crisis reminds us that the *Apologia* consists to a very great extent of lengthy quotations from private letters as well as published works, and this sets in relief the limpid tone of the narrative, which itself is a kind of connected commentary on those documents. For there is certainly excitement in the *Apologia*, but the difference from Newman's other writings is that the argument and polemic are now recollected at a distance—if not exactly in tranquility, at least in relative detachment.

It is a curious anomaly that the book on which Newman's literary reputation is presumed principally to rest should differ strikingly from his other works of controversy, which give him his distinctive place in the history of English literature. Much of its power lies in the (almost) disconcertingly calm tone of the author's conversational, sometimes even colloquial voice. Flashes of eloquence are rare (and all the more effective for their rarity), for eloquence is excluded nearly as rigorously as explicit self-defense: "I am not setting myself up as a pattern of good sense or any thing else: I am but giving a history of my opinions, and that, with the view of showing that I have come by them through intelligible processes of thought and honest external means." Nor is there any claim that his history will be of any great human interest: "I have no romantic story to tell" (51). Indeed, the *Apologia* is unique among Newman's published works not only in its form and content but also in its style and tone. Nearly all of his writings were "occasional" in the sense of being responses to particular occasions, and of course the *Apologia* is no exception, for it is an extended answer to Kingsley's attack. But what makes the *Apologia* so different is that, with the exception of the last chapter, the actual argument, debate, and polemic are now all in the recorded past tense. And the main "apologia" persuades not by overt argument but by the narration of facts, albeit of past controversies.

It is to the original first two pamphlets, or parts, of the 1864 *Apologia* that we would have to turn to find the polemic that makes Newman probably the greatest controversialist in the English language. He was no doubt correct to omit what would not only have looked unnecessarily aggressive to an audience that had already largely recognized his victory over Kingsley but would have been at best irrelevant and at worst prejudicial to the purpose of the history he wanted to tell in refutation of Kingsley in particular and of the prejudiced Protestant public in general. However, from the literary point of view, one cannot but regret the loss of writing that recalls the exuberant satire that flowered in the years immediately after Newman's conversion, especially in *Difficulties of Anglicans* (1850) and *Present Position of Catholics in England* (1851).

Finally, the *Apologia* contains in the last chapter an important contribution to ecclesiology, part of the development or revival of Catholic theology of the Church, to which Newman contributed so significantly and that would culminate in the Second Vatican Council's constitution on the Church. What Newman is considering in his general defense of the Roman Catholic Church is really the larger question of the relation between authority and freedom. As against the modern assumption that freedom by definition means the absence of checks and limitations (except such as may incidentally be imposed by conflict between opposing freedoms), Newman's case is that freedom demands boundaries and limits; otherwise it degenerates into anarchy and thus destroys itself. The post-Enlightenment outlook assumes the validity of the individual mind seeking truth in a kind of splendid isolation from both tradition and the community of other minds. Now, although Newman did not live to see philosophers of science "cast doubt upon the credentials of science itself as an avenue to truth" (Mitchell 1990, 237), he did seriously challenge the epistemology of the Enlightenment in other areas of human knowledge. And in this last chapter of the *Apologia* he insists that the authority of an infallible Church, far from destroying reason, actually sustains it by protecting it from its own "suicidal excesses" (*Apologia*, 220). Not only that, he argues, but paradoxically the "energy of the human intellect. . . . thrives and is joyous, with a tough elastic strength, under the terrible blows of the divinely-fashioned weapon [infallibility], and is never so much itself as when it has lately been overthrown" (225). Newman claims that the reason for the vitality of Catholic theology is precisely because it has to work within the constraints and discipline of an authoritative Church and that the resulting tension, indeed conflict, far from being debilitating or frustrating, is actually creative and liberating. Newman does not purport to provide any kind of schematic theology for the relation between authority and freedom in the Church, and indeed the whole implication of some of the most rhetorical pages in his writings is that no such blueprint is possible for what, after all, is a living rather than a static relationship. But he does proceed, with pointed historical examples, to show, as against the authoritarianism of the Ultramontanes—at whom this chapter is aimed as much as it is at Kingsley and also at liberal Catholics—how important theology is for the life of the Church. And it is the careful balance with which he asserts both the right of theologians to free inquiry and at the same time the prerogatives of the hierarchical teaching authority that makes his discussion highly pertinent to the perennial problem of reconciling the conservative and the innovative elements in the Church.

CRITICAL RECEPTION

The majority, but not all, of contemporary reviewers thought that Newman had proved his sincerity against Kingsley's accusation but, not surprisingly, were unpersuaded by the doctrinal conclusions he reached. The more generous of such reviewers, however, acknowledged that his position was perfectly reasonable given his premises. Preoccupied as they were with the theological views expressed in the book, they paid very little attention to its literary qualities. There were, however, some exceptions, most significantly the very important review by the prominent critic R. H. Hutton in the secular *Spectator*, who called Newman "not only one of the greatest of English writers, but, perhaps the very greatest master of . . . sarcasm in the English language" (1864, 206). Although no Catholic, Hutton also admired Newman as a thinker. The friendly response of Anglican reviewers was no doubt influenced by the way Newman spoke of former Anglican allies and opponents alike.

For further reading, Martin J. Svaglic's critical edition (1967) contains a useful general introduction, while David J. DeLaura's edition (1968) includes a number of essays on the origin and reception of the *Apologia* as well as criticism. My *John Henry Newman: A Biography* (1988) sets the book within the larger biographical and historical context and also analyzes the contemporary and theological significance of the last chapter.

NOTES

John Henry Newman, *Apologia Pro Vita Sua*, ed. Ian Ker (London: Penguin, 1994). All references are to this edition.

1. That is, apart from Frank M. Turner, *John Henry Newman: The Challenge to Evangelical Religion* (New Haven, CT: Yale University Press, 2002), who rejects both the *Apologia* and the letters as truly representing Newman's real intentions and motives and, in the absence of other primary materials, prefers to substitute his own speculations in place of Newman's later account and the contemporary letters that support it.

2. See Linda H. Peterson, *Victorian Autobiography: The Tradition of Self-Interpretation* (New Haven, CT: Yale University Press, 1986, 93–119). I cannot, however, agree with her unconvincing parallel between Augustine's mother, who was profoundly involved in his conversion, and Newman's mother, who (unlike his grandmother and aunt) cannot be said to have had any significant effect on his religious development or indeed any sympathy with it.

WORKS CITED

DeLaura, David J., ed. 1968. *Apologia*. New York: W. W. Norton.

Hutton, R. H. 1864. "Father Newman's Sarcasm." *Spectator* 37 (February): 206–08.
Ker, Ian. 1988. *John Henry Newman: A Biography*. Oxford: Clarendon Press.
Mitchell, Basil. 1990. "Newman as Philosopher." In *Newman After a Hundred Years*, ed. Ian Ker and Alan G. Hill, 223–46. Oxford: Clarendon Press.
Newman, John Henry. 1888. *Verses on Various Occasions*. London: Longmans, Green, and Co.
———. 1956. *Autobiographical Writings*, ed. Henry Tristram. London: Sheed and Ward.
———. 1978. *The Letters and Diaries of John Henry Newman*, vol. 1, ed. Ian Ker and Thomas Gornall, S. J. Oxford: Clarendon Press.
Svaglic, Martin J., ed. 1967. *Apologia*. Oxford: Clarendon Press.

BIBLIOGRAPHY

Cockshut, A. O. J. *The Art of Autobiography in 19th and 20th Century England*. New Haven, CT: Yale University Press, 1984.
Helmling, Steven. *The Esoteric Comedies of Carlyle, Newman, and Yeats*. Cambridge: Cambridge University Press, 1988.
Houghton, Walter E. *The Art of Newman's "Apologia."* New Haven, CT: Yale University Press, 1945.
Peterson, Linda H. *Victorian Autobiography: The Tradition of Self-Interpretation*. New Haven, CT: Yale University Press, 1986.

— Ian Ker

John Henry Newman [1801–1890]

Loss and Gain, The Story of a Convert and Callista, A Sketch of the Third Century

PLOT SUMMARIES

John Henry Newman's two novels *Loss and Gain, The Story of a Convert* (1848) and *Callista, A Sketch of the Third Century* (1855) can be understood in a number of ways: as early Victorian fiction, as extended Catholic apologetic essays, as controversialist polemics, as religious glosses and commentaries, and as autobiographical and confessional conversion stories. They are neither the best of Newman's extensive body of writing nor first-rate literature. Rather, their primary importance and interest are as intense Catholic reworkings and refocusings of themes and ideas already expressed in similar popular English Protestant literature of the nineteenth century.

Because one of Newman's primary forms of expression was the written and preached sermon, these novels contain extensive passages that partake of that same form, monologues, extended meditations and reflections on religious ideas, and the intellectual and emotional reactions of the primary characters to these. Often, these passages freeze the movement and development of the story line, becoming a collection of religious set pieces in which Newman demonstrates his command of a wide variety of ideas and themes. Some of these arguments no longer have the intensity and importance that they had for the nineteenth-century reader. In this sense, the novels are dated both in style and content, with the language of romanticism, verging on sentimentality, often a barrier for the contemporary reader. Yet, these novels still have substance and importance within the broader context of Catholic literature.

The central plot of both novels is that of religious and spiritual conversion, portrayed as an extended and complex process rather than as an immediate event. This was an experience that Newman knew well, beginning with his early commitment to an acceptable evangelical Christianity while an undergraduate at Trinity College, Oxford, in 1817, continuing through his participation in the Tractarian Movement of the 1830s and 1840s while a fellow of Oriel College and a vicar of St. Mary the Virgin University Church, and finally culminating in his "going over" to Rome in 1845. Constant parallels exist between Newman's own conversion experience and that of the principal character of each novel, Charles Reding in *Loss and Gain* and Callista in *Callista*, as they struggle with religious truth.

Newman matches his characters in both novels, establishing early on a model of protagonist and antagonist with the antagonists pulling intellectually, emotionally, and spiritually at Reding and Callista. This created balance allows the author to use a scholastic method in the development of the plot, pronouncing an idea, then answering that idea in both a positive and a negative manner. While this process results in a continually honed set of definitions and debates, it also becomes somewhat strained and dry, in particular as the story line moves toward the conversion of the protagonist, which is to a degree somewhat anticlimactic in the broader scheme. It is evident that Newman the controversialist found in this model ready expression of all points of view.

In *Loss and Gain*, Newman is on very familiar ground as he depicts Oxford University, his academic and spiritual home, in the prolonged process of reforming itself while the whole of the English nation was simultaneously reforming itself. He first conceived of the story while in Rome following his ordination as a Catholic priest in 1847, while awaiting the papal brief that would authorize him to establish the first English Congregation of the Oratory of St. Philip Neri, the religious institute of which he had become a member. Although often not to his taste or sensibilities, Newman's time in Rome provided him the opportunity to reflect on his decision to part from friends and position by converting on his knees before the Passionist priest Father Dominic Barbari at Littlemore in the early hours of October 8, 1845. He was now able to use the form of the novel to transmit the realities of his own religious struggle and conversion, a genre through which he believed others might come to understand his decision and perhaps be influenced in their own similar decisions.

The young man Charles Reding is unformed and unsure of mind and spirit as he enters Oxford, soon to be exposed to a bewildering variety of religious opinions typical of the lax, mid-nineteenth-century High Anglicanism most often characterized as a latitudinarian indifferentism. In typical Oxford common-room exchanges, often continued in extended walking conversations in and around Oxford, Reding is confronted by a series of character types, including Dr. Brownside, the character who portrays Dr. Renn Dixon Hampden, whose appointment in 1836 as the Regius Professor of Divinity provided the Oxford Tractarians with a focused cause; Fairborn, the sum of all evangelical types; Bateman and White, of Anglo-Catholic persuasion; Vincent, the moderate who fears and avoids all parties; and Lord Newlights, of no fixed religious principle. Besides these characters, who can be viewed as typical of the wide variety of Oxford religious opinions, there are other characters more directly related to Reding, in particular Carlton, who is usually understood as portraying John Keble, whose trumpet-call 1833 sermon on national apostasy Newman considered to be the beginning of Tractarianism. In fact, some aspect of Newman's voice can be found in all of his characters.

As the academic year moves forward, determined by its own punctuations of events and traditions, Reding is pushed and pulled toward his ultimate conversion, as his life of the mind evolves into the emotions of the human soul engaged in its journey toward truth and final things. The tensions in the story result from the successive stages of this journey. As the perennial questions with which the Anglican community of the time collectively struggled are debated, Reding becomes intellectually shaken in his inherited trust in the Church of England and eventually comes to see neither its Anglo-Catholic revival nor its traditionally understood position as *via media* as adequate or real. It is then that he must strike the ultimate balance between loss and gain: loss of academic recognition; of ordination and career within the established church; of family; and, most wrenching, of friends; but gain of ultimate truth and peace. Reding crosses over to Rome, and the final short chapter of the novel records his words, paraphrasing Saint Augustine, to his best friend Willis, now the Passionist Father Aloysius: "[Y]ou have taken the better betimes, while I have loitered. Too late have I known Thee, O thou ancient Truth; too late have I found Thee, First and only Fair" (*Loss and Gain*, 296–97). The conversion process is complete, and the novel ends with the smell of incense and the sound of bells.

As Newman's scholarly life, and by extension his spiritual life, began with the study of the Church Fathers and the various heresies they confronted, in particular the widespread Arian heresy, it was natural for these elements to have a profound influence on his second novel, *Callista*. The entire structure and drive of this novel is far different from that of *Loss and Gain*, while the central plot of conversion remains. The plot of *Callista* concentrates on the last phases of the early Christian Church before clear lines of orthodoxy had been established by ecumenical councils beginning with the First Nicaean Council in the year 325. It is an intellectually vibrant and diverse community characterized by a lax Christianity in the process of becoming respectable, yet with clashing extremist positions existing within the community. Roman persecution continued to provide the blood of martyrs, ultimately demanding that Callista herself joyfully join in the physical sufferings of Jesus Christ. Newman develops a unique and direct narration of the concept of martyrdom, viewing it as a matter neither to be sought nor to be avoided but to be ecstatically endured as the highest Christian duty.

Callista lives in the town of Sicca, in Roman provincial North Africa. Newman describes the setting in Eden-like terms. She is a Greek who is a successful maker of pagan images, an activity, however, that increasingly leaves her with a sense of impropriety and wrongdoing. With Agellius, her suitor, and Juba, his brother, Callista gradually responds to the rather opaque teachings of Bishop Caecilius. She is described as being about midway in the process of search and inquiry: neither a Christian nor a pagan, her ambivalent condition will necessarily be solved through the realities of the Decian persecutions of the mid-third century. The argument raised in favor of an established paganism is that with which Newman was familiar at Oxford: duty toward a national religion. In unredeemed paganism, Newman understood the fallacies involved in religious arguments based on the notion of the importance of stability for the larger society.

As in *Loss and Gain*, the characters in *Callista* represent the variety of religious opinions involved in the intense circumstance of a declining Roman pagan orthodoxy now confronting the rising but unfocused realities of early Christianity. This is not a time of tolerance or mutual acceptance but one of heated emotions within and between the two, which give rise to either/or responses and reactions. Callista struggles with the actualities of a protracted conversion, the dividing of family and friends, and the intensity of those who experience the first heady taste of new beliefs seen through the supposedly now-opened eyes of the soul.

When Callista grasps the truth of faith, the conflicting perspectives and parties fade into unimportance and unreality and a light of great intensity fills her. In her martyrdom, her conversion is fulfilled as she cries out to her one and only love, Jesus. Newman concludes the work by using the voice of Saint Cyprian, who died in the year 258, in the eulogy for Callista: "A Greek had come to Africa to embellish the shrines of heathenism . . . and to strengthen the old ties which connected genius with sin. . . . But yesterday a poor child of earth, and today an inhabitant of the heavens. . . . But yesterday tossed about on a sea of opinion, and today entranced in the vision of infallible truth and immutable sanctity" (*Callista*, 209). Again in this novel, the process of conversion is fulfilled by worldly losses but one true heavenly gain. This time, however, the last image is of altars within churches wherein are enshrined the bones of martyrs that will be revered by future generations.

MAJOR THEMES

Newman was the author of serious literature designed to edify rather than entertain: well-defined university sermons, expositions of religious ideas and themes for an educated public audience, apologetic essays, and expositions of controversial topics. As a literary form, the English novel of his time was still in the extended process of gaining validity, developing from frivolous themes to those of a more serious nature. For example, serious religious themes can be found in the two novels of Prime Minister Benjamin Disraeli (1804–1881), *Coningsby, or the New Generation* (1844) and *Sybil, or the Two Nations* (1845), both passionate expositions of political ideas. It is the evolution of the novel that provides the broader context for Newman's fiction.

The central theme of religious conversion is strictly delineated by Newman in a traditional Catholic definition as a concise and direct movement toward the ultimate truth, the fullness and completeness of which is found only in the Roman Catholic Church. This is not a wandering or relative process with any number of acceptable outcomes. Undergirding the process is the always-present theme of human free will, formed and informed by the teaching function of the Church. Individual free will, when properly exercised, leads to essential choices that fulfill the human longing for holiness through which alone ultimate union with the divine can be achieved, a theme found throughout Newman's writings. Charles Reding and Callista come to understand this proper exercise of the free will, which results in the conversion of doubt and flawed belief. Newman also made specific use of this theme of free will and choice in his poem "The Dream of Gerontius" (1865), in which the knight's deathbed experience is a fulfillment of the search for truth. When the beatific vision is finally achieved, Gerontius expresses the same faith as Reding: "Now let me die, since I have seen Thy Face." Here is the ultimate expression of an individual's free will fulfilled, one who willingly leaves behind all that transitory life and earth might offer and holds firm to that which is permanent and true.

Developing from this central theme of conversion are three comparative topics used by Newman in both novels and through which he attempts to prove the theological and historical validity of the Roman Catholic Church, as contrasted to the compromised and confused nature of the Protestant tradition in general and

Anglicanism in particular. In his contrasting of reality with unreality, consistency with inconsistency, and substance with externals, Newman slices through the structure of the much-vaunted Anglican *via media* and his own contemporary Oxford Anglo-Catholic revival, neither of which he sees as adequate or ultimately valid. Charles Reding and Callista inhabit worlds in which these comparative topics provide the framework for the plots. These are worlds separated by some sixteen hundred years of history, yet they share a commonality that can only be found in a Church that likewise shares that extended time frame. Callista acts out her role in a world in which religious boundaries are not yet set and defined and in which orthodoxy and heterodoxy compete for the minds and souls of believers, but also within which the substance of truth can be understood. For Reding, Oxford is a religious microcosm of this same sixteen hundred years, in which definitions, dogmas, and controversies have been milled so fine as almost to have lost substance. Callista, therefore, inhabits a much more open, less-defined world of religious sensibilities than does Reding, and while these contrasting contexts help to define the two novels as very different from each other, they also share a structure that revolves around these three topics.

To Newman, as voiced by his protagonist Reding, the Roman Catholic Church is, first of all, *real* because it fully manifests the essential four distinguishing marks or characteristics as formulated in the Nicene Creed in the year 325: it is one, holy, catholic, and apostolic in both its history and doctrine. By contrast, the Protestant traditions and opinions, represented by various characters in both novels who attempt to influence Callista and Reding, either only partially manifest these marks or create new marks (such as reformed or evangelical) without valid authority, both of which conditions result in their lack of reality. Second, through his study of the early Church and patristics, Newman discovered that the Roman Catholic Church is fully *consistent* in all of its doctrine, dogma, and teaching, establishing and maintaining these four marks within a defined structure of Scripture and tradition, both of which are equally necessary for validity, one of the results of consistency. Both Callista and Reding confront inconsistency, one in a proto-Protestant manifestation, the other in a fully developed Protestantism. Protestant inconsistency is demonstrated best in the conflicting and confusing variety of denominations and beliefs of which Protestantism is collectively composed. These result in doubt and heresy more than truth. And finally, the *substance* of the Roman Catholic Church is to be found in its complete complement of the seven Scriptural sacraments, each consistent and interrelated; in its priesthood, consecrated, celibate, and historical; and in its authoritative voice expressed through a papacy stemming from apostolic succession and augmented by valid Church councils. Protestant expressions, by contrast, are formalized externals lacking in any agreed-upon substance—merely form without content. Newman uses this triple model of comparative topics in *Loss and Gain* to distinguish the true Catholic Church from counterfeit denominations and in *Callista* to distinguish Christianity from paganism and, by extension, orthodox Christianity from heresy.

There are no cleverly orchestrated surprises in the novels' plots, as the story line for each is direct almost to the point of dullness. Nevertheless, the novels share an intensity of purpose and development. The characters are finely drawn, with a basic contrast between those who manifest the healthy unity of a Catholic mentality and those with a confused Protestant personality, vaguely Christian but also intensely secular. To Newman, character was more significant than plot, with the latter serving the former and based on the individual's human search for certainty.

It is in the human heart of the main characters that Newman expresses his firm belief in the intuitive or nonrational approach to religious faith, for it is through the emotions seated in the heart that truth is perceived and understood. This stress upon the emotions shows Newman as a romantic writer, one who does not break with classical and Christian traditions but rather reworks them in order to capture the essence of the experience of religious conversion. The novels culminate in final conversion scenes that are almost beyond verbal expression as the human heart gains union with divine love, an inevitable ending for Newman who, when he was ordained a cardinal, selected as his motto a phrase from Saint Francis de Sales (1567–1622), "*Cor Ad Cor Loquitur*" (Heart Speaks to Heart)—the highest form of conversation. While the love interest of most Victorian novels was human and profane, for Newman the goal was supernatural love, a divine love that overflowed in the hearts of converts to the Catholic faith.

Because it is the lighter of the two novels, with a certain level of sophisticated humor, *Loss and Gain* may be the most accessible of Newman's works for those not familiar with his writings. This novel likewise tends to be more static and less dynamic than *Callista*, which is the more profound and well constructed of the two. *Loss and Gain* has a certain transparent character to it, while *Callista* tends to be more dense and opaque, requiring more attentive reading. When read several times, the two novels manifest most clearly that they are interrelated, actually two installments of the same story. As Newman was moving into the final phase of his own conversion process, he preached a heartfelt sermon on September 26, 1845, in Littlemore known as "The Parting of Friends." Here, he explained that conversion demands even the leaving of friends, which to him represented the ultimate loss. It is this same loss that Reding and Callista embrace that they might defeat this world and gain the next.

CRITICAL RECEPTION

The critical reception accorded Newman's two novels has varied greatly, as with that given most of his works, from almost ecstatic commentary, to unkind attacks on his person, to studied indifference. At the time of the novels' publication, a clear divide could be noted between a positive Catholic critique and a negative Protestant one. The mid-nineteenth-century English Catholic convert community in its various publications tended to hang onto every word Newman produced, often investing works such as his novels with a depth of ideas not really present in the text. On the other hand, those of the English establishment mentality, both within and without the Anglican church, often dismissed the novels as being disingenuous products of an evidently disingenuous mind.

A central problem involved in this early critical reaction is that both novels were produced in the context of what, to many, was a dangerous development: the continuing Catholic emancipation and the reestablishment of a papal presence in England. Beginning with parliamentary legislation in the late eighteenth century and culminating with the Catholic Emancipation Act of 1829 (which, interestingly, Newman opposed at the time), the legal restrictions applied to the Roman

Catholic Church and its faithful in the mid-sixteenth century were eliminated. With the restoration of an English Catholic hierarchy by Pope Pius IX in 1850, a real threat was perceived by much of establishment England, in particular as this was related to the "Irish question" and Irish immigration into the industrial cities of the English midlands. It was one thing to have a somewhat quiet and scattered recusant group that had lost most of its post-Reformation intensity but quite another to have Catholics busily converting good nominal Anglicans and then boasting of this accomplishment. Newman became the very symbol of this threat, with his novels supposedly hammering home Roman errors.

Both *Loss and Gain* and *Callista* were written partly in direct response to other novels that presented negative critiques of the supposedly frightening prospect of conversion to Rome along with critiques of Newman and everything for which he stood. While Newman was in Rome completing his priestly incardination into the Roman Catholic Church, Elizabeth Harris, a convert herself who had subsequently left the Catholic Church and was now questioning whether Newman and his group of converts would not soon follow, published *From Oxford to Rome: And How It Fared With Some Who Lately Made the Journey* (1847). Newman was constantly forced to confront the kind of doubts expressed in this work about his sincerity in conversion and his lack of honesty in general. He penned *Loss and Gain* as an answer and, later, summed up all his defense in his masterful *Apologia Pro Vita Sua* (1864), perhaps his finest piece of autobiographical writing. Interestingly, the notion that Newman was disingenuous or dishonest persists in writings about him today, most recently in Frank M. Turner's weighty *John Henry Newman, The Challenge to Evangelical Religion* (2002).

In the critical exchange of his day, Newman's greatest continuing nemesis was Charles Kingsley (1819–1875), a man who later became professor of modern history at Cambridge and who was the immediate progenitor of the *Apologia*. Kingsley wrote the novel *Hypatia, or New Foes With Old Faces* (1851, 1853), in which he condemned the ignorance and fanaticism of the orthodox members of the early Church in Alexandria and, by extension, the Roman Catholic Church of his own era. Newman's answer to this challenge was *Callista*, with its alternative vision of the early North African Church—confused, perhaps, but still possessing a sense of love and conviction. This pattern of responding novels was typical of mid-nineteenth-century literature: as both a criticism of and an answer to the other, each created a type of sustained dialogue that often lasted as long as the authors lived.

Ever the precise author, Newman continued to revise and edit his works, both those written as an Anglican and later as a Roman Catholic, bringing to print new editions of his two novels and keeping the titles current with his reading and critical audiences. After his death in 1890, Newman's fiction appealed to increasingly smaller audiences. As the body of critical studies on Newman's other writings increased, especially in academic and Catholic circles, the novels tended to be forgotten, although they were continually reprinted in new editions with introductions and commentary by a wide variety of authors and editors over succeeding generations. During this time, what critique there was of the novels most often dismissed them as a specific type of Catholic revival literature, a Catholic romanticism tending toward sentimentality in both theme and language. However, this was also the fate of most nineteenth-century religious novels, Catholic or not, which were viewed, in general, as both outmoded and outdated.

With the development of a twentieth-century Catholic revival, perhaps best witnessed in the 1935 canonization of Thomas More and John Fisher, two six-teenth-century figures who exemplified temporal loss for spiritual gain, Newman's writings in general and his novels in particular were given a new reading with new tools of literary criticism. The novels were no longer understood merely as a type of *apologia* but rather as useful literature of both depth and substance with wider appeal than simply their Catholic plots and themes. As the body of Victorian literature became critically reassessed in a more positive way, so Newman's novels were given new readings by a new generation of scholars.

This twentieth-century literary criticism that gave serious attention to Newman's novels culminated in the 1970s with two definitive and generally accessible studies, *Gains and Losses: Novels of Faith and Doubt in Victorian England* by Robert Lee Wolff (1977) and *The Victorian Historical Novel, 1840–1880* by Andrew L. Sanders (1979). These works provide the broader literary and social context for the novels, in particular that of the hundreds of popular religious novels written in the nineteenth century. Moving well beyond the contemporary sectarian perspectives to which the novels previously were subjected, these two literary scholars present a well-defined and integrated understanding of Newman's fiction.

Wolff's volume is the introductory study for the Garland Reprint Series of 121 religious novels published between 1823 and 1903 that express a variety of themes and ideas reflecting the "complex Victorian religious scene" (1977, 8). Concluding this work is a fine, brief bibliographical note (513–16) of the essential studies evaluating the Victorian literary world. Out of the basic group of these novels, Wolff clusters twenty-seven as Catholic and anti-Catholic works, within which Newman's novels are critiqued. To Wolff, Newman was "a man of the keenest intellect but of over-riding emotion, even mysticism" (20), the interaction among which determined novels that "were too subtle, too intellectual, too profound, then as now, for the ordinary novel reader" (72). Without a close and attentive reading, Newman's novels tend to remain obscure to the modern reader, making allusions to things that have now vanished.

Wolff gives the theme of human sexuality as found in Newman a sympathetic reading, beginning with a direct debunking of the commonly held idea that Newman was at least subconsciously a homosexual, a view expressed by some modern biographers. "Such an interpretation," Wolff insists, "overlooks the emo-tional language between persons of the same sex, which arouses thoughts in post-Freudian minds that sometimes were not present and sometimes were strictly suppressed in pre-Freudian minds" (46–47). Rather than the homosexual theme, Wolff finds more useful in understanding Newman and his novels the theme of sexual abstinence as it relates to the essential human quest for holiness. This is a view that does not resonate well with today's readers in an atmosphere of sexual freedom, but it was of central importance to Newman.

For Wolff, the central problem in Newman's novels was his inability "to fictionalize and still make credible and poignant to the general novel-reading public some of the major religious questions of the day" (72). A reason suggested for this is that Newman's novels are responses to other novels that already had set the issues and the dimensions of ideas involved. Given this circumstance, Wolff still concludes his analysis of Newman in a positive manner. While he maintains that *Callista* "moves with a speed and certainty and power far more certain than the pace of *Loss and Gain*" (71), the former novel already described as being "one of the best historical novels of the entire nineteenth century" (62), he continues to insist that *Loss and Gain* is "extraordinarily significant" (60) because of its treatment of Catholic themes and its often overlooked comic dimension.

In contrast to Wolff's wide-ranging comparative study of most of the religious novels of the nineteenth century, Andrew L. Sanders in *The Victorian Historical Novel* has written a more tightly focused study of a limited number of representative historical novels. Using a forty-year period, 1840 to 1880, he evaluates those novels that he identifies as having been written under the influence of Sir Walter Scott's "Waverley" novels and their portrayal of romantic historical fiction. As *Loss and Gain* is not directly a historical novel except in its varied allusions to the development of Christianity, Sanders makes only oblique reference to it by way of contrast to *Callista*, suggesting that "It is at times almost as if Sicca were the Oxford of *Loss and Gain* translated through time and space like a populous Holy House" (1979, 143).

Recreating the literary context in which Newman wrote *Callista*, Sanders uses the larger national religious revival of nineteenth-century England as an evaluative structure, keying into the influence of the Oxford Movement, with its stress on the ancient Christian Church and the romantic cult of the Middle Ages. "If it produced no supreme masterpiece," he proposes, "it at least made three prominent churchmen [Charles Kingsley, Nicholas Wiseman, and John Henry Newman] into popular novelists and into apologists in fiction for the divergent causes they found themselves defending" (121). For Sanders, all three of these writers are somehow united against the malicious negative portrayal of the early Christian Church presented by Edward Gibbon (1737–1794) in his rationalist historiography, *The Decline and Fall of the Roman Empire* (six volumes, 1776–1788).

Nicholas Wiseman (1802–1865), as Cardinal Archbishop of Westminster and primate of the recently reestablished English Catholic hierarchy, had initiated a project for a "Catholic Popular Library" to instruct the faithful about the Church, for which he had written the first volume, *Fabiola; or, The Church of the Catacombs* (1854). It was as the twelfth volume in this series, and in answer to Kingsley's *Hypatia*, that Newman wrote *Callista*, a work that Sanders finds to have both significant literary and historical dimensions. In particular, he is impressed with Newman's vivid account of the swarm of locusts that descends on Sicca, seeing it as "the most memorable section of the novel, and one of the most striking passages in Newman's entire *oeuvre*" (141). Although Newman himself is understood by Sanders to be a signal literary figure of his time, *Callista*'s literary importance is limited by its evident failings. "In spite of its grand underlying themes," Sanders early on concludes, "*Callista* remains a disappointing novel, awkward and unrealized even as an account of the changing spiritual perceptions which lead characters from doubt to certainty and through the difficult process of conversion" (140). This is somewhat similar to Wolff's analysis of *Loss and Gain*, in which he concludes that even after tracing Charles Reding's pilgrimage of conversion to the Church of Rome, the reader still "cannot be sure *why* he has taken the final step or why he takes it when he does" (1977, 53).

In the final analysis, although Newman's novels have serious flaws as literature, they retain importance as studies of Catholic themes and expressions of interesting syntheses of religious and secular ideas. It is these final dimensions that result in the novels having an established place in the canons of both Catholic and Victorian literature.

NOTE

John Henry Newman, *Loss and Gain, The Story of a Convert* (Oxford: Oxford University Press, 1986) and *Callista, A Sketch of the Third Century* (London: Burns and Oates, 1962). All references are to these editions.

WORKS CITED

Sanders, A. L. 1979. *The Victorian Historical Novel, 1840–1880*. New York: St. Martin's Press.

Turner, Frank M. 2002. *John Henry Newman, The Challenge to Evangelical Religion*. New Haven, CT: Yale University Press.

Wolff, Robert Lee. 1977. *Gains and Losses: Novels of Faith and Doubt in Victorian England*. New York: Garland.

BIBLIOGRAPHY

Chadwick, Owen. *The Victorian Church*. Vols. VII and VIII of *An Ecclesiastical History of England*, ed. J. C. Dickinson. London: Oxford University Press, 1970.

Church, R. W. *The Oxford Movement, Twelve Years: 1833–1845*. 1891. Reprint, Chicago: University of Chicago Press, 1970.

Fraught, C. Brad. *The Oxford Movement: A Thematic History of the Tractarians and Their Times*. University Park: Pennsylvania State University Press, 2003.

Gilley, Sheridan. *Newman and His Age*. London: Darton, Longman, and Todd, 1990.

Ker, Ian. *John Henry Newman, A Biography*. Oxford: Oxford University Press, 1988.

———, ed. *Newman and Conversion*. Notre Dame, IN: University of Notre Dame Press, 1977.

Rowell, Geoffrey. *The Vision Glorious, Themes and Personalities of the Catholic Revival in Anglicanism*. Oxford: Oxford University Press, 1983.

Ward, Wilfrid. *The Life of John Henry Newman*. London: Longmans, Green, and Co., 1912.

— Gerald Michael Schnabel

Kathleen Norris [1947–]

The Cloister Walk

BIOGRAPHY

An eclectic religious heritage paved the way for the ecumenism Kathleen Norris now practices. She was heir to two very different strands of Protestantism (Methodist and Presbyterian) through her grandparents. According to Norris's description in her book *Dakota: A Spiritual Geography* (1993), this was a severe and pietistic inheritance. Her paternal grandfather, Reverend John Luther Norris, had a conversion experience at a revival meeting and then became a preacher. He and his wife Beatrice raised seven children and served seventeen Methodist churches in the Great Plains region over the course of thirty-two years (100). Although her maternal grandfather, Frank Totten, a medical doctor, is described as less devout than his wife, Norris depicts his wife Charlotte's faith as uncompromising. That faith remained a force in her granddaughter Kathleen's life.

Born to John Heyward Norris, a professional musician, and Lois Ferne (Totten) Norris, a teacher, on July 27, 1947, in Washington, D.C., the young Kathleen suffered early on from a mysterious ailment. Over the years, her mother recounted to her the constant care and prayers that the Sisters of Charity at the local Catholic hospital devoted to her. Because she was an infant so near death, Norris later suggests the possibility that these caring nuns may have secretly baptized her as a Catholic. When she was seven, Norris was taken to visit the doctor whose progressive use of penicillin had saved her life when, at six months of age, she still weighed only twelve pounds. That doctor described her as a "fighter" with a strong will to live. However, the familiarity with medical staff and apparent ease with medical procedures that Norris displayed as a baby gave way to her later childhood experience of nightmares and fear of people who wore all-white clothes (*The Cloister Walk*, 87–88). Norris would, aptly, wrestle with the label of "fighter."

Around this age, Norris had her second vital encounter with Catholicism. Because she had a Catholic friend in the first grade, she wanted to convert. This longing met with resistance from her family, especially from her father. His main appeal to her at that time was the restrictions that being Catholic would impose on her, specifically the books and movies that would then be forbidden to her

(*Dakota*, 91). It was his belief, a common one among some Protestants, that the pope could simply tell Catholics what they could or could not read or watch. When refused a rosary of her own, Norris went so far as to borrow a necklace to use for prayer, mumbling the words because she did not know exactly what she was supposed to say (90–91). She did, however, experience a variety of Protestant church services throughout her early childhood and adolescence, including stints at a United Church of Christ and a Congregational church, the latter in which she was confirmed (91). Norris describes her early church experiences as an odd mixture of loving to sing and dress up and chafing at having to follow certain rules.

During this time, Norris was also developing a love of the English language, primarily because she was good at spelling. She writes that her experience with poetry in school followed the "ordinary track"; that is, she had an innate love of it as a child through nursery rhymes but that love was all but gone by the eighth grade due to the school's systematic use of poetry as penmanship exemplars and the fact that its study involved a "deciphering" of "hidden meanings" that frustrated her (*The Virgin of Bennington*, 104–5). Also by this time, the family that she describes as having moved often ended up in Hawaii, where they remain to this day. Many of her new classmates in that state had been together since they first set foot in school, making Norris feel very awkward and isolated. In response to her feelings of loneliness and alienation, Norris took pride in her academic abilities and created a refuge by losing herself in books and music. She mentions figures as diverse as Søren Kierkegaard and Bob Dylan as favorites of hers at age sixteen (*Virgin*, 2–3). She attended a prep school on a scholarship, and the end of her high school education also brought about her exile from church attendance for the next twenty years (*Dakota*, 92).

Norris chose Vermont's Bennington College at least in part because it did not require a stringent core curriculum (she felt very deficient in math) and because it was a women's college. Distracted in high school by the perceived necessity to socialize and have a boyfriend in order to fit in, she hoped that the new setting Bennington provided would be free of such impositions and that it would be a place where she felt less isolated for her academic interests (*Virgin*, 2, 3). Admittedly, she had no idea of Bennington College's reputation, which, in the late 1960s, was tantamount to "bohemian." Her discomfort in these new surroundings accentuated her isolation, and in response, she admits becoming the stereotypical image of "nunnish—quiet, withdrawn, and obviously virginal" (10). This demeanor led to the nicknames she would carry throughout her college years, "Norris the Nun" and "The Virgin of Bennington," the latter of which she uses as the title of the latest of her four autobiographical books to date. She graduated from Bennington with her bachelor's degree in 1969.

In a subchapter of *The Virgin of Bennington* fittingly titled "Synchronicity," Norris chronicles how she met her husband, fellow poet David J. Dwyer. This meeting occurred during the chaotic years after college graduation when she worked as an arts administrator at the Academy of American Poets in New York City. She refers to her position there as the "ideal job" (43). On the fringe of the Andy Warhol crowd, she rubbed elbows with both those who were the elite in the artistic world and those less established artists who would become the elite. She describes the decadent lifestyle that had entangled her: "[m]y life had become bifurcated. Part of me still wanted to be the good kid I had been brought up to be, the Sunday-school girl formed in the Protestant work ethic. But I had grown attracted to what was forbidden, all the things the good girl had been denied" (93). Since she was caught up in a lifestyle of cyclical partying, meeting Dwyer helped stabilize her relationships. The death of her maternal grandmother in 1973 precipitated Norris's move to the Dakotas, further removing her from the setting of some self-destructive ways of life. Not wanting to sell off the family farmland in Lemmon, South Dakota, which included the house her grandparents had built in 1923, she and Dwyer decided to move to the tiny town (population 1,600) temporarily until they decided what to do with their sudden and unexpected inheritance. Norris and Dwyer married in 1977. Some thirty years after their initial move, the couple remains in Lemmon. Referring to this region as a "crucible," Norris insists that the Dakota setting has been formative in both her spiritual growth and her writing. Her first autobiographical work, *Dakota: A Spiritual Geography*, relates the experience of her first years in Lemmon, where she kept body and soul together through a "crazy quilt of jobs": freelance poet, memoirist, and editor; manager of the family ranch corporation; itinerant guest poetry teacher; and even cable television installer (1993, 4).

Norris came to prominence as an author first as a poet and then as a memoirist. Her volumes of poetry include *Falling Off* (1971), *From South Dakota: Four Poems* (1978), *The Middle of the World* (1981), *How I Came to Drink My Grandmother's Piano: Some Benedictine Poems* (1989), *The Year of Common Things* (1990), *The Astronomy of Love* (1994), *Little Girls in Church* (1995), and *Journey: New and Selected Poems, 1969–1999* (2001). In the tradition of many women autobiographers, Norris's life is confined not within the bindings of a single volume but sprawls out over a number of works that blur the distinction between traditional modes of confession and creative nonfiction. While each of these in a large sense concerns the author's spirituality, *Dakota* focuses on the interplay between Christianity and a sense of place; *The Cloister Walk* on sacrament; *Amazing Grace* (1998) on language; and *The Virgin of Bennington* on coming of age.

It was as an itinerant teacher that Norris first made contact with the Benedictine Order, the community that has so inspired and shaped her spirituality and her writing. During her residency at a Catholic school while sponsored by the North Dakota Council on the Arts, she was housed in a small Benedictine convent. In addition, during her intense, early years in South Dakota, Norris not only reconnected with the Presbyterian heritage bequeathed her by her grandmother but also enjoyed visiting a nearby Benedictine monastery. She describes herself as returning again and again until finally the monks asked her if she had ever considered becoming an oblate or lay associate of the order. Her protests that she was both a Protestant and a woman did not dissuade them, and she took vows as an Benedictine oblate in 1986. She later spent two nine-month terms with the Institute for Ecumenical and Cultural Research at the Benedictine St. John's Abbey and University in Collegeville, Minnesota. *The Cloister Walk* is a record of the insights she gathered during her time spent at that abbey.

PLOT SUMMARY

Conjuring images from sources as diverse as *The Sound of Music* and Ann Radcliffe's eighteenth-century gothic novels, the title of Norris's second autobiographical work, *The Cloister Walk*, identifies her subject matter but does not immediately signal to the reader the depth of the contemplation she applies to her subject. Technically a walkway within the confines of a religious community, the word "cloister" derives from both the French word for "partition" and the Latin word for "closing up." A "cloister walk" denotes spiritual seclusion and meditation, and it may also connote a clerical procession, as into Mass. During one such procession that Norris describes in *The Cloister Walk*, she reveals the circuitous nature of the journey that has brought her back to an appreciation of Church liturgy and hence back into a relationship with God.

The Cloister Walk is less a plotted story than a marking of the passage of time and an expression of insight. Norris does not create a chronology of the two periods she spent at St. John's Abbey; rather, she organizes her thoughts in the Catholic way in terms of the liturgical year. She refers to her book as an "immersion into a liturgical world" in which she tries to "replicate for the reader the rhythm of saints' days, solemnities, and feasts that [she] experienced" at the Abbey (*Cloister*, xix). Norris arrives at St. John's during Ordinary Time; her anticipation builds as Advent approaches, continues through Christmastide to Epiphany, after which she returns, as does the Church, to Ordinary Time. In order to recreate this rhythm, Norris often uses saints' days for her chapter titles: the first dated chapter is "September 3: Gregory the Great," for example, and the last is "August 28: Augustine." A particular date, however, does not necessarily correspond with the events of an actual day in her life but rather with a certain pursuit of understanding on a particular religious personage or sacred theme. Norris does, at times, focus on the recovery of some saints, such as an attempt to reconcile Saint Jerome with feminism or the mystic Mechtild of Magdeburg with the modern Church. But many chapters bear only enigmatic titles, like "Dreaming of Trees," in which only a reading of the contents discloses the subject.

MAJOR THEMES

A consideration of the major themes of *The Cloister Walk* should begin with "rules" in every sense of the word. From Norris's earliest religious memory, side by side with her love of sacred music has been the weighty impact of the sense of rules she must follow. "From the Protestants," she writes, "I got a list of rules that were not to be broken and I naively thought that as long as I wasn't breaking those rules, sin was not much of a problem for me" (125–26). Yet some of these rules place a burdensome load on the carrier, a load, in fact, too heavy for one of Norris's aunts: she committed suicide after the birth of a child born out of wedlock. Even Norris's religiously dutiful grandfather could not always comply with the rules set down by some congregations of believers: he was fired from a Methodist church in 1919 for playing dominoes because the church prohibited gambling (128). With this sense of restriction as the backdrop for Norris's spiritual quest, it is both ironic and surprising that she should wind up embracing a Catholic order that boasts a world-famous set of rules, the Rule of Saint Benedict. In fact, on her first encounter with the Benedictines, when they were housing her during her guest teaching, she fully expected to be judged and found lacking. One sister, with a wry sense of humor, played on this expectation by asking Norris, "Would you like to read our Rule? Then you'll know if you've done something wrong" (6). After reading it, of course, Norris appreciated the joke. The Rule of

Saint Benedict is not at all written, nor should it be read, in a spirit of condemnation; it is, rather, known for being reasonable and humane, not harsh.

Throughout her writing, Norris comments on the remarkable flexibility and applicability of Benedict's Rule, which was written around 530, to modern life. From time to time, in both *Dakota* and *The Cloister Walk*, she points out the benefit of the Rule to community life. She finds the small farming communities of the Great Plains, for example, to have a number of similarities with the religious, cloistered Benedictines. These small communities, however, do not have the advantage of a set of rules of engagement or, as is sometimes needed, an abbot or prioress to intervene in disagreements (*Dakota*, 62). On the other hand, one of the similarities between the two groups is what the Benedictines call the "vow of stability"—a lifelong commitment to one's physical place. While the ranchers and farmers of the prairie do not have to take such a vow officially, as the Benedictines do, the very nature of their setting often imposes it, especially in terms of education, occupation, and economy. They are members of their community for life, like it or not. "Memories are long in the western Dakotas," Norris writes, and not always to the benefit of a community's members (xiv). Old grudges fester and seep. Without a common set of rules, as with the Benedictines, the community has no obligation to "accommodate their more troubled members" (*Cloister*, 20). Because of this initiative on the part of the monks and nuns, the Benedictine communities take on the nature of a healthily working family, notwithstanding the foibles of the various family members.

Both types of communities, Dakota's small towns and the Benedictine Order, are also known for their hospitality. Norris recounts numerous examples of generous hospitality on the parts of both. While the people of the plains are not expected to "receive all guests as Christ" (*Dakota*, 112), they often do as Christ admonished and go the extra mile for guests when only one mile is required. However, the fact that there is a guest/host relationship embedded in these acts of hospitality implies that there are always insiders and outsiders to the community. Within a Benedictine community, on the other hand, a novice at least knows the requirements to gain entry and, upon taking final vows, is considered a full-fledged member, even if inexperienced. Norris makes clear that this is not the case in the Dakotas. As an example, she studied the Rule of Saint Benedict under the direction of a monk for a period of three years and then, as a layperson, vowed to follow the Rule to the best of her abilities. She was then accepted as a member, a Benedictine oblate, and welcomed into that community. However, as she relates, she and her husband have lived in Lemmon, South Dakota, for over thirty years, on land belonging to her family for nearly a hundred years, yet they are still, at times, treated as outsiders because they were not born and raised there. Norris attributes this alienation to an understandable mistrust of outsiders, built over many generations, and to a severe resistance to change. Her writing suggests that this wariness toward outsiders is an unfortunate by-product of the residents' unofficial vow of stability.

In spite of their differing "entrance exams," the various religious communities of the plains also share an experience of diversity with their Benedictine neighbors. Due to dwindling populations, disinterest in organized, traditional religion, and financial desperation, a number of towns, such as Hope, South Dakota, now have just one church building that must house a number of different denominations.

Since Hope Church is the only church in town and everyone is welcome, and because the congregants are all, due to proximity, neighbors, the congregation has a strong emphasis on serving the community (162). There is something very "catholic" about the ways in which these Protestant churches are now operating in remote areas. By embracing such diversity within a single community, these one-room churches echo both the Catholic Church, itself housing myriad practices, and Benedictine monasteries and convents, which attract a great many individual personalities.

Continuing her comparison between the two sets of communities, Norris highlights how they differ in their respective emphases on the importance of ceremony and ritual. Meeting times and prayer format are prime examples. Conventional Protestants meet once every Sunday, with the more pious members also gathering for a midweek service. By contrast, the Benedictines, through the Liturgy of the Hours, gather for "offices," or prayer, throughout the day, every day, under the theory that the body should be doing something and where the body goes it eventually brings the mind along with it. Although both parties would endorse an attention to the presence of God around the clock, the structure of Benedictine life lends itself far more readily to the practice. Certainly, there is the inherent difference of theology between the two communities, but in general Catholic worship is more scripted and regimented, even to prescribing when participants will sit, stand, or kneel. Most Protestant worship is not so regimented. In Protestant prayer meetings, for example, members are often free to call out specific prayer needs of their own or of others and to pray aloud in their own words. Benedictine tradition, however, supports using God's words with which to pray to God, specifically the Psalms. The people praying allow the Psalms to take them into prayer, to God himself. In general, Norris finds that the Catholic tradition honors authority and uses appropriate channels of worship over the Protestant tradition of individual expression.

Norris, though remaining Protestant, deeply values the practices of Catholicism. Serving as an oblate in the Benedictine community demonstrates her commitment to both the order itself and the principles of Catholicism undergirding it. She appreciates the unhurried deliberation that ceremony quite naturally and gracefully imposes on an otherwise hectic schedule (*Cloister*, 267). This slower pace encourages meditation and worship and, not coincidentally, creativity. "Good liturgy," she asserts, "is a living poem, and ceremony is the key"; it serves "like an icon, a window" (266). Opening this window has drawn her attention to a spiritual perspective that has enhanced her writing immeasurably. She thus describes her time at St. John's Abbey as "gestational" (267) and attributes a newfound creative proliferation to it (3).

For Norris, visual and creative perspectives are vitally linked to sound and hearing. Apparently, along with faith, inspiration "comes by hearing and hearing by the Word of God" (Rom. 10:17). The first word of the Rule of Saint Benedict, in fact, is an emphatic "Listen." Benedict's Prologue to the Rule then continues, naturally enough, in the language of the Psalms, beseeching the reader to "incline thine ear" to the precepts of Christ. This emphasis on listening is played out, in the Benedictine Order, in the practice of *lectio divina*, or "holy reading." This daily meditation on Holy Scripture, especially the Psalter, takes place in private as well as in public venues and becomes for the Benedictines a way of life (*Amazing*

Grace, 281). While she is with the Benedictines, Norris allows the sung, chanted, and spoken words to sink deep into her and resonate and resurface in new forms (*Cloister*, 144–45). One of the monks tells her that her writing in response to the holy offices was in itself a form of *lectio* (144). The Psalms, in particular, appeal to Norris because they address the hard stuff of life—anger, disappointment, bitterness, and rage—as well as exult in praise. The Benedictine emphasis on the Psalter allows a truer representation of real life than some Christians want to admit. According to Norris, when we read through the Psalms we as humans tend to recoil from the intensity of many of the emotions expressed therein (96). But a "tidy" religion does not encompass the expanse of human experience. And so we have the Psalms and along with them an example of the conversion of all human experiences into praise (96).

Norris's position as both inside and outside Catholicism affords her a unique view of and appreciation for the two greatest divisions of western Christianity, that of Catholic and Protestant. *The Cloister Walk* becomes a vehicle for a great movement toward ecumenism, promoting a better understanding between the two faiths. Still, what remain murky in her writing are the particulars of theology: she does not address, for example, difficult and contentious aspects of religious practice, such as how Catholics and Protestants regard the taking of communion. As if to answer this charge, Norris reminds readers of the words of another Benedictine, Aidan Kavanagh, O. S. B., who in his work *On Liturgy* states that "orthodoxy first means right worship, and only secondarily doctrinal accuracy" (*Amazing Grace*, 209). Norris attempts to bridge the great divide between Protestantism and Catholicism with attention to these faiths' common goal of serving the Lord Jesus Christ and feeding his sheep. Her unique dual religious perspective allows her to do so with success. As she writes in *Dakota*, "[T]his is who I am: a complete Protestant with a decidedly ecumenical bent. I never got that rosary when I was seven, but a friend gave me one when I'd been a Benedictine oblate for nearly five years" (91).

CRITICAL RECEPTION

Perhaps her ecumenism, in part, accounts for Norris's success as a memoirist; popular reception of her memoirs has been tremendously positive. The reader base she garnered with her first such work, *Dakota*, has only increased with subsequent publications. Both *The Cloister Walk* and *Amazing Grace* have been on the *New York Times* best-seller list, and *The Cloister Walk* was a *New York Times* Notable Book of the Year. Because her works are so recent, and because the academy is slow to recognize new or popular works, these books have not yet received the critical attention that they warrant. While she may be referred to extensively in relation to other writers, Norris has yet to be the solitary focus of sustained critical work.

Certainly, Saint Augustine would be counted among Norris's predecessors by virtue of their shared genre. However, Norris also writes in the tradition of the best and earliest women autobiographers. Heir to the first woman autobiographer in English, Margery Kempe, Norris examines the impact of God on her life. Like Lillian Hellman, her memoirs are contained not within a single volume but distributed among several volumes, each boasting a distinct focus. Norris is also often aligned with Annie Dillard because of her attention to the details of nature and with Annie Lamott because of her attention to the particulars of faith. Her literary influences also include Emily Dickinson, Thomas Merton, and Denise Levertov. Saint Benedict himself may have the chief seat among them. The acknowledgment Kathleen Norris gives to the variety of influences on her writing is one more reflection of her ecumenical process. It is that ecumenism that casts such a unique light on the Catholicism of her faith and practice.

NOTE

Kathleen Norris, *The Cloister Walk* (New York: Riverhead, 1996). All references are to this edition.

WORKS CITED

Norris, Kathleen. 1998. *Amazing Grace: A Vocabulary of Faith*. New York: Riverhead.
————. 2001. *Dakota: A Spiritual Geography*. Boston: Houghton Mifflin.
————. 2001. *The Virgin of Bennington*. New York: Riverhead.

BIBLIOGRAPHY

Leigh, David J., S. J. *Circuitous Journeys: Modern Spiritual Autobiography*. New York: Fordham University Press, 2000.
Weaver, Wendy A. "Journeys toward Hope." *Logos: A Journal of Catholic Thought and Culture* 5, no. 4 (Fall 2002): 124–34.
"What I Took Home from the Cloister." *U. S. Catholic* 62, no. 10 (October 1997): 8–12.

— **Wendy A. Weaver**

Flannery O'Connor [1925–1964]

Wise Blood

BIOGRAPHY

Mary Flannery O'Connor was born in Savannah, Georgia, on March 25, 1925, the feast day of the Incarnation. (Later, when she was seventeen, she dropped the "Mary.") She was descended from Irish Catholic great grandparents who had immigrated in the early to mid-nineteenth century. Several of them were the first Catholics to establish their family lines in the Protestant American South. This fact has a symbolic significance. The deeply religious Flannery was to live her entire life—except for two or three years in her early twenties spent in Iowa, Connecticut, and New York—amid an overwhelmingly Protestant culture. That situation, in turn, is reflected in her fiction as a whole, which is insistently religious—fed, she repeatedly insisted, on Catholic dogma and doctrine—but with only a few, minor exceptions contains no Catholic characters.

An only child, Flannery spent her childhood in Savannah, moving when she was thirteen to the old state capital, Milledgeville. Except for those few years in her twenties, this was to be her home for the rest of her life, first in Milledgeville itself and later on a dairy farm, run by her mother, just outside of town. Her father, a real estate agent and appraiser, died when she was fifteen of lupus, an incurable, wasting disease of the immune system. O'Connor's earlier education was in Catholic schools, but she enrolled in public schools for her latter years in high school and her college years at Georgia State College for Women (later renamed Georgia College). She was active in school affairs, excelling in drawing and other visual arts.

O'Connor had also begun writing at an early age, but, by her own admission, she did little serious reading (being mainly influenced by the humorous tales of Poe) until she enrolled, at age twenty, in the prestigious graduate program in creative writing at the University of Iowa. There she read intensively, especially in the modernist authors, and in due course she became recognized as an especially gifted writer herself. After receiving her master of fine arts degree in 1947, she began publishing her stories with increasing regularity while also working on her first novel, *Wise Blood*. After six years of work and much revision, the novel finally appeared in 1952, to mixed reviews. Even more than O'Connor's later work, it met with considerable bafflement. That is not surprising, since its tone is a mixture of the comic and the ghastly and the (purportedly) Catholic message is rendered entirely in a Protestant cultural idiom. Much the same things were true of her first collection of stories (better received by the critics), *A Good Man Is Hard to Find* (1955), and her second novel, *The Violent Bear It Away* (1960). A fourth book, the brilliant short-story collection *Everything That Rises Must Converge*, was published in 1965, a year after O'Connor died.

The turning point in Flannery O'Connor's life was the diagnosis, revealed to her in 1952, that, like her father before her, she too was suffering from lupus. Her entire way of living was drastically affected. The wider life she had begun to lead was cut short, and the remaining twelve years of her life were a struggle against the debilitating effects of the disease, which marred her good looks and eventually reduced her to using a cane or crutches. She was not totally isolated; in the last decade or so of her life she made brief visits to many midwestern and eastern cities, mainly in connection with readings and speaking engagements, and even took a short trip to Europe. She also continued to add friends to those she had made earlier, meeting them in person or by correspondence. These included some of the foremost figures on the mid-twentieth-century American literary scene: her dear friends Robert and Sally Fitzgerald, Caroline Gordon and her husband Allen Tate (also her good friends), Robert Lowell, Elizabeth Hardwick, Robert Giroux (one of the most influential of American editors), Peter Taylor, Randall Jarrell, Malcolm Cowley, Van Wyck Brooks, Elizabeth Bishop, Katherine Anne Porter, Eudora Welty, and Cleanth Brooks. And her illness had one fortunate by-product: the wonderful letters she wrote to friends both famous and not. These letters reveal a serious but utterly unpretentious person, deeply and thoughtfully committed to her faith, her art, and the relationship between them, but consistently modest and never pompous. Moreover, like many of her short stories, her letters can be hilariously funny, partly owing to her mastery of back-woods idiom but mainly because of her laid-back but incisive sense of irony. These heroically cheerful letters give mere hints of the devastating symptoms of lupus.

The year 1964, leading up to O'Connor's death in a Milledgeville hospital on August 3, witnessed a final brave struggle to go on writing and revising her work to the very end. She was not one of those writers who, although dying young, seem to have accomplished as much as they ever would have accomplished. On the contrary, when she died, Flannery O'Connor had just come into her full powers as a writer. Her early death was a grievous loss.

PLOT SUMMARY

Hazel ("Haze") Motes, from the tiny hamlet of Eastrod, Tennessee, came from sternly evangelical Protestant forebears, especially his late mother and grandfather. The latter was a circuit preacher whom Haze often accompanied on trips, the preacher holding forth from atop his car, sometimes using Haze as a prop and calling him a "mean sinful unthinking" boy (*Collected Works*, 11) for whom Jesus had nonetheless died. One formative experience from Haze's boyhood involved his gazing at a carnival exhibit of a naked woman in a coffin. His mother, sensing this sin of Haze's, had struck him and reminded him that Jesus had redeemed him. "I never ast him," Haze had replied (36). He then did penance for his guilt by walking miles with stones in his shoes.

As the novel opens, Haze has recently returned from World War II, in which he was wounded, only to find Eastrod a mere ghost town. He therefore travels by train to the distant southern city of Taulkinham. Having rejected the orthodox Christian beliefs in the Fall, Redemption, and Judgment, Haze intends to preach a new church, the Church Without Christ, based on the denial of those central doctrines and indeed of the very concept of sin. In this church, "the blind don't see and the lame don't walk and what's dead stays that way" (59). On his first night in Taulkinham he visits a prostitute, Mrs. Leora Watts, whose name he found advertised among men's-room graffiti. Prior to this visit he was a virgin.

On his second night in Taulkinham, Haze meets, in front of a street booth, three of the novel's main characters: Asa Hawks, a street hustler/preacher pretending to be blind; his daughter and assistant, Sabbath Lily Hawks, who is in her early teens; and Enoch Emery, an eighteen-year-old boy who has recently come to Taulkinham and works as a guard at a city park. Enoch tells Haze of his boyhood, spent mainly as an inmate of the Rodemill Boys' Bible Academy and as the unwilling ward of a woman social worker whom Enoch finally frightened away by going into her bedroom with his pants down. Dragooned by the Hawkses into passing out evangelical pamphlets, Haze instead begins to harangue a crowd, preaching his anti-Christian message. The crowd reacts with indifference. Throughout the novel, crowds will generally react that way to Haze's message, or at most with mild irritation.

Haze buys an old, ratty, comically decrepit Essex automobile, from atop which he will do his preaching of the Church Without Christ. He drives to the park where Enoch Emery works. Enoch has become obsessed with a three-foot-tall humanoid mummy that is kept in a glass case in the park MVSEVM (the simple Enoch pronounces this sign as "muvseevum"). He shows the mummy to Haze. When a woman also examines the exhibit, Haze flees in a rage, felling Enoch with a stone thrown at his head. When Enoch comes to, he feels in his alertly sensitive, instinctual "wise blood" that he has been entrusted with a large mission.

Haze rents an upstairs room in the boarding house where Asa and Sabbath Hawks live. The landlady, taking him for a preacher, asks him whether his church is "foreign"; "He said no mam, it was Protestant" (60). Dropping in on the Hawkses, Haze is nonplussed because Asa Hawks (a "preacher") makes no effort to "save" him. To affirm his purposeful lack of morality, Haze resolves to seduce the "innocent" Sabbath; ironically, she resolves at the same time to seduce Haze and then marry him, since her father has grown tired of her company. We learn at this point that, in the past, Asa Hawks had once advertised that, to affirm Christ, he would publicly blind himself with quicklime. He had lost his nerve, however, and though scarring his face had left his sight intact.

On a trip to the country, Sabbath tries to give herself to Haze sexually, but he flees from her in anger. She also explains that she is illegitimate, stating, as if quoting a Scriptural text, that "A bastard shall not enter the kingdom of heaven" (67). She thus implies that she has nothing to lose by sinning. Haze at first rejects such prejudice against illegitimacy but soon comes to reflect on the "truth" that even in his new church a bastard cannot be saved.

Convinced by his instinctual wise blood that the mummy is part of a vast mystery and that he has a high mission, Enoch renovates his shabby room. He pays special attention, by painting it gold, to a "tabernacle," or "ark," in the form of a cabinet in a washstand, originally designed to contain a slop jar. Hearing Haze preach the need for a "new jesus . . . without blood to waste" (80), Enoch immediately declares that his mummy fits the bill. He decides to steal it from the exhibit case in the museum.

Sabbath Hawks tries again, unsuccessfully, to seduce Haze, in his room. Preaching once more in public, Haze is joined by a man in his audience, Hoover Shoats (alias Onnie Jay Holy), a hustler-preacher-guitarist who credits Haze with having delivered him from despair. Shoats now does some preaching on his own, of a "Holy Church of Christ Without Christ" (based on the Bible but up to date, he boasts), and starts to collect money from the crowd. Haze, enraged by this attempt to turn his own antireligious message into a pseudo-pious one and to make money from the notion of the "new jesus," repudiates Hoover, to the latter's disgust. Soon thereafter, Hoover, too, begins to preach from a car, in rivalry with "the Prophet" Haze. Hoover exhibits his new jesus in the form of a man, Solace Layfield, who is the visual double of Haze.

That night, Sabbath finally succeeds in seducing Haze. They are both "filthy," she tells him; doesn't he want to learn to like being filthy? "Yeah," he dully answers (95).

Having stolen the mummy and kept it overnight in his "tabernacle," Enoch sets out in the rain to deliver it to Haze. On the way, he takes shelter under a movie marquee, where Gonga, a film gorilla, arrives to make a personal appearance. Enoch shakes hands with the man impersonating the gorilla: "It was the first hand that had been extended to Enoch since he had come to the city. It was warm and soft" (102). He is stunned and outraged, therefore, when the "gorilla" tells him to go to hell. Enoch then delivers the mummy to Haze's house, where Haze is lying sick after his night with Sabbath. She receives the mummy from Enoch. Enchanted with it, she cradles it maternally, reflecting that she "had never known anyone who looked like him before, but there was something in him of everyone she had ever known, as if they had all been rolled into one person and killed and shrunk and dried" (104). She presents the mummy to Haze, who shatters it against the wall and throws the skin out a fire escape doorway. Sabbath, angered in her turn, calls Haze a killjoy who didn't "want nothing but Jesus" (107). He wants nothing but the truth, Haze replies.

Enoch, persuaded that the new jesus is going to reward him, tracks down the imitation gorilla, attacks him in his truck, and dresses himself in the gorilla suit, burying his old clothes.

In his Essex, Haze overtakes Solace Layfield's car, forces him to get out of it and to shed his clothes, and then deliberately runs over him. Before dying, Solace confesses his sins, in the manner of a penitent in the confessional.

Haze now decides to take his preaching to a new city. At a filling station on his way out of Taulkinham, Haze tells the attendant that the Jesus who died for our sins is "too foul a notion for a sane person to carry in his head" (116). On the road to his new city, Haze is stopped by a trooper, who taunts Haze and, for no reason that is explicitly stated, wrecks the old Essex by pushing it off an embankment. Stunned, Haze walks back to Taulkinham, on the way stopping to buy a bucket and some lime. He intends to blind himself.

Having put out his eyes with the quicklime, Haze lives thereafter in a torpid trance, mainly going for long walks, his shoes filled with gravel and glass. He has to "pay," he explains to his landlady: "It don't make any difference for what" (125). She, having taken an interest in him, arranges for Sabbath to be sent by Welfare to a house of detention. Conceiving the idea of marrying Haze, partly for his military pension money, the landlady proposes to him. He responds by hurriedly going out, in bitter wintry weather. The police later find him, near death, in a drainage ditch. One of them strikes Haze with a billy club. He dies in the squad car on the way back to the rooming house. The landlady, contemplating Haze's face composed in death, thinks of him as a distant pinpoint of light at the end of a tunnel.

MAJOR THEMES

If authorial intention means anything, we need to address the Catholic content of *Wise Blood*. O'Connor insisted that only a Catholic could have written it. Yet none of her religious vision, in *Wise Blood* or in her other fiction, is expressed by way of the machinery and explicit idiom of Catholicism. Her stories and novels present almost no Catholic characters, and none who are important. Indeed, she seems to have felt that to introduce Catholic characters would mean the loss of her control as a writer. "[I]t takes some doing to put a Catholic in a novel," she once wrote to Caroline Gordon Tate (September 11, 1952; *Collected Works*, 899). Perhaps she believed that, orthodox Catholic that she was, she would have felt impelled to chasten the extravagance of heresy and blasphemy if it came from the mouths of Catholic characters. In any case, she concentrates in *Wise Blood* on those theological themes that are shared by both Catholics and the Protestants whose spiritual lives she wrote about. "Let me assure you," she wrote in one of her letters,

> that no one but a Catholic could have written *Wise Blood* even though it is a book about a kind of Protestant saint. It reduces Protestantism to the twin ultimate absurdities of The Church Without Christ or The Holy Church of Christ Without Christ, which no pious Protestant would do. And of course no unbeliever or agnostic could have written it because it is entirely Redemption-centered in thought. Not too many people are willing to see this, and perhaps it is hard to see because H. Motes is such an admirable nihilist. His nihilism leads him back to the fact of his Redemption. (to Ben Griffith, March 3, 1954; 923)

In the headnote she added when the novel, first published in 1952, was reprinted ten years later, O'Connor described very explicitly what she was doing, or trying to do. Her aim was to write a variation on what we might call the "Hound of Heaven" pattern, whereby grace pursues even, and perhaps especially, the sinner who desperately attempts to flee from or reject it. This intention is closely consistent with what O'Connor identified as her main thematic preoccupations: the Christian pattern of the Fall, Redemption, and Judgment. "The gist of the story," O'Connor wrote about *Wise Blood* in a letter, "is that H. Motes couldn't really believe that he hadn't been redeemed" (to Helen Greene, May 23, 1952; 897). Haze, she wrote in another letter, "is saved by virtue of having wise blood," which in his southern religious tradition has to serve as the "means of grace" (to John Hawkes, September 13, 1959; 1107). A consistently acidulous critic of secular liberalism, O'Connor advanced this interpretation of the world and of the novel, half defensively, half truculently, in the 1962 headnote:

> That belief in Christ is to some a matter of life and death has been a stumbling block for readers who would prefer to think it a matter of no great consequence. For them Hazel Motes' integrity lies in his trying with such vigor to get rid of the ragged figure [Jesus] who moves from tree to tree in the back of his mind. For the author Hazel's integrity lies in his not being able to. (1265)

This explanation, even if we accept it at face value (as we probably should), still leaves us with problems. How, we can ask ourselves, is the scheme just outlined actually realized in the novel? What narrative events, crises, or turning points move the novel in the direction the author claims to have intended? How much of *Wise Blood* communicates directly and literally, how much only by way of pure symbolism? On the novel's symbolism O'Connor sometimes commented explicitly, as when she glossed the significance of the mummy stolen by Enoch Emery and delivered to Haze: "That Haze rejects that mummy suggests everything. What he has been looking for with body and soul throughout the book [that is, the new lower-case jesus, emptied of religious significance] is suddenly presented to him and he sees it has to be rejected, he sees it ain't really what he's looking for. I don't regard it in any abstracted sense at all" (to "A," July 23, 1960; 1130). If this last sentence is a denial of symbolic intention, it is especially puzzling, since the immediately preceding sentences affirm the symbolic intent, especially when we recall the elaborate pains Enoch takes to house the mummy in a sanctuary, or "tabernacle." We cannot take this mummy incident merely as naturalistic narrative with symbolic overtones; the incident has no meaning *other* than the symbolic. Likewise with Haze's blinding of himself: O'Connor explained that Haze "does not come into his absolute integrity until he blinds himself"; in doing so, she states, he "turns entirely to an inner vision" (to Carl Hartman, March 2, 1954; 920, 921). Would these meanings be communicated by the text itself, without the author's own glosses?

Some of these glosses by O'Connor suggest—which may startle many readers—a kind of upbeat ending. We cannot ignore her emphatic plea, in the 1962 headnote, that we read the novel as comedy: "The book was written with zest and, if possible, it should be read that way. It is a comic novel about a Christian *malgré lui*, and as such, very serious, for all comic novels that are any good must be about matters of life and death" (1265). Many of O'Connor's short stories— the marvelous "Revelation," for example—are masterpieces of comedy, indeed hilarious comedy, but the occasional comic gleams in *Wise Blood* would seem to be totally eclipsed by the sordid and ghastly. It is possible, of course, that O'Connor understood "comedy" in a sense like Dante's, wherein an infernal vision of evil is ultimately resolved into a vision of salvation. Analogously, Haze's blinding of himself, his reversion at the end to the habit of severe penance (walking with stones and glass in his shoes, as he had done in his boyhood after looking at the sex show and being chastised by his mother), and his death of exposure in a drainage ditch could be signs of spiritual progress, of a salutary conversion. But if so, should we not get at least a suggestion of the convert's typical experience of elation, or at least of illumination? (What exactly is the *content* of the "inner vision" that Haze is said to gain through blinding himself?) There is no trace of joy in the denouement of *Wise Blood*; the ending is, in tone, closer to total depression and despair. Haze's climactic act has been to commit a brutal murder. On the following day, he is still convinced, as he tells the gas station attendant, that Jesus' death for our sins is "too foul a notion for a sane person to carry in his head" (116). The only significant event that intervenes between Haze's utterance of this sentiment and his blinding of himself is the wrecking by the police trooper of Haze's automobile (an act of purely symbolic meaning, for which no naturalistic motive whatsoever is assigned). Where and whence is the illumination?

Flannery O'Connor insisted that she was a Catholic writer, that her stories were "watered and fed by Dogma" (to Thomas Mabry, March 1, 1955; 930), and, as we have seen, that only a Catholic writer could have written *Wise Blood*. She found the popular southern forms of Protestantism particularly useful for her purposes, as dramatically more direct than Catholicism while being doctrinally similar to it on the most fundamental matters:

> Wise blood has to be these people's means of grace—they have no sacraments. The religion of the South is a do-it-yourself religion, something which I as a Catholic find painful and touching and grimly comic. It's full of unconscious pride that lands them in all sorts of ridiculous religious predicaments. They have nothing to correct their practical heresies and so they work them out dramatically. If this were merely comic to me, it would be no good, but I accept the same fundamental doctrines of sin and redemption and judgment that they do. (to John Hawkes, September 13, 1959; 1107)

Nevertheless, in many respects O'Connor's writing, and especially *Wise Blood*, is highly untypical of Catholicism. She recognizes that a serious respect for the body is part of the Catholic viewpoint, but for her this emphasis on the body would seem to imply, almost exclusively, a need for penitential bodily suffering (blinding oneself, putting broken glass in one's shoes). Bodily pleasures, especially sex, are never treated as pleasurable by O'Connor, and this is emphatically true in *Wise Blood*, in which an aversion to sex, and the use of sex for joyless pragmatic purposes (Sabbath's attempt to get a husband) or for symbolic purposes (Haze's decision to assert his immorality by seducing Sabbath), are characteristic. O'Connor emphasized that she was a cradle Catholic who could not look at Catholicism as a convert might, and perhaps this accounts for the joylessness and near lovelessness of her version of the faith, as these keynotes emerge in her letters and, even more, as they inform her fiction. She never experienced the convert's sense of discovering an exalted new world. Her creative gift, O'Connor once explained, takes a religious form because of the Church's teaching, "not because of a personal perception or love of God. . . . When I ask myself how I know I believe, I have no satisfactory answer at all, no assurance at all, no feeling at all. I can only say with Peter, Lord I believe, help my unbelief. And all I can say about my love of God, is, Lord help me in my lack of it" (to "A," August 2, 1955; 944). These sentiments unquestionably reflect a sincere spiritual humility, but they can equally well be read as expressing the compulsive, ultimately fear-ridden psychology that, for many Catholics, is their subjective experience of the faith.

The Redemption, as O'Connor said more than once, was at the heart of her fiction, but in *Wise Blood* she seems to reverse the usual weight given to that doctrine. For Catholics as for Protestants, the Redemption (literally, a "buying back" or "paying back") was performed by Jesus on behalf of sinful humankind. But in *Wise Blood* it is the human being who, through penance and suffering, must repay Jesus. Asked by the landlady, near the end of the novel, why he puts rocks in his shoes, Haze says, "To pay." "Pay for what?" she asks, to which he replies: "It don't make any difference for what. I'm paying" (125). As an explanation for this resolve, it will not do to observe that "paying" is part of the Catholic (as opposed to Protestant) doctrine of penitential, purgatorial satisfaction of justice, for in Catholicism that satisfaction implies doing penance for, and thereby partially expiating, actual sins committed. But what Haze thinks of himself as paying for is the metaphysical state of sinfulness (a more typically Protestant preoccupation), of the state of being "unclean." In other words, what he feels guilty about is original sin itself: "If I was in sin," he tells Asa Hawks, "I was in it before I ever committed any" (29). But neither Catholics nor Protestants believe that original sin, the primordial state of fallenness in itself, can be atoned for in one's human person by any kind of penitential suffering or other "works."

CRITICAL RECEPTION

When *Wise Blood* was first published in 1952, most reviewers were baffled or repelled. The nonplussed reviewer in the *New York Herald Tribune Book Review* wondered where the author could go thereafter; *Time* noted the novel's harsh sarcasm and brutal irony; the *New Yorker* also called the novel brutal and its characters brutes; the *New York Times Book Review* called its people nonhuman; the *Saturday Review* found it repulsive (Whitt 1995, 1, 2, 15). Almost no reviewer read the novel as any kind of religious affirmation. As O'Connor's religious beliefs and her claims to have had a religious intent in her novels and stories became more widely known, her own statements came to be standard guidelines dictating specifically Catholic interpretations. Such religious readings have constituted the mainstream of O'Connor criticism, including criticism of *Wise Blood*. (More than three dozen books and almost countless articles have been written about O'Connor, one of the most closely studied American authors of the twentieth century.) Among critics who, in varying ways and degrees, affirm her religious vision are Robert Drake (1966), who notes O'Connor's distrust of intellectual liberalism; John R. May (1976) and Sister Kathleen Feeley (1972), who see the author largely in light of biblical traditions and techniques; and John F. Desmond (1987), who combines religious exegesis with analysis of O'Connor's imagery, style, and artistry. Frederick Crews, in an influential essay on O'Connor and the critics, lists in one of his endnotes eleven book-length Christian readings of the author (1992, 202, no. 16).

Many critics recognize O'Connor's very dark vision, as she herself apparently did, as integral to the dynamics of Redemption she is so deeply concerned with, but other critics are less sympathetic. Martha Stephens (1973) is repelled by O'Connor's view of life as exclusively squalid and ugly (cited in Kreyling 1995, 19). Josephine Hendin sees the final state of Haze, in *Wise Blood*, as not so much religious illumination as nihilism (1970, 54). O'Connor's friend John Hawkes

(1962) found her to be overly receptive to the diabolical (cited in Crews 1992, 155–56). Frederick Crews called her a Manichean (155), and even Ralph C. Wood (1988), in a well-informed theological commentary on the author, saw her as bordering on a heterodox Jansenism, a seventeenth-century Catholic heresy related to Calvinist severity (cited in Crews 1992, 152–55).

Attempts have been made to see O'Connor outside the religious and theological framework. For example, James M. Mellard (1989) substitutes for the great theist Other in O'Connor's work the Other as defined by the psychoanalytic unconscious.

Miles Orvell (1972) and Frederick Asals (1982) have written more balanced treatments of O'Connor, seeing her as less rigidly ideological and as fruitfully divided between alternatives such as religious parochialism and a more inclusive vision (cited in Crews 1992, 163–64).

NOTE

Flannery O'Connor, *Wise Blood*, and quotations from selected letters in Flannery O'Connor, *Collected Works* (New York: Library of America, 1988, 1–131 and 865–1234). All references are to this edition. Used by permission of Farrar, Straus and Giroux, LLC: Excerpts from *The Habit of Being: Letters of Flannery O'Connor* edited by Sally Fitzgerald. Copyright © 1979 by Regina O'Connor. Excerpts from *Wise Blood* by Flannery O'Connor. Copyright © 1962 by Flannery O'Connor. Copyright renewed © 1990 by Regina O'Connor.

WORKS CITED

Asals, Frederick. 1982. *Flannery O'Connor: The Imagination of Extremity*. Athens: University of Georgia Press.

Crews, Frederick. 1992. "The Critics Bear It Away." In *The Critics Bear It Away: American Fiction and the Academy*. New York: Random House.

Desmond, John F. 1987. *Risen Sons: Flannery O'Connor's Vision of History*. Athens: University of Georgia Press.

Drake, Robert. 1966. *Flannery O'Connor: A Critical Essay*. Grand Rapids, MI: Eerdmans.

Feeley, Sister Kathleen. 1972. *Flannery O'Connor: Voice of the Peacock*. Foreword by Caroline Gordon. New Brunswick, NJ: Rutgers University Press.

Hawkes, John. 1962. "Flannery O'Connor's Devil." *Sewanee Review* 70: 395–402.

Hendin, Josephine. 1970. *The World of Flannery O'Connor*. Bloomington: Indiana University Press.

Kreyling, Michael, ed. 1995. *New Essays on Wise Blood*. Cambridge: Cambridge University Press.

May, John R. 1976. *The Pruning Word: The Parables of Flannery O'Connor*. Notre Dame, IN: University of Notre Dame Press.

Mellard, James M. 1989. "Flannery O'Connor's *Others*: Freud, Lacan, and the Unconscious." *American Literature* 61: 625–43.

Orvell, Miles. 1972. *Invisible Parade: The Fiction of Flannery O'Connor*. Philadelphia: Temple University Press.

Stephens, Martha. 1973. *The Question of Flannery O'Connor*. Baton Rouge: Louisiana State University Press.

Whitt, Margaret Earley. 1995. *Understanding Flannery O'Connor*. Columbia: University of South Carolina Press.

Wood, Ralph C. 1988. *The Comedy of Redemption: Christian Faith and Comic Vision in Four American Novelists*. Notre Dame, IN: University of Notre Dame Press.

— Brian Wilkie

Flannery O'Connor [1925–1964]

Short Stories

MAJOR THEMES

Flannery O'Connor, frequently importuned by budding authors for professional advice, always gave the same answer: write about what you know. This was the advice that she herself followed, and thus her stories are regularly in the idiom of the American South, frequently enacted by a mother and daughter, and always permeated by the Catholic worldview.

O'Connor's creative production is comparatively small, determined partially by her death at thirty-nine but more importantly by the author's assiduous correction and revising. An insistently Catholic writer, O'Connor not only knew this vision of the world intellectually but was also one with it, just as she was one with the ethos of the South. This combination of religion and culture, itself unusual and tension-filled given the fundamentalist Protestant heritage of the South, is the origin of the striking particularity of O'Connor's Catholic perspective. In that perspective, the interpenetration of the spiritual and material worlds is everywhere marked by the grotesque. Tapping an ancient tradition of Catholic theology and aesthetics, O'Connor employs the grotesque as the means by which the divine enters the world, shattering human self-satisfaction, arrogance, and vanity. In O'Connor's stories, divine grace touches the main character in a moment of violence that demolishes all of the crutches and clichés by which the character has lived.

In some stories, the character is blameless except for his or her participation in the human condition, and the moment of violence signifies at once the loss of childish innocence and the possibility of salvation, the reality of original sin and the greater reality of its redemption.

Such is the dynamic of "The Turkey," an early story that formed part of O'Connor's master's thesis at the University of Iowa. While one dare not suggest allegorical readings of an author who has so tartly responded to overinterpretation of her work, the presence of two brothers in "The Turkey," the elder stereotypically bad, the younger stereotypically good, suggests the presence of the Cain and Abel trope. Ruller enacts his innocence in a game of cowboy and rustlers in which good and evil are clear and simple, and Ruller, the hero in his own childish game, champions the former, lassoing and putting an end to the criminal career of the imaginary cattle rustler, Mason.

The complex and revealing interweaving of the fictional and the real is accomplished by the appearance of a wounded wild turkey that Ruller, abandoning his imaginary epic, sets out to capture. Mentally savoring the adulation he will receive when he arrives home with the prey, Ruller reveals through interior monologue the family tension in which his domineering mother's preference for his older brother, Hane, drives him to seek approbation from his rather ephemeral father. He seeks attention and praise in all the ways of the not-so-innocent child: he says he is lonely when his father asks about his activities, he fakes a limp when he knows the father's gaze is on him; he even goes so far as to imitate Hane, given his brother's success in getting attention:

"Oh hell," he said cautiously.

Then in a minute he said just, "Hell."

Then he said it like Hane said it, pulling the e-ull out and trying to get the look in his eye that Hane got. Once Hane said, "God!" and his mother stomped after him and said, "I don't want to hear you say that again. Thou shalt not take the name of the Lord, thy God, in vain. Do you hear me?" and he guessed that shut Hane up. Ha! He guessed she dressed him off that time.

"God!" he said. (*Complete Stories*, 46)

Ruller begins a riot of blasphemy, out there alone in the woods, experimenting with the only kind of evil he knows, the fundamentalist fear of words. He imagines smoking and playing pool, like Hane, and getting his pious grandmother's full attention by offering her some "booze!"

But when Ruller succeeds in capturing the turkey, now dead from exhaustion, he deduces that this is a sign from God that he is the chosen one, that he is "unusual," even more unusual than Hane, and, renouncing his brief sinful past, he prepares to accept the mantle of righteousness that has been offered him. His growth in pride is rapid: "He wondered if God could think he was a very unusual child. He must" (49).

Soaking up the surprise and admiration of the people on the street, Ruller parades the turkey over his shoulder through the town center, only vaguely aware of the gang of "country kids" who have picked up his trail. Ruller is preoccupied with the hope of encountering a beggar or some other occasion that will permit him to exercise the magnanimity appropriate to one chosen by God. But on the outskirts of town the country kids, led by the "spitter," catch up with our hero, snatch the turkey, and leave him astonished and terrified in the darkening street. Like all of O'Connor's villains, these thieves play a crucial part in the economy of salvation, transforming the young Ruller's conventional and insipid ideas of good and evil, as well as his part in them, into an unspeakably genuine perception of the reality of sin, the Something Awful that ends the story: "He began to run. He ran faster and faster, and as he turned up the road to his house, his heart was running as fast as his legs and he was certain that Something Awful was tearing behind him with its arms rigid and its fingers ready to clutch" (53).

Unlike Ruller, Mrs. Hopewell, the nagging mother in "Good Country People," is no childish innocent discovering the true nature of evil. She is the embodiment of the cliché, filled with self-righteousness and conventional virtues that she attempts to impose on the sardonic daughter she has fatuously named Joy. Anything but joyous, this Doctor of Philosophy has renamed herself Hulga, a name she feels best expresses her searing intellectual realism as well as affording a portion of vengeance against her mother. Although addicted to the gloomy world view of existential philosophers, the origin of Hulga's nihilism is the hunting accident that caused the loss of her leg. An atheist and resolute debunker of Mrs. Hopewell's saccharine moralism, Hulga believes herself to be her mother's opposite, one of those intellectuals "who see *through* to nothing!" (287). She has reverence for one thing only, her wooden leg, which she has made into a kind of pagan idol: "She was as sensitive about the artificial leg as a peacock about his tail. No one ever touched it but her. She took care of it as someone else would his soul, in private and almost with her own eyes turned away" (288).

Mrs. Hopewell's idolatry is of another kind: she cherishes her comforting clichés about proper behavior and proper people, or "good country people" as she calls them, a term that excludes most of humanity and particularly the human "trash" whom she despises. Her hypocrisy begins to manifest itself with the visit of a Bible salesman, Manley Pointer, to whom she lies about having a Bible by her bedside. She is on full display in her self-image as a shrewd manipulator of her fellow human beings: "Mrs. Hopewell had no bad qualities of her own but she was able to use other people's in such a constructive way that she never felt the lack" (272).

The supreme irony of the story emerges with the reader's gradual realization that Hulga's hard-bitten intellectualism is every bit as trite and clichéd as her mother's moralism. Mother and daughter are finally seen as more similar than dissimilar in their self-serving and self-aggrandizing beliefs. The real difference between the two occurs at the end of the story, when Hulga is offered saving grace. Her decision to seduce the rustic Bible salesman is motivated both by an iconoclastic loathing of his seeming innocence and piety and, O'Connor suggests ever so slightly, by sexual desire repressed by pretentious intellectualism. Hulga's moment of grace arrives high up in the hayloft, the conventional locus for rural seduction, in the form of one of the most unconventional seductions in literature. Like many of O'Connor's villains, Manley Pointer is the instrument of God's grace, providing Hulga with the possibility of really *seeing through* to the sham that is her posturing life. Spectacularly beating Hulga at her own game of nihilistic narcissism, Manley opens his Bible—hollowed out in both the metaphoric and literal senses—to display his collection of pornographic playing cards, a bottle of whiskey, and a box of condoms; he then proceeds to turn the tables on his would-be seducer but in a way that, with all her cynicism, she could never have anticipated. Having yielded to his blandishments and allowed him to take off her leg, Hulga now begs Manley to put it back on: "'Not yet,' he murmured, setting it on its foot out of her reach. 'Leave it off for a while. You got me instead'" (289).

By identifying the prosthetic limb with the demonic Manley, O'Connor makes of him a kind of mirror in which Hulga suddenly sees herself in all her self-absorption, shallowness, and negativity. Driving the lesson home, Manley Pointer takes her wooden leg and disappears down the ladder and out of the barn with his trophy, snarling at his astonished victim: "'And I'll tell you another thing, Hulga,' he said, using the name as if he didn't think much of it, 'you ain't so smart. I been believing in nothing ever since I was born!'" (291). Stripped of all of her self-delusions, with pride in her deformity demolished, and the very emblem of all of this, her wooden leg, stashed in his valise with a Bible at each end, Hulga-Joy is now afforded the possibility of true understanding of the nature of the human condition and thus of sin and redemption.

There is considerable similarity between Mrs. Hopewell and the Grandmother of "A Good Man Is Hard to Find," Flannery O'Connor's singularly most acclaimed story. Much to the irritation of her rude, nasty grandchildren, the Grandmother is the embodiment of the sentimental. Her clichés cluster around the myth of an antebellum South, with columned mansions and happy, grateful, watermelon-eating "pickaninnies." She continually makes herself the center of this idyll, but the dreadful little nuclear family of her son, Bailey, is completely estranged from this myth as from all others. Like Mrs. Hopewell's, the Grandmother's moral range begins and ends with appearances: good manners, proper dress, and pride of origin. Her moral atrophy tends to diminish the reality around her to "cuteness," as we see in her comments about the poor blacks of the rural South: "'Oh look at the cute little pickaninny!' she said and pointed to a Negro child standing in the door of a shack. 'Wouldn't that make a picture, now?'" (119).

During a trip to Florida, a destination she disparages, the Grandmother convinces the family to make a detour to an old plantation mansion she once visited as a girl. Some distance down the isolated dirt road an accident sends the car and the family into a ditch. Soon there arrives a car with three men inside who turn out to be the escaped criminals, led by the so-called Misfit, whom the Grandmother warned against so as to prevent the trip to Florida. The Grandmother blurts out her recognition of the Misfit, whom she feels "she had known . . . all her life," (126), sealing the fate of her family as well as her own. The procession of the family members, one after the other, into the nearby woods is punctuated by the sound of periodic pistol shots and paralleled by a dialogue between the Misfit and the Grandmother that forms the heart and meaning of the story. For all of her belief in her own goodness, it is clear that she is concerned mainly with her own safety: "'You wouldn't shoot a lady, would you?'" (127). As the gruesome parade of her loved ones to the killing woods continues, her panic rises, and she uses one ploy after another to save herself. The Misfit is, she is sure, not of "common blood"; he's from a "good family," she can tell. Hearing the first two shots, the Grandmother's desperation deepens, and she uses what she believes is her trump card in the game to save her own skin: "'Do you ever pray?' she asked. . . . 'If you would pray,' the old lady said, 'Jesus would help you'" (129, 130).

The Misfit does not pray, but he does believe in Jesus. Like Manley Pointer, the Misfit represents pure evil, both of them figures who make manifest the reality of original sin and divine grace. The Misfit's belief in Christ contrasts explosively with the Grandmother's belief in him. Hers is the easy, sentimental religious view of the world that provides reassurance to her shallowness; his is the unshakable and uncompromising realization that Jesus, Son of God, did come into the world, did raise the dead, and did provide the means of overcoming sin: "'And He shouldn't have done it. He thown everything off balance'" (132). The Misfit rejects Jesus and all he stands for; he recognizes the tremendousness of the truth of the Incarnation and the redemptive love of God and has made his own choice against it. In the last moments of her life, the Grandmother also recognizes this enormity for the first time and seems to move to embrace it:

> The grandmother's head cleared for an instant. She saw the man's face twisted close to her own as if he were going to cry and she murmured, "Why you're one of my babies. You're one of my own children!" She reached out and touched him on the shoulder. The Misfit sprang back as if a snake had bitten him and shot her three times through the chest. (132)

The Misfit articulates the antitheology of the modern disbeliever in a way far more complete than other O'Connor villains, even Manley Pointer. Before killing her, the Misfit explains to the Grandmother that Jesus has ruined the easiness of a simply material world of time by creating access to the eternal spiritual world, because now one has to either commit oneself wholly to him or wholly against him:

> "If He did what He said, then it's nothing for you to do but throw away everything and follow Him, and if He didn't, then it's nothing for you to do but enjoy the few minutes you got left the best way you can—by killing somebody or burning down his house or doing some other meanness to him. No pleasure but meanness," he said and his voice had become almost a snarl. (132)

O'Connor's perspicuous critique of modern society reveals that few disbelievers go as far in their convictions as the Misfit and that most believers, like the Grandmother, are really make-believe believers content to observe the social conventions that include religion, as long as religion is kept in its place (usually locked away in the attic with Mrs. Hopewell's Bible). The horrifying experience of the Grandmother checkmates all of her pretenses and forces her to look directly into the nature of real evil and real good. It is the Misfit who understands how deeply she has seen: "'She would of been a good woman,' the Misfit said, 'if it had been somebody there to shoot her every minute of her life'" (133).

So as not to leave the impression that O'Connor's stories are always as grim as those so far discussed, let us end with one that dramatizes a different kind of antihero, one still beleaguered by a doting mother but whose comeuppance is far less violent. In "The Enduring Chill," O'Connor has one of her favorite targets in a potent satire on pretentious intellectuals and self-proclaimed artists. Asbury Porter Fox, who has published nothing since graduating from college and going to live as a writer in New York, has come home to Timbersboro with chills and a fever and full of self-dramatization about his impending death. He even thinks he has discovered a kind of justice in his untimely demise: "He had failed his god, Art, but he had been a faithful servant and Art was sending him Death. He had seen this from the first with a kind of mystical clarity" (373).

Asbury toys with religion in the same way that he toys with art, and at the height of his self-dramatization he asks his desperate mother to call a priest to his bedside, "'Preferably a Jesuit,' he said, brightening more and more" (371). He does this primarily to irk his southern Protestant mother but also because he recalls meeting a Jesuit at a lecture on Vedanta, a man who impressed him because he appeared worldly, intellectual, and ironic—but most of all because he seemed to take Asbury seriously. Awaiting the intellectual excitement of a dialogue with a Jesuit, Asbury regards the dreary walls of his bedroom:

> Descending from the top molding, long icicle shapes had been etched by leaks and, directly over his bed on the ceiling, another leak had made a fierce bird with spread wings. It had an icicle crosswise in its beak and there were smaller icicles descending from its wings and tail. It had been there since his childhood and had always irritated him and had sometimes frightened him. (365–66)

The image of the bird, along with the concept of the chill, turns out to be the controlling metaphor of the story.

What the Timbersboro Jesuit, Father Finn, lacks in intellectual repartee he makes up for in bluster and directness. In a splendidly comic exchange between the patient and the priest, Asbury's narcissism and delusions of intellectual grandeur are ground to dust, the first step in his therapy:

> "This place is incredibly dreary. There's no one here an intelligent person can talk to. I wonder what you think of Joyce, Father?"
>
> The Priest lifted his chair and pushed closer. "You'll have to shout," he said. "Blind in one eye and deaf in one ear."
>
> "What do you think of Joyce?" Asbury said louder.
>
> "Joyce? Joyce who?" asked the priest.
>
> "James Joyce," Asbury said and laughed.
>
> The priest brushed his huge hand in the air as if he were bothered by gnats. "I haven't met him," he said. "Now. Do you say your morning and night prayers?" (375)

The preposterous dialogue has Father Finn insisting that Asbury pray to the Holy Ghost. "'The Holy Ghost is the last thing I'm looking for!'" Asbury insists. "'And He may be the last thing you get,' the priest said, his one fierce eye inflamed" (376–77). Devastated by the priest's deflation of his intellectual pretensions, Asbury next attempts to find meaning in his social and moral superiority. Recalling his pleasure at patronizing his mother's black farm hands by condescending to smoke with them, he now calls for them to gather at his bedside for a last egalitarian smoke. Asbury attempts to draw the men into a deep conversation about death, hopeful of some African mystical insight in place of the failed attempt at Jesuit insight, but every insistence on his imminent demise is politely rebuffed by the farm hands, who assure him he looks fine, that he'll be up and around soon, and that he "'ain't even sick!'" (379). As a commemoration of their original bonding, Asbury offers one of them a cigarette, but, misunderstanding, the man takes the whole package and puts it in his pocket. So much for the cliché of the last smoke!

The final blow comes with the results of Asbury's blood tests, which proclaim, ironically, the worst news of all: he is not going to die. With all the supports of his narcissistic self-delusions gone, Asbury falls back on his pillow and stares up at the ceiling. He feels a new kind of chill, one that O'Connor describes as warm; he perceives again the water stain image of the fierce bird that now seems to be coming down upon him: "A feeble cry, a last impossible protest escaped him. But the Holy Ghost, emblazoned in ice instead of fire, continued, implacable, to descend" (382).

The reader is never allowed to see whether or not the character, blessed with a final moment of grace, takes advantage of it. The principal point for O'Connor is not to draw out the character in psychological ways but to dramatize the nature and working of divine grace, a much greater challenge for any writer. Her themes are constant—the human condition, sin and redemption, the shallowness of modern culture. On this last theme, both religion and politics fall into her cross hairs: easy, sentimental religiosity and easy, self-serving liberalism. In many of her stories, the antagonists each embody one of these failings, and conflict between them produces not a synthesis but a wholly new position: genuine spiritual understanding potentially yielding authentic ethical commitment.

Such is the case in "Good Country People," in which both the smug superiority of Mrs. Hopewell and Hulga's overweening radicalness are so satirized that the reader cannot help but perceive the tougher but more honest way. In "A Good Man Is Hard to Find," the Grandmother's "niceness," with all its insensitivity to others, and the Misfit's nihilism collide to create a vision in which both are seen as grotesquely intertwined. In "The Turkey," even Ruller's childish egotism and facile virtue have the odor of pride about them, and his encounter with the poor whites he disdains produces a similar breakthrough in understanding. In "The Enduring Chill," Asbury's fashionable self-loathing and rejection of his origins O'Connor takes as the hallmark of political liberals, especially white northern liberals, who denigrate their race, their origin, and their religion (when they still have one) in order to advertise their support of blacks and other minorities. Asbury's patronizing of his mother's black employees embarrasses them; their own traditional values are offended by his disrespect of his mother, and the self-dramatized artist in turn scoffs at their good manners and conventional politeness. However, O'Connor also perceives the same hypocrisy and superficiality in the racism of her southern neighbors, in whom condescension and self-righteousness fit easily together. Her stories are filled with characters whose own high opinion of themselves is supported solely by their contempt for their social inferiors, including all blacks and all so-called "white trash." O'Connor's principal satiric goal is to yank that support away.

Flannery O'Connor is not, however, merely a satirist—nor is her view of life ultimately a satirical one. She knocks away the hollow supports of the petty and foolish, but she does not demonize them. Nor does she preach to the reader, suggesting alternative behaviors to the shallow, self-serving ones she satirizes. O'Connor seems to have the genuine Catholic confidence that everyone who comes to see the truth, whether willingly or not, will love it and embrace it. The fullest expression of O'Connor's social and religious world view is found, perhaps, in her portrayal of Mrs. Turpin, the racist "wart hog from Hell" of the story "Revelation," who at the story's end is granted an eschatological vision:

A visionary light settled in her eyes. She saw the streak as a vast swinging bridge extending upwards from the earth through a field of living fire. Upon it a vast horde of souls were rumbling toward heaven. There were whole companies of white trash, clean for the first time in their lives, and bands of black niggers in white robes, and battalions of freaks and lunatics shouting and clapping and leaping like frogs. And bringing up the end of the procession was a tribe of people whom she recognized at once as those who, like herself and Claud [her husband], had always had a little of everything and the God-given wit to use it right. She leaned forward to observe them closer. They were marching behind the others with great dignity, accountable as they had always been for good order and common sense and respectable behavior. They alone were on key. Yet she could see by their shocked and altered faces that even their virtues were being burned away. (508)

CRITICAL RECEPTION

For a writer whose output amounts to thirty-one short stories and two novels, Flannery O'Connor has provoked a vast amount of critical commentary. It falls roughly into two camps: those who greatly admire her writing but either cannot comprehend her Catholicism or just cannot abide it; and those who admire O'Connor's writing and see her Catholicism, as she herself did, as the very source of its greatness. Another version of this divide opposes those who describe O'Connor as a southern writer whose religious preoccupations are at best irrelevant, at worst harmful, to her art and those who locate her greatness exclusively in her Catholicism and who see her southernness as incidental. O'Connor would be quite perturbed with this since she insisted on the indivisibility of her talent and the equal contributions of her religion and her home.

Those who would downplay O'Connor's Catholicism sometimes accuse her of being subconsciously a Manichean fundamentalist whose southern Protestant culture overcame her avowed Catholicism in her writing—like Milton, who was, it was once claimed, of the devil's party without knowing it. Indeed, the American writer John Hawkes (1985) accuses Flannery O'Connor of just that—being of the devil's party (she denied it) in the sense that her work depicts two distinct human options: the religious one and, for lack of a better term, the secular-materialist one. Hawkes feels that O'Connor's rendering of characters who take the second option makes them more persuasive and sympathetic than her religious characters.

There are variations on this general view. In 1970, Josephine Hendin (*The World of Flannery O'Connor*) tried to make a case for O'Connor's work being the product of the author's unresolved psychological issues and claimed that this, not religion, is the ground of O'Connor's artistic energy. Hendin has a low opinion of O'Connor and sees her as an artistic failure. Perhaps the most determined of such critics is Joanne Halleran McMullen, whose *Writing Against God* (1996) attempts a sweeping revisionist reading that sees O'Connor's Catholicism as detracting from her artistic strengths. The most recent turn in O'Connor scholarship is the entry of feminists and Bakhtinians, neither of whom have much sympathy for the author's religious convictions. Katherine Hemple Prown's *Revising Flannery O'Connor* (2001) is one of the most recent studies with feminist concerns. A good idea of the direction of both schools can be had from *Flannery O'Connor: New Perspectives*, edited by Sura P. Rath and Mary Neff Shaw (1996).

The school that sees O'Connor as a great American writer whose vision is sustained by the Catholic religion she so loyally adhered to is, perhaps, best represented by Kathleen Feeley, one of the early critics doing serious and sensitive scholarship on O'Connor as a Catholic writer. She sees O'Connor's art as a whole, produced by a talent in which faith and art were one. Her book *Flannery O'Connor: Voice of the Peacock*, originally published in 1972, was reedited in 1982. David Eggenschwiler's *The Christian Humanism of Flannery O'Connor*, also published in 1972, likewise centers on O'Connor's Christianity as the interpretive key to her work. Martha Stephens' *The Question of Flannery O'Connor* (1973) is a work along the same general lines that takes Christianity as the major factor in O'Connor's writing. Stephens sees O'Connor as an example of the modern, European Christian tradition and in the spiritual and artistic company of such English-speaking writers as T. S. Eliot and Graham Greene and such continentals as Georges Bernanos and François Mauriac. The most recent contribution to this school is George A. Kilcourse Jr.'s *Flannery O'Connor's Religious Imagination* (2001), a thorough and persuasive discussion of the ways in which Catholicism directly affected O'Connor's writing and how an understanding of Catholicism illuminates her fiction. Also recommended is Henry T. Edmondson's highly accessible and interesting *Return to Good and Evil* (2002).

NOTE

Flannery O'Connor, *Flannery O'Connor: The Complete Stories* (New York: Farrar, Straus, and Giroux, 1971). All references are to this edition. Used by permission of Farrar, Straus and Giroux, LLC. Copyright © 1971 by the Estate of Mary Flannery O'Connor.

WORKS CITED

Edmondson, Henry T., III. 2002. *Return to Good and Evil: Flannery O'Connor's Response to Nihilism*. Lanham, MD: Lexington Books.

Eggenschwiler, David. 1972. *The Christian Humanism of Flannery O'Connor*. Detroit: Wayne State University Press.

Feeley, Sister Kathleen. 1982. *Flannery O'Connor: Voice of the Peacock*. New York: Fordham University Press.

Hawkes, John. 1985. "Flannery O'Connor's Devil." In *Critical Essays on Flannery O'Connor*, ed. Melvin J. Freidman and Beverly Lyon Clark, 92–100. Boston: G. K. Hall.

Hendin, Josephine. 1970. *The World of Flannery O'Connor*. Bloomington: Indiana University Press.

Kilcourse, George A., Jr. 2001. *Flannery O'Connor's Religious Imagination*. New York: Paulist Press.

McMullen, Joanne Halleran. 1996. *Writing Against God*. Macon, GA: Mercer University Press.

Prown, Katherine Hemple. 2001. *Revising Flannery O'Connor*. Charlottesville: University of Virginia Press.

Rath, Sura P., and Mary Neff Shaw, eds. 1996. *Flannery O'Connor: New Perspectives*. Athens: University of Georgia Press.

Stephens, Martha. 1973. *The Question of Flannery O'Connor*. Baton Rouge: Louisiana State University Press.

BIBLIOGRAPHY

Cash, Jean W. *Flannery O'Connor: A Life*. Knoxville: University of Tennessee Press, 2002.

Di Rienzo, Anthony. *American Gargoyle: Flannery O'Connor and the Medieval Grotesque*. Carbondale: Southern Illinois University Press, 1993.

Montgomery, Marion. *The Trouble with You Innerlekchuls*. Front Royal, VA: Christendom Press, 1988.

O'Connor, Flannery. *The Correspondence of Flannery O'Connor and the Bernard Cheneys*, ed. C. Ralph Stephens. Jackson: University Press of Mississippi, 1968.

————. *The Habit of Being: Letters of Flannery O'Connor*, ed. and intro. Sally Fitzgerald. New York: Farrar, Straus, and Giroux, 1979.

————. *Mystery and Manners: Occasional Prose*, ed. Sally and Robert Fitzgerald. New York: Farrar, Straus, and Giroux, 1969.

— David Williams

Walker Percy [1916–1990]

Lancelot

BIOGRAPHY

Walker Percy was born in Birmingham, Alabama, in 1916, the son of a prominent lawyer who could trace his lineage back to the Percys of Northumberland and a mother (Martha Susan Phinizy) who had French Catholic ancestors. At age thirteen, Percy was orphaned, together with two brothers, when his father committed suicide and his mother died a few years later in a mysterious car-drowning. The three boys were adopted and raised by William Alexander Percy, a distant kinsman from Greenville, Mississippi. He was a distinguished planter-lawyer-poet as well as an ex-Catholic who had lost his faith and become something of a Stoic. This noble man was to have a deeply shaping influence on Percy, providing him with a sterling example of the highly moral and cultured person who lives utterly without the aid of Christian faith. Will Percy's memoir, entitled *Lanterns on the Levee* (1941), is an essential book for understanding Walker Percy's own life and work.

After finishing high school in Greenville—where the future Civil War historian and novelist Shelby Foote became his lifelong friend—Percy studied first at the University of North Carolina in Chapel Hill, where he took his bachelor's degree in chemistry with high honors. He then received his M.D. degree from Columbia University, concentrating in pathology, although he seriously considered psychiatry as his specialty. Yet Percy spent three of his Columbia years undergoing psychoanalysis, a sign that he was a deeply troubled fellow, a man who would not be satisfied with the worldly success he was already winning. During his residency in pathology at Bellevue Hospital in New York City, as he was doing research on the cadavers of tuberculosis victims, Percy himself contracted the disease. He spent his long recuperation reading philosophy, theology, and fiction, especially the work of Dostoevsky and Tolstoy, Sartre and Camus—but also that of Thomas Aquinas. These artists and thinkers probed the human condition, Percy discovered, in ways that made him wonder whether he was meant to be a writer rather than a physician.

Percy would, in fact, never practice medicine at all, although he would retain the diagnostician's impulse, as he once said, "to thump the patient and to find out what's wrong." Having gradually recovered from tuberculosis, Percy remained personally at sea, not knowing what to do with himself. He was a young man still wandering, both spiritually and geographically. He finally found clarity for his life when, in 1947, he married Mary Bernice ("Bunt") Townsend, a nurse. Not long thereafter, they were both received into the Roman Catholic Church as converts. They eventually settled in Covington, Louisiana, across Lake Ponchartrain from New Orleans. There Percy spent the remainder of his life working as an essayist and novelist. He died in 1990 and is buried beneath a plain gravestone alongside the monks of a nearby Benedictine abbey.

Percy published six novels: *The Moviegoer* (1961), *The Last Gentleman* (1967), *Love in the Ruins* (1971), *Lancelot* (1977), *The Second Coming* (1980), and *The Thanatos Syndrome* (1987). He also penned three volumes of essays: *The Message in the Bottle* (1975), *Lost in the Cosmos: The Last Self-Help Book* (1983), and *Signposts in a Strange Land* (edited by Patrick Samway and published posthumously in 1994). Jay Tolson's *Pilgrim in the Ruins* (1992) remains the indispensable biographical study of Percy.

PLOT SUMMARY

Lancelot is the first-person narrative of Lancelot Andrewes Lamar, a lawyer confined in a psychiatric prison, the so-called Center for Aberrant Behavior. There he is visited on five occasions by a man named Percival, a psychiatrist-priest who was Lamar's boyhood chum and who has remained his lifelong friend. Percival has taken the priestly name of Father John, and he listens silently as Lance unburdens himself. In bits and pieces, Lance gradually reveals his life story, recalling the important things that he has both done and left undone, whether for good or ill. The attentive Father John speaks not a word during Lance's long rambling monologue until the very end, when he utters two syllables: *Yes* twelve times and *No* once. Such a narrative would seem incapable of holding the reader's interest, but it is in fact one of Percy's most gripping works.

The novel begins on All Souls Day, November 1, the Day of the Dead. From the start, Percy suggests that Lancelot Lamar is a dead soul and that he does not belong among the blessed dead. The novel's epigraph is taken from Dante's *Purgatorio*, a passage wherein Beatrice Portinari—the ideal love of Dante's life—explains that she descended from heaven to hell, there summoning the Latin poet Virgil to lead Dante through all the regions of the damned as the only possible way to rescue Dante from his wretched condition. Lance has intimations that he too has been living in hell. Yet he is convinced that he is about to venture on a new path to a paradisal existence. In fact, Lance divides his adult life into two periods. He is exceedingly angry about having lost the best years of his life to what Percy calls "everydayness"—to the empty and thoughtless routines that occupy most middle-class souls. But now Lance believes that he has entered into a revolutionary new phase, having found a radical kind of moral and spiritual excellence that will characterize the remainder of his days.

Lance confesses that he became strangely alive upon discovering that his daughter Siobhan is illegitimate and that her real father is her mother's lover, a moviemaker named Merlin. This startling discovery sets Lance on what he calls his "quest," his determination to discover the nature of evil, to prove that sin really exists. If it does not, he argues, then neither does God exist. As the novel makes increasingly evident, Lancelot Lamar is not a conventional hero; he is an antihero. He is not a splendid but a sordid soul, a man who seeks redemption by plumbing the depths of evil. He is not a noble knight in search of the Holy Grail but an ignoble cuckold seeking unholy proof of God's existence. He is, in sum, one of Walker Percy's most complicated characters.

The novel ends with Lance's recollection of the burning of Belle Isle, his country estate. It is an apocalyptic fire of final judgment set by Lancelot himself, as he incinerates his decadent wife Margot, her new lover Jacoby, and two other people. Percy's plot makes no conventional Aristotelian movement from beginning through middle on to end. The novel's progression deals, instead, with Lance's increasingly violent denunciations of our age and with his equally violent remedy against its evils. As in none of his other novels, Walker Percy requires a decision of his audience: we must make our own judgment of Lance's brilliant rant. His confession to Father John rivets our interest because it forces us to ask whether Lance is making a moral advance or a moral regression, whether he possesses revolutionary religious insight into the horrors of our age or whether he has committed new and worse horrors of his own. As Lance says to his friend Percival, so does Percy declare to his readers: "You must decide ... for yourself" (*Lancelot*, 160).

MAJOR THEMES

Lancelot is Percy's least Catholic novel, at least in the overt sense of the term. The protagonist of both *Love in the Ruins* and *The Thanatos Syndrome* is a self-confessed "bad Catholic" named Dr. Thomas More who is on his way back to faith. *The Last Gentleman* ends with a climactic Catholic baptism, and *The Moviegoer* recounts Binx Bolling's gradual return to the Church after many years of self-abandonment. Although Percy did not want to be called a Catholic novelist—lest he be cut off from the larger secular audience he sought to address— these four novels have an undeniably Catholic quality. Lancelot Andrewes Lamar, by contrast, is no sort of Catholic; in fact, he is no kind of Christian at all. The only Catholic character to appear in *Lancelot* is Father John, a shadowy figure with a hooded, sorrowful look, and he speaks but two words. Does this mean, then, that the novel has no seriously Catholic dimension?

Not if we remember that Walker Percy described himself as a Catholic existentialist. By examining human life itself—by plumbing the complications and contradictions of our own existence—Percy believed that we can find irrefutable evidence for the reality of the triune God. There is no necessity to begin with overt Christian claims about human nature and destiny in order to demonstrate that we are God-shaped and God-starved creatures. Our very own selfhood, when rightly fathomed, reveals that we have inclinations and longings that can be satisfied only by the God who has become flesh in Israel and Christ and the Church.

Yet it was not through Gabriel Marcel or some other modern Catholic thinker that Percy became an existentialist. On the contrary, he owed his Christian conversion largely to Søren Kierkegaard, especially to his essay entitled "Of the Difference Between a Genius and an Apostle" (1962). "Here I am a Catholic writer living in Louisiana," Percy confessed, "and yet the man to whom I owe the greatest debt is this great Protestant theologian" (Lawson and Kramer 1985, 127). It may seem odd that Percy, the Kierkegaardian, would become a Catholic. Yet the human desire for God can turn dangerously subjective and even demonically delusory—this is one of the chief themes of *Lancelot*—unless it is grounded in the objective authority of the Church's magisterial teaching and the transcendent reality of its sacraments. The life of utter transparency before God can be found, Percy concluded, only in the Roman Catholic Church.

Even so, he remained profoundly indebted to the eccentric nineteenth-century Danish theologian-philosopher-poet. Kierkegaard taught Percy that human existence is inexorably double-sided and dialectical. The human self is an uneasy synthesis of both angelic aspirations and bestial desires—of vertical and heavenly possibilities on the one hand and horizontal and earthly limitations on the other. We teeter on the edge of the narrow divide between these contrary impulses, either plunging into a swinish life of the senses or else soaring into an equally false life of abstract spirituality. We live miserably sinful lives, Percy discovered, by trying to become either apes or angels when we are meant to be neither.

Nothing other than a faithful existence, Percy argues, can unite and reconcile the conflicting qualities that constitute our fallen selfhood. Yet Percy feared that traditional approaches to Christian faith have been worn slick from overuse, like coins whose faces are no longer legible. He sought, therefore, to mint the old terms afresh. He likens our fallen species, for example, to a shipwrecked man on an unknown island, a castaway who should be looking for news that might help him find his way back home. What he needs to receive is what Percy calls "news from across the seas"—that is, the Good News of the transformed life to be found in the Kingdom of God. Our great temptation, Percy argues, is to remain content with what he calls "island news" (*The Message in the Bottle*, 140)—with all the standard strategies for settling down and living at ease amidst the wreckage of modern life, or else with the various therapies that provide temporary contentment amidst permanent misery. Percy often confessed that he wrote out of a sense of rage at these strategies and therapies and that his real inspiration was anger. Yet he also remained confident that our homing instinct for God cannot be permanently suppressed and denied. Sooner or later we will become damnably unhappy in our allegedly paradisal life of comfort and conformity. We will blessedly fail to settle for a shipwrecked existence.

Lancelot Lamar knows that he is a castaway because he lives in an age of "interest" (*Lancelot*, 21)—a term that Percy borrows from Kierkegaard. Lance argues that we have abandoned the categories of good and evil for assessing both people and events. We respond only with "curiosity" and "interest"—or else with boredom. "Everything and everyone's either wonderful or sick," Lance declares near the novel's end, "and nothing is evil" (139). An aesthetic word such as "wonderful" or a therapeutic term such as "sick" serves to silence all moral and religious judgments about our lives. These terms also indicate our cool detachment from almost everything, even the most horrible things. A newspaper headline declaring that a plane crash has killed three hundred people causes us to declare our delicious horror, says Lance (22). We are strangely excited and energized by such catastrophes because they render us splendidly if temporarily serious but without requiring any fundamental change in our lives. The burning of Belle Isle occurs, for example, during a terrible hurricane, when the various members of the movie-making set gather for an all-night party, celebrating the thrill of safe danger.

An age of interest is also what Kierkegaard called a Talkative Age (1962, *The Present Age*, 69). Everyone has an opinion about everything, Lance notices, but no one has convictions about much of anything. Our talkative times have an abhorrence of silence and thus an obsession with news, especially the hourly news reported on radio and television. Even during the 1960s, when everyone awaited the latest account of a race riot or an assassination, the news left one exactly and comfortably as one was—and thus all the hungrier for a fresh report of further disasters. "I lived for the news bulletin," Lance confesses, "the interrupted program, the unrehearsed and stumbling voice of the reporter" (72).

A culture obsessed with interest and talk and news is also a moviegoing culture. Film has become the chief determiner of our lives, Lance argues, for it is the ultimately cool medium for keeping the real world at bay. Lance's second wife Margot is a telling example of a movie-determined life. Having become the bored mistress of Belle Isle, she has taken up acting in her late thirties. Most of Lance's recollections of their marriage concern the movie that she and her friends recently filmed near the Lamar home. The silliness of its plot and the triteness of its theme are not the real cause of Lance's contempt. He is angry mainly because various members of his family—as well as the local townspeople—have adopted the qualities and gestures of film stars as their only means for achieving a sense of identity. Yet these actors are themselves empty souls. Lance describes Dana, for example, as having perfect blonde hair, perfect physical features, perfect bodily movements: "He was an idiot but he had grace. He was a blank space filled by somebody else's idea" (146–47). Although he means only to sigh out his own lament, Lance also utters the American creed: "Jesus Christ, the movies" (206).

Nowhere does the religious emptiness of our culture become more evident than in Lance's account of our sexual *mores*. His first marriage was a typically American union. Lucy Cobb was the ideal girl of his youthful dreams, a lovely tennis-playing virgin, a perfect Georgia belle who bore him two children. Yet Lucy remained so angelically unreal to Lance that he can now remember her only as a dancer swirling in a bell jar (119). Her early death meant almost nothing to him. Margot Reilly, the daughter of a West Texas oilman, is by contrast a thoroughly vital and voluptuous woman. In Kierkegaardian terms, she is as bestial as Lucy was angelic. Her pudendum served as his Holy of Holies, "the ark of her covenant" (171). Now in furious retrospect, Lance can discern the fraudulence of his worship. In the absence of transcendent moral and religious referents, he argues, sex becomes our only divinity—the ultimately right and real thing, our true and only heaven. "What else is infinity," he asks, "but a woman [having] become meat and drink to you, life and your heart's own music, the air you breathe? Just to be near her is to live and have your soul's own self" (129). Like a latter-day version of Saint Augustine before his conversion, Lance declares that he once "lived for love" (167). So great was Margot's transformation of his life—since all his desires converged and found their satisfaction in her—that he calls her "a Texas magician" (82).

Having been brought up to believe that only the male seeks sexual pleasure, Margot has shown him that women often crave it no less than men. Among all the animal species, he observes, only the human female is capable of remaining in a state of perpetual estrus—in the heat of constant sexual desire (223). So long as Margot found Lance sexually appealing, they created a splendid erotic universe all unto themselves. They joined what would seem forever put asunder: the heavenly and the brutish. Their sexual transports made them at once angels and beasts. Yet their sexual splendor was short-lived, since Margot valued Lance as little more than a project akin to her house-redecoration schemes. He was a temporary attraction eventually to be left behind for a more fascinating sexual partner. In an age of "interest," Lance concludes, there can be no lasting love.

Lance confesses that he no longer knows what love means. He knows only that, when their bodies were ecstatically joined, they fulfilled the literal meaning of the word "ecstasy": they stood outside themselves (21). Yet he wants to fathom the nature of their "possession." Was it divine or demonic? Into what realm did their sexual glory deliver them? Lance's bitter conclusion is that untempered craving for sexual rapture is nihilistic at its core, for it has replaced the worship of God with nearly nonstop copulation. Yet Lance is himself no believer. On the contrary, he is a virulent God-denier and antihumanist. If there is a deity, he concludes, God is the one who is guilty of the original sin, for he created our species not only to become thinking reeds, as Pascal declared, but also to live as mobile genitals: "The great secret of the ages is that man has evolved, is born, lives, dies for one end and one end only: to commit sexual assault on another human being or to submit to such assault" (222).

Both a lecher and a victim of lechery, Lance is determined to begin a revolution that will cleanse our culture of its moral filth. He prophesies the coming of a New Man and a New Woman who will abandon our hopelessly dead past. Lance believes that he can enter this radically new world with Anna, a once-idealistic social worker who occupies an adjacent cell at the psychiatric prison. She has become a psychotic mute after being sodomized and gang-raped by the same ghetto youths whom she had sought to serve. Lance hopes that Anna—as a sort of virgin-in-reverse, ironically purified by multiple rapes—will join him in creating an entirely new way of life. It will be a world wherein men and women honor rather than assault each other. They will enjoy the plain things once again, asking simple questions and attending to simple needs, remaining close but also keeping a slight distance. Lance sees himself as a latter-day prophet, therefore, waiting and watching and preparing to preside over the violent birth of this courtly new world.

He prophesies that this chivalrous world will be morally clean if also morally violent. Its severe ethical excellence will resemble that of ancient aristocratic societies, where there once prevailed "a stern code, a gentleness toward women and an intolerance of swinishness, a counsel kept, and above all a readiness to act" (157). Ladies and gentlemen will again be lauded: "There will be virtuous women who are proud of their virtue and there will be women of the street who are there to be fucked and everyone will know which is which." The best of the men, Lance adds, "will be strong and brave and pure of heart. . . . The others can whore-monger and screw whom they choose. But we will prevail" (178–79). This drastic revolution will begin, Lance maintains, in the Shenandoah Valley of Virginia, not only because Anna owns property there but also because the cavalier spirit once prevailed there, if all too briefly.

Lance is a trenchant critic of the contemporary Catholic Church no less than of contemporary American culture. He laments to Father John, for instance, that the Church once possessed the necessary spiritual vigor to have prevented the "milksoppery" of the modern world. The dauntless spirit of the Crusaders, the architectural daring of Mont Saint-Michel, the once-fierce devotion to the Virgin Mary, the warlike zeal of the Christ who brought not peace but a sword— these virile Catholic virtues could still inspire a New Age of moral and religious rectitude. Yet Lance complains that the Church has abandoned its own excellences (157). "Now," he laments, "you've gotten rid of your Lady and taken the sword from Christ" (177). The Catholic Church now mirrors the world's own Laodicean lukewarmness. Lance finds the accommodations of the post-Vatican II Church to be summed up in the guitar-strumming, ass-wiggling nuns who, as he acidly observes, would look better in the monastic habits they have rejected than in the J. C. Penney pantsuits they have adopted.

What, then, is Lance to do? He decides that, as his name indicates, he alone must lance the moral abscess (236). Like a contemporary Ulysses returning to slay Penelope's suitors, he burns down Belle Isle in order to stop the sexual outrages occurring there. Yet Lance does not seek to justify his deadly action by comparing it to the wrecking of a crematoria-bound train loaded with Jews, nor even by likening it to the murder of abortionists. He acts entirely from personal animus: to halt the debauchery of Margot and three of her companions. The revolt he hopes to spark—reviving the ancient aristocratic virtues—remains a distant and secondary concern. Lance is not seeking to cleanse the entire American sty but rather to cast out the several swine who have inhabited his own household.

Why does Father John, a priest whose business is to shrive sin, remain silent during Lancelot's confession that he has become a vitriolic murderer? It becomes increasingly evident that Percival is allowing Lancelot to draw up his own bill of self-indictment. Although he regards himself as the scourge of his age, Lance is in fact its moral mirror. He wields the wicked sword of the same moral nihilism that he despises. This irony is most subtly suggested in his repeated visions of a mysterious woman holding a white camellia, a symbol of the moral purity he is determined to restore. As Lance's clear surrogate for the Virgin Mary, these spectral appearances demonstrate Percy's conviction that every denial of sacred reality creates is own idol in reverse. The Knights of the White Camellia are, in fact, one of the South's most virulently racist organizations. While Lance has revealed no latent racism—apart from his casual use of racial epithets—Percy suggests that Lance's moral righteousness resembles the "final solution" advocated by the Nazis or Klansmen.

Lance also contradicts himself when he complains that ours is an age lacking in passion and conviction. Despite his rage, he himself stands coldly aloof from life. He has a scientist's obsession with *knowing*. Instead of confronting Margot with his fear that she has been unfaithful to him, thus violating their covenanted relationship, Lance seeks scientific proof of her infidelity. He cannot credit his suspicion that Siobhan is illegitimate until her blood type demonstrates that she is the product of a sexual tryst. In his obsession with distant matters rather than realities close at hand, Lance even compares himself to an astronomer. So callously unfeeling is this abstracted soul that, after committing quadruple murder, Lance experiences not a moment of guilt. His only negative recollection of the event is that bits of fiberglass got under his collar and caused his neck to itch.

So do Lance's protests against the debilitating effects of television and the movies—their power to make us feel remote from the actual events we are watching—ring terribly hollow. Lance himself is a film creature through and through. In order to justify his moral fury against the cohabitations occurring in the baboon colony at Belle Isle, he employs his black friend Elgin to make videos of Margot and her lovers as they are coupling. Lance cannot believe until he *sees*. The botched tapes of the various sex-making scenes—where dark becomes light, and light becomes dark—cinematically reflect the moral reversal that they so badly record. These lurid movies might have been lifted straight from Dante's *Inferno*, but Lance remains opaque to such ironies, since he is concerned only to document his wife's whoring.

Lance's burning of Belle Isle is the final proof that he is altogether as evil as the age he despises. He often boasts of his freedom, his ability to act boldly, while others remain paralyzed by their moral uncertainty. Lance thus prizes the Bowie knife that one of his ancestors used to kill a man who had crossed him. Hence also his pride in having straddled the copulating Jacoby and Margot, crushing what Shakespeare called "the beast with two backs" before slitting Jacoby's throat and then igniting the methane that burned his wife and three other souls to death. Yet Lance performs his deeds of murderous righteousness only after numbing himself with drugs. He can act only after pharmaceutically abandoning his own sense of identity and responsibility. The drugs made him feel angelically invisible, as if he were floating in the air, utterly distanced from his body.

Even Lance can discern the satanic quality of his deed. Having struck the match that explodes the house and throws him free of the flames, he describes himself as "wheeling slowly up into the night like Lucifer blown out of hell, great wings spread against the starlight" (246). The dispeller of demons has become the prince of darkness. The lives he has destroyed count absolutely nothing for him, since he returns to the conflagration only to search for his lost Bowie knife.

The moral and religious upshot of *Lancelot* would seem to be singularly unedifying and to have little if any Catholic quality at all. Yet this is a deeply Catholic novel. Percy offers the almost silent priest, Father John, as his Catholic answer to Lancelot's homicidal rectitude. His name seems deliberately to echo the Johannine Gospel, the one that emphasizes the self-abnegating love that Lancelot lacks. Despite his short Dantesque fuse for the evils of our time, Percy also possessed an Augustinian patience with human sinfulness. If, as Augustine taught, sin is fundamentally a turning away from the triune God as the source and goal of our lives—and consequently a turning toward ourselves as our own be-all and end-all—then sooner or later evil will reveal its pathetic if also horribly destructive futility. An enormous forbearance is required to let sin declare its own bankruptcy: a firm conviction that God will not abandon his people to their sorry self-destruction. Father John possesses this forbearance. He does not need to condemn the self-condemning Lancelot. Instead, he allows the impenitent killer to lynch himself with his own rope.

Lance's self-appointed role as the executioner of sexual miscreants reveals the nihilism at work in his scheme to recover the morally pristine world once inhabited by true ladies and gentlemen: he must kill in order to make alive. Out of pure destruction, he will bring pure creation. This is precisely the logic animating many major political reformers of the past century, from Hitler and Stalin to Mao and Pol Pot. Raking clean the moral and religious muck, they attempted to create a hygienic new world. The results are well known. More people were killed by violent means in the twentieth century than in all previous centuries combined, roughly 180 million. This figure does not include the millions of surgical and nonsurgical abortions that were also performed. What makes *Lancelot* such a remarkable novel is that, already in 1977, Percy had discerned the terrible truth that Pope John Paul II would elaborate in *Evangelium Vitae* (1995): our age of vaunted human liberties and civil rights is in fact a "culture of death."

It was for good reason that Walker Percy called his novel a cautionary tale. Percy himself was given to Lance's kind of spleen, being fully agreed that ours is an age of monstrous personal no less than political evils. He was thus tempted not only to share Lancelot's kind of rage but also, as himself something of "a liberal gone sour" (181), to embrace his frightful idea of redemption. In this work, therefore, Percy performs the satirist's ultimately faithful act: he satirizes himself. He offers a salutary warning that the lecherous moral degradation of late-modern American life could spark a reactionary response. If Lancelot Lamar were to find followers, they could foment a bloody revolution that would garner both political and religious support. And they would have good cause, as the novel demonstrates, even if their solution were far deadlier than the disease.

What, if anything, does *Lancelot* suggest by way of a solution to the evils that Lance so brilliantly articulates? The answer lies in his grim admission, at the very end, that his soul has a core akin to the center of an onion: there is none. Lance confesses, moreover, that his spiritual emptiness makes him feel terribly cold. "Why," he asks Father John, "did I discover nothing at the heart of evil? There was no 'secret' after all, no discovery, no flickering of interest, nothing at all, not even any evil" (253). Lance's admission that he found a zero at the core of sin is a precise delineation of Saint Augustine's teaching on evil—that it is not something transcendently real but frightfully unreal, that it occupies not a proper but an alien place in God's good creation, that it is *privatio boni*—the absence and displacement of the good.

Lance's confession of spiritual frigidity provides the opening that Father John needs. Having remained completely mute, the priest at last speaks, if only two words. His grunted negatives and positives force Lance to make still more inquiries of the priest, until finally Father John gets the last word: "*Yes*" (257). Percy requires the reader—in a stroke of artistic genius—to supply the meaning of Father John's thirteen monosyllables. Lancelot himself begins to fathom the listening priest's silence. He surmises that Percival has not spoken because he has himself been unwilling to hear, to receive anything other than "island news." Yet Lancelot is right to want a radically new kind of life.

The essence of their clipped exchange seems to be this: the American experiment in freedom, lately understood as the liberty to decide one's life utterly without regard to received traditions or transcendent norms or communal considerations, has come to its end. It has collapsed of its own inherent contradiction, since the very idea of society implies both constraints and obligations that persons do not choose but assume. There must be a fresh start for our entire culture, but it will not come by recasting the old Enlightenment ideal of individual autonomy in new dress. Our radical refounding will occur in one of two ways: either through some version of Lancelot's violent and reactionary recourse to ancient aristocratic ideals, or else by way of Father John's decision to return to the service of the Church. There is no middle way between the extremes.

Yet Percy is careful not to make art a vehicle for the saving of souls. Not one of his novels ends with the protagonist making his way to a confessional or collapsing on his knees before a crucifix. It is the sacramental witness of the Church, not novels, that produces authentic conversions. Thus does *Lancelot* have a quiet, modest, and yet ever so powerfully Catholic climax. Having previously served as a psychiatrist—thus dispensing "island news"—Percival has decided to return to Alabama to work as an ordinary parish priest. This may seem to be a pathetically small response to the gargantuan evils that Lance has both discerned and denounced. Yet the novel makes precisely this subtle and outrageous claim: the Church is the only lasting answer to the perennial ills of our species. In an unknown town located in an undistinguished state, Father John will begin doing utterly unheralded work: preaching the Gospel, celebrating the sacraments, shriving the souls of ordinary sinners, giving hope to the living no less than praying for the dead. The transformed common life enabled by this "news from across the seas," Percy suggests, is the only answer to our culture of death.

Because Father John's renovated life is not intended for himself alone, it may also extend to Lancelot Andrewes Lamar. The priest seems to have been driven back to the Church precisely because of his encounter with his friend's raging righteousness. Lancelot has taught Percival that the late hour is exceedingly late, the times are exceptionally evil, and thus real hope is desperately needed. And Lancelot has admitted that he is immensely cold. He is a soul who shivers in the midst of his shipwrecked life and our castaway culture. Because Percival's final word to him is not chilly negation but warm affirmation, he may yet join his old priest-friend aboard the one true ship.

CRITICAL RECEPTION

The Moviegoer and *Love in the Ruins* both won the National Book Award, and *The Last Gentleman* was a runner-up for this prize, the most prestigious American literary honor. Yet *Lancelot* has not received the high critical acclaim given to Percy's first three novels. Joyce Carol Oates, herself a major American writer of fiction, calls the plot "tired and contrived," complains of "the empty rhetoric that fills page after page," and concludes that *Lancelot* is "one of the most disappointing novels I have read in recent years" (quoted in Bloom 1986, 64, 67). Jay Tolson, by contrast, describes *Lancelot* as Percy's "darkest, most infernal novel." He suggests that it must have been produced from a hellish condition that Percy himself had perhaps endured. The novel possesses the apocalyptic anger, Tolson argues, that the comic vision of Percy's earlier work had too easily ignored (1992, 362–63).

Lancelot has left critics confused at worst, partially convinced at best. Many of them have assumed, quite wrongly, that Percy stands in full accord with Lance's vitriolic denunciation of American decadence. Few have caught the subtlety of Father John's sly willingness to remain silent. Even readers who have discerned Percy's intentions are still not persuaded that the way to reveal demonic brilliance is to display its full fury. Yet this very desire for fiction that is comforting and uplifting makes precisely Percy's point: an age of moral softness is especially susceptible to Lancelot's moral callousness. That critics have been vexed by *Lancelot* makes its harsh caveat no less crucial, its quiet Catholic summons all the more requisite.

NOTE

Walker Percy, *Lancelot* (New York: Farrar, Straus and Giroux, 1977). All references are to this edition.

WORKS CITED

Bloom, Harold, ed. 1986. *Walker Percy: Modern Critical Views*. New York: Chelsea House.

John Paul II, Pope. 1995. *Evangelium Vitae*. Available at www.vatican.va/holy_father/john_paul_ii/encyclicals/

Kierkegaard, Søren. 1962. *The Present Age and "Of the Difference Between a Genius and an Apostle."* New York: Harper Torchbooks.

Lawson, Lewis A., and Victor Kramer, eds. 1985. *Conversations with Walker Percy*. Jackson: University Press of Mississippi.

Percy, Walker. 1975. *The Message in the Bottle*. New York: Farrar, Straus and Giroux.

Percy, William Alexander. 1941. *Lanterns on the Levee: Memoirs of a Planter's Son*. New York: Alfred A. Knopf.

Tolson, Jay. 1992. *Pilgrim in the Ruins: A Life of Walker Percy*. New York: Simon and Schuster.

BIBLIOGRAPHY

Gretlund, Jan Nordby, and Karl-Heinz Westarp, eds. *Walker Percy: Novelist and Philosopher*. Jackson: University Press of Mississippi, 1991.

Lawson, Lewis A. *Following Percy*. Troy, NY: Whitson, 1988.

Tolson, Jay, ed. *The Correspondence of Shelby Foote and Walker Percy*. New York: Doubletake, 1997.

— Ralph C. Wood

Alexander Pope [1688–1744]

Essay on Man

BIOGRAPHY

From the years before his death until our time, Alexander Pope has been the subject of biographies and commentaries written by friends, enemies, literary figures, and scholars. George Sherburn summarizes the early commentaries in the preface to his biography of Pope (1934, 1–26). Just as these first critics do, subsequent commentators, including two of the most important Pope scholars, George Sherburn and Maynard Mack, fail to acknowledge the authentic Roman Catholicism that informed Pope's life. Reflecting the Enlightenment and post-Enlightenment assumptions that only the unlearned or superstitious take Catholicism seriously, biographers did not, and many still do not, accept that a man of Pope's talent could be an authentic believer. This dominant and unquestioning assessment of Pope's religious convictions by his contemporaries and by subsequent biographers ignores the virulence of the English penal laws of his era and underestimates the price that this ambitious man paid to remain a Catholic. Serious reflection on the nature of the penal laws governing the life of the Pope family leads the objective observer to reject the opinion that Pope's motivation for remaining a Catholic was merely filial piety, a commonly propounded explanation (see, for example, Sherburn 1934, 214–15; Spence 1966, no. 351; and Mack 1985, 26–27).

Throughout Pope's lifetime, not one penal law was repealed. Even during the reigns of the Stuarts, new ones were enacted. The unpredictability of enforcement of the laws only made life more difficult for Catholics. The earliest laws forbade them to move more than five miles from home without a written license, be present at court, exercise any rights of patronage, send their children abroad to be educated, occupy any public office, or attend Mass. Those who would not acknowledge that it was Parliament's province to decide heresy and to enjoin on them the obligation to repudiate such heresy were felons and excommunicates. Those who accepted the authority of the Bishop of Rome and all Roman Catholic clergymen were guilty of high treason. Pursuivants who caused a priest's arrest or the discovery of persons at Mass—indeed at any Catholic event—received bounties. In the seventeenth century, even more penal laws were enacted, the most notable of which was the Test Act: all members of Parliament had to take oaths of allegiance and supremacy, declare against transubstantiation and the Mass, and call any invocation to Mary or the saints superstitious and idolatrous (today only the English sovereign takes a form of this oath).

With the ascendancy of William and Mary to the throne, fresh disabilities and penalties against Catholics were passed, including their being forbidden to keep firearms or ammunition (reflecting the prevailing suspicion of Catholics being traitors), own a horse of more than five pounds' value, live within ten miles of Westminster, purchase property, conduct any type of school, and, again, attend Mass. Catholics were specifically excluded from occupying the throne and were subject to double, sometimes triple, taxation. Moreover, the bounties for discovering priests and catching Catholics at Mass were increased.

Although most biographers accept Pope's negative view of his formal education in schools and from tutors (Sherburn 1934, 38–40; Mack 1985, 47–52), another reading is quite reasonable. Some of the Catholic clergymen and laity who tutored him were alive in his adult years. Biographer Francis Thornton notes, "He would be bound in honor to protect them. If they tutored him or taught him his religion, and he readily admitted it, the admission alone provided sufficient grounds for the law to proceed against them" (1952, 32). From Pope's words we know that these tutors were Jesuits or trained by Jesuits. In addition to their influence, Pope's pious parents shaped his religious sensibility. In a letter responding to Bishop Atterbury's expression of sympathy to Pope on his father's death, in which Atterbury attempts to persuade Pope "towards improving that Accident to your Own ease and Happiness" (Sherburn 1956, I, 451), that is, to become a member of the Church of England, Pope writes a tactful refusal of the bishop's offer. In the course of his reply, Pope says that he had read his father's "collection of all that had been written on both sides [Protestant and Catholic controversial literature] in the reign of King James the second: I warm'd my head with them, and the consequence was, that I found my self a Papist and a Protestant by turns, according to the last book I read" (I, 453–54). He adds toward the end of the letter, "I am not a Papist, for I renounce the temporal invasions of the Papal power . . . I am a Catholick, in the strictest sense of the words . . . I have a due sense of the excellence of the British constitution. In a word, the things I have always wished to see are not a Roman Catholick, or a French Catholick, or a Spanish Catholick, but a true Catholick" (I, 454).

This letter is one of the major sources for the characterization of Pope's Catholicism as superficial. However, Pope's remarks about renouncing the papal invasions and upholding the British constitution are somewhat disingenuous. He is distinguishing himself from the caricature of Catholicism held by the English, including Bishop Atterbury. And what he is saying is completely in keeping with influential works that would have been in his father's library as described above. Catholic doctrine is clear in *A Papist Mis-represented* by John Gother (1685). Author of the English catechism, Gother declares (as he does in the catechism), "That it is no part of his *Faith* to believe that the *Pope* has *Authority* to dispense with his *Allegiance* to his Sovereign. . . . that this Doctrine, appertains to the *Faith* of his *Church*, and is to be believ'd by all of that *Communion*, is a malicious *Calumny* a down-right *Falsity*" (24). In his subsequent pamphlet, *Papists Protesting*, Gother further asserts "The Subjects of the King of *England* lawfully may, without the least breach of any *Catholic Principle*, renounce, (even upon Oath,) the Teaching or Practicing the *Doctrine of deposing Kings* Excommunicated for Heresie, by any Authority whatsoever, as repugnant to the *fundamental Laws* of the Nation" (1687, A 2). There is no conflict, then, between being a loyal Englishman and a faithful Catholic.

That this greatest poet of his generation often wrote and spoke about his faith with ambiguity is understandable given the times. Moreover, throughout his life he refused offers to convert, fending off such suggestions with charm and grace. The result was a lifelong sense of oppression (see, for example, Sherburn 1956, I, 246–47, 335–37, and 342) and the particularly painful realization that he would never be poet laureate. For an ambitious man and one whose health was always fragile, such facts belie the notion that filial piety alone kept him in the Church.

But filial piety was not a minor part of Pope's character. All of his commentators acknowledge the religious convictions of Pope's father, Alexander Pope (1646–1717). A convert to Roman Catholicism, he lost his first wife in childbirth, leaving him with a daughter and a short-lived son. Similarly devout was his second wife, Edith Turner (1642–1733), a Catholic from Yorkshire (Mack 1985, 31–34). Into this home Pope was born on May 22, 1688, when his mother was forty-five. In that same year, his father, having accumulated a comfortable fortune in the textile trade, retired from his business. This was a prudent decision, for after the Glorious Revolution (1688–1689) under the new monarchs William and Mary, the enforcement of both the old and new penal laws was more vigorous. However, despite a major law that banned Catholics from living in London, the family did not move to Binfield near Windsor Forest until 1700. During his London years, Pope was tutored by priests and attended two Catholic schools. After the move from London, his assiduous reading and self-directed study, probable instruction from visiting priests, and frequent conversations with cultivated neighbors constituted his education. In addition to developing his intellectual abilities, the young Pope began to draw and eventually paint (Mack 1985, 51, 91), skills that he practiced throughout his adult life. During these years of adolescence, however, Pope's health deteriorated, resulting in fragility, migraines, and a pronounced curvature of the spine that was the object of lampoons by vicious and envious rivals throughout his life. Despite his claiming that his problems resulted from too much study, most twentieth-century commentators attribute his curvature and stunted growth (he was no more than four feet six inches tall) to a form of tuberculosis (Sherburn 1934, 43).

Pope's public life began quietly with Tonson's publication of his *Pastorals* (1709). After the publication of his *Essay on Criticism* (1711), his skills as a satirist and his poetic style were widely acclaimed, although he was attacked from some quarters. As the decade passed, he wrote poetry, successfully translated Homer, and enjoyed friendships with prominent literary, ecclesiastical, and political contemporaries. Among these friends was a group of Tories, fellow members of the Martinus Scriblerus club, notably Jonathan Swift, John Gay, Thomas Parnell, and Dr. John Arbuthnot, physician to Queen Anne. In addition, the Earl of Oxford, Bishop Atterbury, and Lord Bolingbroke befriended him. On the other hand, during these early years Joseph Addison, a prominent Whig, moved from supporting Pope's poetry to being a subtle and influential traducer of Pope's character and work.

Two years after his beloved father's death (1717), Pope ultimately moved his aged mother and nurse out of London to Twickenham on the banks of the Thames, an estate that he planted with gardens and a grotto that were imitated widely in his lifetime and celebrated through the nineteenth century. What enabled him to develop this home was the successful sale of subscriptions for his translation of Homer (issued from 1715 through 1726). He became a relatively wealthy man, honored for his skills as translator and poet by a variety of literary figures, including Voltaire. Nonetheless, Pope was also the object of attacks and criticism. The criticism of his edition of Shakespeare (1725) seems to have more substance than the comments that followed the publication of the first version of the *Dunciad* (1728). Anonymously published but clearly his work, this latter text was his response to vicious personal attacks, attacks that would persist throughout his life.

Among the many major events of 1733 was the death of Pope's mother, a loss he greatly mourned. He had published the first three parts of *Essay on Man* earlier in the year but did not issue the fourth part until 1734. The poem was published anonymously. Pope wrote to Swift that "I had not the least thought of stealing applause by suppressing my name to that 'essay': I wanted only to hear the truth" (Sherburn 1956, III, 438). By the time he acknowledged his authorship, the poem had been praised far and wide. The remaining years of the 1730s were marked by more publications, interactions with friends, a worsening of his health, and an uproar about the "alleged heterodoxy of the *Essay on Man*" (Mack 1985, 733).

In the 1740s, as his health continued to decline, Pope was busily revising his canon with the assistance of William Warburton, generally considered to be an overreaching and poor collaborator but one whose defense of Pope's *Essay* is part of the story of its critical response. In his last years, Pope wrote his most tragic satire, a work that ultimately became the fourth book of the revised *Dunciad* (1743). His final illness was marked by hallucinations, moments of lucidity, loving comments, and persistence in his religion. On the evening of May 30, 1744, Pope died peacefully, surrounded by loving friends who paid tribute to him as a true and loyal man. To this day, doubts about the sincerity of his Catholicism, even on his deathbed, persist. Joseph Spence quotes Pope's response to his friend Nathaniel Hooke, who had suggested sending for a priest: "I do not suppose that [the presence of a priest] is essential, but it will be right" (1966, 268 no. 654). In his edition of Spence, James Osborne adds to Spence's account an anecdote from Joseph Warton, a later editor of Pope's works. After revealing his anti-Catholic bias by attacking Hooke as "a bigoted Papist," Warton says, "And such was the fervor of his [Pope's] devotion, that as Cheselden, the surgeon, who was present, related to Dr. Hoadley, he [Pope] exerted all his strength to throw himself out of his bed, that he might receive the last sacraments kneeling on the floor" (268).

SUMMARY

Essay on Man, a long poem of 1,304 lines divided into four "epistles," is written in iambic pentameter. The very first edition of the work contains Pope's prose arguments in which he explains the topic and gives a summary of the contents of each epistle to follow. The argument preceding Epistle I, "Of the NATURE and STATE of MAN, with respect to the UNIVERSE," begins with his limiting his poem to studying "Man *in the* Abstract." He contends that man is proud, impious, absurd, and unreasonable when he questions his place: "*That throughout the whole visible World, an Universal* Order *and* Gradation *in these is observ'd, which causes a* Subordination *of Creature to Creature, and of all Creatures to Man.*" The argument of Epistle II, "Of the NATURE and STATE of MAN, with respect to HIMSELF as an INDIVIDUAL," asserts that "*The Business of Man* [is] *not to pry into* God, *but to study* Himself." Pope describes "*His two Principles,* SELF-LOVE *and* REASON," calling "*both necessary,*" with "SELF-LOVE *the stronger.*" He contends that there is a "PREDOMINANT PASSION" in each man that directs him to his purpose and gives rise to virtue as well as vice, both of which are "*joyn'd in our* Mixt Nature." He says these passions are universally distributed and work to the good of society and the individual.

The argument preceding Epistle III, "Of the NATURE and STATE OF MAN with respect to SOCIETY," instructs the reader that its subject is "*The* Whole Universe *one System of* Society." The author then explains that "*Nothing is made wholly for* itself, *nor yet wholly for* Another." In this epistle he describes instinct and reason and claims that the "*Origin of* True Religion *and* Government [is] *from the same Principle, of* Love. . . . [the] *Origin of* Superstition and Tyranny [is] *from the same Principle, of* Fear." He then adds, "Self-Love [is] *operating to the* Social *and* Publick Good." Finally, in his argument to Epistle IV, "Of the NATURE and STATE of MAN, with respect to HAPPINESS," Pope explains that he examines happiness in terms of its being the "*End* of all men, and attainable by all." After looking into various ideas about the nature of happiness and the nature of calamities, he concludes by insisting that "no man [is] happy without Virtue . . . VIRTUE ONLY constitutes a Happiness, whose Object is *universal,* and whose Prospect *eternal,* the perfection of which consists in a *conformity* to the *Order of Perfection,* here, and in a *resignation* to it, here and hereafter."

MAJOR THEMES

Pope's letters reveal that he was working on *Essay on Man* for several years. In June 1730, he wrote to Jonathan Swift, "Yet am I just now writing (or rather planning) a book, to make mankind look upon this life with comfort and pleasure, and put morality in good humour" (Sherburn 1956, III, 117). In a letter to John Caryll dated December 1730, Pope describes his work in composing a poem in which he is "writing on human life and manners, not exclusive of religious regards" (III, 155). In a later letter to Caryll about the supposedly unknown author of *Essay on Man*, Pope states that despite certain phrases being unorthodox, "contrary to what I think his intention," the author is "quite Christian in his system" (III, 354). In his biography of Pope, Mack does not abandon his doubts about Pope's commitment to Catholicism (1985, 739–41). In his edition of the poem, he asserts that the "attitudes [in the poem] generated by deism, eighteenth-century sociality, and Roman Catholicism come together" (lxxiv–lxxv). Mack contends that "In the Roman church, man may be and indeed is a pilgrim working out his own salvation . . . in terms of a vast and authoritative social and religious whole" (lxxiv). But despite his scholarly excellence in analyzing Pope's work and life, Mack does not understand Pope's Catholicism or the impact it had on the author's formation. Moreover, despite his index's list of references, echoes, and quotations from Augustine and Thomas Aquinas found in the *Essay*, Mack does not grasp the significance of their presence in a poem written in a time of anti-Catholicism by a poet who was widely known to be a Catholic.

What makes the poem Catholic is Pope's sacramental vision, formed by Scripture and tradition. Pope sees the world as a sign of God's love: "Look round our World; behold the chain of Love" (*Essay on Man*, III.7). Interfering with man's grasp of this love is pride, a pride that refuses to submit to the Creator. In the opening of Epistle I, Pope, in a metaphor, explains what he will do in the poem: "Expatiate free o'er all this scene of Man; / A mighty maze! but not without a plan" (5–6). He then states that his purpose is to "vindicate the ways of God to Man" (16)—apparently, that is, to compose a theodicy.

In this vindication, Pope's words frequently echo the Bible, not surprising given the biblically based apologetics with which he was familiar from childhood. Moreover, many surveys of post-Reformation Catholic apologetics belie the stereotype of Catholics as ignorant of the Bible. In his edition of the *Essay*, Mack points out many references in the poem to the Old Testament, the Gospels, and the Epistles. He specifically cites the eighteenth-century critic W. L. Bowles, who "compares the apostrophes spoken to Job from the whirlwind" to Pope's words in Epistle I.31–34 (Index 172). However, neither Bowles nor Mack considers the implication of Pope's echoing of God's words at the end of the Book of Job: "Where were you when I founded the earth? Tell me, if you have understanding. Who determined its size; do you know? Who stretched out the measuring line for it? Into what were its pedestals sunk, and who laid the cornerstone, while the morning stars sang in chorus and all the sons of God shouted for joy?" (Job 38:4–7). In *Essay on Man*, when the poet rather than the Lord admonishes those who demand that creation be different than it is, that human nature be altered, and that man should understand all, the poet establishes his ethos as a serious and clear-sighted speaker who deserves attention:

> Presumptuous Man! The reason wouldst thou find,
> Why form'd so weak, so little, and so blind! (I.35–36)
> . . .
> Go, wiser thou! And in thy scale of sense
> Weigh thy Opinion against Providence (I.113–14)
> . . .
> All this dread ORDER break—for whom? for thee?
> Vile worm!—oh Madness, Pride, Impiety! (I.257–58)

Pope concludes Epistle II with a similar statement: "Tho' Man's a fool, yet God IS WISE" (294). In Epistle III, Pope's questions share the same tonal resonance: for example, "Has God, thou fool! work'd solely for thy good" (27). Similar is his epithet for those who prefer vice to virtue: "Oh blind to truth" (IV.93). Pope reminds his readers that Job's answer to the Lord is the proper one for all mankind: "I know that you can do all things, and that no purpose of yours can be hindered. I have dealt with great things that I do not understand; things too wonderful for me, which I cannot know" (Job 42:2–4).

Not only did the Bible influence Pope; so too did his education at the hands of Jesuits and those trained by them. Moreover, these teachers were important in shaping his religious attitudes throughout his life, as were other order and secular priests, his learned father, and friends who were practicing Catholics. Implicit in Catholic discussions, instruction, and controversy is the thought of the great Doctors of the Church, notably Augustine and Thomas Aquinas, whose vision of the world is sacramental. In the following passage can be seen just one of many reverberations of Augustine's *Confessions* and Aquinas's *Summa Theologica* in the *Essay*:

> Hope springs eternal in the human breast:
> Man never Is, but always To be blest:
> The soul, uneasy and confin'd from home,
> Rests, and expatiates in a life to come. (I.95–98)

Later in the poem, Pope insists that

> For him alone, Hope leads from goal to goal,
> And opens still, and opens on his soul,
> 'Till lengthen'd on to Faith, and unconfin'd
> . . .
> Hope of known bliss, and Faith in bliss unknown. (IV.341–43, 346)

These lines recall Augustine's quotation from Romans: "our salvation is founded upon the hope of something. Hope would not be hope at all if its object were in view" (1961, XIII 13, 319). And Aquinas, in one of his many passages on hope, writes that "the object of hope is a future good, difficult but possible to attain" (1947, II 17 a 1, 1242–43).

The many passages in the *Essay* that describe the plenitude and hierarchy of creation also echo Augustine and Aquinas as they see the world in sacramental terms. Augustine states of God, "You created, not because you had need, but out of the abundance of your own goodness" (XIII 4, 313), and Aquinas writes,

> [God] brought things into being in order that His goodness might be communicated to creatures, and be represented by them; and because His goodness could not be adequately represented by one creature alone, He produced many and diverse creatures, that what was wanting to one in the representation of the divine goodness might be supplied by another. For goodness . . . in creatures is manifold and divided; and hence the whole universe together participates in the divine goodness more perfectly, and represents it better than any single creature whatever. (I Q.47 A1, 246)

Pope's passages on the great chain of being, with its variety and beauty, resonate with these Doctors' words:

> See thro' this air, this ocean, and this earth,
> All matter quick, and bursting into birth.
> Above, how high progressive life may go!
> Around, how wide! How deep extend below!
> Vast chain of being, which from God began,
> Natures aethereal, human, angel, man,

Beast, bird, fish, insect! what no eye can see,
No glass can reach! From Infinite to thee,
From thee to Nothing! (I.233–241)

Pope's telling humans to abandon the idea that all other beings are made exclusively for them, as if other beings' lives have no intrinsic worth, is also congruent with Catholic teaching:

Has God, thou fool! work'd solely for thy good,
Thy joy, thy pastime, thy attire, thy food?
Who for thy table feeds the wanton fawn,
For him as kindly spread the flow'ry lawn.
Is it for thee the lark ascends and sings?
Joy tunes his voice, joy elevates his wings. (III.27–32)

Another implication here is the importance of the great chain of being, the ancient Greek philosophers' world vision that was adapted by Christians as early as the third century. Its hierarchical description of human beings emphasizes man as the rational animal:

Far as Creation's ample range extends,
The scale of sensual, mental pow'rs ascends:
Mark how it mounts, to Man's imperial race,
From the green myriads in the peopled grass. (I.207–10)

Augustine attributes "man's power to judge all things . . . [and] his rule over" the animals to human intelligence (XIII 23, 332–33). Aquinas, in one of his many investigations of reason, notes that "the need of reason is from a defect in the intellect, since those things in which intellective power is in full vigor, have no need for reason" (II–II 49 a 5, 1404). Pope praises reason as intrinsic to human nature, particularly in Epistle II, but he too sees reason in man as imperfect. He often points out how flawed and blind it is: "reas'ning but to err" (II.10); "What Reason weaves, by Passion is undone" (II.42).

Similarly, Pope's attacks on human pride follow the tradition of Christian morality. Augustine contends that had "Adam not fallen away from" God, mankind would have not been "buffeted by the storms of its pride" (XIII 20, 329). He warns against "the savage monster pride" (XIII 21, 330) and asserts that "the arrogance of pride, the pleasures of lust, and the poison of vain curiosity are the impulses of a soul that is dead" (XIII 21, 331). Aquinas describes pride as "the appetite for excellence in excess of right reason" (II–III 162 a 1). Both emphasize the corrosive effect this primary sin has on the soul. Ironically, in his apparent theodicy, Pope demonstrates that the call for a vindication of God's justice is the result of human pride. He argues that to think that one can comprehend God and his works is to ask a "part" to "contain the whole" (I.32):

Know then thyself, presume not God to scan;
The proper study of Mankind is Man.
Plac'd on this isthmus of a middle state,
A being darkly wise, and rudely great. (II.1–4)

Moreover, he opens Epistle III by stating that the "great truth" that "The Universal Cause / Acts to one end, but acts by various laws" must be grasped despite pride (1–4).

Many other lines in *Essay on Man* reveal a poet whose vision is Catholic at a time when to be so was to ensure exclusion, criticism, attacks, and possible legal penalties of all kinds. Pope was indeed a man of the eighteenth century, one who absorbed some of its presuppositions. These, however, did not compromise his fundamental Catholicism. James Osborne adds to Spence's account of Pope's death the words of the Benedictine Edward Pigott, who gave Pope the last rites: "he had Pope's Directions to declare to everybody that Pope was very sorry for everything he had said or wrote, that was against the Catholic Faith" (1966, 269).

CRITICAL RECEPTION

Essay on Man has been an object of praise, attack, and mixed criticism since its publication. As noted, Pope published it anonymously, hoping that he would get an objective reading. Mack states, "Until 1738 its reception in England had been overwhelmingly favorable. Its author had been here or there censured for addressing the poem to a bad man, namely Bolingbroke, but not for his doctrine. On the Continent . . . the *Essay* enjoyed an extraordinary popularity" (1985, 736). In *Lives of the English Poets*, Samuel Johnson notes that both positive and negative reviewers "thought him [the anonymous author] above neglect: the sale increased, and editions were multiplied" (1967, 162). However, Dr. Johnson, like most of Pope's contemporaries, overestimated Bolingbroke's contribution to the poem. And even as Dr. Johnson praised the poetry in the *Essay*, insisting, "the order, illustration, and embellishments must all be Pope's" (163), he contended that the poem's form hid its "evil tendency" (164)—that is, Bolingbroke's influence. Henry St. John, Viscount Bolingbroke, became Pope's friend in the 1710s. His controversial actions, conflicts, and belief in Deism formed the bases for the many negative depictions of him and of any persons who were influenced by him. Thornton describes how the "legend" of "Pope's complete dependence upon Bolingbroke" has been difficult to correct (1952, 199). Contributing to that difficulty were letters that Bolingbroke wrote; for example, in a letter to Swift, Bolingbroke asked if Pope had talked "to you of the noble work which, att [*sic*] my instigation, he has begun," and then outlined the poem (Sherburn 1956, III, 213–14). Also contributing to the legend is Pope's dedication of the *Essay* to Bolingbroke. Similarly problematic are the speaker's direct addresses to Bolingbroke in which Pope honors him, particularly the lengthy peroration (IV.373ff).

Not only did Dr. Johnson overestimate Bolingbroke's role in the poem, but he also ignored the inaccuracy of the French versions of the poem. These mistranslations were the bases for Jean Pierre de Crousaz's attack on the *Essay*. Moreover, Johnson takes no notice of William Warburton's defense of the poem (1967, 164 ff). Unfortunately, Johnson's assessments of the poem and of Crousaz's attack have persisted in the intervening centuries. However, recent critics have accepted Pope's self-defense and, labored though it is, Warburton's defense of the poem. For example, Mack's account offers a careful interpretation of the reasons behind these attacks on the *Essay*. He attributes the reversal from praise to condemnation exemplified in Crousaz's attack to "a translation of the poem into French verse" in which J. F. du B. Du Resnel "undertook to confer on the *Essay*" philosophical systems that were "in fashion." Mack observes, "To this end, a multitude of passages in the poem were deleted, others added, still others transposed, expanded, or contracted, and the whole was so altered, despite extensive omissions, as to [make the work] unrecognizable as Pope's" (1985, 736). He further notes, "Despite its egregious faults, the attack was damaging"; Crousaz's tactics "were ideally suited to alarm the orthodox and give a handle to the poet's enemies" (737). Equally persistent is the notion that Pope is a Deist, an "accusation [that] has lingered on, gathering force with the years since Pope's death" (Thornton 1952, 180). The content of Crousaz's attack is the ultimate source for that persistence.

Clearly, *Essay on Man* has been the subject of philosophical and theological analysis since its publication. At the same time, as is evident in Dr. Johnson's remarks, the work's poetic form has also been the subject of continual criticism. Much of the criticism has been positive; the most negative periods were during the romantic (Byron was an exception) and the Victorian ages. In the early twentieth century, poet and critic T. S. Eliot wrote a vindication of Pope's canon in "John Dryden" in *Selected Essays, 1917–1932* (1922) and in his introduction to *Selected Poems* (1928). In the introduction to his 1950 edition of the *Essay*, Mack contends that the poem reflects its Renaissance predecessors in subject and in structure (xlvii ff). Moreover, he calls Pope's subject one of "magnitude and range" (lxxiii) and reminds readers that the work "is a public, social, and classical poem" (lxxiv), facts that have import in understanding its diction and arrangement.

Many hundreds of critical responses to the poem exist, interpreting and criticizing its ideological, aesthetic, political, and philosophical premises. Most of these have denied the work's religious significance. However, Pope's own assessment of the contents of the *Essay* most strongly supports the position that the poem is essentially a Catholic one. In a famous letter to Louis Racine, who had attacked the *Essay*, Pope argues that he is being censured for principles that he never held: "my Opinions are intirely [*sic*] different from those of Spinoza; or even of Leibnitz; but on the contrary conformable to those of Mons. Pascal & Mons. Fenelon: the latter of whom I would most readily imitate, in submitting all my Opinions to the Decision of the Church" (Sherburn 1956, IV, 416).

NOTE

Alexander Pope, *An Essay on Man*, ed. Maynard Mack (Twickenham Edition, London: Methuen, 1950). This edition is recommended.

WORKS CITED

Aquinas, Saint Thomas. 1947. *The Summa Theologica*, trans. Fathers of the English Dominican Province. New York: Benziger Brothers.

Augustine, Saint. 1961. *Confessions*, trans. R. S. Pine-Coffin. London: Penguin.

Gother, John. 1685. *A Papist Mis-represented and Represented*. London.

———. 1687. *Papists Protesting*. London.

Johnson, Samuel. 1967. *Lives of the English Poets*, ed. George Birkbeck Hill. 3 Vols. New York: Octagon Books.

Mack, Maynard. 1985. *Alexander Pope A Life*. New York: Norton.

Sherburn, George, ed. 1934. *The Early Career of Alexander Pope*. Oxford: Clarendon Press.

———. 1956. *The Correspondence of Alexander Pope*. 5 Vols. Oxford: Clarendon Press.

Spence, Joseph. 1966. *Observations, Anecdotes, and Characters of Books and Men Collected from Conversation*, ed. James M. Osborne. Oxford: Clarendon Press.

Thornton, Francis Beauchesne. 1952. *Alexander Pope: Catholic Poet*. New York: Pellegrini and Cudahy.

— C. N. Sue Abromaitis

Katherine Anne Porter [1890–1980]

Ship of Fools

BIOGRAPHY

Born on May 15, 1890, in Indian Creek, Texas, Katherine Anne Porter was destined to live the life of a bohemian writer, traveling from state to state and from country to country in search of a satisfying life. Her travels began at the age of two, when she and her siblings left Indian Creek after their mother died and went to live with their grandmother in Kyle, Texas. Nine years later, after her grandmother's death, the family moved again to San Antonio, Texas with their father. Katherine and her sister had the opportunity to attend the Convent of the Child Jesus in New Orleans, where Katherine was introduced to the Catholic faith. As one critic states, "She was greatly drawn to Catholicism. Its physical grandeur and intriguing rituals were a constant source of wonder" (Lopez 1981, 22).

At sixteen, Porter married John Henry Koontz, a German Catholic, and she converted to Catholicism when she was twenty. The marriage ended in divorce after nine years, and Porter traveled to Chicago, where she tried acting in addition to writing for the local newspaper. These potential careers ended unsatisfactorily and she returned to Dallas. There she contracted tuberculosis and spent twelve months in a rest home before resuming her writing career and her travels. While working as a journalist for the *Rocky Mountain News* in Denver, Porter became a victim of the dreaded influenza outbreak of 1918. She survived, and her experiences with this illness were described vividly in one of her most acclaimed stories, *Pale Horse, Pale Rider* (1939).

Next, Porter traveled to Greenwich Village, where she met other aspiring writers and artists who encouraged her to continue writing. At this point in her life she made the decision to move to Mexico, a choice that proved very influential for her narratives. Her first major short story, "María Concepcíon," set in Mexico, was published in 1922 in *Century Magazine* when she was thirty-two. For the next decade, she traveled between New York and Mexico many times, with side trips to Texas (where she renewed her connection with the past) and Bermuda for five months (where she finally completed some of her most creative and successful stories). Her memories of Texas and Mexico again influenced her work with the publication of *Flowering Judas and Other Stories* in 1930. Many of her stories were interpreted in terms of the moral values of Catholicism even though Porter herself by this time was no longer a practicing Catholic. In 1925, Porter was married briefly to Ernest Stock, but her restlessness doomed the relationship.

Mexico continued to play a key role in Porter's development as a writer. In 1931 she won a Guggenheim Fellowship to study in that country. While there, she met her third husband, Eugene Pressley, an official at the United States embassy. Together they embarked on the voyage that would become the inspiration for Porter's much-anticipated novel, *Ship of Fools*. The S. S. *Werra* left from Veracruz, a dusty town on the eastern coast of Mexico, traveled to Bremerhaven, a major port in Germany, with stops at Havana and Tenerife, Spain. Porter kept a journal throughout the voyage detailing the behavior of her follow passengers, which provided the background for the epic novel. However, the novel was not published until 1962, thirty-one years after the voyage.

Once in Europe, Porter and Pressley traveled throughout Germany, France, and Spain before finally settling in Paris, where they were married in 1933. The union lasted for three years, at which point the couple returned to the United States and finally divorced in 1937. While living in the South, Porter met and married Albert Eskine Jr. Once again, the marriage was not successful, and the couple separated in 1940. It is generally agreed that the 1930s were Porter's most productive and creative years.

From 1938 to 1962, Porter led the life of a successful writer. She published *The Leaning Tower* in 1944, and then eighteen years elapsed before the appearance of *Ship of Fools*. In the meantime, she received many awards, including another Guggenheim Fellowship, a Ford Foundation grant in literature, and the O. Henry Memorial Award. In addition, she became writer-in-residence at a number of prestigious colleges in the United States and Europe. With the publication of *Ship of Fools* in 1962 and the subsequent release of a film based on the novel in 1965, Porter finally achieved the financial security and independence she had lacked throughout her life. She settled in College Park, Maryland, and published *The Collected Stories of Katherine Anne Porter* in 1965. This volume contained all of her short stories, twenty-seven in total. It won a Pulitzer Prize and the National Book Award for fiction.

After a long and adventurous life, Porter died on September 18, 1980, at the age of ninety. At her request, her ashes were returned to Indian Creek, Texas, and buried near her mother's grave in the local cemetery.

PLOT SUMMARY

Ship of Fools was published in 1962, but the events that inspired the novel actually occurred thirty-one years before, when Katherine Anne Porter sailed on a German ship called the S. S. *Werra* from Veracruz, Mexico, to Bremerhaven, Germany. Attempting to incorporate all of the passengers and events of the voyage into the novel proved a daunting task. As a result, the novel has a chaotic quality as the author moves from character to character and narrative to narrative in no particular order.

The ship provides the unifying factor for a frame story reminiscent of Chaucer's *Canterbury Tales*. Porter herself said that she was inspired by the medieval text *Das Narrenschiff* (Ship of Fools) written by Sebastian Brant in 1497 (1944). Brant's ship of fools was a Christian allegory describing the passage of human souls through life. Porter's *Ship of Fools* follows this pattern of presenting the imperfections of the characters as they strive to succeed in an unknowable and unfeeling universe. Porter employs an omniscient point of view, allowing the reader to eavesdrop on the secret thoughts of the passengers. This point of view also permits the author to move randomly from one event to the next, emphasizing the arbitrary nature of existence.

The narrative is divided into three sections, each with a title and epigraph. The first is called "Embarcation" and is followed by the question, "Quand partons-vous vers le bonheur?" (When do we sail for happiness?), a quotation from Baudelaire. In this section, the author introduces the forty characters and one old bulldog who will occupy the *S. S. Vera* (*vera* means "truth") for twenty-seven days. The characters are from various countries and social classes and literally do not speak the same language. Germans predominate, but Mexicans, Spaniards, Americans, and others are also on board: in other words, here we have a microcosm of humanity. The scene at Veracruz has an undertone of despair and darkness as the characters attempt to negotiate the heat, noise, pushing, and general chaos of the crowds. Once on the ship, the passengers are disheartened to learn that they must share their tiny, airless cabins with strangers. This plot device allows the author to reveal the pettiness and snobbery of many of the characters from the beginning of the voyage.

Although each character has a somber story to confess, several passengers are revealed in more depth. These include the ship's Captain Thiele, an authoritarian German who feels superior to most of the others onboard; Dr. Schumann, the ship's doctor and a Catholic, who is dying of a heart ailment; Herr Professor Hutten, his wife, and their old, white bulldog; Herr Karl Glocken, a hunchback who looks like a gargoyle; Herr William Freytag, a German with a Jewish wife; La Condesa, a once-beautiful political exile being deported to Tenerife who is also a drug addict; William Denny, a lustful Texan; Mary Treadwell, a bitter, forty-six-year-old divorcee; David Scott and Jenny Brown, Americans and would-be artists who cannot find happiness in their love; and a zarzuela, or gypsy, company of four men, four women, and two children, who will be responsible for many of the conflicts on board the *Vera*. In addition, eight hundred seventy-six migrant workers inhabit the dark, dank steerage area, a huddle of nameless humanity in contrast to the pampered passengers on the upper decks. At the end of part one, the voyage has begun, the passengers have been introduced, and they are slowly and reluctantly beginning to converse with each other.

Part two is entitled "High Sea" and is followed by the epigraph "Kein Haus, Keine Heimat," a song by Brahms translated as "No House, No Home." In this section of the novel, the likes, dislikes, and prejudices of the passengers and crew are dramatized. In particular, the antisemitism of the captain and members of the German community onboard are highlighted through one particular event. Herr William Freytag is a German of impeccable heritage who has married a Jewish woman. As a result of this union, he is asked to leave the captain's table and dine with others. The bitterness of this event begins to affect Freytag's resolve as he vacillates between his desire to be treated as a respected German and the resentment of being treated unfairly because of his wife. He begins a flirtation with Jenny, the young American artist, but they both know that this interlude cannot resolve their problems.

Another doomed relationship takes place between Dr. Schumann and La Condesa. She is a world-weary woman condemned to exile in Tenerife. On this, her last voyage, she and the doctor fall in love, but their previous lives interfere and the relationship ends in despair. The doctor can only try to relieve her distress by supplying her with drugs. A married man, the doctor, too, is condemned to inaction, both physically and spiritually. He has terminal heart disease and is inhibited in his love for La Condesa by his adherence to orthodox Catholicism, which prohibits divorce.

As in life, the spectrum of humanity continues to unfold in no particular order. The married couples begin to argue while the single men attempt to seduce the zarzuela women. The two zarzuela children, Ric and Rac, are responsible for one of the more heinous events on the ship. They throw the old dog Bébé overboard. One of the men in steerage, an artist who carves wooden figures, jumps into the sea to rescue the dog. Although the dog is saved, the man drowns. Porter's irony in narrating this occurrence is strikingly poignant. Later, the dog's owners, Herr Hutten and his wife, cannot even remember the name of the man who gave his life for their animal.

Part three is called "The Harbors," and here Porter inserts a quotation from Saint Paul: "For here have we no continuing city." The souls in steerage, poor and jobless, are freed from their bondage on the ship only to face more problems at home. A pivotal scene takes place when La Condesa departs. The doctor cannot free himself from his constricting past and finally rejects her. Later, when the doctor sends her a note offering his help, she does not reply. Missed opportunities for happiness are quite common on the ship of fools. Meanwhile, the upper-class passengers prepare for a party given by the zarzuela company, a supposedly festive gathering that turns ugly as the passengers reveal their inhumanity toward their fellow travelers. Arguments and hostile feelings are finally exposed as fights break out among the men while would-be lovers quarrel and separate. The most violent expression of frustration and rage occurs when the lustful and drunk Denny mistakes Mrs. Treadwell for one of the Spanish prostitutes. Mrs. Treadwell loses all control as she beats Denny unconscious with her high-heeled shoe. This event would also seem humorous except that by now any veneer of civilization has been trampled by the emotions of the moment.

The novel ends on a somber note as the passengers disembark at various ports to uncertain futures. In Bremerhaven, the weather is overcast and foreboding, perhaps symbolizing the future barrenness of Nazi Germany. The voyage has revealed all of the conflicts that plague humanity—those of class, nationality, gender, religion, and love. Porter closes with a description of a blind boy, cleaning his trumpet and repeating in a whisper, "'Grüss Gott, Grüss Gott,' as if the town were a human being, a good and dear trusted friend who had come a long way to help him" (Ship of Fools, 497). "It's a pleasant Christian greeting," Herr Freytag had stated earlier in the book (89). Porter's final image suggests that humanity perseveres in spite of being fools.

MAJOR THEMES

At the time, Katherine Anne Porter did not realize her 1931 journey on the *S. S. Werra* would provide the inspiration for her famous novel *Ship of Fools*. Porter kept a journal of her experiences—the people aboard ship, the activities—and attempted to write a cohesive account of the many individual dramas that took place on the twenty-seven day voyage. In spite of publishing an occasional piece about the crossing, she did not complete the novel until more than thirty years later. By this time, nations and cultures had undergone such violent changes that the narrative assumed an air of prophecy and irony.

Porter's dilemma revolved around the vast number of characters she wanted to include in her epic. Should each character be given equal status, and were all of the stories worth narrating? How much detail and description were necessary? In addition, she wanted to imbue her saga with a moral depth rather than simply presenting a series of vignettes about stereotyped characters such as "cold" Germans, "passionate" Mexicans, "frivolous" Americans, and "greedy" Jews, to name but a few. She found her narrative device in Brant's *Das Narrenschiff* ([1497] 1944). In the work's frontispiece, she informs the reader, "When I began thinking about my novel, I took for my own this simple almost universal image of the ship of this world on its voyage to eternity." And, by inference, all humanity is also on this voyage. Porter invites the reader on the human journey through life, a life filled with injustice, guilt, sadness, evil, and despair.

There are no heroes on the ship of fools, only those trying to negotiate living in an uncertain world. The passengers on the ship are a microcosm of humanity—old, young, sick, healthy, rich, poor, male, female, Christian, Jewish—all with a personal view of morality tempered by their culture and their past. Nationalism plays a central role as individual tensions on the ship mirror the international situation that, in the 1930s, was about to explode around the world. Porter also casts a critical eye on organized religion. The dying doctor, for example, tries but cannot escape his Catholic orthodoxy, while the three Mexican priests on board are merely figureheads offering little spiritual consolation to the poor in steerage. The Protestants detest the Jews, and the one Jewish person on board is portrayed unsympathetically. He hates Catholics but, in an ironic twist, sells religious articles to Christians. In short, Porter represents the world of modern-day fools, those who in spite of their religious indoctrination act as hypocrites and do not recognize their folly. As Sebastian Brant recorded in the prologue to *Das Narrenschiff*:

> All lands in Holy Writ abound
> And words to save the soul are found . . .
> So many that I feel surprise
> To find men growing not more wise
> But holding writ and lore in spite.
> The whole world lives in darksome night
> In blinded sinfulness persisting. ([1497] 1944, 57)

While Porter herself, despite having converted to the faith as a young woman, later rebelled against orthodox Catholicism, many of her stories reflect Catholic moral values. *Ship of Fools* is no exception. Love, betrayal, sacrifice, and salvation—or, better said, the lack of these—are underlying themes in the novel seen through a kaleidoscope of modern life. The characters "yet will not own to folly's name" (Brant [1497] 1944, 57), preferring to believe in their own virtue and goodness. However, what they perceive as righteousness is, in reality, selfishness and cruelty. No longer as simple as Brant's late medieval world, in which right and wrong were cemented in a common Christian moral creed, Porter's modern world is filled with ambiguity and doubt.

Before choosing the final title, *Ship of Fools*, Porter experimented with three others: "The Promised Land," a biblical allusion used ironically; "No Safe Harbor," a title that closely reflects the characters' dilemmas; and "The Land That Is Nowhere," an apt reference to the plight of twentieth-century humanity betrayed by broken relationships, hypocritical religion, and false social values. The voyage on the *S. S. Vera* is both literal and symbolic. As the ship sails from the sunny climate of Mexico to the cold, barren port of Bremerhaven, the passengers begin to discover the darkness and depths of their own hearts, and these individual, secret emotions reflect the atrocities to come on a world scale with the advent of World War II.

Porter infuses the novel with Christian references that both support the allegory and subvert it. The author states, "The port town of Veracruz is a little purgatory between land and sea for the traveler" (3), and the reader is immediately aware of the implications of such a religious reference for the voyagers. If Veracruz is purgatory, then the voyage itself is, by implication, a type of hell. One is reminded of the plight of Dante's lost souls as they are heaped into Charon's boat and rowed across the River Acheron to their fate. The blistering hot day adds to the chaos and pandemonium of the embarking passengers as they attempt to flee the burning sun and reach the safety of the ship, only to find that it does not provide the comfort they expected. A supernatural glow, perhaps indicating the judging finger of God, is cast over the ship as it departs for open water: "Though it was still broad daylight, the August sun, dipping into the far horizon, threw a burning track over the waters which ran like oil in the wake of the ship" (44). The scene in steerage adds to the sense of hell. Reminiscent of medieval illustrations depicting nameless masses of humanity, the description is vivid and unworldly: "Hundreds of people. . . . lay in the film of water just lifting their heads now and then . . . and in the abominable heat a strange mingled smell of vegetation and animal rot rose from them" (73). Clearly, Porter is taking the reader on a mystical voyage into a Dantesque type of Inferno.

Not even the three Mexican priests on board can save the suffering souls. Although they believe in traditional teachings about damnation and salvation, they are powerless. But among the forty crew and passengers on the upper decks (reserved for the more prominent social classes), one person emerges as a potential savior. The Catholic German, Dr. Schumann, seems friendly, cultured, and confident. He exemplifies the rational and charitable person unencumbered by prejudice. Perhaps, as a doctor, he can heal not only the physical but also the spiritual. Dr. Schumann "believes in God, the Father, Son and Holy Ghost and the Blessed Virgin Mother of God finally, in a particularly forthright, Bavarian way" (113). However, in a touch of irony, the doctor is dying of a heart ailment and cannot even rescue himself. In spite of his orthodox Catholic beliefs and the comfort he takes in them, his strict adherence to traditional dogma prevents him from attaining the love he desires—he is, indeed, perishing from heart sickness or lack of love. He falls in love with La Condesa, but his conscience prevents him from breaking his marriage vows. Thus failing to heal La Condesa spiritually, he can only provide her the physical comfort of drugs that helps her numb the sadness of the world. But he, too, craves consolation: "He lay down with his rosary in his fingers and began to invite sleep, darkness, silence, that little truce of God between living and dying" (121).

In the midst of daily pettiness, bickering, and scheming among the passengers, one selfless act occurs, albeit with tragic consequences. The entire incident is steeped in irony as one of the people among the masses in steerage sacrifices his life to save Herr Hutten's dog. In this act, Porter demonstrates the Christian imperatives of pure love and self-sacrifice, but with a negative outcome. A man dies for a dog and the sacrifice is futile. The poor martyr, a woodcarver, emerges from the anonymity of steerage and throws himself into the sea in a useless attempt at heroism. The woodcarver's parallels to Christ the carpenter and the fact that his self-sacrifice is unappreciated make him, perhaps, a type of Christ figure. In this incident, Porter highlights class differences between upper-class and lower-class passengers and the indifference to such heroism and goodness demonstrated by the wealthy. Herr Hutten, reflecting pride in his German ancestry, believes his dog to be better than some of the people on board the ship. After the nameless man dies rescuing their dog, the Huttens are uncomfortable and cannot understand why anyone would perform such a selfless act. They decline to attend the man's funeral and refuse to even remember his name. But the Catholic immigrants in steerage are not generous and understanding either. Even the burial of the wood-carver is not dignified, as a riot breaks out because one man mocks the Christian ritual and is severely beaten by others for his lack of respect.

The inability to achieve satisfying love in the modern world is one of Porter's primary motifs throughout her fiction. Love that requires sacrifice and commitment has been subverted by selfishness and lust. Most of the characters in *Ship of Fools* are involved in relationships that reflect guilt, unkindness, and despair. The search for authentic love is a universally human one, transcending nationality and social class. Even when love seems to elevate the human spirit above the mundane, the forces of society inevitably cause friction and doubt. For example, Herr Freytag is a German of "pure blood" who commands respect. However, when the others discover that he is married to a Jewish woman, he is exiled from the captain's table. Eventually, this conflict of the public versus the private begins to wear away his commitment to love his wife and preserve his marriage. He begins to resent his wife and the negative impact of their marriage on his social status.

For another passenger, Frau Schmitt, whose husband has just died, the happiness of marriage has turned into despair, and she wonders, "I am tempted though I know it is a sin sometimes to ask myself—what is life but that, after all" (29). Others on the ship look for satisfaction in the physical, lusting after the four attractive Spanish prostitutes who take full advantage of the situation. Inevitably, this evil leads to violence, as William Denny, a Texan, mistakes Mrs. Treadwell for one of the Spanish dancers and is viciously attacked. His behavior unleashes a darkness in Mrs. Treadwell of which she was previously ignorant.

But the novel's focal point in terms of failed love is the relationship between Jenny Scott and David Brown. Porter modeled these characters on herself and Eugene Pressley, her third husband. Their relationship, as mirrored in the novel, was a mix of antagonism and affection. Jenny and David alternate between bickering and forgiving, never finding peace. When they are not arguing, each bestows on the other a pet name, Jenny "Angel" and David "Darling." However, these sweet names are simply ironic since neither Jenny nor David is an angel or a darling. Instead, they deliberately taunt each other, releasing the latent cruelty in their personalities. David is adrift in the modern world, unable to believe in any kind of religious tradition: he "didn't like the words soul, God, spirit, spiritual virtue, especially that one, and love" (55). Jenny knows that they will never spend their lives together but remains with David anyway, caught in the grip of alternating love and hate. It is clear that they will never be ready for a pure and unselfish love.

But Porter does not despair completely of her characters attaining lasting love. A bride and groom are also on the voyage, and they keep their distance from the other passengers. After boarding the ship, they "stood leaning together looking toward the sea" (20), providing the passengers with the romantic scene of two lovers contemplating their new and happy life together. Throughout the novel they are shadowy figures, shades of what love can be. Herr Freytag speaks of the bride to Jenny, "She has just the right look . . . Eden just after the Fall. That little interval between the Fall and the driving out of that tricky jealous vengeful old God" (92). The implication is that this couple, too, will soon experience the inevitable negative aspects of a love relationship but, for now, they are blissfully excluded from the darkness surrounding them and the other passengers.

The existence of evil, both its insidious horror and its banality, is one of Porter's major Catholic themes. Evil, she insists here, as Jesus did, springs not from outside forces but from the lusts of the human heart. The characters in *Ship of Fools*, like many modern people, do not think of themselves as sinful. But they subtly cooperate in acts of petty injustice that are the wellsprings of greater and greater evil. For example, the upper class easily and unthinkingly participates in the exclusion and excoriation of others less fortunate. Most of them, as Germans, are extremely proud of their nationality and refined heritage. As a matter of course, they all agree to dismiss Herr Freytag from the captain's table once they discover that his wife is Jewish. But these passengers do not realize the extent to which their personal act of prejudice will eventually escalate. Reading *Ship of Fools* with a knowledge of Hitler's atrocities, one can only marvel at the blindness that these characters exhibit. Even Frau Schmitt, a Catholic, agrees with the decision to ostracize the Freytags, for national pride and social acceptance take preference over the tenets of her faith. Such seemingly minor—and mindless— acts of superiority and cruelty are but a foreshadowing of what the passengers will eventually encounter once they reach Bremerhaven. In fact, Porter includes a chilling reference to the Holocaust when the Spanish workers join the ship in Cuba. Watching the pathetic crowd of outcasts flooding into steerage, Herr Rieber comments, "I would do this for them: I would put them in a big oven and turn on the gas" (59). When Frau Schmitt pales at this suggestion, Herr Rieber and his companion Lizzi "left the atmosphere of Frau Schmitt's moral disapproval for the freedom of the bar" (59). The irony is that while Frau Schmitt apparently disapproves of the extreme notion of gassing innocent people she nevertheless does nothing to prevent Herr Freytag's exile from the captain's table. Porter emphasizes the fact that "small" acts of unkindness and prejudice are but the beginning of great acts of pure evil—both proceed from the same source, the darkness in the human heart.

In the final analysis, *Ship of Fools* is an allegory of humanity's tenuous voyage through life in the modern world, a life without God or authentic religious and moral values that Porter describes as a type of hell. The traditional symbolism of the ship landing at a safe and secure port is no longer feasible. Instead, the passengers must seek their own destiny in an uncertain and ever-changing world. The prejudices of nationalism, social class, gender, and age have determined and affected their behavior while on board and have made each voyager even more insecure than when they embarked. As they exit the *Vera*, Saint Paul's words, the epigraph for the final section of the story, echo strongly and ironically: "For here have we no continuing city" (361).

Porter's work is not easy to categorize. The various narratives in *Ship of Fools* reflect Porter's ideas subtly rather than obviously. In other words, her subject is what lies beneath the surface. With so much seeming despair and evil infiltrating the novel, how can this work be considered Catholic? In spite of the negativity, Porter explores the Christian virtues of love, truth, and self-sacrifice. However, she does not rely on the tenets of faith and salvation characteristic of traditional Christianity. Instead, she dramatizes mankind's constant struggle with evil in the modern world. The voyagers on Brant's *Das Narrenschiff* were part of the medieval landscape, embedded in the dogma of good and evil even as they, too, battled the temptation of sin. Yet, in that past world, eternal salvation was promised to those who persevered on their earthly voyage. Porter's characters, conversely, are seemingly abandoned on their journey. Several attempt to rely on orthodox Catholic teachings—Dr. Schumann and the woodcarver in steerage—particularly the belief in self-sacrifice. Porter presents their dilemmas objectively, so readers must decide if the sacrifices are worth the tragic human consequences. This infusion of religious undertones is apparent throughout the novel as she incorporates Catholic terminology to describe the conflicts on board the *Vera*. The juxtaposition of Catholic ideals and human realities reinforces the dilemmas that individuals face in a complex twentieth-century world dominated by the pressures of nationalism, gender, and race.

Porter also explores the concept of love, the foundation of Christianity, in its various manifestations, from idealistic, newlywed optimism, to a widow's lament for her deceased husband, to the selfishness of Jenny and David that prevents them from fulfilling their need for love. Her characters search for the joy of human love with limited success. Is the ideal of Christian love impossible in a world filled with war, prejudice, and selfishness? Porter does not give in to despair. While traditional Christian morality may be threatened, she has sympathy for those voyagers who are adrift at sea without "a continuing city." As Robert Penn Warren reminds her readers, "In the face of the great and pitiless and dehumanizing mechanisms of the modern world, what [Porter's] work celebrates is the toughness and integrity of the individual" (1980, 10).

CRITICAL RECEPTION

By the time she published *Ship of Fools*, Katherine Anne Porter was in her seventies and had had a long and colorful career. Her reputation as a short-story writer was solid, with her meticulously crafted narratives being compared to those of Henry James, Katherine Mansfield, and James Joyce. Her style—terse and understated, with controlled characters and emotions—was clearly suited to the short-story genre. It is no wonder, then, that she had problems completing this episodic novel, which required an extended albeit disjointed narrative and the interaction of forty characters. Porter took over thirty years to compile the vast amount of material and organize it into a cohesive and coherent epic. The literary community had patiently waited for the novel, and when it appeared the critical reviews were initially enthusiastic. *Ship of Fools* was chosen as a Book-of-the-Month club selection and became a best seller. In addition, the novel was adapted for the screen and made into a successful film. The royalties from the book and film allowed Porter to live out her life free of debt.

However, the fact that the book was commercially successful also exerted a negative influence on some of the reviews. The literary community of the era favored writers who perfected their craft instead of creating best-sellers. As a respected writer, Porter was held to high standards of technical mastery and carefully structured prose, and a number of critics expressed disappointment in a novel that appeared to move chaotically and randomly from character to character and scene to scene. As John Hardy reported in his critical study, *Katherine Anne Porter, Ship of Fools* seemed formless, whereas the author was famous for her formal perfection. To Hardy, the novel lacked sequence and general "coherence of action" (1973, 115). In addition, the narrative style seemed monotonous, with no heroes or climactic action; it was simply a recounting of vignette after vignette about those on the ship. This sense of disorder, some critics decided, could be attributed to the fact that Porter did not write the novel as a unified whole but in "batches and binges" (Lopez 1981, 183) over a period of thirty years. Critics noted that perhaps her talent and style were not suited to the genre of the novel, because *Ship of Fools* read more like a series of short stories than a sustained, organized narrative. The work simply did not seem to conform to a rigorous definition of a literary novel. However, critics conceded that Porter's typical themes and motifs were present here. In their book *Katherine Anne Porter*, George and Willene Hendrick commented, "She has constantly dealt with the chaos of the universe and with the forces within man and within society which have led to man's alienation" (1988, 137).

Upon its appearance, *Ship of Fools* was critiqued in many noted newspapers and magazines of the day, including *Newsweek, The Saturday Review, Commentary, The New Yorker,* and *The New York Times.* The review in *Newsweek* praised the story, stating "Katherine Anne Porter has produced a work of ragged power and myriad insights, a book of the highest relevance to the bitterness and disruption of modern civilization" (Lopez 1981, 289). Mark Schorer's review in *The New York Times* echoed the sentiments of those who praised the universal depth of the work: despite the surface action of the plot "all the time, with any great work of art, something larger is in the air, and we know that we are on another ship as well, another voyage, sailing to another border" (1962, 23). Howard Moss also cited Porter's unique viewpoint: "We are impressed not by what Miss Porter knows. Neither heartless nor merciful, she is tough. Her virtue is disinterestedness, her strength objectivity" (1979, 160). In light of this praise, a negative evaluation by Theodore Solotaroff in *Commentary* seems unduly harsh.

Solotaroff wrote, "*Ship of Fools* is simply what it is: an account of a tedious voyage to Europe three decades ago that has been labored over for twenty years by a writer who, later in life, is venturing, hence revealing, little more than misanthropy and clever technique" (1962, 286).

Some prominent writers, including Granville Hicks, Eudora Welty, and Robert Penn Warren, did not share Solotaroff's stinging criticism of the novel. Instead, they offered more balanced appraisals of Porter's work, taking into consideration the novel's weaknesses as well as its strengths. Writing for *The Saturday Review*, Granville Hicks stated that *Ship of Fools* "shows that Miss Porter is one of the finest writers of prose in America," but he also acknowledged that the book "for all its lucidity and all its insights, leaves the reader a little cold. There is in it, as far as I can see, no sense of human possibility" (1962, 15). Porter's friend and fellow writer Eudora Welty emphasized the author's moral outlook: "All the stories she has written are moral stories about love and the hate that is love's twin, love's injustice and enemy and death. Rejection, betrayal, desertion, theft, roam the pages of her stories as they roam the world" (1966, 268). Finally, Robert Penn Warren, a lifelong admirer of Porter's work, wrote of his personal reaction to *Ship of Fools* in the introduction to *Katherine Anne Porter: A Collection of Critical Essays*: "The general argument is that the book is not flawless, even if I, personally, find no fault with its general scheme and even if, by and large, the writing is of an excellence not admitted by all readers" (1979, 16).

It may be time for a reevaluation of *Ship of Fools* in light of recent trends in fiction. No longer is a novel criticized for failing to follow a certain structure and, in light of postmodernism, the very definition of a novel is subject to interpretation. Episodic stories with many characters are now popular and successful. Heroes are no longer required for a riveting tale, and beginnings, middles, and endings are optional in twenty-first-century fiction. In 1962, on the cusp of the movement to revolutionize many of the accepted norms in society, a move from a certain innocence to experience—and to cynicism—Porter was criticized for presenting a story with no admirable characters. According to Robert Penn Warren, "More than one critic has complained that there are not enough nonfools on the ship" (1979, 16). However, readers now are quite familiar with characters who struggle with but never quite manage to rise above their imperfections. In addition, the terror of the utter complacency and pettiness of Porter's passengers read in light of twentieth-century atrocities has deepened in the last forty years.

In a 1995 critical reassessment, fifteen years after the author's death, Mary Gordon reaffirmed that Porter's writing resisted categorization. *Ship of Fools*, she stated, has a kind of greatness: "Porter is a master: [she has] the ability to describe gestures and manners, to use them as a nest in which to enclose a statement of general, even metaphysical, significance" (1995, 17). Both Gordon and Robert Hosmer believe that Porter's emphasis on love in the modern world is crucial to her works' appeal. Writing in *Commonweal*, Hosmer quotes from a letter Porter once wrote to her nephew, assessing her life: "All life worth living is difficult; nobody promised us happiness; it is not a commodity you have earned or shall ever learn. It is a by-product of brave living and it never comes in the form we expect, or at the season we hoped for or as a result of our planning for it" (1991, 267).

NOTE

Katherine Anne Porter, *Ship of Fools* (Boston: Little, Brown, 1962). All references are to this edition.

WORKS CITED

Brant, Sebastian. [1494] 1944. *Das Narrenschiff*. Translated as *The Ship of Fools* by Edwin H. Zeydel. New York: Dover Publications.

Gordon, Mary. 1995. "The Angel of Malignity: The Cold Beauty of Katherine Anne Porter." *New York Times Book Review* (April 16): 17–19.

Hardy, John Edward. 1973. *Katherine Anne Porter*. New York: Frederick Ungar.

Hendrick, George, and Willene Hendrick. 1988. *Katherine Anne Porter*. New York: Twayne.

Hicks, Granville. 1962. "Voyage of Life." *Saturday Review* 45 (March 31): 15–16.

Hosmer, Robert E., Jr. 1991. "One Fixed Desire." *Commonweal* 118 (April 19): 266–67.

Lopez, Enrique Hank. 1981. *Conversations with Katherine Anne Porter: Refugee from Indian Creek*. Boston: Little, Brown.

Moss, Howard. 1979. "No Safe Harbor." In *Katherine Anne Porter: A Collection of Critical Essays*, ed. Robert Penn Warren, 155–61. Englewood Cliffs, NJ: Prentice Hall.

Schorer, Mark. 1962. "We're All on the Passenger's List." *New York Times Book Review* (April 1): 23–24.

Solotaroff, Theodore. 1962. "*Ship of Fools* and the Critics." *Commentary* 34 (October): 277–86.

Warren, Robert Penn, ed. 1979. *Katherine Anne Porter: A Collection of Critical Essays*. Englewood Cliffs, NJ: Prentice Hall.

———. 1980. "The Genius of Katherine Anne Porter." *Saturday Review* 7 (December): 10–11.

Welty, Eudora. 1966. "The Eye of the Story." *Yale Review* 55 (Winter): 265–74.

BIBLIOGRAPHY

Bloom, Harold, ed. *Modern Critical Reviews: Katherine Anne Porter*. New York: Chelsea House, 1986.

Givner, Joan. *Katherine Anne Porter: A Life*. New York: Simon and Schuster, 1982.

Libermann, M. M. *Katherine Anne Porter's Fiction*. Detroit: Wayne State University Press, 1971.

West, Ray B., Jr. *Katherine Anne Porter*. Minneapolis: University of Minnesota Press, 1968.

— Kathleen Jacquette

J. F. Powers [1917–1999]

Morte d'Urban

BIOGRAPHY

At the height of his career, in the mid-twentieth century, J. F. (James Farl) Powers was one of the most admired writers on the American literary scene, appreciated particularly by a large and widely varied assortment of other professionals. Powers was a writer's writer if there ever was one. Painstakingly deliberate, he produced a body of work that, although small, is of consistent high quality. Personally, he was reserved and saturnine except among close friends, avoiding publicity and often taking a contrarian attitude toward prevailing cultural values and trends. (He was a conscientious objector during World War II, and in later years he took a dim view of the reforms promoted by the Second Vatican Council.) For the last quarter century of his life he almost disappeared from public view, although the republication of his works in 2000 in the New York Review of Books Classics series helped restore his fame. His most characteristic fiction describes the lives of priests—not their inner spiritual lives but rather their workaday routine. A cradle Catholic, he defined the relation of his faith to his art inconsistently, sometimes accepting the label of Catholic author and at other times resisting it as overly narrow.

Powers was born in 1917, of solidly middle-class parents, in Jacksonville, a town in southern Illinois rather like the hometown of Harvey Roche, the protagonist of *Morte d'Urban*. After an almost archetypically normal boyhood, he moved with his parents to Chicago at the very nadir of the Great Depression. Over the decade from 1935 through the end of World War II, Powers managed to take a few college classes but mainly bounced around from one low-paying job to another, in sales, as a chauffeur, as a clerk at the Chicago Historical Society, and in a bookstore. His politics were those of the Catholic left, and his first publications were in Dorothy Day's offbeat but influential *Catholic Worker* (annual subscription price: one cent). Influenced by retreats he went on in the early 1940s, he became a pacifist, refusing to be drafted during the war and consequently serving a prison term for thirteen months. In 1946, he married Elizabeth Wahl, a gifted author in her own right. The couple had five children.

Powers's first important story, and one of his best, was "Lions, Harts, Leaping Does," which probes the thoughts of a guilt-ridden dying priest. This anticipated his later work in that it centers on a priest, but it is atypical because it explores the priest's spiritual condition. Most of the later stories about priests, along with the two novels to come (*Morte d'Urban* [1962] and *Wheat That Springeth Green* [1988]), are concerned not with the inner religious life but with the workaday conditions of the clergy and with ecclesiastical politics, often treated in a vein between the grim and the hilarious. At rather widely spaced intervals, brilliant short-story collections appeared: *Prince of Darkness* in 1947; *The Presence of Grace* in 1956; *Look How the Fish Live* in 1973. Many of Powers's admirers, and Powers himself at times, considered such short fiction to be his best work. The high point, however, of what fame he achieved came when *Morte d'Urban* won the National Book Award in 1963.

Powers lived for several periods in Ireland, but he never earned enough from his writing (not voluminous in any case) to support his family, and his bread-and-butter occupations over the latter part of his life consisted of college appointments to teach creative writing. (Characteristically, out of artistic principle he declined a chance to turn *Morte d'Urban* into a Hollywood movie.) Having taught briefly at such places as Marquette, the University of Michigan, and Smith, he finally settled permanently at St. John's College (later University) in Minnesota. After surviving his wife by eleven years, he died in 1999.

PLOT SUMMARY

Morte d'Urban's protagonist, Father Urban, is the central consciousness through most of the novel. Readers should recognize, however, that Urban's point of view, especially his dim assessment of other people, is sometimes considered a distorting lens.

The time is the 1950s. The main character is a fifty-four-year-old priest named Father Urban (born Harvey Roche). He was the son of a golf course greenskeeper in a southern Illinois town where Catholics such as Harvey were a fringe minority. As a caddy, the boy observed the social world from below. In his midteens, Harvey ran away from home under the wing of Father Placidus Hartigan, a charismatic, cosmopolite priest zestfully comfortable in the secular world. Influenced by the priest's membership in the Clementines, a (fictional) order of priests, Harvey entered its seminary and was ultimately ordained, in 1933, as Father Urban. It later became clear that Father Placidus was unique, the only member of the undistinguished Clementine order who rose above the level of mediocrity.

When the novel opens, the middle-aged Father Urban, too, has proved an exception among the Clementines: tall and handsome, supremely self-confident, spellbinding as a mission preacher, hedonist in taste and habits, and ambitious to lift the Clementines above their ingrained mediocrity. He aspires to attract a "higher type" of converts, especially "worldly executives" (*Morte d'Urban*, 17, 18). Father Urban has recently begun to influence Billy Cosgrove, a rich vulgarian who, despite moral shortcomings (which Father Urban intends to correct, but only in due time), becomes a financial patron of the Clementines. Billy donates to the order a fashionably located office building as the new Chicago headquarters of the order.

Reporting to headquarters after a tour of preaching, Urban discovers with dismay that he has been taken off the preaching circuit and, along with a stolidly pious priest named Father John (Jack), has been posted to a remote site near Duesterhaus, Minnesota. This reassignment to the boondocks is a severe blow to Father Urban, who had hoped to rise to the elected post of provincial of the Clementine order. At Duesterhaus the Clementines have acquired a rundown property, formerly a poorhouse and then a sanitarium for alcoholics, which has recently been donated to the Clementines by Mrs. Thwaites, a crabbed old widow fearful for her eternal salvation. Fathers Urban and Jack join the existent staff of two: the rector Father Wilfrid (Wilf) plus a lay brother sycophantically allied with him. Their first job, under Father Wilf's plodding and penny-pinching leadership, is to make the place (newly named St. Clement's Hill, or, informally, the Hill) minimally livable and usable as a retreat center. Urban, accustomed to metropolitan amenities, finds himself billeted in a severely underheated bedroom and subjected to a regime of menial labor as an untalented handyman, working under a rector who agonizes over the extra cost of a person-to-person phone call and economizes by buying cheap paint.

The Clementines of Duesterhaus sometimes help out with the weekend confessions and Masses at the nearby St. Monica's parish. Through such brief escapes from the Hill, Father Urban begins to win back some of his former celebrity. Especially successful is an address to the Commercial Club of the nearby town of Great Plains; here his skills in public relations come in handy, mainly when he sides with the local merchants against Father Wilf's objections to the commercialization of Christmas. Urban has now "put the Hill on the map for a lot of people who really mattered in the community" (99). Requests for speaking engagements snowball. Billy Cosgrove also reemerges, donating to the Hill an elaborate Christmas crèche and a color television set, to which Father Wilf, despite some feelings of guilt, becomes addicted. Father Urban having become a credit to the Clementine community, Father Wilf takes a more favorable view of his public career.

When the pastor of St. Monica's, Father Phil, and his friend Monsignor Renton, an official of the diocesan cathedral, take off for a few months of winter vacation in Florida, Father Urban is put in charge of St. Monica's church and parish. He has begun to feel like a real priest again—neither a star circuit preacher nor a Duesterhaus drudge. His tenure at St. Monica's is spectacularly successful: he is popular with the parishioners, the local nuns, and the rectory housekeeper. He sponsors lay activities, wins over the new curate to active pastoral work, undertakes a census of parishioners, and, despite inertia on the part of Father Phil, projects a new church building to accommodate the swelling local Catholic population. That plan is derailed when news arrives from Florida: Father Phil has had a fatal heart attack on the golf course. Father Urban tactfully manages the obsequies for the never-very-popular pastor and begins to nourish hopes that he will be named the new pastor of St. Monica's.

An exciting new development occurs: land adjacent to the Hill has come on the market. Father Urban conceives the idea of acquiring the land, turning it into a golf course, and using the course to attract wealthy businessmen as retreatants—instead of the tightfisted ethnic types who have heretofore been the center's clientele. Billy Cosgrove's help and money are enlisted, and the property is deemed eminently suitable for a golf course. Father Urban goes to Chicago and persuades the Clementines' chapter to endorse the project. Under Urban's supervision, the golf course rapidly emerges as a first-rate facility.

Father Urban's good fortunes, ascendant until now, will henceforth decline. He is severely disappointed when the bishop decides not to appoint him rector of St. Monica's. Administrative problems also arise in connection with the golf course (who should be permitted to play it?). The problems do not seem insuperable, but a storm cloud appears when the bishop (who, the Clementines fear, may co-opt the Hill facility and convert it into a diocesan seminary) makes a spectacle of himself by his wretchedly bad golf, his mood not improved by giggles from a woman looking on. Father Urban is also rebuffed in attempts to win over the clergy and influential laity of the adjacent diocese of Ostergothenburg.

Things really plunge downhill when an informal but intense golf competition arises: the bishop, who has been taking lessons, shows up one day with his golf coach, a scholarly young priest named Father Feld who, like Father Urban, is an excellent golfer. An intensely symbolic foursome shapes up: the bishop and Father Feld on one side against, on the other side, the pastor of the local Presbyterian church and Father Urban. Father Urban's "team" is about to win the match when he is beaned by a golf ball erratically struck by the bishop. Urban has to be hospitalized and never fully recovers from this head injury.

After a recuperative stay with Mrs. Thwaites, whom he alienates by trying to mediate a petty dispute about money between her and a mistreated servant, Urban returns to the Hill. Billy suddenly invites him to go along on a fishing trip to northern Minnesota that turns out to be a disaster. Billy behaves offensively, especially by making unseemly passes at the resort owner's comely wife in the very presence of the husband and Father Urban. The last straw is an attempt by Billy to wantonly drown a deer that the fishing party encounters on the lake. Father Urban obviates this piece of cruelty by revving up the boat. This marks the end of the relationship with the affronted Billy, who departs in fury, forcing Urban to take a bus home.

While changing buses on the way, he meets Sally Hopwood, the attractive married daughter of Mrs. Thwaites. Sally drives Urban back to her mother's estate and then takes him by boat to a miniature castle on an island in the lake. There they have a few social drinks, and Sally forces Urban to recognize that he has no real friends. He begins to imagine in detail the cosmopolitan life he might have lived had he not become a priest. She tries to entice him into a nude swim and doffs her clothes. When he declines the gambit, she huffily motors off in the boat, leaving him stranded on the island. He has to swim to land, in the process catching a bad cold. Monsignor Renton picks him up and drives him home.

Anticlimactically, Father Urban is elected provincial of the Midwest chapter of the Clementines; ironically, they have belatedly come to believe that he is the person to restore their failing fortunes, Billy Cosgrove having evicted them from their posh quarters in Chicago. But Father Urban is not what he used to be. On the outs with Billy, he is powerless to help. He has also grown reclusive and subject to periodic attacks of severe head pain. (His need to be alone in such crises earns him a reputation for piety.) The local radio station cancels the Clementines' regular radio broadcast. Even the elm trees at the novitiate die of disease, for which Father Urban gets the blame, although the real cause was neglect by the previous administration. As for the Hill, it appears that the bishop, with Father Feld, is going to take it over as a seminary after all. Father Urban is troubled; no longer the worldly peripatetic, he has come to think of the Hill as home.

MAJOR THEMES

Morte d'Urban is in some ways the most "Catholic" of novels, steeped entirely in matters not only Catholic but clerical. The very few characters who are not priests or religious function in the plot exclusively in relation to the institutional Church: as rich lay financial patrons, wives active in parish affairs, and the like.

It is also the novel's Catholicism that poses the most difficult interpretative challenges. The book wholly avoids doctrine and theology, unless one counts a brief discussion of the problematical passage in the Gospel for the Eighth Sunday after Pentecost (Luke 16:1–9) in which Jesus recommends befriending the mammon of iniquity (229–31); but this episode is significant less as theology than as development of the pervasive theme of worldliness, as embodied in Father Urban. The Catholic ambiance consists entirely of the routine of clerical life: the hierarchical relationships within religious orders and dioceses, the relation of these to each other as regards authority and power, the home life of rectories and chapters, and the logistics of pastoral duties, such as hearing confessions, saying Mass, and preaching missions.

The main challenge arising out of the novel's Catholicism is its rather dismal picture of the Catholic culture. Is there any piece of imaginative literature, one might ask, by a Catholic or a non-Catholic, more likely to discourage conversions to Catholicism or vocations to the Catholic priesthood? Day-to-day Catholic life has rarely been depicted as so dispiriting—reversing the widespread, more-or-less anticlerical tradition wherein the Church embodies a corrupt form of glamour (one thinks of Stendhal, Thackeray, and Robert Browning). Except for Father Urban himself, the characters in *Morte d'Urban* tend to be excruciatingly dull: either dim-witted or stolidly uninteresting or both. The most obvious cases in point are Father Wilf, concerned doggedly and almost exclusively with the physical repair of the property at the Hill, and Father Jack, a woodenly humorless model of narrow-focused piety.

How are we to take this novel, so dispiriting but at the same time so infectiously readable? The two readiest options would seem to be as satire or as a less mordant mode of pure comedy. Let us consider first this latter option—keeping in mind, of course, that the comedy often has bite even when it does not reach the level of serious satire.

Some of the lighter-weight comedy is linguistic and literary, exemplified by Father Jack's earnest efforts at literary composition, which illustrate Catholic provincialism at its most suffocating. His most ambitious enterprise is "a *scholarly* children's edition of *Le Morte d'Arthur* by Sir Thomas Malory" (256), tidied up for Catholic edification. Can one avert scandal, Father Jack agonizes, by showing that Launcelot and the Lady Elaine were married? Cannot the love between Launcelot and Guenevere also be shown, by careful reading of the texts, to be unsinful? (316–18). In much the same vein is a version of the Robin Hood story, "with a Catholic twist," being composed by Mrs. Thwaites's son Dickie. The story is to be transferred to the Reformation era so that the rich from whom

Robin steals are Tudor-era despoilers of the monasteries. Maid Marian is to end up in a nunnery. "'As a nun?' inquired Father Boniface. 'Yes,' said Father Urban, and this, he could see, was very good news to Father Boniface and to others [among the Clementines] who might have thought that Maid Marian was just doing time in a nunnery" (201). Father Boniface, the provincial of the order, had written a pamphlet, too, on mercy killing, which had not gone over big but is being reissued with an updated cover: "Father Urban wasn't fooled by the flashy new cover, nor, he thought, would the big dealers, the priests and nuns who could make or break a pamphlet, be fooled by it" (28). ("Make or break?" We're talking here about that slightest of media, the tiny booklets displayed on racks in church vestibules.) Father Louis, like Father Urban a former disciple of the flamboyant Father Placidus, had been expelled by the Jesuits because of "a run-in with his confessor over the value of St. Ignatius's 'Exercises' as prose" (198).

Sometimes the humor is broader, indeed farcical. The barely running pickup truck that represents the Hill's whole fleet of transportation is almost a source of pride to Father Wilf (44–45). Brother Harold aspires to create sacred art; in the meantime he is taking a correspondence course in show-card lettering (53). Father Jack comes home from an assignment at a parish rectory wearing another priest's trousers, which have to be exchanged for his own through silent subterfuge (112–27).

Jokes like these are "Catholic" ones, but they do not bite very deep. The more typical, and more significant, comic episodes are more darkly satiric. It is not at all obvious, however, who or what is the satiric target. In many respects the target seems to be the Church itself, or rather its institutional mechanisms. For one thing, hardly any of the novel's clergy seem to be in positions in which they belong and can perform well, Father Urban being only the most obvious case in point. Only when, at the end of the novel, he has lost all his typical fire, initiative, and leadership skills is he installed in the position of provincial to which he has aspired. He had, in fact, for several years been nonplussed by *Time* magazine's rating of the Catholic Church as second in efficiency only to Standard Oil (117).

It is precisely such sentiments, of course, that seem to direct the satire against Father Urban as a kind of (more sophisticated) ecclesiastical Babbitt; like golf, Standard Oil and *Time* were standard mid-century symbols of American materialism. Father Urban has been presented from the outset of his priestly career as an Apostle to the Affluent. He envisages the public lounge of the order's new headquarters in Chicago, a gift from Billy, as potentially a kind of tastefully furnished university club, a well-appointed, soft-sell lure to potential converts, especially converts "of a type badly needed and generally neglected—the higher type" (17).

Addressing businessmen in Minnesota, he dissociates himself from standard clerical complaints about the commercialization of Christmas. His rationale is characteristic: "Charity toward all, even when a few sharks get in among the swimmers, is always better than holier-than-thou singularity. That, roughly speaking, was the mind of the Church" (107). His most sustained project is to turn the Hill into a retreat house, resort-style, with the golf course as the primary draw of a classier clientele than "the ham-and-sausage-supper types" the Clementines have been attracting (189). Visiting the order's Chicago headquarters, he pitches the idea in a similar vein: "Father Urban said it was high time somebody considered the plight of the one man for whom the Church was perhaps doing too little" and for whom a first retreat at, say, a Trappist monastery would be a pretty deep plunge (198–99). One of the novel's climactic turning points is the episode in which Father Urban, nearing symbolic victory in the great golf match against the bishop and Father Feld—described in mock-epic language as a kind of medieval trial by combat—is seriously injured by the bishop's errant shot. The point, it would seem, is to give Father Urban a poetically just, excruciatingly banal, comeuppance.

The trouble with this reading of the novel as satire directed at Father Urban's tendency to cultivate mammon is in the contrast between him and the other people in the book. Father Urban is not only the most interesting and intelligent person in the novel; he is also the most attractive and, arguably, even the one most dedicated to his priestly function. His taste for glamour, like the earlier described chumminess of his mentor Father Placidus with the cast of Victor Herbert operettas, may seem unspiritual, but it also represents an authentic elevation of taste, an attunement with beauty, when compared with, say, Father Wilf's and Mrs. Thwaites's addiction to daytime television. Father Urban's delight in driving Sylvia Bean's neat little Barracuda sports car may seem materialistic, but are we really to see its counterpart, the ludicrous flivver that Father Wilf has coaxed back into life, as a balancing symbol of laudable asceticism? Whatever else Father Urban may be, he is after all a kind of artist. Are we really to consider that bad?

Even measured by religious standards—or at least by the standard of pastoral effectiveness that is this novel's closest approach to a religious ideal—Father Urban excels. His brief tenure as interim pastor of St. Monica's is, in pastoral terms, a triumph, infusing unprecedented energy into the life of the parish. (Interpreters who see Father Urban as achieving an admirable quietist piety at the end of the novel need to consider whether the sole duty of a priest is to refine his inner life.) Some of Urban's accomplishments are conditioned by his unique style and charm. For example, he makes life easier for the school nuns by lending them a car for shopping and sometimes giving them money: "'Buy yourself some cigars, Sister.' [The nuns] all loved him" (163–64).

To see *Morte d'Urban* primarily as a satire directed at Father Urban, then, is not a very satisfying reading of the novel. Perhaps it would be better to see it as a version of tragedy. The general tone of the book, a combination of the mordant, the sardonic, and the farcical, would seem inconsistent with the high seriousness one associates with tragedy, but if we allow for that variable the novel does have a kind of tragic pattern, the kind that centers on human waste resulting from a missed vocation. Indeed, missed vocations constitute much of the novel's human background; but this is especially true of Father Urban, who makes a good priest but whose achievements in that role, in the teeth of the limitations imposed by his banal circumstantial and human environment, show all the more clearly how much he might have accomplished in a more appropriate vocation.

The downward turning point of the tragic curve is Urban's head injury on the golf course. Before that incident, despite a setback or two, things had been looking up for him; thereafter, nothing works out. The novel looks far back in time, to the boyhood of Harvey Roche, who was sociologically on the wrong side of the tracks in his Illinois home town, an outsider in several ways including, especially, his religion. A pattern close to that of Fitzgerald's Gatsby is discernible: like

James Gatz's discovery of the gorgeousness of life when he happens on Dan Cody's yacht, Harvey's first "conversion" is to glamour itself. That the glamour is embodied in the high-living Father Placidus Hartigan—a priest—is less important than the glimpse itself of a larger, freer world than the boy has known. (Perhaps significantly, Father Placidus recalls Monsignor Darcy, the cosmopolitan priest who serves as Amory Blaine's mentor in Fitzgerald's first novel, *This Side of Paradise*.) The uniqueness of Father Placidus constitutes an early tragic twist; the boy has happened upon the only priest in the Clementine order who is at all out of the ordinary, a lonely eminence that ultimately will define Father Urban's status as well. Nevertheless, Harvey persists in the seminary, and it is fitting that, when ordained, he takes a priestly name that suggests urbanity.

For most of his career, before the opening of the novel, Father Urban manages somehow to combine his priestly vocation with his taste for glamour and the theatrical. This is a *tour de force*, however, succeeding despite severe frictional drag from the institutional bureaucracy of the Church. Eventually, this friction will prove too much for him; his ultimate installation as provincial, at a time when he can do neither himself nor the order any good, is the final cruel, tragic irony. During their tête-à-tête on the island, Sally Hopwood tells him that he really has no friends—a fact that he recognizes, with a shock, as true (301). One of the focal points of the novel is Urban's elaborate fantasy of the life he might have lived in the world:

> in some kind of business you could breathe in, perhaps heavy machinery, much of it going overseas, lots of travel, meeting fellows like Haile Selassie and Farouk's father, whatever his name was, and operating out of a spacious office on Michigan Avenue, high up, with a view of the lake, walnut paneling, Persian carpets, furnished with gifts from potentates and dictators of the better sort, a tree at Christmas, efficient rosy-cheeked girls in white-collared dark dresses, Irish girls hired for the purity of their vocables, and himself hardly ever there. (302)

This vision, which continues for two more pages, is heavily colored by the novel's extravagantly ironic tone, but it also suggests a tragically unexplored dimension of life, the life that for Harvey Roche/Father Urban was channeled into the priesthood at an impressionable time in adolescence and, the die having been cast, put thereafter to sadly limited use, human or divine.

CRITICAL RECEPTION

Almost everyone agrees that *Morte d'Urban* is funny, and most readers find it at least partly satiric, although the target of the satire—Father Urban? the Church? the priesthood?—has been variously identified. Critics disagree, however, on three matters not distinctly separable from one another: the religious dimension of the novel; the tone of its portrayal of Father Urban and the other characters; and the question of whether the book works as a novel or is merely episodic.

Is *Morte d'Urban* a Catholic novel? Even if we assume—as may not be true—that Powers achieved what he was aiming at in the book, we are left hanging, because his statements are inconclusive. He once said, in an interview, "Philosophically,

I am a Catholic writer" (quoted in Weber 2001, 1). At another time, however, he insisted that *Morte d'Urban* was no more "a book about and for Catholics than *Wind in the Willows* is a book for animals" (quoted in Ritter 1998, 1). On still another occasion, in a 1988 interview, he stated, "There isn't anything the Church can do that it hasn't already done to disillusion me," although he then added, rather opaquely, "but I still think it's *it*" (quoted in Derbyshire 1999, 4).

William Gass declared, "I cannot imagine a book in which religious feeling would be more conspicuously absent" (Gass 1962, 182–83; reprinted in Evans 1968, 77). Saul Bellow considered the novel spiritually thin, and Peter De Vries, denying that Powers was a religious writer, said that his priests practice "their profession, not their religion" (cited in Weber 2001, 4, 5). Powers has also come in for some acidulous clerical criticism—for example, by the Redemptorist priest Thomas Rowan—for allegedly portraying priests contemptuously in *Morte d'Urban* (Rowan 1963, 291–94; reprinted in Evans 1968, 101–05). (One recalls Powers's extravagant admiration for James Joyce, not exactly a model for pious edification.)

Many readers have taken a different view. Thomas Merton (1962) argued that the latter part of the novel rises above clinical satire to portray the "death" of Father Urban as that of "a superficial self leading to the resurrection of a deeper, more noble and more spiritual personality" (quoted in Evans 1968, 95). Marie J. Henault saw in the novel "the great theme of individual salvation. The death of Urban is the saving of him" (Henault 1963, 292; reprinted in Hagopian 1968, 127). The novel has also been defended on the score of its accuracy and moral realism. Flannery O'Connor conceded that Powers's Catholics are "vulgar, ignorant, greedy and fearfully drab" but added that "Mr. Powers doesn't write about such Catholics because he wants to embarrass the church; he writes about them because, by the grace of God, he can't write about any other kind" (quoted in Weber 2001, 4).

The reading of the novel as religious or not depends closely on readers' view of Father Urban in relation to the other characters. One standard view is to see most of the other priests—especially Father Boniface (the Clementine order's provincial) and Fathers Wilf and Jack—as repellently narrow. The central questions are whether Father Urban's worldliness is attractive or not and also whether or not it serves authentic religious ends. Some critics, including F. W. Dupee (1963), Phoebe Adams (1962), and Thomas Curley (1962), view Urban sympathetically, largely because they see him as surrounded and hampered by mediocre or contemptible colleagues. Other critics view Urban's urbanity as a serious spiritual flaw for which he must (and, in the opinion of most of them, does) atone, ultimately achieving humility and a deeper spirituality at the cost of his worldly self-assurance and proud cockiness. Included in this group of critics are Marie J. Henault (1963) and John V. Hagopian (1968). For Hagopian, this view of the novel has to filter out a misleading distraction occasioned by the narrative point of view, which for most of the novel is the distorted and contemptuous viewpoint of Urban himself. Only in the concluding chapter, Hagopian contends, does the viewpoint become more neutral, thus redressing the balance between Urban and the other clerics, showing the latter as worthy priests, not the incompetent buffoons Urban had encouraged us to take them for (1968, 124–34).

To view the novel in this way would seem to redeem it from charges that it is episodic or otherwise invertebrate, as was alleged by Gass (1962), Granville Hicks (1962), and Martin Price (1962). Hagopian and Henault take the opposite view, that the novel is organically structured. For most such defenders of the novelistic coherence, the turning point is the episode in which Urban is injured by the bishop's errant golf shot and thus enters on the process of spiritual renewal. Even readers who see the denouement differently—as, for example, depicting Urban's tragic failure—can see the same episode as a turning point, thus vindicating the novel's structure but in the interests of a different interpretation.

NOTE

J. F. Powers, *Morte d'Urban* (Garden City, NY: Doubleday, 1962). All references are to this edition.

WORKS CITED

Adams, Phoebe. 1962. "Reader's Choice." *Atlantic Monthly* 210 (November): 134–36.

Curley, Thomas. 1962. "J. F. Powers' Long-Awaited First Novel." *Commonweal* 77 (October 12): 77–78.

Derbyshire, John. 1999. "*Sub Specie Aeternitatis*: J. F. Powers, 1917–1999." *The New Criterion Online* (September), www.newcriterion.com/archive/18/sept99/powers.htm.

Dupee, F. W. 1963. "In the Powers Country." *Partisan Review* 30 (Spring): 113–16.

Evans, Fallon, ed. 1968. *J. F. Powers*. St. Louis, MO: B. Herder Book Co.

Gass, William. 1962. "Bingo Game at the Foot of the Cross." *The Nation* 195 (September 29): 182–83. Reprinted in Evans (1968), 77.

Hagopian, John V. 1968. *J. F. Powers*. New York: Twayne.

Henault, Marie J. 1963. "The Saving of Father Urban." *America* 108 (March 2): 290–92.

Hicks, Granville. 1962. "The Foibles of Good Men." *Saturday Review* 45 (September 15): 21.

Merton, Thomas. 1962. "*Morte d'Urban*: Two Celebrations." *Worship* 36 (November): 645–50. Reprinted in Evans (1968), 95–100.

Price, Martin. 1962. Review of *Morte d'Urban*. *Yale Review* 52 (December): 263–67.

Ritter, Peter. 1998. "J. F. Powers: The Sins of the Fathers." *City Pages: The Online News & Arts Weekly of the Twin Cities* 19, no. 927 (September 9), www.citypages.com/databank/19/927/article5972.asp.

Rowan, Thomas, C. S. S. R. 1963. "*Morte d'Urban*: A Novel about Priests." *Homiletic and Pastoral Review* 63 (January): 291–94. Reprinted in Evans (1968), 101–5.

Weber, Ronald. 2001. "Men of the Cloth." *Notre Dame Magazine Online* (Winter), http://www.nd.edu/~ndmag/w2000_01/weberw00.html.

— Brian Wilkie

Jessica Powers [1905–1988]

Poems

BIOGRAPHY

Jessica Powers, born in February 1905 in Mauston, Wisconsin, to parents of Scots-Irish heritage, lived until August 1988, her life spanning the turbulent twentieth century. As Powers's biographer Dolores Leckey explains, "Catholicism was a central point" (1992, 25) in both Powers's paternal and maternal ancestry. Other dominant influences on Powers's life included family, the farming community with much shared ancestry, and the season of winter: "Winter in all its forms, spiritual, emotional, intellectual as well as meteorological, runs through her writing. She learned to live sparely, esthetically, deliberately, daringly, deeply in Wisconsin. It was winter that vibrated through her being like music" (3).

Powers's childhood, in the rich farmland of southwestern Wisconsin, was marked by suffering: her seventeen-year-old sister Dorothy died of tuberculosis when Powers was eleven, and both of her parents were dead before Powers was twenty. Powers spent one year at Marquette University in the journalism school, but she had to return to the Mauston, Wisconsin, area because of her mother's failing health and lack of finances. During the Marquette year, since the journalism department shared many connections with the English department, Powers had opportunities to study, read, and write poetry and to foster her fledgling interests in the literary world.

At eighteen, Powers and her cousin Mary Walsh went to Chicago, another literary environment, where they lived lives dominated by clerical work during the day and enlivened by hours of reading in public libraries in the evening. Again this entry to the literary world had to be aborted when Powers faced a bout with tuberculosis, which worried her family, given Dorothy's death, and prompted a return to the rural setting of the Cat Tail Valley. Even after her health improved, the pursuit of a literary career still eluded Powers because when her mother died, Powers was destined to be a farm housekeeper until 1937, when her brothers had married and assumed management of the family farms.

Much of the poetry of this period of Powers's life, the natural contemplative period, is nature poetry and much was unrefined; however, suffering and loss worked for Powers as they did for Emily Dickinson, one of the poets whom Powers read and admired, providing poignant images and fertile material for poetry. Several poems from this early period of Powers's writing were published in Wisconsin newspapers and magazines.

Knowing intuitively that she needed kindred spirits for her poetic growth, Powers, once she was free of family responsibilities, moved to New York for its rich cultural ambiance. Despite her inexperience with urban life and amid the dire poverty raging during the Depression years, she found New York City in the 1930s a rich, supportive environment, particularly for Catholic writers. Founded in 1931 by editors of the three most prestigious Catholic publications, *America*, *Commonweal*, and *The Catholic World* (Leckey 1992, 76), the Catholic Poetry Society had headquarters in New York City; its purpose was to foster the Catholic poetic movement and advance American art and culture. Given this impetus for Catholic writers, Jessica Powers met publishers like Frank Sheed and Maisie Ward; she formed a friendship with Clifford Laube. Although Powers already had had some poetry published in the *New York Times*, these contacts would promote the publication of selected works.

For most of these New York years, Powers lived with philosopher Anton Pegis and his wife, Jessica; she had met the Pegises during her year at Marquette University. Ultimately, her continuing exploration of the inner life and the influence of the Carmelite spirituality of John of the Cross and Teresa of Avila led her to a Carmelite monastery in Milwaukee. As a direct result of a retreat guided by Father Charles Connors, a Jesuit, Powers wrote to Mother Paula at the newly established Milwaukee monastery asking for admission (Leckey 1992, 105). Powers had doubted she could join the Carmelites, being then thirty-one, very poor, and not in the best health given the family history of tuberculosis, but Mother Paula, who had read Powers's poetry, saw in her the spirit that would be consonant with Carmelite life. On June 24, 1941, Powers entered the Carmelite monastery, eventually receiving the name Sister Miriam of the Holy Spirit. This name, too, shapes the poetry and the inscape of her life: "The dominating force in the life and poetry of Jessica Powers is the doctrine of Divine Indwelling, the life of the Blessed Trinity within her soul" (Geigel 1961, 55). Indeed, the next forty-seven years of that life were never without rigors and never without the "acres of God's mercy" that she continued to till and reproduce in poetry.

As she described it, Powers's purpose in writing was to sing all praise and thanksgiving for our "good God's loving mercy." In keeping with that wish, her final work, *Selected Poetry of Jessica Powers*, which she compiled with editors Bishop Robert Morneau and Sister Regina Siegfried and completed in 1988 just before her death, opens with poems under the theme of the mercy of God and ends with "Doxology," a poem praising the Trinity. Powers wrote over four hundred poems, nearly three hundred of which have been published in a variety of periodicals, including *America*, *Commonweal*, and *Sign*. In all likelihood she would have written and published more poetry, but during some of her years as a contemplative nun she did not have the leisure and for a time she did not believe, much like her poetic compatriot, Gerard Manley Hopkins, a Jesuit priest, that writing poetry was consistent with her vocation as a contemplative nun.

Powers's other books of poetry include *The Lantern Burns* (1939), *The Place of Splendor* (1946), *The Little Alphabet* (1955), *Mountain Sparrow* (1972),

Journey to Bethlehem (1980), and *The House at Rest* (1984). Published in 1989 by Sheed and Ward, *Selected Poetry of Jessica Powers* was reissued in 1999 by ICS Publications. In the introduction to this volume, editor Robert Morneau writes,

> Jessica Powers is an artist, painting in words the movements of the heart, the aspirations of the soul, the homelessness of a pilgrim people, the joys and sufferings of the mystic, the song and dance of those in love, the beauties of creation. The reader of her verse will pause for a deep look into the solitude of God's presence, will be drawn, through wonder and awe, to sigh before the voluminous garments of God's mercy [a reference to Powers's poem "The Garments of God"], will smile at the poet's claim that inebriation occurs in the name of courtesy to a God who offers too much potent goodness. (xiii–xiv)

(Morneau's last line here refers to another of Powers's poems, "But Not With Wine.")

These themes of Powers's poetry are grounded in spiritual experiences, not limited to the Catholic or to the cloistered nun but extending to the contemplative level of human nature. The contemplative in Jessica Powers's poetry is evidenced on three levels, paralleling the three major geographical locations and poetic periods of her life. These three levels I identify as the "natural contemplative"—dominating Powers's Wisconsin farm years from 1916 to 1937 and presenting poetry primarily of the external world; the "poetic contemplative"—most evident from 1937 to 1941, when Powers was truly a social justice mystic; and the "monastic contemplative"—seen from 1941 to 1988, the years Powers was a Carmelite nun. Because her poetry can reach the human heart and speak to the common journey of humanity, her writings remain contemporary and worth exploration. *Selected Poetry of Jessica Powers*, which includes many later revisions of earlier poems, provides a rediscovery of Jessica Powers, and for many to whom she was unknown, an introduction to the poetry of a twentieth-century mystic.

MAJOR THEMES

Jessica Powers continues the tradition of the celebration of nature that many of America's eighteenth- and nineteenth-century writers began. Powers, however, brings contemporary readers a sense of mysticism and of the place of contemplative religious life, a particular gift to religion and literature in America. Powers's rendering of the paradoxical imagery of inner and outer geography is precisely why she has a voice that needs to be heard by contemporary readers in a world so advanced scientifically and technologically yet facing voids that can only be satisfied in the realm of the spiritual.

The American landscape, and specifically the Wisconsin of rich glacial soil and topography composed of plains, stream-cut plateaus, and large areas of erosion-worn bluffs, was unlike any geography known to European mystics. The expansiveness of the United States and its relative wilderness remaining uncharted in the waning decades of the nineteenth century provided a unique mystical world for a woman with the vision to fathom that world and with the sense of a poet to convey what she saw. Furthermore, Powers had a distinct sense of winter, the kinds of winters known firsthand from life in the upper Midwest. Powers captures this metaphor of winter, this harsh, cold season demanding strength of will and firm belief in the return of spring, as a unique metaphor for the spiritual life. Lines from her poem "Wisconsin Winter" demonstrate the metaphor:

> Climate, declared a holy man, can be
> a purification;
> climate, atonement for the sins of all.
> Taken with love, or even resignation,
> it can make potent pleading for God's grace.
>
> Snowflake and snowdrift, ice and icicle,
> frost on the wall, frost on the windowpane,
> frost when my breath edges a scarf with lace:
>
> These are the coins of silver we collect
> for others and ourselves. It may well be
> that this year will yield fortunes we can pour
> into the treasury... (*Selected Poetry*, 164)

The speaker in this poem makes concrete the theological concepts of sin and atonement in linking these with the winter that Powers knew in all its dimensions. The role of the contemplative is to be in such total union with the divine that the human person becomes illuminator and intercessor of divine love. Living in the harshness of winter with love or even resignation, the speaker asserts, is a "potent pleading for God's grace"; such metaphors most clearly define Powers's ability to integrate the spirituality of her Carmelite predecessors with the natural landscape and philosophical and spiritual climate she knew best in rural Wisconsin.

Two poems, "Petenwell Rock" and "Old Bridge," provide representative examples of Powers's early period of imagery solidly based in the natural surroundings. At the Petenwell reservoir, a twenty-five mile drive from Powers's home, "a huge rock guarded the dance hall like some pre-historic monolith" (Leckey 1992, 56). In "Petenwell Rock," the speaker is not unlike Powers, who on her first visit lingered outside the dance hall, absorbing the energy of the stars and dance rhythms alike (56). The speaker is attending a country dance; leaving the dance, she muses,

> ... Out of a long black road there bloomed this bright
> portion of revel, near
> a tall pine-wreathed rock, as certain as a wall.
>
> ... where dancers swayed like songs, and music bellowed
> its anger against grief; and laughter flying
> fell on my ears like sounded waterfall.
>
> But overhead the whip-poor-wills were crying,
> crowding all loneliness into one cry,
> and a great rock maintained a wise old silence,
> lifting its strength into the starlit sky.
>
> O silver loneliness!
>   O golden laughter!
> O grief that only loneliness should last!
> Madness will die, and youth will hurry after.

Into some shadowed past
dancers will bow like dust; laughter will crumble,
while still beneath the silver of the moon
for loveliness and joy that died too soon
these plaintive birds will cry,
and this tall rock will watch with calm indifference,
holding itself aloof against the sky. (103)

The mood is not unlike that expressed in the poetry of Edwin Arlington Robinson or Robert Frost; the American landscape is evident in both. Powers, though, possessed a growing spirituality that would move beyond the physical world's indifference. Her inner restlessness would be sated only by that which would endure longer than the great rock that maintained its silence.

"Old Bridge," a second poem highlighting the landscape of Powers's home, opens with the speaker recalling childhood fears that the "ogre wait[ed] under it [the bridge]" and ends with the acknowledgment that the childish fears are fled in the wisdom of experience, "yet I find / that worse than ogres are the dark shapes crouched/lurking beneath the bridges of my mind" (104). The speaker's anxieties are dissipated when she goes "bold enough to peer and pry, seeking the monster, finding peace instead." Even in this early work, Powers articulates powerful human experiences like those when we must confront the dark shapes within.

"The Granite Woman," written in 1929, exemplifies the ways the natural world blended seamlessly for Powers into the metaphysical. This brief lyric portrays a woman whose mind "[that] bore earth's agony so long" and who is no stranger to the rough demands of physical toil. The poem's final stanza exclaims, "Her heart that shut its doors on love's wide calling / that was as granite where the storms begin, / would break beneath the weight of petals falling / out of the music of this violin" (62). Here the inner life of the future contemplative is evident in the "heart that shut its doors on love's wide calling"; the solitary heart, though, even in its granite steeled against suffering, when permeated by the love of the Beloved and the tempering of suffering, can break under the weight of petals falling. The granite woman provides an apt metaphor for the American woman of the late 1920s and of the onset of the Great Depression, the woman who so often needed to serve in stoic perseverance.

Viewed in this way, Jessica Powers emerges as a New World mystic, as Regina Siegfried defines the mysticism seen in the United States. Powers repeatedly uses the landscape of America with its vastness and variety as a metaphor for the relationship of humans to the divine. This portrayal of the physical world as a conduit to the metaphysical is one of the New World mystics' primary characteristics. Siegfried includes Powers along with others such as Annie Dillard, Ralph Waldo Emerson, the Quakers, and the Shakers as being "rooted in the ordinary with a consistent, conscientious seeing of the sacred" (1993). Herein lies another of the distinctive gifts of Powers to American literature. Jessica Powers lived first as a child of a farming family; eventually she became a Carmelite nun, living a cloistered life for over forty-seven years in the Carmel established first in Milwaukee and later in Pewaukee, Wisconsin. Her life in the convent, seemingly hidden from the world, was ordinary; her blending of the mysticism of the natural world based in the distinctive Wisconsin landscape with the mysticism of Catholic and

Carmelite spirituality yielded poetry. This poetry voices the feminine, the agrarian, the woman religious, and the "new world" of the twentieth-century United States.

During the years of her urban experience in New York and Chicago, Powers wrote a number of significant poems; these blended the images she witnessed in the streets and in a nation on the verge of entering World War II with her developing Carmelite spirituality. In the poem "Human Winter," the speaker struggles with the insufferable coldness with which humans treat one another: "So chilled am I by this presence of human winter / I cannot speak or move" (113). The poem is rich in winter imagery—the "wind of inclement glances," "their frost too subtle to forestall," and "[W]ords fall in slow icy rain and freeze / upon the heart's sudden dismantled trees." The winters in nature were part of the fabric of Powers's experience; her inner eye translated these natural winters to express coldness on the metaphysical level. "Human Winter," composed in 1939 or 1940 before Powers entered Carmel, maintains an immediacy of imagery enlivened through the contemplation of nature, of the external world.

In "The Master Beggar," Powers employs the extended metaphor of God as a beggar on the corner. Powers sees, though, in the ordinary of life, in the homeless and poor wandering the New York streets, a Master beggar, Jesus of Nazareth. The speaker asks the great question of the spiritual life, "Jesus, my beggar, what would You have of me?" In answer to her own question, the speaker ultimately realizes, "I too would be a beggar. Long tormented, / I dream to grant You all and stand apart / with You on some bleak corner, tear-frequented, / and trouble mankind for its human heart" (23). Here, as in "Human Winter" and also in "The Masses," in which the speaker asserts, "my passion was to be / mother of the masses, claiming by some small right of anguish / this piteous and dear humanity" (90), the compassion of the true contemplative dominates the imagery. Here, too, Siegfried's characterization of New World mystics as those going beyond a privatized spirituality into a communal context is evident.

In one further social justice theme, Powers offers the paradox of the contemplative in response to war. It was 1941 when she entered a Carmelite monastery in Milwaukee; in that same year, Thomas Merton became a Trappist monk and Dorothy Day set herself up in an unpopular role as a prophetic witness endorsing pacifism and renouncing United States mobilization plans for war (Kappes 1994, 61). Powers's poem "This Generation of War," from *The Place of Splendor* (1946), gives both a poet and future contemplative nun's response.

> Now is the moment most acceptable
> To enter the soul's peace, to rise and go
> Into the vast illuminated silence
> Of regions that the saints and mystics know.
>
> Let it be said of us: They found God dwelling
> Deep in their souls to which they fled from pain.
> Let it be written on the stones they grant us
> When peace shall deign to walk the earth again:
>
> These found the hidden places of the tempest
> In the soul's fastness, in its long sweet lull,
> A generation of the inward vision
> Whose outward glance became intolerable. (*Place of Splendor*, 34)

That vision of the outer world in the midst of World War II was indeed "intolerable"; Powers, Merton, and others entering contemplative life chose prayer as an answer to the rising tide of world aggression. They found the hidden places of the tempest in "the soul's fastness." And as "they found God dwelling deep in their souls" they became, like Powers's speaker in "The Little Nation," "citizen[s] of love, / that little nation with the blood-stained sod / where even the slain have power"; they were of "the only country / that sends forth an ambassador to God" (*Selected Poetry*, 39).

Particularly during her years as a Carmelite nun, Powers lived within a rather limited external geography, so that the natural environment was interior. The interior world, a rich one for the mystic poet, engendered Powers's strongest images. A frequent one is the thousand acres of God as compared to the small or limited acre of human beings. A Carmelite nun who knew and lived with Jessica Powers (Sister Miriam), first as one of her novices, describes how the importance of those acres never stopped being paramount for Powers:

> Her entry into Carmel was, within the literal, natural truth, into a small house on Wells St. in Milwaukee that had been remodeled to serve as a convent. Thus, the "refectory" [dining room] was also the kitchen and the council room. Each of the other rooms, in other words, doubled and/or tripled in service. . . . The grounds, incidentally, were also quite limited to a modest backyard, hardly offering space to roam and explore like Cat Tail Valley. . . . She adjusted beautifully, but not without pain. Her adjustment was possible because her inner world was expanding due partially to and probably triggered by the experience of having her own surroundings contracting. (unpublished letter to the author from Sister Mary Joyce King, O. C. D., August 3, 2002)

Robert Morneau, who besides coediting *Selected Poetry* has written extensively on Powers's poetry, suggests in his essay "The Spirituality of Jessica Powers" (1990, 159) that readers can apply the following words of Richard Sewall in a description of Emily Dickinson likewise to Jessica Powers:

> There is a paradox here, of course. She [Emily Dickinson] knew very well that the landscape of the spirit—the inner life—needed a tongue, and no one surpassed her in getting at its truth. She is simply saying, "There's no need to tell you I love you; while I breathe, I do." It is when she says, "I tell you what I see," that she describes her purpose as a poet of both lives, inner and outer. As the poet of the inner life, her dedication to this kind of truth led her to insights of the most penetrating kind, epiphanies of the moral and spiritual life; as poet of the external world, she caught its evanescences and its permanent realities with matchless precision. (1974, 611)

Powers also knew very well that the "landscape of the spirit—the inner life—needed a tongue." In a 1970 letter, she wrote, "We waste time (well, not really waste) in doing all the dull mundane duties, and beautiful thoughts are laid aside, thoughts that could change lives and lift up the world."[1] While Powers may not have "told out her inner journey" with the forthrightness of Dickinson, and without the terse, compact verse that so typifies Dickinson's unique style, Powers offers a voice of twentieth-century inscape, voicing the landscape of the spirit.

Gerard Manley Hopkins coined the word "inscape," a term that best describes the mystic and contemplative sides of Jessica Powers's poetry. W. H. Gardner, in the introduction to *Gerard Manley Hopkins: Selected Poems and Prose*, presents Hopkins's definition of inscape as "a name for that 'individually-distinctive' form (made up of various sense-data) which constitutes the rich and revealing 'oneness' of the natural object" (1953, xx). Hopkins expresses this meaning of inscape in his Sonnet 34: "Each mortal thing does one thing and the same: / Deals out that being indoors each one dwells" (Gardner 1953, 51). Powers grounds her poetry and sense of inscape in the Catholic monastic world, as the titles of several of her poems evince: "The House at Rest," "The Place of Splendor," "Doxology." In each poem the motif recurs: "God fills my being to the brim / with floods of His immensity. / I drown within a drop of Him / whose sea-bed is infinity" (*Selected Poetry*, 191).

Carmelite spirituality is exemplified most clearly in John of the Cross and Teresa of Avila. These spiritual founders of the Carmelite order speak of the "dark night of the soul" and the demand of surrender to a love greater than any human love. The primary means of achieving the surrender and the ultimate union with the divine love is the contemplative life. Powers's poem "This Trackless Solitude" displays the path and guides for the spiritual odyssey:

> Deep in the soul the acres lie
> of virgin lands, of sacred wood
> where waits the Spirit. Each soul bears
> this trackless solitude.
>
> The Voice invites, implores in vain
> the fearful and the unaware;
> but she who heeds and enters in
> finds ultimate wisdom there.
>
> The Spirit lights the way for her;
> bramble and brush are pushed apart.
> He lures her into wilderness
> but to rejoice her heart.
>
> Beneath the glistening foliage
> the fruit of love hangs always near,
> the one immortal fruit: *He is*
> or, tasted: *He is here.* (6)

As the poem continues, Powers expresses the primary reason for the journey: Love. She concludes with lines that again reinforce the inscape discovered: "The soul that wanders, Spirit led, / becomes, in His transforming shade, / the secret that she was, in God, / before the world was made" (6). Much of the poem's imagery—the acres of the soul, the brambles and brush, the glistening foliage— appears repeatedly in her poetry and reflects her rural Wisconsin background. The Spirit, "Love," is the compelling force and the ultimate and "immortal fruit." Only those who "enter in" or who can be lured into wilderness will find the ultimate wisdom. And the journeyer must know that this is "trackless solitude," an image appealing to several senses, particularly auditory. Inscape of soul is won through the paradoxes of emptying, suffering, and of journeying to desert places.

Powers learned these spiritual demands in probing and imitating the lives of Teresa of Avila and John of the Cross.

The image of tracklessness, as in the poem "This Trackless Solitude," appears frequently in Powers's poetry. In addition to this metaphor of unchartability, apt to both the American landscape and the inner spirit of humans, there is the anguish of the soul in search, which Powers explored in "Night of Storm":

> *The times are winter.* Thus a poet signed
> our frosty fate. Life is a night of snow.
> We see no path before us, nor behind;
> Our faithless footprints from our own heels blow.
> Where can an exile out of heaven go,
> with murk and terror in a trackless place
> and stinging bees swept down upon his face?
>
> *Or what is else? There is your world within.*
> and now the soul is supplicant: O most
> wretched and blind, come home! Where love has been
> burns the great lantern of the Holy Ghost.
> Here is His light, review your world of frost:
> a drifting miracle! What had been night
> reels with unending eucharists of light. (36)

This poem exemplifies the range of Powers's imagery that simultaneously blends the natural and the metaphysical worlds. The "trackless place" and "stinging bees" are concrete realities of the physical world and address the challenges of the journey; the "great lantern of the Holy Ghost," the calling homeward, and the night that "reels with unending eucharists of light" express profoundly the metaphysical world that rarely can be communicated except through symbolic, poetic language. Note the winter metaphors as well: "Life is a night of snow / We see no path before us, nor behind; / Our faithless footprints from our own heels blow."

When, to exterior perception, Powers in her years as a Carmelite nun might have appeared close to God, her poetry identifies the dark night of the suffering that she experienced in the rigors of the Carmelite life of poverty, the cloister, the extensive hours of prayer, and the manual labor. One of her most significant poems, "The Garments of God," captures Powers's experience and articulates the integral relationship of poetry and faith, a relationship that the prioress who encouraged her to write recognized in Powers:

> God sits on a chair of darkness in my soul.
> He is God alone, supreme in His majesty.
> I sit at His feet, a child in the dark beside Him;
> my joy is aware of His glance and my sorrow is tempted
> to nest on the thought that His face is turned from me.
> He is clothed in the robes of His mercy, voluminous
>   garments—
> not velvet or silk and affable to the touch,
> but fabric strong for a frantic hand to clutch,
> and I hold to it fast with the fingers of my will.

Here is my cry of faith, my deep avowal
to the Divinity that I am dust.
Here is the loud profession of my trust.
I need not go abroad
to the hills of speech or the hinterlands of music
for a crier to walk in my soul where all is still.
I have this potent prayer through good or ill:
here in the dark I clutch the garments of God. (21)

The repetition of the word "clutch," with the harsh consonants linguists label "affricatives," conveys a sense of the speaker's dark night; at the same time, the speaker reiterates Powers's sense of God's mercy. The garments of God are strong fabric for "a frantic hand to clutch." They can be held with the "fingers of [one's] will." This poem was first written in 1945 and was revised in 1984, only four years before Powers's death. Its themes bookend her spiritual journey in Carmel.

Powers's poetry in her final period exhibits what T. S. Eliot recognized as the strength of the tradition of mysticism: "It does not presuppose merely an interior and personal experience, but also a rigorously austere and impersonal understanding or grasp of the Truth" (quoted in Murray 1991, 27). "Pure Desert," another poem of this period, displays many images of self-abnegation leading to ultimate fulfillment. The poem's headnote, from Padre Pio, states "The more one runs in the spiritual life the less tired one gets":

This is pure Gobi desert, you declare;
I see, past sandstorms (of exaggeration)
and rage of flesh at ghostly motivation,
pink health invade your prayer.

Pure desert, you complain, though now you walk
where once had shuffled through the arid miles.
Sighting a day of flight, I shelve my smiles
and share your pilgrim talk.

All true ascesis as a desert lies:
hot wind, hot sand, no water, and no way.
The ego agonizes through each day.
Freedom is when it dies.

I coax you onward: soon, first breeze of bliss;
soon, sun that scorches cooled to sun that warms.
Your youth will dance when shady lanes lock arms
with each green oasis. (154)

Again the images are powerful: hot wind, hot sand, no water, no way, and arid miles, and the repetition of "pure desert." Louis Martz, in *The Poetry of Meditation*, describes the kind of poetry that Powers has engendered as

intense, imaginative meditation that brings together the senses, the emotions, and the intellectual faculties of man; brings them together in a moment of dramatic, creative experience.... Meditative style, then, is "current language heightened," molded to express the unique being of an individual who has learned by intense mental discipline, to live his life in the presence of divinity.[2]

As Martz speaks of the "'current language heightened,' molded to express the unique being of an individual," he is articulating another description of inscape exemplified in Powers's poetry.

CRITICAL RECEPTION

Particularly because Jessica Powers has only become more widely known since the 1989 publication of *Selected Poetry of Jessica Powers*, criticism of her work is limited. Previous to her entrance to Carmel, reviews of her poetry appeared most often in Catholic periodicals. Since the mid-1980s, Regina Siegfried (1993) and Robert Morneau (1990) have both written extensively on Powers; both have approached the works primarily from the theological perspective, although Morneau has done comparative studies of the poetry of Emily Dickinson, Gerard Manley Hopkins, and Jessica Powers. The Jessica Powers Symposium, held at Marquette University in August 1989, produced a collection of criticism from a range of backgrounds, including Carmelite spirituality. The works from the Symposium are housed, as are the majority of the Jessica Powers papers, in the Archives of Marquette University. I have published two examinations of Powers's poetry: "The Paradox of Contemplation: The Poetry of Jessica Powers" (1998) and "Who Speaks for Winter? Jessica Powers: Poet and Mystic" (2002).

NOTES

Jessica Powers, *The Selected Poetry of Jessica Powers* (Washington, DC: ICS Publications, 1999), and *Place of Splendor* (New York: Cosmopolitan Science and Art Services, 1946). All references are to these editions. All copyrights, Carmelite Monastery, Pewaukee, WI. Used with permission.

1. Unpublished letter to Sister Regina Siegfried, February 14, 1970 (Jessica Powers Papers, Marquette University Archives, Milwaukee, WI).

2. Sister Regina Siegfried cited these words of Martz from *The Poetry of Meditation* (New Haven, CT: Yale University Press, 1954) in a lecture as part of the August 26, 1989, symposium on Jessica Powers held at Marquette University. The text may be found at www.spondee.net/JessicaPowers/interprt.html.

WORKS CITED

Gardner, W. H., ed. 1953. *Gerard Manley Hopkins: Selected Poems and Prose*. New York: Penguin Books.

Geigel, Winifred F. 1961. "A Comparative Study of the Poetry of Jessica Powers and St. John of the Cross" (master's thesis, St. John's University, Collegeville, MN).

Kappes, Marcianne, C. S. T. 1994. *Track of the Mystic: The Spirituality of Jessica Powers*. Kansas City, MO: Sheed and Ward.

Leckey, Dolores R. 1992. *Winter Music: A Life of Jessica Powers*. Kansas City, MO: Sheed and Ward.

Morneau, Robert F. 1990. "The Spirituality of Jessica Powers." *Spiritual Life* 36 (Fall): 150–60.

Murray, Paul. 1991. *T. S. Eliot and Mysticism: The Secret History of Four Quartets.* New York: St. Martin's.

Sewall, Richard B. 1974. *The Life of Emily Dickinson.* New York: Farrar, Straus, Giroux.

Siegfried, Regina, A. S. C. 1993. "New World Mystics: The Wisdom of Jessica Powers and Others" (audiocassette). Liguori, MO: Redemptorist Pastoral Communications.

Warner, Mary, S. S. N. D. 1998. "The Paradox of Contemplation: The Poetry of Jessica Powers." *Christianity and Literature* 47 (Spring): 295–307.

———. 2002. "Who Speaks for Winter? Jessica Powers: Poet and Mystic." *Renascence* 54, no. 4 (Summer): 235–46.

BIBLIOGRAPHY

Boudreau, Richard. "A Meadow Moreover: The Wisconsin Poems of Jessica Powers." In *Jessica Powers Symposium: Proceedings of the Symposium in Milwaukee, Wisconsin, August 26, 1989*, 8–13. Milwaukee, WI: Marquette University, 1989.

Kavanaugh, Kieran. "Jessica Powers in the Tradition of St. John of the Cross: Carmelite and Poet." *Spiritual Life* 36 (Fall 1990): 161–65.

Morneau, Robert F. Introduction to *Selected Poetry of Jessica Powers*. Kansas City, MO: Sheed and Ward, 1989.

———. *Jessica Powers: Mantras from a Poet.* Kansas City, MO: Sheed and Ward, 1991.

———. *A Retreat with Jessica Powers.* Cincinnati, OH: St. Anthony Messenger Press, 1995.

Nuns of the Pewaukee Carmel, Wisconsin. "Sister Miriam of the Holy Spirit, O. C. D." *Carmelite Digest* 4 (Summer 1989): 8–12.

Siegfried, Regina, A. C. S. "Jessica Powers: The Paradox of Light and Dark." *Studia Mystica* 7 (Spring 1984): 28–45.

— Mary Warner

Piers Paul Read [1941–]

A Season in the West

BIOGRAPHY

Piers Paul Read, the English novelist, writer of investigative nonfiction, and biographer, is the third son of the poet and critic Sir Herbert Read and his wife Margaret, nee Ludwig. He was born in Beaconsfield, in Buckinghamshire, in 1941, but the family soon moved to Yorkshire, his father's native county, where he spent his childhood and adolescence and was educated by Benedictine monks at Ampleforth College. After reading history at St. John's College, Cambridge University, he spent two years in Germany, working briefly in publishing, and joined the *Times Literary Supplement* as a subeditor on his return to England. In 1967 he married Emily Booth, and they have two sons and two daughters. Read's first novel, *Game in Heaven with Tussy Marx*, was published in 1966, followed by *The Junkers* (1968), *Monk Dawson* (1969), *The Professor's Daughter* (1971), *The Upstart* (1973), *Polonaise* (1976), *A Married Man* (1979), *The Villa Golitsyn* (1981), *The Free Frenchman* (1986), *A Season in the West* (1988), *On the Third Day* (1990), *A Patriot in Berlin* (1995), *Knights of the Cross* (1997), and *Alice in Exile* (2001). He has also written a number of works of nonfiction and plays for television and radio, and he is currently working on the authorized biography of an eminent fellow Catholic, the recently deceased English actor Sir Alec Guinness. Piers Paul Read is a past Chairman of the Catholic Writers' Guild (the Keys). A Fellow of the Royal Society of Literature, he sits on its council and that of the Society of Authors. He is an active Catholic layman who has served as governor for two Catholic schools in London, where he lives, and is on the English board of the international Catholic charity Aid to the Church in Need.

PLOT SUMMARY

The action of *A Season in the West* takes place very largely in the London of the 1980s. Josef Birek, a young Czech dissident writer, has crossed through Yugoslavia into Austria, asking the British embassy there to allow him to go to England. His British admirers support him, and his English translator, Laura

Morton, who has also written an essay on his work and has a job at the Comenius Foundation, a London institution for Czech exiles, is both delighted and slightly alarmed by his imminent arrival. A nice, but rather naive, well-preserved thirty-nine-year-old woman with three children, married to a merchant banker, she is as thrilled as if the hero of a favorite novel were coming to lunch next day. They meet at the airport, and Laura is struck by what, in her essay, she called "the poetic certainty of his unabashed naivety" and his childlike fascination with the new world around him. She is much more interested in the connection between his stories and his private life than in his political beliefs, and she wonders how long it will be before she can broach such personal matters. At the reception given for him at her rather grand London house, Birek is the center of attention because, although most of the Mortons' rich friends have no real interest in a Czech dissident, he wants to know all about their lives. He explains the constant tension in Czechoslovakia between professional conscience and the demands of the regime, made in the name of the Marxist-Leninist ideology no one has believed in since the 1968 rising. Laura tells him that the translator only knows what the author chooses to reveal, but what little she knows only makes her want to know more. At this stage, he is keener to talk about various types of freedom to the Mortons' social and banking acquaintances, pointing out that the Church is the leader of the opposition in his country and that despite all its faults he remains a Catholic.

In the Mortons' sexually rather free-wheeling circle of friends, one particular serial seducer, Charlie Eldon, is making an unhurried, deliberate, and calculated play for the rather guileless Laura. The sexual politics of her circle are counterpointed by the play for power in Birek's Czechoslovakia. Both his grandfather and his father have been dissidents in their own way and to some degree, which perhaps accounts for his rather odd ideological and philosophical position.

Wandering around London on his first night alone in the city, Birek is amazed and intoxicated by its wealth and cosmopolitan nature and disturbed by its heartless overt commercial eroticism. The next day, he is invited to lunch by Charlie Eldon and meets the inner circle of a group of rich and posturing English writers who talk about nothing but money and sex, their book deals, the women they have had, and sexually transmitted diseases.

After a superficial interview at the Home Office, and thanks to Laura's blandishments and the efforts of Charlie Eldon, who still hopes to seduce her, Birek is granted political asylum and a publisher is sought for his novel. Eventually Laura, in a mixture of maternal tenderness and vague amorousness, persuades her husband to let the young man stay in their London house, using the bedroom of their son Johnny, who is away at boarding school. He moves in, enchanted by the contrast between their home and the squalid hostel he has lived in. Laura, busy on the translation of his novel, needs to consult him frequently. The meetings lead to lunch together while Francis, her husband, is at work, and discussion of the emotions of Birek's characters lead to erotic wonderings.

At Risley, the family country house where they spend some time, a local woman friend suggests to Laura that Francis has a mistress. As a kind of unspoken riposte, she decides to ask Birek down for a weekend. On the evening of their return home, at a time when the young Czech is lonely and his thoughts are turning more and more toward her, Birek overhears a minor domestic quarrel and realizes that Laura is glad to see him. With a light kiss, she invites him down to Risley for the following weekend.

Later, when they are back in London, she returns one afternoon from a lunch date and comes to his room, ostensibly to tell him, as gently as possible, that the agent for his novel has turned him down and the potential publisher is not interested. Author and translator console each other with gentle caresses, and the inevitable result, the first of many such rapturous occasions, is cunningly and connivingly brought about. The pair gradually become careless, however, and suspicions are aroused in friends. Charlie Eldon, in fact, is well aware of what is happening, as Laura half-delightedly knows. So too is her husband, who has no more idea what to do about the situation than he has about the dangers thrown up by a major upheaval in the banking world. Laura even becomes jealous of her fifteen-year-old daughter Belinda, who flirts bashfully with Birek, afraid of the humiliating contrast between her own no longer totally youthful features and body and the girl's adolescent beauty.

With the family safely out of the way at Risley for the summer, Laura goes home frequently, having established a routine of visits to the Comenius Foundation followed by a picnic lunch with Birek in her library and sex upstairs. Gradually, their love turns from passion to an affectionate melancholy. Birek develops a deep distaste for Laura's rich friends. At a smart party at Diston, the country house of a couple Laura knows, he drinks heavily to cope with his intense loneliness and boredom. Some guests pretend to take him for a waiter and he is ordered about as a joke. Very drunk, he finally vomits into a silver dish half full of scrambled eggs.

The affair slowly cools, and Laura's teenage children continue to refer to Birek, who has accompanied them on the family holiday on Corfu, as "the waiter." Once they are all back in London, Birek moves out into a cheap apartment, found and paid for by Laura through the Comenius Foundation. Sex between them becomes rapid and almost casual. Birek loses all his attraction as a social asset, since his novel is unpublishable, and his romantic status as a lover to be discreetly paraded on social occasions is consequently lessened. The last straw is when Laura's Mercedes is vandalized outside his squalid apartment. In her anger and disappointment, Laura stops paying Birek's rent and writes to say that she will not see him any more. The postage, she reflects, is the last sum of money she will ever spend on him. He tries to contact her and finds that she has left the country. He is dunned for arrears of rent and goes to ground, wretched, lost, penniless, and miserable.

In his early days in London, Birek had once attended, more by accident than design, what he had thought was a Catholic Mass but was in fact a Church of England service, receiving and turning down afterward, in the parish hall, a distinctly odd invitation to lunch. He goes back again, is given a great deal of mulled wine and invited once more to a louche all-male lunch, and is the appalled victim of an attempted but unsuccessful homosexual seduction. His not very robust Catholicism fades, he finds prayer impossible, and he breaks off relations with the Comenius Foundation. He attempts to jump under an underground train but is saved by a compatriot, a driver at the Czech embassy, who recognizes his face from pictures in the papers. He attacks the West at a press conference, returns to Czechoslovakia, and is as useless and unhappy there as he had been in England. Laura is piqued by her return to the dull and virtuous role previously thrust upon her, and she vainly tries to renew Charlie Eldon's interest in her. She grows abrupt with her husband, Francis, who realizes that once their youngest child, Lucy, is a year or two older, he will have to do without any gestures of human affection.

MAJOR THEMES

From a structural and thematic point of view, *A Season in the West* is a straightforward and unproblematic work, and the ordinary reader with no particular literary pretensions sees immediately and clearly what it is about and how it is presented. The topic is the ancient one of desire transcending barriers of culture, class, nationality, and wealth, of an affair between a woman enjoying the privileges provided by power, money, and prestige and a young, poor, but attractive man from a very different background. In older European terms, it is that of the princess and the peasant, or in modern American terms, that of the uptown matron and the younger downtown boy, or the woman from a background of old money and a young immigrant. The situation is presented, described, and analyzed in a straightforward way in a well-written, articulate, and unpretentious narrative style, without the fashionable indeterminacy characteristic of certain kinds of modern fiction. It is, in the old-fashioned and nonpejorative sense of the phrase, a good read, an interesting narrative that carries the reader along with it and into the minds and emotions of the characters.

Read is a workmanlike writer, a very competent storyteller with a sharply achieved setting and a deft depiction of social markers, and he uses dialogue effectively to achieve this. The approach, too, is old-fashioned in that it posits an omniscient narrator (a term Read himself actually uses in the novel) who knows and can say what the characters think, feel, and do. There is no need to wonder what Laura, Birek, Francis, Charlie Eldon, and others are experiencing, feeling, and planning, as the author makes their sexual, emotional, and social stances and reactions clear. There is no mystification, no troubling ambiguity. Within the limits of the information provided by the text, we know what is going on. We can of course wonder about aspects of personalities or actions that are not revealed by the narrative or authorial comment, but that is another matter. We have abundant authorial indications, statements, and comments, ranging from observations about a whole range of important and less central characters to the geographical, social, economic, and cultural background of the story, including reflections on market and command economies, Marxist ideologies, and the failings of all three. The novel has a specific, amply described, and fully presented setting. The characters do not move in an individual vacuum but perform social and, in a sense, political, economic, and ideological roles.

The background to their personal relationships is there, but it does not hide, or entirely explain, or assume a greater importance than their individual destinies. A Marxist critic once said that Thomas Hardy's *Tess of the d'Urbervilles* was not the story of an individual young woman but a study of the decline of the English peasantry in the late nineteenth century. Applied here, that kind of simplistic ideological stance would rule out any balanced reading of *A Season in the West*. The background heightens and illuminates the personal situations rather than replacing or dominating them. One thing it does add to the novel, however, is an element of the fable: that is, of a tale that conveys a lesson through a fictional narrative.

Indeed, one very striking quality of Read's writing is its concern with moral themes and perspectives. To a degree, his novels are explorations of the moral lives of his characters and the results of their choices. In this novel, it is Laura's husband and her lover who both reflect on their personal morality and change as a result of it. They are self-critical, increasingly self-questioning and anguished, and they begin to see their lives and destinies in a new way, whereas the fragrant and ladylike Laura seems merely peeved by the situation her actions have led her into. It is important to remember that the novel is called *A Season in the West* and primarily concerns a young, naive Czech dissident rather than Laura's adulterous affair. Although the affair is interestingly and convincingly presented, it is not really the main matter of the novel, which explores other psychological and moral situations and conflicts rather more than the more purely erotic or amatory ones. What it shows, with varying degrees of depth, is the moral development of three different people, and Laura's is the least noticeable. Her story is interestingly and convincingly presented, but it is not Read's sole or perhaps even main concern. There is also the effect of the affair on Birek, which is a contributory cause of his decline and the ultimate loss of the autonomy and freedom he had hoped to find in the West. Read's main concern here is a reflection on the moral life in terms of a specific individual destiny. A moral concern does not, of course, necessarily entail showing meritorious characters coming to impeccably correct conclusions and leading exemplary lives. It can involve something very different from preaching and edifying or instructing by pious exhortation. Moral confusion, mistaken actions, and misguided searching are as legitimate a field of reflection, imagination, and portrayal as praiseworthy progress and enlightenment. The still, sad music of humanity we hear in compelling literature is perhaps more moving in novels involving failure than in those concentrating on success. Since only the wildest optimist would dismiss the adage that it is not given to men to succeed but only to fail honorably, it is not surprising that one of the paradoxes of literature is its fascinating concern with our weaknesses and struggles. Through comment and more indirectly through the words and thoughts of his characters, Read gradually removes the false glamour from Laura's affair and the various other illicit sexual activities in the novel. He also offers a sharp criticism of the opposing ideologies of the East and West. A bonfire of the vanities need not, as we know, be a dull matter. It can often have a sharp and stimulating edge that is more effective than a merely uplifting message.

To some, *A Season in the West* might seem a cynical novel, an ironic tale by a disenchanted and rather world-weary author. It is certainly less than sanguine about society, politics, human motivation and relationships, and contemporary culture, aims, and mores. In the case of the Western characters, any real morality is replaced by a narrow social and sexual code based on habitual practices and a sense of tradition and clan loyalties. Nor are there any powerful aspirations beyond a love of possessions and the preservation of the very satisfactory status quo. Faith, hope, and charity seem to have little or no meaning in the world of the Mortons and their peers. Their Eastern European counterparts in the higher apparatchik echelons of the dying Marxist system, though seen at second hand through Birek's description and with an authorial gloss, are no better.

At one level, the story of a short adulterous affair between a gullible and naive young man and a rather older woman who uses him for her own ends (for her pleasure, her social and sexual status as a woman with a rather appealingly foreign and exotic lover, capable of arousing interest and envy in her female acquaintances) is apparently no more than an amoral if very competent study of sexual psychology. The depiction of the growth, ripening, and decline of desire and satisfaction in two disparate people is set against an amoral but civilized, or at least wealthy and socially acceptable, background of uncaring materialism. The author distances himself from his characters and their background, or at least has little sympathy with their predicament. Yet all is not black. Francis, Laura's cuckolded husband, has the makings of a social conscience, as we see in his anxious self-questioning with regard to the activities of the merchant bank he directs, and he certainly has a desire to see his wife happy (he has allowed her to take a job with the Comenius Foundation, and to save his marriage and his children's happiness he is willing not to take any action on his suspicions about her infidelity). She may use others in the furtherance of her own objectives, as she uses Birek, her children, and her husband, but he does have some thought for her. Birek, young, weak, isolated, and in some ways an inept failure who, in the end, returns to Prague and joins the system he despises, is at least aware of his own failure and humbled by it. Even though Laura remains what she has always been, a charming and attractive but rather unimpressive and spoiled female, there are occasional short-lived and easily suppressed glimmers of self-knowledge, but without any deep self-criticism.

Reactions to the novel will vary. It is fairly easy to see that alongside the picture of an adulterous affair it contains both an ironic, sharp, and unsentimental critique of British (and by extension western) life and society in the late twentieth century and a reflection on that other pole of the sensibility of the time, the cultures and political structures of Eastern Europe. That is fine and no doubt provides an interesting and fruitful source of material for the kind of serious literature any intelligent author might produce. But Read is a particular kind of author. His mind and imagination are informed by a Catholic awareness and understanding of human life in all its aspects. In other words, he is a Catholic writer. Yet although many modern novelists who are also Catholics, such as François Mauriac, Georges Bernanos, G. K. Chesterton, and Sigrid Undset, have accepted that particular label, several others, such as Graham Greene and Heinrich Böll, have not. Presumably the latter two wished to avoid the accusation of writing from a predetermined ideological position, of consistently and overtly putting across the party line or being limited by a ready-made and imposed frame of reference. In connection with *A Season in the West*, it is difficult to say to what extent Read is a Catholic writer in the narrower sense in which Greene dismissively used the term or simply a writer who happens to be a Catholic and in whose work there may be nothing or very little overtly "Catholic." Elsewhere, Read has certainly produced fiction that is more noticeably steeped in evident Catholicism, in which the minds, emotions, and decisions of the characters are deeply influenced by their faith, whether they reject it, temporize with it, or grope blindly toward it. *Monk Dawson*, *A Married Man*, and *On the Third Day* are examples. *A Season in the*

West, however, as well as being the product of a Catholic mind and sensibility, is "catholic" with a lowercase "c" in the sense of universal, a sensibility that includes all that which is not Catholic in the doctrinal or ecclesiastically defined sense. It is the duty of the Church to show us how to live, but it may be the duty of the Catholic writer to show us how deep and almost invincible nonculpable ignorance may be and to help us understand the pathos and anguish of life without faith and the sacraments.

Read has suggested that *A Season in the West* perhaps conveys his Catholic "take"' on life more succinctly than some of his other novels. The overtly Catholic element, in terms of references, ideas, beliefs, practices, sensibilities, and a general frame of reference, varies considerably from novel to novel, and it is hardly a major presence here. There is no trace of any real religious sense or feeling in Laura. Even when the aggressively pious vicar of Risley hectors her on the nature and seriousness of Baptism for her children, there is no religious reaction. All she feels is a strong distaste for his bad manners in raising the topic in such a way. It is also difficult to assess what Birek's Catholicism, firmly proclaimed during an argument at the reception for him at Laura's London home, actually means to him. It certainly does not seem to exercise his mind or inform his sensibility or engage him to any marked degree. He maintains that he is a Catholic because the Church teaches the truth, to which he adheres despite her faults. His feelings about the affair seem to be a compound of adolescent sexuality, idealized worship, and childish dependence, and there is little evidence of any serious conflict between adulterous desire and faith, or any suggestion that he has suspended his religion temporarily to avoid the conflict. Even his confusion, shame, and sense of guilt at the attempted homosexual seduction after the rich luncheon are the products of an immature mixture of mild temptation and strong repulsion rather than any objective sense of right and wrong. Are we to take his Catholicism as being vestigial, merely formal, superficial, or an adolescent fantasy? There is no sense of faith informing a life, or even offering an opposing view of the promptings of the flesh or the ways of the world. No other character, Czech, British, or American, seems to have any kind of religious belief. A reflection on the nature of this particular novel might provide the basis for a reasoned, coherent, and perceptive view of that important aspect of Read's work.

It might be fruitful to consider this work very briefly alongside that thematically similar but otherwise very different Catholic novel, Graham Greene's *The End of the Affair*. Both are works by well-known Catholic authors, both deal with an adulterous affair, both are set in twentieth-century London, both have as central figures a married woman with an assured social background and a lonely writer who is to some extent an odd man out, and both involve the end of a liaison and the characters' reflections on it. Yet Greene's novel is full of Catholic allusions. His heroine is a baptized Catholic, although unaware of it for most of her life, and keeps a diary recording her feelings, ideas, longings, and decisions as she tries to express them in terms of her rediscovered love for God and her fellow human beings. Read's *A Season in the West*, however, is devoid of any such Catholic gloss by a character and contains very few references to Catholicism or attempts to live it. The theme is similar, but the approach, development, and treatment vary. Greene's novel is a reflection on sanctity and a growing awareness of God in both the main characters. Read's novel, on the other hand, could perhaps most accurately be seen as a convincing picture of the world without God, without even a sense of or a vague longing for the spiritual, of the kind of life François Mauriac called "that life which is not Life," of the desert of an existence with no external spiritual focus but only invalid ones such as Mammon or Marxism. It might, however, be taken for an illustration of Augustine's famous dictum in his *Confessions*: "*Fecisti nos ad te et inquietum est cor nostrum donec requiescat in te*" (Thou hast created us for Thyself, and our heart is not quiet until it rests in Thee), where Laura is more like Flaubert's Emma Bovary than Greene's Sarah.

If *A Season In the West* has a fault, it is perhaps an overemphasis on informing the reader. The omniscient author tells too much and lacks the catechetic virtue of economy with the truth. Its attraction lies in its clarity of narration, its sense of real people, and its pity for our vanities and self-delusions and the dissatisfactions they bring, and in the clarity, economy, and effectiveness of an intelligent, articulate, decent writer who suggests the need for wisdom by the portrayal of folly, the need for truth by the presentation of deceit, the need for charity by the lack of real love, and the need for hope by a picture of its absence. There is an added bonus. In this study of sexual maneuvers, desire, adultery, and passion, there is no explicitly described sex. Read does not write pornography, nor does he suggest the need for it by its absence. In this, as in other ways, his working methods are in agreement, no doubt unconsciously and on the basis of personal perceptions rather than authoritative ideological directives, with the advice once given by Pope Pius XII that the Catholic creative writer or artist should not make sin attractive or present it as if it were not sin or present it in appealing or sensual terms.

What most Catholic writers and critics seem to ask for in fiction is intelligence, imagination, perception, and occasionally, profundity and aesthetic competence. What they want is writing that tells the truth as the writer perceives it, and that is what they ask of themselves. That truth is a personal one, caught in its quiddity and idiosyncrasy and revealed effectively to the reader. It is not generally a vision of a better type of social organization or the end of history but a vision of fictional lives in the here and now. Paradoxically, perhaps, the teaching Church has no official literary theory or doctrine and has not seen literature as part of a sustained effort to convert the world. Apart from Cardinal Newman, few modern popes or bishops have written on literature, seeing it largely as an ennobling human activity with no necessary didactic function.

Sin is not attractive in *A Season in the West*. The natural desire that the two lovers feel for each other is in itself to some degree attractive, although it is blemished by selfishness and manipulation. The adultery, lying, manipulation, and cheating that are part of the use to which it is put are not. A gift, promised by Laura exclusively to one person, her husband, is cheapened and degraded by her adultery. In other words, there is nothing wrong with sexual desire in itself and properly used. Laura and her actions are not interesting because she is a free spirit determined to escape from a marriage typified by routine and boredom but because she is an attractive woman who gains sympathy as well as provokes a rueful pity when she gets her life into a muddle. Birek, the dominated rather than the dominant partner throughout the brief liaison, also arouses as much irritation as pity, given his ineptitude and indecisiveness. They are both lost children rather than determined sinners, weak and irresolute rather than exalted, and following their own rebellious wills.

CRITICAL RECEPTION

Read's fiction has always received favorable attention in the more civilized sections of the British press, and reviews of his novels as they appeared have tended to range from the respectful to the enthusiastic.[1] To date, there has been no book devoted to the whole of his work, but articles on his writing in general and on individual novels have frequently appeared in the Sunday broadsheets, the *Times Literary Supplement*, and other serious weeklies for almost forty years. However, perhaps a list of the major prizes Read has won for his novels (two of which, *A Married Man* and *The Free Frenchman*, have been adapted for BBC television) gives a good idea of the critical reputation his fiction has very quickly gained and still enjoys. *The Junkers* won the Sir Geoffrey Faber Memorial Prize, *Monk Dawson* the Hawthornden Prize and the Somerset Maugham Award, and *A Season in the West* the James Tait Black Memorial Prize. In addition, his nonfiction has also attracted very favorable attention, and *Alive*, his account of the survival of a group of young men after a plane crash in the Andes, described by Graham Greene as a masterpiece of narration, was made into a film in 1992.

NOTES

Piers Paul Read, *A Season in the West* (London: Random House, 1988). All references are to this edition.

1. Among Read's other novels, particularly recommended are *Monk Dawson*, *A Married Man*, and *Alice in Exile*. His most interesting works of nonfiction are possibly *Alive* (1974), *Quo Vadis? The Subversion of the Catholic Church* (1991), and *The Templars* (1999). His article "Decline and Fall of the Catholic Novel" (*The London Times*, March 29, 1997) is also of interest.

BIBLIOGRAPHY

Cambridge Guide to Literature in English. Entry on Piers Paul Read's works, 779. Cambridge: Cambridge University Press, 1993.

Crowe, Marian E. "A Modern Psychomachia: The Catholic Fiction of Piers Paul Read." *Christianity and Literature* 47, no. 3 (Spring 1998): 309–29.

Read, Piers Paul. Interview by Valerie Grove. *The London Times* (May 28, 1993): 16

Whitehouse, J. C., ed. *Catholics on Literature*. Dublin: Four Courts Press, 1997.

Woodman, Thomas. *Faithful Fictions: The Catholic Novel in British Literature*. Milton Keynes, England, and Philadelphia, Open University Press, 1991.

— J. C. Whitehouse

Christina Rossetti [1830–1894]

Poems

BIOGRAPHY

Born on December 5, 1830, in London to an Anglo-Italian family that brought together several different elements of religious culture, Christina Georgina Rossetti created a unique poetic voice in synthesizing those elements, although the theology she practiced gave her work its primary depth and color. The richness and variety of her metaphysical ideas, expressed in lyric and dramatic poetry that ranges from the sonnet to the dream vision, are also shown through a less well-known but simultaneously multilayered set of prose works. The imagery that conveys her ideas is always concrete: whether Rossetti's persona speaks in first or third person, or multivocally as in some of her poetic dialogues, Rossetti always emphasizes the importance of explaining spiritual concepts through material and sensory analogies. Although her work has been controversial because of both its adherence to orthodox Christianity and the equally individualistic (even mystical) manner in which that adherence is expressed, it vigorously communicates the tensions inherent in the choices made by the self-struggling person either to maintain his or her identity or to deliberately seek fragmentation. Because Rossetti makes the account of that struggle so vivid, her poetry and prose may be appreciated both by those who share her understanding of Christianity and by those who stand outside of it.

Rossetti was the fourth of four children in the family; her mother, Frances Polidori Rossetti, had been a governess before marrying Gabriele Rossetti, a political exile from Italy and a professor of Italian at King's College. Rossetti's oldest sibling, Maria Francesca, became a writer and eventually an associate in one of the first Anglican sisterhoods, All Saints. Dante Gabriel, her second sibling, both wrote poetry (*The House of Life* was one of his most famous works) and painted several important Pre-Raphaelite works as part of this artistic movement. William Michael, the second youngest in the family, published criticism and biographies of his siblings' and parents' work and lives.

The first publication of Christina Rossetti's work was a collection titled *Verses*, privately published by her maternal grandfather in 1847. In 1849, the newly formed Pre-Raphaelite Brotherhood, which included Dante Gabriel Rossetti as one of its charter members, began to publish a magazine called *The Germ*. It lasted for only four issues but published a few of Christina Rossetti's poems under a pen name. In 1850, Rossetti wrote her first prose fiction, *Maude*, but it remained unpublished until William Michael Rossetti released it posthumously in 1897. In 1854 she attempted to volunteer for the battle-zone hospital established by Florence Nightingale in the Crimea but was turned down because she was considered too young. From 1857 to 1863, she published a series of encyclopedia entries in the *Imperial Dictionary of Universal Biography*; these were her first works widely read outside her circle of family and close friends. In 1859, Rossetti, who never married, began a ten-year stint working as a volunteer at a home and vocational school for ex-prostitutes, St. Mary Magdalene's Penitentiary for Fallen Women (D'Amico 1999, 104). In 1861 her poem "Up-hill" was published by *Macmillan's*, her first contribution to a major literary magazine. The next year saw her first general success with a volume of poetry, *Goblin Market and Other Poems*. The title poem, written in a style accessible to both children and adults, has gained current critical recognition as one of her most important works. In 1866, Rossetti published a second collection, *Poems*, through Roberts Brothers in Boston, the first time she had worked exclusively through a United States publishing firm.

In 1872 and 1874, respectively, Rossetti published a collection of poetry and a set of prose tales aimed at a juvenile audience. *Speaking Likenesses*, a book of three interlocked prose fables for children that included both realistic and "grotesque" characters, was not a success, but *Sing-Song*, a collection of poems readily understood by children but also readable as allegory on an adult level, sold extremely well. In 1881, Rossetti published another important collection of her poetry, *A Pageant and Other Poems*. A notable achievement in this collection is her "crown" or interlocked group of fourteen sonnets, titled *Monna Innominata*, which translates into "My Lady Unnamed" or "My Lady Nameless." Written from a woman's point of view, these sonnets are the first such series in English to reflect on the lives of the women who were celebrated but not named in the sonnet sequences written by the male poets of the Renaissance. Like *Goblin Market*, *Monna Innominata* has received recent critical attention.

In 1881, another kind of creative work by Rossetti, religious writing, saw its first success. The Society for Promoting Christian Knowledge, the chief publisher of religious works by Anglo-Catholics, published a work of Rossetti's titled *Called To Be Saints: The Minor Festivals Devotionally Studied*. Although prose related to the minor festivals of the Anglican church makes up the bulk of this book, *Called To Be Saints* consists of multiple layers of poetry and prose. In 1883, her dual commentary on the Decalogue and the two "great commandments" given by Christ, *Letter and Spirit: Notes on the Commandments*, was published by the same Anglican publishing society. It was followed by the London publication of her book of devotional personal essays, *Time Flies: A Reading Diary*, in 1885. A year later, this book was also released in Boston for the American market.

As Rossetti gained literary success, she suffered a number of significant losses in her personal life. In 1876, her sister Maria Francesca died after spending only two years as a professed associate of All Saints convent. Her brother Dante Gabriel died in 1882, and her mother Frances, with whom she was very close, died in 1886. Christina Rossetti would outlive her mother by only eight years, and the loss was visible in her prose and poetry. The last prose work published in her lifetime, *The Face of the Deep* (1892), is a commentary on the Apocalypse that employs both of these modes of discourse, and both, as Diane D'Amico has pointed out, are used in this text to enshrine mothers (1999, 119, 144). The last collection of Rossetti's poems to appear in her lifetime bore the same simple title as her first, *Verses*.

In 1892, Rossetti underwent surgery for cancer, but by 1893 the cancer had returned and spread (Bell [1898] 1971, 165, 167). She died on December 29, 1894, a few weeks after her sixty-fourth birthday.

MAJOR THEMES

Discussion of the themes in Rossetti's poetry would be incomplete without a study of some of the influences surrounding her in a family whose culture both absorbed and expressed a multiplicity of divergent views. Nothing could be further from the truth than to portray Rossetti as a monoglot speaker, expressing a single theme in her religiously inflected arguments. Although it is true that one form of Anglicanism, the Anglo-Catholicism of the late nineteenth century, was the form of faith that Rossetti, the actual historical character, believed, practiced, and depicted in much of her work, the variety of roles she played as part of the Polidori-Rossetti family gave her a wide and practical experience of how different philosophical positions could coexist, whether confrontationally or peacefully. The Catholic Christianity of her poetry is one of the unifying threads that runs through it, but that statement must be qualified in several ways to provide a useful insight into Rossetti's work.

First of all, while Rossetti's views concurred with those of the Roman Catholic Church in many respects, and at least one of her poems eulogizes the famous convert from High Church Anglicanism to Roman Catholicism, John Henry Newman, she adhered to Anglo-Catholicism herself, as far as can be known from her writings. Although in a few of her poems Rossetti openly acknowledges the divide between Roman Catholicism and Anglo-Catholicism, at least one of them, in *Called To Be Saints*, contrasts the lesser grace of Mary with the fuller grace of Christ in a way that might be considered heterodox in a Roman Catholic context (1881, 193). Second, Anglo-Catholic doctrine is not sharply defined or distinguished from most other forms of Christianity in Rossetti's poetic texts. Certainly, Catholic doctrine forms part of the background to her writing, but most of her metaphysical poetry in the 1911 collection of her poems could be, on its surface, the expressed perspective of any orthodox Christian of the period. The only notable exceptions to this rule are the series of poems that celebrate the decisions of women to enter the religious life of either the cloister or the convent. Many Protestants of the nineteenth century might have regarded such a decision with pity at best or suspicion at worst, but Rossetti portrays it as a way in which a divided or shattered personality may regain some of its integrity. "The Convent Threshold," "Soeur Louise de la Misericorde," and "An Immurata Sister," all told from the perspective of those taking vows, justify the need of the speakers to do so (*Poems by Christina G. Rossetti*, 71, 120, 122).

Finally, even the poems that draw from Christian imagery to articulate themes and practices familiar to Christians of any denomination do not, in general, portray a Christianity unchallenged by competing perspectives, whether from the rebellious soul itself, from the sensual temptations of the outer world, or even from people of other faiths (as in "Christian and Jew" [90]). For the most part, the central figures in the poems move toward a more Christian world view than was theirs before, but the process of struggling through the options they are given is not always a linear progression. Although the individuals in Rossetti's poems share a general search for Christian truth and usually find it, the way it is found changes with each poem. In that sense, while Christian faith and practice provide a common goal and achieving it provides a common experience that can be said to unify Rossetti's poetry, the allegiance to Christianity in the poems is a complicated one.

In considering the question of major themes in Rossetti's work it is necessary first to consider other elements that are present in the context of her formation as an author and then to explain how they are related to the question of her poetry's Catholic Christian thought. Somewhat unusual in the nineteenth century, Rossetti's family embraced an eclectic mix of doctrines. Her maternal grandmother and grandfather exemplify this family trait: Anna Louise Pierce was a practicing Anglican when she married Gaetano Polidori, a Roman Catholic (Packer 1963, 2). Rossetti's mother Frances, the youngest of the daughters in the Polidori family, had two wedding ceremonies when she married Gabriele Rossetti, one Anglican and the other Roman Catholic (5). Gabriele Rossetti, however, showed little evidence of adherence to any organized religious group. His research on Dante Alighieri seems to have been partially concerned with tracing possible influences of Freemasonry on the poet, and this may reflect his own quasi-religious beliefs. His occasional use of religion as material for poetry can also be seen in his volume of religious verse, *L' Arpa Evangelica*, published late in his life. According to Mackenzie Bell, the volume's title translates as *The Evangelic Harp*, and Bell further quotes William Michael Rossetti on his father's beliefs: "in religion he was mainly a freethinker, but tending in his later years to an undogmatic form of Christianity" ([1898] 1971, 6). Still, a large part of Gabriele Rossetti's work was designed, in his son's words, "to prove that Dante, Petrarch and other great writers, were in reality anti-Christians" (quoted in Packer 1963, 5). His wife, who maintained her Anglican beliefs to the end of her life, seems to have understood at least one of her husband's books as a tract against Christianity; according to Packer, she "burned every copy she could find of his *Amor Platonica*, the most anti-Christian of all" (5).

Since so many theological perspectives were represented in the household, the Rossetti children, including Christina, had choices modeled for them for both their personal spirituality and the aesthetic influences they drew from each tradition. Packer's simple, gendered division of the four Rossetti children into the "irreligious" William Michael and Dante Gabriel and the "devout" Christina and Maria (5) is a good beginning for an understanding of Rossetti's beliefs. However, her personae in both her poetry and prose represent a much less conventional set of beliefs than the word "devout" might connote. Much of her metaphysical poetry, like John Donne's and George Herbert's before hers and the roughly contemporary works of Gerard Manley Hopkins, centers around the idea of the soul as wrestler: either it overcomes various temptations to turn away from God or it contends with God himself. In either case, the orthodox perspective confronts its opposite, and the tension of religious opposition is woven into the poetry.

For example, in "The Convent Threshold" (*Poems*, 71) the poem's subject speaks about the resistance she encounters in seeking refuge in the convent. Her human lover, while posing a threat to her religious life ("Your eyes look earthward, mine look up") still attracts and tempts her. "How long shall stretch these nights and days?" she asks, and she still desires to "turn earthwards with a pitiful pang" for her lover's sake. The force attempting to turn the speaker away from the religious life is not simply externalized in the form of the lover's behavior. Most of the poem centers on the speaker's internal struggle between acceptance of religious life without her lover (so that she may experience eternal love) and her despair of ever achieving that acceptance:

> I woke and prayed against my will,
> Then slept to dream of you again
> At length I rose and knelt and prayed
> . . . through the dark my silence spoke
> Like thunder. (76)

Without mentioning the name of God, these lines focus on a conflict with him. Another poem, "Weary in Well-Doing," tells of the same kind of internal conflict, albeit much more simply and directly:

> I would have gone; God bade me stay
> I would have worked; God bade me rest.
> He broke my will from day to day,
> He read my yearnings unexpressed,
> And said them nay. (292)

While the poem cries out to Christ at the end— "When will it be / That I may let alone my toil / And rest with thee?" —there is no certain answer to the question or resolution to the tension of the conflicted soul. "The Convent Threshold" at least provides a possible resolution in its closing lines. The speaker, after recounting her "struggle" with her emotions, envisions her lover with her in the afterlife, "safe within the door" of "Paradise" (76). The suffering entailed in the speaker's renunciation of earthly love has (at least in the speaker's view) worked toward the possibility of perfecting her relationship with her lover in a heavenly realm.

The poetic tradition of the lover and beloved working out the sanctification of their love through renouncing its earthly fulfillment can be seen in authors from whom Rossetti claimed her literary descent. For example, Dante's *Commedia*, one of the foundational works of the Italian literary tradition, draws dramatic energy from the progress the central figure makes toward eventual reunion with his beloved, Beatrice, in the *Paradiso*; the loss of their earthly love helps make possible the fulfillment of perfected love for Dante and Beatrice. Because Rossetti uses this poetic tradition in a similar way, her poetry may be connected to Catholicism in both a doctrinal and a literary sense. Going beyond the idea of suffering as generally redemptive, Rossetti's texts portray the power of suffering to make an individual fit for heaven, closely analogous to the function of Purgatory in

Roman Catholic doctrine. In this sense, the version of Catholic religious thought portrayed in Dante may also be seen as basic to Rossetti's poetics. The Catholicism ingrained in the texts written by one of Italy's national poets is very much a part of Rossetti's work. Her authorial identity as both Anglo-Catholic and Anglo-Italian is shown in part through her identification with Dante and his religious thought.

In "Dante, An English Classic" ([1867] 1998), an article for *The Churchman's Shilling Magazine*, Rossetti claims a preeminence for Italy as *the* most important modern nation in terms of classicism in literature. "Viewing the matter of nationality exclusively as one of literary interest . . . a wise man might choose not unwisely to be born an Italian, thus securing Dante as his elder brother, and the 'Divina Commedia' as his birthright," she wrote (Kent and Stanwood 1998, 168). Although Rossetti, in this statement, may seem to privilege the Italian elements of her creative heritage without reference to doctrinal perspectives, further reading suggests that she is also discussing how emphasis on different elements in Dante's work might suggest a variety of religious viewpoints. Rossetti used her own family members' interest in Dante to explain this possibility:

> My father Gabriele Rossetti in his . . . Analytical Commentary on Dante's Hell, has left . . . to fellow-experts a theory. My sister, Maria Francesca Rossetti, has in her "Shadow of Dante" eloquently expounded the Divina Commedia as a discourse of most elevated Christian faith and morals. My brother Dante has translated with a rare felicity the "Vita Nuova" . . . and other minor (poetical) works of his great namesake. My brother William has . . . rendered the Inferno into English blank verse. (175)

While at first glance her admiration for Dante seems to have more to do with nationalistic and familial ties than with religious faith, her sister Maria's appraisal of Dante's *Commedia* as a "discourse of most elevated faith and morals" is characteristic of Christina Rossetti's own regard for the poet. In one of the prose passages in her work that applies specifically to Catholic doctrine, Rossetti describes Dante's Purgatory as a place of "finite pain, assured hope" (188).

One of Rossetti's most famous poems, *Monna Innominata*, both celebrates the influence of Dante and Petrarch on the literary tradition of the sonnet sequence and characterizes the world of the sonnets as one in which "finite pain" and "assured hope" coexist. The epigraphs to all fourteen of the sonnets in this sequence, in fact, are taken from Dante and Petrarch. Rossetti's headnote to the poems first explains how the sonnet sequence connects with the literary tradition of the two poets and then expands the genre through the device of an unnamed woman speaker who has already had a sequence of sonnets written to her. The speaker's inability to be united with her beloved, hinted at in the headnote ("the barrier between them might be . . . held sacred by both, yet not such as to render mutual love incompatible with mutual honor" [*Poems*, 54]), causes her pain, yet in sonnets twelve and thirteen she expresses hope for her beloved's happiness and confidence in God's will for him. Such hope allows her a kind of joy as well: "And you companioned I am not alone" (66). In *Monna Innominata* Rossetti portrays the mingling of pain and hope as an experience of purification, similar to that which she sees in Dante's Purgatory.

Even *Monna Innominata* and "The Convent Threshold," however, are less reflective of Catholic theology and Catholic literary tradition as represented by Dante's *Commedia* than "From House to Home," one of Rossetti's long narrative poems. Like "The Convent Threshold," this poem illustrates its speaker's journey from the joys of earthly love, through purification in response to losing that love, to reunion with her lover in the beatific vision. Yet its literary similarities to Dante's famous work and its metaphysics are more detailed than those in both *Monna Innominata* and "The Convent Threshold." Like the *Commedia*, "From House to Home" relates a set of dream visions: "The first was like a dream through summer heat / The second like a tedious numbing swoon" (103). In fact, it is a vision within a vision. The speaker of the poem characterizes the first as her "castle of white transparent glass" and her "earthly paradise . . . / That lured [her] from the goal" (103). The loss of her lover and her resultant near-death experience, when "life swooned from" her (107), initiates the second vision: a woman, whom the speaker recognizes as a symbol of her own soul, drinks the "cup" (109) of suffering. The second woman is rewarded for her acquiescence in drinking the cup, first by "new wine and virgin honey," making it "sweet indeed" (109). Finally, she is judged worthy of the heavenly vision of God, where "multitudes . . . in bliss" rank "tier beyond tier" and "each face look[s] one way . . . towards its Sun of Love" (110). This beatific vision, similar to that in Dante's *Paradiso*, is filled with the reunions of earthly beloved as well, although Christ is their primary focus: "Hands locked dear hands never to sunder more" (111). This section of the vision ends with the woman who "drank the loathsome cup" united with her earthly lover: "The lost in night, in day was found again; / The fallen was lifted up" (111). Returning to her narration drawn from the first vision, the speaker concludes that she "would not . . . / Rebuild [her] house of lies" (obviously a reference to the fragile "glass castle") but that her "soul shall walk in white" (111). The woman of the second vision is specifically identified with the speaker of the first: "*This* cup is loathsome, yet He makes it sweet" (112; emphasis mine). The speaker closes by affirming that she will "stay upon [her] God" (112). In this poem, a specifically Catholic view of being purged through suffering is clearly stated through the voices of a chorus of "spheres and spirits" (107). "How long? yet founded on the Rock / She shall do battle, suffer and attain," one of the spirits calls out to the other (109)—and great victory or "attainment" through suffering is achieved here. The poem's references to a spiritual audience for the "battle" also accord with the Catholic belief that both angels and the blessed dead witness and share in the struggles of those on earth. The direct discourse of the spirits that might belong to either or both of those categories distinguishes this poem from *Monna Innominata* and "The Convent Threshold," in which such voices are not heard.

Dante's Catholic poetics are one of several religious influences that can be traced in Rossetti's work. Another was the influence of "religious aestheticism" through the Pre-Raphaelite movement; in her poetry, the return to medieval and folkloric images and themes (given visual expression in paintings by William Holman Hunt, Ford Madox Ford, and Dante Gabriel Rossetti) is verbally represented for its audience. Although some critics in recent decades have made light of Rossetti's connection with the Pre-Raphaelite Brotherhood, her work, like theirs, uses forms and techniques associated with the "legendary" past.

The Pre-Raphaelite Brotherhood's return to either an archaic or a timeless past, found variously in early English ballads and newer poems (such as Keats's "The Eve of St. Agnes") that revisited their style and theme, in religion and the literature surrounding it, or in subjects drawn from medieval history, is portrayed in some of Rossetti's most famous works. Her poem "Goblin Market," which has received, arguably, the most critical attention, exemplifies this part of the Pre-Raphaelite Brotherhood aesthetic in its material presentation, its genre conventions, and the subject matter of its story. Published in 1862, the poem was illustrated with woodcuts by Dante Gabriel Rossetti that portray both human and goblin characters in medieval dress. The poem has the deceptively simple, repetitive, and alliterative diction of a ballad: "Morning and evening / Maids heard the goblins cry / Come buy our orchard fruits / Come buy, come buy" (3). The story, while complex in interpretation, is easily understandable on the surface; both the complexity and the apparent simplicity of it are typical of the folk legend. Two sisters are tempted to eat fruit sold by the goblins. One purchases the fruit at the cost of a physical token (a lock of hair) while the other avoids the goblins until her sister falls ill. The illness can only be cured by the juices of the fruit, which forces the virtuous sister to attempt its acquisition. Although the goblins try to compel her to eat it, they do not succeed but merely cover her face with its juices. Her sister is cured by a kiss that allows her to taste the fruit again, but this time the taste repels rather than tempts in order for her to revert to her state of innocence. The poem ends with both sisters teaching their children about the supportive power of sisterhood.

The simple plot of "Goblin Market" complements the poem's multiplicity of mythic themes. As Pre-Raphaelite paintings often do, the poem takes archetypal stories and reworks their imagery. The two major story structures that blend here are the story of the temptation and fall of the first sister and the quest of the second to save the first from the consequences of that fall. These two structures have obvious parallels with those in Genesis and the Gospels, respectively, yet they also reflect the tradition of the heroic romance. The rich doublings and crossings of biblical and traditional Christian imagery with that of the chivalric romance are particularly evident in the scene in which the virtuous sister is assaulted by the goblins (17). The iconography makes this part of the poem easy to read in the context of Catholic thought. Diane D'Amico points out that comparing Lizzie to a "lily in a flood" and a "fruit-crowned orange tree" invokes the iconographic associations of lilies and orange blossoms with the Virgin Mary (1999, 74). The symbolism connecting Lizzie, the orange tree, and the Virgin Mary is particularly powerful because Mary's "crown" is dependent on "the fruit of [her] womb." Lizzie is also compared to "a beacon ... alone / In a hoary roaring sea." A traditional name for Mary, the Stella Maris or "star of the sea," may be reflected in the imagery here; D'Amico also notes that the beacon, a source of light, may refer to the light of Christ (75). The final simile in this passage, "like a royal virgin town," is filled with densely packed meanings. The "royal virgin town" will only receive the monarch that has a right to it; the reference to Mary's obedience to God and willingness to receive Christ in her womb is not difficult to derive from the chivalric symbol. Mary herself, because of her obedience, is a "royal virgin" in her relationship to the King of Kings. Finally, the image of the "town" as the locus displaying the monarch's power recalls images of the perfected

Jerusalem associated with the eternal reign of God in the last book of the New Testament. In a Catholic reading of this symbolism, the New Jerusalem, the Church Triumphant, and Mary are all associated with each other. In this seemingly simple narrative poem, some of the conventions drawn from the aesthetic of the medieval romance and the ballad become the vehicles for powerful explorations of Christian doctrine.

CRITICAL RECEPTION

In recent years, critical analysis has changed with regard to Rossetti's works, and this shift is typified in the response to "Goblin Market." Rossetti's originality in representing the heroic quest for redemption in a feminine rather than a masculine context has brought this poem to the center of current critical interest. Along with interpretations such as Packer's, which positions "temptation" at the "thematic core of 'Goblin Market'" (1963, 142), other readings, such as D'Amico's, highlight Rossetti's celebration of "[a] woman's spiritual power not only to resist sensual temptations but also to help those who have not been able to do so" (1999, 80). While critical commentary at various times in the past frequently stressed the painful or distressing aspects of Rossetti's work (and life), some criticism today has diverted attention from biographical explanations of her poetry while at the same time affirming rather than denying the power of her female speaker/subject.

The notion that Rossetti's emotional pain is the font of her poetic genius can be traced at least as far back, in inchoate form, to her brother William Michael's biographical and critical writings. William Michael Rossetti related the Italian poetry written by Rossetti in her early thirties, *Il Rosseggiar Dell' Oriente*, to her "feelings" for one of her suitors, Charles Bagot Cayley (Packer 1963, 163–64). He implied that the pain Christina experienced in rejecting Cayley caused her to begin writing these poems. For her part, Packer accepts that "it is true that the poem [*sic*] evinces most unmistakably the state of Christina's feelings" (164), but she proposes a different romantic source as their cause. In considering Rossetti's poems as chronicles of her romantic affairs, Packer follows not only William Michael Rossetti but also such famous literary historians as Virginia Woolf and F. L. Lucas (D'Amico 1999, 3).

However, a separate strand of Rossetti criticism has begun to emerge in more recent years that values her poems in a way sharply differentiated from that of the earlier critics. Rossetti's Anglo-Catholicism is now seen as informed by and informing a specific kind of poetic aesthetic, not simply contributing to her individualized expression of emotion. In one of the earliest works to reevaluate metaphysical nineteenth-century poetry in this way, *Victorian Devotional Poetry: The Tractarian Mode*, G. B. Tennyson defines what he refers to as "Tractarian Poetics" (1981, 12). He explains that authors such as John Keble, one of the writers of the *Tracts for the Times* series that shaped both Anglo-Catholicism and the Oxford Movement, drew ideas for fashioning poetry from the theological beliefs delineated by the *Tracts*. In particular, Tennyson claims that the doctrine of analogy as Keble expressed it enriches the significance of mimesis in poetry because it focuses on the idea that all sense-objects can serve to teach concepts concerning the invisible spiritual world (53–56). In describing Rossetti as "the true inheritor of the Tractarian devotional mode in poetry" (198) and noting that "her most Tractarian element is her very approach to poetry itself as a way of seeking the Deity . . . [and as] the expression of intense religious longing" (202), Tennyson replaces the image of Rossetti as lone mourner with that of Rossetti as a participant in the tradition of the metaphysical poets.

In a later critical text that affirms the power of Rossetti's faith on her poetry, *Christina Rossetti: Faith, Gender, and Time*, Diane D'Amico extends Tennyson's approach to Rossetti. As a poet working within the Anglo-Catholic tradition, Rossetti as an author was able to transcend the categories imposed by gender roles in creating the characters in her poems, states D'Amico. Her poetry's central figures speak as "preacher, psalmist, Christian disciple, and even . . . priest . . . with voices that have power and meaning for all readers, male or female" (1999, 15). This authority to speak in a variety of constructed voices paradoxically contributes to Rossetti's ability to celebrate the role of the feminine in Christian doctrine. Since she "reaches beyond herself and beyond the feminine sphere of her time" (15), her authoritative voice can serve as a corrective to one-sided portrayals of female figures in Scripture. To D'Amico, Rossetti's faith allows her the freedom to speak about femininity without necessarily reflecting a personal bias—only that of her persona. Rossetti's ability to create speaking subjects who cannot all be categorized through simple gender designations does not mean that she tries to obliterate the consciousness of her actual authorial identity as woman and poet. Rather, it signifies her confidence in her vocation as a creative woman author, even to the point where she does not necessarily seek to represent the self unmediated by artistic distance.

While the emotional impact of Christina Rossetti's poetry has never been questioned, its creative value has, not least because of her works' apparently simple, vivid, and exciting diction. As noted, recent readings of her poetry, however, have centered on her ability to create imaginative texts stemming from the Anglo-Catholic aesthetic. This recognition of her heritage and ability as a metaphysical poet serves to strengthen the appreciation of her poetic genius.

NOTE

Christina Rossetti, *Poems by Christina G. Rossetti* (Boston: Little, Brown, 1911). All references are to this edition.

WORKS CITED

Bell, Mackenzie. [1898] 1971. *Christina Rossetti: A Biographical and Critical Study*. New York: Haskell.

D'Amico, Diane. 1999. *Christina Rossetti: Faith, Gender, and Time*. Baton Rouge: Louisiana State University Press.

Kent, David A., and P. G. Stanwood, eds. 1998. *Selected Prose of Christina Rossetti*. New York: St. Martin's Press.

Packer, Lona Mosk. 1963. *Christina Rossetti*. Berkeley and Los Angeles: University of California Press.

Rossetti, Christina. [1867] 1998. "Dante: An English Classic." In *Selected Prose of Christina Rossetti*, ed. David A. Kent and P. G. Stanwood, 169–73. New York: St. Martin's Press.

———. 1881. *Called To Be Saints: The Minor Festivals Devotionally Studied.* London: Society for Promoting Christian Knowledge.
Tennyson, G. B. 1981. *Victorian Devotional Poetry: The Tractarian Mode.* Cambridge, MA: Harvard University Press.

BIBLIOGRAPHY

Proctor, Ellen A. *A Brief Memoir of Christina G. Rossetti.* London: Society for Promoting Christian Knowledge, 1895.
Rossetti, Christina. "Dante: The Poet Illustrated Out of the Poem." 1884. In *Selected Prose of Christina Rossetti.* ed. David A. Kent and P. G. Stanwood, 174–190. New York: St. Martin's Press, 1998.
———. *The Works of Christina Rossetti*, intro. Martin Corner. Ware, England: Wordsworth Poetry Library Edition, 1995.

— **Maria Keaton**

Dorothy L. Sayers [1893–1957]

The Man Born to Be King

BIOGRAPHY

Dorothy L. Sayers is best known for her detective fiction about aristocratic amateur Lord Peter Wimsey, but she was also a prolific dramatist, poet, translator, and essayist who displayed a devout Anglican Christianity in almost all of her work. The only child of Reverend Henry Sayers, the headmaster of Christchurch Cathedral Choir School, and Helen Leigh Sayers, she was born in Oxford on June 13, 1893, then moved at age four to Bluntisham Rectory, Huntingdonshire, in the fen country. Tutored privately by her father and a tutor, she learned Latin, French, and German, which led to a lifelong facility with languages. At fifteen she entered the Godolphin School, a boarding school in Salisbury, where she participated in musical and dramatic activities, and in 1912 she won a Gilchrist scholarship to Oxford University's Somerville College.

Sayers excelled there and formed a reputation for idiosyncratic ideas and style, all the while forging strong friendships and again performing in musical and dramatic productions. In 1915 she earned a first-class bachelor of art's degree, and then in 1920 a master's degree in modern languages, one of the first women to graduate from Oxford. After college, Sayers taught languages for two years at Hull High School for Girls but longed for a fuller, more intellectually satisfying life. So she returned to Oxford and worked as an editor at Blackwell's, a firm that promoted the work of young poets and that published her poetry collections, *Op. I* and *Catholic Tales and Christian Songs*. At Oxford, Sayers was part of a circle of intellectuals that included Eric Whelpton, a war veteran, with whom she fell in love, and in 1919 Sayers left Blackwell's to follow him to the École des Roches in the French region of Normandy. While teaching there, she began to write crime fiction, partly to make money and partly because she was fascinated with the genre's possibilities.

Sayers returned to England and worked for nine years as a copywriter at Benson's advertising agency in London, living in Bloomsbury among the progressive artists and political thinkers of the 1920s. In 1924, she secretly gave birth to an illegitimate son, John Anthony, but his father, Bill White, took no responsibility for him. John was raised by Sayers's cousin Ivy Shrimpton, and he knew his mother only as "Cousin Dorothy" throughout his childhood, even after Sayers's 1926 marriage to Oswald Fleming, a World War I veteran and writer who refused to adopt her son.

While their marriage was not passionate, Sayers and Fleming remained together until his death in 1950. Sayers was by now very successful as a detective fiction writer, having published such popular novels as *Murder Must Advertise* (1932) and *Gaudy Night* (1935). In 1931 she quit her job at Benson's and moved to the village of Witham in Essex to write essays, speeches, plays, and verse translations during her final twenty-six years. These include the popular play *Busman's Honeymoon: A Detective Comedy in Three Acts* (1939) as well as several Christian dramas, such as *The Zeal of Thy House* (1937) and *The Just Vengeance* (1946). She also penned *The Mind of the Maker*, a complex theological essay that connects the artist's creative act with the Holy Trinity, and a verse translation of Dante's *Divine Comedy*, finished by her friend Barbara Reynolds after Sayers's sudden death in 1957 of a thrombosis.

Alzina Stone Dale calls Dorothy L. Sayers "one of the great popularizers of Christianity" (1979, 79) in the twentieth century. Sayers communicated the Christian message through many mediums in a direct, engaging style to a world that she refused to consider "post-Christian."

PLOT SUMMARY

Dorothy L. Sayers's *The Man Born to Be King: The Life of Christ in Twelve Dramatic Episodes* was first performed on the BBC in 1941 and 1942. It consists of twelve radio plays in two or three short acts that each dramatize the narrative of the New Testament in contemporary English. The plays utilize a mixture of the four Gospels' chronology and theology, and each presents a discrete unit of Christ's life and teachings, with "notes" that explain salient aspects of the characters and plot and instruct actors and technicians. "The Evangelist" narrates each play, describing the time and place and introducing the plot and scene changes, usually in abbreviated New Testament language.

The first play, "Kings in Judaea," recounts the Nativity story, with an emphasis on Herod's political position as the king of potentially rebellious Jews under Roman rule. Visited by three "wise men," African kings whose astrological knowledge has led them to seek in Bethlehem "him that is born King of the Jews" (*The Man Born to Be King*, 32), Herod intends to kill the child and force the rebels out into the open. The Magi, warned of danger by an angel, determine not to return to Jerusalem. Herod orders the murder of all male children in Bethlehem aged two and younger, but Jesus and his family escape to Egypt.

The second play, "The King's Herald," focuses on John the Baptist; it also introduces Judas Iscariot as his follower and shows Judas's first meeting with Baruch the Zealot (Sayers's one wholly invented character), who leads a Jewish independence movement. John baptizes Jesus, realizing that Jesus is "the promised Messiah" (62). Jesus goes into the wilderness and fasts for forty days, and Herod's soldiers take John the Baptist to jail.

The third play, "A Certain Nobleman," depicts the wedding at Cana, Mary's difficult position as the mother of a son both human and divine, Jesus chasing the merchants out of the temple, the parable of the flowers, and Jesus saving the son of a "certain nobleman" from Capernaum. All of this exemplifies Jesus' rising reputation as well as the growing opposition to his influence.

The fourth play, "The Heirs to the Kingdom," presents the parable of the steward, Judas's first meeting with Jesus, Matthew and Simon's stories of their first encounters with Jesus' divine power and goodness, and a meeting of the Jewish priests to discuss the problem of Jesus' popularity. Jesus preaches to a crowd whose members argue about his identity and motives; he then encounters the Roman centurion Proclus, whose faith that Jesus' word alone will heal his servant amazes Jesus. Finally, Jesus learns of the death of John the Baptist.

The fifth play, "The Bread of Heaven," demonstrates the power to heal that Jesus has given his disciples and their sense of being overwhelmed by the needy. Baruch plants the seed of Judas's betrayal by implying that Jesus may be motivated by vanity, and Judas declares he would kill Jesus if this proved true. Jesus performs the miracle of the loaves and fishes, and the crowd proclaims him King of the Jews, although Jesus protests. As the disciples leave in a boat, they see Jesus walking toward them on the water, pronouncing in Hebrew God's name, "I Am" (142). Jesus renames Simon Peter the "rock," the one who will hold the keys to the kingdom of heaven and be the Church's foundation.

The sixth play, "The Feast of Tabernacles," begins with Caiaphas ordering the arrest of Jesus and Jesus' insistence that they will go quietly to Jerusalem for the feast. Eunice, a servant girl, describes to Claudia, Pilate's wife, how Jesus healed her daughter's fits. Jesus tells the inhospitable Samaritans the parable of the talents and teaches the disciples the Lord's Prayer. John, Peter, and James recount with amazement the Transfiguration. Caiaphas sees that Judas will be their instrument for killing Jesus, and Jesus preaches on the temple steps.

In the seventh play, "The Light and the Life," Jesus tells Martha the story of the prodigal son to explain why Mary has "chosen the better part" in her vivid love of life and deeper devotion to Jesus. Jesus brings Lazarus back to life, and the Sanhedrin, the highest court and council of ancient Jews, resolves to have him arrested and executed.

The eighth play, "Royal Progress," emphasizes the tragic treachery of Judas's egotism in his belief that Jesus has "sold" himself for earthly power. Here Sayers inserts a crucial plot device. Baruch the Zealot sends Jesus a message: if Jesus rides into Jerusalem on the war-horse Baruch will make available, then Baruch will know that Jesus will fight for his revolutionary cause; if he rides an ass's colt, Baruch will wait for a "bolder Messiah" (203). Jesus tells the parable of the rich man and the beggar and explains to a scoffing Judas that Mary acts charitably when she anoints him with expensive perfume. Jesus rides into Jerusalem on the ass's colt and preaches to the crowd. Judas agrees to betray Jesus, misinterpreting Jesus' words and action as plots to take over as the Jewish king and overthrow Roman rule.

The ninth play, "The King's Supper," which Sayers calls "the focal point for the whole series of plays" (225), portrays the Last Supper and Judas's betrayal. Jesus performs the first Eucharist with the bewildered disciples, telling them that he is "the way, and the truth and the life" (241). Caiaphas orders Jesus' arrest, stressing the haste with which he must be tried and executed, and he convinces Pilate to ratify immediately the sentence against Jesus since there might be a nationalist uprising. Agonized, Jesus waits in the Garden of Gethsemane as the disciples struggle to stay awake; although they fight the soldiers when they come, the disciples then flee as Jesus is led away.

The tenth play, "The Princes of this World," portrays the travesty of Jesus' trial, Peter's denial, and Judas's self-hatred and suicide. Caiaphas initially accuses Jesus of blasphemy, but when Pilate refuses to have him executed for this Jewish insurrection Caiaphas changes the charge to treason against Rome. Pilate then sends Jesus to Herod, who sends him back; and Pilate washes his hands of Jesus' case and gives him to the bloodthirsty crowd demanding his crucifixion.

The eleventh play, "King of Sorrows," dramatizes the Crucifixion. Mary, mother of Jesus, Mary Magdalene, Mary Cleophas (here presented as the Virgin Mary's undefined "sister"), John, and Baruch reflect on Jesus' life and death. Dysmas, the thief, has a partial revelation that Jesus will be his salvation, and Jesus asks John to look after Mary after he dies. Claudia relates her dream of the death of God under Pontius Pilate; Proclus talks with Balthazar, who tells him that the man dead on the cross is the "child that was born King of the Jews" in Bethlehem. Jesus' body is placed in a tomb with a stone at the entrance.

The twelfth play, "The King Comes to his Own," portrays Jesus' final appearances on earth to Mary Magdalene, Mary Cleophas, Salome (James and John's mother), and the disciples. The guards describe their experience of earthquake and shock during the Resurrection. Peter affirms to Jesus three times that he loves him, and Jesus then tells Peter to feed his "sheep." After forty days, Jesus leads them to the Mount of Olives and instructs them to "go and teach all nations" the Christian truth (339).

MAJOR THEMES

The Man Born to Be King takes its title from John 18:37. When Pilate asks Jesus if he is a king, Jesus replies, "You say that I am a king. For this I was born, and for this I came into the world, to testify to the truth. Everyone who belongs to the truth listens to my voice." This passage, and the title itself, convey the gist of Sayers's points in this dramatization of the New Testament. Sayers stresses in her preface and notes to individual plays that this is a human drama, one that happened in a historical time and involved real people. As such, she focuses on the individuals in the New Testament, and their reactions to Jesus and his "kingship" and teaching drive both the plot and the theology.

The "world" that Jesus repeatedly names in John's Gospel and in Sayers's plays is both the earthly "kingdom" Jesus establishes among incipient Christians and the heaven of the Father to which this world leads. Like John, the Gospel narrative that Sayers follows most closely, the plays underline the tragic irony of the players' mistaken focus on Jesus' role in this world. Jesus' apparently blasphemous claim to be the Messiah, the man born to be king, motivates unbelieving Jews to insist on his crucifixion; and Pilate's fear that any such claim constitutes treason against Rome convinces him to comply. They fail to see the magnitude of Jesus' divine kingship, a dominion far more real than any political authority he might claim. Yet of course the Crucifixion leads to the Resurrection and the commencement of Jesus' real sovereignty; hence, Sayers's statement in the preface that "[s]hort of damnation ... there can be no Christian tragedy" (11). Sayers's technique of placing the New Testament story within political and historical contexts accentuates her message that these were real events and real people, comprehensible to and even congruent with contemporary people and circumstances. The world that Jesus invokes includes Gentiles as well as Jews, women and children as well as men. Sayers wants the audience to see themselves in these players and to recognize that Christianity, while indeed "the way," is not a comfortable ride but a steep and stony path that requires intense personal effort. Each major actor in her drama can choose sin or salvation, and each has a unique understanding of Christ's purpose. Jesus and Judas, antitheses of each other and exemplars of virtue and sin, respectively, particularly embody this choice, but every person evinces this fundamental point.

The Man Born to Be King retells the story of Jesus Christ from Scripture, and as such its Christian themes are "catholic" rather than specifically "Catholic." It focuses on the Incarnation as the vehicle and symbol of God's grace and thus on Jesus' humanity, which exists paradoxically with his divinity. The world's only hope for even partially comprehending God's mysteries lies in the contemplation of his most fundamental intervention in human history and of Christ's atonement as humanity's means to salvation. Consequently, Sayers also emphasizes free will and the responsibility each individual bears for his or her salvation. Finally, Sayers wants her audience to understand Jesus' point that the first two commandments—to love God and neighbor—are the most important and override any temporal personal or political purposes.

Three particular emphases in *The Man Born to Be King*, however, show Sayers's sympathy with specific aspects of Catholic doctrine. First, the plays painstakingly show Peter's development from fumbling, irresolute disciple to Christ's human heir apparent. As such, they reinforce the importance of structure and obedience within the incipient Church as well as the Scriptural basis for the papacy. Second, the plays reiterate the parts of Christ's teaching that emphasize good works as well as faith as the path to salvation. Third, Judas's sin of pride creates the conditions and motivation for his betrayal. With this literary choice, Sayers endorses Saint Thomas Aquinas's abhorrence of pride as the worst of the vices, an overweening sense of self that makes people contemptuous even of God.

Many critics agree that the plays center on Judas and that his characterization is Sayers's most effective creation. The Gospels report but do not explain the reasons for Judas's betrayal (with the exception of John, who attributes Judas's evil actions to Satan). Sayers provides specific motivation within a particular context by making Judas that familiar political animal, an intelligent, fiery revolutionary who fights for national autonomy against an oppressive imperialistic power. But despite Judas's political cause, one with which many might sympathize, Sayers emphasizes that his pride—like Satan's, to whom he is implicitly compared—is predictably born of his superior intellect and ability. This ironically leads to "a deeper corruption than any of the others are capable" (52). Judas cannot achieve the humility necessary for a true Christian life and understanding, since he sees "only with his intellect and not with his heart" (52).

Sayers's audience in the early 1940s (as well as twenty-first-century people only too cognizant of the fruits of rigid ideologies) would have grasped immediately that Judas is the man who must follow his ideas over the plain facts of the case—like Fascists whose adherence to political doctrine allows them to justify atrocities. For instance, Judas understands that women and children will be very important followers in the new religious movement since they bring in husbands and extended family. But he does not see, as Jesus later explains to the perplexed disciples, that holiness means "to love, and to be ruled by love" (71) and that to follow Jesus means to give up "everything that may stand in the way" (67). Sayers explains that Judas represents the risk posed by all intellectuals because of their innate skepticism and potential vanity—they can be "the greatest saints or the greatest sinners"—but that they must be "let in" to the fold despite the danger (101).

Sayers points out that Judas's imagination and brilliance allow him to see Jesus' potential political power among Jews as well as "the meaning of sin and redemption"; he can also see and fear, unlike the other disciples, the "paradox by which all human good is corrupted as soon as it comes to power" (52). But Judas clearly deceives himself when he insists that Jesus has failed to live up to his own high standards by pursuing earthly power and glory, a deception Baruch the Zealot will exploit to the full. Baruch is another recognizable figure across all centuries: the radical who will use any means necessary to overthrow a perceived tyranny. Baruch, who has no interest in religion but a passionate hatred for Roman rule, wants to use the crowd's love of Jesus to inspire a Jewish revolution against Rome, and he has the shrewdness to recognize and exploit Judas's motive for betrayal. Declaring that Judas's sin is the same as Adam's, "[i]ntellectual dishonesty springing from intellectual pride," Baruch explains that through "specious arguments" Judas will convince himself that Jesus must be stopped (116) even though Baruch himself fears that Jesus may be incorruptible. Caiaphas, another proud man who cares more for maintaining his powerful position within the status quo than for promoting truth, also seizes on Judas's ideas and suggests that Judas is doing Jesus a favor by bringing him to death, since afterward the people will only remember his miracles and teachings. Ironically, Judas speaks truthfully when he says "The Son of Man must die before he can save" (221). But he mistakenly asserts that he will then be the instrument of Israel's salvation, and he takes thirty pieces of silver as if to prove a concrete motivation that downplays the magnitude of his betrayal, one Judas knows but denies to himself.

Sayers explains that Judas is the "egoist" who hates God, and it is Judas's insecurity about his personal part in Jesus' ministry that underscores his growing mistrust. When he agrees to help Baruch, Judas justifies his treachery partly by saying that Jesus did not listen to him as much as to the less gifted disciples. Most of the disciples worry at some point about their respective relationships to Jesus and their places in what they peevishly see as a hierarchy of state. But only Judas is rude and unpleasant, hinting at his sense that Jesus wishes power and glory rather than righteousness, especially when Jesus washes the disciples' feet. After the miraculous feeding of the five thousand, Judas, rather than expressing awe, wonders sarcastically if Jesus plans in fact to become king. Even before his suicide—when he realizes that Jesus is in fact incorruptible and that he has "murdered the Christ of God for hate" (266)—Judas compares himself to Jesus. Bemoaning the awfulness of God's "innocence" compared to his own sinfulness, Judas can neither accept Christ nor hide from the knowledge of his forgiveness. While he sees the truth, he chooses to turn away from it, stubbornly seeing his relation to Jesus as a personal contest he has lost.

The staunch believer "John Evangelist," as Sayers familiarly names him, contrasts with the selfish, political Judas. Sayers gives John a stutter to contrast Judas's smooth articulate speech—what Catherine Kenney calls the language of the dealer and politician (1990, 238)—that Judas mocks in the second play, choosing to belittle John and imply his own superiority. But John's stutter and shyness emphasize his overwhelming and immediate faith. Judas's intellect allows him to see some truths, but he follows tortured reasoning in order to translate them, mistakenly, into worldly terms. Conversely, John sees more clearly than the other disciples that Jesus has been sent by God; he does not need to think before he sees and believes, and he never wavers in his simple but profound faith. At the Transfiguration, it is John who instantly recognizes that Jesus had not changed but that they had gained the ability to see him "as he always is" (161).

Most importantly, John completely lacks Judas's pride. After the Resurrection, he understands that Jesus appeared to the women and to Peter rather than to him because they needed the visitations more. Likewise, he does not resent the fact that the Church is to be founded upon Peter, and he understands that Peter's less personal connection to Jesus will ensure a less exclusive "catholic" church. John also understands Jesus' point that the greatest are those who perform the greatest service to others; he does not seek praise for his works but performs them out of the love that Jesus stresses must precede any faith.

In fact, John can love as the proverbial child loves, which is proved by his relationship with his brother and fellow disciple James. Sayers takes some pains to show little brother John allowing big brother James to protect him affectionately. This goes against the typical presentation of the brothers as the "sons of thunder" in order to bolster Jesus' point at the Last Supper that the world will know the disciples because they love one another (239). Above all, John adores Jesus as both God and man, and this special friendship develops Jesus' love for John, noted several times in John's Gospel. As Janice Brown says, the disciples become "friends of the Kingdom" not because they avoid sin but because their "choice and their goal is simply to Love and to 'follow'" (1998, 276) Jesus, an actual human individual as well as God.

Matthew also loves Jesus simply, and while he is a more flawed person than John, he too lacks Judas's egotism and intuits immediately the importance and truth of Jesus' teaching, having been "swept off his feet by [Jesus'] heavenly kindness and beauty of mind" (100). While Matthew's experience as tax-gatherer would logically make him the disciples' treasurer, he gladly relinquishes the role to Judas, cheerfully admitting that the temptation to pilfer would be too great. (Judas, of course, would never have made such a self-deprecating point.) Thomas, the famously doubting disciple, represents those whose faith needs more "proof" than others, in spite of Jesus' assertion that those who believe without seeing are blessed. As such, he frankly represents ordinary people who struggle with and question the extraordinary claims of Christianity. Yet Thomas's final leap of faith contrasts powerfully with his former skepticism, and Sayers calls "convincing" the fact that of all the actors in this drama it is Thomas in the last play who makes "the one absolutely unequivocal statement . . . of the divinity of Jesus" (315).

Peter, recipient of the keys to the kingdom of heaven, is also ironically the only disciple besides Judas who truly forsakes Jesus. Yet Peter can face his faults and accept forgiveness when Jesus offers him another chance, since—again, unlike

Judas—his zealous faith and love overcome his shame and his worry about what Jesus and others will think of him personally. For this reason, Jesus singles Peter out as a leader, asking him twice at the end of the last play if he is a "friend" and if he loves him "a little" and entreating Peter to follow him. Peter honestly and endearingly replies, "Look in my heart—my cowardly, faithless heart—and read there how I love you" (339).

Through such detailed characterizations, Sayers aims to show "the words and actions of actual people engaged in living through a piece of recorded history" (5). Sayers's boldest move, however, is to depict Christ the Messiah as "God-in-his-thisness" as well as Jesus, "*this* Man, *this* person, of a reasonable soul and human flesh subsisting, who walked and talked then and there, surrounded, not by human types, but by those individual people" (5). From the first, the reverent Magi offer their gifts to the Christ child in the hope that love will now coexist with wisdom, power, and sorrow, and Mary voices the belief that Jesus "is the answer to all riddles" (40). When Jesus preaches to disciples and crowds at key moments, his powerful biblically based language accentuates his divinity and his unmistakable difference from those to whom he speaks: his status as "king" of a world more profound than any they have contemplated.

Still, he is a man, and Sayers emphasizes his sheer physical suffering as well as the responsibility for humanity's sins that he, of all individuals in history, must bear. As Jesus carries the cross, his followers implore *him* to comfort *them*, and Sayers includes vivid details to force her audience to realize the brutality of Jesus' death. The soldiers jeer and kick; and just as Jesus asks God to forgive these people who "don't know what they are doing," the stage directions read, "His voice breaks off in a sharp gasp as the mallet falls. Fade out on the dull sound of hammering" (295). John Thurmer points out that Sayers includes the sum of all that Jesus says in the four Gospels, going from "forgiveness and concern for others" to "agonies of despair and pain . . . to triumph . . . and resignation," and that "none of the four gospels actually tells *this* story" (1993, 82). In short, Jesus displays the full range of human emotion. His faith, and even—especially—his divinity, do not erase his pain. Sayers also shows Jesus' foreknowledge as incomplete, although it coexists with his absolute surety in God as Father of himself and all people. This pertains particularly to Judas; while Jesus knows that one will betray him, only gradually does he come to see that it will be Judas. Jesus shares vulnerability with everyone, and this even includes a susceptibility to pride. Jesus describes Satan's temptations in the wilderness as a struggle with his "other" self, a self who taunts him to use his powers both to prove his divinity and to gain power and glory.

Yet the point is that frail humans can triumph in spite of the temptations and contempt of the world if they maintain fidelity to God. Jesus repeatedly warns his disciples that only if they are willing to lose life will they gain it, that they must suffer before gaining salvation, and that faith must precede all recognition and comprehension of Jesus' parables. He particularly admonishes them not to focus on the miracles as proof of his divinity and to recognize that they are not to be used for the sake of converting nonbelievers. Most of all he focuses on love for God and humanity, and in fact Sayers highlights the message of Matthew 25 in the play "Royal Progress," in which it is paraphrased in full. Jesus debates with a crowd of Jews and claims that those who will inherit the kingdom of his Father are those who "showed kindness to the humblest of [his] brother-men" because "when [they] neglected [his] brother-men, they neglected [him]" (214).

And of course most of the men and women Jesus meets are not living this way. Throughout the cycle, it becomes clear that although Jesus is a Jew preaching primarily to Jews, his teaching is for everyone—Jew, Gentile, man, woman, or child—and that all people are equally sinners and equally qualified for salvation. Jesus tells the disciples that he is their only means of eternal salvation and that those who see him have seen God, but even they understand this only vaguely. Yet others who have no particular knowledge of Jesus or any standing within the community believe immediately. When Jesus tells the parable of the ten brides-maids, stressing that they must watch for the Son of Man—an oft-repeated phrase that deliberately links Jesus to the Messiah prophesied in the Old Testament—the wedding guests' surprise and incomprehension parallel the foolish girls' lack of preparation for Christ. The one exception is the old rabbi, who rapturously sees that it may not be too late for him "to behold the Kingdom" (85); likewise, Benjamin of Capernaum's faith that Jesus will save his dying son brings him to recognize that Jesus' "word is the living truth" (95). Certainly, Sayers shows Mary Magdalene, Mary Cleophas, and Martha as true believers, and she carefully develops the character of Claudia, Proclus's wife, as a pagan who nevertheless has the "typically feminine" ability to drive "straight through laws and regulations to the essential: good men should not be hanged" (232). This contrasts with Pilate, who also sees Jesus' goodness but fears too much for his political position—like Judas and Caiaphas—to eschew selfishness and save him.

Some of the men in power, however, are presented sympathetically and realisti-cally as people who stand up for their beliefs even as they participate in Jesus' demise. Sayers warns in her notes about Herod that "we must forget . . . the traditional picture of a semi-lunatic monster" (25–26) and instead recognize that Herod's political and military strategy of accepting Rome's authority has kept peace for thirty years. Joseph of Arimathea, a member of the Sanhedrin that condemns Jesus, nevertheless speculates that Jesus meant to enlarge Israel "to take in all the world" (296), and Nicodemus recognizes that they have "slain the Lord's anointed" (328). Proclus—the decent Roman guard whose servant Jesus cures early in the cycle and who appears as the "centurion" at the Crucifixion—represents, as Janice Brown (1998) suggests, those heirs of the kingdom who will form the future Church.

Sayers fleshes all these people out from Gospel passages that she claims have grown dull from repetition and have turned into stylized, reverent ritual removed from everyday existence. A realistic treatment of Jesus' life and sayings, she believed, would force her audience to recognize the New Testament not only as the spiritual pinnacle of human history but as the central fact of their own lives. Like Flannery O'Connor, Sayers wants to shock readers and listeners into experiencing freshly the truths of Christianity, employing "modern speech and a determined historical realism" (7) rather than the "insipid" rendering that "pious hands" have inflicted (21). In fact, critics have claimed that Sayers's radio plays paved the way for the later hit musical plays *Jesus Christ Superstar* and *Godspell* as well as for such controversial films as Martin Scorsese's *The Last Temptation of Christ* (all of which present Judas and the political situation very similarly). Certainly, the fact that *The Man Born to Be King* has been rebroadcast many times since its debut in 1942 attests to its popular and religious appeal to Christians of all denominations.

CRITICAL RECEPTION

The best and most thorough analysis of *The Man Born to Be King* remains Sayers's own introductions to the cycle and the individual plays. She discusses her dramatic techniques as they relate to Christian theology; each character's place in the drama as well as her interpretation of their relationships to Christ and his teachings; and the challenges of presenting the New Testament to an apathetic and frankly ignorant modern audience. Among the several Sayers biographies, Barbara J. Reynolds's *Dorothy L. Sayers: Her Life and Soul* (1993) does the most thorough job of describing the artistic disagreements, the public disapproval, and the censorship problems involved with personifying Jesus Christ that Sayers and the BBC encountered when producing the plays for "The Children's Hour."

Two important full-length studies of Sayers examine *The Man Born to Be King* as her most important dramatic work. Catherine Kenney details Sayers's development as a Christian artist and thinker and discusses important characters in the play cycle as both modern and biblical types who struggle as Christians with the earthly "conflict between the mind and heart" (1990, 240). Janice Brown approaches Sayers's theology through her literary use of the seven deadly sins and is one of the few critics to examine each play sequentially. Brown shows in detail their emphasis on the human suffering that results from sin and that "the evil of Sin must be *redeemed* into good" (1998, 262) through love of Christ and adherence to his teaching.

Among critical essayists, John Thurmer (1993) provides the most detailed theological analysis, explaining the ways in which Sayers conflates and highlights specific parts of the Gospels, discussing her characterizations of Judas and Jesus, and connecting the plays to *The Mind of the Maker*. Terrie Curran claims that *The Man Born to Be King* reveals "Sayers' most ambitious manifestation of the Christian aesthetic" of "art as actualization . . . art [as] the word made flesh" (1979, 68) and discusses the ways in which the plays effectively employ theological archetypes, historical imagination, and contemporary realism to convey the shock of Jesus' death and resurrection. Alzina Stone Dale places Sayers's attempt to "flesh out an existing tale" (1979, 80) within the tradition of Christian play cycles, showing the parallels between Sayers's cycle, mystery plots, and the stories of a legendary hero like King Arthur, another man "born to be king."

NOTE

Dorothy L. Sayers, *The Man Born to Be King* (New York: Harper and Brothers, 1943). All references are to this edition.

WORKS CITED

Brown, Janice. 1998. *The Seven Deadly Sins in the Work of Dorothy L. Sayers*. Kent, OH: Kent State University Press.

Curran, Terrie. 1979. "The Word Made Flesh: The Christian Aesthetic in Dorothy L. Sayers' *The Man Born to Be King*." In *As Her Whimsey Took Her*, ed. Margaret P. Hannay, 67–77. Kent, OH: Kent State University Press.

Dale, Alzina Stone. 1979. "*The Man Born to Be King*: Dorothy L. Sayers' Best Mystery Plot." In *As Her Whimsey Took Her*, ed. Margaret P. Hannay, 78–89. Kent, OH: Kent State University Press.

Kenney, Catherine. 1990. *The Remarkable Case of Dorothy L. Sayers*. Kent, OH: Kent State University Press.

Reynolds, Barbara. 1993. *Dorothy L. Sayers: Her Life and Soul*. New York: St. Martin's Press.

Thurmer, John. 1993. "The Greatest Story, or From Mystery to Mystery." *Seven* 10: 77–95.

BIBLIOGRAPHY

Brabazon, James. *Dorothy L. Sayers: The Life of a Courageous Woman*. New York: Scribner, 1981.

Brunsdale, Mitzi. *Dorothy L. Sayers: Solving the Mystery of Wickedness*. New York: St. Martin's Press, 1990.

Coomes, David. *Dorothy L. Sayers: A Careless Rage for Life*. Oxford: Lion Press, 1992.

Durkin, Mary Brian, O.P. *Dorothy L. Sayers*. Boston: Twayne Publishers, 1980.

Hitchman, Janet. *Such a Strange Lady: An Introduction to Dorothy L. Sayers*. New York: Harper, 1975.

Hone, Ralph E. *Dorothy L. Sayers: A Literary Biography*. Kent, OH: Kent State University Press, 1979.

— **Ann V. Norton**

Elizabeth Ann Seton [1774–1821]

Letters of Mother Seton to Mrs. Julianna Scott

BIOGRAPHY

Saint Elizabeth Ann Seton, wife, mother, educator, and founder of the Sisters of Charity, was born Elizabeth Ann Bayley on August 28, 1774, in New York City, during the great political upheaval of the American War of Independence. This "daughter of the American Revolution" was born to Anglican parents of prominence. Her father, Dr. Richard Bayley, born in Connecticut and descended from a family of the landed gentry of Norfolkshire, England, was educated in England as a physician. He was the first professor of anatomy at King's College, now Columbia University, and was highly regarded for his work as the first health officer of New York City. His work and efforts on behalf of the sick at the Quarantine Station on Staten Island caused him to be held in high regard. While ministering to poor immigrants, he died of typhus.

Elizabeth's mother, Catherine Charlton, the daughter of an Anglican minister of Staten Island, New York, died when Elizabeth was three years old. Dr. Bailey remarried. Her stepmother, Charlotte Amelia Barclay, was the daughter of Andrew Barclay and Helen Roosevelt, whose father was the founder of the Roosevelt dynasty in America.

While Elizabeth's education was conducted primarily by her father, to whom she was quite devoted and who cultivated in her the subjects of French and music as well as basic studies, she had a natural propensity for prayer and introspection and those practices in the Anglican Church that had been retained from Catholicism. For example, she loved the Bible, especially the Psalms, and Saint Thomas à Kempis's *Imitation of Christ*, and she longed to receive the body and blood of Christ in communion. She held Saint Augustine in especially high regard since she was born on his feast day, August 28. These devotional practices and religious beliefs grew deeper as she matured. Elizabeth was fifteen years old when George Washington became the first president of the United States. At age nineteen, this "belle of New York" society became engaged to William Magee Seton, the eldest son of William Seton, a wealthy New York merchant and descendant of the famous Scottish Seton family. Like Elizabeth's father, William was also educated in England and had traveled extensively. They married on January 25, 1794, in

St. Paul's Church, New York, and lived for a while with William's father, a widower with children. One of the children, Rebecca Seton, became Elizabeth's "Soul's Sister" as they went about on missions of mercy and were known as the "Protestant Sisters of Charity" (*Letters*, 14; Dirvin 1975, 65). When William's father died in 1798, Elizabeth assumed responsibility for the household and soon began her own family with William that consisted of five children: Anna Maria, William, Richard, Rebecca, and Catherine. In 1803, her husband's poor health required a sea voyage to Leghorn, Italy, a journey that took nearly seven weeks. Their eldest daughter Anna Maria accompanied them on this voyage. They were eventually quarantined in the Lazaretto, a detention hospital near the town's port and a damp, windy, and smoky place. At one time, Elizabeth feared that Anna Maria would also die before the quarantine was lifted. During this time, she kept a detailed journal for her sister-in-law Rebecca in which she confided the increasing severity of William's illness and her honest feelings about this time of confinement, sickness, and physical and emotional anguish. For example, on November 24, 1803, she wrote:

> We pray and cry together until fatigue overpowers [William], and then he says he is willing to go. Cheering up is useless; he seems easier after venting his sorrow, and always gets quiet sleep after his struggle. A heavy storm of wind which drives the sprays from the sea against our window adds to his melancholy. If I could forget my God one moment at these times, I should go mad; but He hushes all. "Be still and know that I am God your Father." (Dirvin 1975, 118)

Indeed, her letters to close friends and relatives, excerpts from her Leghorn journal to Rebecca, and her spiritual relationships with her husband's friends, the Filicchis, sustained Elizabeth during this dark time.

William died on December 27, 1803, in Pisa. Elizabeth and Anna Maria remained with the Filicchi brothers, Antonio and Filippo, and their families for some time, during which Antonio and Amabilia Filicchi instructed Seton in the tenets of the Catholic Church and in Allan Butler's *Lives of the Saints*. Delayed by her daughter's illness and then by her own, she sailed for home and reached New York on June 3, 1804. Her sister-in-law and "Soul's Sister" Rebecca died the next month.

Perhaps three qualities, in particular, endear us to Elizabeth Seton: her honest expression of what was occurring in her life; her natural ability to cultivate friendship as an art form; and her practical spirituality that found God in the midst of people and daily occurrences. She corresponded frequently with three female companions of her youth, Julianna Sitgreaves Scott, Eliza Craig Sadler, and Catherine Dupleix, as well as with the Filicchi brothers and their families and various ministers. She was truly "Mother" to her family and friends in her solicitude toward them and concern for their well-being. The word "Mother" became more than a title later in her life; it served as an appositive of her devotion and loyalty.

On Ash Wednesday, March 14, 1805, Seton was received into the Catholic Church, and on March 25 she received holy communion as a Roman Catholic for the first time. She kept the journal of her conversion for Amabilia Filicchi, who initially led her into a Catholic parish church and taught her the significance of the symbols of Catholicism. She penned the anxieties, doubts, and alienation that she experienced when many family members and friends attempted to dissuade her from converting, and she confided to Julianna Scott that she "could go almost mad at the view of the conduct of every friend I have here, except yourself" (Dirvin 1975, 171). Her soul's journey to God, expressed in her letters and journals, parallels the dark night of the soul experience—purgation, illumination, and union with God. Her decision to convert from Anglicanism to Roman Catholicism occurred at a time when she and her children could have profited by the financial and emotional support of her Protestant relatives and friends, but her desire to join the Catholic Church strengthened her resolve to practice her religious faith.

Seton's solicitude toward her own children and children in general impelled her to be concerned for their educational and spiritual needs. Excitedly, she wrote a letter to her friend Julianna Scott, dated May 6, 1805, stating that she had "entered into an engagement with an English gentleman and his wife [the Whites] to assist them in an English seminary" (*Letters*, 127), a school for boys in the suburbs of New York, but the rumors that this was merely a proselytizing scheme, as well as a lack of administrative acumen, forced the school to close. In November 1806, the founder of the Sulpician order, Father William Dubourg of St. Mary's Seminary in Baltimore, Maryland, met Seton in New York and suggested opening a school for girls in Baltimore. Her own boys were brought to St. Mary's College, and she opened a school next to the chapel of St. Mary's Seminary. Bishop John Carroll of New York urged Seton to move to Baltimore. Father Matignon, Boston's first priest and pastor of Holy Cross Church, spoke prophetically when he said to her, "You are destined, I think, for some great good in the United States, and here you should remain in preference to any other location" (199). (She was also considering a move to Montreal, Canada.)

Seton left her home in New York and sought to fulfill the will of God in Baltimore. Her progression in the spiritual life is evident in this passage she wrote toward the end of her journey from New York to Baltimore:

> Tomorrow, do I go among strangers? No. Has an anxious thought or fear passed my mind? No. Can I be disappointed? No. One sweet Sacrifice will unite my soul with all who offer it. Doubt and fear fly from the breast inhabited by Him. There can be no disappointment where the soul's only desire and expectation is to meet His adored Will and fulfill it. (166)

The "great good" to which Seton was destined was the institution of Catholic elementary education in the United States. In a letter of October 10, 1808, to Julianna Scott, she presented her "terms" for board and tuition for the little school on Paca Street that accommodated seven pupils: four boarders and her own three girls. She wrote, "They are 200 dollars per year; extra accomplishments which require the assistance of Masters, as music, drawing, etc., are paid separately" (173). And on December 6, 1808, she wrote that she was

> [a]t five in the afternoon (as soon as school is over) seated gravely with a slate and pencil, with a Master of arithmetic stuffing [my] brain with dollars, cents, fractions, and actually going over the studies both in grammar and figures which are suited to the school better than the mistress. So it is. And you may well imagine there is very little time for writing; even at this moment the pen is falling from my hand, so completely is nature wearied. (174–75)

In a letter to Father Dubourg, who supported her efforts to institute a school in Baltimore, she wrote that her intention was to make her school different from the current "mixed schools, in which ornamental accomplishments are the only objects of education; we have none that I know where their acquisition is connected with, and made subservient to, pious instruction—and such a one you certainly wish yours to be" (Dirvin 1975, 219).

Simultaneous with founding the school, Seton gathered women together to teach the children, with the intention of "forming a permanent institution" (221). In another letter to Julianna Scott, dated October 3, 1808, she referred to herself as "your poor little Nun" (*Letters*, 170). With the assistance of a benefactor, Samuel Cooper, Seton established a religious community at Emmitsburg, Maryland, "in a beautiful country place in the mountains" (Dirvin 1975, 232). From her youth, she had loved nature, wherein she felt close to God. Under the guidance and rule of Father Dubourg, Seton pronounced vows of poverty, chastity, and obedience on March 25, 1809, and became known as "Mother Seton," since she also assumed the responsibilities and leadership of the community. While the goals she established for the community—assisting the poor, visiting the sick, comforting the sorrowful, clothing the poor, and teaching children—were also marks of the Vincentian order, she adopted and adapted the Vincentian rule and shifted the emphasis from ministry to the poor and sick to education. She remarked in a letter to Julianna Scott dated October 29, 1812, "Our Community is nothing like the religious institutions in Europe" (*Letters*, 222). She continued to wear the attire she had worn since her husband's death in Leghorn:

> a black dress with short shoulder cape, a white muslin cap with crimped border tied under the chin by means of a black crepe band. A rosary was draped from the leather belt that served for a cincture.... A cross hangs from [the beads] engraved with the words "Caritas Christi urget nos"—"The Charity of Christ urges us on," which was the motto given by St. Vincent de Paul to his Daughters of Charity. (Dirvin 1975, 238)

From the challenges and difficulties she encountered she articulated a spirituality that was both temporal and eternal: "Faith lifts the staggering soul on one side, Hope support it on the other. Experience says it must be, and love says—let it be" (280).

The curriculum of her school, St. Joseph's Academy, consisted of reading, writing, spelling, grammar, geography, and arithmetic. The annual tuition was approximately $125; music, needlework, and languages were privately taught for a fee of $5 to $8. The students who could not afford the tuition were supported by those who could pay, which set a precedent for school administration.

Elizabeth Ann Seton, the founder of the first religious community native to America, the first American parish school, and the first American Catholic orphanage, died of tuberculosis on Thursday, January 4, 1821, exhorting her sisters to "Be children of the Church" (Dirvin 1975, 453). In 1959, she was pronounced "Venerable" by the Catholic Church; in 1963, "Blessed"; and on September 14, 1975, she was canonized as the first native-born American saint by Pope Paul VI. As Terence Cardinal Cooke states in his Foreword to Father Joseph Dirvin's biography *Mrs. Seton*, "In Elizabeth Ann Seton, we have a saint for our times . . . a woman of faith for a time of doubt and uncertainty . . . a woman of love for a time of coldness and division . . . a woman of hope for a time of crisis and discouragement" (1975, xiii).

Seton's training in the French language equipped her to translate ascetical French works, including the life of Saint Vincent de Paul, which her sisters often used on days of retreat. Her diaries and correspondences provide a window into the soul of this saint of our time and enrich the canon of nineteenth-century American literature and spiritual autobiography.

MAJOR THEMES

Letter writing was an increasingly popular activity in the eighteenth and nineteenth centuries. Male and female writers popularized the epistolary mode as a literary genre during this time. Elizabeth Seton's style of letter writing more closely paralleled the Pauline letters of the New Testament in their focus on the spiritual progress of both herself and the recipient. Indeed, her sacramental outlook on life reflects the theological belief that a disciplined and evolving vision allows us to see through the life of things into the life of God. Her writings reenact the Pauline doctrine: "Since the creation of the world, invisible realities, God's eternal power and divinity, have become visible, recognized through the things he has made" (Rom. 1:20).

Seton's letters also expressed her ties to her friends and acquaintances that, while not constituting a formal autobiography, convey the high regard in which she held friendship, her ability to express with genuineness and honesty the joys and frustrations of quotidian experiences, the sacramental relationship that exists between the soul and its Creator, and her consistent wish to fulfill the will of God. In particular, her letters to Julianna Scott, her lifelong friend and benefactor in Philadelphia, afford the reader an intimate profile of her friendship, love, faith, courage, magnanimity, and practical spirituality. On September 20, 1809, she wrote to Julianna that "the nearer a soul is truly united to God, the more its sensibilities are increased to every being of His creation; much more to those whom it is bound to love by the tenderest and most endearing ties" (*Letters*, 188). These letters to "Julia" provide the most complete record of Seton's sustained friendship and chronicle her impressions of daily and momentous events. Her writing was therapeutic as she recorded her sorrow at the loss of her loved ones and reassured Julianna and herself of the certainty of eternal life. She gave the name "Gloriana" to Julianna and frequently concluded her letters with a declaration of her affection and love for her "dear Julia." When a woman who had served as a servant neglected to give Seton a letter from Julianna, Seton, upon receiving it, immediately wrote to Julianna, "How it hurts me, my own Julia, that your letter should have been on the way so long before it reached me. . . . You have been suffering, my Julia, really suffering, since the spirit was wounded. What you must have felt in your apprehension for the precious friend and companion of your varied days!" (200–201). Such apologies are frequently seen in her letters, as are remarks of gratitude for money that Julianna often sent to Seton for the care of Seton's family and community and the maintenance of her school. The letters also provide updates on the condition of mutual friends and acquaintances, the weather, Seton's love of nature, and her constant concern about the illnesses and deaths of family and community members. She wrote to Julianna from the bedside of her dying daughter Anna Maria, and a month after her daughter's death expressed, "How true a comfort have I when possessed of such a friend as you are. Dear, dear, little faithful soul!" (218). These correspondences also provide insight into the vagaries of the postal system, as Seton candidly expressed her dismay at the amount of time such mail delivery took and at her own propensity to prolong her letter writing.

While progressing through these letters, the reader perceives the strong bonds that connect these two women. Written in the epistolary mode of the early nineteenth century, these letters reflect the enduring ties of friendship, compassion, and love, and of financial, emotional, and spiritual support, that existed between Seton and Scott. They also solidify the close connection between temporal and eternal friendship. In these letters, Seton expressed her affinity with Catholic theology's definition of the sacrament of the Eucharist as the true body and blood of Christ. This doctrinal point of the Real Presence of Christ in the Eucharist fired her intellect and imagination and impelled her to write about God's immanence in the communion host, in nature, and in quotidian experiences. During Seton's periods of spiritual struggle and conversion, and the establishing of her school and founding of a religious community, she counted on Julianna's sustained friendship and moral support. In a letter dated October 3, 1808, she paid her friend a high compliment: "I might challenge the whole world to produce a friend so sincere and constant as yourself. . . . Dear, dear Julia, what would I not give to put my heart in your hands for a few hours" (170). Later in the letter, she informed Julianna of occurrences at home and her own "pain in the breast which has weakened me so much as to leave me little hope of the health in which you left me. . . . You know my mind which is founded on a confidence in the Divine Goodness; and if death succeeds it, I must put a mother's hopes and fears in His hands who has promised most to the widow and the fatherless" (171). Seton's desire to be reunited with her loved ones who had died and her own increasing illness provided her with a glimpse of heaven that she often alluded to in these letters as "the place where there is no time! Eternity!" (219). Her letters also contain her hope that "we may but pass our dear Eternity together" (225).

What is most remarkable and refreshing about Seton's letters to Julianna Scott and her correspondence in general is their conversational tone. Her use of dashes, exclamation points, and question marks reflects a woman who was intimately passionate about life and who expressed this intensity and zeal through writings that are grounded in reflection and spirituality. Moreover, they reveal her honesty, sincerity, humor, anxiety, hopes, fears, pleas for continued correspondence, and trust in and longing for God and eternity. *The Letters of Mother Seton to Julianna Scott* are of prime importance for an understanding of the mind, character, and spirituality of a woman who exercised a profound influence on America in its early stages of educational and religious development in the nineteenth-century and whose influence continues to be far-reaching. They provide a journal of a soul, with its concomitant "dark night" and eventual conversion experiences.

Seton used the written word most effectively and efficaciously to convey her love and affection for her family and friends, her dedication to her secular and religious vocations, her professional responsibilities to various constituencies, and the rich dimensions of her religious faith. For example, in her letters to her sons William and Robert, Seton discussed family concerns and financial matters, encouraged them in their search for employment and stability, and reminded them to receive the sacraments. In letters she sent to the parents of her students, she provided reports on the conduct of the children, their academic and social progress, and their religious development. A tone of solicitude, assurance, and professionalism permeates these letters, interspersed with concerns for travel, safety, and weather conditions. Letters to the sisters, priests, and the bishop who helped in the establishing of her community underscore the importance of financial accountability and record such practical matters as house cleaning and duty changes. They also provided a vehicle by which Seton released the grief she experienced at the loss of family members and friends, and they served as a source of healing and reaffirmation of God's providence, guidance, and care. Indeed, she even encouraged some of the people to whom she wrote to pen letters of their own to their friends who may have experienced a sorrow or loss, and she often concluded her letters by stating how much she anticipated receiving another missive from them. Some of the letters to her friends exhibit happiness and congratulations on a forthcoming wedding and provide advice on being a good spouse and the awesome responsibilities of parenthood.

Her journals provide another window through which the spiritual dimensions of Elizabeth Ann Seton are revealed. The Leghorn journal that she wrote for her sister-in-law Rebecca Seton chronicles the voyage to Italy with her sick husband, their eight-year-old daughter Anna Maria, the month of quarantine in the Lazaretto, William's suffering and death, and the kindness of the Filicchi family, William's business associates and friends. It is a testament to Seton's deep faith and trust in God during a time of loneliness and trial.

Seton's booklets containing her personal devotions include marginalia—her handwritten prayers and reflections—that cover such topics as God Incarnate, humility, the temporal nature of earthly life, eternity, the love of God, and the necessity of abandoning the self to God's will. She also penned her own prayers and reflections for personal devotion, some of her own composition and some deriving from books she received from the Filicchis or from the notes she recorded on retreat days that were conducted by the priests who visited her community during its establishment. Occasional topics covered in these devotions are love of God, sin, death, judgment, the omnipresence of God, harmony in community, prayer, Mary's virtues, peace, Christmas, fear of God, the charity of Christ, and living in the presence of God. She also provided a plan for an examination of conscience and a daily schedule of a retreat for newcomers. Her writings are practical in their spiritual orientation and profound in their depiction of her interior spirit. They serve not only as literary representations of early nineteenth-century personal recordings but, more importantly, as artful and strategic descriptions of the soul's progress in a life of continual conversion and emerging identity. Like the Catholic religion to which Seton subscribed, her writings are rooted in history and representative of the journey of the Christian disciple. They are true not only because they are biographical recordings of her life but also because they are spiritual records of the Christian disciple.

Seton's letters, journals, meditations, devotions, and instructions to her community provide a rich insight into her times and her spirituality as well as the details of her life as widow, convert, single mother, educator, and religious. They provide a biography of a woman on a lifelong spiritual journey, of continual conversion toward the truth of her existence. Moreover, they furnish an intimate verbal self-portrait of a woman who was not only grounded in the realities of early nineteenth-century American life but also rooted firmly in a God of charity and in her Catholic faith.

CRITICAL RECEPTION

Two Sisters of Charity, Regina Bechtle and Judith Metz, have compiled a three-volume annotated collection of Seton's writings in *Elizabeth Bayley Seton: Collected Writings* (2000, 2002). The thirteen religious congregations that constitute the Sisters of Charity Federation undertook the publication of the complete corpus of the writings of Elizabeth Ann Seton. To date, two volumes of Seton's letters, a substantial collection of meditations, instructions, reflections, copybooks, translations, poems, receipts, and other miscellaneous jottings have been located and published, with ongoing research forthcoming in a third volume. Volume 1 includes Seton's correspondence and journals from 1793 to 1808, Volume 2 from 1808 to 1820, and Volume 3 will include her meditations, instructions, and other writings. These well-researched and documented publications provide unprecedented access to and an updated collection of Seton's writings. Included are listings from the archives of the Sisters of Charity and various repositories in the United States and Canada. These collected works provide rich source material about religious history, women's history, the evolution of religious life and Catholic education in America in the early nineteenth century, and the spirit of Elizabeth Ann Seton herself.

The single volume of *Letters of Mother Seton to Mrs. Julianna Scott* is collected in Monsignor Joseph B. Code's second edition (1960) of his original work (1935). The book contains letters written by Seton dating from 1798, shortly after the death of Julianna's husband, the former Secretary of State of New York, and concludes with a letter dated July 19, 1820, six months before Seton's death. Code intermittently situates these correspondences with critical commentary on Seton's circumstances and provides a transition from one set of letters to the next.

In *Elizabeth Ann Seton: A Self-Portrait (1774–1821): A Study of her Spirituality in Her Own Words* (1986), Sister Marie Celeste Cuzzolina captures the multifaceted nature of Elizabeth Seton by writing a work that is thematic and scholarly in its attention to the facts and in its inclusion of cross-references, an extensive index, and citations from Seton's memoirs, diaries, and correspondences. Much of the documentation is derived from unpublished material in the Vatican archives. Seton's own words serve as chapter titles and describe her evolution from New York society belle, to devoted wife and mother, to founder of the first academy for girls under Catholic auspices in the United States and of the Sisters of Charity. Cuzzolina, who has undertaken the most definitive and extensive treatment of Elizabeth Seton to date, is a Sister of Charity in Greensburg, Pennsylvania, and professor emeritus of modern languages at Loyola University. In 2000, she published *The Intimate Friendships of Elizabeth Ann Bayley Seton: First Native-Born American Saint* and *Elizabeth Ann Seton, A Woman of Prayer: Meditations, Reflections, Prayers and Poems Taken From Her Writings*. Her books have been released in France, Canada, and the United States.

Previous to the publication of Cuzzolina's work, Father Joseph Dirvin wrote *Mrs. Seton, Foundress of the American Sisters of Charity* in 1962 and provided an updated edition to coincide with Seton's canonization in 1975. This biography was written from original sources and provides citations from various letters, correspondences, and notes of Elizabeth Seton. The book focuses primarily on the people who influenced her in the development of her spiritual life, both as an Anglican and a Catholic. It provides an extensive bibliography, an index, and, in the canonization edition, a foreword by Terence Cardinal Cooke (1975), Archbishop of New York, that describes the universal quality of Elizabeth Seton and her appeal to the current generation. In 1990, Father Dirvin also released *The Soul of Elizabeth Seton*, a book of spiritual reading that exemplifies how Seton used Scripture and meditations to become closer to God. Dirvin is also the author of two other saints' biographies, *Louise de Marillac* and *St. Catherine Labouré of the Miraculous Medal*.

In 1976, Annabelle Melville updated her 1951 Hudson River edition of *Elizabeth Bayley Seton 1774–1821*, which in a lucid and readable style furthers the appeal of Seton's spiritual pilgrimage by situating her in early nineteenth-century American society. This study makes a significant contribution to biographical studies on Seton; it also provides visual appeal in its color portrait cover of the subject as well as eight pages of photographs.

Leonard Feeney's revised biography, *Mother Seton: Saint Elizabeth of New York* ([1947] 1975), suggests the complexities of Seton's relationships with the ecclesiastical officials and the challenges of establishing two institutions simultaneously: a school and a religious community. In 1938, Feeney also published *Elizabeth Seton: An American Woman, Her Story*.

Quite a few other resources now available underscore the universal appeal of Elizabeth Seton. Julie Walters, an author of several children's books, wrote *Elizabeth Ann Seton: Saint for a New Nation* (2002), which is aimed at young adults and highlights the events that shaped Seton's character and spirituality. Elaine Murray Stone's *Elizabeth Ann Seton: American Saint* (1993), written for juvenile audiences, is a biography that focuses on Seton's deeds and contributions to American Catholicism. Various videotapes and even musical cantatas also underscore the appeal of this first American-born saint to a wide audience.

NOTE

Elizabeth Ann Seton, *Letters of Mother Seton to Mrs. Julianna Scott*, ed. Msgr. Joseph B. Code (Baltimore, MD: Chandler Printing Co., 1960). All references are to this edition.

WORKS CITED

Bechtle, Regina, and Judith Metz. 2000, 2002. *Elizabeth Bayley Seton: Collected Writings*. 2 vols. New York: New City Press.
Cooke, Terence Cardinal. 1975. Foreword. In Joseph I. Dirvin, C. M. *Mrs. Seton: Foundress of the American Sisters of Charity*, 2nd ed., xiii. New York: Farrar, Straus, and Giroux.

Cuzzolina, Marie Celeste, S. C. 1986. *Elizabeth Ann Seton, A Self-Portrait (1774–1821): A Study of Her Spirituality in Her Own Words*. Libertyville, IL: Franciscan Marytown Press.

———. 2000. *Elizabeth Ann Seton: A Woman of Prayer: Meditations, Reflections, Prayers and Poems Taken From Her Writings*. Lanham, MD: University Press of America.

———. 2000. *The Intimate Friendships of Elizabeth Ann Bayley Seton: First Native-Born American Saint, 1774–1821*. Lanham, MD: University Press of America.

Dirvin, Joseph I., C. M. 1975. *Mrs. Seton: Foundress of the American Sisters of Charity*. 2nd ed. New York: Farrar, Straus, and Giroux.

———. 1990. *The Soul of Elizabeth Seton*. San Francisco: Ignatius Press.

Feeney, Leonard. 1938. *Elizabeth Seton: An American Woman, Her Story*. New York: America Press.

———. [1947] 1975. *Mother Seton: Saint Elizabeth of New York (1774–1821)*. 2nd ed. Cambridge, MA: Ravengate Press.

Melville, Annabelle M. [1951] 1976. *Elizabeth Bayley Seton: 1774–1821*. 2nd ed. New York: Scribner's.

Stone, Elaine Murray. 1993. *Elizabeth Ann Seton: American Saint*. New York: Paulist Press.

Walters, Julie. 2002. *Elizabeth Ann Seton: Saint for a New Nation*. New York: Paulist Press.

BIBLIOGRAPHY

Melville, Annabelle M., and Ellin M. Kelly. *Elizabeth Seton: Selected Writings*. Sources of American Spirituality Series, vol. 5. New York: Paulist Press, 1987.

Seton, Robert. 1869. *Memoir, Letters and Journal of Elizabeth Seton: Convert to the Catholic Faith, and Sister of Charity*. 2 vols. New York: P. O'Shea Publisher.

— Mary Theresa Hall

Henryk Sienkiewicz [1846–1916]

Quo Vadis?

BIOGRAPHY

Henryk Sienkiewicz's life often eclipsed those he created for his fictional characters, both in vividness and in passion. Henryk Adam Aleksander Pius was born on May 5, 1846, into an impoverished noble Polish family of Lithuanian Tatar descent. His background thus exemplified the multinational identity that characterized Poland in the sixteenth and seventeenth century, the epoch that later brought Sienkiewicz great fame. But as colorful as his lineage was, his relationships with women were the stuff of which novels are made. Engaged to Maria Keller in 1874, he was spurned by her parents, who found the "beautiful and eloquent, charming and witty" Sienkiewicz entirely unsuitable as a husband (Narkowicz 2000, 16). The engagement was dissolved by Maria's father in a letter to Henryk while the latter was on a visit to Paris. In 1876, Sienkiewicz left for the United States, where he spent two years in the company of the beautiful actress and internationally famous *femme fatale* Helena Modrzejewska, by then Countess Chlapowska. At that time, he was a journalist commissioned by the *Gazeta polska* to report his observations in a series of "travel letters." She was a renowned Shakespearean actress who became famous in the United States under the name Modjeska. The couple spent two years in an experimental utopian commune in Anaheim, California. The experiment and the union proved unsuccessful, but for Sienkiewicz, Helena Modrzejewska remained forever a passionate memory and the ideal of feminine beauty.

On his return to Europe, Sienkiewicz traveled to Italy, where, in Venice, he met Maria Szetkiewicz. They married in 1881, and she is said to have been the love of his life. His letters offer a glimpse of their happy life together, completed by the birth of their two children and their obvious love for each other. However, the family bliss was cut short when Maria died of tuberculosis four years into the marriage. In 1888, Sienkiewicz next proposed marriage to his distant cousin Maria Babska, but he broke the engagement off shortly thereafter. Instead, he married Maria Romanowska-Wolodkowicz, a woman twenty-seven years his junior. She left him while they were honeymooning in Italy. In 1899, Sienkiewicz attempted a marriage proposal to Maria Radziejewska but was unsuccessful. Finally, in 1904, he married his cousin Maria Babska after all. She proved the ideal companion for the restless writer. Maria was actively engaged in Sienkiewicz's philanthropic works while sheltering him from the petty troubles of everyday life. She fiercely protected his memory after his death.

Apart from troubles of the heart, Sienkiewicz's entire life was deeply marked by the political realities of his time. He was born almost fifty-one years after Poland's political collapse and its final partition among Russia, Prussia, and Austria. And, like most of his contemporaries, he was raised on the idea of patriotic duty, watching two generations of his family fight for independence and dreaming of one day seeing Poland regain its statehood. Sienkiewicz died on November 15, 1916, just two years before that wish was realized.

For 125 years, Poland had existed only in hopes and dreams. Literary and cultural trends were inextricably linked to a political discourse on the future of Poland and its struggle for independence. The writers and poets of the romantic generation proclaimed a fiery, belligerent patriotism calling for armed uprisings, which were then brutally put down by the occupying powers. In their political idealism, they believed in the struggle against all oppressors, and they often traveled the continent fighting and dying in foreign battles. They failed to consider the context of Poland's geopolitical realities, and their sacrifice brought no political gain but merely repeated the cycle of defeat and deep despair. The political sufferings and fall of Poland were verbalized theologically by the Romantics. The term "Polish messianism" was coined to express the belief that the political humiliations, reversals, and defections served a higher purpose. After the bloodily crushed November Uprising of 1831, Adam Mickiewicz, the leading writer of the Polish romantic period, wrote, "And on the third day the soul will return to the body, and the nation will rise up from the dead and liberate all of the peoples of Europe from captivity.... And just as bloody sacrifices on earth came to an end with the Resurrection of Christ, so wars in Christianity will cease with the resurrection of the Polish nation" (1884, 7). Polish messianism ascribed to Poland a particular historical role, that of a martyr who would bring about the renewal of Europe. Analogies were drawn between the martyrdom of Christ and the dismemberment of Poland, between the Way of the Cross and exile to Siberia—with parallels seen between the mockery and disrobing of Christ and the partition of the mother country. The correlation between politics, literature, and religion was rooted in the realities of nineteenth-century Poland. The Church and, to some extent, the theater were the only places where the Polish language was allowed to be used without constraints. In other public areas—from schools to workplaces—Poles were subject to Germanization and Russification by their occupiers. It was a natural development, therefore, to see religion and literature as the mainstays of Polish identity. It was unavoidable for both areas to become politicized and entwined in the struggle for independence, especially in the romantic period.

Sienkiewicz was not alien to the ideals of romanticism, particularly to Polish messianism, and traits of it appear in his writing, notably in *Quo Vadis?* However, after witnessing the January Uprising of 1863 and the executions and massive deportations that followed, Sienkiewicz came to view the new positivist movement, based on the ideals of enlightenment and progress, as more appropriate and ultimately more successful. The movement cultivated reason, education, and the advance of science and learning as a means to a responsible, just, and independent society. Sienkiewicz's early novellas and essays clearly reflect these precepts. They expose the romantic ideal of a nationwide struggle against foreign villains as false in the face of social injustice within the nation itself. For example, in *Charcoal Sketches* (*Szkice weglem* [1880]), an impoverished, uneducated peasant considers equally oppressive the landlord, the Church, and the tsarist officials. The protagonist of *Bart the Victor* (*Bartek Zwyciezca* [1882]) is forced to fight in a war that does not concern him. *Janko the Musician* (*Janko Muzykant* [1880]) is the story of a peasant boy whose musical talent cannot but go to waste. And the main character of *The Lighthouse Keeper* (*Latarnik* [1882]) is an emigré with nothing left but nostalgia. However, Sienkiewicz was also very aware of the dangers inherent to tendentious literature. Politically engaged writing led, in his opinion, to shallowness, stereotyping, and banality.

In 1883, Sienkiewicz's writing seemed to change. In May of that year, installments of the novel *By Fire and Sword* (*Ogniem i mieczem* [1884]) began to appear in the daily newspaper *Slowo*. With this work, Sienkiewicz turned away from contemporary topics and toward history. *By Fire and Sword* was to be the first novel in a trilogy set in the seventeenth century, a time when Poland was sovereign, mighty, and successful in battle. At the time of publication, Sienkiewicz included the now-famous comment that the goal of his writing was to "uplift the spirit" (753). At a time of national despair, this motto struck a chord. *By Fire and Sword* was an instant success. The story of the great Cossack revolt, filled with dynamic depictions of rivalries, duels, ambushes, kidnappings, daring escapes, and rescues, proved immensely popular with the reading public. This novel was followed in 1886 by *The Deluge* (*Potop*), based on the Swedish invasion of Poland, and in 1888 by *Pan Michael* (*Pan Wolodyjowski*), based on the wars with the Ottoman Empire. These works sealed Sienkiewicz's fame and fortune. In fact, the trilogy was almost obligatory reading in all parts of occupied Poland. It also had a devoted following among the Polish immigrants to the United States, who, anonymous and insignificant in their new country, wished to remember a Poland that was proud, important, and relevant.

The impact of these novels was best described by Stefan Zeromski, one of the greatest Polish writers, in his "Journals" (*Dzienniki: Wybor* 1980). Zeromski recounts the story of a friend who was waiting at a small town post office one day along with two dozen shoemakers, storekeepers, farmhands, and other simple folk. They were all waiting for the *Slowo*. Once the mail arrived, the post office clerk began to read out loud from the daily installment of *The Deluge*. All those people had waited for hours, away from their work, just to hear Sienkiewicz's story. People who had hardly ever read a book in their lives could not spend one day without his trilogy of novels. And for that, Zeromski said, Sienkiewicz should be thanked.

The main topic of the trilogy—the Polish wars of the seventeenth century—had religious overtones. The battles with the Cossacks and the Polish-Russian wars were conflicts with Eastern Orthodoxy. The Swedish invasion was waged as a religious war by the Protestant Swedes, who destroyed religious symbols, killed priests, and sought support from Polish Protestants. The wars with the Ottoman Empire were against Muslims. Sienkiewicz emphasized this correlation between the defense of the state and of religion. The main characters of the novels are, somewhat simplistically, divided into the good (mostly Poles and Catholics) and the bad (foreigners and infidels). The high points of the novels are often composed around religious symbols, as in the battle of the monastery at Jasna Góra in *The Deluge*. This theme of religion as being at the core of national survival is emphasized throughout the trilogy and finally culminates in the writing of *Quo Vadis?*

Critics, though divided on the merits of Sienkiewicz's novels, hailed his mastery of language and style. Sienkiewicz seemed to draw from many different techniques of historical novel writing. For example, he combined Walter Scott's style of situating his fictional main characters in a background of authentic, historic events with the optimism and pathos of the Homeric epic tradition. He also blended Alexander Dumas's dynamism with the romantic traditions of storytelling. Out of this mélange, Sienkiewicz created his own unmistakable style. And it was rendered in a language masterfully stylized to the particular historical epoch. To this day, Polish dictionaries use quotations from his works to illustrate word usage.

Sienkiewicz was a prolific writer, and the complete edition of his works runs to sixty volumes. These works include the hugely popular *Teutonic Knights* (*Krzyzacy* [1900]), the children's book *Through Desert and Jungle* (*W pustyni i w puszczy* [1912]), and the psychological novel *Without Dogma* (*Bez dogmatu* [1891]). But it was the 1896 publication of *Quo Vadis?* that brought Sienkiewicz international acclaim. The novel was translated into more than fifty languages and sold millions of copies within the first few years. The English translation sold 800,000 copies in one year alone, and the French translation outsold the works of the most popular French writer, Émile Zola. To this day, *Quo Vadis?* remains the most popular Polish book abroad.

In 1905, the Royal Swedish Academy awarded Sienkiewicz the Nobel Prize in Literature for *Quo Vadis?* The Academy's presentation citation began:

> Whenever the literature of a people is rich and inexhaustible, the existence of that people is assured, for the flower of civilization cannot grow on barren soil. But in every nation there are some rare geniuses who concentrate in themselves the spirit of the nation; they represent the national character to the world. Although they cherish the memory of the past of that people, they do so only to strengthen its hope for the future. Their inspiration is deeply rooted in the past, but the branches are swayed by the winds of the day. Such a representative of the literature and intellectual culture of a whole people is the man the Swedish Academy has this year awarded the Nobel Prize. He is here and his name is Henryk Sienkiewicz. (*Nobel Lectures* 1999, 12)

This citation eloquently put into words what Sienkiewicz's readers found in all of his historical novels: the hope for a future. The fact that his role was recognized by the Royal Swedish Academy made that hope realistic. By the time he received the Nobel Prize, Sienkiewicz was the most popular and beloved writer in Poland. In 1900, he was presented with a manor house and estate, paid for by voluntary donations collected throughout the country. It was a gift from the nation to celebrate his years as a writer and to thank him for uplifting the nation's despairing spirit.

But Sienkiewicz was not one to settle down. He had traveled extensively during his life. After losing the family estate, the Sienkiewiczs had moved to Warsaw, where Henryk took up university studies. He lived in the United States and throughout Europe—in Paris, Lvov, Venice, Rome, Vienna, and on the Adriatic coast. He stayed at times in Brussels and Ostend, and he toured England, Italy, and Switzerland. He visited Romania, Bulgaria, Turkey, Greece, Egypt, and Zanzibar. On his travels, Sienkiewicz researched his historical novels meticulously. While visiting Rome in 1894, he met the painter Henryk Siemiradzki, famous at the time for his paintings of ancient Rome. Sienkiewicz was awed by Siemiradzki's highly realistic canvases showing the stunning opulence and beauty of the imperial court as well as the haunting depiction of Christian martyrdom. He was struck by the contrast between these two worlds, and when Siemiradzki showed him the inscription "Quo Vadis?" on the pediment of a roadside chapel, the idea for a novel took seed. To research *Quo Vadis?* Sienkiewicz toured Rome with Tacitus's *Annales* in hand. He visited all of the sites he later described in the novel and compared them with Tacitus's references. He visited museums and studied the latest academic and archaeological research on ancient Rome. He read extensively in Latin prose and poetry to learn everything he could about the ancient Romans, from their religious rites to their food preferences. As a consequence, it was often said that his portrayal of supposedly immoral pagan Rome is much more appealing than that of the virtuous but pallid community of Christians.

At the onset of World War I, Sienkiewicz moved to Vevey in Switzerland, where, together with the famous pianist and later prime minister of Poland, Ignacy Paderewski, he headed the Red Cross Committee for the Assistance to War Victims in Poland. Sienkiewicz died in 1916 and was buried in Vevey. In 1924, in a lavish ceremony, his remains were moved to St. John's Cathedral in Warsaw.

PLOT SUMMARY

Marcus Vinitius, a young Roman patrician and soldier on his return from a campaign in Armenia, pays his uncle Petronius a visit. At his side, the reader enters the splendors of ancient Rome. Petronius (an historical figure) is a reputed aesthete at Nero's court, a writer, thinker, and *arbiter elegantiarum*, one who has the last word in matters of manners and good taste. With Petronius, the beautiful and indulgent existence of a Roman patrician comes lavishly to life. Because he spent the preceding night at a palace reception, he is exhausted. He rises at noon and idles the rest of the day as he is bathed and massaged by a retinue of, by his own count, nearly four hundred slaves, each with a different skill. Even Marcus Vinitius, the warrior, is not indifferent to the joys of this life and joins his uncle in the daily routine.

Marcus comes to tell his uncle the story of Lygia Callina, whom he met while recovering from an injury at the house of her Roman family. She is as beautiful as she is mysterious, and Marcus wants to possess her. He is enamored with the daughter of a Barbarian king. Callina arrived in Rome as a hostage to ensure that the warriors of her father, the king of the Lygians, do not cross the Roman border. But as Vinitius will gradually discover, her power is more profound. She is a Christian, and her staunch beliefs will expose the weakness of Nero's empire— the spiritual emptiness masked in breathtaking splendor.

Callina had been taken in and raised by Aulus and his wife Pomponia, who is secretly a Christian. The couple are widely respected for their righteousness and modesty, and their household is famous for its extraordinarily respectful treatment of slaves and for its quiet and peaceful happiness. Life in Aulus's house stands in stark contrast to that of other patricians, where divorce, adultery, and debauchery are the norm, where masters are inhumane and slaves immoral, and where the reification of human beings is rampant and cruelty is to be expected. But Callina's life is different.

As a king's daughter Callina cannot be Marcus's slave, and as a Christian she will not become his lover. Marcus thus solicits Petronius's help to devise a plan whereby Callina, the royal hostage, is to be taken to Nero's court. There, Petronius will use his influence to ensure that she is given to Marcus as a gift by the emperor. For Nero sees himself as a most accomplished poet and singer, a role that enables Petronius, who flatters him, to be one of his favorites. But the cunning plan backfires. Deeply disgusted by the court, Callina escapes with her Lygian servant Ursus, a man of mild temper but Herculean strength, and goes into hiding within the secretive Christian community. She disappears without a trace.

Thus begins Marcus's long search for Lygia Callina, which will lead him into the Christian community, into her life, and into her religion. At first, Marcus relies on tricks and betrayal to find Callina. He employs the learned scoundrel Chilon Chilonides, who pretends to be a Christian in order to win the community's trust and get close to her. But when tricks, bribes, and forcefulness fail, Marcus has no choice but to rely on honesty. After witnessing a sermon by Saint Peter the Apostle, he is wounded in an effort to kidnap Callina and finally surrenders to her to be treated and healed, in body and soul. Marcus's journey culminates in a confession of love for Callina and in his baptism.

Meanwhile, Callina disappears again and Marcus joins the emperor on a trip to Antium. There, the court receives word that Rome is burning. The capital is destroyed. Nero needs a scapegoat, and as Petronius is losing influence at the court, his nemesis, Tygellinus, the brutal imperial councilor and prefect of the Praetorian guard, persuades the emperor to blame the Christians. The persecutions begin. Callina is imprisoned with other Christians, and Marcus's efforts to free her fail. As she lies ill, she bids farewell to Marcus and begs him not to give up his faith.

Bloody spectacles take place in the arenas as Christians are devoured by wild animals. Nero surpasses himself in gory pageants: mass crucifixions are ordered, as are "life torches"—Christians tied to poles and set on fire to light the emperor's gardens. But in all the chaos and bloodshed, one soul is saved: Chilon Chilonides confesses that Rome was burned on Nero's orders. He converts and begs for forgiveness. Saint Peter baptizes him and gives him absolution. As torture and agony reign, Chilon dies a martyr.

Death holds sway everywhere, and it seems invincible. Marcus becomes an undertaker to be closer to Callina, to have a chance to see her one last time. And Callina's time comes—she is tied to a bull and chased into the Colosseum. As the audience cheers the new game, there seems to be no hope left. But her faithful servant Ursus never leaves her side, and he displays his legendary strength by wrestling and killing the bull with his bare hands. Awed, the audience requests that they both be spared, and the emperor reluctantly yields to the wishes of the crowd and sets them free. Marcus and Callina are finally reunited.

Urged to do so by the faithful, the apostle Peter flees Rome. But on the Via Appia he meets Christ walking toward him. To his question, "*Quo vadis,*

Domine?"—"Where are you going, Lord?"—Christ replies, "Since you are leaving my people, I am going back to Rome, to be crucified again." Ashamed of his cowardice, Peter returns to Rome and is himself crucified.

The end is near, and terror reigns at Nero's court. Seneca and Petronius are ordered to commit suicide. As Nero's world crumbles, his soldiers revolt against him. The emperor returns to Rome, where the Senate's verdict awaits him. Charged with parricide, Nero is condemned to die, but he chooses suicide out of fear of execution. At the last moment, he hesitates and Epaphroditus, his servant, helps him to die by his own hand.

MAJOR THEMES

In order to comprehend the strong and lasting impact of *Quo Vadis?* one has to realize that Sienkiewicz's novel represents the climax of a subgenre that emerged in the nineteenth century. Archaeological discoveries of ancient Rome and early Christianity inspired authors to translate these findings into monumental historical epics. The four seminal novels in this subgenre were Edward Bulwer-Lytton's *The Last Days of Pompeii* (1834), Cardinal Wiseman's *Fabiola; or the Church of the Catacombs* (1854), John Henry Newman's *Callista, A Sketch of the Third Century* (1855), and Lewis Wallace's *Ben Hur* (1880). While Bulwer-Lytton indulged in an elaborate portrayal of a decadent society, the Anglo-Irish Cardinal Wiseman assembled most of the motifs and figures, based on archaeological discoveries, that would make *Quo Vadis?* the representative best-seller of the genre. In *Fabiola*, a Christian virgin is pursued by a pagan lover, and the treachery of the heathen contrasts with the virtuous conduct of Christians in a world filled with abominable villains and temptations. John Henry Newman, in *Callista*, developed what was to become, of course, the major theme of his life: the story of conversion. In terms of best-seller status, *Quo Vadis?* was rivaled only by former American Major-General Wallace's *Ben Hur*. Benefiting from his experience of horrific battle casualties in the American Civil War, Wallace's portrayal of the persecution and sacrifice of martyrs did not lack realistic detail. However, the fact that *Quo Vadis?* was in a popular genre of the period is but the short answer to the novel's long-lasting success. The long answer must factor in the premises that led the author to combine in virtuoso fashion various traditions and techniques to construct his powerful story. Unlike these other writers, Sienkiewicz was a skilled journalist and researcher who had become a master craftsman of narration equal to a Tolstoy, Dumas, or Scott in writing historical novels about his country's national heritage. A religious novel, *Quo Vadis?* reached out beyond a nineteenth-century interpretation of the national past of Russia, France, or Scotland. It provided a bridge to biblical times.

The title incident of the novel, as referred to in the last sentence of its Epilogue, goes back to a brief anecdote in the apocryphal *Acts of Saint Peter* in which Peter encounters Jesus on his way out of Rome and is then redirected toward his true destiny, crucifixion. This and other apocryphal texts that were not included in the biblical canon were generated during the last quarter of the second century for a specific need of popular piety. The beleaguered Christian communities, mostly of minority status in a heathen world, thirsted for stories involving New Testament figures performing miracles and resisting the evils of pagan power.

Numerous episodes in *Quo Vadis?* involving descriptions of mass torture, like being thrown before wild beasts, find their source in these apocryphal narratives. This is also the case for familiar Christian themes like virgins vowed to celibacy and chaste matrons spurning pagan suitors and husbands and enduring persecution as a consequence. The powerful dynamics of these tales of early Christian heroism translated easily into the contemporary diaspora situations of other European nations, where the main threat was not from Russia but from the dominant Protestant majority culture. A further element was the *fin de siècle* spirit that permeated other European nations at the time of publication. The end of the nineteenth century was characterized by an overpowering feeling of decadence against which Catholicism reacted with a very confrontational attitude. Identification with early Christians provided a sense of mission, conversion, and tradition with which popular piety could easily identify.

And then there is the secondary consideration that Sienkiewicz was a master storyteller who could make the numerous interludes in which the story is interrupted by catechetic discussion about articles of faith palatable to a wider audience. He was also very clever in translating nineteenth-century political conflicts into early Christian confrontations. For example, most of the novel's important secondary figures, such as Lygia Callina's giant servant Ursus, are members of ethnic minorities.

Probably the most intriguing narrative element of *Quo Vadis?* is the fact that, while the apostles Peter and Paul are sketched with great virtuosity, creating authentic effects, the real hero of the novel is Petronius. This hedonistic yet stoic aristocrat, with all his ambivalence, is the work's most colorful character. His love affair with the slave Eunice is far more moving than the eventual union of the chaste Lygia Callina with Marcus Vinitius. The last scene of the novel is probably the most moving and transgresses the boundaries of traditional religion. In an act of supreme defiance, Petronius assembles his friends for a last symposium and commits suicide with his beloved, but not before berating and ridiculing the Roman emperor as a tasteless and incompetent idiot. And the portrayal of the decadent Roman society provides far more interesting reading than the episodes in which virtuous but rather bland Christians reiterate the basic tenets of their faith. Sienkiewicz also had no hesitation in employing very dramatic, sensual effects. For example, at the end of chapter ten, when Callina is abducted, Marcus vents his sexual frustration by having the culpable slaves whipped: "there rang groans and whistling of the whip. These sounds lasted almost until morning" (*Quo Vadis?*, 95). And Nero's deviant behavior is often very openly described. In chapter thirty-one, for example, the reader is introduced to the outlandish excesses of an imperial orgy and its aftermath: "Darkness fell on many parts of the groves. Everywhere was heard the sound of laughter, shouts, whisperings, or the panting of both sexes. Rome had never seen its like" (262).

Very often, individual episodes and scenes are staged as if they were, like many modern novels, written for a film script. Sienkiewicz skillfully blends narrative with reflections, and *Quo Vadis?*'s seventy-four chapters contain several gems that are quite unforgettable. The most famous scene, of course, is the near martyrdom in the Colosseum that turns into a triumph for the Christians when the crowd, awed by Ursus's heroic feat, forces an unwilling emperor to grant clemency. But there are many more episodes that let Christian teaching and moral values come to life—and not merely as banal illustrations of catechism answers. When Marcus Vinitius hires the most famous gladiator, Croto, to kidnap Callina, Ursus kills him in a spectacular way (chapter twenty-two); and two chapters later the reader receives the explanation that it is acceptable to kill in self-defense. In spite of using the repertoire of stereotypes of popular novels, Sienkiewicz manages to stay clear of stale predictability. The intellectual climax is, of course, the conversion of Marcus Vinitius. In chapter thirty-nine, he narrates in a love scene with Callina how he had witnessed a debate between Saint Paul and Petronius in which Paul could not convince the pagan of the higher truth of the Christian faith. Yet Petronius conceded, "O little Jew, but I wouldn't care to be matched against you in debate" (313).

There are still other reasons why *Quo Vadis?*, together with *Ben Hur*, did not sink into oblivion like their seminal predecessors. These two novels are teeming with characters that transcend a simple black-and-white depiction of the confrontation between a Christian and a pagan world. *Quo Vadis?*, like the trilogy of novels that came before it, was written with a purpose. It was meant to let its Polish readers find solace and hope in the past and to uplift their spirits by giving them pride and inspiration for the future. Three distinct elements within the novel are clearly designed to accomplish that aim: the portrayal of the Lygians, the use of Christian mythology, and the suggestion of Poland's role as the messiah of the nations.

A vague Polish connection is introduced early in the novel with the characters of Lygia Callina and her servant Ursus. Sienkiewicz describes the Lygians as inhabitants of a land between the rivers Oder and Vistula. This clearly meant Poland and was immediately recognized as such by Polish readers. We know from Sienkiewicz's letters that he based the Lygians on the historical tribe of the Lugiones. In the nineteenth century, it was believed that the Lugiones were Slavs. And even though we know today that their origin was most likely Germanic, there is an emotional bond that still retains its full effect. Sienkiewicz created an emotional kinship between the reader and the historically distant characters by providing them with a common lineage.

Callina and Ursus also show familiar traits endearing them to Polish readers. Ursus is a giant of a man with exceptional strength. When asked about it, he replies that among the Lygians there are "many more like him" (65). To many Polish readers, this alluded to the medieval chronicle of Gallus Anonimus who described Polish warriors as having exceptional strength, with one Polish warrior being worth ten warriors of any other nation. Sienkiewicz's Ursus thus reminded readers of the legendary Poles of ages ago. Callina adds to this familiarity by bearing a name that was, and still is, fairly common in Poland. When the pair appears in the arena of the Colosseum, their struggle also carries a thinly veiled symbolism: Callina representing Poland is tied to the horns of an *ur germanus*, a German bull. Ursus, representing the Polish people, fights the beast with bare hands and wins through sheer will and determination. Thanks to his loyalty and readiness for sacrifice, both Lygians are freed. Allusions of this kind, designed to circumvent censorship, were readily interpreted by Sienkiewicz's original readers.

But what made *Quo Vadis?* even more popular was the deeper symbolism carried by the novel's main Christian theme. History teaches us that in the confrontation between the mighty Roman Empire and an obscure religion embraced by people on the fringes of society, the invincible fell and the powerless prevailed and reshaped the world. Sienkiewicz made this historically astonishing outcome realistic by creating a contrast between the formidable but morally corrupt Romans and the destitute but spiritually powerful Christians. By going back to the roots of Christianity, by introducing Christ and the apostles into the novel, Sienkiewicz reminds the reader that Christendom is not only a religion but a community of people living with a common goal. For Poles, this rang true not only on the spiritual but also on the political level. With the exception of Austria, the occupying powers were of different Christian denominations than the mostly Catholic Poles. Their political struggle was thus given sacral overtones. Sienkiewicz wrote in a letter, "The idea of the victory of the spirit over secular power attracted me as a Pole" (*Listy*, 1977, 126). The persecution of the Christians for their beliefs depicted in *Quo Vadis?* delivered a symbolic comment on the forced Germanization and Russification of Poles, on their persecution for being Poles in their own country. Spirituality and religion thus became part of the political goal of freedom and statehood.

The martyrdom of Christians depicted in *Quo Vadis?* also represented hope. If the early Christians could keep faith in their darkest hour, if through mass arrests and executions they could prevail and ultimately rise to conquer an empire, then Poland could too. However, Sienkiewicz made it very clear that the Christians prevailed through a moral force and a strict code of conduct based on love, altruism, and rectitude. True to his positivist beliefs, Sienkiewicz delivered a memento to his countrymen that victory and statehood would come only to those who aspired to a just society. The occupation will be exposed as immoral in the face of spiritual opposition. So those confident in their faith and conduct should not despair, as their optimism is well founded.

Underlying the idea of martyrdom is the conviction that true victory comes to those who were chosen to suffer by no fault of their own and who are ready to give their lives for a higher purpose. Just as the early Christians in *Quo Vadis?* were chosen to suffer and die and thereby expose the immorality of the Roman Empire, causing it to disintegrate and vanish, so too Poland should accept its messianic role, for its plight would outrage the world and cause the occupying empires to crumble.

Sienkiewicz would never know that the descendants of his imagined Lygians would indeed live to see the day when Prussia, the Austro-Hungarian Empire, and the empire of all the Russias would vanish one by one. But his contemporary readers would have been even more astonished that in 1980 a new moral force rose in Gdansk and confronted another totalitarian imperialism. And in this confrontation, too, the empire crumbled and the new Ursus remained to form a statehood for Poland. Clearly, the timelessness of *Quo Vadis?* and its relevance to so many generations of readers has gone beyond its author's intentions. What Sienkiewicz did was give his readers Saint Paul's words to carry on their journey: "I have fought a good fight, I have finished my course, I have kept my faith."

CRITICAL RECEPTION

One mark of *Quo Vadis?*'s critical success is the fact that it has been translated over the years into many other forms of narration. In 1899, Wilson Barrett, the

English actor and playwright, adapted the novel for the stage. The first of many adaptations, it played on several stages in England and Poland. In 1900, another version by A. Walewski was staged in Lvov. The most successful dramatic version, adapted by Emile Moreau, was staged in Paris in 1901. It ran for 167 performances.

In 1902, Jan Styka created a panoramic painting of *Quo Vadis?* that was hugely popular in Warsaw and was later exhibited in Paris. His illustrations of scenes from the novel can be seen in the recent American edition of *Quo Vadis?* published in 2000.

In 1909, Jean Nogues composed an opera entitled *Quo Vadis?* with a libretto by Henry Cain. This work played with great success in Paris, then in Nice, and later in Berlin, London, and finally Vienna, where Sienkiewicz himself saw its twenty-fifth performance.

In 1909 and 1910, two more versions were staged in France, one by Georges Ducis and the other by C. Trioniller Marcuset. That same year in Prague, a stage adaptation by Karl Hoffman met with great acclaim. Also in that year, Feliks Nowowiejski composed an oratorio based on the novel that met with much success in Germany and was then turned into an opera in Italy by G. Marucello. In the United States, five stage adaptations of *Quo Vadis?* were produced, and one of them was so successful that it was subsequently taken to London.

The first movie version of the novel came out in 1901. In 1923–24, the famous Italian writer Gabriele d'Annunzio codirected a second film. But it was the opulent production of Sam Zimbalist, directed by Mervin Leroy, that introduced this powerful story to a new audience in 1951. The filming took place in Rome. In his autobiography, *Dear Me* (1977), Peter Ustinov, who played a brilliant Nero, recalls quite a few amusing anecdotes illustrating the dilemma that accompanied the filming. From the beginning, the decadent features of a Roman society in decline were far more impressive and dramatic than the virtuous episodes of Christian piety. A recent remake (1985, directed by Franco Rossi), starring Karl Maria Brandauer as Nero and Max von Sydow as Saint Peter, confirms this kind of modern stereotyping. Focused primarily on the antics of Nero, the movie provides a dysfunctional postmodern story line, leaving the roles of Petronius, Lygia Callina, Ursus, and Marcus Vinitius by the wayside. Finally, in 2001, the first Polish version of *Quo Vadis?* was filmed under the direction of Jerzy Kawalerowicz.

NOTE

Henryk Sienkiewicz, *Quo Vadis? A Story of Faith in the Last Days of the Roman Empire*, trans. Jeremiah Curtin (1896; rev. ed. with an introduction and afterword by Joe Wheeler; Wheaton, IL: Tyndale House, 2000). All references are to this edition.

WORKS CITED

Mickiewicz, Adam. 1884. *The Books of the Polish Nation and the Polish Pilgrimage*, trans. Krystyna Lach Szyrma. London.

Narkowicz, Liliana. 2000. "Szwajcarskimi Sladami Henryka Sienkiewicza." *Nasza Gazeta* 26, no. 462: 16–17.

Nobel Lectures: Literature 1901–1995, vol. 1. Singapore: World Scientific Publishing Co., 1999.

Sienkiewicz, Henryk. 1884. *Ogniem i mieczem: Powiesc z lat dawnych.* Warsaw: Keller.

———. 1891. *With Fire and* Sword, trans. Jeremiah Curtin. Boston: Little, Brown & Co.

———. 1977. *Listy*, ed. J. Krzyzanowski. Warsaw: PIN.

Ustinov, Peter. 1977. *Dear Me.* Boston: Little Brown & Co.

Zeromski, Stefan. 1980. *Dzienniki: Wybor*, ed. Jerzy Kadziela. Wroclaw, Krakow: Zaklad Narodowy im. Ossolinskich.

BIBLIOGRAPHY

Dybciak Krzysztof, ed. *Henryk Sienkiewicz: Szkice o tworczosci, zyciu i recepcji.* Siedlce: Instytut Fililogii Polskiej, 1998.

Giergielewicz, Mieczyslaw. *Henryk Sienkiewicz.* New York: Twayne, 1968.

"Henryk (Adam Aleksander Pius) Sienkiewicz." In *Twentieth-Century Literary Criticism*, vol. 3, ed. Sharon K. Hall, 421–32. Detroit: Gale Research, 1980.

Krzyzanowski, Jerzy R. "Henryk Sienkiewicz." In *Contemporary Authors: A Bio-Bibliographic Guide*, vol. 134, ed. Susan M. Trosky, 440–46. Detroit: Gale Research, 1992.

Schmidt, Josef. *Quo vadis?—woher kommst du? Unterhaltungsliterarische konfessionelle Apologetik im Viktorianischen und Wilhelminischen Zeitalter.* Canadian Studies in German Language and Literature, vol. 39. Bern: Peter Lang, 1991.

— Josef Schmidt and Edyta Laszczewska

Muriel Spark [1918–]

Memento Mori

BIOGRAPHY

Born in Edinburgh on February 1, 1918, Muriel Sarah Camberg attended James Gillespie's School for Girls, where she studied English literature, classical languages, French, and physics. She later took a course in précis writing at Heriot Watt College while tutoring students at the Hill School in order to pay for a secretarial course. In 1937 she traveled to Southern Rhodesia (now Zimbabwe) and married Sydney Oswald Spark; the marriage broke down (it was later annulled) and Spark sailed to London in 1944, accompanied by her son, Samuel.

In London, Spark went to work for British Intelligence, writing anti-Nazi propaganda. At the end of the war, she parlayed her long-standing interest in poetry (at the age of nine, she rewrote "The Pied Piper of Hamelin"; at the age of twelve, she won the Sir Walter Scott prize for one of her poems) into a job as general secretary of the Poetry Society and editor of *Poetry Review*. In 1952 she published her first book of poems, *The Fanfarlo and Other Verse*. Spark continued to write poems—publishing *Collected Poems I* (1967) as well as *Going Up to Sotheby's* (1983)—and although she still writes poems (New Directions Press will publish an edition of collected and new poems in 2004) she has devoted most of her energies to writing fiction.

Technically, Spark's professional career as a fiction writer began in 1951, when her remarkable short story "The Seraph and the Zambesi" was selected from nearly 6,000 entries in the London *Observer's* newspaper contest; in the course of a literary career now spanning more than fifty years, she has continued to write short stories, publishing several collections, most recently *The Complete Short Stories of Muriel Spark* (2001), a gathering of forty-one tales.

The string of Muriel Spark's novels—now including twenty-one books—began with *The Comforters* in 1957. While every one of her novels is remarkable for its invention, insight, brilliant economy of means, and icy satiric thrust, a number stand out: *Memento Mori* (1959); *The Prime of Miss Jean Brodie* (1961), an international best-seller that became a hit stage play with Vanessa Redgrave and an award-winning film with Maggie Smith; *The Girls of Slender Means* (1963);

The Driver's Seat (1970), made into a film with Elizabeth Taylor; *Loitering with Intent* (1981); *A Far Cry from Kensington* (1988); *Symposium* (1990); and *Aiding and Abetting* (2000).

Spark has also written critical and biographical works on Emily Brontë, John Masefield, Cardinal Newman, and Mary Shelley; stories for children; stage and radio plays; essays on diverse topics; and the first volume of an autobiography, *Curriculum Vitae* (1993).

Muriel Spark moved from London to New York in 1962 when William Shawn, editor of *The New Yorker*, gave her an office at the magazine's headquarters. In 1968 she moved to Rome, drawn there for several reasons, most prominently its place at the center of the Church. In the late 1970s she settled in Tuscany, where she lives today with her companion and assistant, Penelope Jardine, in a converted rectory hidden within olive groves. She has recently completed a stage play and her twenty-second novel, *The Finishing School*.

Spark has received numerous awards, including honorary degrees from the universities of Strathclyde, Edinburgh, St. Andrews, and Oxford; in 1993 she was made a Dame of the British Empire. Other honors include appointment as Commandeur de L'Ordre des Arts et des Lettres by the French government, honorary membership in the American Academy of Arts and Letters, the David Cohen British Literature Prize for lifetime achievement, the Ingersoll Foundation's T. S. Eliot Award, the Edmund Campion Award, and the Boccaccio Europa Prize for European Literature 2002.

PLOT SUMMARY

Set in 1950s London, Muriel Spark's third novel, *Memento Mori*, focuses on the lives of two groups of aged people: the first, a loosely connected set of men and women in their late seventies and early eighties, some wealthy, most artists of one sort or another; the second, the aged female residents of a state-run nursing home. Thirty or forty years previous, members of the first group were caught in a web of affairs, blackmail, bigamy, literary high jinks, and country house capers. The two groups are linked by the presence of a former ladies' maid/companion, Jean Taylor, recently retired to the nursing home and suffering horribly from rheumatoid arthritis. Actually, a third group, never individualized, enters the picture as well: a group of very aged "senile cases" moved into a corner of the Maud Long Ward, home to Taylor and twelve other patients, known to the staff as "grannies." The members of the first group receive identical anonymous telephone messages, "Remember you must die"; each hears a different voice, suspects a different perpetrator, and responds in distinctive fashion. In the process, past lives emerge from the shadows and old feuds are rekindled, with shocking consequences. By the novel's end, the voice's warning, heeded or not, crackles everywhere and Death has come for all.

MAJOR THEMES

Any discussion of Muriel Spark as a "Catholic writer" must begin with attention to her conversion, an experience of profound consequences for her as a person and an artist. Reared in a home with a Jewish father and a Christian mother, young Muriel Sarah Camberg and her brother Philip were nominally, although not fervently, Christian. In a recent, rather public dispute with her son, an Orthodox Jew who claims that both his maternal grandparents were Jews, Spark and her brother have both dissented vigorously, and a recently discovered marriage certificate verifies their claim.

On May 1, 1954, after a brief time as an Anglican, Spark was received into the Roman Catholic Church by Father Philip Caraman, Jesuit confidant of Evelyn Waugh, at the Society's Farm Street church. Although notably reticent on the subject of her conversion, Spark has written or spoken of it, often elliptically, in "How I Became a Novelist" (1960), in "My Conversion" (1961), and most "fully" in 1992, in *Curriculum Vitae*, the first installment of her autobiography.

"My Conversion," an interview converted to an essay by another hand, adds some dimension to the account. Spark dismisses the idea that her friendship with Roman Catholics led her to the Church (quite the opposite, in fact). She credits Cardinal Newman as instrumental. Furthermore, she is at pains to say that her conversion was "an instinctive rather than an intellectual experience" (1961, 59). With characteristic reticence, she suggests a connection between conversion and success as a novelist, opining, "I think there is a connection between my writing and my conversion, but I don't want to be too dogmatic about it. Certainly, all my best work has come since then" (59). But it is in "How I Became a Novelist" that she makes it clear. After a period of illness, and having written nothing for almost a year, she observes that she "entered the Roman Catholic Church—an important step for me, because from that time I began to see life as a whole rather than as a series of disconnected happenings" (1960, 683). Like the American writer Flannery O'Connor, with whom she has striking kinship as artist and believer, Spark rejects the notion that Catholicism cramps her creativity.

In *Curriculum Vitae*, with what some critics have called maddening brevity, she devotes a mere two hundred words to the subject:

> When I am asked about my conversion, why I became a Catholic, I can only say that the answer is both too easy and too difficult. The simple explanation is that I felt the Roman Catholic faith corresponded to what I had always felt and known and believed; there was no blinding revelation in my case. The more difficult explanation would involve the step by step building up of a conviction; as Newman himself pointed out, when asked about his conversion, it was not a thing one could propound "between the soup and the fish" at a dinner party. "Let them be to the trouble that I have been to," said Newman. Indeed, the existential quality of a religious experience cannot be simply summed up in general terms. (1992, 202)

For Spark, conversion fixed her personal and aesthetic bearings and imparted a sure sense of this world—and another, beyond. All of her fictions are grounded in her faith, although none of them could be considered polemic or propaganda; rather, in their point of view, sacramental dimension, eschatological perspective, and transfigurative power, each represents a stunningly modern take on the ancient form of parable.

Two more brief remarks, both taken from later interviews, substantiate matters. Speaking about her conversion to Stephen Schiff, Spark characterized it as "the first philosophical integrity I've ever known. And it united a lot of disintegrating factors. It gave me a ground and something to measure from—'the still point in the turning world,' as Eliot said" (1993, 40). Six years later, when asked how she viewed her conversion forty-five years later, she responded, "the same way I did then: it changed my life" (personal conversation with me, March 1999).

The Comforters (1957) launched Muriel Spark's career as a novelist. An enthusiasm for strong narrative line connects her poetry and short fiction to her novels, but the transition was effected by her conversion. Favorable reviews encouraged Spark to write a second novel, *Robinson* (1958), and then, as she tells it,

> I decided to write a book about old people. It happened that a number of old people whom I had known as a child in Edinburgh were dying from one cause or another, and on my visits to Edinburgh I sometimes accompanied my mother to see them in hospital. When I saw them I was impressed by the power and persistence of the human spirit. They were paralyzed or crippled in body, yet were still exerting characteristic influences on those around them in the world outside. I saw a tragic side to this situation and a comic side as well. I called this novel *Memento Mori*. (1960, 683)

Memento Mori appeared in 1959 to nearly unanimous critical praise; even those critics who did not quite get the point admired its abundant literary virtues— economy, wit, dialogue, and character. And indeed, to judge from sales then and now, readers have shared the critics' sentiments.

On the narrative level, the novel yields considerable pleasures indeed, revolving as it does around the mystery of anonymous telephone calls, each echoing the same message, "Remember you must die," received by a group of geriatric Londoners at mid-twentieth century. The cast of characters/recipients is varied, rich, and interesting, with figures like Godfrey Colston (age eighty-seven), a penurious, self-absorbed, spiteful, and jealous curmudgeon with a passion for staring at ladies' garter tops; his wife, Charmian Piper (age eighty-five), a retired "lady novelist" enjoying a revival of her work; and Godfrey's sister, Dame Lettie Colston (age seventy-nine), a retired prison visitor and busybody. The Colston set includes a number of long-standing friends, relations, and help, most near or well into their ninth decades. One of these stands out: Jean Taylor (age eighty-two), once Charmian's maid, later her companion, now retired to a nursing home.

The novel is concerned with more than the simple fact of the calls, however: it carefully details the reactions of all recipients, and the responses are nearly as varied (and eccentric) as the women and men themselves. Although each message is the same, the gender, age, and accent vary wildly, according to the recipient. To one, it's a barrow boy calling; to another, it's a cultured, middle-aged man; to another, it's "a common little fellow, with his lisp" (*Memento Mori*, 101). Most are terrorized, although none to the degree of the elevated paranoia experienced by Dame Lettie. To Charmian, "It is surprising how variously people react to the same thing" (188); but not to Muriel Spark. Nor to Charmian Colston or Jean Taylor, for neither one is put off by the call she receives. Both identify the caller as "Death himself." Both embrace the message as a salutary reminder.

No matter the interpretation or attribution, all die in the end. Each character is dispatched with clinically descriptive precision: for example, "Lettie Colston . . . comminuted fracture of the skull; Godfrey Colston, hypostatic pneumonia; Charmian Colston, uraemia; Jean Taylor, myocardial degeneration" (224). And so *Memento Mori* ends. Read on this level, some readers are dissatisfied. While the novel follows some of the conventions of the mystery novel genre as practiced by G. K. Chesterton and Agatha Christie, including the grand gathering of all the suspects in one room to crack the case, *Memento Mori* remains a whodunit without a "who" for those who do not buy into the notion of death as the caller does. And to someone like John Coleman, who reviewed the novel for the *Spectator*, those last two pages inventorying the dead are nothing less than "a sort of satanic prize giving" (1959, 447).

Yet not so, ultimately, for on a deeper level the puzzling questions of *Memento Mori* can be answered, but only by apprehending the novel's crucial grounding in the absolutes of faith. In its form, substance, and implied intent, Muriel Spark's *Memento Mori* reflects, indeed embodies, the distinctive perspective that can only be termed "Catholic." This contemporary parable partaking of the ancient meditative tradition set forth in its very title is an invitation to share that perspective, be converted, and ultimately be summoned to challenging and life-changing faith. Whatever other Catholic writers might choose to do, for Spark the novel is no place for apologetics, polemics, or propaganda; nor is it the place for catechizing or hagiography or romantic visions. Her fictional world is often cold, hard, alienating, violent, and dislocating, populated with any number of vile, double-dealing characters (some of the worst of them Roman Catholics). It is a place where suffering obtains for nearly everyone, where the supernatural coexists with the natural, or as Spark herself once put it, "they are implicit in each other" (Glavin 1988, 223). Conversion and redemption are manifest realities; the redemptive efficacy of suffering is a manifest reality.

Spark's deliberate use of literary convention only to overturn it explains part of her larger purpose. The path to a deeper understanding of the novel begins with Spark's own words. Two sources offer particularly relevant remarks or present concerns. In an interview with Frank Kermode, Spark asserted:

> I don't claim that my novels are truth—I claim that they are fiction, out of which a kind of truth emerges. And I keep in my mind specifically that what I am writing is fiction because I am interested in truth—absolute truth—and I don't pretend that what I'm writing is more than an imaginative extension of the truth—something inventive . . . what I write is not true—it is a pack of lies . . . there is absolute truth, in which I believe things which are difficult to believe, but I believe them because they are absolute. (Kermode 1963, 80, 81)

And the aforementioned "My Conversion" provides information enabling us to move from the epistemological and theoretical plane to the literary and analytical: "Fiction to me is a kind of parable. You have got to make up your mind it's not true. Some kind of truth emerges from it, but it's not fact" (1961, 63). Simply put, objective and form as set out by the writer herself supply grounds for asserting that *Memento Mori* is a parable, one of the oldest literary forms extant and, although not original to Jesus, certainly most often associated with him and his public ministry. The parable is a crisp, vivid, economical narrative form, grounded in details of ordinary life so as to construct plausible character and plot, only to overturn the ordinary into the extraordinary. The parable often constructs a realistically plausible situation, establishing a certain level of comfort for the listener/reader, only to deconstruct that world, to unsettle the listener/reader, who is called to see things from another vantage point, the ultimate or eschatological angle. The distortions (often rhetorical), tensions, and apparent contradictions of the parable can be resolved only from that point of view, toward which the listener/reader must occasionally be shocked or violently dislocated.

In its eschatological emphasis, purpose, and essential literary characteristics, *Memento Mori* is indeed a parable. In its form, the novel certainly qualifies: in a little more than two hundred pages, Spark constructs a vivid, engaging narrative set in a recognizable place and time. In its seamless construction interweaving the natural and the supernatural, the parable illuminates the human condition in all of its complexities and tensions while positioning the listener/reader at a moment of existential choice. Furthermore, essential to the parable is a certain obliquity; in the words of W. H. Auden, "what is obliquely meant is, and must be, different for every reader" (1962, 6).

The key to *Memento Mori* appears before chapter one even begins: Spark has chosen three epigraphs on the subject of old age. The first, taken from Yeats's poem "The Tower," mourns the absurdity of a "[d]ecrepit age that has been tied to me"—tied like a can to a dog's tail. The second comes from Thomas Traherne's "Centuries of Meditation": "O what venerable and reverent creatures did / the aged seem! Immortal Cherubims!" The third reprints an excerpt from *The Penny Catechism*: "Q: What are the four last things to be ever remembered? A: The four last things to be ever remembered are Death, Judgment, Hell, and Heaven."

These three excerpts offer three distinct perspectives on aging and dying: the first rails against the ravages of time (an attitude personified in a number of the novel's characters); the second is no more than a clichéd piety, ironically mocked by Spark in the course of *Memento Mori*; but the third, with its contextu- alizing of irreversible process within an eternal and eschatological perspective, is the distinctive, Catholic point of view that shapes the whole novel. Those char- acters who see the world that way, with acceptance and detachment, are three: Charmian Colston, Jean Taylor, and Henry Mortimer.

When Charmian's caller tells her, "Remember you must die," she answers "Oh, as to that, for the past thirty years and more I have thought of it from time to time. My memory is failing in certain respects. I am gone eighty-six. But somehow I do not forget my death, whenever that will be" (*Memento Mori*, 128). Immediately afterward, she becomes "strong and fearless" (129), empowered in both body and spirit. Jean Taylor never receives a call herself—indeed, she does not need to, for she has achieved the perspective from which all human life and its inevitable suffering are to be viewed. She too acquires strength and courage, enabling her to do what must be done to free others from moral tyranny. When the time comes to reveal Charmian's extramarital capers, she reflects, "There is a time for loyalty and a time when loyalty comes to an end" (175), before proceeding. But when others tell her of their calls, she identifies the caller as Death, without hesitation and with absolute conviction. She herself has formed the habit of seeing things this way much earlier in life, for as she opines, "it is difficult for people of advanced years to start remembering they must die. It is best to form the habit while young" (39).

It may come as a surprise that the third member of the trio is retired Inspector Henry Mortimer, an agnostic, but in this novel there is no Roman Catholic monopoly on insight. Called in to solve the mystery of the caller's identity, Mortimer confides to his wife, "And considering the evidence, in my opinion, the offender is Death himself" (144). It is Mortimer who makes the point with fullness and emphasis to the terrified members of the Colston set gathered at Mortimer's home at Kingston-on-Thames:

> If I had my life over again I should form the habit of nightly composing myself to thoughts of death. I would practice, as it were, the remembrance of death. There is no other practice which so intensifies life. Death, when it approaches, ought not to take one by surprise. It should be part of the full expectancy of life. Without an ever-present sense of death life is insipid. You might as well live on the whites of egg ... Now, one factor is constant in all your reports. The words, "Remember, you must die." It is, you know, an excellent thing to remember this, for it is nothing more than the truth. To remember one's death is, in short, a way of life. (153–54)

The implied Scriptural injunction, "let him who has ears listen," that concludes Mortimer's remarks is not heeded, to judge from the varied, sometimes willful and obtuse, responses of the group. Only after his guests have departed do we learn that Mortimer himself has also received the call, and more than once; to judge from his insight and subsequent conduct, it has brought him strength and courage—along with equanimity.

Detachment is the paradoxical and ironic accompaniment essential to the privileged perspective endorsed. What some have criticized about Spark's fiction—the cold, clinical separation between creator and character—is integral to the eternal/eschatological perspective; as John Updike has observed, "detachment is the genius of her fiction" (1961, 161). That same detachment creates not a "satanic prize-giving" (Coleman 1959, 447) but an ethic essential and fundamental to Spark's aesthetic. In a recent essay, she has stated, "I have learned that happiness or unhappiness in endings is irrelevant. The main thing about a book is that it should end well, and perhaps it is not too much to say that a book's ending casts its voice, color, tone and shade over the whole work" (2001, 6). And how appropriate it is that the eschatological ends the novel—isn't that the point of the whole exercise, to see the end in everything?

Vision, detachment, perspective, ultimate serenity, even rejoicing are the distinctive qualities of *Memento Mori* and indeed of all Muriel Spark's fiction. To those who have found the novel's geriatric subject matter gruesome, grisly, even grotesque, let Fleur Talbot, the protagonist of a later novel (*Loitering with Intent* [1981]) and something of a surrogate for the author herself, respond: "But you must understand that everything happens to an artist; time is always redeemed, nothing is lost, and wonders never cease" (116).

In an extraordinary and moving meditation on Piero della Francesca's "Madonna del Parto," a rare fresco showing a pregnant Mary in the foreground, Spark has observed, "this lady has no problem, she has a purpose" (1984, 103).

Certainly, this is so for Muriel Spark. When a minor character, Mr. Rose, who has received the call, comes to the great gathering of all recipients at Mortimer's house, he asks, "The question is, who's the fellow that's trying to put the fear of God in us?" (*Memento Mori*, 155). The answer is clear, and it is no man: it is Muriel Spark, crafter of contemporary parables par excellence.

CRITICAL RECEPTION

Immediately upon publication, *Memento Mori* was reviewed in the most prominent critical venues on both sides of the Atlantic. In Britain, Graham Greene was said to have declared that the novel "delighted me as much as any novel that I have read since the war" (quoted in Schiff 1993, 37). Evelyn Waugh chimed in with praise of his own, followed by V. S. Naipaul's glowing review in the *New Statesman*, praising "the easy economical narrative, the continuing invention . . . the well-cut dialogue, the controlled tone" in this, "a brilliant, startling and original book" (1959, 452). Most other reviews followed suit. In *The Twentieth Century*, Barbara Lucas (1959) linked Spark to Iris Murdoch and Ivy Compton-Burnett and offered a perceptive, positive bit of character analysis. An anonymous review for the *London Times* (March 26, 1959), while offering little more than plot summary, lauded Spark's style and wit; likewise, an unsigned review in the *Times Literary Supplement* (April 17, 1959). Most British reviewers were of like mind: they gave Spark's novel high marks for style and wit but offered no consideration of its religious dimension beyond one or two noting that *Memento Mori* might be read as a contemporary take on the medieval morality play.

Two reviewers blundered about and revealed a real lack of understanding. Anthony Quinton's misreading of the book is amusing; while covering himself by noting that *Memento Mori* is "an exceedingly adept book," he observed that Charmian is "a kind of senile Virginia Woolf" and concluded that the book is "a gratuitous curiosity" (1959, 85). John Coleman acknowledged that the novel is "compellingly well done," presenting what "is really an astonishing series of studies in senility," but his reading of the ending, as noted above, is off point (1959, 447).

In later pieces by Bernard Bergonzi and W. H. Auden, Spark's novel received its due. Bergonzi's essay in *The Listener*, while focused on other novels, describes *Memento Mori* as "one of the most original novels for many years" (1963, 416). Auden's perceptive and detailed reading of the novel as a morality play in *The Mid-Century* (1962) established a critical foundation for further work.

Much the same lines can be traced in the response of American critics. Several may be taken as typical. In an undocumented cover blurb, Tennessee Williams offered his estimate of the writer and her work: "a marvelously witty English writer—her best, I think, is *Memento Mori*, which is chillingly brilliant." In *The New York Times Book Review* of May 17, 1959, Robert Phelps set Spark in the tradition of Chesterton, Greene, and Waugh, further noting that this "daffily hilarious work . . . should disappoint only readers without moral imagination" (1959, 5). In *The Atlantic*, Phoebe Adams lauded Spark's construction of character and the "infallibly comic" effect of the novel (1959, 81). And in a lengthy review in *The New Yorker*, Whitney Balliett focused, like other reviewers, on Spark's considerable skills at characterization in the novel he called "a celebration of death" (1959, 127). Not surprisingly, reviewers in journals with religious affiliation did tend to consider the religious dimension, but surprisingly, none really went beyond categorizing the novel as a morality play or, as James Finn did, as a modern representative of the medieval "how to die" manual (1959, 525).

In subsequent decades, *Memento Mori*, and indeed all of Muriel Spark's work, has attracted readers and writers of the first rank. Among those who have written extensively are Frank Kermode (1963), David Lodge (1985), and John Updike (1961). Deeper exploration of *Memento Mori* in book-length studies of the writer has been accomplished by Peter Kemp (1974), Alan Bold (1986), Ruth Whittaker (1982), Allan Massie (1979), and Joseph Hynes (1988). Together, these writers and scholars have given Spark her due, establishing a solid critical foundation for future work on this writer once described by David Lodge as "the most gifted and innovative English novelist of her generation" (1985, 1).

NOTE

Muriel Spark, *Memento Mori* (New York: New Directions, 2000). All references are to this edition.

WORKS CITED

Adams, Phoebe. 1959. "Reader's Choice." *The Atlantic* 204, no. 2 (August): 81.
Auden, W. H. 1962. "A Disturbing Novelist." *The Mid-Century* 39 (May): 5–8.
Balliett, Whitney. 1959. "The Burning Bush." *The New Yorker* 25, no. 17 (June 13): 127–30.
Bergonzi, Bernard. 1963. "The Novel No Longer Novel." *The Listener* 70, no. 1799 (September 19): 415–16.
Bold, Alan. 1986. *Muriel Spark*. Contemporary Writers Series. London: Methuen.
Coleman, John. 1959. "Borderline." *The Spectator* no. 6822 (March 27): 447.
Finn, James. 1959. "Death and Old Age." *Commonweal* 70, no. 21 (September 18): 524–26.
Glavin, John. 1988. "Muriel Spark's Unknowing Fiction." *Women's Studies* 15: 221–41.
Hynes, Joseph. 1988. *The Art of the Real: Muriel Spark's Novels*. Rutherford, NJ: Fairleigh Dickinson University Press.
Kemp, Peter. 1974. *Muriel Spark*. Novelists and Their World Series. London: Paul Elek.
Kermode, Frank. 1963. "The House of Fiction: Interviews with Seven English Novelists." *The Partisan Review* 30 (Spring): 61–82.
Lodge, David. 1985. "Marvels and Nasty Surprises." *New York Times Book Review* (October 20): 1, 38–39.
Lucas, Barbara. 1959. "*Memento Mori* by Muriel Spark." *The Twentieth Century* 166 (September): 213–15.
Massie, Allan. 1979. *Muriel Spark*. Edinburgh: Ramsay Head Press.
Naipaul, V. S. 1959. "Death on the Telephone." *New Statesman* 57, no. 1463 (March 28): 452.
Phelps, Robert. 1959. "In the Lengthening Shadow." *New York Times Book Review* (May 17): 5.
Quinton, Anthony. 1959. Review of *Memento Mori*, by Muriel Spark. *London Magazine* 6 (September): 84–88.

Review of *Memento Mori*, by Muriel Spark. *London Times* (March 26, 1959): 15.
Review of *Memento Mori*, by Muriel Spark. *Times Literary Supplement* (April 17, 1959): 221.
Schiff, Stephen. 1993. "Muriel Spark Between the Lines." *The New Yorker* 69, no. 14 (May 24): 36–43.
Spark, Muriel. 1960. "How I Became a Novelist." *John O'London's* 3 (December 1): 683.
———. 1961. "My Conversion." *The Twentieth Century* 170 (Autumn): 58–63.
———. 1981. *Loitering with Intent*. New York: Coward, McCann and Geohegan.
———. 1984. "Spirit and Substance." *Vanity Fair* 47, no. 12 (December): 103.
———. 1992. *Curriculum Vitae*. Boston and New York: Houghton Mifflin.
———. 2001. "The Writing Life." *Washington Post Book World* (March 11): 6.
Updike, John. 1961. "Creatures of the Air," review of *The Bachelors*, by Muriel Spark. *The New Yorker* 37, no. 33 (September 30): 161–67.
Whittaker, Ruth. 1982. *The Faith and Fiction of Muriel Spark*. New York: St. Martin's.

BIBLIOGRAPHY

Baldanza, Frank. "Muriel Spark and the Occult." *Contemporary Literature* 6 (Summer 1965): 190–203.
Hengest, Philip. "Muriel Spark." *Punch* 245, no. 6412 (July 31, 1963): 175–76.
Hosmer, Robert E. "Muriel Spark: Writing with Intent." *Commonweal* 116, no. 8 (April 21, 1989): 233–41.
Leonard, Joan. "Loitering with Intent: Muriel Spark's Parabolic Technique." *Studies in the Literary Imagination* 18, no. 1 (Spring 1985): 65–77.
Mallon, Thomas. "Off Its Rocker," review of *Aiding and Abetting*, by Muriel Spark. *The Atlantic* 287, no. 2 (February 2001): 124–25.
Manning, Gerald F. "Sunsets and Sunrises: Nursing Home as Microcosm in *Memento Mori* and *Mr. Scobie's Riddle*." *Ariel* 18, no. 2 (April 1987): 27–43.
Price, Martin. "The Difficulties of Commitment: Some Recent Novels." *Yale Review* 48, no. 4 (Summer 1959): 595–604.
Richmond, Velma. *Muriel Spark*. New York: Ungar Publishing, 1984.

— **Robert Ellis Hosmer Jr.**

Edith Stein [1891–1942]

Essays on Woman

BIOGRAPHY

Born in Breslau, Germany (now Wroclaw, Poland) on October 12, 1891, Edith Stein has been called one of the greatest women of the twentieth century. Her parents, Siegfried and Augusta, were devout Jews. Edith was the last of their seven surviving children. After Edith lost her father as an infant, her mother became her great love and ideal image of womanhood. Although a businesswoman, Augusta Stein was the heart of the home. The family spoke and prayed in German, and a respect for all religions was one of Augusta's tenets.

Although fascinated by her mother's religious fervor, the teenaged Edith dropped Jewish religious rite and prayer and left school. Then, by study, she mastered the time lost and, in Breslau in 1911, became one of the first women to attend a German university. Here she first read the New Testament. In 1913, Stein arrived at the University of Göttingen, where she studied under Edmund Husserl, who taught in the philosophy department and who founded the major philosophic movement of phenomenology. The phenomenological method examines a phenomenon and arrives at certitude with no preconceived theories; judgments are reduced to evidence gained through personal consciousness and intuition. At the university, Stein found herself among brilliant intellectuals, many of whom were spiritually inclined. The religious revival of the time included a number of philosophers who were Jewish converts to Christianity. One of these, Max Scheler, maintained that religion and ethics were consistent with phenomenology, and Stein's mentor Husserl also analyzed spiritual realities. Some thirty years prior to Stein's studies at Göttingen, Pope Leo XIII had named Saint Thomas Aquinas the patron of Catholic education. Although a Lutheran, Husserl was influenced by Aquinas's metaphysics, telling his students that phenomenology "converges towards Thomism and prolongs Thomism" (de Mirabel 1954, 73). While considering herself an atheist at the time, Stein was awed by the Christian faith and knew she had to come to grips with it as a phenomenon.

Stein left school in 1914 during World War I to nurse soldiers infected with contagious diseases. Then she returned to writing her doctoral dissertation,

On the Problem of Empathy (1989), under Husserl's direction. She herself was an empathetic person, and she refers to this spiritual quality, the basis of human relationships, as putting oneself into another's shoes. When one of her teachers, Adolf Reinach, was killed in 1917, Stein visited his widow, Anna, to help arrange Reinach's papers. This visit proved to be the turning point in Stein's life. Former Jews, husband and wife had converted to Christianity and were baptized Lutherans. Despite keen sorrow over her husband's death, Anna displayed a calm presence. Witnessing Anna's serenity, Stein writes that her unbelief was shattered, her belief in Judaism paled, and the Cross loomed high.

A brilliant intellectual, Stein published her dissertation in 1917 and went on to write other phenomenological studies, including *Sentient Causality* and *Individual and Community*. Her interest in political structure and human rights produced *Eine Untersuchung über den staat* (The State). By 1921, she had become a believing Christian, but she did not know what denomination to join. A reading of Saint Teresa of Avila's autobiography brought her into the Catholic Church. As she prepared for baptism, she studied the works of Thomas Aquinas. She was baptized on New Year's Day in 1922. Stein then taught at St. Magdalena College for Women in Speyer, where she started her analysis of woman's psyche in order to best educate her students. From 1928 to 1932, she lectured to groups of academic women who made up the Catholic Women's Movement, a movement supported by the Church. Through her lectures and a series of published articles, Stein became widely known as an advocate for women's rights. These lectures and articles were later collected as *Essays on Woman*. Stein's hearers at the time often described her simplicity, warm loveliness, affability, gentle but subtle humor, self-control, and detachment.

The dual paths of phenomenology and Thomism intersected in Stein's very being: the relationship between the two disciplines fascinated her and, as a result, she wrote *Husserl and Aquinas: A Comparison*, a work that became a seminal, enduring contribution to scholarship. She also translated from English the letters and journals of Cardinal John Henry Newman and from Latin Aquinas's *de Veritate*, which she developed into a phenomenological commentary on Thomism. In 1932, she was the only woman invited to the Thomistic Society convention held in France. Emphasizing that Husserl's intuitive extrication of essence is like the Thomistic abstraction, she was highly praised for her part in the discussion.

In 1932, Stein was teaching at the Scientific Institute of Pedagogy in Münster. Although Hitler was audible throughout Germany at the time, Stein attacked Nazi ideology publicly and challenged her Nazi students. When Hitler seized power the following year, Stein wrote to Pope Pius XI asking for a personal interview and requesting that he publicly stop Hitler's bigotry. She warned that silence was indefensible and that Catholics would soon be attacked as well as Jews. Her request was denied. This letter, recognized by Holocaust historians for its early, unique action when most were silent, was publicized in 2003, creating world interest.

Because of her Jewish blood, Stein lost her teaching position. She was now free, therefore, to act on the desire she had had since baptism to pursue a religious vocation. In October 1933, she entered the Carmelite Order in Cologne, taking the name Sister Teresa Benedicta of the Cross. Her decision was made with much agony, for she had to part from her family, who were scandalized by her action, particularly at a time when Jews were being attacked. Rather than emigrate to safety, Stein offered her life for world peace, Germany's deliverance from National Socialism, the contrition of Nazi sympathizers, and the safety of her fellow Jews. Putting herself in the shoes of suffering humanity, she was convinced that prayer in union with the crucified Christ would redeem a brutalized world. The Carmel represented love in a world of hate. No earthly joy could equal her spot before the tabernacle, where she fervently believed Christ was present.

In the Carmel, advised to return to writing, Stein started her autobiography *Life in a Jewish Family* ([1933–35] 1986) to counteract the Nazi caricature of the Jews with a faithful account of Jewish humanity. She also completed *Finite and Eternal Being* in nine months, so great was the strength she derived from monastic life.

In April 1938, Stein disclosed her Jewish identity when refusing to vote for Hitler in a mock election. After *Kristallnacht* that November, the nuns feared for her safety and smuggled her out of Germany to the Echt Carmel in Holland. Much of her joy disappeared as she learned more about Nazi atrocities; members of her family escaped, but a sister and a brother were deported to a concentration camp. Stein's poetry at the time evinces stark pain: she wishes she could help those in the war, yet she knows that, in union with the Passion of Christ, she can heal and console those who suffer on both sides. Disciplining herself, she wrote *The Science of the Cross* and *Ways to Know God*.

The deportation of Dutch Jews began in 1942. As protest, a Pastoral Letter was read from all pulpits on July 26 of that year. As reprisal for that letter, all Jews who had received Catholic baptism were arrested on August 2. The Echt Carmel had tried to move Stein into Switzerland, but she refused to go without her sister Rosa, who was with her and who had also become a Catholic. When arrested, Stein was heard to say to Rosa, "Come, let us go for our people" (Oben 2001, 60). The prisoners were taken first to Dutch camps. Freed Jews witnessed to Stein's courage and loving care for the Jewish women and children there, and a guard testified that she seemed like a saint as she went among them, radiant in her privilege of serving. The sisters were gassed on arrival at Auschwitz on August 9, 1942. Edith Stein was beatified in 1987 and canonized in 1998. The following year, Pope John Paul II declared her one of the co-patronesses of Europe. Her feast day is August 9.

MAJOR THEMES

In *Essays on Woman*, Stein writes as a Christian philosopher, analyzing woman and comparing her to man in her roles and relationships. Using theology and philosophy to reveal the person in God's creation, she writes that faith is superior to both of these disciplines and closer to divine wisdom.

Stein presents Thomistic themes and uses the phenomenological method to attain an understanding of the essence of woman, man, and the human person. She analyzes both *what* one is (our essence) and *that* one is (our existence) and confirms both in God's essence and existence. She also applies ontology, the science of divine being and created beings. She takes us on an exciting quest of what woman *can be*. "We are trying to attain insight into the innermost recesses of our being," she writes; "we see that it is not a completed being but rather a being in the state of becoming, and we are trying to achieve clarity relative to that process" (*Essays on Woman*, 88). Stein accomplishes this study through an anthropological journey using the basic truths of Christianity—creation, original sin, redemption, and holiness—to address woman and man in their original, fallen, and redeemed natures.

Adam and Eve were harmonious with God in a community of love. But they denied God's authority and the Fall brought about death and loss of grace. With the human person's faculties now in chaos—the senses turned against the spirit, and the will against reason—human nature became prone to error and inclined to evil. Woman becomes subordinate to man and quarrels arise regarding roles and relationships. Animal life now menaces human life. However, humanity recovers its innocent nature through union with Christ. "To begin with, where do we have the concrete image of total humanity? God's image walked amongst us in human form, in the Son of Man, Jesus Christ," states Stein (258). Christ is the *total* image of God, and the Virgin Mary the perfect *human* image. But man and woman image God only partly. Created as two species, each gender has its own meaning and reflects the triune God differently; that is, God as being, Christ as divine wisdom, and the Holy Spirit as love. As Stein puts it, "Each finite creature can reflect only a fraction of the divine nature; thus, in the diversity of His creatures, God's infinite unity and oneness appear to be broken into an effulgence of manifold rays" (118).

The closer one is to God, the more perfect is his or her image. God forms this image in us: "Just as *an inner form resides* in the seed of plants, an invisible force making a fir tree shoot up here and a beech there, there is in this way an inner mold set in human beings which urges the evolution into a certain direction and works towards a certain *gestalt* in blind singleness of purpose, that of the personality which is mature, fully developed, and uniquely individual" (130). The unique seed in each human being is Christ. Christ did not restore original nature but planted the seed for human salvation in each soul by his act of redemption. The more man and woman share in Christ's redemptive action, the clearer they will hear the voices of God and nature, and the more rightly they will relate to each other. Prayer and the reception of Holy Communion are vital aids here.

Each person has the free choice to adopt or deny an attitude or action and to accept or reject divine grace. In right reason, a person acts with integrity and cooperates in forming his or her being according to God's plan. The highest act of freedom is total surrender to God: the soul, empty of self and directed in total love to his will, is filled with happiness, courage, and vitality. The surrender of the Father and Son to each other in a free act of love prefigures the surrender of God and a person, or a person and another person, in the Holy Spirit. Thus are we able to participate in co-redemption with Christ, our highest duty and privilege. A person may achieve this high state if he or she is harmonious within the self, but most humans live as torn vessels merely reacting to inner and outer pressures.

The rational, free person is consciously responsible for others and enacts positive values. One cannot understand persons without knowing their values; these designate personal being and are the basis of communal life. International peace cannot be won, for example, unless justice exists in each country. This means that each person must act in justice, which is a natural law written by God into each person's nature. Communication is a communal factor; identification with others establishes the concept of "we" instead of "me." Thus, communication holds the key to peace and understanding between groups of people. This means that the study of languages, the beauty and exactness of speech, is a vital issue. "To be able to express oneself appropriately is thus something which belongs essentially to perfected humanity," writes Stein (231).

Stein's feminism presents woman as a human being, a person, and a female integrated into one being. In her lectures and writings, including those in *Essays on Woman*, Stein contributed to advancing woman's roles as the intellectual leader of the Catholic Women's Movement throughout Europe. Her focus was on woman's education. To Stein, the male-dominated nineteenth-century educational system treated woman merely as an *"ornament of the domestic hearth"* (166). As I stated in my article "Edith Stein as Educator," "[T]he high school girl . . . of the early twentieth century was expected to be docile, manageable, have pretty manners, and know next to nothing of mathematics, history and the natural sciences" (1990, 114). In 1919, attendance at school became authorized for girls up to eighteen years old. Recognizing that a woman's psyche differs from a man's, Stein stressed the need for a Catholic education geared specifically toward girls.

A hallmark of Stein's philosophy of woman is her emphasis on woman as a unique person. God created man and woman to be one; yet, in reality, they are two, for each has his or her own distinct soul. Woman is to be what God intends her to be, to go her own way, and to perform her special contribution. Each woman is predisposed with special abilities and is called to fulfill her own vocation. Stein understands woman according to the Aristotelian-Thomistic concept that states that "form is the spiritual essence of the body." This "essence" accounts for woman's body structure and purpose. Stein states, "Of course, woman shares a basic human nature, but basically her faculties are different from men; therefore, a differing type of soul must exist as well" (*Essays on Woman*, 45). However, Stein differs from Aquinas in his concept of woman as a "helper in the work of generation" but deficient in "intellectual operation" (*Summa Theologica*, 1947, 1, 92, 1). Rather, to Stein, woman can perform any type of job that a man can: she is in no way "deficient" in her intellectual capabilities. However, Stein maintains, it is necessary to know woman's essential nature to investigate what professions she is *particularly* suited for.

What, then, is woman's essential nature? The scientific method capable of answering this question is a cognitive one that can grasp the universal structure of a concrete object—that is, its essence. It combines the phenomenological method of intuition and the Thomistic method of abstraction. To examine the species under consideration, a woman's soul, Stein first identifies the major types of woman as maternal, erotic, romantic, level-headed, and intellectual. She then draws from three types of womanhood found in literature: Ingunn Steinfinnsdattar from Sigrid Undset's epic novel *Olav Audunssøn* ("The soul of Ingunn, this child of nature, is like land untouched by the plough," Stein comments [*Essays on Woman*, 90]); Nora from Ibsen's play *A Doll's House*, a woman who realizes that she must first be a person and a human being before she can be a spouse and a mother; and Goethe's protagonist in *Iphigenie*, a woman who represents pure humanity and the eternal feminine. About these types of women, Stein writes,

> I believe, just as long as they are types of women, we will always find fundamentally the compulsion to become what the soul should be, the drive to allow the

latent humanity, set in her precisely in its individual stamp, to ripen to the greatest possible perfect development. The deepest feminine yearning is to achieve a loving union which, in its development, validates this maturation and simultaneously stimulates and furthers the desire for perfection in others . . . such yearning is an essential aspect of the eternal destiny of woman. It is not simply a human longing but is specifically feminine and opposed to the specifically masculine nature. (94)

In Stein's analyses of gender through differential psychology, man is oriented to intellectual, objective, and creative performance. The center of woman's being, on the other hand, is the emotional life by which she grasps the specificity and value of others. This permits woman to have a personal approach that "is objectively justified and valuable because actually the human person is more precious than all objective values . . . And behind all things of value to be found in the world stands the person of the Creator who, as prefiguration, encloses all earthy values in Himself and transmits them." "It is the *whole person* about whom we are speaking," Stein continues, "*that* human being in whom God's image is developed most purely, in whom the gifts which the Creator has bestowed do not wither but bloom" (256). This wholeness of being protects woman against the weakness typical of man, an excessive drive for vocational excellence. To Stein, woman's union of body and soul is more intimate than man's: her soul is present in her entire being and greatly affected by her bodily condition. This is God's gift to her for the purposes of motherhood and human development. Thus, man and woman strive in different ways not only to perfect human nature but to do so as an image of God: woman by working toward the harmony of all her faculties and man by a greater development of specific ones.

God's call is revealed in Scripture, past history, and present times. The Book of Genesis tells us to image the Creator, to be fruitful, and to master the earth. This command, states Stein, differs for man and woman. Primary for man is lordship over the earth and secondary is procreation and the raising of young; primary for woman is the bearing and fostering of children and secondary is lordship over the earth. Originally, woman was given to man as a companion and helpmate, enjoined to stand by his side over all creatures: "*Eser kenegdo*, a helper as if vis-à-vis to him" (196). Man and woman were to complement each other in body and soul, as one hand complements the other. But with the Fall came concupiscence, the domination of man over woman, humans' loss of sovereignty over the earth, suffering for the purpose of survival, and woman's pain in childbirth.

Stein challenges Saint Paul's version of the gender relationship, protesting that his view of man's sovereignty over woman is seen through fallen nature rather than original or redeemed nature. Paul's counsel for woman's silence in the assembly and insistence that her salvation is attained only through child bearing (1 Tim. 2:11–15) cannot be counted as major teachings about the sex relationship, states Stein. Rather, Paul is confused between the divine and human aspects and the Old and New Laws. Women were Christ's friends; their spirituality was as important to him as was that of men. Moreover, Stein points out that Paul also declares that "*there is neither male nor female. For you are all one in Christ Jesus*" (69).

In her analysis, Stein also presents the negative aspects of woman's nature. Woman can be violently inclined toward possessions and becomes an easy prey to the desire for an easy life. "There is a bit of defiance in each woman which does not want to humble itself under any sovereignty," she writes. "In each, there is something of that desire which reaches for forbidden fruit" (119). Reaching for wholeness of being and total humanity, woman may strike out in too many directions, with the result that her efforts become peripheral and her abilities fragmented. A young girl may become obsessed by pleasure, clothes, and love affairs. A selfish wife may control her family and concentrate purely on her own desires. Hysteria may result if such excess is wedded to idleness. On the other hand, woman's exaggerated interest in others may cause a morbid curiosity, a desire to literally confiscate them. An unrealistic urge to protect may alienate others. Degeneracy of a woman's person comes about through "vanity, desire for praise and recognition, and an unchecked need for communication" (47). Hyperemotionalism prevents the guidance of her reason and prudent activity of her will. Moreover, such spiritual and moral decline may be accompanied by a swift descent into carnality. Woman surrenders herself more easily than man, but it is perverse when she becomes enslaved by passion for another human being. Only God satisfies total surrender; given freely to him, the soul paradoxically wins total freedom.

By contrast, the ideal qualities of woman's soul are quietness, warmth, clarity, emptiness of self ("O Lord God, take me away from myself and give me completely to you alone" [134]), an expansiveness that welcomes all, self-containment (the lack of need to go searching to appease inner drives and an imperviousness to outer confusion), and a readiness to serve God's will rather than her own. These qualities are not separate but form a united whole in a well-developed soul.

"Woman's nature is determined by her original vocation of *spouse and mother*," Stein states, but she insists that such motherhood may be in both the physical and spiritual realms (132). Woman gains by disclosing and nurturing the hidden richness within others, for example, and when she helps to relieve others' inner burdens. Her special gift for reading souls derives from her spiritual maternity. The marital union implies the union of souls as well; the fruit of the couple's self-giving is the child. Women who tend to children help them to be formed as cells in the Mystical Body of Christ. To Stein, a married woman's greatest responsibility is to form her child's moral and spiritual being: teaching the truths of faith, keeping the home atmosphere pure, leading the child to sacramental and liturgical life, and struggling to develop God's image in herself, her husband, and her child. Stein urged mothers to stay home with small ones, for mothers best instill trust and confidence in their children and intuitively recognize their needs. Yet if she must augment the family income or if her abilities demand outside employment, a mother has the right to work outside the home.

In her discussion of marriage, Stein lauds Pope Pius XI's encyclical *Casti Connubii* (1930) for its concept of marriage as involving blessed offspring, fidelity, and sacrament. The institution of marriage can only be saved by the teachings of the Catholic Church, Stein maintained. The rhetoric of National Socialism pointed women to "*kirche, küche, kinder*" (church, kitchen, children) yet did not preclude the Nazis from creating farms where young girls were urged to donate their bodies for the bearing of Aryan babies. Rather, faith demands

rejection of a social order and of education which deny completely woman's unique nature and particular destiny, which disclaim an organic cooperation of the sexes and organic social patterns but seek rather to consider all individuals as similar atoms in a mechanistically ordered structure . . . and, above all, are lacking completely in any supernatural orientation. (206)

Yet Stein also challenges the Church to reexamine its concept of marriage in light of modern research methods that impact health care and education. "It is necessary to come to an understanding of all these trends on the basis of Catholic thought," she writes. "The traditional Catholic handling of these questions or, indeed, the traditional disregard for them could and should be revised if it is to meet the challenging questions of the time" (150).

Stein upholds the right of a woman to choose the vocation best suited to her. Virginity of soul is true of the married woman as well as the single and religious: it is the pure love present in her service, a sharing in Christ's love. Young women more suited to single life than to marriage are those who possess less sexual drive and who enjoy solitude and meditation. Even those who prefer marriage will find their feminine nature best fulfilled as companion and spouse of Christ if their will is offered up to God. No one who loves and is loved can be lonely or joyless; she belongs to the great community of lovers of God and will know the reciprocity of such love. All women who serve God attain their full personal stature; it is in his service that all faculties are developed harmoniously. Whether married or single, women in secular life can influence their agnostic friends and colleagues, who may be even more open to them than to women in religious habit.

There is no better source than objective work to counteract woman's negative qualities. Certain attitudes help to form woman's professional ethos. "Thus the divine life entering the being surrendered to God is love, ready to serve, compassionate, awaken and foster life; it corresponds thoroughly to what we have found to be the professional ethos required of woman" (53): "[T]here is no profession which cannot be practiced by a woman" (49). Professions previously considered "masculine," such as engineering, law, medicine, and politics, are well suited to woman's psyche. In fact, women are vital to public economy, health, and morality: "when women themselves are once again whole persons and when they help others to become so, they create healthy, energetic spores supplying healthy energy to the entire national body" (260).

No matter what vocation she chooses, woman needs prayer and liturgy to sustain her vitality and stamina. Silence, solitude, and meditation energize service to others. Christ's presence in the tabernacle lends quietude, peace, and the help of a friend. Grace won becomes "a living power of God within us, which we interweave into our professional life" (253). If one does not have the time to go to Mass, one does not have the time to go anywhere else. Woman's own needs become unimportant in the face of the Lord's business, which becomes her own. Stein states, "It is most important that the Holy Eucharist becomes life's focal point . . . the great events of the cosmic drama concerning the fall of man and redemption are renewed again and again in the life of the Church and in each human soul. And this will be permitted to happen again and again in the struggle of light over all darkness" (125–26). She asks, "In this *womanhood* devoted to the service of love, is there really a divine image? Indeed, yes. . . . Thus we can see the prototype of the feminine being in the Spirit of God poured out over all creatures" (200).

Stein inquires, what is the Catholic Church's philosophy of woman? In today's Church, there is no equality between woman and man, yet there is also no official definition—"ex-cathedra"—of woman's place in the Church. To Stein, Christ and his Church need woman. Throughout history, religious women have always been involved in the ministry of education, and women of the past have exercised an "intense apostolate as confessors and martyrs" as well as consecrated deaconesses (83). Will the modern changes in Church structure facilitate a law in this direction? Stein refers to Aquinas's remark that "Man is the source and end of woman" (180) and rebuts it by stating that woman's life is not for man alone. Each person has a unique meaning in his or her humanity, individuality, and gender. The fact that Mary chose virginity shows that woman is independent of man and cannot be defined solely through her relationship to him. The Church relies on tradition regarding the possible ordination of women, and it is doubtful that women will ever be welcomed as priests because Christ was born as man. But surely women will be called more and more to serve in the Church through teaching and pastoral work. Stein leaves the question open: "The Church as the kingdom of God in this world should reflect changes in human thought. Only by accepting each age as it is and treating it according to its singular nature can the Church bring eternal truth and life to temporality" (169). Rather than insisting on tradition, the Church should allow women to employ fully their talents and abilities.

Based on her philosophy, Stein worked toward a complete change in the educational structure of her day for women. Education involves the forming of a soul. Spiritual predispositions and faculties are shaped through motivation; the soul's qualities cannot be trained but only given the freedom and opportunity to develop. God alone changes nature. An objective education based on discipline and reason helps women to curb their compulsions, augment their intellect, and control their moods and reactions. It also encourages right values and actions. Yet women's emotional responses must also be valued, for they provide a personal view, self-knowledge, relation to others, and recognition of values. Since the girl cannot know her future beforehand, education should prepare her for possible roles as wife, mother, single woman, or religious. Stein suggests that a general education for domestic women or women who do not opt for professional life should activate practical intelligence and encourage a larger view of life that will help shape the world. Girls who wish to enter the work force should be transferred to a vocational school and there receive appropriate training. Girls preparing for university-level studies should be made familiar with abstract and scientific subjects as well as the arts—indeed, all the achievements of the human mind.

Stein was also a pioneer in sex education. She maintained that mothers have priority as teachers when their daughters reach puberty but that many mothers are unable to assume this role. A detached teacher may be better able to disclose the sacred meaning of marriage and motherhood. Sixty years before the Church considered sex education, Stein wrote, "The setup of a genuinely Catholic broad-minded approach to marriage and sexuality and the educational principles to be derived from this should therefore be considered as an urgent problem in contemporary education. This means the education of all youth, including young girls" (150).

Because grace determines a person's inner formation, religion is the essential core of any education. An early start is best, for truths of faith and personal sanctity work together. In the becoming of "another Christ," one's potentialities become actualities. Only pure nature can image God. Through the concept of Mary standing with Christ, a young girl understands what union with transcendental power means. "Only the girl who has understood the grandeur of virginal purity and union with God will fight earnestly for her purity," states Stein (248). The truths of the faith have the power to stir feminine emotions in a positive way, inspiring women to perform works of love: "Were each woman an image of the Mother of God, a *Spouse of Christ*, an apostle of the divine Heart, then would each fulfill her feminine vocation no matter what conditions she lived in and what worldly activity absorbed her life" (54). Religious education is the direct obligation of the Church as "universal teacher" in accordance with her "supernatural maternity" (211).

Salvation history is understood by viewing humanity as one being in the process of becoming; each person has a role and meaning in the being's growth through time. Humanity is Christ's Mystical Body since he died to redeem all. To perfect humanity, each person must become fully developed as a unique being. Yet, it is in the glory of heaven alone that one's full stature as a woman, man, or child of God is perfected.

CRITICAL RECEPTION

The publication of *Essays on Woman* spurred a furor of articles—secular, religious, feminist, and philosophical—and inspired numerous dissertations, conferences, and retreats. Internationally, the book can be found classified under such wide-ranging categories as feminism, Christianity, Judaism, phenomenology, philosophy, theology, and even law. As Father Emmet Costello writes (1999), "Edith Stein was a most brilliant and versatile intellectual and it would seem that her most original and seminal contributions to modern thought are her *Essays on Woman*."

Formal reviews of the book have been quite positive. In a 1990 edition of *The Thomist*, Marian Brady writes, "One would hope that these essays will be read widely and carefully by both women and men, as they offer serious, basic thoughts and insights which everyone concerned with present-day feminism should consider" (1990, 383). A review in *Spiritual Life* states, "one cannot help but be fascinated by the precision and clarity of [Stein's] thoughts. She was one of the intellectual giants of her day, yet at the same time an extremely practical and pragmatic thinker" (Quitslund 1987, 172). And Prudence Allen, in *The Review of Metaphysics*, concludes that "This newly revised edition . . . is a valuable text. . . . Stein's style is light and for the most part non-technical. . . . The essays should be of interest to academic philosophers as well, however, because they contain some of Stein's original thought and some brilliant intuitions about new ways to approach the question of woman's identity" (1998, 181).

A number of studies have been written about the considerable influence of Stein's feminism on the thinking of Pope John Paul II. In his October 1, 1999,

Apostolic Letter, John Paul wrote of Stein, "Particularly significant for her time was her struggle to promote the social status of women; and especially profound are the pages in which she explores the values of womanhood and woman's mission from the human and religious standpoint" (6).

My book, *Edith Stein: Scholar, Feminist, Saint* (1988), presents a concise introduction to Stein's feminism, and my *The Life and Thought of St. Edith Stein* (2001) is an updated account of the saint's biography and major thought.

NOTE

Edith Stein, *Essays on Woman*. Vol. 2 of *The Collected Works of Edith Stein*, ed. Lucy Gelber and Romaeus Leuven, O. C. D., trans. Freda Mary Oben (rev. ed., Washington, DC: ICS, 1996). All references are to this edition. Used by permission. Copyright © 1987, 1996, Washington Province of Discalced Carmelites, ICS Publications, 2131 Lincoln Road, N.E., Washington DC, 20002-1199, www.icspublications.org.

WORKS CITED

Allen, Prudence, R. S. M. 1998. "Edith Stein's *Woman*." *The Review of Metaphysics* 52, no. 1 (September): 180–81.

Aquinas, Saint Thomas. 1947. *The Summa Theologica*. Trans. Fathers of the Dominican Province. New York: Benzinger Brothers.

Brady, Marian, S. P. 1990. "Freda Mary Oben's *Edith Stein: Scholar, Feminist, Saint* and Edith Stein's *Essays on Woman*." *The Thomist* 54, no. 2 (April): 379–83.

Costello, Emmet P., S. J. 1999. "Saints Popular and Relevant." http://www.webvertisers.au.com/costello/books/saints/stein.html.

de Mirabel, Elizabeth. 1954. *Edith Stein*. Paris: Editions du Seuil.

John Paul II. 1999. Apostolic Letter Issued *Moto Proprio* Proclaiming Saint Bridget of Sweden, Saint Catherine of Siena, and Saint Teresa Benedicta of the Cross Co-Patronesses of Europe. October 1, http:www.carmelites.ie/Archive/johnpaul1oct1999.htm.

Oben, Freda Mary. 1988. *Edith Stein: Scholar, Feminist, Saint*. New York: Alba House.

———. 1990. "Edith Stein as Educator." *Thought* 65, no. 257 (June): 113–26.

———. 2001. *The Life and Thought of St. Edith Stein*. New York: Alba House.

Quitslund, Sonya A. 1987. Review of *The Collected Works of Edith Stein*: vol. 2, *Essays on Woman*. *Spiritual Life* 33, no. 3 (Fall): 171–76.

Stein, Edith. 1986. *Life in a Jewish Family*. Vol. 1 of *The Collected Works of Edith Stein*, ed. Lucy Gelber and Romaeus Leuven, O. C. D.; trans. Josephine Koeppel, O. C. D. Washington, DC: ICS.

———. 1989. *On the Problem of Empathy*. Vol. 3 of *The Collected Works of Edith Stein*, ed. Lucy Gelber and Romaeus Leuven, O. C. D.; trans. Waltraut Stein. Washington, DC: ICS.

— Freda Mary Oben

Jean Sulivan [1913–1980]

Eternity, My Beloved

BIOGRAPHY

Jean Sulivan, French Catholic priest and author of thirty books of fiction and nonfiction, is the *nom de plume* of Father Joseph Lemarchand, who chose his authorial name in homage to the hero of Preston Sturges's film, *Sullivan's Travels*, who embraces solidarity with the poor. Jean Sulivan was born in 1913 in Montauban, a small village in rural Brittany, where, as a child, he felt "perfectly in communion with the earth" (Sulivan 2000, 45). Soon after his birth, his father died in one of the first battles of World War I. Sulivan grew very close to his mother, Angela, whom he memorializes in his moving memoir *Anticipate Every Goodbye*. Through his traditionally, deeply pious mother, Sulivan "came to understand [his] relationship to the Church" (68), a relationship that, although vexed by Sulivan's rejection of institutional conformity and coercion, was faithful until his death in 1980 as a result of an automobile accident in the Bois de Boulogne.

As a seminarian, Sulivan first embraced and then recoiled from the tightly knit, scholastic order that marked his studies. But a sympathetic superior allowed him to read books by "Jacques Maritain, Gabriel Marcel, Heidegger, Kierkegaard, Gilson, de Lubac, and Congar. Such writers were not then normally available to seminarians" (Maher 1994, 1). Sulivan was ordained in 1938, taught literature and philosophy at the Catholic lycée in Rennes, and was soon after appointed chaplain of that city's university. He became a leader in the cultural world of Rennes, founding a film club, newspaper, library, and lecture series that featured some of the foremost French Catholic writers of the time, including Gabriel Marcel, François Mauriac, Emmanuel Mounier, and Jean Danielou. Although he himself had always wanted to write and had already run a magazine in Rennes, it was not until mid-life that Sulivan came into his own as a writer. He published his first novel, *Le voyage interieur*, in 1958, at the age of forty-five. Upon its publication in 1964, his third novel, *Mais il y a la mer* (*The Sea Remains*), proved a success. It won the Grand Prix Catholique de literature, and Sulivan was acclaimed as the "new Bernanos," a role he found confining: "[A]ll of a sudden, there I was, obliged to defend myself, to produce sworn evidence to the fact that

I was a bona fide Catholic" (Sulivan 2000, 86). He accepted the prize, chiefly to please his mother, but silently vowed that thereafter he "would keep [his] distance from the literary establishment by adopting the means that would allow me to talk freely" (89). His sympathetic bishop supported his calling to write and freed Sulivan from his pastoral responsibilities. Thus, for the last fifteen or so years of his life, Sulivan focused upon his vocation as a writer and lived in relative anonymity in Paris.

If Sulivan's mother gave him the gift of his relationship with the Church, she also modeled for him an experience of faith released from institutional consolations and boundaries. Near death, she unexpectedly refused the signs and sacraments that had nurtured her lifelong faith. In her death, Sulivan discerned the abandonment of Christ, stripped and forsaken. Paradoxically, she became "a sign" for her son "that He existed": "I knew through you of His presence" he tells her in his memoir (120). *Car je t'aime, o eternite!* (*Eternity, My Beloved* [1966]) is the first novel Sulivan wrote after his mother's death.

Sulivan continued residing and writing in Paris, publishing numerous works not yet translated into English. As Eamon Maher relates, Sulivan "was killed in a hit-and-run [accident] as he was coming out of the Bois de Boulogne on one of his interminable walks. [He is] buried in the family plot in Montauban, Brittany, beside his mother to whom he was so attached" (personal correspondence with me, October 19, 2003).

PLOT SUMMARY

The hero of *Eternity, My Beloved* is a Catholic priest named Jerome Strozzi, whose character is based upon a real-life priest, Auguste Rossi, whom Sulivan knew in Paris. Strozzi's story is told in elliptical and fragmentary form by a jaded, cultured narrator named "Sulivan." The novel focuses upon Strozzi when he is already in his fifties. In brief sketches we learn that Strozzi has enjoyed a rural childhood in close communion with nature. He is liked and respected as a child, but nevertheless he is expelled from public school for an act of public protest against a teacher's injustice. In Catholic school, he does especially well in math and science. Sympathy for the misery of others and a desire for adventure draw him toward the priesthood—as does his expulsion from the polytechnic institute for still another protest against a professor's injustice. In the seminary, he appreciates the mathematical certainties of scholastic theology; after ordination, he teaches math for thirteen years in a Catholic high school in Thoissy. In Fribourg, Switzerland, he serves as superior of the seminary and also as a go-between for Resistance correspondence smuggled out of Nazi-occupied France. He is betrayed, declared *persona non grata* in Switzerland, and—now over fifty years old—sent back to France.

Bereft of an official parish, Strozzi wanders the streets and finds work for young people in the seedy Pigalle neighborhood of occupied Paris. He begins ministering to the poor and to the prostitutes, pimps, and gangsters who also live there. In one crucial scene, he arrives at a German police station to attest to the character of two sisters arrested for marching with the tricolor French flag on the Champs Elysess. His presence and persuasion secures their release. One late night later, he falls asleep on the metro, misses his stop, and, penniless, stays at the sisters' family home for the night: soon after, the family disavows its business of prostitution and becomes conventionally, even insistently, pious. After the war, Strozzi continues to serve his "parishioners" by becoming associated with Abbé Godin, who appears as a character in the novel. Godin's *Mission de France* publicized the Church's disconnection with the working class and led to the formation of the worker priest movement (1944–1954), in which well over a hundred French and Belgian priests were given permission to dispense with their cassocks and take ordinary jobs with the aim of reaching estranged Catholic laborers. By the late 1950s the Church had withdrawn support for the movement, which it saw as compromising the traditional priestly role.

At this point in the novel, Strozzi is in his mid-sixties and resists returning to that role. In consequence, he is told by his provincial superior to leave the religious community on which he has depended for food and shelter. Now "he had come to experience humiliation in his flesh and blood. . . . Now he was stripped bare without having wished it" (*Eternity, My Beloved*, 80). Yet Strozzi responds without resentment, with the joy of an interior freedom in his heart. He finds an apartment in Pigalle, only now "[gives] up wearing his cassock" (80), and continues to serve his parishioners even after brutal beatings by neighborhood thugs and continued criticism by Church superiors. One woman, Elizabeth, a prostitute for twenty years, is dramatically transformed by Strozzi's presence; she moves to a town on the Mediterranean, where she meets the narrator and serves others much as Strozzi does in Paris. By the end of the novel, Strozzi emerges as a saint—but in the sense that Jean Sulivan describes sanctity in his spiritual journal, *Matinales* (*Morning Light*): "Saints, whether officially recognized or not, have not sought happiness merely in the hereafter, but in the kingdom here and now on behalf of concrete men and women who were their neighbors" (1988, 69).

MAJOR THEMES

Since Jean Sulivan's breakthrough 1964 novel, *The Sea Remains*, contains important Catholic themes that recur in *Eternity, My Beloved* and throughout his later works, it is appropriate to begin the discussion of his major themes with a look at that novel. *The Sea Remains* tells the story of a Spanish cardinal, Ramon Rimaz, who retires by the sea and sheds his long-worn mask of prestige. The story's themes involve a spiritual wisdom grounded in the Incarnation and kenosis of Jesus Christ and its implications for the Church. Sulivan recognizes the Church's need for institutional embodiment. As a character in the novel puts it, "the gospel couldn't be delivered to the world in its pure essence. If the soul were without a body, there would no longer be a soul" (*The Sea Remains*, 24). Yet tension can emerge between Incarnation and kenosis. If the Church inhibits the working of the spirit through its body of dogma, or confuses spectacle with inspirited ritual, it can allow power to demolish kenosis and embodiment to petrify. The Church can easily forget its fundamental role as "servant of the Gospel," as Sulivan puts it in *Morning Light* (1988, 27). As servant, he continues, the Church ought to "allow the Word to make its way within human consciousness" (92). If, in the quest for conceptual coherence, it attempts "to keep the lid on that sparrow-hawk, the Holy Spirit" it "yield[s] to the temptation of an imperialistic unity" (93). Likewise, if it covers itself too snugly with the trappings of power and prestige, it grows deaf to the Gospel's call to poverty. In *The Sea Remains*, Cardinal Rimaz reflects on this tension in a homily:

> Of course he remained convinced that the Church needed a firm and independent base in order not to dissolve in people's consciousness: there were lots of examples to demonstrate the illusion of those who had wanted to rely solely on their inspiration. But little by little, he said, he had come to think that the social power of the Church could be the cause of its spiritual weakness, just as a mass membership could go hand in hand with profound alienation. The Church itself ought to be poor and humble, without waiting to be crucified. People were able to be poor and humble for themselves, and rich and proud for the Church. (1989, 100)

Rimaz utters these words—"as discreet as a feather brushing a windowpane" (100)—late in the novel, in retirement and near the end of an interior journey through humiliation and self-discovery. In an Augustinian search through memory, he recollects those moments when the conflict between his role as Church leader and servant of the Gospel was most clearly cast into relief. He remembers his mother stepping into "the immense paneled rooms of [his] Episcopal palace," and asking, stunned, "'How can it be? We were . . . and you, because you . . . Is this what the Gospel. . . ?'" (44). He recalls the authoritative challenge of a young Chinese priest: "'Juan Ramon, are you a successor of the apostles or the director of a corporation?'" (56). Now, with "all his real power . . . withdrawn" (9), he recognizes the futility of a life founded on external reverence and regard as opposed to an interior vitality. In anger and humiliation, he orders his housekeeper to burn the ecclesiastical memorabilia she has lovingly gathered.

But here, at his lowest point, Rimaz's interior journey takes a hopeful, restorative turn. On long walks along the seashore, he attends closely to the physical reality surrounding him—water, beach, grass, boulders, the faces and bodies of other people. As he enters into relationship with an unlikely array of others—for example, a small child, a painter and her imprisoned lover, his niece and her Marxist boyfriend, a poor fisherman—he emerges from solitude. Gradually, he rediscovers his deepest self and his vocation: "To his endless amazement, by discovering the world he entered into the understanding of the gospel" (81).

Like the Gospels, which are his inspiration, Sulivan's work is rich in paradox. In *The Sea Remains*, Rimaz must lose himself before he finds himself; in his recovery of childhood he achieves maturity; in accepting the limit of death he discovers his greatest joy. In *Morning Light*, Sulivan avows his Gospel-rooted preference for the marginal and the powerless, the last that shall be first—the rebel, reject, and vagabond. But in this journal his pokes at the pompous and powerful veer close to sarcasm and heavy-handed judgment. Here, paradox can deteriorate into dialectical opposition and can become just another assertion of power: "There is no hope for someone like that," he writes of the person who tells others "he's praying, that he's been praying, or is about to pray." Immediately aware of his objectifying self-assertion, however, Sulivan recovers paradox and humility in his next sentence: "Of course, he might be a saint; language is deceptive" (1988, 138).

In *The Sea Remains*, Sulivan relinquishes such power in his refusal to inscribe its plot with a clear-cut authorial preference. The character one least suspects emerges, possibly, as most Christlike: Juan Gonzalez, a traditionally pious, rich, right-wing landowner. In a remarkable scene—one that anticipates the film *Jesus of Montreal*—the powerful landowner plays the part of Christ in the town's version of the Passion Play: "[P]erhaps . . . he becomes, by grace, humble and poor, one with Him under this cross" (1989, 113). "[P]erhaps" he too inspires the culminating kenotic step of Cardinal Rimaz (104). As a novelist, Sulivan sustains the radically disruptive spirit of paradox. Appropriately, Denise Levertov, in a book jacket quotation for the 1989 publication of *The Sea Remains*, praised Sulivan's novel as "polyphonic," a word that the Russian literary theorist Mikhail Bakhtin uses to describe Dostoevsky's artistic rendering of his character's internal freedom, their unpredictability and "unfinalizability." So too Sulivan. In each of his characters, Sulivan deeply respects "the mystery of conscience and ambiguity of human actions" (69). He relinquishes authorial omniscience and control over them. His authorial "perhaps" regarding their motivations suggests a position alongside rather than above them. Thus, his polyphonic creation partakes in kenosis.

Sulivan's fractured style—even more evident in his later work—further evinces his relinquishing of tight authorial control. Although ultimately beautiful in form, *The Sea Remains* often proceeds by hints, ellipses, premonitions, and fragmentary images, a process especially evident in his later novel *Eternity, My Beloved*. These techniques also recur in *Morning Light*; although that book is rich in challenging ideas, Sulivan refrains from imposing a restrictive coherence or "order" (1988, 85) upon them. Taking the path of Meister Eckhart and the Tao, he resists what he calls "the dominant thought of the West, which invites us to knowledge, to power, to take, to possess" (11).

Nietzsche is among the authors who most impressed Sulivan; in *Morning Light*, Sulivan writes of Nietzsche's apophatic potentialities: "By breaking words open and unveiling the mechanisms of attachment, [Nietzsche] can bring us to rejection, but he may also leave us more open to what is coming" (16). But how might the Christian literary imagination respond to Nietzsche's searing critique of Christian love? In his *Genealogy of Morals*, Nietzsche unmasks "*caritas*" as "*ressentiment*": the fearful weak envy the courageous strong and assert their will to power with "faith" in eternity and with the belief that the charitable meek will inherit bliss while the strong are turned empty away. For Nietzsche, Christianity denies life: the would-be saint infects the present with venomous and vengeful dreams of the future. *Eternity, My Beloved* takes its title and epigraph from Nietzsche: "I have never found the woman by whom I would want to have a child, except this woman that I love—for I love you, eternity my beloved." The novel can be read as a respectful reflection on and persuasive refutation to Nietzsche's rejection of Christian love as life-denying.

The protagonist of *Eternity, My Beloved*, the priest Strozzi, loves and ministers to his *outre* parishioners without pronouncing the doctrinal certitudes or judgments that can mask an assertion of power motivated by resentment. "Profoundly attentive to what was going on" (*Eternity, My Beloved*, 67), he simply receives and gives friendship. He "sit[s] with others in silence for a whole hour, even two" (84); when he does utter words, "he speaks to everyone as equal to equal, totally oblivious of pity" (86). In so doing, he "never stop[s] fighting for life against death" (76). In the course of the novel, Strozzi emerges as an image of the Jesus who befriended the spurned and who proclaimed, "I came that they may have life, and have it abundantly" (John 10:10).

The narrator, Sulivan, like Nietzsche, is himself a "master of suspicion," and the narrator's own transformation provides one of the key dramatic strands of the novel. At first, the narrator distrusts Strozzi's serene celibacy amidst the prostitutes he befriends. In these friendships, relaxed and affectionate as they are, Strozzi practices a purposeful asceticism (another practice in which Nietzsche spies life-denying resentment). Strozzi renounces lust, but he also relinquishes any desire to impose principles or control over his friends. In his "passion to help life succeed" (102) he looks calmly, openly, and hopefully at the person before him and practices an asceticism of attentiveness, an attentiveness he insists is "essential" to every human relationship (101), especially marriage. Like Freud, the narrator yearns "to explain [Strozzi's serenity] as a mechanism, to unmask an illusion" (93). In Dostoevsky's *The Brothers Karamazov*, Rakitin reduces the spiritually transformative encounter between Grushenka and Alyosha Karamazov to machinations of power and lust; similarly, the narrator of *Eternity, My Beloved* initially suspects the intent behind the image of the prostitute Paquerette on Strozzi's lap. Unlike Rakitin, however, the narrator is gradually able to understand that Strozzi was "[t]he first man who had ever looked on her as a human being" and that her family's "regeneration" "starts from this point" (31). By the end of the novel, he realizes the folly of his anxiety to reduce and "explain everything psychologically" (117). He begins to understand Strozzi's celibacy, to recognize the paradox that "in order to give assistance to life, it was necessary to keep yourself, to some degree, outside of life. It was the love of life that kept him from entering its stream. Out of love for life he had chosen the appearance of death" (95). Strozzi is the corn of wheat that dies to bring forth much fruit.

And Strozzi's friendships with the women clearly do bear fruit. For Paquerette, for example, Strozzi becomes "The first man with whom she had walked and talked who did not brush against her or touch her, and did not lecture her—which is really just another way to touch and deceive you, and treat you like an object" (31). Paquerette, along with her family, soon renounces prostitution, and, as the narrator reports with the self-satisfied irony that marks the earlier sections of his narration, she becomes a "rigid moralist. . . . a lay catechist in her parish" (35). Elizabeth, also a prostitute, later becomes a kind of Saint Jeanne de Chantal to Strozzi's Saint Francis de Sales. With Strozzi, she helps a grieving man find his daughter who had been about to be caught up in the underworld of the sex trade. Also like Strozzi, Elizabeth begins to visit her neighbors, enacting a charity that is "discreet, unobtrusive, unaffected" (65).

One of Jean Sulivan's recurring themes is the way in which words and conceptual formulations can sap vitality from their referents. For example, Strozzi believes that "charity" is "the most beautiful word on earth" yet "strik[es] it out of [his] vocabulary" because of the "sanctimonious air" it has for others (97). As narrator, Sulivan strives to find a language that describes Strozzi's charity "without turning it into a catechism lesson, without making it either pretentious or superficial" (65). The novel's style is often aphoristic, but the aphorisms aim to awaken the reader from conventional habits of thought, much like the parables of Jesus do. For example, reflecting on the strange moment in which Jesus curses the barren fig tree when it's not the season for figs, the narrator writes, "Men and women are made for the unexpected and the impossible—the Gospel keeps reminding us of this" (129). Indeed, the novel's narrative development often breaks off unexpectedly, creating a fragmented form that Sulivan claimed was necessary to reflect, in Joseph Cunneen's words, "the brokenness of our world" (1986, 119). At times, however, the reader wishes that scenes of Strozzi's personal encounters with others had been more fully and tangibly rendered or that more narration had been included. Some of these scenes are striking: for example, when Strozzi visits the smoky, airless room of Arlette, a destitute eighty-six-year-old woman whom he embraces as "mother . . . daughter . . . sister" (*Eternity, My Beloved*, 117), or when Strozzi is touched on the shoulder by an official of the Church that has kept its distance from him: "Strozzi never forgot that hand. Although it didn't promise any particular help, still, it was a maternally caring hand" (123). These scenes give a strong sense of human reality to Strozzi's characterization, and a novel with as incarnational a vision as this warrants even more flesh-and-blood embodiment.

However, Sulivan the narrator anticipates such criticism and defends his attenuated renderings: "I could have made up scenes, livened everything up; it would have filled hundreds of pages. My publisher would have been delighted—a sure best seller" (83). Instead, he gives his readers a narrative that requires—and proves worthy of—an attentive, laborious remembering of the fragments of Strozzi's life. Gradually, like the narrator, the reader discerns a Christological pattern in that life. In his self-emptying attention to others, Strozzi imitates Christ and "serve[s] life" (145). In Strozzi, Sulivan the author has created an unforgettable character whose loving engagement with the world reflects that of the One who said, "I am the life."

Throughout the novel, Sulivan's vision can be described as sacramental and analogical: he depicts a physical world that mediates grace and points often to the reality of the divine. For example, Strozzi accompanies Paquerette into a bar, and the narrator sees in this scene an image of Jesus with the Samaritan woman at the well (26). Similarly, Strozzi, sitting with Paquerette in a movie theater watching *Les enfants du paradis*, touches her left shoulder with his right hand, and the narrator discerns this "rapid gesture" to be "light as a sacrament" (26). Moreover, Strozzi's close friend Elizabeth also begins to see the world sacramentally: like Strozzi, she starts to find in every meal an image of the Last Supper (62). For Strozzi, the divine image is present everywhere, as he explains to the narrator toward the end of the novel: "As I've often told you, I instinctively see Jesus, Son of God, in every human being. God has no other image except the face of a person, every person" (125).

In an especially perceptive discussion of *Eternity, My Beloved*, Joseph Schwartz concludes with insightful reflections on the novel's Catholic dimension:

> Sulivan's subject is religion, particularly Roman Catholicism. Why is it central to his life and his understanding of civilization? Quite simply, the desire for the absolute, which Christianity has in common with other religions, is the way to understanding reality. Order, as [Paul] Claudel made clear to Sulivan, is the overarching expression of the nature of being, especially the order given to reality by the four last things—death, judgment, heaven, hell. "[He is] a priest, visible and invisible, of the catholic, apostolic, and Roman church, visible and invisible" ([*Eternity, My Beloved*] 130). What is amazing is the way that Strozzi

calls on his Mother, the Church, every time he is in a crisis. When challenged by Sulivan [the narrator] to tell him what he knows about God, he answers: "What the Bible and the Church tell us" (124). But we must note also that Strozzi scolds his Mother for becoming too institutionalized and too formal. He is eager in his way to rehumanize the Church and will be a troublemaker if necessary to make his point. He does not in any way undermine theology or the moral law, only insisting that "we interiorize them enough to forget them" (128).

Searching for parallels in American culture, I find that the older priest, the hero, is very much like Dorothy Day, and that the younger priest, the narrator/author Sulivan, resembles [Walker] Percy. In words that Percy would recognize and approve, Sulivan says: "Someone has to cry out. That's my job, to be the town watchman, the one who alerts the public" (123). (Schwartz 2001, 377)

In all his later works, including *Eternity, My Beloved*, Sulivan continued to discern the divine presence among the dispossessed, rebellious, and rejected. But unlike many of the heroes portrayed in the media of the 1960s and 1970s, Sulivan's rebels are not motivated by the fulfillment of desire. As Patrick Gormally writes, "For Sulivan, there is no way in which the Christian can reconcile the desire for glory—or, for that matter, desire in any form—with the liberating message of Christianity. [Sulivan's] characters, members of an underground fraternity, learn not to actively seek the object of their desire, detaching themselves from any conscious quest apart from the quest for meaning" (1985–86, 429). The earthy paradoxes of the Gospel, the scandal of the kenotic Christ, infuse Sulivan's work and lend it its sustaining spirit of freedom, hope, and joy.

CRITICAL RECEPTION

Although most of Sulivan's books have been published in Paris by the prestigious Gallimard press, only four of them have been published in English translation: *Morning Light*, in 1988; *The Sea Remains*, in 1989; *Eternity, My Beloved*, in 1998; and *Anticipate Every Goodbye*, in 2000. The critical reception of *Eternity, My Beloved* has been very positive since it was first published in France in 1966. Robert Conard called it "A novel of profound passion. . . . In cobbling together the story of a man's life from snippets of dialogue and tidbits of information, Sulivan anticipates the technique of Heinrich Böll in his Nobel Prize novel, *Group Portrait with Lady*. . . . The translation [by Sister Francis Ellen Riordan] faithfully captures Sulivan's language and the introduction [by Joseph Cunneen] provides an informative overview of Sulivan's life and oeuvre" (1999, 335). In his review in *Christianity and Literature* (2001), Joseph Schwartz was similarly positive, although he commented upon "the harshness of [Sulivan's] style" in the novel:

As reporting, *Eternity, My Beloved* reads like a work in progress, like a rehearsal instead of a performance, in which the reader becomes the actor working out the meaning of his being in a search for the absolute. The conventional novel form is seriously fractured by the presence of both author and narrator. In *Eternity, My Beloved* there is no carefully constructed plot, no development of character, no climax, and very little action. There is instead much meditation and explanation. (2001, 377)

In *America*, John Breslin, S. J., made similar observations but wrote, "Strozzi's combination of anti-bourgeois sentiment, Gospel conviction and humility prove irresistible. . . . He is regularly roughed up by the pimps whose business he threatens, and is reported to the chancery by virtuous Christians whose wayward pleasures he subverts" (2000, 27). In a *London Tablet* review of the novel, Eamon Maher applauded the "wonderful descriptions of encounters between Strozzi and his ecclesiastical superiors, who want him to adopt a more conventional ministry" (1999, 1113), and in *The Irish Times*, Patrick Gormally argued that "The broaching of the impossible is precisely what makes Sulivan an important writer of Christian inspiration" (1999, 67). Denise Levertov, in her quotation on the book jacket for *The Sea Remains*, called Sulivan "one of the great Catholic novelists of our time." And Elie Wiesel, on the same book jacket, exhorted "Listen to the voice of Jean Sulivan: you will be enriched by its poignant quest for beauty and humanity."

NOTE

Jean Sulivan, *Eternity, My Beloved*, trans. Sister Francis Ellen Riordan (St. Paul, MN: River Boat Books, 1999). All references are to this edition. Used by permission of River Boat Books. Portions of this article are drawn from my reviews of Sulivan's work first published in *The Cresset* in October 1992 and in Christmas/Epiphany 2000–2001; used by permission of *The Cresset*. Quotations from Joseph Schwartz's review of *Eternity, My Beloved* used by permission of *Christianity and Literature*. I wish to express my gratitude to Joseph Cunneen for his editorial suggestions in response to an earlier version of this essay and to Monica Kunecki for her research assistance.

WORKS CITED

Breslin, John, S. J. 2000. Review of *Eternity, My Beloved*, by Jean Sulivan. *America* 183, no. 8 (September 23): 27–29.

Conard, Robert. 1999. Review of *Eternity, My Beloved*, by Jean Sulivan. *Choice* 37, no. 2 (October): 335.

Cunneen, Joseph. 1986. "Jean Sulivan: Writing as a Vocation." *America* 154, no. 6 (February 15): 117–20.

Gormally, Patrick [Padraig O Gormaile]. 1985–1986. "A Stray in the Profession: Rebellion in the Work of Jean Sulivan." *Cross Currents* 35, no. 4 (Winter): 423–33.

———. 1999. Review of *Eternity, My Beloved*, by Jean Sulivan. *The Irish Times* (July 3): 67.

Maher, Eamon. 1994. "The Rebel Novelist Priest Who Liked to Buck Tradition." *The Irish Times* (April 4): home news section, 1.

———. 1999. Review of *Eternity, My Beloved*, by Jean Sulivan. *The London Tablet* (August 14): 1113.

Schwartz, Joseph. 2001. Review of *Eternity, My Beloved*, by Jean Sulivan. *Christianity and Literature* 50, no. 2 (Winter): 375–78.

Sulivan, Jean. 1988. *Morning Light: The Spiritual Journal of Jean Sulivan*, trans. Joseph Cunneen and Patrick Gormally. Mawah, NJ: Paulist Press.

———. 1989. *The Sea Remains*, trans. Robert A. Donahue Jr., and Joseph Cunneen. New York: Crossroad.

———. 2000. *Anticipate Every Goodbye*, trans. Eamon Maher. Dublin: Veritas.

BIBLIOGRAPHY

Gormally, Patrick [Padraig O Gormaile]. "Jean Sulivan écrivain chrétien. Une nouvelle conception du rôle de l'écrivain." Dissertation, University de Toulouse-le-Mirail, 1980.

Guillemin, Henri. *Sulivan ou la parole libératrice*. Paris: Gallimard, 1977.

Lebrun, Claude. *Invitation à Jean Sulivan*. Paris: Le Cerf, 1981.

Majault, Joseph. *L'évidence et le mystère*. Paris: Le Centurion, 1978.

— Paul J. Contino

Henry Suso [c. 1295–1366]

Exemplar

BIOGRAPHY

Henry Suso was a fourteenth-century Dominican whose life experiences and teachings inspired generations of lay and religious men and women also seeking to attain for themselves a closer relationship with God. Suso's name commonly appears today in German as Heinrich Seuse, a form advocated by the Catholic historian Father Denifle, who published the first volume of his edition of Suso's works in 1876 and who himself adopted the friar's name on his reception into the Dominican Order. The Latin form Suso has again gained currency in recent years. Along with Meister Eckhart and John Tauler, Suso is regarded as a key figure in the mystical movement that flourished in the late Middle Ages in German-speaking territories.

Around 1295 or 1297 Suso was born into a wealthy family in or near the town of Constance, located on the lake of the same name on the Swiss-German border. The child was strongly influenced by his mother, whose family name Sus or Süs—in German, *süß* means "sweet" or "dear"—he later adopted. Unsuited because of poor health for the life of a knight, the vocation of his father, the boy decided to pursue a religious life and entered the local monastery at the age of thirteen. A donation by his family may have facilitated his acceptance into the religious community at such a young age; later, as a student, Suso still expressed regret and shame at the thought that his initiation into the religious life might have been tainted by simony. At the age of eighteen, Suso underwent a spiritually life-changing experience; it was at this point in his life that his devotion and service to God took on new meaning.

After obtaining a basic education in Constance, the Dominican's studies may have taken him to Strasbourg before he was chosen to attend the *studium generale* in Cologne in 1324 or 1325. It was at the renowned school in the North that Suso probably studied with Meister Eckhart until the great teacher's death in 1327. Once he had completed his studies, Suso returned to the monastery in Constance and assumed the position of lector. Around 1330, the friar faced charges of heresy, the result of which was the loss of the lectorship. Ultimately nothing came of the charges, and Suso was appointed prior, a position he held until 1334.

As part of his religious vocation, Suso engaged in numerous ascetic practices. Through fasting and inflicting physical pain upon himself, he sought to imitate the example of Christ (*imitatio Christi*) and deny himself worldly comforts, thereby focusing his attention more fully on his relationship with God. Suso continued the acts of penance and suffering until the age of forty, when he felt himself called by God to abandon them and to embrace the life of an itinerant preacher.

For much of the subsequent decade, Suso traveled throughout southern Germany and northern Switzerland, preaching to lay and religious persons. He made the acquaintance of Friends of God (*Gottesfreunde*), individuals seeking to enhance their relationship with the Divine through meditation and imitation of the apostolic life, and he served as spiritual adviser to beguine communities (beguines were women who were devoted to the religious life but who took no permanent vows; they engaged in handiwork to support themselves) as well as nuns in the houses of the Dominican province of Teutonia. The friar developed a special spiritual relationship with Elsbeth Stagel, a nun and later the prioress of the Dominican convent in Töss near Winterthur in northern Switzerland; she came to play a pivotal role in the recording of his writings. Suso also enjoyed the friendship of Henry of Nördlingen, whose relationship with the Dominican nun Margaretha Ebner was similar to that between Suso and Stagel. Both men served as confessors and confidants to the women in their care and engaged in correspondence with them.

Like most of the Dominicans in Constance, Suso supported the pope in the latter's conflict with Emperor Louis of Bavaria, which came to a head in 1338 and 1339. When Suso and other friars loyal to the pope refused to acquiesce to the emperor's demands that they reinstate the public worship banned by the pope, they were forced to leave Constance, although most friars returned by 1349. During the period of exile, Suso was transferred to Ulm, where he remained until his death in 1366.

In 1831, Pope Gregory XVI beatified the Dominican. Blessed Henry Suso's feast day in the Dominican Order is March 2.

SUMMARY

In the years before his death, around 1362 or 1363, Suso undertook the editing of his writings for publication; such an edition prepared by the author himself is known in German as an *Ausgabe letzter Hand*. The friar's efforts yielded the *Exemplar*, which consists of four works: *The Life of the Servant*, *The Little Book of Eternal Wisdom*, *The Little Book of Truth*, and *The Little Book of Letters*.

In the prologue, Suso briefly characterizes the purpose of each of the works; as the title of the collection indicates, they are filled with and are themselves meant to serve as examples or models for spiritual behavior. Originally the author did not intend to allow the first work, autobiographical in nature, to be published during his lifetime, but he later decided it would be prudent for it—as well as the other writings—to be written under his supervision and distributed while he was yet alive so that he could explain and defend the work, if necessary. Suso's writings, especially *The Little Book of Eternal Wisdom* and *The Little Book of*

Truth, were quite popular during his lifetime, and in the prologue he notes that unauthorized manuscripts of the works had begun to appear in German-speaking areas as well as in other lands (*Exemplar*, 57). Recalling the controversies that had arisen between Meister Eckhart and the Church hierarchy concerning the master's teachings, Suso was justified in his concern about the spread of versions of his writings that might be inaccurate. The prologue also addresses the issue of orthodoxy: Master Bartholomew, a superior of the province of Teutonia, gave his approbation for the circulation of the first part of the *Exemplar*. Although he died before further sections were added, he appeared to Suso in a vision, providing a posthumous ecclesiastical *imprimatur*. The prologue concludes by identifying the potential audience and purpose of the *Exemplar*: "Anyone who would like to become a good and blessed person and share special intimacy with God, or whom God has singled out by severe suffering—which he is accustomed to do with his special friends—such a person would find this book to be a comforting help" (59).

The *Life of the Servant* has been regarded by some scholars as the first autobiography in German, although it is written in the third person. The chronicle serves as a source of details concerning Suso's life and is composed of two parts. The first part (chapters 1–32) deals with noteworthy events in the life of the "servant of Eternal Wisdom" (*Diener der Ewigen Weisheit*), Suso himself; the second part (chapters 33–44) also relates personal anecdotes about the servant, but they are presented in the context of responses to questions posed by Elsbeth Stagel or advice Suso wishes to impart. The prefatory comments to the *Life* describe how the work came to be written. A holy person, understood to be Stagel, was seeking spiritual consolation and guidance, which Suso provided during his visits to Töss and in letters to her and the other sisters. Stagel secretly recorded her confessor's words. When Suso discovered the "spiritual theft" (63), he confiscated the notes she had at that time and burned them. However, a message from heaven warned him not to continue to destroy the writings; what was not burned constitutes the *Life*, with additions presumably by Suso himself after Stagel's death around 1360.

The events related in chapters 1–32 are not presented in chronological order but rather according to certain themes or to points Suso wishes to make regarding the sufferings and struggles of a servant of Eternal Wisdom. The central idea in the spiritual journey is detachment from people and things that can distract one from service to and contemplation of God. The most significant and dramatic way in which Suso attempts to achieve detachment manifests itself in the castigations of the flesh he inflicts upon himself from the ages of eighteen to forty. He describes how he inscribes the name of Jesus over his heart with a stylus. He wears a penitential shirt and an iron chain and uses a door for a bed. Most graphic are the descriptions of the nail-studded cross Suso carries on his back for eight years. Suso relates the disciplines of the flesh to aspects of the imitation of Christ: for example, when he scourges himself with thorns, it reminds him of the scourging Christ suffered before the Crucifixion.

At the age of forty, the Dominican is commanded to give up the external penitential exercises and move to a more advanced school, a higher level of detachment. This level is characterized by the ruination of his reputation, suffering by others on his account, and abandonment of the servant by everyone, including God. When he sees a doormat in the mouth of a dog, he recognizes that his fellow friars will abuse him just as the dog drags and tosses the doormat (chapter 20). Suso relates how the prediction subsequently becomes reality. He is accused of being a thief, a heretic, and a poisoner. He is shamed by the behavior of his sister, a wayward nun whom he eventually is able to lead back to pious ways. His own life is put in peril when he encounters a murderer and when he is swept away in the waters of the Rhine. Taxed to the limit by these experiences, Suso speaks to God within himself and offers all his suffering to God. The first part ends with the servant finally content and at peace.

The second part of the *Life* is directed to Elsbeth Stagel, who had inquired of Meister Eckhart about lofty intellectual matters but did not fully understand the answers. Here, Suso offers practical and specific advice that Stagel can more easily comprehend. The first step on her spiritual journey is confession, with Suso serving as her intercessor. When Stagel reveals that she has been imitating Suso's spiritual practices by mortifying her own flesh, the friar admonishes her to stop. Different acts of suffering are expected from different individuals, and Suso views Stagel's illnesses as the suffering God expects her to bear. The friar relates additional episodes of suffering in his life, including how his reputation was marred when he was accused of fathering a child. As Suso directs Stagel to a higher level of understanding, he continues to focus on detachment from material things and from the external senses. The *Life* concludes with Stagel's death and Suso's vision of her as she enters into the naked Godhead.

The *Little Book of Eternal Wisdom*, one of the most popular devotional tracts in the late medieval mystical tradition, consists of three parts. In the first two parts, Suso as the servant of Eternal Wisdom converses with Eternal Wisdom herself about the role of suffering in the spiritual life and about the individual's behavior toward God. The suffering of Christ on the cross and Mary's suffering at the Crucifixion are the examples that Suso imitates in his own spiritual journey. Eternal Wisdom describes how the journey of the soul progresses: "The more the soul freely goes out of itself in detachment, the freer is its ascent; and the freer its ascent is, the farther it enters into the wild wasteland and deep abyss of the pathless Godhead into which it plummets, where it is swept along, and to which it is so united that it cannot want otherwise than what God wants" (243). The freedom leads to a clearer comprehension and praise of God. The third part of the *Little Book of Eternal Wisdom* comprises one hundred meditations, brief statements presented in groups of five or ten, presenting aspects of Christ's passion for contemplation. Between the groups are prayers of petition that the servant recites. About twenty-five of the meditations are directed to Mary.

Much shorter than its predecessor, the *Little Book of Truth* presents the next step on the spiritual journey; here, Suso seeks discernment, an understanding of inner detachment. In an allegory in the form of a dialogue, Suso, now as disciple, speaks with the personification of Truth. Truth describes how a person loses himself and attains oneness with the first Exemplar, the eternal being given to creatures. Having been granted insight, the disciple undergoes a dramatic change. As he struggles to comprehend the union, he engages in a series of questions and answers with the Word, and he also engages in a debate on the distinctness between the creature and God with an individual identified as the "wild one."

The *Exemplar* concludes with the *Little Book of Letters* (*Briefbüchlein*), a condensed version of Suso's correspondence with his spiritual children, primarily

Stagel. The intent is to refresh the spirit. The letters offer straightforward advice, often directed at a specific audience, such as novices and individuals in authority in the religious community. The arrangement of the letters reflects the progression in the spiritual life from a beginner through one increasing in understanding to a spiritually mature individual; in letter 10, Suso recalls the three steps toward mystical union—purification, illumination, and perfection—outlined by Dionysius the Pseudo-Areopagite in the fifth and sixth centuries.

In addition to the works included in the *Exemplar*, several other writings by or attributed to Suso have survived. The *Large Book of Letters* (*Großes Briefbuch*) is a more extensive collection of missives from which the compilation in the *Exemplar* was excerpted. Four sermons are included in Karl Bihlmeyer's 1907 edition of the German works (1961), although today only two are generally deemed genuine. There is one surviving manuscript of the *Minnebüchlein* (*Little Book of Love*), a tract in three chapters consisting of prayers and meditations on the suffering of Christ; its authenticity also is uncertain.

In contrast to Meister Eckhart, whose extant corpus includes numerous nonvernacular works, only one work in Latin by Suso survives: *The Clock of Wisdom* (*Horologium sapientiae*) is a greatly expanded and modified version of the *Book of Eternal Wisdom*, written with a theologically more sophisticated audience in mind.

MAJOR THEMES

Suso's name often appears together with the names of two other men associated with the mystical tradition in fourteenth-century Germany, and each man in the triumvirate has been accorded a distinct role. Meister Eckhart is the philosopher, John Tauler the preacher, and Henry Suso the lyric voice.

The poetic nature of Suso's prose is indeed its most remarkable aspect, with the *Little Book of Eternal Wisdom* serving as the best example of the Dominican's lyric abilities. His native Swabia was home to the Hohenstaufens, at whose court the tradition of courtly love, *Minnesang*, flourished. Suso's works are replete with themes and language found in German courtly poetry; for this reason, scholars have accorded the Dominican the epithet of the *Minnesänger* among the German mystics. Although the language is reminiscent of worldly literature of the time, the content maintains its spiritual focus. Suso serves not a noble lady of the court but rather the lady of heaven, Eternal Wisdom. Nonetheless, the suffering that the knight of the court and the servant of Eternal Wisdom each bear on account of their love of a lady is similar; the suffering is necessary and ennobling. The words of the servant could just as easily be those of a knight at court: "Look, a noble soul thrives in suffering as beautiful roses do in the sweet dew of May. Suffering gives one wisdom and makes one a tested person. A person who has not suffered—what does he know?" (*Exemplar*, 248). Another explicit comparison between worldly knights and spiritual ones in the service of Eternal Wisdom concerns the prize sought of the ladies by their admirers: "Beautiful, comely, eternal Wisdom, whose riches of grace find no equal in all the lands, if only my soul could receive a ring from you!" (172). For Suso, the ring of spiritual knighthood is an eternal prize, higher than anything attainable on earth.

Suso's love imagery also draws on the Bernardian tradition and ultimately on that of the Song of Songs, as do the works of many German women mystics of the Middle Ages. However, whereas the women compare themselves to the bride of Christ, Suso engages in role reversal and occasional amorphous gender identity to characterize the love relationship with the Divine. In the *Life* he frequently adopts the persona of a knight in service to his beloved lady, Eternal Wisdom. However, in the *Little Book of Eternal Wisdom*, Eternal Wisdom identifies herself with Christ; as a consequence, Suso associates himself with Mary, desiring like the grieving mother to hold the crucified Christ in his lap. The reversal of gender roles is exemplified in manuscript illustrations as well (Hamburger 1998, 435–37).

Nature and elemental imagery is prevalent in the Dominican's works; in his descriptions he evokes colors, smells, and sounds that allow readers to comprehend his point in as concrete a manner as possible. Prominent are red roses, which represent Christ's suffering and sacrifice. The friar asserts that rose-colored blood gives life, whereas the plucked red roses offer no fragrance, no sustenance or nurturing of the soul. Suso occasionally juxtaposes red roses with white lilies, symbolizing purity—just as the *Minnesänger* contrasts the red lips of the noble lady with her white skin in his idealized portrait of her.

Suso's appeal to the senses as he describes the spiritual journey is another characteristic more reflective of the experiences of the women mystics than those of his male counterparts. It is primarily through hearing and seeing that Suso is directed inward. One impetus for inner contemplation is singing. When Suso hears music or sings, both text and melody console and inspire him. Sometimes the singing is part of the Divine Office; on other occasions it emanates from heavenly voices. The beauty of the songs of heaven moves him to tears (*Exemplar*, 72).

Likewise, the friar's contemplation of images often turns his thoughts inward. The images he describes are the linguistic equivalent of the devotional pictures, the *Andachtsbilder*, that gained popularity among both lay and religious persons in the later Middle Ages. Suso himself acknowledges the significance of the illustrations alongside words, noting that he had a chapel decorated with pictures and pious sayings for devotional purposes; he also carried with him the image of Eternal Wisdom, which he placed on the windowsill of his cell (137). A series of miniatures accompany many manuscripts of the *Life*, and colored engravings were included in the first printed edition as well (Colledge and Marler 1984, 301); these depict, for example, "Seuse as Suffering Servant" and "The Mystical Way." It is assumed that the manuscript images were prepared under Suso's direction, thus allowing his readership to meditate upon the pictorial representations as he did. Jeffrey Hamburger examines in detail the Dominican context of the images and the significance of the works of art for Suso's didactic purposes (1998, 197–232).

Some descriptions in Suso's writings are reminiscent of sculptures common in women's religious communities in southern Germany in the fourteenth century. Because the friar is writing primarily for the edification of his female spiritual charges, it is not surprising that his writings resonate with images familiar to the religious women. Examples include the scourged Christ and the pietà (*Exemplar*, 91, 265). The most well-known sculpture is the group of Christ and Saint John; it is distinctive of monastic communities in German-speaking areas in the fourteenth century, where the mystical tradition was particularly strong. The image derives from the reference in John 13:23 to the disciple whom Jesus loved who leaned on his bosom. For the mystics, the intimate pose of Christ and John, often with Christ's arm around the disciple, mirrors their sought-for relationship to God, that between the chosen one and the Divine. In the *Life*, Suso describes how the soul of the servant is seated next to God, inclined at his side, and embraced by his arms (73). The identity of God is coalesced with that of Eternal Wisdom, a female personification, thus allowing Suso to assume the role of the male lover. The same image is presented in the *Little Book of Eternal Wisdom* (281).

It is perhaps ironic that Suso's writings are filled with images and language that appeal to the senses and that sensual experiences figure so prominently in his spiritual journey. Throughout the *Exemplar*, Suso advocates withdrawal from the senses, characterizing their influence as detrimental to the beginner seeking detachment (330). Such paradoxes are common enough in the writings of the mystics, who attempt to convey their experiences by the only means available: language and commonly understood images. The inadequacy of language is apparent in the repetitive wordplay Eternal Wisdom resorts to as she attempts to characterize detachment: "It is detachment above all detachment to be detached in one's detachment" (234). In the prologue to the *Little Book of Eternal Wisdom*, Suso laments the linguistic limitations that mystics face: "Unlike as it is to hear for oneself the melody of sweet strings being played rather than merely to hear someone describe it, just so dissimilar are the words that are received in pure grace and flow out of a responsive heart through a fervent mouth to those same words written on dead parchment, especially in the German tongue" (209).

For Suso, Church rituals are integral to the spiritual journey. The Mass itself and especially the songs sung on specific feast days or as part of the Divine Office inspire the friar. Among the sacraments, confession and penance serve important functions. Suso identifies confession as the first step toward a closer relationship with God (134). Through confession, Suso reinforces the pivotal role of the priest as confessor and intercessor. Penance manifests itself externally and internally: in self-inflicted punishments of the body and in the anguish of the mind with the searching and questioning by the soul. The sacrament of communion, central to many of the visionary experiences of the women mystics, is mentioned less frequently. Whereas the religious women can only partake of the Eucharist, Suso frequently serves the wafer and the cup. While carrying out this duty, he probably has less of an opportunity to meditate on their significance.

The function of the *Exemplar* is overwhelmingly didactic. Through examples from his own life, Suso guides the reader on a spiritual journey, characterized by a progression from the beginner who cannot see beyond external things in the material world to the person detached from the physical world and focused inward. The author makes his work accessible to readers by including personal anecdotes and by bringing his own doubts and concerns to the fore when he in the role of servant and disciple engages in dialogue with Eternal Wisdom and Truth. The letters reflect the admonitions and advice Suso imparted specifically to the Dominican women in his care.

Because the *Exemplar* for the most part is intended for an audience lacking theological training, Suso limits the discussion of philosophical ideas. However, in the *Little Book of Truth* he undertakes an examination of the key concepts of speculative mysticism, especially concepts introduced by Meister Eckhart. The *Little Book of Truth* is Suso's earliest work, probably dating from his final days as a student in Cologne. In fact, the *Little Book of Truth* has been described as an apology for Meister Eckhart (Christensen 2001, 551); in the tract, Suso contrasts ideas presented in the Eckhartian doctrine with those adopted by the beghards (members of lay brotherhoods formed on the model of beguine communities—that is, without permanent vows but who commonly supported themselves by begging; by the fourteenth century their reputation had deteriorated dramatically and they frequently were associated with heretics) and the Brethren of the Free Spirit (individuals inspired by mystical ideas and ideals but vehemently opposed to ecclesiastical authority; many of their beliefs were considered heretical). The friar employs Eckhartian terms such as the "ground" (of the soul) (*grunt*) and "breakthrough" (*durchbruch*) in his discussion of the distinction between the created and the Creator and the nature of the Trinity. Although Suso attempts to avoid the difficulties Eckhart encountered with Church superiors, it is probable that the publication of the *Little Book of Truth* gave rise to the accusations of heresy leveled against him as his student years in Cologne came to an end. The visions and anecdotes that dominate the contents of the rest of the *Exemplar* proved less controversial.

Suso's writings incorporate the ideas not only of Meister Eckhart but also of other luminaries of the faith. He cites in particular the writings of the Desert Fathers, whose sayings he had painted in the chapel in Constance so that he could meditate more easily on them (*Exemplar*, 137–39). Suso makes reference to the Church Fathers as well.

In all of his writings, Suso focuses his devotion on Christ, in particular the suffering of Christ on the cross. The friar demonstrates special devotion to the name of Jesus, incising the monogram IHS into his flesh above his heart. Second in importance is Mary, who serves as mediatrix and as an example of the suffering mother. Unlike many other fourteenth-century Germans in the mystical tradition, Suso seldom makes mention of other saints.

CRITICAL RECEPTION

The number of extant manuscripts gives evidence to the popularity of Suso's writings during his lifetime. By far the most well-known work was the *Little Book of Eternal Wisdom*, which survived in full in some 180 manuscripts; in addition, the "One Hundred Meditations," the third part of the book, was transmitted separately in more than 100 manuscripts. As Dominican communities underwent a period of reform in the fifteenth century, known as the Observance, Suso's writings were read with renewed interest. Manuscripts of his works were translated into various languages in the centuries after his death. Suso's writings also resonated with the German mystics of the baroque era, especially Jacob Boehme and Gerhard Tersteegen.

The first printed editions of the Dominican's works appeared at the end of the fifteenth and the beginning of the sixteenth centuries. With the Catholic revival in the early nineteenth century, the first modern editions of Suso's writings began to appear. At the end of the nineteenth century, there was renewed interest in the medieval German mystics. Critical editions of many works in the tradition appeared, among them the critical edition of the *Exemplar*, published in 1907 by Bihlmeyer (1961). In 1966, in commemoration of the 600th anniversary of Suso's death, a collection of essays edited by Ephrem M. Filthaut appeared in Germany that renewed interest in the mystic's life, teachings, and writing style and the manuscript tradition of his works. The end of the twentieth century witnessed another renaissance in the study of mysticism, in Germany as well as in the United States. Frank Tobin's 1989 English translation of the *Exemplar* and two sermons appeared in the Paulist Press Classics of Western Spirituality series, which makes medieval religious texts accessible to a broader audience.

Much less controversial than the works of Meister Eckhart, Suso's writings nonetheless have sparked numerous debates over the years. A central controversy in Suso scholarship continues to be the question of the authorship of the vita. Despite the claims in the first chapter of the *Life*, it is unclear how much of the text may be attributable to Stagel and how much is the product of Suso's editing. In order to evaluate Stagel's contribution, scholars have compared the *Life* and Stagel's sister-book, *The Lives of the Sisters of Töss* (*Das Leben der Schwestern zu Töß*) with regard to style and content; results have been inconclusive. More recently, Stagel's authorship of the sister-book (a collection of *vitae* of blessed sisters in a given community, recorded by their contemporaries or by subsequent generations to attest to the sanctity of the individuals and to promote the renown of the house) has been called into question, making the nun's role in the composition of the *Life* even more difficult to ascertain. Frank Tobin has summarized the authorship debate to date (1999, 118–35); his reexamination of the issue reveals that the relationship between Suso and Stagel can be regarded as a collaborative one, although there is a conflation of the historical nun and the idealized image of her that Suso presents in his writings.

Just as the image of Stagel is stylized to serve the didactic purposes of Suso's writings, so too is the characterization of the servant less than realistic. Because the plausibility of some incidents in Suso's life is suspect, it has been posited that the *Life* should be classified as fiction and legend rather than (auto)biography. In particular, the friar's patient suffering, his perseverance under all types of adversity, and the miraculous events and experiences related in the *Life* suggest an (auto)hagiographic appeal, with the servant as a saintly model, the holy "exemplar."

Among the miraculous events recounted in the *Exemplar* are numerous visionary and ecstatic experiences. In this regard, too, Suso's writings are more akin to the revelations of and the sister-books by women mystics of the period, who often relate visions and experiences of spiritual union. Suso's visions often are characterized as either in or out of the body, like those of Saint Paul in 2 Corinthians 12:2. In some visionary experiences he encounters friends and relatives; on other occasions he sees and converses with heavenly beings. He is given knowledge of unknowable things in the future: for example, the nature of heaven, hell, and purgatory (*Exemplar*, 74). Other experiences are very personal: for example, the bejeweled golden cross on his heart that emanates light (71). Although Suso is presumed to have been active as a preacher for many years, only two sermons can be attributed to him with any certainty. It has been suggested that the friar may not have preached as many sermons as others charged with the *cura monialium* (spiritual care of the nuns) or that the congregation, commonly nuns, was not interested in recording them. However, the paucity of extant homiletic texts is less puzzling if one considers that the missives in both the *Little Book of Letters* and the *Large Book of Letters* are more like sermons than letters in the modern sense. Most betray characteristics of thematic sermons: they begin with a motto, biblical in origin, and they are developed according to a clear structure, employing various methods of *amplificatio*, especially numbered points (Stoudt 1998, 95–116). Thus, although the majority of the sermons themselves are no longer extant, their spirit has been preserved in the letter collections.

Scholars at the end of the nineteenth century argued that the *cura monialium* was a burden to the Dominican friars and a distraction from more meaningful work. Recently, the relationships that developed between the religious male and the female charges have been viewed in a more positive light. The friendship between Suso and Stagel clearly served their mutual benefit, and the continued popularity of Suso's writings attests to the enduring nature of his message of love for and devotion to Christ.

NOTE

Henry Suso, *The Exemplar*. In *Henry Suso, The Exemplar, with Two German Sermons*, trans. Frank Tobin (Classics of Western Spirituality Series. Mahwah, NJ: Paulist Press, 1989). All references are to this edition.

WORKS CITED

Bihlmeyer, Karl, ed. [1907] 1961. *Heinrich Seuse: Deutsche Schriften*. Stuttgart: Württembergische Kommission für Landesgeschichte. Reprint, Frankfurt/Main: Minerva.

Christensen, Kristin M. 2001. "Mysticism." In *Medieval Germany: An Encyclopedia*, ed. John M. Jeep, 549–53. New York and London: Garland Publishing.

Colledge, Edmund, and J. C. Marler. 1984. "'Mystical' Pictures in the Suso 'Exemplar' Ms Strasbourg 2929." *Archivum Fratrum Praedicatorum* 54: 293–354.

Filthaut, Ephrem M., ed. 1966. *Heinrich Seuse: Studien zum 600. Todestag, 1366–1966*. Cologne: Albertus Magnus.

Hamburger, Jeffrey E. 1998. "Medieval Self-Fashioning: Authorship, Authority, and Autobiography in Suso's *Exemplar*." In *The Visual and the Visionary: Art and Female Spirituality in Late Medieval Germany*, 233–78. New York: Zone Books. Also published in *Christ Among the Medieval Dominicans: Representations of Christ in the Texts and Images of the Order of Preachers*, ed. Kent Emery Jr., and Joseph Wawrykow, 430–61. Notre Dame Conferences in Medieval Studies VII. Notre Dame, IN: University of Notre Dame Press, 1998.

———. 1998. "The Use of Images in the Pastoral Care of Nuns: The Case of Heinrich Suso and the Dominicans." In *The Visual and the Visionary: Art and Female Spirituality in Late Medieval Germany*, 197–232. New York: Zone Books. Originally published in *The Art Bulletin* 71 (1989): 20–46.

Stoudt, Debra L. 1998. "Heinrich Seuse's Sermons: Homiletic Tradition and Authenticity." In *Medieval Sermons and Society: Cloister, City, University*, ed.

Jacqueline Hamesse, Beverly Mayne Kienzle, Debra L. Stoudt, and Anne T. Thayer, 95–116. Textes et Études du Moyen Âge, 9. Louvain-la-Neuve: Fédération Internationale des Instituts dÉtudes Médiévales.

Tobin, Frank. 1999. "Henry Suso and Elsbeth Stagel: Was the *Vita* a Cooperative Effort?" In *Gendered Voices: Medieval Saints and Their Interpreters*, ed. Catherine M. Mooney, 118–35. Philadelphia: University of Pennsylvania Press.

BIBLIOGRAPHY

Clark, James M. *The Great German Mystics: Eckhart, Tauler and Suso*. Oxford: Blackwell, 1949.

Haas, Alois M. *Kunst rechter Gelassenheit: Themen und Schwerpunkte von Heinrich Seuses Mystik*. 2nd ed. Bern and New York: Peter Lang, 1996.

———, and Kurt Ruh. "Seuse, Heinrich OP." In *Die deutsche Literatur des Mittelalters: Verfasserlexikon*, ed. Kurt Ruh, 2nd ed., vol. 8, 1109–29. Berlin: de Gruyter, 1992.

Stoudt, Debra L. "Heinrich Seuse." In *German Writers of the Renaissance and Reformation 1280–1580*. Vol. 179 of Dictionary of Literary Biography, ed. James Hardin and Max Reinhart, 265–75. Detroit: Gale Research, 1997.

Tobin, Frank. "Coming to Terms with Meister Eckhart: Suso's *Buch der Wahrheit*." In *Semper idem et novus. Festschrift for Frank Banta*, ed. Francis G. Gentry, 321–44. Göppinger Arbeiten zur Germanistik, 481. Göppingen: Kümmerle, 1988.

— Debra L. Stoudt

Teresa of Avila [1515–1582]

The Interior Castle

BIOGRAPHY

Teresa Cepeda y Ahumada was born in Avila in 1515 during the most intense and glorious period of Spanish history: the country had finally been reconquered from the Moors in 1492 and was being reunited under the crown of Ferdinand and Isabella. During the resulting campaign of Christianization, Muslims and Jews were expelled from Spain except for those "*conversos*" who accepted Baptism. Teresa descended from one of these *conversos*. The struggle with the Moors in the Mediterranean would peak in the naval victory of Lepanto in 1571.

At home, the Spanish Inquisition watched over the success of the Christianization project. It was wary of the new spiritual movements flourishing among Franciscans, *alumbrados*, and *beatas*—women like Isabel de la Cruz, who was condemned in 1525. Access to many books of the kind Teresa loved to read would be prohibited in 1559 by the *Index* of Inquisitor Valdes.

Across the Atlantic, Spaniards were in the process of conquering the Americas, newly discovered by Isabella's emissary, Christopher Columbus. By 1521, Cortez completed the conquest of Mexico. Seven of Teresa's brothers spent their careers in that country.

In 1519, the Spanish King Charles I was elected Holy Roman Emperor, as Charles V. At the Diet of Worms, two years later, he branded Martin Luther an outlaw. From then on, Spain was locked in a fierce struggle with the growing Protestant movement, engulfing the heart of Charles's empire in bloody fighting. By the time Teresa was twenty, in 1534, Ignatius Loyola had founded the Jesuit order. Teresa would find among young Jesuits the most helpful of her spiritual directors.

This background is necessary to understanding Teresa. Far from being an escape into the quiet of monastic existence, her life vibrated to all these contemporary currents. Hers was a *hidalgo* family (from the lower nobility), descended from a rich *converso* who had married into the low nobility. Teresa quickly demonstrated that the same blood ran in her veins as in her *conquistador* brothers. When she was eight, she ran away from home with one of them in order to "buy cheaply the happiness of enjoying God" (*The Book of Her Life*, 1976–85, chapter 1, 4); that is, the two children hoped to conquer heaven at one stroke by being martyred by the Moors. But Teresa's father caught them and brought them back home. He intended Teresa to develop a more staid spirituality: their household was equally concerned with eternal salvation as with the preservation of the family's honor. But Teresa balked at this education. Along with her mother, she sought delightful recreation in reading tales of chivalry, deceiving her father. Teresa soon learned to make the best of her feminine charms, and she began responding to a young cousin's admiration. When she was sixteen, her mother having died, her worried father sent Teresa to an Augustinian convent to protect her honor from her passionate temperament and to give her the proper formation for a society woman.

Teresa left the convent at eighteen because of her first serious illness. Decisions had to be made about her future. She was so "anxious not to be a nun" because of the "trials and distress" of this life that she "asked God not to give her this vocation" (3, 2). Yet she was also afraid of marriage, having observed her mother's difficulties as a wife and mother. This conflict lasted three months, during which she decided "little by little" that being a religious was "the best and the safest state," so she "determined to force herself to embrace it" (3, 5). In 1535, against her father's will, Teresa decided to join one of her best friends as a Carmelite. For the second time, she stole away from home accompanied by a brother, and the doors of the Convent of the Incarnation closed on her. There, society women lived a relaxed religious existence in which liturgies alternated with parlor conversations, prayer with festivities. None of the aristocratic nuns ever worked. Teresa discovered, to her astonishment, that all of the things of religious life delighted her. "The dryness of her soul" was transformed into "the deepest tenderness" (4, 2). Her health, however, quickly deteriorated; once again, she had to leave the convent. An uncle she visited gave her the Franciscan Osuna's *Third Alphabet*, a book on the prayer of recollection. She immediately followed that path. Within nine months she had been granted the prayer of quiet and even of union. Just in time! From 1538 to 1543, she would need to practice it. Her terrible nervous illness was only made worse by the "harsh cures" imposed on her (4, 6). She went into a three-day coma in the middle of it only to wake up paralyzed and on the verge of being prepared for burial. Eventually, she was able to get up again, but she suffered all the rest of her life from headaches, illnesses of the throat, and weakness of the stomach and of the heart.

For the next ten years, Teresa led a pleasant but ambiguous life in the Convent of the Incarnation. She was spending an inordinate amount of time in the parlor, in spiritual conversations with "worldly" friends. Amidst these distractions, she abandoned mental prayer, "until one day, entering the oratory, I saw a statue put away there. It represented the much wounded Christ. . . . Beholding Him, I was utterly distressed in seeing him that way . . . I felt so keenly aware how poorly I thanked Him for those wounds that, it seems to me, my heart broke" (9, 1). From then on, Teresa's "captivity in the shadow of death" ended and her life in the hands of God truly began. She received grace after grace in prayer. These graces manifested themselves physically, in ecstatic raptures. Tongues began to wag. Her spiritual directors did not understand what was happening and tried to discourage her: they feared that the devil was at work. They also worried about potential heretical leanings when they discovered that she was reading Franciscan spiritual writings suspected of illuminism. In desperation, Teresa turned to young Jesuits for direction. They led her wisely through her most intense moments, until 1554, when she became the penitent of Father Alvarez. He, by contrast, feared the worst and told her to insult her visions, which he thought must come from the devil. Desolate, she obeyed. But when he finally asked her to stop mental prayer, she revolted. Christ told her to transmit his displeasure: this was tyranny. This stormy time reached its climax in the transverberation, the experience of the piercing of her heart by an angel, of 1560.

Teresa was now on fire. The Protestant reform, all over Europe, was challenging the Catholic Church. Frustrated in her great impulse to help souls so terribly endangered, she decided that the only thing she could do for God from her convent was to "keep her rule as perfectly as [she] could" (32, 9). Concretely, this would imply helping reform her order: there were too many comings and goings at the convent for the serious practice of contemplative life. After many discussions, Teresa decided to found a small convent for young women in which mental prayer would be practiced and the original Rule followed, in strict poverty: "Contemplating Christ on the cross, so poor and so naked, I could not patiently accept the idea of being rich" (35, 3).

With *"muy determinada determinacion"* (*The Way of Perfection*, 1976–85, chapter 21, 2) she set out on her first foundation. Twelve remarkable young women offered to join it; they would eventually become lights of the Counter Reformation. But, to achieve their common dream, Teresa had to brave the bishop, the provincial of the order, her prior at the Convent of the Incarnation, the town's nobility, and even the city council of Avila, which complained that the new convent overshadowed the city's fountain. Her "very determined determination" brought fruit: on August 24, 1562, the nuns settled in the new convent of San José. For five years, Teresa lived there with her young wards a life of terrible poverty and ecstatic prayer, spinning wool and writing. Her first effort to transmit her experience was *The Book of Her Life* (1555). Because it related the extraordinary favors God had granted her, her confessor refused to let her show it to her nuns, for whom it had been intended. Consequently, they begged her to write another treatise for their use. This resulted in *The Way of Perfection* in 1566.

In 1568, a new call came. At San José, one lived for the Church, which was not only shaken to its roots by the swelling Reformation but was also facing immense new fields of mission. In a time like this, "when the world was on fire," Teresa chafed at being "a women and wretched and incapable of doing any of the useful things [she] desired to do in the service of the Lord" (1, 2). She and her nuns "were occupied in prayer for those who are defenders of the church and for preachers and for learned men who protect it from attack" (2, 2). The general of the Carmelites, Father Rubeo, passing through Avila, was struck by Teresa's intense way of life. He ordered her for the sake of the Church to found as many convents as she had hairs on her head.

Teresa would never again have peace. "Sleep no longer, sleep no longer. There is no peace on earth" (*Poems*, 1976–85, 406). For fourteen years, she would crisscross Spain on horrendous roads in all types of weather. By the time she died, she had established sixteen new "dovecotes" for her sons and daughters. With each foundation, the decrepit buildings they could barely afford would challenge to the limit Teresa's extraordinary practical ability to transform pigsties into monasteries. But worse, she would have to wage battles of will, of patience, of courtesy, and of intelligence with the powerful forces intent on destroying the Discalced Carmelites. The threat of the Inquisition was constant. John of the Cross, who had helped her launch her first convent for men and had been a marvelous spiritual director for her nuns, was kidnapped, imprisoned, and beaten for months for the sake of her reform.

Throughout this harassing life, Teresa put herself in God's hands, obedient to his every word and enjoying his sweetness. In 1572, she had become Christ's bride and was now totally at his business: "From now on you will look after My honor . . . as My true bride. My honor is yours, and yours Mine," he had told her (*Spiritual Testimonies*, 1976–85, chapter 31, 402).

Political tensions around Teresa's foundations kept getting worse. By 1577, all seemed lost. The General Chapter of the Carmelites demanded that she stop founding convents and condemned her to remain henceforth cloistered in a convent of her choice. She picked San José in Toledo. There, except for an overwhelming correspondence, she enjoyed a respite of relative peace. "I am becoming a religious," she wrote, delighted, to Maria de San José (*Letters of St. Teresa of Avila*, 1980, 348). This exile gave her the chance to write *The Interior Castle*.

The internecine struggle among the Carmelites was finally brought to an end by the intervention of King Philip II and the pope. In 1581, the General Chapter of the Carmelites allowed the Discalced Carmelites their full independence. Teresa could now die. She gave a few last guidelines to her nuns: "Do nothing routinely, let every act of yours be heroic! Desire greatly. Even when one cannot realize such desires, they are very profitable" (976). Fittingly, she died on the road, exhausted, on October 4, 1582, as she was passing through her foundation of Alba de Tormes at the call of the duchess of Alba, who wanted her present at the birth of her child. Her last words were "At last, Lord, I die a daughter of the Church." By 1614, this controversial daughter of the Church was beatified by Pope Paul V, in 1622, she was canonized by Pope Gregory XV.

SUMMARY

Teresa began writing *The Interior Castle* in 1577, on the instruction of her spiritual director, Jeronimo Gracián, who was also Visitor of her order. The Inquisition had sequestered *The Book of Her Life*, the story of her spiritual development, which she had written in 1561 for the nuns of her first reformed foundation. But the precious teachings on prayer it contained could still be transmitted through a new book describing the same experience without referring to herself. This would make it less questionable by authorities wary of "illuminist" nuns.

Teresa later told her biographer, Fray Diego de Yepes, that a vision had given her the organizing conceit of the book. She had been meditating on the beauty of a soul in grace, and as she launched into writing, she was granted a luminous image: that of a crystal castle with seven rooms, at the center of which dwelt God himself. The whole was filled with his radiance, until dark stinking vermin from outside invaded the place, filling it with smoke. This radiant vision structures the "plot" of *The Interior Castle*. It describes the soul's progression through the spiritual quest, once one has decided to enter into oneself in response to a divine call to recollection. Teresa charts the exploration that follows, as the seeker is mysteriously drawn from one mansion to the next, toward direct encounter with God present at the very center of the soul. Stage by stage, Teresa describes the different experiences one can expect to have on the way.

Entering the first room is frustrating: "It may be flooded by divine sunlight, but one's eyes are so full of dust that one can hardly open them" (*The Interior Castle*, chapter 1, 14). One therefore tends to see nothing there but darkness, one's own darkness. In the second mansion, the soul struggles with the "slimy venomous reptiles" she has allowed to enter here with her, unaware. In the third mansion comes a period of quiet and arid security without excitement. Here, the seeker is conscientiously doing all the right things. The divine water of spiritual sweetness flows into the soul, but it is carried there by meditation and intellectual effort as by a long pipe system. Teresa describes this as a noisy experience. In the fourth mansion, however, the water comes directly from its source at the center of the soul's basin, a spring which is God. This spring fills the basin from its very core and its waters overflow the whole self, stretching it in the process. In the fifth mansion, the soul busies herself identifying with Christ; she invests herself fully in all the gifts he left to his Church. In the process, she loses all personal identity, as a silk moth spins a cocoon out of herself and disappears in it. At this point, fully hidden in God, the soul dies to herself, only to wake up transformed into a little white butterfly. No longer does anything of her previous life attract her. Wild with desire, the butterfly/soul now seeks a new resting place, seeding joy wherever she passes. She can now access the sixth mansion, that of the Betrothal. Here, she will be battered by a storm of passion. It is a period of anguish and ecstasy, when the Beloved calls, reveals himself, and flees; a time of "delectable torture" (6, 6). While she lives in this mansion, no one understands her any longer, not even herself. For here the soul has totally lost control; she is tossed about by waves of desire for her lover's unpredictable favors. Finally, God takes pity on his betrothed and brings her into the seventh mansion, where the spiritual marriage is consummated. Here, the triune God comes to dwell with the soul. From then on, she will experience his stable presence. It will never vanish again. Her beloved and she can no longer ever be separated, having become one, as Christ promised his disciples when he said "I am in them." This union is exceedingly lucid, peaceful, and simple—even practical. "It is time you took upon you My affairs as if they were your own. I will take your affairs upon Myself," Christ says here (7, 2). The great mystical quest thus ends in a life of service; the soul is by now miraculously capable of being at once Mary and Martha.

"Although when I began to write what I have set down here it was with great reluctance, as I said at the beginning, I am very glad I did so now that it is finished and I think my labour has been well spent, though I confess it has cost me very little. . . . Considering how few opportunities you have of recreation . . . I think it will be a great consolation for you . . . to take your delight in this Interior Castle, for you can enter it and walk about in it at any time without asking leave from your superiors" (Epilogue, 234). Thus concludes the book. When it was finished, on November 29, 1577, Teresa wrote Father Gaspar de Salazar: "This work is my best, for it speaks only of Him" (*Letters of St. Teresa of Avila*, 1980,

500). Bound in red, the original manuscript is now in the Seville Carmel, set in a reliquary shaped like a castle.

MAJOR THEMES

The Interior Castle gives us direct access to Teresa's spiritual experience. It is the antithesis of bookishness: spontaneous, colorful, full of disconnected observations, digressions, and exclamations. Here, Teresa thinks as she writes, searching for the right word and image to transmit her insights, often to the point of exasperation. She disliked writing and begged her spiritual director to be allowed to get on with her spinning and go to choir like the other sisters instead. It was only for the sake of her sisters that she agreed to obey Gracián, who had ordered her to write the work. Writing brought her terrible headaches, but she persisted: should one give up work "one day because our head aches, another because it was just now aching, and three more so that we won't ache again," we would never do anything, as she had earlier stated in *The Way of Perfection* (1976–85, chapter 11, 6).

Teresa thirsted to orient souls to Christ, to guide others to perfection. *The Interior Castle* is such a guide; hence its practicality. It offers experienced advice on the life of prayer to readers of every kind, at any level of spiritual maturity. It calms the exalted and urges on the sluggish.

Evidently, Teresa invents nothing; she reveals generously what she went through herself and what she has observed through two decades as *Madre* of her nuns. But she transmits all this experience with great respect for her readers' personal spiritual paths, reminding them that her advice is not binding. She herself had suffered too much from the dogmatism of her spiritual directors. "No soul which practices prayer whether little or much, should be subjected to undue constraint or limitation," she wrote (*The Interior Castle*, chapter 1, 2). All of this gives the book its great emotional impact: it is a one-on-one conversation with the reader, passionate and bracing, peppered with exclamations, apologies, laughter, and tears. Teresa always loved conversing about God. Her highly contagious delight in this exchange with her nuns and with us is evident in every line of the book.

In *The Interior Castle*, Teresa proves herself to be the best of teachers, mixing doctrine with the testimony of her own successes and failures. She never hides her ignorance, but she does not downplay the certitude of what she has lived through. And she does not hesitate to test her insights against those of Moses or Augustine. But this book transmits something more than the experience of a great educator. It also gives the wind of inspiration: "I write as mechanically as birds taught to speak, which, knowing nothing but what is taught them . . . repeat the same things again and again," Teresa warns us in the introduction (Prologue, 24). Repeatedly, as she attempts to describe supernatural realities, she hesitates, commends herself to the Holy Spirit, and "begs Him from this point onward to speak for me, so that you may understand" (4, 1). Paradoxically in this lucidly structured book, each chapter feels a bit hectic. Teresa knows it but cannot do otherwise: "Consider these things carefully, though they are in rather a jumbled state; I cannot explain them better; the Lord will make them clear to you" (3, 1). Teresa tries anything as she takes a stab at describing the indescribable. The reader shares her struggle to find the words, the images, and the analyses that will unlock the mysteries of the life of prayer as she knows it, and then her radiant relief when the words and images are given to her. She, too, is exploring with us what happened to her, and she is dazzled at what she sees at though for the first time.

Among the themes that stand out in *The Interior Castle*, the foremost is the absolute gratuity of spiritual joys. All initiative in the spiritual life is God's. Try all we will, "we cannot squeeze a drop of this joy out of ourselves" (4, 2). On the one hand, Teresa warns those intending to follow her into the castle of the soul that trying to force our way in will not work: "we cannot enter by any effort of our own" (5, 1). We must wait on the Lord. On the other hand, she rails at the sluggish "with this habit of always serving God at a snail's pace!" (3, 2). This receptivity is rooted in the one necessary virtue: the kind of humility only self-knowledge can bring. No theme recurs more often in this text: "I was wondering once why Our Lord so dearly loved this virtue of humility; and all of a sudden . . . the following reason came into my mind: that it is because God is sovereign Truth and to be humble is to walk in truth" (5, 10). Just the same, humility must not become an obsession. We must remember that "the soul must sometimes emerge from self-knowledge and soar aloft in meditation upon the greatness and majesty of its God . . . one can have too much of a good thing and believe me we will rise to much greater heights by thinking upon the virtue of God than if we stay on our own little plot of ground" (1, 2). This explains the puzzling combination of humility and daring that pervades this book. Teresa's sense of our "great dignity and beauty" surfaces throughout *The Interior Castle*, which offers its reader a heady cocktail of obedient receptiveness and passionate audacity.

Another theme often surprises those who read this book merely to thrill at descriptions of Teresa's extraordinary mystical experiences. She stresses again and again her ambiguous attitude to her own "favors" and "raptures." Although arousing appetite for the joys she hints at by rhapsodizing about them, she also sternly warns against the danger of desiring them. "There are many saintly people who have never known what it is to receive a favor of this kind" (6, 9), she points out. The book, in fact, concludes on the following thought: "We should desire and engage in prayer, not for our enjoyment, but for the sake of acquiring this strength which fits us for service" (7, 4). "I am Yours and born for you; What do You want of me?"—the leitmotif of her poem entitled "In the Hands of God" is ultimately the leitmotif of *The Interior Castle* (*Poems*, 1976–85, 377).

This book is a mine of advice about prayer; but its astonishing success with the public at large is probably due less to its spiritual teachings than to the access it gives to Teresa's fascinating personality. Four and a half centuries after her death, fresh as the day on which she sat down to write, we hear in these pages the voice of one of the greatest saints of the Church, of one of the most heroic women ever. We meet in these pages, as though still alive, the proud Castilian who fought all her life against the tyranny of honor and who would achieve that all-conquering humility that total abandon of the self in God alone can give. Here is the sister of *conquistadores*, whom nothing could scare, for whom no physical effort was too great. Here speaks the "ignorant nun" who fearlessly faced off the Inquisition to affirm women's spiritual equality because she knew the Church needed their peculiar gifts. "I see that these are times in which it would be wrong to undervalue virtuous and strong souls, even though they are women," she had cried out in *The Way of Perfection* (1976–85, 3, 7). *The Interior Castle* indeed demonstrates beyond doubt that there was once, at least, a woman capable of reaching the highest states of holiness.

Few are those who can resist the charm of the supple, tender, audacious, realistic, and indomitable personality that jumps out at the reader from every line of this book. Indeed, it makes holiness seductive, as Teresa herself did through her very presence. For Teresa's holiness was astonishingly balanced: her wild and limitless desire did not blind her to the need for patient, prudent progression toward her goal. Full of common sense, she respected the reality of incarnate existence. She recognized the need to consult others to avoid error. She rejected all excesses, ascetic or ecstatic. But this did not keep her from calling her wards— indeed every person—to accompany her on the most daring of quests, that for God himself. Her indomitable decisiveness was only surpassed by her self-abandon into the hands of her Lord. Such was the secret of her indestructible cheerfulness.

"I die, Lord, a daughter of the Church." Such were Teresa's last words. *The Interior Castle* demonstrates how she managed to become and remain a model daughter of the Church she so loved. Her willingness to lay bare her soul to her confessors and to obey her superiors, humbly and joyously, is evident. But equally so is her ability to do this without ever losing her inner freedom or obfuscating her message. Obedience, she had written in *The Way of Perfection*, usually lessens the difficulty of things that seem impossible (1976–85, chapter 32). There is no better teacher of humble service to God, here and now, in the most practical as in the most august circumstances, than *The Interior Castle*. And there is no better proof that total self-fulfillment is the fruit of such abnegation.

The love of this dedicated daughter, her humble obedience and prophetic daring, did not remain unheeded. On September 27, 1970, Pope Paul VI pronounced Teresa a Doctor of the Church along with Catherine of Siena, the first two women raised to this honor.

CRITICAL RECEPTION

Teresa's writings have been popular from the day of their publication to the present. Except perhaps for Cervantes, no author is as widely known in Spain as Teresa. Her books were first copied to be distributed within her order, but they were soon published for their practical utility in the training of religious. They circulated all over Europe, with the resulting inevitable textual errors. Luis de Léon's first edition of *The Interior Castle* (1588), for example, contains quite a few changes from the original manuscript.

Teresa's works have been translated into twenty-one languages. *The Book of Her Life* was the first to be translated into English, in 1611 by William Malone, an Irish Jesuit priest exiled in Antwerp. *The Interior Castle* had to wait until 1675.

After a lull of nearly two centuries, interest in Teresa revived after 1850. Between 1914 and 1924, a complete definitive edition in Spanish was published by P. Silverio de Sta. Teresa, including 450 of the saint's letters. English Benedictines then published their version of *The Interior Castle* and of the letters, thus contributing to the heightened interest in Teresa in England. Today, the most widespread version of *The Interior Castle* is a translation by the scholar E. Allison Peers dating from 1944. But the Institute of Carmelite Studies in Washington launched a new English version of Teresa's collected works in 1976, translated by Kieran Kavanaugh and Otilio Rodriguez, O. C. D.

Contemporary criticism of Teresa's work is abundant. Much of it is feminist in nature, stressing the centrality of gender issues in her work, as for example Alison Weber's *Teresa of Avila and the Rhetoric of Femininity* (1990). Gillian T. W. Ahlgren's *Teresa of Avila and the Politics of Sanctity* (1996) points out that we must "decode" Teresa's message in defense of the spiritual experience of women visionaries if we wish to do her justice.

Many of Teresa's critics have traced her unique contribution to the development of the notion of the "self." John Welch has compared her experience with Jung's in his *Spiritual Pilgrims: Carl Jung and Teresa of Avila* (1982). Jacques Lacan, Julia Kristeva, and Luce Irigaray all have given psychoanalytic meanings to her mystical experience; Carole Slade comments on them in *St. Teresa of Avila, Author of a Heroic Life* (1995). Francis Gross studied Teresa's psychological development from crisis to crisis in the light of Erik Erikson's categories in *The Making of a Mystic: Seasons in the Life of Teresa of Avila* (1993).

Other critics focus on Teresa's context. Some explore the impact on her work of the religious renewal that vitalized the sixteenth century in Spain as in the rest of Europe: for example, Jody Bilinkoff in *The Avila of Saint Teresa: Religious Reform in a Sixteenth-Century City* (1989) and Antonio Perez Romero in *Subversion and Liberation in the Writings of St. Teresa of Avila* (1996). Mercedes Camino emphasizes Teresa's socioeconomic milieu, in particular the new urbanization, in *Practicing Places: St Teresa, Lazarillo and the Early Modern City* (2001).

There are, of course, numerous biographies: Marcelle Auclair's is a classic, dating from 1953, but more recent ones keep appearing. Teresa's life clearly fascinates women. To name but a few: Victoria Lincoln's novel-like *Teresa: A Woman* (1984); Shirley du Boulay's *Teresa of Avila* (1991); and Cathleen Medwick's excellent *Teresa of Avila: The Progress of a Soul* (1999).

Naturally, spiritual analyses of Teresa's work as that of a mystic and saint abound, most of them by Carmelites. Elizabeth Ruth Obbard's *La Madre, the Life and Spirituality of Teresa of Avila* (1996) stresses the originality of the Carmelite way. Some explore practical aspects of her teaching on prayer, such as Sam Anthony Morello's *Lectio Divina and the Practice of Teresian Prayer* (1994).

For a more specific focus on Teresa's written works, one can turn to Ruth Burrows's *Interior Castle Explored: St. Teresa's Teachings on the Life of Deep Union with God* (1981) or to Mother Tessa Bielecki's *Teresa of Avila: Mystical Writings* (1994), which deals with *The Way of Perfection* as well as *The Interior Castle*. An interesting exploration of Teresa's poetry has appeared recently: Suzan McCaslin's *The Altering Eye* (2000). The latest study of *The Interior Castle* is Peter Bourne's *St. Teresa's Castle of the Soul: A Study of the Interior Castle* (1995).

Those seeking a quicker and more general introduction to her spirituality will enjoy two simple and clear approaches to Teresa's way to God: J. Mary Luti's *Teresa of Avila's Way* (1991) and Mother Tessa Bielecki's wonderful *Teresa of Avila: Ecstasy and Common Sense* (1996).

NOTE

Teresa of Avila, *The Interior Castle*, trans. E. Allison Peers (New York: Doubleday, 1989). All references are to this edition.

WORKS CITED

Ahlgren, Gillian T. W. 1996. *Teresa of Avila and the Politics of Sanctity*. Ithaca, NY: Cornell University Press.

Auclair, Marcelle. 1953. *St. Teresa of Avila*, trans. Kathleen Plond. New York: Pantheon.

Bielecki, Mother Tessa. 1994. *Teresa of Avila: Mystical Writings*. New York: Cross-road/Herder and Herder.

———. 1996. *Teresa of Avila: Ecstasy and Common Sense*. Boston: Shambhala.

Bilinkoff, Jody. 1989. *The Avila of Saint Teresa: Religious Reform in a Sixteenth-Century City*. Ithaca, NY, and London: Cornell University Press.

Bourne, Peter. 1995. *St. Teresa's Castle of the Soul: A Study of the Interior Castle*. Long Beach, CA: Wenzel Press.

Burrows, Ruth, O. C. 1981. *Interior Castle Explored: St. Teresa's Teachings on the Life of Deep Union with God*. London: Sheed and Ward.

Camino, Mercedes. 2001. *Practicing Places: St. Teresa, Lazarillo and the Early Modern City*. Amsterdam and Atlanta: Rodopi.

du Boulay, Shirley. 1991. *Teresa of Avila*. London and Toronto: Hodder and Stoughton.

Gross, Francis. 1993. *The Making of a Mystic: Seasons in the Life of Teresa of Avila*. Albany: State University of New York Press.

Lincoln, Victoria. 1984. *Teresa: A Woman*. Albany: State University of New York Press.

Luti, J. Mary. 1991. *Teresa of Avila's Way*. Collegeville, MN: Liturgical Press.

McCaslin, Suzan. 2000. *The Altering Eye*. Ottawa: Borealis Press.

Medwick, Cathleen. 1999. *Teresa of Avila: The Progress of a Soul*. New York: Knopf.

Morello, Sam Anthony. 1994. *Lectio Divina and the Practice of Teresian Prayer*. Washington, DC: ICS Publications.

Obbard, Elizabeth Ruth. 1996. *La Madre, The Life and Spirituality of Teresa of Avila*. New York: Alba House Books.

Romero, Antonio Perez. 1996. *Subversion and Liberation in the Writings of St. Teresa of Avila*. Amsterdam: Rodopi.

Slade, Carol. 1995. *St. Teresa of Avila, Author of a Heroic Life*. Berkeley: University of California Press.

Teresa of Avila. 1976–1985. *The Book of Her Life*. In *The Collected Works of St. Teresa of* Avila, trans. Kieran Kavanaugh and Otilo Rodriguez, O. C. D. 3 vols. Washington, DC: ICS Publications.

———. 1976–1985. *Poems*. In *The Collected Works of St. Teresa of* Avila, trans. Kieran Kavanaugh and Otilo Rodriguez, O. C. D. 3 vols. Washington, DC: ICS Publications.

———. 1976–1985. *Spiritual Testimonies*. In *The Collected Works of St. Teresa of* Avila, trans. Kieran Kavanaugh and Otilo Rodriguez, O. C. D. 3 vols. Washington, DC: ICS Publications.

———. 1976–1985. *The Way of Perfection*. In *The Collected Works of St. Teresa of* Avila, trans. Kieran Kavanaugh and Otilo Rodriguez, O. C. D. 3 vols. Washington, DC: ICS Publications.

————. 1980. *The Letters of St. Teresa of Avila*, trans. E. Allison Peers. New York: Sheed and Ward.

Weber, Alison. 1990. *Teresa of Avila and the Rhetoric of Femininity*. Princeton, NJ: Princeton University Press.

Welch, John. 1982. *Spiritual Pilgrims: Carl Jung and Teresa of Avila*. New York: Paulist Press.

— Janine Langan

Thérèse of Lisieux [1873–1897]

Story of a Soul

BIOGRAPHY

From Pius X, who in 1914 privately declared her the greatest saint of modern times, to John Paul II, who in 1997 publicly proclaimed her a Doctor of the Universal Church, Thérèse of Lisieux has been honored by virtually every pope since her death. The numerous titles she holds as a Doctor of the Church[1] reflect the diverse facets of Thérèse's message, as emphasized by the popes in their writings and homilies over the years. Who was this young woman who appeals to so many people of all ages and races, as witnessed still today in the enthusiastic and prayerful reception given to the recent visits of her relics throughout the world?

Born in Alençon, France, on January 2, 1873, Thérèse was the ninth child of Louis and Zélie Martin, a pious middle-class couple who in their earlier years had both longed to enter monastic life. Thérèse, the youngest of their five daughters who survived childhood, became the family pet and her father's "little Queen." Raised in a solid Catholic atmosphere, she claims to have never refused God anything from the age of three and a half. With the death of her mother, the saint's naturally happy and outgoing nature became extremely sensitive and introverted. Shortly after Madame Martin's death, the Martin family moved to Lisieux to be near the girls' uncle, Isidore Guérin, and his family. Thérèse spent a sheltered childhood largely in the company of women, associating with almost no one other than her extended family. Both Pauline and Marie, her eldest sisters, became "mothers" for the little Thérèse and were responsible for her education up to the age of eight and a half. Thérèse's formal education at the Benedictine abbey, which was to last a short five years, was sheer misery for her, as she was unaccustomed to mixing with children who had different family backgrounds and interests. About the time that Thérèse began her studies at the abbey, another traumatic experience occurred. Her beloved Pauline entered the Carmelite convent in Lisieux on October 2, 1882. Saddened by the loss of her elder sister, whom she looked upon as a second mother, Thérèse fell victim to a strange illness the nature of which has intrigued scholars.[2] Miraculously cured by seeing a statue of the Blessed Virgin smile at her, Thérèse was soon plagued by scruples and doubts about the extraordinary nature of her cure.

Thérèse's First communion and confirmation were grace-filled events bringing the young girl closer and closer to transforming union with Christ. The Christ child's gift of a Christmas "conversion" in 1886 restored her naturally happy nature and gave her the courage to embark on her journey of love. Determined now to enter Carmel at the age of fifteen, Thérèse found no obstacle, including the objections of her uncle and a disappointing visit to the bishop of Bayeux, too great to surmount. A pilgrimage to Rome even found her with her hands on Pope Leo XIII's knees begging him for permission to enter the monastery. She had no illusions about monastic life, for had not the scenic beauty of the Swiss Alps, viewed on the way to Rome, led her to reflect upon how easy it would be to become self-centered and forget the goal of her vocation? Thérèse finally received permission to enter the Carmelite monastery in Lisieux on April 9, 1888, experiencing at that moment a sense of profound peace that would remain with her for the rest of her life in spite of her suffering. She received the habit in January 1889 and made her religious profession in September 1890. But although Thérèse was a professed religious, she asked to remain in the novitiate. This was a sacrifice on her part, as it meant that she would be obliged to spend her entire religious life in a position of inferiority. Added to this self-imposed trial was the ever-present cross of community life shared with a group of women whose family backgrounds and education were far different from hers. Life in the monastery was rendered even more complicated by having a prioress, Mother Gonzaga, who tended to be domineering and hotheaded. But one of Thérèse's most difficult trials was certainly that of seeing her beloved father become a victim of dementia and being aware that local gossip judged her entry into the monastery to be responsible for his condition.

Although some of the Carmelites in Thérèse's monastery wondered what they could possibly say about her after her death, Therese's autobiography, *Story of a Soul*, testifies to an heroic sanctity consisting in fidelity to God in the "little" things of daily existence, such as suffering out of love from the cold, hunger, fatigue, illness, hurt feelings, jealousy, pettiness, and the thoughtlessness of others. It also took great courage and strength of character on the saint's part to overcome what she herself calls her extreme sensitivity. Over the course of time, Thérèse reached a full understanding of her vocation to love and made an Act of Oblation to Merciful Love on Trinity Sunday, 1895. From Easter 1896 until her death a year and a half later, she went through a trial of faith in which she no longer experienced God's presence but in spite of which she continued to radiate joy and sing God's praises. Desiring to save sinners, she willingly offered herself as a victim of holocaust to divine love. She lovingly accepted her physical suffering and trial of faith on behalf of unbelievers and sinners, especially Father Hyacinthe Loyson, a Carmelite priest who had left the Catholic Church. Her body entirely consumed by tuberculosis, Thérèse entered "life" at the age of twenty-four on September 30, 1897.

PLOT SUMMARY

A little over a century ago, in a Carmelite monastery in Lisieux, France, four blood sisters were reminiscing about their childhood days when one of them suggested that their youngest sister write her memories of her childhood. The latter thought the idea amusing until a third sister who happened to be the prioress at the time ordered her to write the story of her life. And so Thérèse of Lisieux came to write *Story of a Soul*, the spiritual adventure of a young woman who, from her early childhood days, believed herself destined to become a great saint.

In *Story of a Soul*, Thérèse recounts her cooperation with God's grace and the discovery of her vocation to be love at the heart of the Church. She offers her readers a contemporary interpretation of the Gospel call to holiness and of God's infinite love for humanity. We discover here the rich treasure of her spiritual doctrine, which at times seems to lie buried in certain vestiges of late nineteenth-century French romanticism, unattractive to today's reader. Nevertheless, Thérèse shows us how we can live in our own daily lives the spirit of childhood in our attitude to God, who desires us to approach him with childlike love and confidence, the call to merciful love, and the joyful acceptance of suffering. This threefold nature of Thérèse's spirituality is found throughout the three manuscripts that constitute *Story of a Soul*.

In Manuscript A, Thérèse reflects on the graces received from her birth until her Act of Oblation to Merciful Love. As a small child, she learned from her parents and sisters how to give and receive love. Her father was a perfect model of God as a loving father. But this picture of a happy, loving family stands in stark contrast to the physical and emotional suffering that entered Thérèse's life at the age of four and a half with the death of her mother. She relates how during this trial and others, such as serious illness, scruples, and the entry into Carmel of her sisters Pauline and Marie, she tried to accept her weakness and depend on God's power. Regarding what she calls her Christmas "conversion," which took place in 1886, Thérèse describes how God accomplished for her in an instant what she herself had been unable to do in ten years. She broke loose from the bonds of selfishness, desiring only to love others and forget herself. She relates how reflecting upon an image of Christ's suffering on the cross shortly after her conversion led her to understand his thirst for souls and to experience her own desire to save sinners from eternal damnation. It was at this time that she started to pray fervently for the conversion of the great criminal Henri Pranzini. Thérèse's already deep spirituality was enhanced by the reception of the sacraments for the first time. Special graces received at her First communion and confirmation show the saint as already experiencing the high states of prayer described by Teresa of Avila. Overcoming the obstacles preventing her from entering Carmel, Thérèse concludes Manuscript A with a glimpse of how she lives on a supernatural level the joys and sufferings of everyday life.

Perhaps the most beautiful section of *Story of a Soul* is Manuscript B, in which Thérèse attempts to explain her "little doctrine" to Marie. Her explanation reveals that she did not find her vocation as a cloistered nun to be completely fulfilling, for she longed at the same time to be a warrior, a priest, an apostle, a doctor, and a martyr. Searching sacred Scripture for an answer, Thérèse found the solution to her spiritual quest in Saint Paul's writings on the Mystical Body. Since love includes all vocations, Thérèse will be love at the heart of the Church. Her weakness, she states, gives her the confidence to offer herself as a victim of love. While following the teachings of Saint Paul and the idea of John of the Cross that love is repaid by love alone, Thérèse was, at the same time, breaking away from the image of a God of fear still prevalent in the Jansenist-inspired spirituality of her day.

In Manuscript C, Thérèse describes the trial of faith she was to undergo for the last eighteen months of her life. She exposes her moral anguish caused by the temptations to doubt the existence of God and heaven while at the same time suffering with almost no relief from tuberculosis, which was virtually incurable in her day. But rather than yield to such temptations, Thérèse heroically continues to suffer and abandon herself to God with confidence and love.

The Centenary edition of *Story of a Soul*[3] concludes with an epilogue written by Pauline and other eyewitnesses to the saint's suffering and death. Its contents include sections from *Her Last Conversations* (1977), which, along with her letters (*General Correspondence*, 1982, 1988), are indispensable to anyone wishing to have a solid grasp of Thérèse's message.

MAJOR THEMES

The work of a spiritual genius, *Story of a Soul* testifies to the fact that Thérèse possessed a spiritual maturity far beyond her years. Only two months before her death, she realized that *Story of a Soul* would be published posthumously and that her real mission would then begin. Since all three manuscripts are simply reflections on her spiritual growth written at the request of a specific person, it is not surprising that love, respect, and the desire for truth motivate the saint's attitude toward each one. She finds it difficult to communicate her spiritual thoughts about events with which these readers are familiar. With Pauline, she reminisces about family happenings that were sources of grace for her. But, Thérèse wonders, is she giving her sister too many details? She has no time to reflect on her writing, she states, and since she must use the language of earth to speak of heavenly concepts, she will speak with the simplicity of a child. Similarly with Marie, Thérèse describes her powerlessness to speak of heaven's secrets in human terms. Will Marie, she asks, find the explanation of her little doctrine incomprehensible and her expressions exaggerated? Thérèse apologizes to Mother Gonzaga for her digressions, telling her that she is not writing a literary work. She claims that she must be boring her prioress, who should, perhaps, consider keeping the manuscript for amusement in her old age and then use it to relight her fire.

Throughout *Story of a Soul*, Thérèse endeavors to give a clear explanation of the spiritual truth God has revealed to her. She will on occasion reread something composed the day before, consider it to be poorly written, but refuse to change it because it is the truth. Her work proved consistent with her life, for only a few hours before her death she affirmed, "I never looked for anything but the truth" (*Story of a Soul*, 270). Her concern for presenting spiritual truth in simple language can be noted in the structure, themes, and figurative language found in her work.

The structure of *Story of a Soul* rests on the three major themes of Thérèse's little doctrine. Although all three are present in each manuscript, Manuscript A centers more on the spirit of childhood, Manuscript B on the call to love, and Manuscript C on the trial of faith. Thérèse's autobiography can be compared to an open book in which Manuscript A faces Manuscript C. At the heart of the book, holding the other two parts together, Manuscript B reveals love to be the way to abandon ourselves to God as our heavenly Father and to accept the trials of life. Thérèse's little way thus offers a fresh look at the Gospel message of Christ's love for humanity in his coming to us as a child and his death on the cross.

Thérèse shares with us her growing understanding of these themes as she progresses toward transforming union with God. Manuscript A, with its description of her childhood, provides an ideal setting for explaining the loving parent-child relationship between God and humanity. God resembles a human father who knows our weakness and wants to help us. In Manuscript B, Thérèse pictures herself as the child of the Church. Since she is too little to perform heroic deeds like her older brothers and sisters, the great saints, she asks only to give and receive love. She rejoices in her weakness, which gives her the courage to offer herself as a victim to God's merciful love. In Manuscript C, Thérèse proclaims like Saint Paul, "I am not disturbed at seeing myself *weakness* itself. On the contrary, it is in my weakness that I glory" (224).

The theme of love exists at the heart of Thérèse's teaching on the spirit of childhood. Her Christmas conversion, described in Manuscript A, taught her how to love others, particularly sinners and unbelievers. Rejecting fear of God, she declares, "with *love* not only did I advance, I actually *flew*" (174). In Manuscript B, her love of God deepens when she realizes that her vocation is "LOVE," and in Manuscript C, Thérèse's love is so great that she continues to love even when she no longer perceives God's presence. As her trial of faith intensifies, so too does her sole desire to love "to the point of dying of love" (214).

Suffering, the third major theme, appears in the first pages of Manuscript A with Thérèse's reflection, "I had to pass through the crucible of trial and to suffer from my childhood in order to be offered earlier to Jesus" (30). As time passes, Thérèse acquires a spiritual attraction for suffering. Confirmation brings her the strength to suffer the martyrdom, which would soon begin. During her pilgrimage to Rome, she discovers her vocation of suffering for priests. In Carmel she comes to understand that Christ's real glory was in his hidden suffering, and from this comes her desire to suffer and be forgotten. Manuscript B finds Thérèse speaking in veiled terms about her trial of faith as the "storm" raging in her soul since Easter 1896. Desiring to suffer martyrdom, she compares herself to Joan of Arc, "like Joan of Arc, my dear sister, I would whisper at the stake Your Name, O Jesus" (193). Thérèse's difficulty in explaining her trial of faith in Manuscript C indicates her intense suffering. Satan even tempts her to doubt the existence of God and eternity by saying to her, "rejoice in death which will give you not what you hope for but a night still more profound, the night of nothingness" (213). Thérèse says nothing more about the darkness surrounding her soul for fear of blasphemy. Her happiness lies in not enjoying the thought of heaven so that God will give unbelievers the grace to believe. Although her moral anguish lasts the rest of her life, she continues to sing God's goodness and mercy to her. Her last written words, "I go to Him with confidence and love" (259), are far more than a simple conclusion to her spiritual journey, for they are the lived testimony of a spiritual giant.

Although Thérèse claims to have had little time to reflect on her writing, she does at times use figurative language to reinforce her three major themes. Two such literary devices are her description of dreams or visions she has had and her use of visual imagery. Thérèse declares that her dreams are far from being mystical and that she does not attach much importance to them. There is, nonetheless, a certain mystical quality about them, reminding the reader of accounts of dreams and visions in biblical literature and in medieval French works such as *La Chanson de Roland*. A religious interpretation can be assigned to Thérèse's dreams and visions in that they seem to point out to her the heights of sanctity to which she is being called and to warn her about the intense suffering she must endure along the path to sanctity.

The first example of such a dream took place when Thérèse was four years old. She never forgot this dream, in which she came upon two terrifying little devils playing in the garden behind her home. She found it strange that they seemed more frightened of her than she was of them. Thérèse did not consider this dream as anything out of the ordinary, but might we not consider it as a prophecy that she would spend her heaven in doing good upon earth? The young saint recounts a second dream or vision she had a short time later, when her father was away on a trip. Looking out into the garden, she thought she saw a man dressed like her father except that he was more stooped and his face seemed to be covered with an apron. Thinking that their father had returned home early and wanted to tease Thérèse, she and her sisters searched the garden but could find no one. It was not until years later when her father, suffering from dementia, used to cover his face with a handkerchief that she realized the prophetic nature of this childhood vision. Farther on in Manuscript A, Thérèse recounts how the Blessed Virgin miraculously cured her from a strange and serious illness she had at the age of ten. A statue of Mary placed near the young girl's bed seemed to come to life and the Blessed Virgin smiled at her. At that same instant, Thérèse's suffering vanished. This vision of Mary highlights the important role that she would play in the saint's life, for having no earthly mother, Thérèse truly regarded the Blessed Virgin as her heavenly mother.

Two other significant dreams occurred after Thérèse entered the monastery. The first of these was a dream she had shortly after Mother Geneviève's death.[4] *Story of a Soul* shows Thérèse's deep affection for Mother Geneviève, whose spirituality closely resembled her own. In the dream, Mother Geneviève wills her heart to Thérèse, thus symbolizing the young saint's vocation of being love at the heart of the Church. The description of the second prophetic dream is found in Thérèse's letter to Marie. In this dream, the saint finds herself at dawn in a type of gallery, where she sees three Carmelites wearing their mantles and long veils. Sensing that they are visitors from heaven, Thérèse longs to see the face of one of them. Her joy is immense when she recognizes one of the Carmelites as Mother Anne of Jesus, the foundress of the French Carmel, who tells her that God will come for her shortly and that he is very pleased with her. The prophecy came true, for Thérèse died a little more than a year later.

In *Story of a Soul*, Thérèse writes in simple language using visual imagery familiar to her readers to explain the profound spiritual concepts of her little doctrine. Her images fall into several categories, such as nature, daily life, combat, and science. They form a reliable pattern in which a specific image reflects at one point the weakness of a little child whose sole ability is to love and at another the heroism needed to endure suffering.

Nature is the image of Thérèse's soul. Christ is seen as the Divine Gardener, and the differences in human beings are symbolized in the variety of flowers in his garden. No two flowers are the same, but each one is beautiful in its own way. The saint herself is the little white flower named in the subtitle and symbolized in the flower her father gives her on the day she begs his permission to enter Carmel. Flowers also represent the little sacrifices Thérèse makes out of love. She has no other way to prove her love for God "than that of strewing flowers" (196). Like spring flowers that germinate under the snow before blossoming forth in the sun, so too must Thérèse, the little flower, endure "the winter of trial" (30). In Carmel, Mother Gonzaga's attempts to humiliate her become life-giving water for the little flower who is "too weak to take root without this kind of help" (206).

Influenced no doubt by the French romantic poets such as Alphonse de Lamartine, Thérèse compares the state of her soul to images of nature such as the weather and the sea. The torrential downpour on the day of her visit to the bishop of Bayeux symbolizes the "diamonds" of tears she "bestows" upon the bishop before the day is over. Nature too, Thérèse recalls, was sad on the day of her audience with Pope Leo XIII: "the sun dared not shine and Italy's beautiful blue skies, covered with dark clouds, never stopped crying with me" (136). Darkness and thick, penetrating fog represent the saint's interior state of solitude and distress during her trial of faith. But nature also reflects the joy that is part of the saint's spirituality. God's grace appears at times as a ray of light in a storm. The sea represents the joys and pleasures of childhood. Thérèse's first glimpse of the sea at Trouville on the English Channel speaks to her of God's grandeur and power. The "little white flower" rejoices that on the day she received the habit nature, too, was robed in white.

Other images of nature portray Thérèse's acceptance of her littleness in God's eyes. She and her sisters are compared to doves leaving the paternal nest. In Manuscript B, the saint's trial of faith is symbolized in the allegory of the little bird longing to fly toward the divine sun. Attacked by a storm, it believes that nothing exists except for the clouds surrounding it. Like the little bird refusing "to weep over its misery and to die of sorrow" (198), Thérèse also remains joyful and confident, believing that Christ, the "Adored Eagle" (199), will eventually take her up to heaven. In Manuscript C, Thérèse describes herself as an "obscure grain of sand trampled underfoot by the passers-by" (207). She accepts her imperfections, knowing that God will perform wonders for her. She depends on him to the extent that she must borrow his love in order to love him properly because her love is so infinitesimal that "it is not even like a drop of dew lost in the ocean" (256).

The saint's concept of her littleness is further revealed in images relating to daily life. Nostalgic memories of happy afternoons spent with her father in the country are filled with the beauty of wild flowers and the songs of birds and also with reflections on the brevity of life. Recollections of her father's love and tenderness provide the metaphor for the road leading to divine love: "this road is the *surrender* of the little child who sleeps without fear in its Father's arms" (188). Children's toys furnish other images of the saint's spirituality. When Léonie offers her toys to her younger sisters, telling them to choose what they want, Thérèse chooses everything, thus foreshadowing her desire for all vocations. Toy imagery also appears in her desire to be Jesus' toy, "a little ball of no value which He could throw on the ground, push with His foot, *pierce*, leave in a corner, or press to His heart" (136). The same little ball also symbolizes Thérèse herself in her sister Céline's Christmas gift to her of a little boat in which the Christ child is asleep with a little ball beside him. The word "abandonment" is printed on the side of the boat. Thérèse's joy consists in lovingly abandoning herself to God's will. Another image of daily life is seen in her trial of faith in which she pictures herself sitting down to eat at a table soiled by unbelievers, whom she calls her "brothers." To describe her role as assistant mistress of novices, Thérèse uses a familiar object from one of her occupations in the monastery. She compares herself to a paintbrush, a "*very small brush*" (235), that Jesus uses to paint the details on the canvas representing the souls of the novices entrusted to her care.

In contrast to these familiar images of daily life are images of combat, in which the spiritual life is pictured as a battlefield. On Christmas Eve, Christ made Thérèse strong, arming her for battle, and from that moment on she has "walked from victory to victory" (97). Inspired by Joan of Arc, she longs to be a warrior and a martyr. Prayer and sacrifice become her only weapons, and daily life in the monastery becomes the battlefield on which she and her sisters struggle together for the King of Heaven. Acts of virtue, such as enduring one of the sisters making a disturbing noise during meditation, become "little struggles" (249).[5] Suffering is referred to as being "in combat" (249).[6] "The heavenly militia" (222) comes to her aid, but when the "battles" become too violent, Thérèse flees the battlefield "like a deserter" (223). As assistant mistress of novices, she views her duty to correct the faults of the novices as "a war to the death" (239) in which she is "like the watchman observing the enemy from the highest turret of a strong castle" (239). When the possibility of being sent to a monastery in Indo-China arises, Thérèse views the situation as simply an order from the "Divine General" (216) to go to another battlefield. Combat imagery thus highlights the saint's attempts to practice heroic virtue.

Images dealing with scientific discoveries and phenomena symbolize Thérèse's yearning to reach God and to remain confident in spite of the darkness enveloping her soul. Her continued belief in the existence of heaven during her trial of faith resembles Columbus's belief in the existence of the New World. She has no other "compass" (178) than that of her abandonment to God's will. Jesus himself is the "luminous Beacon of love" (195) guiding her to the "shores of heaven" (178). Further metaphors from the scientific domain are the "fulcrum" and the "lever," symbolizing God and the prayers used by the saints to lift the world (258). Thérèse's metaphor of iron being attracted by fire and becoming penetrated by it reflects her desire for total union with God. Having seen elevators in the hotels during her trip to Rome, Thérèse searches for "a little way, a way that is very straight, very short, and totally new" (207) to reach God quickly. She discovers in sacred Scripture passages portraying God as a mother caressing her child, and she writes, "The elevator which must raise me to heaven is Your arms, O Jesus" (208).

Finally, contrasting images of Christ appearing throughout *Story of a Soul* highlight the major themes of Thérèse's spirituality. The divine child, only an hour old, offers her his strength on that memorable Christmas night, while in her father's suffering she sees "the adorable Face of Jesus [that] was veiled during His Passion" (47). Christ's weakness as a newborn infant and his strength in his Passion thus become fused together to reinforce Thérèse's major themes of the spirit of child-hood, the call to love, and the acceptance of suffering.

CRITICAL RECEPTION

The message contained in the spirituality of Thérèse of Lisieux is judged by many who have reflected seriously on it to be a vital one for our times. One of the first people to recognize the importance of her message was her sister Céline, who believed her younger sister's message to be so crucial that if she had had to choose between having Thérèse canonized or having her message officially recognized by the Church she would have chosen the latter.

In 1898, exactly one year after Thérèse's death, the first edition of *Story of a Soul* was published. The forty or so editions and translations of the autobiography printed in the first half of the twentieth century contain Pauline's numerous corrections and editorial changes. In 1956, François de Sainte Marie, a Carmelite scholar, prepared the first facsimile edition based on the authentic manuscripts. From 1969 to 1988 a team of Lisieux Carmelites collaborated in preparing a critical edition of Thérèse's complete works, the English editions of which are published by ICS Publications.

Among the first to spread Thérèse's message to the world were French soldiers who came in contact with the Allied armies in the trenches of World War I. Since then, *Story of a Soul* has had a tremendous influence on people from all walks of life, such as the singer Edith Piaf and Dorothy Day, the founder of the Catholic Worker movement, whose theology of nonviolence, according to Ann Laforest, resembles Thérèse's spirituality (2000, 105). Thérèse's trial of faith has even been compared to that of historical figures such as Martin Luther and Nietzsche. Her spirituality has had an impact on the life and work of several French authors, including François Mauriac and Georges Bernanos, who, throughout his writings, refutes the popular sugar-sweet image of Thérèse, declaring her instead to be the herald of a message of hope for our times.[7] Much of the earlier writing and iconography has given a false image of Thérèse that has since been corrected by those who have clearly understood the urgency of her message. Over the years, scholars have begun to explore the heroic virtue lying behind the saint's outmoded nineteenth-century images and style and to reveal the richness and accessibility of her spirituality for our times.

The first such study of Thérèse's spirituality was undertaken by André Combes (1950) in the late 1940s. A few years later, the Carmelite scholar François Jamart (1961) described the essential characteristics of Thérèse's little way in his classic work on her spiritual doctrine. But the best scholarly work on the saint has appeared since 1970. The German-Swiss theologian Hans Urs von Balthasar (1980) has produced various theological studies on Thérèse highlighting the timeliness of her message. In 1947, Marie-Eugène Grialou, a Carmelite priest, referred to Thérèse as "Doctor of the Mystical Life" in conferences that have since been published in *Under the Torrent of His Love* (1995). René Laurentin's major work on Thérèse, *Thérèse de Lisieux: mythes et réalités* (1972), destroys pious myths regarding the saint and points out the heroic reality of her life. Unfortunately, this work has not been translated. Jean-François Six has furnished three in-depth studies of the saint's childhood (1972), her life in Carmel (1973), and the last eighteen months of her life (1998). In an informative study, Àngel de les Gavarres (1999) shows the rapport between Thérèse's words and those of John of the Cross and Teresa of Avila, thus proving that her spirituality is based on the Gospel call to holiness. Finally, Conrad de Meester and Guy Gaucher, both members of the Carmelite team that produced the critical edition of Thérèse's works, have written outstanding volumes on the reality of her life and how she discovered and developed her little way. De Meester's work, *The Power of Confidence* (1998), is a masterpiece outlining Thérèse's discovery of the path leading to confidence and love, while Gaucher's work, *The Story of a Life* (1987), is considered by the Lisieux Carmelites to be the best biography of Thérèse to date.

NOTES

Thérèse of Lisieux, *Story of a Soul*, trans. John Clarke, O. C. D. (Washington, DC: ICS Publications, 1972). All references are to this edition.

1. The titles of Thérèse's doctorate appear in Camilo Maccise's and Joseph Chalmers's *A Doctor for the Third Millenium: Letter from the O. C. D. and O. Carm. General Superiors on the Occasion of the Doctorate of Saint Thérèse of Lisieux* (Rome: Casa Generalizia O. C. D., 1997). Ann Laforest comments on the significance of these titles in the epilogue to her work, *The Way to Love* (2000, 131–35).

2. Many scholars consider Thérèse's illness to have been some type of hysteria or neurosis caused by Pauline entering Carmel. For the young girl, her older sister's leaving home represented the loss of a second mother. Kieran Kavanaugh provides a more recent interpretation of Thérèse's illness in his foreword to Àngel de les Gavarres's work: "a most recent study in French by the psychiatrist Dr. Robert Masson concludes that Thérèse's 'strange' illness showed all the symptoms of tubercular encephalitis and are unexplainable by the other theories of hysteria or neurotic regression that have been proposed" (1999, x–xi).

3. The ICS edition of *Story of a Soul* is the English translation of the Centenary edition of Thérèse's autobiography, *Histoire d'une me: manuscrits autobiographiques* (1972).

4. Mother Geneviève was one of the Carmelites who founded the Lisieux Carmel.

5. The French word "combat," obviously a battle term, seems stronger than the English translation "struggle."

6. A stronger translation for the French "*au sein du combat*" might be "in the midst of battle."

7. For evidence of Thérèse of Lisieux's presence in Georges Bernanos's works, see my book, *Georges Bernanos' Debt to Thérèse of Lisieux* (1996).

WORKS CITED

Combes, André. 1950. *The Spirituality of Saint Thérèse*, trans. Msgr. Philip E. Hallett. New York: P. J. Kennedy.

de les Gavarres, Àngel. 1999. *Thérèse, The Little Child of God's Mercy*, trans. Michael Gaughan. Washington, DC: ICS Publications.

De Meester, Conrad, O. C. D. 1998. *The Power of Confidence*, trans. Susan Conroy. New York: Alba House.

Dorschell, Mary Frances. 1996. *Georges Bernanos' Debt to Thérèse of Lisieux*. Lewiston, NY: Edwin Mellen Press.

Gaucher, Guy, O. C. D. 1987. *The Story of a Life*, trans. Sister Anne Marie Brennan. New York: Harper and Row.

Grialou, Marie-Eugène, O. C. D. 1995. *Under the Torrent of His Love: Thérèse of Lisieux, a Spiritual Genius*, trans. Sister Mary Thomas Noble. New York: Alba House.

Jamart, François, O. C. D. 1961. *The Complete Spiritual Doctrine of Saint Thérèse of Lisieux*, trans. Walter Van De Putte. New York: Alba House.

Laforest, Ann, O. C. D. 2000. *The Way to Love: Thérèse of Lisieux*. Franklin, WI: Sheed and Ward.

Laurentin, René. 1972. *Thérèse de Lisieux: mythes et réalités*. Paris: Beauchesne.

Six, Jean-François. 1972. *La véritable enfance de Thérèse de Lisieux: névrose et sainteté*. Paris: Éditions du Seuil.

———. 1973. *Thérèse de Lisieux au Carmel*. Paris: Éditions du Seuil.

———. 1998. *Light of the Night: The Last Eighteen Months in the Life of Thérèse of Lisieux*. Notre Dame, IN: University of Notre Dame Press.

Thérèse of Lisieux. 1972. *Histoire d'une me: manuscrits autobiographiques*. Paris: Éditions du Cerf et Desclée de Brouwer.

———. 1977. *Saint Thérèse of Lisieux: Her Last Conversations*, trans. John Clarke, O. C. D. Washington, DC: ICS Publications.

———. 1982, 1988. *General Correspondence*, trans. John Clarke, O. C. D. 2 vols. Washington, DC: ICS Publications.

von Balthasar, Hans Urs. 1980. "The Timeliness of Lisieux," trans. C. Latimer. *Carmelite Studies* 1: 103–21.

— **Mary Frances Dorschell**

J. R. R. Tolkien [1892–1973]

The Lord of the Rings

BIOGRAPHY

J. R. R. Tolkien's life was deeply permeated, spiritually and psychologically, by his Catholicism. John Ronald Reuel Tolkien was born in 1892 in South Africa to a Protestant family. His father, Arthur, had only recently brought his family to Africa, hoping to advance more rapidly in his banking career than was possible back home in England. While on a visit to relatives in England, Tolkien, then six, his younger brother, Hillary, and his mother, Mabel, learned that Arthur had suddenly taken ill and died. Mabel, choosing to stay in England, became the most important influence on the young Tolkien. This influence deepened after Mabel converted to Catholicism. Mabel's relatives disowned her and her sons, causing both psychological and financial hardship.

When Tolkien was twelve, his mother died. Later in life, Tolkien called her a "martyr," feeling that she had been mistreated by her Protestant relatives. He concluded, however, that her death was divinely purposeful to ensure that her two sons would remain committed to the Catholic faith. The Church was emotionally as well as spiritually fulfilling: it became for him, literally, "Mother Church." The veneration he felt for his own mother transformed into a deep, lifelong gratitude and closeness to the Mother Mary. Later his own wife, Edith, experienced the same alienation from her distant relatives when she converted to Catholicism prior to their marriage. Tolkien perceived a pattern of conversion, sacrifice, and alienation around his religious beliefs; this stood to strengthen, rather than challenge, his faith.

Before her death, Mabel came to rely on the generosity of a Catholic priest, Father Francis Xavier Morgan. Upon her death, she left her boys in his care in order to ensure that they would be brought up Catholic. Father Francis turned out to be an excellent choice, taking great care in his responsibilities to the two orphans. He selected one of their distant relatives to care for them, chosen primarily because she was not anti-Catholic; when she showed herself distant and unloving (she burned their mother's effects, not thinking the boys might like some memento), the good Father placed the boys in a boarding house near the rectory. Here, Tolkien, at age sixteen, met another orphan, nineteen-year-old

Edith Bratt. The two bonded for obvious reasons and soon began to share food and frequent outings to tea shops.

Father Francis, however, forbade the relationship until Tolkien turned twenty-one. Although the young Tolkien had developed strong feelings for Edith, he complied with Father Francis's wishes; the two lovers parted with an understanding that they were informally spoken for. Ronald focused on his schooling while Edith moved some distance away to live with relatives. She became involved with the local Protestant church and even became interested in the local young men. After three years with almost no communication between the two, Edith was pleasantly surprised to hear that Tolkien planned to renew and formalize their relationship when he turned twenty-one. Two complications were speedily addressed. First, Edith replied by letter that she was engaged to someone else, although Tolkien persuaded her without much difficulty to break off the engagement. Second, Edith was not yet a Catholic. For his sake she converted, although she never felt completely comfortable as a Catholic, and she often chose to stay at home as Tolkien took their children to daily Mass. Edith's inability to understand her husband's deep emotional commitment to the Church produced conflict in their marriage.

Shortly after they were married, Tolkien and Edith were again separated because of World War I. In fact, the endurance of love through separation later became a theme in two of Tolkien's best-known love stories: that of Beren and Lúthien (from *The Silmarillion*) and that of Aragorn and Arwen (from *The Lord of the Rings*). To alleviate the boredom of military life (and then to fill his time as he recovered from a lengthy bout of trench fever), Tolkien began writing stories in the style of Norse and Icelandic mythology as an outgrowth of a hobby, a linguistic interest in developing an artificial language for elves. Knowing that language development takes place in a context of geography, society, and history, as ultimately reflected in that language's literature, Tolkien produced a mythology for the elves. He viewed this work as "subcreation"; that is, as making an imaginative world as realistic as our own world. The "sub" aspect of this creation acknowledges that a writer mirrors his own Creator and functions in his image. This writing, the history of Middle-earth, came to be Tolkien's lifelong obsession and eventually produced *The Lord of the Rings*.

After the war and a brief stint working for the *Oxford English Dictionary* and as a lecturer at the university in Leeds, Tolkien was hired to a professorship in Anglo-Saxon at Oxford. Within a year he met a newly hired tutor, C. S. Lewis, and the two soon discovered they shared an interest in mythology and medieval literature. Lewis joined Tolkien's Coalbiters club, with the purpose of reading Old Icelandic sagas in the original language. After this goal was achieved, the two chose to continue meeting with a group of like-minded friends as The Inklings, this time with the goal of reading one another their own writings. Tolkien soon learned that Lewis loved to hear stories read aloud, and thus he found an eager audience for his Middle-earth writings.

While reading manuscripts was the stated purpose of The Inklings, discussions were wide ranging, philosophical, heated, and humorous, further stimulated by tea, tobacco, and alcohol. Tolkien once suggested that an eavesdropper would likely assume from the extent and energy of the discussion that The Inklings were bitter enemies. Yet three characteristics formed a common bond among members: a preference for the values of past ages (namely, classical pagan and medieval Christian), a preference for masculine friendships, and a belief in Christian theism. Tolkien, in fact, was central to Lewis's conversion from atheism to Christianity, although Tolkien remained disappointed throughout his life that Lewis refrained from embracing Catholicism.

One of the manuscripts Tolkien read to The Inklings was *The Hobbit*, begun and abandoned in 1930, then finished in 1936 with the encouragement of a publisher who had read the unfinished draft. After *The Hobbit* appeared in 1937, the publisher suggested a sequel. Tolkien thus began work on *The Lord of the Rings*, not completing it until 1949, after which it remained unpublished for five more years. Tolkien credited Lewis with motivating him to continue work on the novel as it grew in complexity during and after World War II, although Tolkien was also notorious for ignoring the extensive revisions Lewis suggested for the book.

The Lord of the Rings confused reviewers, who did not know how to react to such a massive yet coherent narrative having no apparent connection to literary modernism. Sales were light at first, but an inexpensive, unauthorized edition appeared in the United States in 1965, making the book a cult classic on university campuses. When an authorized United States edition appeared, Tolkien began to realize some significant profits. He published a few short stories and essays but spent most of his remaining time on his first love, the stories of Middle-earth's "First Age." These were the same stories he had begun during World War I, but Tolkien continually added to them, reshaped them, and retold them. Although ostensibly preparing those stories for publication, Tolkien had lost his motivation and ability to focus on such a massive project. Not until several years after his death in 1973 did his son Christopher collect and finalize the stories into *The Silmarillion* (1977).

PLOT SUMMARY

The Hobbit, although a self-contained narrative, is often considered a prelude or introduction to the *Ring* trilogy. Hobbits are a short people who populate The Shire in Middle-earth, a world of Tolkien's own invention, although based on the land of Fairie and, to some extent, the continent of Europe. The story focuses on one hobbit, Bilbo Baggins, who through the manipulations of the wizard Gandalf accompanies thirteen dwarves (Tolkien's preferred spelling) on a quest to recover a treasure-filled kingdom overrun years before by a dragon. Along the way Bilbo discovers, apparently by accident, a ring with the power to make the wearer invisible. Bilbo uses the ring to aid the dwarves and himself, but never for malicious purposes.

Although finding the ring is merely an incident in *The Hobbit*, it becomes the central point of conflict in the *Ring* trilogy. The story begins several decades after the end of *The Hobbit*. Bilbo, now very old, lives in retirement in The Shire with his ring, his share of the dragon horde, and an adopted nephew, Frodo. An urge to travel has overtaken Bilbo, and he plans to leave The Shire indefinitely, perhaps permanently, on his one hundred and eleventh birthday. Gandalf convinces him to transfer possession of his magic ring to Frodo, ostensibly because Bilbo will no longer have a use for it; secretly, Gandalf suspects that the ring possesses a longer history and greater power than hitherto known.

Gandalf eventually learns that the ring was forged thousands of years before by Sauron, an evil being of great power. With the ring, Sauron had hoped to control other rings of power created for good purposes and distributed to elves, dwarves, and men. Sauron's quest for power resulted in war. He and his minions were miraculously defeated in battle with the combined armies of men and elves. Isuldur, a human king, removed Sauron's ring and claimed it as his own. Isuldur was later attacked and killed by orcs (wholly evil life forms bred by Sauron as soldiers and servants) while swimming across a river. The ring remained lost for thousands of years until discovered, again apparently by accident, by Smeagol (commonly called Gollum), a creature ancestrally related to hobbits. Gollum used the ring for evil, and its magic power soon possessed his will, although also (like Bilbo) lengthening his life span. Gollum had misplaced the ring moments before Bilbo found it on his adventure with the dwarves.

The reappearance of the ring takes on great urgency since Sauron, in hiding for millennia, has reappeared, consolidating his power and searching for his lost ring. Gandalf fears that the ring will allow Sauron to enslave all living creatures in Middle-earth. Yet, as Gollum had exhibited, to use the ring extensively will pervert the wearer to evil. Thus, the free peoples of Middle-earth are in grave danger: if Sauron finds his ring, he will ascend to an inexorable dictatorship; yet if the ring is used against Sauron, the wearer will ascend to an inexorable dictatorship in Sauron's place. Gandalf believes that the only solution is to destroy the ring, although the only fire in Middle-earth hot enough to accomplish that task burns in Mount Doom, a semidormant volcano in the middle of Sauron's territory.

Gandalf also believes that finding the ring, first by Gollum and then by Bilbo, was not an accident. Both the evil magic within the ring and the good magic from outside Middle-earth have worked to cause the ring's discovery. Those outside powers have placed the ring into the possession of a hobbit; Gandalf's study of hobbit nature leads him to conclude that their strong common sense makes hobbits remarkably immune from the vices of greed and lust for power through which the ring perverts its wearers. Thus, Gandalf does not accept possession of the ring for himself, even when Frodo begs him to. Instead, Gandalf suggests that Frodo is destined to keep possession of the ring, at least until a meeting of representatives of Middle-earth's free peoples can decide together how to respond to Sauron's growing power.

Frodo embarks on a perilous journey to Rivendell, where Elrond, a learned leader of the elves, may keep him safe. On this journey, Frodo is accompanied by three other hobbits: his valet, Sam, and two cousins, Merry and Pippin. Their adventures bring them into contact with a wide variety of characters, including frightening black riders on horseback who chase them and a weather-beaten loner named Strider who protects and leads them. At Rivendell, Frodo meets Bilbo and Gandalf (who had been held captive by a fellow wizard, Saruman, and thus prevented from accompanying and protecting Frodo and his friends). Frodo also learns more of the ring's history and that Strider, whose given name is Aragorn, is a descendant of Isuldur and thus royalty. A Council of Elrond decides that, indeed, the ring must be destroyed, and when no great warrior volunteers to perform the deed, Frodo volunteers. Elrond chooses eight companions for Frodo: Gandalf,

Aragorn, Frodo's three fellow hobbits, and representatives of the three primary free peoples of Middle-earth, Legolas the elf, Gimli the dwarf, and Boromir the man. Thus, the Fellowship of the Ring is born.

The Fellowship travels with no definite plan other than to get closer to Morder, the land of Sauron. Gandalf leads the group until a Balrog in the Mines of Moria kills him. Aragorn then takes the lead, although dissent regarding the group's ultimate objective becomes apparent as Boromir speaks of taking the ring to his hometown, Minas Tirith, and using it to defend against Sauron. The dissent leads to the breaking of the Fellowship when Boromir attempts to take the ring from Frodo by force, followed by an attack from enemy orcs. Frodo and Sam set out on their own toward Mordor with the ring. Boromir is slain defending Merry and Pippin, who are then taken captive by the enemy; Aragorn, Legolas, and Gimli pursue the enemy to free the captive hobbits.

The narrative then splits into two strands, one following Frodo and Sam, the other centering on the rescue of the captured hobbits. Merry and Pippin's captors are not servants of Sauron but of Saruman, the wizard-gone-bad. Saruman has set himself as an antagonist of Sauron, but he is seeking power for himself and thus unwittingly serving Sauron's evil purposes. Saruman believes that Merry and Pippin possess the ring. Before the captives can be handed over to Saruman, men of Rohan attack their captors. In the confusion, the two hobbits escape and enter a forest where they meet Fangorn, an Ent. As shepherds of the trees, Ents live thousands of years and are physically very powerful, although generally patient and slow to anger. Saruman's vast building projects have required wood for furnaces, and thus the Ents are moved to action when the hobbits describe Saruman's treachery. The Ents surround and destroy Saruman's base, making him a captive in his own marble tower.

Meanwhile, Aragorn, Legolas, and Gimli pursue Merry and Pippin to Fangorn Forest. Instead of encountering Ents, they find Gandalf, resurrected from the dead and returned to Middle-earth as an indestructible being. They accompany him to Rohan, where Gandalf heals the King and musters the army against Saruman. While the Ents are destroying Saruman's headquarters, the men of Rohan narrowly defeat Saruman's forces. Gandalf and his allies then rush to Minas Tirith, the city closest to Sauron's domain, where he will likely make his first attack.

Sauron's army is led by nine ringwraiths, the ghosts of men long ago perverted by Sauron, the very same black riders who earlier pursued Frodo and his friends. An old proverb had predicted that the head ringwraith could be killed by no man, yet in a terrible battle before Minas Tirith he is destroyed by a woman (the niece of the King of Rohan) and a hobbit. All of Sauron's army is then routed, although Sauron himself remains in power in Mordor. With Gandalf's guidance, the leaders of the conquering alliance decide that their only option is to boldly face Sauron, even though they have no chance of defeating him. They realize that their only hope is the destruction of the ring; by openly facing Sauron, they might keep his focus off his own kingdom, giving Frodo and Sam greater opportunity to sneak into Mordor unnoticed.

All this time, Frodo and Sam have been approaching Mordor on foot, completely unaware of what has befallen their comrades. They acquire a most unlikely guide, Gollum, who lost the ring to Bilbo and who has lusted after and searched for it ever since. While Gollum is not a trustworthy guide, he is one of only a few characters who have entered and left Mordor. Frodo and Sam's adventures include lengthy marches with few rations, avoiding capture by the enemy, and battle with a giant spider named Shelob.

Abandoned by Gollum, who had hoped that the giant spider would kill the hobbits and allow him to reclaim the ring, Sam and Frodo arrive at the volcanic pits of Mount Doom at the very moment that Gandalf leads the forces of good to the gates of Mordor. Battle erupts at the gates as Frodo decides he is unwilling to part with the ring. Gollum reappears and seizes this opportunity to regain the ring by biting it off Frodo's finger. Gollum loses his balance and falls into the fiery pit, destroying both himself and his ring. This in turn destroys Sauron, whose power was invested in the ring. Without their leader goading them on, Sauron's troops give up or run away.

Aragorn is installed as king over the united realms of Middle-earth. Peace, prosperity, and freedom reign. The hobbits return to The Shire as respected leaders. Ultimately, Gandalf, Bilbo, and Frodo leave Middle-earth, a privilege commonly reserved only for the elves.

MAJOR THEMES

J. R. R. Tolkien's *The Lord of the Rings* is one of the most successful literary works of the twentieth century. Although Tolkien's publisher feared the book would have at best a small reading audience, it has become a long-term best-seller with a large, diverse, and devoted audience. Its significance can be measured by its impact. *The Lord of the Rings* has been translated into more than ten languages. Dozens of Middle-earth societies have formed, paying homage to the world of which Tolkien wrote. The story has been recreated as both animated and live-action feature films. Most impressively, it has spawned an entire literary genre, that of fantasy writing.

The success of the *Rings* is especially surprising considering its length. The book exceeds 1,500 pages and is published as three volumes, *The Fellowship of the Ring*, *The Two Towers*, and *The Return of the King*. Furthermore, to fully grasp the story, readers should also engage Tolkien's *The Hobbit*, which introduces relevant characters and situations, and *The Silmarillion* and related writings. These latter volumes develop an extensive and contradictory mythology comparable to Icelandic sagas; characters in *The Lord of the Rings* refer to characters and events from this mythology as though from a common cultural heritage. This gives the book impressive depth, as if there must be more stories somewhere in the background, all of which impinge upon Tolkien's primary narrative.

The story's depth makes Tolkien's invented world feel both real and wonderful. Yet many readers, especially those who hear of Tolkien's strong commitment to the Catholic Church, are surprised when that invented world seems completely free of religion. Although it has been accused of being a non-Christian or even an anti-Christian work, *The Lord of the Rings* directly reflects Tolkien's theistic world view and more specifically his deeply held Catholic faith.

While *The Lord of the Rings* gives no indication of any organized religion in Middle-earth, the book contains many themes and images compatible with a Catholic world view. Tolkien himself avowed that the book is both religious and Catholic in nature, although this only became clear to him as he revised his manuscript. Most obvious of the book's religious themes is the death and resurrection of Gandalf. He dies to save the people he is leading; at his death, he descends for a time into the lowest pits of Middle-earth; then he comes back to life in superhuman form. While Gandalf is not a healer, he does possess special powers. He claims he was sent to earth as a servant of an even higher power. After his death, he is associated with the color white. Yet, although Gandalf is a Christ figure, he is not Middle-earth's Christ, since he makes no claims to be a creator or savior of Middle-earth.

Gandalf is also central to one of the book's major themes, that of mercy or pity. Although Gandalf first appears as a crotchety, easily angered old man, he espouses a strategy of patient acceptance of the shortcomings of others. He recognizes that those without the advantages of longevity, knowledge, and power may yet have strengths necessary for the defeat of evil. This can be seen when Gandalf first explains the horrible history of the ring to Frodo. The young hobbit remarks, "What a pity that Bilbo did not stab that vile creature [Gollum], when he had a chance!", to which Gandalf responds, "Pity? It was Pity that stayed his hand. Pity, and Mercy: not to strike without need. . . . [Bilbo] took so little hurt from the evil, and escaped in the end, because he began his ownership of the Ring so. With Pity" (*The Fellowship of the Ring*, 92).

Humility is equally rewarded. While Gandalf struggles to practice this virtue, hobbits are by nature self-deprecatory. These creatures, based on an idealized impression of the British common person, have too much good sense and love of the everyday to grow self-important. Thus, Frodo and Sam are amazed at the esteem bestowed on them by Aragorn and Gandalf after completing their mission. As hobbits, they perceive that they did what they must rather than something heroic. Then, after receiving praise and honor, they eagerly return to a quiet life in The Shire.

Other virtues reveal themselves as ultimately triumphant while vices and sins lead ultimately to destruction. Such is the case when Gollum's lust for the ring leads to his falling into a pit of fire, although ironically his action saves Frodo from falling prey to the irresistibly strong evil toward which the ring leads its wearer. Sauron, the chief of evil figures, like Lucifer, suffers first and foremost from pride. This, combined with lust for power and control, leads to his destruction. Gandalf suggests the plan for destroying the ring because he believes that Sauron will never conceive that a good person might wish to renounce the ring rather than embrace its power.

While these themes are fully compatible with a Catholic world view, they are not overt references to Catholicism. They could just as easily be attributed to western European humanism. To understand more fully the impact of Catholicism on *The Lord of the Rings*, one must turn to *The Silmarillion* and Tolkien's lesser known Middle-earth writings. The first two sections of *The Silmarillion*, "Ainulindalë" and "Valaquenta," are creation myths offering a snapshot of Tolkien's Middle-earth cosmology. Here we learn that Middle-earth was sung into existence by Eru Ilúvatar. He was aided by the Ainur, beings of great power, but not themselves capable of creating something out of nothing. Some of the Ainur became smitten with this new world and begged Eru's permission to mold and shape it. Eru granted them authority as caretakers of Middle-earth, thus distancing himself from his creation. Fourteen of the most capable of these Ainur were given a greater authority and called the Valar; an unknown number were assigned a lesser status as Maiar, serving under the Valar. The Valar and Maiar simultaneously fulfilled their own created natures and served Eru by forming, shaping, and influencing Middle-earth.

From this summary, several Catholic influences appear. First, Tolkien's world is monotheistic; Eru, like the Christian God, is ultimately in charge. The Ainur are his powerful servants, or angels. Yet the granting of authority to the Valar and Maiar mirrors the earthly authority granted not only to angels but to Christ, the saints, and the Church leadership. Similarly, the Valar are intermediaries between Eru and his created beings on Middle-earth.

Tolkien further complicates this cosmology in a manner both different from and similar to Catholic tradition. Besides the fourteen Valar, a fifteenth Ainur of equal power desired to influence Middle-earth. He was Melkor, intended by Eru to be the head Vala (the singular form of Valar) but who instead introduced discord into the singing of Middle-earth. Melkor was the Satan figure, created good by Eru but becoming bad through the exercise of pride. Melkor and his Maiar followers battled the Valar for the control of Middle-earth. The introduction of Melkor was a literary necessity for Tolkien since he desired to create a pseudomythology. Melkor's presence created strife among the Valar, such conflict being necessary for gripping literature. Yet the conjunction of this cosmic strife with the distancing of Eru from his creation produces a cosmology that appears multitheistic to many residents of Middle-earth, akin to Greek or Norse mythology. That is, while maintaining an overarching monotheism, Tolkien creates a world that appears to be controlled by "the gods," who are themselves in conflict.

The results of this conflict are apparent in *The Lord of the Rings*. Sauron, forger of the ring, was among the rebellious Maiar and second in command to Melkor. Thus, Sauron is not a creature of Middle-earth but from outside that world. Gandalf, too, becomes more than just a wizard. "Olórin I was in my youth in the West that is forgotten," he says after his resurrection (*The Two Towers*, 353). The "Valaquenta" describes Olórin as the wisest of the Maiar, having learned pity from the Vala Nienna. Thus, Gandalf, Saruman (the traitor wizard), Sauron, and even the Balrog who kills Gandalf are all hierarchically equal; all are (or were) Maiar, second-rank angels, and all would have been colleagues, perhaps even friends, when Eru first conceived of Middle-earth. This realization adds tragic depth to the conflicts within *The Lord of the Rings*.

This early Middle-earth mythology provides insight into the forces at work behind the rediscovery of the ring. Gandalf exclaims to Frodo that the ring itself was seeking its maker, yet "behind that there was something else at work, beyond any design of the Ring-maker. I can put it no plainer than by saying that Bilbo was *meant* to find the Ring, and *not* by its maker" (*The Fellowship of the Ring*, 88). While such a statement might at first sound fatalistic, once Tolkien's cosmology is understood, the "will" driving Bilbo into contact with the ring is revealed as the Valar themselves. Although unwilling to eliminate the ring on their own (such overt control would be outside the will of Eru), they are careful to ensure that the ring comes into the hands of good rather than evil.

Remaining books of *The Silmarillion* survey Middle-earth's early history. "Quenta Silmarillion" ("The History of the Silmarils") relates events from the First Age. Opening chapters describe the strife between Melkor and the Valar.

Eventually the "children of Eru," elves and men, appear in Middle-earth. The elves first awaken in wondrous amazement upon seeing the stars, created by the chief female Vala, Varda, who they call Elbereth (Star Queen). They remain fascinated by light, especially the stars, and thus hold Varda in special reverence. Her elevation parallels traditional Catholic veneration of Mary (although Tolkien also endorsed a Marian association with Galadriel). Thus, when Frodo is attacked at Weathertop Mountain by a Black Rider and shouts "O Elbereth Gilthoniel" (*The Fellowship of the Ring*, 263), he unwittingly utters a prayer, the Middle-earth equivalent of a "Hail Mary." Although much more complex in its history, a similar spiritual and historical dimension can be found for the Phial of Galadriel that Frodo and Sam use to defend themselves from the spider Shelob (herself a descendent of an underling of Melkor). These direct parallels with Tolkien's Catholic beliefs may explain his annoyance at the complaint made by some critics that *The Lord of the Rings* contains no religion.

CRITICAL RECEPTION

Few authors have addressed at length the impact of Tolkien's Catholicism on *The Lord of the Rings*, although both biographies and critical assessments indicate the significance of his religious faith to his life. Among the best studies are the following four collected in Joseph Pearce's *Tolkien: A Celebration* (1999). Charles Coulombe's "*The Lord of the Rings*—A Catholic View" suggests that Tolkien's writing was influenced by Catholic culture (as separate from Catholic religion and theology). Colin Gunton's "A Far-Off Gleam of the Gospel: Salvation in Tolkien's *The Lord of the Rings*" emphasizes the parallels between Tolkien's book and the Christian tradition of atonement. Sean McGrath, in "The Passion According to Tolkien," examines the theme of renunciation that pervades both Christianity and *The Lord of the Rings*. And Joseph Pearce's "Tolkien and the Catholic Literary Revival" argues that Tolkien should be understood as an overtly Catholic writer in the same way as John Henry Newman and G. K. Chesterton, rather than as a writer who happens to be Catholic.

Joseph Pearce has himself written at greater length on the connection between Christianity and Tolkien in *Tolkien: Man and Myth* (1999). As the title implies, this book is partly biographical, emphasizing the importance of his religious belief to Tolkien. At the same time, it strongly connects those beliefs to elements in the novel. Clyde S. Kilby has discussed generically Christian elements of *The Lord of the Rings* in "Mythic and Christian Elements in Tolkien" (1974). Also of interest is the chapter "Tolkien as Christian Writer" in Kilby's *Tolkien and the Silmarillion* (1976). Kurt Bruner and Jim Ware's *Finding God in the Lord of the Rings* (2001) is a slim and largely superficial volume meditating on Christian themes in Tolkien's work. The standard biography of Tolkien, by Humphrey Carpenter (1977), addresses at length the importance of Catholicism to his life and the conflicts it caused within his marriage.

NOTE

J. R. R. Tolkien, *The Lord of the Rings* trilogy: *The Fellowship of the Ring, The Two Towers, The Return of the King* (New York: Ballantine, 1965). All references are to this edition.

WORKS CITED

Bruner, Kurt D., and Jim Ware. 2001. *Finding God in the Lord of the Rings*. Wheaton, IL: Tyndale House.

Carpenter, Humphrey. 1977. *Tolkien: A Biography*. Boston: Houghton Mifflin.

Kilby, Clyde S. 1974. "Mythic and Christian Elements in Tolkien." In *Myth, Allegory and Gospel*, ed. Edmund Fuller, et al., 119–43. Minneapolis, MN: Bethany Fellowship.

———. 1976. *Tolkien and the Silmarillion*. Wheaton, IL: Harold Shaw.

Pearce, Joseph, ed. 1999. *Tolkien: A Celebration (Collected Writings on a Literary Legacy)*. North Pomfret, VT: Trafalgar Square.

———. 1999. *Tolkien: Man and Myth*. Fort Collins, CO: Ignatius Press.

Tolkien, J. R. R. 1937. *The Hobbit*. New York: Ballantine.

———. 1977. *The Silmarillion*, ed. Christopher Tolkien. New York: Ballantine.

— **Candice Fredrick and
Sam McBride**

Sigrid Undset [1882–1949]

Kristin Lavransdatter

BIOGRAPHY

Writing in exile in the United States in 1942, two years after the Nazi invasion of Norway, Sigrid Undset recounts poignantly her memories of Norwegian Christmases, for in Norway "it is Christmas Eve that is the greatest and the most sacred time in all the year" (*Happy Times in Norway*, 25). She describes the Christmas tree, the telling of the Christmas story, the beauty of the manger scene, the burning candles, and the gift and warmth of her family life. Someday soon, she hopes and believes, the "forces of evil" will be banished from Norway and the world, and in Norway "we will be able again to offer up to the wild birds of our woods and mountains the sheaf of grain at Christmas in front of our windows—the sacred gift of some thousands of years of Norwegian history to the powers of life and fertility, whatever name our ancestors gave to the Good Spiritual Forces watching over our home" (ix). Undset's love of nature, of Norway, and of ancestry's ongoing presence center in the "Good Spiritual Forces" that bless life and combat evil. Her conversion to Roman Catholicism in 1924 deepened and crystallized these preoccupations.

Sigrid Undset was born in Kalundborg, Denmark, in 1882, to a Danish mother and a Norwegian father. She was a bright and self-described headstrong, independent child. Her father, Ingvald, from Trondheim, was an archeologist well known for his book *The Beginnings of the Iron Age in Northern Europe*. Her mother, Anne Charlotte Gyth, held highly rationalistic views—she was "skeptical about everything," Undset later recalled ("Sigrid Undset," 1942, 1432)—yet questioned many of the "advanced" ideas of the time. This habit she shared with her daughter. Indeed, when she attended a progressive school headed by Ragna Nielsen, an ardent feminist who was extremely kind to her, Sigrid showed far greater interest in painting than in her academic studies and was skeptical of certain progressive aspects of the school even as she affirmed its equal treatment of girls and boys. Undset indicated her lack of interest in attending the university and in becoming a teacher. Yet in her own way she demonstrated the womanly independence Ibsen's dramas were then representing—indeed, in 1913 Norway became the first European nation to extend women the vote—by her interest in and affinity for the Norwegian past, particularly the past of the Middle Ages. "I think the reason why I understand our own time so well, or see it so clearly," she wrote in 1919, "is because ever since I was a child I had some kind of living memories from an earlier age to compare with it" (quoted in Brunsdale 1988, 3).

Undset's family had moved to Christiana (now Oslo) shortly after Sigrid's birth, and her nearly mystical affinity for Norway's past was nurtured by her reading with her father of the Old Norse and Icelandic sagas, including *Njal's Saga*, which she read in 1893 at the age of eleven. Its narrative greatly impressed her by its vision of moral struggle and responsibility, fate, and influences both pagan and Christian, resonating with the presence of both Odin and Christ. Her reading of *Njal's Saga* in her grandfather's library changed her life, she said later, and its stark intensity, psychological realism and depth, and moral conflicts would be reflected in her imagination and her writing, especially in *Kristin Lavransdatter*.

For Undset, the year 1893 also proved negatively pivotal. Her father's death left an immense void. It also left the family in poverty. At sixteen, Undset began work in an electrical engineer's office, where she remained for ten years. During this time, she continued to read and write and published two books. In 1905, she completed a novel set in the thirteenth century, but it was rejected. In this same year, Norway declared its independence from Sweden and Haakon VII was crowned King at Trondheim. Undset published her first novel, *Mrs. Marta Oulie*, in 1907, and in 1909 she published *Gunnar's Daughter*. Two years later, her novel *Jenny* became immensely popular in Norway.

In 1912, two years before the outbreak of World War I, Undset married Anders C. Svarstad, a painter, and they moved first to England, then to Rome. Svarstad had three children from a prior marriage, and in 1913 their son Anders was born. They also had a daughter, Tulla, born in 1915, and a second son, Hans, in 1919. Undset's familial responsibilities intensifying, strains developed between her and Svarstad, and in 1919 she and her children moved to Lillehammer. In 1922, the couple mutually agreed to divorce. In 1924, their marriage was annulled—the Church had refused to recognize Svarstad's divorce from his first wife—and Undset was received into the Roman Catholic Church. She had been made an agnostic, she said, by the liberal Protestantism in which she was educated, and so she looked back to an older and original Christianity in the hope that it held some truth. We often do not wish to discover truth, she insisted, for we prefer to cling to our illusions. But she had journeyed too close to truth's abode in researching the stories of the saints, or "God's friends," as the saints are called in the Old Norse narratives of Catholic times. She had become persuaded that "these queer men and women" were, in fact, the "only sane people" in western civilization. Their eccentricity rightly offended contemporary trends and smugness, for they seemed to have grasped "the true explanation of man's undying hunger for happiness—his tragically insufficient love of peace, justice, and good-will to his fellow-men, his everlasting fall from grace" ("Sigrid Undset," 1942, 1433). In this light—their light—she experienced conversion.

Undset published the trilogy, *Kristin Lavransdatter*, from 1920 to 1922, and the tetrology, *The Master of Hestviken*, from 1925 to 1927. She continued to care for her family and to write throughout the later 1920s and the 1930s. In

1928, she was awarded the Nobel Prize for Literature, and she donated the financial portion of the prize to the Norwegian Authors' Association. In 1934, her autobiographical *The Longest Years* appeared, as did *The Saga of Saints* (1934). Hitler's rise to power and the gathering war clouds cast dark shadows, and in 1939, the year the Nazis invaded Poland, these deepened with the deaths of her mother and of Tulla, her twenty-four-year-old daughter. In 1940, Nazi bombers devastated Lillehammer. Undset was forced to escape, and her son Anders was killed as his machine gun unit fought Nazi troops. Arriving in Sweden penniless, she was taken in by friends. She journeyed first to Moscow, then to Siberia and Japan, and finally to San Francisco. Later, she lived and wrote in Brooklyn, New York.

In 1937 a Norwegian Fascist newspaper had denounced Undset for her early and powerful attacks on Hitler and antisemitism, and in 1940 the Nazis banned and destroyed her books. She continued to condemn Hitler's savagery, to champion freedom, courage, and democracy, and to attack totalitarianism in all its guises. For the war's duration she worked for the Norwegian Information Service in America. In 1942, she recounted her escape from the Nazis in *Return to the Future* and spoke of her hopes for Norway's and the world's children through her spirited memories in *Happy Times in Norway*.

Upon her return to Norway at the war's end in August 1945, Undset's health had weakened. As Tiina Nunnally writes, she "had endured great personal losses, and her home in Lillehammer would never be the same. The Germans . . . chopped up for firewood . . . her father's desk, at which she had written *Kristin Lavransdatter* and all her other novels. Although Undset continued to write . . . her artistic zeal and physical strength were spent" ("Introduction," *The Wreath*, xix). Despite her failing health, Undset participated in rebuilding the ruins of the Hammer Cathedral near Lillehammer and worked on a biography of Saint Catherine of Siena and several essays on the sacredness of life and the importance of communality. Although Doubleday rejected her book on Saint Catherine, it was published in Norwegian in 1947 and in English in 1954. For her long service to Norway and the world in working for freedom and against materialism and totalitarianism, King Haakon in 1947 awarded Undset the Grand Cross of the Order of Saint Olaf.

When Sigrid Undset died on June 10, 1949, says Charlotte Blindheim, for her family it was "like having a solid anchor cut away" (quoted in Brunsdale 1988, 123). She was laid to rest between her children in a cemetery near Lillehammer, with an epitaph declaring her to be, notes Brunsdale, "like Kristin Lavransdatter, 'a loyal handmaiden of the Lord'" (123).

PLOT SUMMARY

Kristin Lavransdatter consists of three novels that appeared in consecutive years: *The Wreath* (*Kransen*), originally translated as *The Bridal Wreath* and published in 1920; *The Wife* (*Husfrue*), first translated as *The Mistress of Husab*y, published a year later; and *The Cross* (*Korset*), published in 1922. Set in fourteenth-century Norway, the novels delineate Kristin Lavransdatter's external fortunes and afflictions and the depth of her interior life as she grows from childhood to adulthood, from her early years to the time of her death. In this growth, Kristin seeks not only earthly love but the salvation wedded to the deepest gift of love.

The Wreath

The setting of this novel clearly reflects Undset's love of Norway's mountains, fjords, and forests. As Brunsdale rightly notes, her decision to live and write in rural Lillehammer rather than in Oslo, the city where she had lived, accentuates nature's power and mystery in her life and work: "The harmony of her daily round at Lillehammer, one of Norway's loveliest natural settings, must have heightened [her] awareness of her Norwegian heritage, and at the same time, as she raised her eyes to the Dovre mountains beyond, her Creator must have seemed constantly near" (1988, 65). As a child, Kristin is absorbed by nature's beauty and the safety of her home at Jorundgaard, especially as this safety is assured by her father's presence and love. Yet in a moment alone in nature, she experiences terror as well as wonder in glimpsing the mysterious image of a "dwarf maiden" who offers her a wreath of golden flowers. The "wreath" Kristin later accepts is her own powerful will rather than selflessness, but here, awed and frightened, she enters a church and confers with a monk, Brother Edvin, who illuminates for her the ongoing battle between God and the devil. In the cathedral, she sees radiant pictures of Jesus and Mary, Saint Nicholas carrying a child, and Saint Kristina: "It was like standing at a great distance and looking into heaven" (*The Wreath*, 32). Brother Edvin speaks to her of Christ's mercy and his suffering love embodied in the cross.

This scene takes place close to Advent; the liturgical year frames the novel and Kristin's growth and conflicts. She loves her father Lavrans and her more melancholy mother Ragnfrid, who grieves over the deaths of three sons and over the seeming distance between her and Lavrans. An adolescent friend falls tenderly in love with Kristin, but another man violently assaults her. Kristin comes to recognize that love can take the form of compassion, or *caritas*, true charity, as in the eternal wreath Brother Edvin offers her, or *cupiditas*, self-absorption and pride, the wreath she embraces when she pursues her own desires to the exclusion of all other values and responsibilities.

Betrothed at fifteen in an arranged marriage to a young man named Simon, Kristin instead begins a passionate and reckless affair with Erlend Nikulausson, a charismatic older man. As Kristin breaks her engagement to Simon and indulges her psychological and sexual desire for Erlend, Erlend in turn seeks to break away from Eline, a married woman with whom he has had several children. Eline dies, and Kristin and Erlend's complicity in betraying her and in her death engender deep guilt. Kristin, now pregnant with Erlend's child, knows no peace, and her youthful innocence gives way to restlessness, betrayal, and despair. Her father Lavrans reveals to Kristin his own guilt for past sins, and Kristin faces within and without a darkening world of moral conflict, acute con- science, and mortal pain—and most important, a world that seems starkly unforgiving.

The Wife

Undset dedicates this second novel of the trilogy to her father Ingvald, and in it she continues to delineate the complex, often tormented relationship between Kristin and Erlend and its reverberations for their families. Unlike Lavrans's farm, Erlend's manor at Husaby reflects an elaborate history of nobility and aristocracy, toward which Kristin's ambivalence and skepticism are striking. Elsewhere, Undset insisted that the Norwegian army had always been a people's army and that Norwegians "had always had greater freedom than people . . . in Denmark and Sweden. There the peasants were subjects of powerful proprietors and noblemen, but in Norway the peasants had never been serfs" (*Happy Times in Norway*, 87–88). In this light, Kristin's attitude toward strong social hierarchy and class distinctions, even when the symbols of nobility are impressive, is both negative and impatient, especially when she experiences firsthand the careless neglect, filth, and squalor of the manor itself.

Torn by inner conflict, Kristin walks twenty miles through the snow to Saint Olaf's shrine—the shrine of Norway's patron and only native saint. She seeks forgiveness for her doubts of Erlend's love for her, the pain she has inflicted on her father, and her fierce pride. Erlend and Lavrans have made their peace, Kristin has given difficult birth to a son, and through it all she wavers between self-righteousness and a penitential heart. Always, suffering and grace are interwoven, and Brother Edvin's assurance of Christ's mercy for even the deepest sins echoes in her mind and heart even when her heart cannot believe or embrace this assurance fully.

This familial narrative of sin and forgiveness, transgression and grace, at once divine and earthly, moves through the dynamic between Erlend and Kristin. As she bears more children, she devotes herself to them so intensely that she further alienates Erlend and her father, who is dying. Feeling confined and belittled, Erlend leaves home on a voyage to defend northern Norway, and despite his imprisonment and torture for taking part in a political conspiracy, he retains his honor. But Kristin, refusing to acknowledge his true heroism and willingness to sacrifice, distances herself from him, in large measure because in her eyes he cannot compare in virtue and steadfastness to her father.

The Cross

Erlend has lost his manor and lands and has come to live at Jorundgaard, the setting in which *Kristin Lavransdatter* begins. He continues to be judged by Kristin in light of her love and admiration for her father, Lavrans. "Self-exiled" to a small farm still belonging to him, Erlend returns to defend Kristin from the accusation that he did not father their youngest child, who has died. He dies in the fight. Still distanced from Erlend in death and still denying her share of responsibility for this distance, Kristin vows to make one more pilgrimage, this time communally with other pilgrims, to do penance. Arriving at the convent in Rein, Kristin has a vision of her friend and companion in life, Brother Edvin, offering her the sacramental bread of love and forgiveness. After a dream in which Erlend and her father appear and after experiencing a high Mass following her dream, Kristin feels a deep solidarity with these "destitute and suffering people," many of whom are seriously ill (*The Cross*, 383). She prays with and for them and, in the end, sacrifices her life for another. Enveloped at once by the plague and God's mercy, tended to by the sisters and by Ulf, an old servant of her father's household, Kristin sees in the symbol of her wedding ring, marked with the holy sign of the Virgin Mary, a sign of her salvation. Significantly, she gives away the ring before she dies, her only remaining possession now a cross her father had given her. Kristin had remembered and done penance for her betrayals and had also remembered all the gifts she had given and been given. Now with all stripped away to her soul, it is as if she recalls, with Isak Dinesen's minister from *Babette's Feast*, a story set in nineteenth-century Norway, that "The only things . . . we may take with us from our life on earth" are "those we have given away" (1993, 51). For all Kristin's physical and psychological suffering and pain, here redemption, true charity, and divine forgiveness have the last word.

MAJOR THEMES

Even as a child, says Undset, she despised all conquerors and all rule by force and terror. Although many of her friends idealized Napoleon, for example, she found him appalling, as she found appalling the excessive violence of her Viking ancestors. Although not a pacifist in the tradition of her friend Dorothy Day—Undset believed individuals and nations sometimes had to fight against those who set out to dominate and enslave others—Undset knew acutely how disastrous an individual's or society's desire to follow powerful and authoritarian leaders can be. This hunger for authority, she insists, clearly thinking of Hitler, Stalin, and others, can lead entire nations to embrace "any ghoulish caricature" of authority. Yet, she continues, she has learned that no earthly power and authority of force can be valid. The "only Authority" humanity can submit to without warping itself is "His whom St. Paul calls *Auctor Vitae*—the Creator's toward Creation" ("Sigrid Undset," 1942, 1434).

Her conviction of God's authority and presence in and over nature pervades Undset's vision in *Kristin Lavransdatter*. To be sure, we learn early in the trilogy that the created order may be a source of terror. As a child, Kristin "knew that wolves and bears reigned in the forest, and under every rock lived trolls and goblins and elves, and she was suddenly afraid, for no one knew how many there were, but there were certainly many more of them than of Christian people" (*The Wreath*, 12). In nature's sublime power, then, humanity finds beauty and fear just as these qualities inhabit the forest of the unconscious and the battlefield of human nature on which good and evil conflict. That this human nature is real and perennial and not, as Marxism and other systems would have it, infinitely malleable and even a fiction in light of the primacy of environment remains a central tenet of Undset's faith. She would be amused by the trendy currents of contemporary culture, some of which find her traditional vision archaic, since the popular, chic, and trendy also held a great deal of advertising space in her own time.

But Undset knew that the word "modern" is an extremely old word and that the truths of human nature remain constant in the ancient, medieval, and more recent worlds. She writes that she consistently doubted the ideas of her early education and that for her "liberalism, feminism, nationalism, socialism, pacifism, would not work, because they refused to consider human nature as it really is. Instead, they presupposed that mankind was to 'progress' into something else—towards their own ideas of what people ought to be. Being fostered on pre-history and history I did not much believe in progress" ("Sigrid Undset," 1942, 1433). Accumulated experience and increased knowledge do not mean recent minds will surpass Aristotle, Saint Paul, or Saint Thomas Aquinas, and it is wholly clear that modernity will not mean an exponential growth of virtue and compassion.

To praise you, says Saint Augustine in addressing God in his *Confessions*, is "the desire of man, a little piece of your creation. You stir man to take pleasure in praising you, because you have made us for yourself, and our heart is restless until it rests in you" (1991, 3). Kristin's restless heart keys the dynamism of Undset's trilogy. Often, Kristin knows intellectually what is good and right yet directs her will in the opposite direction. As Saint Paul says agonizingly in Romans, "what I would, that I do not; but what I hate, that do I. . . . For the good that I would I do not: but the evil which I would not, that I do" (Rom. 7:15, 19, Authorized [King James] Version). In this strong light, it is clear that for all of Kristin's sexual passion, her real sin is not such passion but vainglory, self-exaltation, and self-absorption. For Undset, writes Tiina Nunnally, Kristin's greatest sin lies not in succumbing to her sexual desires and yielding "to the amorous demands of her impetuous suitor before they are properly married. Of much greater import is Kristin's decision to thwart her father's wishes, to deny the traditions of her ancestors, and to defy the Church; her worst sin is . . . pride" ("Introduction," *The Wreath*, xv).

Within the family, always an indispensable and sacred community for Undset, individual pride is dangerous in its leading to isolation and to alienating those one loves. Kristin and Erlend, like Kristin's own father and mother, often do not speak intimately with each other but remain lost in their own thoughts, worlds, and, at times, despair. The Catholic vision of communality, the "communion of saints" envisioned as an article of faith in the Apostles' Creed, proves difficult for Kristin—and for many other characters in *Kristin Lavransdatter*—to embrace in actuality rather than theoretically. For this reason, her climactic pilgrimage to Rein is especially powerful and moving: in the church "the radiance of colored sunlight mingled with the glow of candles; the fresh, pungent scent of incense seeped over everyone, blunting the smell of poverty and illness. Her heart burst with a feeling of oneness with these destitute and suffering people, among whom God had placed her; she prayed in a surge of sisterly tenderness for all those who were poor as she was and who suffered as she herself had suffered" (*The Cross*, 382–83). Here, Kristin's compassion is authentic, her empathy not theoretical but experiential. Like Dostoevsky in exile in a Siberian prison, she comes to see her fellow sufferers not as remote strangers but as related, even as members of the Mystical Body of Christ.

The suffering of this Mystical Body, like the suffering of Christ, remains real and concrete throughout *Kristin Lavransdatter*. For Kristin and for others, affliction often comes starkly and implacably: the specter of violence, the early deaths of children, precarious life subjected to sudden crippling and loss. Our hearts are divided and conflicted, Brother Edvin tells the young Kristin, and we must join Christ's suffering to our own. "I fear the Devil," he says, "and love and desire this world like a fool. But I hold onto the cross with all my strength—one must cling to it like a kitten hanging on to a plank when it falls into the sea" (*The Wreath*, 36). In light of the cross, suffering can be redemptive. Says Brother Edvin to Kristin: "It was because of God's mercy toward us that He saw how our hearts were split, and He came down to live among us"—to suffer and love (36).

Throughout the verisimilitude of her settings and psychological delineations of character, Undset's recurring emphasis on the redemptiveness of suffering remains striking. It links her, of course, with the great writers of the twentieth-century Catholic literary renaissance, including François Mauriac, Graham Greene, and Georges Bernanos. Indeed, Graham Greene's citation of Leon Bloy for the epigraph to *The End of the Affair* could have been taken from *Kristin Lavransdatter*: "Man has places in his heart which do not yet exist, and into them enters suffering in order that they may have existence" ([1951] 1962, 6). Yet in order for suffering to redeem rather than to destroy and embitter the soul, Undset insists on the indispensability of accepting moral responsibility for one's actions and their consequences. Then, as now, blaming others for our own pride and transgression is commonplace. Indeed, in a particularly grotesque example of this evasion, Hitler blamed and scapegoated "the eternal Jew" for all the world's evils, including his own, and in his last days in the Berlin bunker wrote a "will" or "testament" indicting the weakness of the German people for the war's apocalyptic disaster. Nowhere does he express any degree of personal responsibility for initiating and continuing the most destructive and genocidal war in history. Throughout *Kristin Lavransdatter*, Kristin and other characters often project their guilt onto others and scapegoat them, refusing to be self-critical and seeking to locate the source of destructive thoughts and actions and the reality of moral judgments everywhere but in their own imaginations, intellects, and hearts. Yet without individual moral responsibility—which Undset finds affirmed and valued amid the violent battles of *Njal's Saga*—and the honesty it entails, one's intellect remains distorted and one's heart poisoned. Absent responsibility, real love and intimacy become impossible.

That Undset finds deeply human values—hard work, courage in the face of death, loyalty, familial love and allegiance—amid the Old Norse gods, eddas, and sagas speaks to her conviction, like Dante's toward the pagan world from which a good and even prophetic figure like Virgil can arise, that God has used the pagan world and its stories as a kind of preparation for the coming of Christ. Undset at one point calls the Viking age "a love poem to a God who remained hidden," and, as Brunsdale aptly puts it, "in the Norse imagination, Thor's hammer, after all, was not so far in shape and meaning from the cross of Christ" (1988, 32). Indeed, the goddess Freya (or Freyr) provides a strong maternal presence in Norse mythology, embodying a protectiveness toward family life and its continuity. And as Virgil was said to have prophesied the birth of Christ despite his living before the event, Freya also is a diviner, initiated wholly into the world of the spirit.

Jacques Maritain and the neo-Thomism and Christian humanism he advanced strongly influenced Undset, and at one point she and Maritain met. We see this kind of deeply sacramental vision in Undset's recognition that even certain misguided pagan ideals can retain a spark of the ultimate truth found only in Christ. Undset's embrace of the mystery of the Incarnation and the need for grace undergirds her valuing of moral responsibility, for moral responsibility alone cannot ensure salvation. As for Kierkegaard, the individual's—and humanity's—need for faith and grace is absolute. For Undset as for Kierkegaard and Maritain, of course, this need is met by God's love, or charity, in his free gift of Christ. And the essence of this love is forgiveness, which, ultimately, lies at the heart of *Kristin Lavransdatter*—God's forgiveness of humanity's original and ongoing sin, and the need for human beings to forgive each other in charity rather than condemning them in judgment. Luther, laboring as an Augustinian monk in his monastery, continued to imagine God as a harsh father and judge even as he wanted to believe in him as a loving and forgiving mother. After finally experiencing Saint Paul's words that we are saved by God's grace and not by our own virtues and merit, Luther said the gates of Paradise had been opened to him. In *The Wife*, Undset draws on this same familial imagery to describe forgiveness. Although we might stray from the path of righteousness, Kristin remembers Brother Edvin saying, Christ's pierced hands continue to stretch out to us, yearning: "Only one thing was needed: that the sinful soul should turn toward the open embrace, freely, like a child who goes to his father and not like a thrall who is chased home to his stern master. Now Kristin realized how hideous sin was. Again she felt the pain in her breast, as if her heart were breaking with remorse and shame at the undeserved mercy" (*The Wife*, 114).

When Kristin as a child sees in church the holy images of Mary and the Christ Child, it is telling that the iconic image of Saint Nicholas is carrying a child. In one of her final essays, a Christmas meditation titled "And What If This Baby Were Not Born?" Undset asks why anyone should care about a tiny infant who is not theirs. If it is unwanted, why not kill it? There is no reason to protect this child, she concludes, "no reason except the whole of Christianity" (quoted in Brunsdale 1988, 112). In *Kristin Lavransdatter*, we are reminded of life's sacredness even or especially amid violence and retribution. For Undset, the constant presence and intercession of men and women saints, "God's friends," signify this divinity, this sacredness. The shrine of Saint Olaf, of course, is pivotal in the narrative. In *Happy Times in Norway*, Undset recounts that many "young Norwegian princes set out as Vikings and came home Christians, eager to convert all the people" to faith in Christ. The last of them, "Olav Haraldson, succeeded. When he fell at Stiklestad in 1030, he had made Norway a Christian land, and he came to be remembered as Saint Olav" (1942, 23). In the Apostles' Creed, as Undset well knew, the "communion of saints" refers not exclusively to the exceptionally holy or the canonized but to the communion of all believers, *justus et peccator*, the saved and the sinful. In this light, Kristin's gazing at and experiencing in church the radiance of the saints and thinking, "It was like standing at a great distance and looking into heaven" (*The Wreath*, 32), signifies, to be sure, the saints' transcendence. Yet as readers we recognize that the saints, like divinity, are also an immanent presence and that the paradoxes of Christianity make great distances near, make the transcendently divine incarnate and concrete, and make saints of all-too-human yet yearning believers.

CRITICAL RECEPTION

The Nobel Prize committee, in choosing Undset for the 1928 award for achievement in literature, crystallized the general reception of *Kristin Lavransdatter*. It proved an immensely popular trilogy of novels. The only critical controversies were generated by the historical accuracy (or inaccuracy) of the novel's portrayal of life in fourteenth-century Norway and by the deep presence and influence of Roman Catholicism on Norway's people. Even in her descriptions of her own Christmas memories, Undset stresses this key condition: "In many places in Norway people have clung to the customs of Catholic times and fasted . . . on Christmas Eve, even though it was four hundred years since the country became Protestant"

(1942, 27). Some critics argued that the ongoing influence of Viking attitudes and values in the fourteenth century would have militated against any deeply religious vision of sin, grace, and redemption. Others, however, argued for the importance of allowing Undset her own interpretation of the place of religion in medieval culture in Norway, and critics pro and con on this question agreed that Undset was in fact a diligent and meticulous researcher of this culture, one whose concern for historical fact and verisimilitude could not be questioned. Furthermore, the ancient Viking world certainly recognized the raging forces of good and evil and the presence of the spirit as palpably real. And before the Reformation, the Catholic Church's authority, vision, doctrines, and presence surely were interwoven with Norwegian culture, just as it is Brother Edvin, whose guiding presence—even after his death—serves Kristin as a constant source and reminder of truth and love.

Whatever the questions over particular external forms of realism in *Kristin Lavransdatter*, it remains true, as Velma Ruch argues, that "much as one must admire Sigrid Undset's skill in the depiction of outer detail, never does she lose sight of the significance of the spirit" (1957, 78). For some secular critics—and in this context, strains of anti-Catholicism do emerge at times—Undset's emphasis on Catholicism appears overly weighty. Yet for others sympathetic to, or at least open to, the seriousness and validity of religious faith and tradition rather than solely to Freud, Marx, and a materialistic naturalism, *Kristin Lavransdatter* awakens echoes of Dostoevsky's greatest novels. Frank O'Malley links Undset to Greene, Mauriac, Bloy, and Bernanos and argues that she "achieves notably what Claudel has termed the Catholic oneness. Her novels fuse magnificently the world of sense and the world of spirit. . . . She affirms everywhere her faith in the redeeming God, in man's tremendous freedom and its tremendous responsibilities, her belief that the central struggle of every human being is . . . the struggle for salvation through the sacramentalism of the Church." Readers, he concludes, "can find nothing more tragic or more effective and beautiful in the literature of the twentieth century than . . . the blundering yet grieving man and woman whose characters were fundamentally religious: Olaf Audunnson, master of Hestviken, and Kristin, mistress of Husaby" (1951, 59–60).

C. A. Brady, writing in *America*, contends that *Kristin Lavransdatter* is an even greater novel than *Anna Karenina*: "From any point of view *Kristin Lavransdatter* must be accounted one of the master novels of the world, the greatest novel ever written by a woman, and possibly, the greatest single historical novel in literary annals" (1949, 402). And H. C. Gardiner notes that Undset in *Kristin Lavransdatter* both addresses and expresses "the total Christian and Catholic integration" of a vision of God and humanity. Unlike many novelists of her time who will be forgotten, Gardiner states, Undset will remain foundational, one of those writers "who have tapped new and vital sources, who have approached the whole problem of the artistic representation of human life with new richness, new depth, new vision" (1954, 161).

The serious writer, says Flannery O'Connor in her essay "Novelist and Believer," begins with the flaw in human nature, "the flaw in an otherwise admirable character":

The novelist doesn't write about people in a vacuum; he writes about people in a world where something is obviously lacking, where there is the general mystery of incompleteness . . . and the novelist tries to give you, within the form of the book, a total experience of human nature at any time. For this reason the greatest dramas naturally involve the salvation or loss of the soul. Where there is no belief in the soul, there is very little drama. (1975, 74)

For most of those readers, critics, and reviewers who believed and believe in the soul's drama, *Kristin Lavransdatter* was and remains a powerful and perennial novel. Indeed, we have a fine recent translation of the novel (by Tiina Nunnally) as well as a film version of *Kristin Lavransdatter* (directed by Liv Ullmann, 1996). For secular readers who dismiss the spirit as vapor, for whom neither humanity's tragic sinfulness nor its redemptive joy is potential or actual, and for whom human nature does not exist, the joyfulness of Kristin's experience presumably is as unreal as its tragedy. Our age, as O'Connor reminds us, often seems without deep feeling, mystery, or the sacramental, and at its worst it is an age that has "domesticated despair and learned to live with it happily" (1975, 70).

A given interpretation of *Kristin Lavransdatter*, then, depends to a degree, as interpretations always do, on the preoccupations and faith—and objects of faith—of the reader. One critic has argued that Undset "consecrated" her life to the study of woman, to which a rejoinder holds that "her whole life instead has been consecrated to the study of the human soul" ("Sigrid Undset," 1942, 1434). Mitzi Brunsdale notes that a great deal of Undset's literary fame has slipped away, an acknowledgment that literary reputations, like all reputations of public figures, are bound to shift and change. But Brunsdale, for her part, acknowledges that Undset writes of woman and the soul—again, of human nature, God, and salvation—and that her literary achievement is lasting and striking: "Sigrid Undset's long pilgrimage from freethinking liberalism to conservative Christianity, at its finest a celebration of Christian humanism that knows no gender, no nation, no century, offers an example of stages on a woman's road to personal salvation, and her incomparable re-creations of medieval Norway" assures *Kristin Lavransdatter* its place "among the world's great literature" (1991, 95). The depth of Sigrid Undset's sacramental religious and moral vision, as well as of her literary achievement, is as striking and profound as their epic breadth.

NOTE

Sigrid Undset, *The Wreath*, vol. 1 of *Kristin Lavransdatter* (trans. Tiina Nunnally; New York: Penguin, 1997); *The Wife*, vol. 2 of *Kristin Lavransdatter* (trans. Tiina Nunnally; New York: Penguin, 1999); *The Cross*. vol. 3 of *Kristin Lavransdatter* (trans. Tiina Nunnally; New York: Penguin, 2000). All references are to these editions.

WORKS CITED

Augustine, Saint. 1991. *Confessions*, trans. Henry Chadwick. Oxford: Oxford University Press.
Brady, C. A. 1949. "Sigrid Undset: Heir of the Volsungs." *America* 81 (July 2): 402.

Brunsdale, Mitzi. 1988. *Sigrid Undset: Chronicler of Norway*. Oxford: Berg.

———. 1991. "Stages on Her Road: Sigrid Undset's Spiritual Journey." *Religion and Literature* 23 (Autumn): 83–95.

Dinesen, Isak. 1993. *Babette's Feast*. In *Anecdotes of Destiny*, 19–59. New York: Vintage.

Gardiner, H. C. 1954. "Sigrid Undset." *Catholic Mind* 52 (March): 161–66.

Greene, Graham. [1951] 1962. *The End of the Affair*. London: Penguin.

Kristin Lavransdatter. 1996. A film in Norwegian with English subtitles, directed by Liv Ullmann. Jar, Norway: Norsk Film AS.

O'Connor, Flannery. 1975. "Novelist and Believer." In *Religion and Modern Literature: Essays in Theory and Criticism*, ed. G. B. Tennyson and Edward E. Ericson, 68–75. Grand Rapids, MI: Eerdmans.

O'Malley, Frank. 1951. "The Renascence of the Novelist and the Poet." In *The Catholic Renascence in a Disintegrating World*, ed. Norman Weyand, S. J., 23–88. Chicago: Loyola University Press.

Ruch, Velma Naomi. 1957. "Sigrid Undset's Kristin Lavransdatter: A Study of Its Literary Art and Its Reception in America, England, and Scandinavia." Dissertation, University of Wisconsin-Madison.

"Sigrid Undset." In *Twentieth Century Authors: A Biographical Dictionary of Modern Literature*, ed. Stanley J. Kunitz and Howard Haycroft, 1431–35. New York: H. W. Wilson, 1942.

Undset, Sigrid. 1934. *Saga of Saints*, trans. E. C. Ramsden. New York: Longmans Green.

———. 1942. *Happy Times in Norway*. New York: Knopf.

— **Thomas Werge**

Evelyn Waugh [1903–1966]

Brideshead Revisited

BIOGRAPHY

Arthur Evelyn St. John Waugh was born on October 28, 1903, the second son of Arthur and Catherine Waugh. Waugh's father was the managing director of Chapman and Hall, a successful London publishing firm; he was also an essayist and reviewer who shared his love of literature with his family. Both Waugh and his elder brother Alec became professional writers. In *A Little Learning* (1964; the first and only volume of his autobiography), Waugh describes himself as a church-loving child, enjoying services and ritual worship. At Lancing (his High Church public school), however, he turned agnostic after a teacher shared with students unorthodox speculations on theological matters.

Waugh enjoyed a successful public school career, winning a scholarship in modern history at Hertford College of Oxford University in 1922. Waugh's experiences there provided many of the situations and personalities that feature in the early sections of *Brideshead Revisited*. Waugh admitted that he was hardly a diligent student; for him Oxford was a world of glamorous living and exuberant companionships: "I regarded Oxford as a place to be inhabited and enjoyed for itself . . . The record of my life there is essentially a catalogue of friendships" (*A Little Learning*, 171, 190). After three years of extravagant living, Waugh left Oxford with a third-class degree and no particular ambitions or plans.

Waugh attended art school briefly before a short career as a schoolmaster, employment that he found discouraging. In 1927, he published a biography of the Pre-Raphaelite painter Dante Gabriel Rossetti, which met with critical success. He married Evelyn Gardner in 1928, despite her mother's protests that Waugh could not support a wife. This marriage would not endure, however; within two years, "she-Evelyn" (as Waugh's wife was known to their friends) announced that she was having an affair with another man, and the couple divorced.

Waugh published his first satirical novel, *Decline and Fall*, in 1928; although receiving mixed reviews, it marks his style for several subsequent (and more popularly successful) novels, including *Vile Bodies* (1930), *Black Mischief* (1932), *A Handful of Dust* (1934), *Scoop* (1938), and *Put Out More Flags* (1942).

Throughout this period, Waugh also published articles on the social scene and international travel.

In 1930, Waugh converted to Roman Catholicism, a decision he explained in his essay "Converted to Rome." He maintained that the present state of European history was chaotic, fractured, and meaningless; the "essential issue" was "between Christianity and Chaos." He turned to the Roman Catholic Church because he saw it as "the most complete and vital form" of Christianity (1983, 104). He later wrote of the compelling Catholic roots of England: "The Catholic structure still lies lightly buried beneath every phase of English life" ("Come Inside," 1983, 367).

Waugh continued his travel writing during subsequent years as well as penning a biography of the English Jesuit saint and martyr Edmund Campion, for which he won the 1936 Hawthornden Prize. After his marriage to Evelyn Gardner was annulled by the Catholic Church in 1936, Waugh married Laura Herbert. They had six children.

Motivated to join the war effort because of Stalin and Hitler's joint aggression against Catholic Poland, Waugh secured a commission in the Royal Marines in 1939. His military career is difficult to characterize definitively, although most accounts present him as resistant to authority and not altogether winning among his fellow soldiers. His term of service, however, produced *Brideshead Revisited*, to which he referred as his "magnum opus" (*The Letters of Evelyn Waugh*, 1980, 176). Its style and subject matter break with the satirical fiction he produced before the war. In a dust jacket "warning," Waugh writes, "There are passages of buffoonery, but the general theme is at once romantic and eschatological. It is ambitious, perhaps intolerably presumptuous; nothing less than an attempt to trace the workings of the divine purpose in a pagan world" (Stannard 1984, 236).

Waugh characterized the novel as a turning point in his development: in his future books he would "attempt to represent man more fully, which, to me, means only one thing, man in his relation to God" ("Fan-Fare," 1946, 56). *Brideshead Revisited* was a popular success in England and America, where it was chosen by the Book-of-the-Month Club. In 1947, Waugh was invited to Hollywood by MGM regarding a possible film adaptation—a plan that foundered because movie executives saw the novel only as a romance and failed to recognize its theological meanings. Waugh refused to agree to a film that would erase the novel's religious import.

During this trip, however, Waugh began work on *The Loved One* (1948), his next successful satiric novel. In 1949 he edited Thomas Merton's *The Seven Storey Mountain* for publication in England, where it appeared under the title *Elected Silence*, and in 1950 he published *Helena*, a novel about Saint Helena. Waugh then began work on the *Sword of Honor* war trilogy: *Men at Arms* (1952), *Officers and Gentlemen* (1955), and *Unconditional Surrender* (1961).

At this time, his health began to deteriorate and he suffered from insomnia, for which he took increasingly risky doses of bromide and chloral. Interruptions of this medication resulted in hallucinations and paranoid delusions—experiences fictionalized in *The Ordeal of Gilbert Pinfold* (1957). Waugh revised *Brideshead Revisited* in 1960, altering chapter and book divisions, slightly modifying some phrasings, and adding a brief Preface that clarified the novel's theme as "the operation of divine grace on a group of diverse but closely connected characters"

(Stannard 1984, 271). His final years were often not happy ones; he grew uneasy with the progressive direction of the Catholic Church and other signs of what he disdainfully referred to as "The Century of the Common Man." He died at home after Easter Sunday Mass on April 10, 1966.

There are numerous sources of information about Waugh's life. Christopher Sykes's *Evelyn Waugh: A Biography* (1975) is the account of a personal friend; it benefits from the warm and intimate knowledge of its subject but is compromised by Sykes's reticence regarding Waugh's less agreeable qualities. Martin Stannard's exhaustive three-volume *Evelyn Waugh* (1984–1992) benefits from published diaries, letters, and memoirs unavailable to Sykes; however, Stannard finds Waugh's religious views intemperate and alien. More sympathetic, Douglas Lane Patey's critical biography, *The Life of Evelyn Waugh* (1998), provides both biographical and theological contexts for Waugh's writings.

PLOT SUMMARY

Brideshead Revisited's Prologue is set during World War II. Charles Ryder, the narrator, is a captain in the British Army, commanding a company of soldiers. He is thirty-nine years old, divorced, disconsolate, and weary of military life. Ryder feels old and unhappy with the future of England as he sees it embodied in his subordinate officer Hooper, whose lower middle-class education failed to introduce him to romance and chivalry. Ryder's regiment travels by night to a large private estate housing soldiers. The house is Brideshead Castle, a place Ryder knows well.

Book one ("Et in Arcadia Ego") begins with Ryder's memory of meeting Sebastian Flyte, whose family owns Brideshead. Ryder recalls that upon arriving at Oxford, he was a conscientious student who behaved respectably and cautiously, embracing the academic culture despite his inclination toward the arts. While Ryder is aware of Sebastian's reputation for refinement and eccentricity—he carries about a teddy bear named Aloysius—he does not meet him until a very intoxicated Sebastian is sick through the open window of Ryder's ground-floor room. To apologize, Sebastian sends Ryder a roomful of flowers and invites him to lunch.

Ryder admits to being "in search of love in those days" and finds Sebastian "magically beautiful" (*Brideshead Revisited*, 31). He is captivated by Sebastian's luxurious lifestyle and boyish charm. Through Sebastian, Ryder meets other upper-class students, including the hearty "Boy" Mulcaster and the decadent Anthony Blanche. Ryder and Sebastian's romantic friendship dominates the novel's early chapters; however, its possible sexual depth is undeclared.

Ryder first sees Brideshead in 1923 with Sebastian when they visit Sebastian's old nurse, Nanny Hawkins. Ryder is enchanted by the baroque architecture of the extensive country house, although Sebastian avoids spending time there; he shows Ryder only the Art Nouveau chapel. Ryder is perplexed by Sebastian's reticence regarding his family, who, he claims, are so "madly charming" (37) that they would steal Ryder's friendship.

As a result of Sebastian's influence, Ryder drinks more, dresses expensively, and decorates his college rooms extravagantly (one embellishment is a human skull bearing the inscription "Et in Arcadia Ego" [I too am in paradise]). His cousin Jasper, also at Oxford, warns against the unwholesome influence of the

Flyte set, but Ryder continues his intimacy with Sebastian because, he reflects, "to know and love one other human being is the root of all wisdom" (45). Anthony Blanche also warns Ryder that the Flyte family is "sinister" (53), capable of corrupting the developing artist in Ryder with their charm.

As a result of his prodigality, Ryder returns home for the long vacation with neither money nor plans. He is soon rescued from spending time with his irascible father when Sebastian invites him to Brideshead. Although elated to visit with Sebastian, Ryder is also moved by his sister Julia's striking resemblance to him; when near her he catches "a thin bat's squeak of sexuality" (76).

Ryder observes Sebastian's devotion to his Roman Catholic faith, contrasting it with his own agnosticism. Sebastian's religion is with him at all times, and he expresses an unaffected belief in the power of prayer. Ryder learns of the other members of the family: Brideshead (Bridey), the elder son, who had wanted to be a priest; Cordelia, the younger daughter, who is devout in her faith although capable of irony in speaking of it; Lord Marchmain, who left home and never returned; and Lady Marchmain, popularly viewed as a saint.

In September, Sebastian and Ryder visit the Byronic Lord Marchmain and his Italian mistress Cara in Venice. When the two friends return to Oxford, they share a more solitary and fragile companionship, and Sebastian, placed by his mother under the observance of a don, feels trapped and morose. During Ryder's visits at Brideshead, Lady Marchmain attempts to win his confidence and obtain his help in conquering Sebastian's advancing dipsomania. She discusses religion with Ryder, joking that "We must make a Catholic of Charles" (126), and she tries to enchant Ryder with "the Alice-in-Wonderland side of religion" (127). Her charms do not win him over, but Sebastian remains suspicious of her influence.

After an especially extravagant drinking binge, Lady Marchmain removes Sebastian from Oxford. Ryder then leaves Oxford himself, without taking his degree, and studies art in Paris. When Ryder next visits the family, he learns that Sebastian has grown increasingly wily in eluding his guardians; Sebastian appears before the family seriously drunk, and there is an explosion that loses Ryder both Sebastian's friendship and Lady Marchmain's trust. After he leaves Brideshead, Ryder learns that Lady Marchmain is ill and that Julia has married Rex Mottram, a social-climbing Canadian who is not a Roman Catholic.

Ryder now tells Julia's story. From the time of her social debut, Julia's position was unstable: as a Catholic, she could not marry into aristocratic Anglican families, and most of the men in her own social milieu failed to interest her. She found Rex attractive for his maturity and his crass but easy social manner. Discovering that he had another lover, Julia's jealousy moved her to agree to a marriage. In order to marry in the Church, Rex determined to convert to Catholicism, but his efforts proved farcical as he showed no engagement with any articles of faith. When Bridey discovered that Rex was divorced, however, the Catholic wedding was called off, and the couple obtained Lord Marchmain's permission to marry in a Protestant chapel. Later in life, Julia recognizes that Rex was not a complete human being: "he was something absolutely modern . . . that only this ghastly age could produce" (200).

Ryder returns to London in the spring of 1926 to defend conservative interests during the General Strike; while there, he learns that Sebastian now lives in

Tangier with a German friend, Kurt, who deserted the Foreign Legion and now depends on Sebastian. Julia contacts Ryder to inform him that her mother is dying and asks him to bring Sebastian home. When Charles arrives in Morocco, however, he discovers that Sebastian's drinking has so weakened him that he cannot travel.

Upon his return, Ryder is asked by Bridey to paint pictures of Marchmain House; this commission will mark the beginning of Ryder's career as an architectural painter. Lady Marchmain's death induces Cordelia to discuss religion with Ryder. She explains that God keeps the faithful on a thread and that, with a twitch, can call them back; she is confident that God will call back Sebastian and Julia in this way. Cordelia grieves over the closing of the chapel at Brideshead after her mother's funeral. The bishop "blew out the lamp in the sanctuary and left the tabernacle open and empty, as though from now on it was always to be Good Friday" (220).

Book two ("A Twitch Upon the Thread") begins ten years later. Ryder has become a successful architectural painter but has been unhappily married to Celia Mulcaster, with whom he has two children. Ryder and Celia are on the way from New York to England; Julia is traveling on the same ocean liner, and during the journey, they begin an affair. Because of a rough crossing, Celia is laid low with seasickness, leaving Ryder free to spend time with Julia. She tells Ryder of her unhappy marriage with Rex and of the child she lost at birth; she admits to a spiritual crisis, believing that she has been punished for marrying Rex.

Once they land, Ryder remains in London with Julia. They spend the next two years together, some of it at Brideshead with Rex. Although they hope to obtain divorces and marry each other, a disruption comes when Bridey announces that he is to marry a widow of "strict Catholic principle" (285), whom he cannot bring to the house while Julia and Charles are there "living in sin." This pronouncement inspires in Julia an hysterical outburst of spiritual sorrows: "Living in sin, with sin, by sin, for sin, every hour, every day, year in, year out" (287).

The fabric of the family begins to weaken. Cordelia returns from Spain, where she has been a missionary, not having found the religious vocation for which she had hoped; she reports that Sebastian is in the infirmary of a monastery in Carthage, where the monks care for him. Kurt has hanged himself, and now Sebastian alternates between drinking binges and monastic devotion.

Lord Marchmain, now very ill, unexpectedly returns to England, and the family discusses the appropriateness of sending for a priest, given Lord Marchmain's apostasy. Despite Julia's ambivalence and Ryder's opposition, Bridey calls in Father Mackay, but Lord Marchmain responds coldly to him. As her father nears death, however, Julia again reinvites Father Mackay, who anoints Lord Marchmain and asks him to give a sign that he is sorry for his sins. Ryder joins the family in praying for a sign; when Lord Marchmain makes the sign of the cross, Ryder acknowledges that this betokens the return of God into the man's life.

After her father's death, Julia informs Ryder that she cannot continue their relationship: "I can't shut myself out from His mercy. That is what it would mean; starting a life with you, without Him" (340). She explains that she has promised God that she will give up Ryder to prove that she is not a hopeless sinner.

The Epilogue returns to Ryder's war experience. The Quartering Commandant gives Ryder a tour of Brideshead, showing him the estate's decayed condition. Ryder visits Nanny Hawkins, who informs him that Julia and Cordelia are serving as nurses in the Holy Land and that Bridey's regiment is also there. Ryder then visits the chapel, which is brighter and in better condition than any other part of the house. The altar lamp is burning again, and in this Ryder sees hope—a sign of God's presence in the sad and war-torn world.

MAJOR THEMES

Brideshead Revisited is complex in its structure, its characterization, and its use of language. The retrospective structure of the novel, in which Ryder (now converted to Catholicism) wistfully recalls his sybaritic and agnostic youth and young manhood, creates a number of unavoidable ambiguities. Importantly, the narrative never explicitly states that Ryder has converted. We have only clues to suggest this: Hooper referring to the "R. C. church" as "more in your line than mine" (17); Ryder admitting that when he visits the chapel in the Epilogue he utters "a prayer, an ancient, newly learned form of words" (350); and the occasional references to God and spirituality that subtly appear in the remembering narrative voice of the older man. Arguably, it is in the Epilogue that Ryder's conversion is most apparent, but that is the briefest section of the novel, and the languorous descriptions of Ryder's "pagan" youth, especially the episodes shared with Sebastian, have a compelling presence in the narrative, not only for the reader but for Ryder himself. He clearly evokes those memories with a fondness that takes on an almost Wordsworthian dimension: "This is the full account of my first brief visit to Brideshead; could I have known then that so small a thing, in other days, would be remembered with tears by a middle-aged captain of infantry?" (40).

Waugh's own statements about the novel further mystify this ambiguity. In one letter, he describes the novel as "a very beautiful book, to bring tears, about very rich, beautiful high born people who live in palaces and have no troubles except what they make themselves and those are mainly the demons sex and drink which after all are easy to bear as troubles go nowadays" (*The Letters of Evelyn Waugh*, 1980, 180). In another letter, he simply states that "the book is about God" (196). However unhelpful Waugh's own comments, the plot moves toward Ryder's grateful acknowledgment of the presence of God in the world, not only symbolized in the altar lamp burning in the chapel but also manifest in Lord Marchmain's return to God in his dying moments. Waugh recounts a personal experience behind this *dénouement* and claims that he "wrote the book about that [real-life] scene" (206). Waugh was present at his friend Hubert Duggan's death, at which Duggan accepted the presence of a priest and the administration of the Last Rites. Lord Marchmain's sign of the cross repeats Duggan's own actions; Waugh remarks, "we spent the day watching for a spark of gratitude for the love of God and saw the spark" (*The Diaries of Evelyn Waugh*, 1976, 553). Ryder, until then an agnostic, is never the same after this occurrence; like Julia, Sebastian, and Lord Marchmain, he turns to God. Book two concludes with an image that captures the spiritual triumph that is not articulated outright: "The avalanche was down, the hillside swept bare behind it; the last echoes died on the white slopes; the new mound glittered and lay still in the silent valley" (*Brideshead Revisited*, 341).

Lady Marchmain presents another complexity for readers, Waugh himself calling her "an enigma" (*The Letters of Evelyn Waugh*, 1980, 185). While she is one of the most devout characters in the novel, she is seen by many to be the cause of the family's troubles. We watch her subtly engineer the supervision of Sebastian at Oxford, treating him in precisely those ways most likely to alienate his affection and trust. Yet, various aspects of the novel identify her as the spiritual core of the family and perhaps of the novel as well. Lady Marchmain is Catholic by birth; Lord Marchmain converts when he marries her, thereby restoring the ancient Catholic roots of the family. It is she who reads the G. K. Chesterton story that provides the image of the twitch upon the thread, representing God's capacity to call back members of the faithful no matter how far they have strayed. And when she dies, the lamp in the chapel at Brideshead is extinguished, establishing a relationship between her life and God's presence there. In a letter to Nancy Mitford, Waugh explained that while he was not on Lady Marchmain's "side," God is (196). The novel's treatment of her suggests that her role in securing salvation for people is more important than her inability to make them happy on earth: "the keynote of new hope . . . is due not least to her insistent, disturbing, infuriating presence" (Stopp 1958, 111).

Waugh's vision of Catholic redemption is not always a comfortable one, but the value structure of the novel insists that the eventual "twitching back" of Julia, Sebastian, and Lord Marchmain, and the conversion of Ryder, are worth the loss of material and sensual pleasures. Moreover, in a world that is deteriorating socially, politically, and morally, Ryder's progressive loves (Sebastian, then Julia, and then God) signal his transcending of worldly involvements in order to accept God in his life. The urgency of this salvation is established through our immersion in Ryder's mounting cynicism and despair. When the novel opens, he declares that "love had died between me and the army" (*Brideshead Revisited*, 3), but we watch love die (or see evidence of long-dead love) between him and everyone closest to him: Sebastian, Ryder Senior, Celia, his children, and Julia. That Ryder accepts the love of God is indeed miraculous. Like Julia, Ryder finally recognizes that "the worse I am, the more I need God" (340), an epiphany that arguably justifies the suffering that every major character in this novel experiences. Such a view is consistent with Waugh's dictum of Catholic observance: "I am very far from good; therefore I go to Church" ("Converted to Rome," 1983, 105). *Brideshead Revisited* shares this recognition that religion serves its greatest purposes in a fallen world.

CRITICAL RECEPTION

The early reception of *Brideshead Revisited* in the press was decidedly mixed. Writing for *The Spectator*, an enthusiastic V. C. Clinton-Baddeley found Ryder to be "gentle, humorous, civilized, entirely likeable" (Stannard 1984, 237) and alleged that Waugh was "brilliant" to use a non-Catholic narrator. This review saw Julia's conversion (and not Ryder's) as pivotal. Henry Reed (1984), in *The New Statesman*, found fault with Waugh's class snobbery but admired the Oxford scenes; he acknowledged the challenge in writing a book about faith for a "pagan" audience of nonbelievers. John K. Hutchens (1984) in his *New York Times* review praised the novel without reservation, appreciating Waugh's moralism and admiring his ability to write "objectively" about Catholicism. The (London) *Times Literary Supplement*, on the other hand, saw no objectivity in the novel's treatment of religion, faulting Waugh as a "Catholic apologist" (Stannard 1984, 234) with a style that is "cramped by a too obviously preconceived idea" (236). Rose Macaulay, in *Horizon* (Stannard 1984, 253), echoed this: "Love, the English aristocracy, and the Roman Catholic Church, combine to liquefy a style that should be dry" (253); she sees the novel as a "partisan" polemic that fails to see the potential for salvation outside membership in one church.

A more hostile review appeared in *The Nation*; Diana Trilling branded the novel as "incoherent," depicting Catholicism as "a religion for well-placed reprobates" (1946, 19). Trilling read the novel as a condemnation of Lady Marchmain's piety, thereby dismissing any political or economic forces responsible for the decay of the aristocracy. Edmund Wilson's *New Yorker* review (1946) applauded the glamorous early sections of the novel but condemned the novel as a Catholic tract and questioned the authenticity of its religious experiences. Wilson, an admirer of Waugh's earlier fiction, alleged that the anarchy that inspired the early satires is now depicted as sin, which Waugh even fears to represent.

Catholic critics also voiced reservations. Joseph McSorley, in *The Catholic World*, expressed distress that readers unfamiliar with Roman Catholicism would take away a "poisoned" impression: "Resentment will be awakened by his picture of Catholics clinging to outmoded traditions and assenting to unintelligible shibboleths" (1946, 470). And in *The Bell*, Donat O'Donnell cataloged the other "pieties" that mingled with Waugh's Catholic piety: English romanticism, nostalgia for youth, snobbery for the upper classes, and conservative politics. O'Donnell accused Waugh of superimposing a Catholic nomenclature on a private religion and concluded that "so fantastic a mind is hardly qualified to make great contributions to Christian thought" (1952, 134). Waugh was moved to respond to this jeremiad, countering that two worldly characters, Celia and Rex, are not sanctified, and that while he is "happiest in the company of the European upper-classes" (Stannard 1984, 270), Catholicism in England is largely a religion of the poor.

Scholarly analyses often reflect and complicate the issues raised in early reviews. James F. Carens, clearly preferring the satirical novels, nevertheless acknowledges that, for Waugh, Catholicism "dissipates [the] obscurity and ambiguity" (1966, 96) of the modern world. Another enthusiast of the early Waugh, Thomas Churchill (1967), traces how metaphorical language "sanctifies" the novel and indicates the ironies in Bridey's callous stupidity resulting in Julia's salvation. Terry Eagleton (1970) regards the novel as a success but admits that it is puzzling because of its inherent paradoxes: simultaneously criticizing and defending the upper class; presenting the Arcadian past as both a developmental stage devoutly to be transcended and as a "golden time" whose passing is mourned; and creating a tension between morality and style that invites readers to conclude that the Marchmain style (and not their faith) moves Ryder to convert.

A. A. DeVitis's monograph *Roman Holiday: The Catholic Novels of Evelyn Waugh* (1956) establishes many of the critical commonplaces for the consideration of Roman Catholicism in the novel: how the Church offered Waugh meaning in a world of disorder and violence; how the earthly loves of Sebastian and Julia are "forerunners" of Ryder's love of God; and how conversion cannot be explained in words so much as plot. Of further critical interest is the relationship between the spiritual and aesthetic dimensions of the novel. For Millo Shaw (1993), Anthony

Blanche may have an unerring eye for aesthetic and social discriminations but he is unable to lead Ryder to spiritual fulfillment; art cannot bring a person to salvation, only religion can, and Lord Marchmain accomplishes that guidance. Other critics do not polarize religion and art so absolutely. Ulf Shönberg (1990) argues that architecture mirrors spiritual development; he reads Brideshead itself as a representation of the Roman Catholic Church. Rodney Delasanta and Mario D'Avanzo propose that Waugh, like Keats in the "Ode on a Grecian Urn," yokes the apprehensions of truth and beauty. Ryder's pursuit of art leads directly to his embrace of religion, and the Flyte family are "vicars of Christ" (1965, 149), bringing Ryder to God. The coherence of the novel is also apparent to Frederick Beaty (1992), who sees the tension between material and spiritual values reflected in the double narrative (past Charles and present Charles); for Beaty, the novel is a *Künstlerroman* framed in a religious matrix, and the narrative shifts from irony and chaos to divine order and control.

Resistant readings also appear in scholarly literature. Robert Garnett reduces *Brideshead Revisited* to a fantasy of aristocratic pleasures with which Catholicism has been amalgamated. In his view, the castle is merely a retreat from the modern world and Catholicism is appealing for its "theatrical Pre-Raphaelite" style (1990, 162). For Valerie Kennedy (1990) the lost paradise of childhood is more compelling for Ryder and the reader than the paradise of religious faith that is gained through Ryder's conversion. Frank Kermode argues that the novel equates aristocratic and Catholic traditions; he distrusts a "reasonable religion" that, for Waugh, "has nothing to do with making or keeping people in the ordinary sense happy" (1962, 172).

Frederick Stopp, in *Evelyn Waugh: Portrait of an Artist*, asserts that Waugh's "presumption" in the novel is literary and not theological: "The spiritual theme is, indeed, simple" (1958, 109), and Ryder's narration of his conversion, suspended between past and future, presents the novelist's greater challenge. Other critics are similarly engaged with the narration's complexity. Laura Mooneyham (1993) and Charles Hallett (1994) share the view that the narrative structure allows readers to apprehend (and accept) the emergence of grace just as Ryder himself does. For David Rothstein (1993), the novel is preoccupied with preserving Catholic memory: Ryder must "get inside" Brideshead because it is a shrine to the Catholic past; as he merges his personal story with the Flyte family story, Ryder is searching for a meaningful existence. Joseph Hynes (1987) explores how the reader follows the narrator's experience of believing that events are moving in one direction only to be surprised by the interventions of providence. Hynes argues that for readers to understand this novel, they must grant Waugh his *donnée*: that salvation is a lifelong struggle.

The *Evelyn Waugh Newsletter* devoted several short articles to narrowly focused issues. John Osborne's "The Character of Bridey" (1993) examines how Bridey represents the dogmatic and formal dimensions of Roman Catholic faith and how his orthodoxy is characterized by a certainty that is often insensitive to others. Osborne's "The Character of Lord Marchmain" (1993) argues that the patriarch's retention of Brideshead demonstrates the covert pull that religious faith retains over his life. Charles Hutton-Brown's "Sebastian as Saint: The Hagiographical Sources of Sebastian Flyte" (1977) teases out the significance of naming Sebastian's teddy bear after Saint Aloysius while also asserting that the sacrifices made by the Flyte children are forms of martyrdom that will lead to the attainment of grace.

In "Remembrance of Things Past: Proustian Elements in Evelyn Waugh's *Brideshead Revisited*," Richard G. Hodgson (1984) argues that, unlike Proust, Waugh understands religion, not art, to be the solution to the problems of modern life. David G. Brailow's "'My Theme is Memory': The Narrative Structure of *Brideshead Revisited*" (1980) explores how the narrative makes apparent the workings of grace so that readers can glimpse a pattern beyond human events. From 1988 to 1990, John W. Osborne (1988, 1989, 1990), Donald Greene (1988, 1989), and John W. Mahon (1989) engaged in a lively *Evelyn Waugh Newsletter* dialogue on the legitimacy of various "clues" in the novel that indicate Ryder's conversion to Roman Catholicism.

Recent criticism often focuses on the immensely popular 1980 Granada television adaptation of the novel. Fred Inglis admires it but finds the theological message irrelevant: "Renunciation of earthly happiness in order to do one's duty to Catholic precepts, themselves a direct apprehension of the presence of God, is almost disappeared from English culture, even among Catholics" (2000, 193). Kingsley Amis's review of the adaptation, "How I Lived in a Very Big House and Found God" (1981), declares that Catholics should be offended by Waugh's slippage from glamour to moral significance.

The success of the adaptation has also resulted in reappraisals of the novel itself. Evelyn Toynton (1998) denounces the book's Catholicism because, she claims, it has no moral content: it is all ritual and mystery with no implications for human relationships. For Frederic Raphael (1995), the novel depicts spiritual "social climbing": only in heaven will Ryder (or Waugh) share the same status that aristocratic Catholics enjoy. Edward Pearce's dismissive "Brideshead Resisted" stimulated defenses of the novel in *Quadrant*. Pearce excoriates the novel as an expression of triumphalist Catholicism, celebrating both class snobbery and "clerico-fascism" (1982, 60). Simon Leys (1982) counters that the novel's religious dimension is so central to its meaning that any critic who ignores it is deaf to the book's purpose; and Ruth Wilson explains that Waugh charitably demonstrates that through pain and suffering even weak and flawed characters (such as Lady Marchmain) can "pass through the eye of the needle to the Kingdom of Heaven" (1982, 65). Douglas Lane Patey's *Life of Evelyn Waugh* traces Waugh's search for a "ground of meaning and value" (1998, xviii) in a bleak and damaged world. Patey explores how Ryder, ascending through hierarchies of love and kinds of beauty, ultimately finds redemption.

NOTE

Evelyn Waugh, *Brideshead Revisited: The Sacred and Profane Memories of Captain Charles Ryder* (Boston: Little, Brown, 1973). All references are to this edition.

WORKS CITED

Amis, Kingsley. 1981. "How I Lived in a Very Big House and Found God." *Times Literary Supplement* (London) (November 20): 1352.

Beaty, Frederick L. 1992. *The Ironic World of Evelyn Waugh*. DeKalb: Northern Illinois University Press.

Brailow, David G. 1980. "'My Theme is Memory': The Narrative Structure of *Brideshead Revisited*." *Evelyn Waugh Newsletter* 14, no. 3: 1–4.

Carens, James F. 1966. *The Satiric Art of Evelyn Waugh*. Seattle: University of Washington Press.

Churchill, Thomas. 1967. "The Trouble with *Brideshead Revisited*." *Modern Language Quarterly* 28: 213–28.

Delasanta, Rodney, and Mario L. D'Avanzo. 1965. "Truth and Beauty in *Brideshead Revisited*." *Modern Fiction Studies* 11: 140–52.

DeVitis, A. A. 1956. *Roman Holiday: The Catholic Novels of Evelyn Waugh*. New York: Bookman.

Eagleton, Terry. 1970. *Exiles and Émigrés: Studies in Modern Literature*. New York: Schocken.

Garnett, Robert R. 1990. *From Grimes to Brideshead: The Early Novels of Evelyn Waugh*. Lewisburg, PA: Bucknell University Press.

Greene, Donald. 1988. "Charles Ryder's Conversion?" *Evelyn Waugh Newsletter* 22, no. 3: 5–7.

———. 1989. "More on Charles Ryder's Conversion." *Evelyn Waugh Newsletter* 23, no. 3: 1–3.

Hallett, Charles. 1994. "A Twitch upon the Thread." *New Oxford Review* 61, no. 9: 19–22.

Hodgson, Richard G. 1984. "Remembrance of Things Past: Proustian Elements in Evelyn Waugh's *Brideshead Revisited*." *Evelyn Waugh Newsletter* 18, no. 3: 1–5.

Hutchens, John. 1984. Review of *Brideshead Revisited*, by Evelyn Waugh. In *Evelyn Waugh: The Critical Heritage*, ed. Martin Stannard, 241–45. London: Routledge.

Hutton-Brown, Charles. 1977. "Sebastian as Saint: The Hagiographical Sources of Sebastian Flyte." *Evelyn Waugh Newsletter* 11, no. 3: 1–7.

Hynes, Joseph. 1987. "Two Affairs Revisited." *Twentieth-Century Literature* 33: 234–53.

Inglis, Fred. 2000. "*Brideshead Revisited* Revisited: Waugh to the Knife." In *The Classic Novel: From Page to Screen*, ed. Robert Giddings and Erica Sheen, 179–96. Manchester: Manchester University Press.

Kennedy, Valerie. 1990. "Evelyn Waugh's *Brideshead Revisited*: Paradise Lost or Paradise Regained?" *Ariel* 12: 23–39.

Kermode, Frank. 1962. "Mr. Waugh's Cities." In *Puzzles and Epiphanies: Essays and Reviews 1958–1961*, 164–75. New York: Chilmark.

Leys, Simon. 1982. "Brideshead Reconsidered, I." *Quadrant* 26, no. 9: 61–62.

Macauley, Rose. Review of *Brideshead Revisited* by Evelyn Waugh. In *Evelyn Waugh: The Critical Heritage*, ed. Martin Stannard, 253–55. London: Routledge, 1984.

Mahon, John W. 1989. "Charles Ryder's Catholicism." *Evelyn Waugh Newsletter* 23, no. 1: 5–7.

McSorley, Joseph. 1946. Review of *Brideshead Revisited*, by Evelyn Waugh. *Catholic World* 162: 469–70.

Mooneyham, Laura. 1993. "The Triple Conversions of *Brideshead Revisited*." *Renascence* 45: 225–36.

O'Donnell, Donat [Conor Cruise O'Brien]. 1952. "The Pieties of Evelyn Waugh." In *Maria Cross: Imaginative Patterns in a Group of Modern Catholic Writers*, 119–34. New York: Oxford University Press.

Osborne, John. 1988. "Hints of Charles Ryder's Conversion in *Brideshead Revisited*." *Evelyn Waugh Newsletter* 22, no. 3: 4–5.

———. 1989. "A Reply to Donald Greene about Charles Ryder's Conversion." *Evelyn Waugh Newsletter* 23, no. 1: 3–5.

———. 1990. "Charles Ryder's Conversion Revisited." *Evelyn Waugh Newsletter* 24, no. 2: 3–4.

———. 1993. "The Character of Bridey." *Evelyn Waugh Newsletter* 27, no. 2: 7–8.

———. 1993. "The Character of Lord Marchmain." *Evelyn Waugh Newsletter* 27, no. 3: 5–6.

Patey, Douglas Lane. 1998. *The Life of Evelyn Waugh: A Critical Biography*. Oxford: Blackwell.

Pearce, Edward. 1982. "Brideshead Resisted." *Quadrant* 26, no. 7: 59–61.

Raphael, Frederic. 1995. "Revisiting Brideshead: A Re-Introduction." *Poetry Nation Review* 21, no. 4: 29–31.

Reed, Henry. 1984. Review of *Brideshead Revisited*, by Evelyn Waugh. In *Evelyn Waugh: The Critical Heritage*, ed. Martin Stannard, 239–41. London: Routledge.

Rothstein, David. 1993. "*Brideshead Revisited* and the Modern Historicization of Memory." *Studies in the Novel* 25: 318–31.

Shaw, Millo L. G. 1993. "Anthony Blanche and Tiresias." *Classical and Modern Literature* 13: 337–51.

Shönberg, Ulf. 1990. "Architecture and Environment in Evelyn Waugh's *Brideshead Revisited*." *Orbis Litterarum* 45: 84–95.

Stannard, Martin, ed. 1984. *Evelyn Waugh: The Critical Heritage*. London: Routledge.

———. 1986. *Evelyn Waugh: The Early Years 1903–1939*. New York: Norton.

———. 1992. *Evelyn Waugh: The Later Years 1939–1966*. New York: Norton.

Stopp, Frederick J. 1958. *Evelyn Waugh: Portrait of an Artist*. Boston: Little, Brown.

Sykes, Christopher. 1975. *Evelyn Waugh: A Biography*. Boston: Little, Brown.

Toynton, Evelyn. 1998. "Revisiting *Brideshead*." *American Scholar* 67, no. 4: 134–37.

Trilling, Diana. 1946. "The Piety of Evelyn Waugh." *The Nation* (January 5): 19–20.

Waugh, Evelyn. 1946. "Fan-Fare." *Life* (April 8): 53–60.

———. 1964. *A Little Learning*. Boston: Little, Brown.

———. 1976. *The Diaries of Evelyn Waugh*, ed. Michael Davie. Boston: Little, Brown.

———. 1980. *The Letters of Evelyn Waugh*, ed. Mark Amory. New Haven, CT: Ticknor.

———. 1983. "Come Inside." In *The Essays, Articles and Reviews of Evelyn Waugh*, ed. Donat Gallagher, 366–68. London: Methuen.

———. 1983. "Converted to Rome: Why it Has Happened to Me." In *The Essays, Articles and Reviews of Evelyn Waugh*, ed. Donat Gallagher, 103–05. London: Methuen.

Wilson, Edmund. 1946. "Splendors and Miseries of Evelyn Waugh." *New Yorker* (January 5): 71–74.

Wilson, Ruth. 1982. "Brideshead Reconsidered, II." *Quadrant* 26, no. 9: 63–65.

— **Paul M. Puccio**

Evelyn Waugh [1903–1966]

Sword of Honor

PLOT SUMMARY

Sword of Honor is the title of Evelyn Waugh's 1965 one-volume recension of three novels of the Second World War: *Men at Arms* (1952), *Officers and Gentlemen* (1955), and *The End of the Battle* (1962; titled *Unconditional Surrender* in Great Britain). Waugh also reissued the three novels separately in 1964; they are known collectively as the "war trilogy." The author's changes in the one-volume work are minimal. As Waugh notes in the preface to *Sword of Honor*, he limited himself mostly to excising the redundancies that serial publication demanded, correcting discrepancies and removing passages that he found tedious on rereading. Because the changes are so minor and because the separate titles are currently more readily available than the one-volume work, this commentary, while treating the trilogy as a unified whole, refers unless otherwise noted to the texts of the individual novels.

Waugh called *Sword of Honor* an attempt to "give a description of the Second World War as it was seen and experienced by a single, uncharacteristic Englishman" (*Sword of Honor*, 9). Guy Crouchback is the last heir of an ancient English Catholic family. He is thirty-five years old, divorced, and living in self-imposed exile at the family villa in Santa Dulcina, Italy, when news of the Russian-German treaty reaches him in August 1939, prompting him to seek a commission in the army.

Guy's father, Mr. Gervase Crouchback, is the humble keeper of the family's proud recusant tradition (uninterrupted in succession from the time of Henry II). Having leased the family estate at Broome to a convent, he lives happily if in reduced circumstances at the Mariner Hotel in Matchet, Somerset. Guy's oldest sibling, Angela, is married to a Protestant, a conservative member of Parliament (and all-around bore) named Arthur Box-Bender. Their son, Tony, is fighting in France. (Tony will be captured at Calais and will spend the entire war as a prisoner.) Two elder brothers, Gervase and Ivo, have died young. Gervase was killed in France in World War I; Ivo died mad, starving himself to death in 1931 at age twenty-six. Uncle Peregrine, Mr. Crouchback's brother, a stuffy but harmless old bachelor with a penchant for heraldry, family history, and bibelots, is Guy's only other living relative.

Also in 1931, Guy's wife Virginia suddenly left Kenya, where the couple had been living during the year since their marriage. By 1939, Virginia is twice divorced (from Guy and from Tommy Blackhouse) and is married to an American named Troy. Mrs. Virginia Troy has recently returned to England without her husband, anticipating the "fun" of wartime London. Guy occasionally sees Captain Tommy Blackhouse at Bellamy's, his London club, the major setting for Waugh's London satire throughout the trilogy. Another Bellamy's member is Lord Ian Kilbannock, a sporting journalist who has gotten himself an air force commission as liaison to the American press. Kilbannock's wife, Kerstie, is Virginia's close friend.

The bulk of *Men at Arms* deals with Guy's training period as a temporary officer in the Royal Corps of Halberdiers from November 1939 to August 1940. Guy's age places him in the position of "uncle" to most of the other recruits. Frank de Souza, literate and wisecracking, is a leftist Cambridge man. The cockney Trimmer is something of a mystery and the only fellow Halberdier whom Guy "definitely dislike[s]" (*Men at Arms*, 55). He will be dismissed from the Halberdiers before the end of training. The corps brigadier is the wildly eccentric Ben Ritchie-Hook, a one-eyed, oft-wounded, oft-decorated, and oft-reprimanded soldier's soldier with a penchant for "biffing" the enemy at all costs.

Guy's bizarre relationship with his fellow "uncle" Apthorpe, an absurdly pompous figure obsessed with his horde of gear and competitive to the point of paranoia, provides Waugh with a major plot device of *Men at Arms*. Apthorpe rises steadily to a captaincy despite signs of alcoholism and mental instability. (In one extended episode Apthorpe engages in clandestine warfare with Ritchie-Hook over the use of Apthorpe's "Thunder-box," a field toilet that is among his most precious possessions.) Meanwhile, Guy struggles to play what he thinks is the soldier's role, doing a creditable job in his official duties but ending up as only a lieutenant and a platoon commander while Captain Apthorpe is given command of a company.

Men at Arms ends with the abortive mission to Dakar in August 1940 and with Apthorpe dead from the effects of tropical disease, hastened, in the opinion of his doctor, by a bottle of whiskey that Guy had supplied. (Guy is unrepentant.) At Dakar, Guy had participated at the urging of Ritchie-Hook in an unauthorized reconnaissance mission, and at the end of the novel, Guy and Ritchie-Hook are on their way back to England to face an inquiry. (Only the intervention of the Prime Minister himself on behalf of Ritchie-Hook will allow Guy to escape the consequence of having "blotted his copy book" [320].)

The second novel in the trilogy, *Officers and Gentlemen*, takes Guy's story forward to the days just after the German invasion of Russia in June 1941. Guy is assigned to Tommy Blackhouse's "X Commando" and reports to a remote Scottish island—the Isle of Mugg—for training. There he settles in among the local pro-Fascist Jacobites, new acquaintances (notably Ivor Claire, a young aristocrat whom Guy will come for a time to admire as "the fine flower of them all" [*Officers and Gentlemen*, 151]), and old (the odious Trimmer has resurfaced as "McTavish," wearing the kilt of a highland regiment). Later in the novel, Trimmer will have a brief affair with an increasingly dispirited Virginia in Glasgow, at which time we learn that Virginia had known Trimmer as "Gustave," the hairdresser aboard the *Aquitania*. Trimmer also plays the main role in a key subplot, becoming a certified "war hero" through his bumbling part in Operation Popgun, a cynical publicity stunt cooked up by Ian Kilbannock to boost the morale of "the People." When Trimmer falls in love with Virginia, Ian convinces her (cut off by her husband, she is dependent on the Kilbannocks' hospitality) to accompany the smitten hero on his publicity tours.

Guy travels with X Commando to Africa and eventually to Crete, where the hellish confusion of that ill-fated episode in British military history is depicted in stark and sometimes hallucinatory detail. The battle's nightmarish quality is rendered in large part through Waugh's depiction of the descent of Major ("Fido") Hound from officious functionary to groveling appetitious straggler. Intimately connected with Hound's demise is the outlandish character Corporal-Major Ludovic, Ivor Claire's Corporal of Horse, a man with a checkered past and literary pretensions who keeps a diary of "*Pensees*." When Hound is missing after the battle, we are to suppose that he was killed by Ludovic. Ludovic also apparently killed a second man, a "sapper" who disappeared from the small fishing boat on which Ludovic (and Guy, among others) made their perilous escape from the beach of Sphakia after the order to surrender was issued on May 31.

Back in Alexandria recovering from his ordeal at sea, Guy learns that Ivor Claire, whom Guy had assumed had followed orders and surrendered with his troops, deserted his men at Crete. When Julia Stitch, Ivor's powerful protectress, presses Guy about his memory of events, Guy realizes that his notebook contains evidence that Ivor knowingly disobeyed the surrender order. Julia intervenes with her politically connected husband to have Guy shipped out to England.

The final novel of the trilogy, *The End of the Battle*, follows Guy from his return to England in the autumn of 1941 through the end of the war. The development of Ludovic's character occupies a considerable portion of the novel. Ludovic, as a young man, had a homosexual relationship with Sir Ralph Brompton, a former ambassador and civilian advisor to the military who functions as a symbol of and mouthpiece for fashionable left-wing political opinion. Sir Ralph is now helping Ludovic break into fashionable literary circles, represented by Sir Everard Spruce (generally regarded as based on Cyril Connolly) and his avant-garde journal *Survival*. As Ludovic becomes increasingly mad (in part because he thinks, mistakenly, that Guy knows his homicidal secrets), his literary work, *The Death Wish*, grows and grows. It will eventually become a best-seller.

Guy spends two years after Crete with his career on hold. He is held back in part by his age, in part because of his exploits in Africa, and in part by the work of one Grace-Groundling-Marchpole, a conspiracy-mad junior counterespionage officer whose "Most Secret" file on Guy weaves a series of coincidences into evidence of pro-Fascist activity. It is only when he is picked by the "Electronic Personnel Selector" as uniquely qualified for work in Croatia that Guy escapes from the bureaucratic limbo of the London Transit Camp. While awaiting posting to a parachute school run by Ludovic (where he will unwittingly—and hilariously—force the guilt-ridden commandant into ever more insane attempts to evade him), Guy receives news of the death of his father. Attending the Requiem Mass at Broome, Guy learns that his father's financial retrenchment had been more successful than anyone had imagined; he has been left with a comfortable inheritance.

Meanwhile, Virginia has been divorced by her American husband and finds herself pregnant by Trimmer. After unsuccessful attempts to procure an abortion, Virginia sets her sights on Guy, who is staying with Peregrine in London while recuperating from a leg injury sustained on his first parachute jump. Guy, to the bewilderment of all, agrees to remarry Virginia and to raise "little Trimmer" as his own.

The major movement of the final section of the novel deals with Guy's sojourn in Croatia as part of the British liaison to the Yugoslavian partisans and especially with his attempts to do what he can for a group of Jewish "displaced persons." In Croatia, Guy witnesses the death of Ben Ritchie-Hook, who is shot while forging ahead single-handedly during an aborted attack staged for the purpose of demonstrating the zeal of the partisans to Allied commanders. The ironic linkage between Ritchie-Hook's sacrifice and Trimmer's Operation Popgun is made explicit by Ian Kilbannock: both events will figure in the press as "classic stories of heroism" (*End of the Battle*, 294). Also while in Croatia, Guy receives news of the deaths of Virginia and Peregrine, killed by a German drone. Virginia, who had converted to Catholicism, had never warmed to "little Trimmer" (baptized Gervase). But she did have the foresight to get the child out of London and into the safekeeping of her sister-in-law, Angela. After Virginia's death, the child is taken off Angela's hands by Eloise Plessington, a member of a prominent Catholic family and childhood friend to Angela. Eloise thinks of the child in part as a diversion for her daughter Domenica, who, having tried the convent and failed, has been showing an alarming aptitude for farming.

In the Epilogue, set at a 1951 reunion of the Commando at Bellamy's, we learn that Ivor Claire finished the war fighting with the Chindits in Burma, earning a medal and an "honourably incapacitating wound" (316). Trimmer has disappeared. Ludovic has bought the Crouchbacks' *castello* in Santa Dulcina with the proceeds of his novel. Tony Box-Bender has entered a monastery, much to his father's embarrassment. Guy has married Domenica Plessington and has settled at Broome. They have no children besides Gervase.

MAJOR THEMES

"The failure of modern novelists," wrote Waugh in 1946, "is one of presumption and exorbitance":

> They are not content with the artificial figures which hitherto passed so gracefully as men and women. They try to represent the whole human mind and soul and yet omit its defining character—that of being God's creature with a defined purpose. So in my future books there will be two things to make them unpopular: a preoccupation with style and the attempt to represent man more fully, which, to me, means only one thing, man in his relation to God. (*The Essays, Articles, and Reviews*, 1984, 302)

Guy Crouchback, as his unprepossessing name suggests, is a decidedly unpresumptuous character. He is as orthodox and observant a Catholic as one is likely to meet in a twentieth-century novel, at least in one not overtly apologetic or proselytizing. Indeed, he is what Waugh called an uncharacteristic Englishman primarily in that he regularly and without irony attends to his relation to God through the ancient forms and teachings of the Catholic Church.

Guy, like his author, would be much more comfortable talking about his soul than his psyche. Like his author, he is a firm believer in the ultimate reality of the supernatural: "Do you agree," he asks an army chaplain, "that the Supernatural Order is not something added to the Natural Order, [that] it *is* everyday life . . . [that] the supernatural is real?" (*Men at Arms*, 99). As unexceptionally formulated and naively unfashionable as Guy's metaphysic is ("Up to a point," answers the wary modern clergyman), it nevertheless underwrites the art of the novel. Waugh's "realism" is grounded throughout in an entirely orthodox view of creation and creatures as, rightly apprehended, charged with supernatural meaning. In another throwaway line that clearly identifies Guy with his author, Guy attributes his somewhat aloof, melancholy sense of humor to an habitual tendency to see the created world *"sub specie aeternitatis"* (under the aspect of eternity) and therefore to see it justly (*Officers and Gentlemen*, 112). Throughout the trilogy, the rituals and sacraments of the Church provide the means for investing the everyday with a significance that points beyond itself. It is on Ash Wednesday, for example, that Guy, still bearing the ash on his forehead, feels himself implicated in "universal guilt" after the brigade receives a dressing down from Brigadier Ben Ritchie-Hook (*Men at Arms*, 155). In many passages, Guy finds material reminders of the spiritual incongruously thrust forth in the least promising places. When he comes across a group of "progressive novelists in fireman's uniform . . . squirting a little jet of water" on the embers of a London club bombed during the blitz, for example, Guy suddenly remembers Holy Saturday services at Downside Abbey and the priest "paradoxically blessing fire with water" (*Officers and Gentlemen*, 4).

Guy habitually marks the passage of time with reference to the liturgical year. He attends Mass regularly and does his best to perform corporal works of mercy. Above all, he is firmly convinced, as was his author, that his "defined purpose" as a creature of God is perfectly well set out in the catechism: he is to know, love, and serve God in this world in order to be happy with him in the next. Neither the "what" nor the "why" of his existence gives him much trouble. The whole question is one of "how": how to discern and live out his vocation, how to be what he was meant to be. It is a question of what form his life should and will take.

In a 1948 review of Graham Greene's *The Heart of the Matter*, Waugh claims that in an age dominated in the public realm by sociology, the spirit of the true artist has turned definitively to eschatology: while "politicians and journalists and popular preachers exhort him to sing the splendours of high wages and sanitation . . . [h]is eyes are on the Four Last Things, and so mountainous are the disappointments of recent history that there are already signs of a popular breakaway to join him" (*The Essays, Articles, and Reviews*, 1984, 360). Guy's religious seriousness saturates the trilogy with an eschatological consciousness. Waugh's narrative derives much of its energy from its protagonist's (and author's) urgent concern, in a time of crisis, to redeem the time—to discern the shape of a meaningful plot within the contingent circumstance of a profoundly disappointing present. For Waugh, as for Frank Kermode, the modern novel is quintessentially a genre in search of a "sense of an ending" and novelists are people bent on discovering in the midst of present confusions the end according to which the beginning and ending of a life (or an epoch) may be brought into "consonance" and thereby "charged with significance" (2000, 46–47). The serious comedy of Waugh's trilogy is generated in large part by Guy's paradoxically wandering progress toward his proper end, a progress through which his true character will emerge parallel with his (and our) ability to discern that end.

As the trilogy begins, Guy is thirty-five years old. Until very recently he has been wandering in the very middle of the dark wood of his disappointments. He has been living for eight years in a physically lovely spot (the Castello Crouchbach in Santa Dulcina, Italy) that belies his inward spiritual wasteland. (Eliot's poem functions allusively throughout *Sword of Honor*.) His failed marriage to Virginia suggests that he misheard that particular call. His disengaged, dispirited response to European political movements, including the rise of the Fascists in Italy, is a common one among conservative Catholics of his generation, for whom the ceding of political power by the Vatican ensured a brutalization of political life and fostered repression under the guise of reform. What does one expect with the pope a virtual prisoner in the Vatican? Guy, living in a kind of self-imposed exile from country and family, is not even much connected with the people of Santa Dulcina. They respect him, but they do not find him *simpatico*. He is conscious of there being "no sympathy between himself and his fellow man" (*Men at Arms*, 14). He even chooses not to go to communion on Sundays with the townspeople, preferring instead to slip into the church on weekdays, when he knows it will be virtually empty.

The initiating event of the plot is Guy's learning, on August 30, 1939, of the alliance between Russia and Germany, sealed in a treaty signed one week before. Guy responds to the news with an explicitly apocalyptic joy, understanding it as a brilliant clarification of the moral order. The invisible evil that has been lurking since the end of the last war steps forth into the light: "[T]he enemy was plain in view, huge and hateful, all disguise cast off" (8). Guy welcomes this unholy union of Fascist and Communist as a sure sign of the commencement of the great battle under two clear standards: Christendom versus the modern atheistic nation state, European culture versus the dehumanizing barbarity of modernity, good versus evil, Christ versus anti-Christ. "It was the Modern Age in arms. Whatever the outcome, there was a place for him in that battle" (8).

Guy enters the war much as Waugh did, as what Martin Stannard calls a "Catholic crusader, aching for adventure and honourable service" (1994, xix) and seeing in England's resistance to Axis powers the last, best hope of Christendom. Before leaving Italy to take up his role in the great fight, Guy visits the tomb of Sir Roger of Waybroke, an English knight known locally as "il Santo Inglese." As he runs his finger along the blade of Sir Roger's sword, Guy prays both for his personal crusade and for "our endangered kingdom" (9). In his zeal, Guy overlooks the symbolic significance of the knight's story. Sir Roger was on his way to Jerusalem during the Second Crusade when he was shipwrecked in Italy. He entered into the service of a local count who promised to assist him on his quest, but he died in that service before he could continue on his way. The sword of honor thus belongs not to a hero of temporal Christendom but to a "man with a great journey still all before him and a great vow unfulfilled" (9). Sir Roger failed in his quest to liberate the Holy Land, perishing instead in some historically insignificant skirmish, probably more a matter of turf or wealth or pride than justice. Nevertheless, Sir Roger is a local "saint," one recognized, even if only within the small world of Santa Dulcina, as having achieved holiness, as having been in the end what he was meant to be. If Guy had been able in 1939 to muse on Sir Roger's peripeteia, he could have read his own future and saved himself from four years of a sort of spiritual tilting at windmills—playing soldier, shuffling from place to place under bureaucratic directives, taking part in some of the more feckless and ignoble operations of the war (at Dakar and Crete). But saving himself, of course, is precisely what Guy must learn (or remember, or learn in his bones) he cannot do. The road to sainthood, Waugh's narrative insists, runs through disillusionment and, crucially, loss of self.

Guy's peripeteia, in its simplest terms, involves a transformation of his model of the Christian, one that arguably marks a similar transformation in Waugh's own thinking and belief during the war years and into the 1950s. In what is probably his earliest public comment on the work, Waugh let slip a reference to what Stannard calls the "grand theme" of *Sword of Honor* when he told an American reporter in 1949 that he wanted to write a World War II novel that would be "about the idea of chivalry" (Stannard 1994, 240). Through most of the course of the first two novels, Guy's view of himself as a Christian knight remains intact, even as he comes gradually to recognize his own limitations and those of his country's leaders. During the long period of training that dominates *Men at Arms*, Guy finds that his age limits him and keeps him at a distance from the men. On the one occasion on which he does enter fully into the camaraderie of the barracks, he wrenches his knee and ends up walking with a cane. His failing eyesight leads both to embarrassment on the rifle range and to his acquiring a monocle that he later will regard with disgust as part of a "disguise." The grinding boredom involved in the long waits between false alarms to battle takes its toll on his patience. Being bested by the clownish Apthorpe is a further source of mortification.

Perhaps most humiliating of all is Guy's disastrous attempt to seduce Virginia. Having gotten the idea that a liaison with her would involve no sin because they are still married in the eyes of the Church, Guy rushes off to London in the full flush of lustful bravado only to meet a stern (and hilarious) rebuke from Virginia: "You wet, smug, obscene, pompous, sexless lunatic pig" (*Men at Arms*, 178). Nevertheless, through it all Guy continues to imagine himself in the image of Sir Roger and other models of chivalry. In passages in *Men at Arms* that were cut from *Sword of Honor*, Waugh perhaps overemphasizes Guy's romantic illusions by having him indulge in daydreams that place him in the role of a character from his boyhood reading, an Edwardian avatar of the medieval knight called "Captain Truslove." Even after the Dakar expedition, during which Guy "distinguishes" himself by leading a reckless and useless reconnaissance raid and after which he is shipped back to England under a cloud of suspicion in the death of Apthorpe, Guy regards his progress as essentially uninterrupted. As *Officers and Gentlemen* begins, Guy imagines his attempts to carry out a charge laid on him by the dying Apthorpe as "an act of *pietas*" and "the beginning of the second stage of his pilgrimage, which had begun at the tomb of Sir Roger" (*Officers and Gentlemen*, 20).

All that will change by the end of the second novel. Guy's conversion to a sadder, wiser, and decidedly less heroic understanding of Christian witness comes in two stages. *Officers and Gentlemen* is a book of bitter disillusionment, *The End of the Battle* a tale of penitential acceptance of a new way of living in the midst of disillusionment and uncertainty.

In *Officers and Gentlemen*, Waugh's focus shifts noticeably from Guy's personal quest to the larger scene. The narrative voice, which is almost exclusively keyed to Guy's consciousness in *Men at Arms*, floats much more freely among characters and points of view in the second novel. The shift is perhaps most notable in the brilliant use of the disintegrating consciousness of Fido Hound as one of several points of view in the portrayal of the debacle at Crete. Other important instances are the long sections devoted to Guy's father, Mr. Crouchback's, life at Matchet (especially his ordeal with the opportunistic proprietors of his hotel) and to Operation Popgun, the ludicrous mission that inflates Trimmer (thanks to Ian Kilbannock's journalistic inflation) into a hero of the "People's War" (allowing Waugh to express his disgust at what he regarded as the larger scale opportunism of left-leaning political elites and their sympathizers in the press). The technique allows Waugh to move Guy off center, to shrink him a bit in relation to the landscape of a political and social scene that is becoming increasingly incapable of assimilation to Guy's romantic outlook.

In the episode dealing with Mr. Crouchback's response to the Cuthberts, Waugh begins to develop Guy's amiable father both as a foil to Guy and as an important agent of his son's conversion. Mr. Crouchback's tale has been one of ever-diminishing worldly status, but he lives patiently with his dog in his two rooms at the Mariner Hotel. When his landlords try to capitalize on the local housing pinch by depriving him of his sitting room, Mr. Crouchback responds with amazing equanimity. He readily cedes this last vestige of worldly respect, citing the needs of those deprived and displaced by the war as having the greater claim: "it's rather selfish keeping both my rooms at a time like this" (44). The Cuthberts' amazed and suspicious response makes Waugh's point: "he's a deep one," says Mr. Cuthbert, "[s]omehow his mind seems to work different than yours and mine" (45). The difference, of course, is the Gospel, the deep source from which Mr. Crouchback's selflessness flows: "He who has two cloaks, let him share with him who has none" (Luke 3:10). In the eyes of the materialist Cuthberts, such a man is too good to be true.

This theme of the displaced person and of the personal obligation of the Christian to those who exist on the fringes of the community—the alien, widow, and orphan of Deuteronomy—will become central to Guy's experience in *The End of the Battle*, especially in his relation to Virginia and in his response to the plight of the Jews in Croatia. For now, Waugh foreshadows the emergence of a new spiritual economy in his portrayal of Mr. Crouchback's small, almost invisible act of faith.

The "bloody mess" of Crete and its aftermath is disillusioning for Guy for a number of reasons. Waugh's vivid descriptions in *Officers and Gentlemen* of the chaos of battle are justly admired as the very antithesis of the jingoistic depictions of the boy's books that Guy seems to have carried with him into adulthood. In this surreal world, good guys and bad guys look alike and nobody seems to know the purpose of the fight. One scene in particular marks the distance between the Guy of 1939 and the Guy who leaves Crete in 1941 on a leaky boat with a one-in-ten chance of survival. During the course of his wandering retreat, Guy descends from a mountain, the view from the top of which reminds him of his prewar vantage point at Santa Dulcina. As he enters the village at the mountain's foot, he comes upon a young English soldier lying dead on a stretcher and watched over by two village girls. The boy's body reminds him of an effigy, which in turn recalls Sir Roger. Standing there with the two girls, silent and helpless together before the mystery of the body, Sir Roger's image superimposed on the image of the dead boy, Guy is at a loss. How does this boy's death relate to the tale of honor that Guy has been telling himself? The narrative matter-of-factness juxtaposed with the strangeness of the scene makes the episode quasi-allegorical. Guy has come down from the mountain of his apocalyptic vision to wander in a world with no clear paths and in which he is virtually powerless. The rocky soil will not even allow him to bury the boy. All that Guy can do is offer a prayer and take the soldier's identity disc with him in hope of bringing the fact of his death to someone's attention, somewhere.

Guy's escape from Crete, his ordeal at sea, and his withdrawal into silence during his convalescence signal, conventionally enough, a spiritual passage through physical suffering. Learning of the desertion of Ivor Claire is a hard blow for Guy, as Ivor had become for him the last embodiment of English chivalric virtue. Most devastating of all, however, is news of the June 1941 invasion of Russia by the Germans and the resulting new alliance between Great Britain and the Soviet Union. This new "apocalypse for all the world for numberless generations" (*Officers and Gentlemen*, 324) awakens him from what he now thinks of as the "hallucination" of 1939: "he was back after less than two years' pilgrimage in a Holy Land of illusion in the old ambiguous world, where . . . gallant friends prove traitors and his country was led blundering into dishonour" (325).

The first part of *The End of the Battle* is dominated by a new symbolic sword, the Sword of Stalingrad, commissioned by the King in honor of the Russian defense of Stalingrad and reverently displayed in Westminster Abbey. For Guy (and Waugh), it is a symbol of political idolatry. Abandoning his belief in the justice of Britain's cause, his "crusade" shifts definitively inward as he tries to find a way to salvage his personal honor.

The End of the Battle has been called a "mystical work" (Stannard 1994, 441). If it deserves that description it is largely because of a phrase of Mr. Crouchback's that resonates throughout the novel: "*Quantitative judgments don't apply*" (*The End of the Battle*, 8; emphasis in text). At the beginning of the novel, Mr. Crouchback sees that Guy is in spiritual peril. He has been talking "awful nonsense" about his role as a soldier who no longer believes in the justice of his cause and especially about the Church and its role in the world. Guy has upset his father by gloating over the surrender of Italy and reading it as evidence that the Church made a mistake in entering into the Lateran treaty of 1929. Rather than suffering the humiliation of recognizing the claims of the secularists, Guy says, the popes should have stayed aloof; they should have "sat it out and then emerged, saying: 'What was all that?'" (5–6). Mr. Crouchback instructs Guy in the vast difference between the Church as temporal institution and as Mystical Body: "The Mystical Body doesn't strike attitudes and stand on its dignity. It accepts suffering and injustice." Has Guy considered "how many souls may have been reconciled and died at peace" because the treaty allowed the Church to function? Then comes the crucial line: "*Quantitative judgments don't apply.*" If only one soul was saved, that is full compensation for any amount of loss of "face." Mr. Crouchback ends the letter saying that he is worried about what will become of Guy after the war. He suggests that he think about returning to Broome and moving into what is known there as the "Lesser House" (8–9).

Guy finally comes down from the *castello* on the mountain to the Lesser House at Broome in two stages, both of which show that he takes to heart his father's lesson about "quantitative judgments." The first stage is his decision to renew his marriage vows, forgive Virginia, and accept Trimmer's baby as his own. His conversion comes during the period of his recovery from a severe reinjuring of the knee that has troubled him since 1939. Lying helplessly in bed at his uncle Peregrine's apartment, tended daily by Virginia, Guy comes to understand that his calling involves a very different kind of sacrifice than he was prepared to make, or rather that what he had thought was a road of sacrifice was really an elaborate and self-serving illusion. (It is amusing to think of Guy in ironic juxtaposition with Saint Ignatius, another soldier who saw the light during a period of convalescence from a leg injury.) Kerstie Kilbannock's response recalls the Cuthberts' bewilderment at Mr. Crouchback's sacrifice; it also serves as the occasion for transforming the book's view of chivalry: "You poor bloody fool . . . you're being *chivalrous*—about *Virginia*. . . . Can't you see how ridiculous you will look playing the knight-errant?" "Knights-errant," Guy responds, "used to go about looking for noble deeds. I don't think I've ever in my life done a single positively unselfish action." To Kerstie's argument that "the world is full of unwanted children. . . . What is one child more or less?" Guy tells her that the difference is, first, that he can do something about this one, if not any others, and second, that only he can do what needs to be done for the child. In short, this is his calling. When Kerstie concludes that he is "insane," Guy silently recalls his father's letter and reflects that "[a]ll differences are theological differences." His calling, because it is utterly unique to him, is bound to be unaccountable to those for whom quantitative judgments continue to be important (195–96).

In the second stage of Guy's conversion, he comes to recognize that not only was his chivalric quest part of a selfish illusion but his following of it has also made him personally guilty for the vast suffering that has been the result of the war. On his last posting in Croatia, Guy sees a group of displaced Jews as presenting an opportunity to "do a single small act to redeem the times" (251). Still not entirely free from self-delusion, Guy at one point sees himself as a Moses figure parting a sea of red tape. By the end of the novel, he has played a minor role in an only partly successful effort to rescue the Jews from the Scylla and Charybdis of the Fascists and the Communists. While most of the Croatian Jews do finally escape to Italy, Guy finds himself unwittingly involved in the disappearance (and probable execution) of the group's spokeswoman, Mme Kanyi, and her husband, having raised the Communists' suspicions by visiting her and by giving her some American magazines. The Kanyis' fate—to be "saved" from the Fascists only to be executed by the Communists—confirms Guy's hard-won conviction that the war, including his own participation in it, has been a perpetuation of evil, a participation in the madness that Waugh calls throughout the novel "the death wish." It is in a conversation with Mme Kanyi that Guy reaches what seems to be in Waugh's view his deepest point of spiritual awareness. "It is too simple," Mme Kanyi says, "to say that only the Nazis wanted War." The Communists wanted it, too, as did many of Mme Kanyi's own people, "to be revenged on the Germans, to hasten the creation of the national state." Talking about what she sees as a "will to war, a death wish, everywhere," she says that even good men were caught up in the madness. Thinking that "their private honour would be satisfied by war," these men accepted "hardships in recompense for having been selfish and lazy." When she asks if there were no such men in England, Guy replies "God forgive me. . . . I was one of them" (305).

From Christian crusader to sinful pilgrim, from soldier to servant, Guy has come a long way. The self-defensive detachment of the Santa Dulcina years gives way to a more compassionate spirit of self-sacrifice as Guy retires at the end to Broome. That Waugh obviously approves of his protagonist's withdrawal from the world is underscored by the use of Guy's nephew, Tony Box-Bender, as a foil. Tony's entrance to monastic life, so embarrassing to his utilitarian father, reflects Waugh's increasing conviction during the postwar years that Europe was on the verge of a new "Dark Age" during which the Church would increasingly withdraw from the active into the contemplative life. As he put it in his preface to his revised edition of Thomas Merton's *The Seven Storey Mountain* (published in 1949 as *Elected Silence*), "the modern world is rapidly being made uninhabitable by the scientists and politicians. . . . As in the Dark Ages the cloister offers the sanest and most civilized way of life." In such a time, the supernatural order demands that "Prayer must become heroic" (quoted in *The Essays, Articles, and Reviews*, 1984, 369).

It is not surprising, then, that Waugh found the Second Vatican Council and its reforms so profoundly painful. Just as he was portraying his comic alter ego as shaking the dust of modernity off his feet, the Church was readying itself for a definitive turn in the other direction, throwing open its doors and encouraging intense engagement with modern ideas. In the preface to the 1965 edition of *Sword of Honor*, Waugh says that he had unintentionally written "an obituary of the Roman Catholic Church in England as it had existed for many centuries. All the rites and most of the opinions here described are already obsolete" (*Sword of Honor*, 9). If that is so, then Guy Crouchback may represent the *fin de ligne*—the end of the line—in more than one sense.

CRITICAL RECEPTION

The three novels that make up *Sword of Honor* were well reviewed as they appeared. Martin Stannard's *Critical Heritage* volume provides a substantial gathering of the most important contemporary critical statements and an excellent critical overview of that response. Often quoted and often seconded is Cyril Connolly's assessment, in a review of the third volume, that the trilogy as a whole is "unquestionably the finest novel to have come out of the war" (Stannard 1984, 430). Virtually all commentators are in agreement that the trilogy represents the most ambitious and serious work of Waugh's career, even if they do not agree on its quality.

As is the case with all of Waugh's novels from *Brideshead Revisited* forward (that is to say, all of the "Catholic novels"), much of the critical reception has been dependent on where one stands with regard to George Orwell's famous claim that Waugh is "about as good a novelist as one can be . . . while holding untenable opinions" (1970, 576). For most critics unsympathetic to Waugh's Catholicism, the novels are at best uneven. "Good Waugh," which is to say the "funny Waugh" of the pre-*Brideshead* books, breaks out occasionally, as in the characterization of Apthorpe, Ben Ritchie-Hook, or Ludovic, but for this group of critics John Raymond's view of *Men at Arms* is pretty standard: the book is "good-tempered Waugh—and therefore Waugh at his second best." Moreover, the Catholicism comes across as mannerist: "must his characters forever be splashing each other with holy water?" (Stannard 1984, 339). Another strong strain in this criticism may be read as carryover from the reception of *Brideshead*; that is, a repetition of the charge of "snobbery" in Waugh's romantic reverence for the old aristocratic virtues, a reverence that is traced to a reactionary tendency bordering on Fascism and to a Catholic love of hierarchy (the Americans Joseph Heller and Gore Vidal may be included here [Stannard 1984, 442–44, 438–42]).

By far the more influential strain issues from contemporary critics, among them Frank Kermode (1962) and Bernard Bergonzi (1961), for whom Waugh is successful not despite his "ideas" (tenable outside of a fictional context or not) but because of them. For these critics, Waugh's Catholicism provides a coherent, strong, and therefore enabling symbolic and mythic vantage point from which the forms of modernity may be viewed and challenged. David Lodge (1971) identifies this vantage point with what he calls Waugh's "myth of decline" and argues that it is at the heart of the trilogy's success as a war novel in that it provides the moral position capable of exposing the follies and destructiveness of progressives and reactionaries alike.

For sympathetic critics, Waugh's major achievement in the trilogy (and indeed in all of the postwar fiction) is what Frederick Stopp called the "delineation of the impact of the supernatural on the natural." For Stopp, Waugh's Catholic novels aim "at neither conversion nor explanation, but rather at the 'hint of an explanation,' a perception of the workings in human life of a kind of cosmic analogy never to be fully resolved in this life" (Stannard 1984, 333–34). Stopp's 1958 study, *Evelyn Waugh: Protrait of an Artist*, develops this insight in what Stannard calls "arguably the subtlest critique of Waugh's work" (324).

Among the several more recent studies of Waugh's fiction, all of which give sustained attention to the trilogy, William Myers's study of "the problem of evil" (1991) is especially worthwhile. David Cliffe's "Companion" (2001) on the World Wide Web is an excellent resource.

NOTE

Evelyn Waugh, *Men at Arms* (Boston: Little, Brown, 1952); *Officers and Gentlemen* (Boston: Little, Brown, 1955); *The End of the Battle* (Boston: Little, Brown, 1962); and *Sword of Honor* (Boston: Little, Brown, 1966). All references are to these editions.

WORKS CITED

Bergonzi, Bernard. 1961. Review of *Unconditional Surrender (The End of the Battle)*. *Guardian* (October 27). In M. Stannard, *Evelyn Waugh: The Critical Heritage*, 423–24. Boston: Routledge and Kegan Paul.

Cliffe, David. 2001. "A Companion to *Sword of Honour.*" *An Evelyn Waugh Website.* http://www.abbotshill.freeserve.co.uk/.

Kermode, Frank. 1962. Review of *Unconditional Surrender (The End of the Battle). Partisan Review* (August 20): 466–71. In M. Stannard, *Evelyn Waugh: The Critical Heritage*, 445–46. Boston: Routledge and Kegan Paul.

———. 2000. *The Sense of an Ending*, 2nd ed. New York: Oxford.

Lodge, David. 1971. *Evelyn Waugh.* New York: Columbia University Press.

Myers, William. 1991. *Evelyn Waugh and the Problem of Evil.* Boston: Faber and Faber.

Orwell, George. 1970. *Collected Essays, Journalism and Letters*, vol. 4, ed. Sonia Orwell and Ian Angus. Harmondsworth: Penguin.

Stannard, Martin, ed. 1984. *Evelyn Waugh: The Critical Heritage.* Boston: Routledge and Kegan Paul.

———. 1994. *Evelyn Waugh: The Later Years, 1939–1966.* New York: Norton.

Stopp, Frederick J. 1958. *Evelyn Waugh: Portrait of an Artist.* London: Chapman and Hall.

Waugh, Evelyn. 1984. *The Essays, Articles, and Reviews*, ed. Donat Gallagher. Boston: Little, Brown.

— Brennan O'Donnell

Simone Weil [1909–1943]

Waiting for God

BIOGRAPHY

Simone Weil was born in Paris on February 3, 1909, the child of nonpracticing Jews. She attended the École Normale Supérieure from 1928 to 1931, after which she became a teacher. In 1934 she took a year off to work in a factory in Paris in an attempt to get to know the working class better, before returning to teaching. In 1935, on a holiday in Portugal, she had a profound religious experience while watching a religious procession in a fishing village. In 1936 she enrolled in the anarchist militia to serve in the Spanish Civil War, but she returned home within a year. On a visit to Assisi in 1937, she had a second religious experience—disillusioned with revolutionary politics, she was turning to religion as the true solution to human ills. While visiting the Benedictine monastery at Solesmes, she had her first mystical experience. In September 1939, the Second World War broke out. The Weil family left Paris for Marseilles just before France surrendered in June 1940. Simone began to consider the possibility of baptism and started to read Hindu scriptures as a complement to Christianity. When a Nazi ban on Jews teaching in state schools was implemented, she worked for a time on a farm. In 1942 she went to the United States, attending Mass every day and continuing to contemplate baptism. She traveled to London in December 1942 to join the Free French under General de Gaulle. In April 1943 she was admitted to Middlesex Hospital suffering from tuberculosis, but she refused treatment and food. She died at Ashford, Kent, on August 24, 1943, moved there by the Middlesex doctors who had grown impatient with her noncooperation and who needed her bed. One local headline read, "French professor starves herself."

MAJOR THEMES

Waiting for God is Simone Weil's best-known book. It is a collection of reflections, letters, and essays examining her spiritual development, her attitude toward God, Catholicism, the Church, Judaism, and Rome, and how best to comply with the will of God. There is a second book by Weil, *Gateway to God* (1974), dealing with the same subjects, to which I also refer in this essay.

The single most important concept in the thought of Simone Weil is that of waiting: it is for her the supreme exemplary act. We should not try to find God but let him find us. *Laisser faire Dieu*: leave everything to him. In *Waiting for God*, Weil ransacks the whole of human experience to find confirmation that the soul must wait for God to come. Only a fool believes that if he keeps jumping up into the air someday he will stay there—there is a law of gravity in matters of the spirit too (*Waiting for God*, 147). A man can move horizontally, not vertically; he cannot ascend to God but must wait for God to come down to him (91, 167). Defying this, he simply constructs yet another blasphemous Tower of Babel. "Never at any moment in my life have I 'sought for God,'" Weil wrote (29). There is no hint of contrition in this statement. The bride must wait for the bridegroom to come, because only then can "the nuptial yes" be spoken (91). When a little boy loses his mother he must not go looking for her; he should stand still and, sooner or later, his mother will find him. The servant must wait by the door, ready to die of hunger or exhaustion, until the master knocks (149). In Weil's emendation of Scripture, it is, significantly, the master who knocks.

But Scripture, too, supplies its confirmations. The lost sheep waiting for the shepherd, the wounded man waiting for the Good Samaritan, the lilies of the field making no effort to be beautiful—Pascal's strenuous exertions to reach up to God are futile idiocies. The passerby does not invite himself to the wedding feast; he need only accept the invitation (148). In the myth of Electra and Orestes, Weil finds a perfect image of the soul and God. Electra does not even know her brother, will not recognize him when he comes. No matter: he will recognize and rescue her. Her vocation is to wait, and she does it to perfection. Nor is this vocation some second best alternative to action: "This waiting for goodness and truth is . . . something more intense than any searching" (149). Do not pester God with your petty petitions; he will act when he chooses and it is sinful to demand more.

This insistence upon waiting is evident in Weil's own much-pondered, forever postponed baptism. She said that she felt born into the faith, but this did not prevent her from thinking of officially converting (32). She was not opposed to baptism in itself. She advised her brother to have his daughter baptized. During her final illness, she hinted to a friend to have her baptized should she ever become comatose—what she shrank from in consciousness she seemed prepared to accept in a coma. Did she want to be Christ's captive, to have it done to her without her having to choose? Yet even when we act in accordance with God's will, we must still act: he will not drag us to the font or into heaven against our will. Weil's critics complain that she had devised a recipe for stasis, standing immobile at the church door, like Bouridan's ass, unable to enter or leave, and attributing her paralysis to God's will. She convinced herself that God "does not want me in the Church" (41)—the implication is that she wants to come in but that he is stopping her. Baptism will come when God wants it. But baptism never came; ergo, God did not want it. For her critics, it is altogether too contrived, too convenient. It is easy to understand Graham Greene's exasperation as he describes Weil standing "at the edge of the abyss, digging her feet in, refusing to leap like the common herd ... demanding that she alone be singled out by a divine hand on her shoulder forcing her to yield" (quoted in Gray 2001, 221–22). That there might be something elitist and snobbish in this she herself admitted in conceding the possibility of "a crazy presumption in claiming that one might be an exception" (*Waiting for God*, 23). She defended her own special vocation not to be a Christian on the ground that a few exceptional sheep must always remain outside. Baptism, it seems, might be all right for humdrum souls, but for the spiritual elite there is another path to salvation.

Weil's own reluctance aside, there were a number of intractable problems in the way of her baptism—as she herself admitted, at least seventeen centuries of Christianity would have to be discarded to make it possible. She was a mystic, and the mystic occupies an ambiguous position within the institutional Church: ecclesiastical suspicion of mysticism is easy to understand. The mystic tends to obliterate the impassable gulf between God and man. Orthodox religion teaches submission to, but not absorption into, God, and it distrusts any hint of a soul vanishing without trace into the abyss of the Godhead. Second, the very function of the Church becomes problematic. The mystic apparently has no need of the Church as irreplaceable mediator between God and his people—in direct communication with God, the mystic needs no mediator and no sacraments. Third, if only God is desirable, then any other love for or attachment to creatures, oneself included, is idolatry. The mystic must purge himself of all selfish desire, including the desire for his own salvation. God must be loved for his own sake, not because he has promised us the bliss of heaven. God must never be debased into a means to serve human needs, not even the need for salvation. We must embrace his will unconditionally and in advance, even if it includes our personal damnation (17).

The potential dangers in all this led the Church to formulate criteria for "allowable mysticism" (see Kolakowski 1982, 98–151). The ontological distinction between God and man must never be eroded—the western idea of a Fall into individual being is irreconcilable with the Judeo-Christian account of creation. The mystic must not dispute established dogma by pretending that he or she receives a superior source of wisdom or claim exemption from the teaching binding upon the rest of the faithful. The mystic's experience cannot be from God if it produces elitism or contempt for the mass of ordinary believers.

It is undeniable that Weil's writings infringe upon the limits of allowable mysticism. The modernists told the Church to stay out of secular, scientific affairs in which it had no competence to speak. Weil told the Church that it had no teaching authority at all, even in religious matters; it should confine itself to the custodianship of the sacraments, which it had no right to refuse to anyone. It has no magisterial role and is of service only to those "mediocre souls" (*Gateway to God*, 106) whose only access to God is through the sacraments. Weil herself loved the sacraments, especially the Eucharist, but she was prepared to forego them if the price was submission to the Church. As for the idea of the Church itself as a sacrament, a channel of grace to mankind, it seems never to have crossed her mind. At times she referred to the Church as the foe, rival, and usurper of Christ (*Waiting for God*, 21–22; *Gateway to God*, 120).

There were other difficulties: Weil believed in incarnations apart from Christ's, insisted that the knowledge of God given to non-Christian people in India was as whole and genuine as that given to Christians, and demanded that the detestable Old Testament be banned from the canon of the Church. The Church taught that there is only one universal Savior and only one true Church founded by that Savior. Christ came to save the world, not just the western hemisphere. He is not a regional redeemer, one savior among many, all equally from God. Christianity is not merely "complementary" to other world faiths. There is not an action of the Spirit distinct from the action of Christ, an economy of the eternal Word (outside the Church) and an economy of the incarnate Word (limited to Christians)—different although complementary routes to salvation. Christ is not simply God's accredited representative in the West, leaving the Spirit to take care of the rest of mankind—he is Lord and Savior of the human race, not merely of one of its subdivisions.

This is what Weil repudiated. For her, Jesus is a savior, not *the* Savior (*Waiting for God*, 139). To Weil, Christianity is a religion for white westerners, which, but for a voracious imperialism, should never have been exported to regions where it was neither wanted nor needed. Weil was openly antagonistic to a missionary Church (*Waiting for God*, 136 ff). Go forth and teach all nations? The truth is that Christ's apostles were simple men who completely misunderstood what he meant (*Gateway to God*, 141), and this blunder was perpetuated by their inheritors. Christianity became an aggressive, intolerant creed because of this totally unjustified claim to a monopoly of truth.

There were far too many good things outside of Christianity that Weil valued and that the Church either slighted or ignored. She pleads the pain of separating herself from the unfortunate hosts of unbelievers, excluded through no fault of their own—how can she embrace redemption with so many left outside? And so, believing in God, she nevertheless defers her own baptism. It is a kind of game she plays with the Almighty: "I hope he will forgive me my compassion" (*Waiting for God*, 55). And if he forgives her for her delay, surely he will not condemn all those who do not believe in Christ because they have never heard his name?

Weil's real quarrel, of course, is not with God at all but with the intolerant Church that has hijacked his name. In her view, it had from the outset been a corrupt institution, contaminated by Judaism before its idolatrous sellout to the Roman Empire, a double defilement. While approving of the New Testament, the mystics, the liturgy, and the Mass, Weil detested the catechism of the Council of Trent and compared the medieval Church of Aquinas to the totalitarian tyranny of Nazi Germany (*Gateway to God*, 120)—she was writing this at a moment when the Nazis were triumphant in Europe. She condemned the excommunication of heretics. She deplored the failure to acknowledge Osiris, Dionysius, Krishna, Buddha, and the Tao as all emissaries of the Holy Spirit, coequal with Christ himself. She boasted that she had never donated so much as a sixpence to the missions (108). The truth is, Weil stated, that there are really two religions, "that of the mystics and the other one" (117)—this description of official Christianity could scarcely be more scathingly dismissive. The Church's so-called "teaching" is merely a veil behind which the real truth is to be discovered by the mystics, herself included (120). All of this plainly violates the limits of allowable mysticism; she clearly claims privileged access to truths denied to the mass of clodhopping believers and divides the Church into two groups, a tiny elite of supersouls elected by God and a host of dull, uncomprehending souls whose meager intellects must make do with the second-rate instruction provided by the magisterium.

Weil's fierce, almost unbalanced detestation of Judaism is relevant here. She repudiates the Gospel claim that salvation comes from the Jews—for her it is corruption that comes from that unwholesome source. The Jews infected Christianity when they persuaded the early Church to accept the idolatrous Old Testament as the word of God. She denied any personal link—racial, religious, or cultural—with Judaism, insisting that her total allegiance was to the Catholic, French, classical tradition. Other Jews shrank from conversion to Christianity as a betrayal of their people. Weil, strikingly, refused baptism because, in her eyes, the Church was altogether too Jewish: not loyalty to Judaism but an aversion to it—this was another reason for avoiding baptism. There are echoes here of Marcion, the Gnostic heretic condemned by the Church in the first century. He believed in two Gods: the inferior God who created the world and who gave the Law to the Jews, and the superior God, the father of Christ, who sent his son to free men from the enslavements of the flesh. Jesus was an unprecedented revelation of the true God; there had been nothing like him in ancient Jewish history. Marcion rejected the entire Hebrew Bible as not simply worthless but as a barrier to salvation. At stake here is a point of continuing crucial importance. Either there is, as the Church maintained in condemning Marcion, a vital continuity between Judaism and Christianity, the old and the new Israel; or, as Marcion insisted, there must be a complete and irreparable rupture between the two. Weil, siding with Marcion, lamented the fact that Christianity had not sufficiently liberated itself from its debilitating Jewish legacy and was, in consequence, corrupted from the start.

Weil could not comprehend how a reasonable mind could regard Jehovah and the loving Father of the New Testament as the same God. To her, Jehovah was simply a mask for Jewish aggression, a tribal deity poorly disguising a lust for power—but no people can become an incarnation of God. Weil's distrust of all collectivities (she even feared the totalitarian connotations of the Body of Christ) made her recoil from the God of Israel. She disliked, too, what she saw as the huckstering, bargaining spirit of Judaism in its dealings with God: if you serve us, we will serve you. For her, it indicates a spiritual crudity completely at odds with a true religious sensibility. *Our* God: it is altogether too sordidly proprietorial.

Weil's antisemitism led her into ill-balanced, prejudiced, sometimes outrageous judgments, zany attempts to detach Christ from Judaism and to reattach him to any other pre-Christian mythology, almost as if it hurt her to confront the inescapable fact that Jesus was a Jew. When she did bring herself to admit this, it was in a way most discreditable to his birthplace. Born as he was to take away the sins of the world, she maintained that it was fitting he should have been born in the most evil place of all, among Jews and Romans. She spins elaborate, farfetched theories to justify her almost irrational antipathy to Judaism and claims that we would all agree with her but for the Hebrew distortion of history. But after reading her eccentric, perhaps perverse, exegesis of the episode of Noah's drunkenness, doubts might legitimately arise regarding who is the real distorter (*Waiting for God*, 177–91). The accepted interpretation of this passage in Genesis is one of literal inebriation. Noah, as first cultivator of the grape, was excusable for not anticipating its intoxicating properties. The real culprit was his malicious son, Ham, who, in flagrant breach of filial reverence, made a show and a joke of his helpless father's nakedness in inviting his brothers to join him in impious mockery. Shem and Japheth refused, however, to look on their father's shame and, eyes averted, entered the tent backwards to cover him with a compassionate cloak. Shem is the ancestor of the Semites, Japheth of the Gentiles (Greeks and Romans), Ham of Canaan (Africans and Asians). The point of the story is the curse laid upon the bad son and the blessing given to the two good sons.

Weil urges us to reject this version as a piece of propaganda invented to justify the illegal, immoral invasion of Canaan and its seizure from the hands of its rightful owners, Ham's descendants—imperialists are adept at concocting excuses for their aggression. Europe, born of Israel and Rome, the evil sons of Noah, is the continent of aggressive imperialism, and it has gone on doing to the sons of Ham in Africa and Asia what the Israelites originally did in Canaan. In Weil's version, Ham is the hero, not the villain, and to justify this conclusion she supplies a fanciful symbolic interpretation of what happened. Noah, she states, was not drunk but divinely inspired, like the inebriates of mysticism. His nakedness was not due to sottishness but was the innocence of prelapsarian Adam and Eve before the shamefulness of sin caused them to cover themselves: the guilty soul disguises itself with carnal garments. Noah's sinful sons covered him after his virtuous son found him gloriously naked—they are the sons who chose to be spiritually blind. Ham is the father of Egypt and Phoenicia, the home of true religion: salvation comes from Africa, not Israel. Shem and Japheth (Israel and Europe) are the villains, the debauchers of religion to this day. They have severed our links with our Ham-inspired past, and their legacy of exploitation disfigures us still.

The same readiness to frog-march texts, overlooking what seems straightforward and literal in favor of an arcane symbolism, is evident in Weil's idiosyncratic reading of the Our Father (*Waiting for God*, 166–77). To Weil, we are not to ask for anything so mundane as literal bread. Indeed, we are not to ask for anything above what has already been given, because the totality of facts—what has already been given—is the will of God; to ask for anything in addition is an insult to God. Embrace things as they are; whatever is, is right—this is what the makers of theodicies, from Leibniz to Hegel, tell us. The perfect petition is to ask for what already exists, not for what does not. We are not to be importunate beggars, pestering God with our inconsequential wants. The aim is to make every accomplished fact, whatever it may be, an object of desire, not simply of acceptance or resignation, but to love necessity, as Spinoza demands (*Waiting for God*, 169). What, one wonders, would she have made of Auschwitz?

Weil pursues her argument with a relentless logic that makes no concessions to common sense or everyday religion. We must love our own past sins, she writes, because they, too, are facts, hence the will of God. But this seems incompatible with the sacrament of reconciliation. How can you at once feel sorrow for sins that you joyfully accept having committed? Even to pray for one's own salvation is presumptuous and suspect. And suppose you end up in hell? You must embrace your own damnation with the same fervor as you would admittance to heaven. The normal sensibility balks at this as an instance of lunatic extremism. Does the God of Christianity will anyone's damnation? Isn't this rather Descartes's demon or the nightmare deity of Calvinism? Not everything that happens is God's will, as he himself makes clear: "I have forbid that they should commit iniquity, but their hearts have undone what my word decreed" (181–82). Far from embracing the totality of facts, we must condemn many of them as an errant abuse of God's gift of freedom.

So fearful was Weil of God being reduced to a mere instrument of human desire that she veered to the opposite perverse extreme: "If I had my eternal salvation placed in front of me. . . . I would not put out my hand so long as I had not received the order to do so" (24–25). This stoic abstention makes sense only on the heretical supposition that God may not want us to be saved, that to desire salvation may be defiance of his will, and that we must not reach out for what is not ours to take. In a similar vein, Weil argues that only Pharisees expect a reward, and Saint Paul, anticipating his crown of righteousness, is for her simply a Pharisee at second remove. To desire one's salvation is to forfeit it; it is to make God a means to an end. Her admiration for Spinoza was increased by his denunciation of the religions of the ignorant, whose view of the afterlife as reward or punishment for behavior here below is an opinion "so absurd as to be hardly worth mentioning" (1989, 223). In any case, why long for a heaven you already possess? Jacques-Benigne Bossuet's chief complaint against the Jansenists—that in their passive acceptance of God's will they made hope redundant—is just as available for use against Weil's thought.

Weil's is a ferociously exacting standard that is far too exorbitant for the great mass of ordinary human beings. She declares that if we help the afflicted because we see Christ in them, our action is contaminated: we have, Pharisee-like, had our reward. We must not see Christ in the wretch we succor—only then is it meritorious, only then will he praise us. We must be genuinely puzzled at this praise—Lord, when did I help you?—to deserve it. Weil's paradoxical reading of Saint Matthew suggests that a non-Christian is much more likely to win this praise than a follower of Christ. Mother Teresa, laboring among the afflicted in Calcutta—she, too, has had her reward.

Weil's meditations on the self similarly transgress the limits of allowable mysticism. In western mysticism, the self and God, even in the closest imaginable union, continue to exist as separate entities. In Weil, this crucial distinction is obliterated: "The soul must finally cease to be, through total assimilation to God" (*Gateway to God*, 41). Annihilation is the desideratum: "We shall be pure good. We shall no longer exist" (44). Practically speaking, there is no difference between atheism and Weil's idea of total absorption: in both you simply cease to be. God will come only when the self departs and leaves a void for him to enter. Underlying this is a suspicion of creation itself. God is "greater" before his creation than after, says Weil, failing, however, to explain why, in that case, he chose to create at all (*Waiting for God*, 102; *Gateway to God*, 97). The Fall is not *from* but *into* creation: the emergence of self, of individual being, is the Fall. "God's great crime against us is to have created us, is the fact of our existence. And our existence is our sin against God. When we forgive God for our existence, he forgives us for existing" (*Gateway to God*, 49–50). And again, "Adam made us believe we have being; Christ showed us that we are non-being" (50). Christ brings not life (as Saint John has him say) but nonbeing. This is an eastern, not a western, idea. If we accept it, we must also accept Schopenhauer's claim to be Christianity's best interpreter in presenting its true message as the boon of individual extinction.

It is no surprise to learn that Weil had no time for the Resurrection. She affirmed her belief in God, the Trinity, the Incarnation, the Redemption, and the Eucharist, but, revealingly, she omits the Resurrection. Thou shalt not be consoled is the first of her commandments. When religion consoles, it is, in her view, a hindrance to true faith. We are not to be lifted above our affliction, and belief in the Resurrection is likely to do this. Freud, too, forbade consolation, but he was an unbeliever; Weil's veto is the more surprising in coming from one who believes. Hers is a lopsided Christianity, all Cross and no Resurrection: we are to suffer but not to rise with Christ. "Our country is the Cross" (*Gateway to God*, 91), she declared, and she refused to leave this country even for the fields of heaven. She deplored the Resurrection as a distraction from what really matters: "if the Gospel omitted all mention of Christ's resurrection faith would be easier for me. The Cross by itself suffices me" (129). A Christian discomfited by the empty tomb—it is a scandal that would have bewildered Saint Paul. If only Christ had been left to rot in the grave, how much more satisfying the story would have been. For Weil, Christianity does not provide a supernatural *remedy* for suffering but a supernatural *use* for it. It supplies yet another excuse to quarrel with Pascal, who discovered in man both greatness and wretchedness. Weil finds only the latter and is content that this should be so. "The Cross produces the same effect upon me as the Resurrection does upon other people," she wrote (130). Is it unfair to detect here a pride in being different from the mediocre herd? She does, after all, refer to "a deplorable puerility in the case of a great many pious and even saintly souls" (130). It is this puerility that lures us into expecting rewards and craving resurrection. She had no such expectations or cravings. The only thing that made her envious was thinking of Christ's crucifixion (*Waiting for God*, 49).

Disconcerting, too, is the alacrity with which Weil takes the side of almost any historical enemy of the Church, including Gnostics, Manichaeans, and Catharists (*Gateway to God*, 61–62). Her admiration for the Catharists and her lament at their defeat as a great cultural calamity for Europe are puzzling. The Cathari (*katharoi* or "pure ones") believed in one God, father of both Satan and Christ. Betraying the supreme God, Satan created the world to hold human souls captive in its materiality. Christ came to deliver these souls from the evil world. The Cathar leaders renounced all physical engagement with this world, rejecting sex, marriage, family, and many different foods, including milk, cheese, eggs, and meat. Catholicism was bound to find Catharism unacceptable. It denied the unity of God as the supreme Creator and repudiated the goodness of creation itself. Catharism, for its part, denounced the attempt, basic to Catholicism, to find spiritual powers in the material world.

By contrast, Catholicism is distinguished as a religion for its celebration of the material world; its enemies have said, and continue to say, that it is altogether too scandalously enmeshed with matter. The most cursory reading of the Gospel shows how deeply rooted Catholic Christianity is in the things of the earth: water, wine, bread, oil. Jesus is forever employing material things to teach spiritual truths. Not only is matter redeemed, it is the means of redemption: we are to be saved by water and wine, bread and oil. Matter itself is a sacrament. From the beginning, the Church has denounced the heresy that matter is unimportant, worse still, vile: that the body is a mere container, a piece of ephemeral trash, in which the soul is briefly imprisoned before its final blessed release into eternity. So odious was this captivity to the Cathari that they accused Mary, Jesus' mother, of complicity with Satan in trying to confine Christ in a body, imprisoning him in her womb. They identified the cross as an instrument of murder, not salvation; body and cross alike are the rightful property of Satan. The Cathari carried this to a logical conclusion. Jesus was not really born of Mary, did not really die on the cross, but wore a phantom body in which matter had no part. All procreation is evil, since it adds to the number of Satan's followers. To assert that grace is conveyed through the material channels of the sacraments is blasphemy. There is no resurrection of the body—the soul's whole effort consists in escaping from this loathsome corporeal captivity.

This oriental nightmare is irreconcilable with Christianity, ascribing, as it does, the whole material creation to an evil power. It is not surprising that the emergence of such teaching in the south of France in the thirteenth century provoked alarm in the Church, causing Pope Innocent III to launch a Crusade against the Albigensian Cathars that ended in their complete defeat. At stake were crucial issues of doctrine, ritual, and society. What is surprising is to find Weil siding with the Cathari and comparing the Catholic triumph to the Nazi conquest of France. It was, for her, another sorry instance of Shem and Japheth, the intolerant imperialists, prevailing over Ham, a victory that brought sterility to the whole Mediterranean basin (*Waiting for God*, 189).

What is Weil doing in this dubious company, she who had such a deep veneration for the Eucharist (which the Cathari denounced as a transaction with Satan) and such a fervent love of the Cross (which they abominated as a device of evil)? There is, admittedly, a link with Catharism in her own aversion to the body and her revulsion to eating as a base and disgusting function. The "pure ones" fasted three times a week and believed that death by fasting (the *endura*) was the holiest death of all, the one in which the power of Satan was most manifestly overcome. Death through illness or senile decay showed Satan still in control. But if you fasted to death, it was not suicide (forbidden by the Cathari), it was you controlling Satan. Why give this wretched body, Satan's slave, a supply of food to keep it alive? There are links here with Weil's own anorexia. Her friends were alarmed by her researches into the possibility of feeding on light to obviate the need for ingesting food—it sounds zany enough to have emanated from Swift's Academy of Lagado—and the tragic conclusion to this obsession was the coroner's verdict of death resulting from a suicidal refusal to take food. Weil's brother denied that she was a suicide, arguing that her stomach had shrunk and that she was so unused to eating that she no longer could eat. But she herself had described how a desire can become an addiction (*Waiting for God*, 153).

Nevertheless, Weil's admiration for the Cathari is perplexing; she surely did not subscribe to their basic doctrine that creation is evil and the world satanic. She blames Christianity for its failure to appreciate the beauty of the natural world (only Saint Francis of Assisi escapes censure) and writes movingly on beauty as God-inspired, a foretaste of eternity here on earth (116). But if the Church slighted the beauty of the world, the Cathari abominated it. Why, then, did she want a Cathar victory? For it was not simply the methods used to defeat them (armed force, Inquisition), but the fact that they were defeated at all—this is what grieved her. True, she disliked the authoritarian medieval Church and cared little for the teaching Church or for dogma in general. But the Cathari, too, had their dogmas and were just as intolerant in promoting them as the Crusaders were in promoting theirs. It seems strange that Weil should have wanted the teachings of these life-deniers to triumph over the tenets of orthodoxy. It is yet one more enigma in the life and thought of this brilliant, bewildering, exasperating, contradictory woman who has some claim to be regarded as the first postmodern theologian.

CRITICAL RECEPTION

The best introduction to the life and thought of Simone Weil is by Francine du Plessix Gray. She also supplies a useful summary of some of the major responses to Weil's work (2001, 221–23). Predictably, these responses have been radically divergent. A number of critics, such as T. S. Eliot, Andre Gide, and Malcolm Muggeridge, have hailed Weil as one of the most important mystical thinkers of modern times. Some Catholics, notably Graham Greene, are exasperated by what they see as her demand to be treated by God as a special case, while others rebuke an alleged pride in her rejection of any need for a mediator between herself and God. Weil's unappeasable hostility to Judaism has provoked an understandable retaliation from Jewish thinkers, a subject thoroughly treated in Thomas R. Nevin's study (1991). The best analysis of her political thought (on Marxism, Nazism, and colonialism) is in David McLellan's account (1989) of her utopian pessimism. Among Weil's warmest admirers are Albert Camus and Pope Paul VI. Camus called her the most penetrating social and political thinker since Karl Marx. And Pope Paul VI named the three most important influences on his own intellectual development as Pascal, Georges Bernanos, and Simone Weil.

NOTE

Simone Weil, *Waiting for God* (London and Glasgow: William Collins Sons, Fontana Books, 1959). All references are to this edition.

WORKS CITED

Gray, Francine du Plessix. 2001. *Simone Weil.* London: Weidenfeld and Nicolson.
Kolakowski, Leszek. 1982. *Religion: If There Is No God.* Glasgow: Fontana, William Collins Sons.
McLellan, David. 1989. *Simone Weil: Utopian Pessimist.* London: Macmillan.
Nevin, Thomas R. 1991. *Simone Weil: Portrait of a Self-Hating Jew.* Chapel Hill: University of North Carolina Press.
Spinoza, Benedict. 1992. *Ethics,* trans. Andrew Boyle, ed. G. H. R. Parkinson. London: Everyman's Library.
Weil, Simone. 1974. *Gateway to God.* Glasgow: William Collins Sons, Fontana.

BIBLIOGRAPHY

Bell, Richard, ed. *Simone Weil's Philosophy of Culture.* Cambridge: Cambridge University Press, 1993.

Breuck, Katherine T. *The Redemption of Tragedy: The Literary Vision of Simone Weil*. Albany: State University of New York Press, 1995.

Coles, Robert. *Simone Weil: A Modern Pilgrimage*. Reading, MA: Addison-Wesley, 1987.

Dunaway, John M. *Simone Weil*. Boston: Twayne, 1984.

Pétrement, Simone. *Simone Weil: A Life*, trans. Raymond Rosenthal. New York: Pantheon Books, 1976.

Plant, Stephen. *Simone Weil*. Ligouri, MS: Triumph Books, 1996.

— **Patrick Reilly**

Antonia White [1899–1980]

Frost in May

BIOGRAPHY

Antonia White often saw herself as an unsuccessful writer, a failed artist who faced a crippling writer's block for much of her professional life. Ultimately, she produced a volume of short stories, more than thirty translations of French works, and, her most well-known works, the four novels *Frost in May* (1933), *The Lost Traveller* (1950), *The Sugar House* (1952), and *Beyond the Glass* (1954). In 1965, she also published *The Hound and the Falcon* (1983), the correspondence with J. Peter Thorp that influenced her reconversion to the Catholic Church. In addition, White was an essayist, a very successful advertising copywriter, and a journalist who wrote for several of the most important periodicals in London. It is telling that White wrote more in her diaries than she did in all of her published works together. The published diaries make up two volumes, although most of White's personal writing remains unpublished. Another volume of unfinished material—including an autobiography—exists in print as well (*As Once in May* [1983]). The four major works are always referred to as "autobiographical fiction"; indeed, it would seem artificial to discuss the characters of *Frost in May* and the three Clara Batchelor novels without referring to the life of their author.

Antonia White lived vividly, sensationally, and, often, tragically. The scenes and impressions depicted in her novels adhere closely to her own experiences, and the fiction portrays relationships that often correspond to White's relationships with her own parents, friends, teachers, husbands, and lovers. *Frost in May* is the first of the four, and it records a young girl's four-year stay at a convent school. The succeeding trilogy continues the tumultuous emotional life of the same girl, now called Clara Batchelor, who struggles with her father's authority, Catholicism, madness, difficult marriages and affairs, and the writing life.

Antonia White was born on March 3, 1899, in West Kensington, England, as Eirene Botting. Her father, Cecil Botting, was a classics master at St. Paul's School, and her mother was Christine White Botting. When Antonia was seven, Cecil converted to the Catholic Church, bringing Christine and his daughter with him. He enrolled Antonia in the Convent of the Sacred Heart in Roehampton when she was nine. White's relationships with her parents were complex and troubled. She regarded her father, in particular, with both love and resentment, and she associated these feelings with her similar feelings for Catholicism. These experiences and emotions provided the subject for much of her fiction. As an adult, however, White often claimed that the profound writer's block she suffered was caused by her father's control over her.

After the convent school, Antonia went to St. Paul's School for Girls, but, rather than pursuing scholarship opportunities at Cambridge, she lighted on several different jobs and diversions in the next few years after graduation. With little desire to seek out a single profession with earnestness, she became a governess for a Catholic family, then taught at a boys' school. She clerked in the Ministry of Pensions and wrote freelance advertising copy. She also began writing for *The Westminster Review*. During this time, Antonia experienced a diminishing of the intense, powerful faith she had felt at Roehampton despite the school's strictures. Her biographer Jane Dunn infers that "it was hard for her to see how to anchor her newly emerging personality in her Catholicism without the external structure and reinforcement of daily rituals and community consciousness" (1998, 57).

White's early adult life brought her years of troubled marriages and bouts of mental illness. With her advertising earnings, she enrolled in the Academy of Dramatic Art in 1919, where she met the men who would become her first two husbands, Reggie Green-Wilkinson and Eric Earnshaw-Smith. White's marriages to these men (1921–1925 and 1925–1929, respectively), who were both homosexual, were marked by periods of intimate friendship between husband and wife as well as episodes of White's declining mental health. White was committed to Bethlem Royal Hospital in 1922, where she remained for nine months. Both marriages were ultimately annulled for nonconsummation, and White officially lapsed from Catholicism in 1926. She married the writer Tom Hopkinson in 1930, after a long engagement to another man, Silas Glossup. Hopkinson acted as father to both of White's children, Susan and Lyndall, although Susan's biological father was Glossup. In 1935, White left Hopkinson and began Freudian analysis.

White always wrote easily while involved with Hopkinson, and he had encouraged her work about her convent school experiences. Throughout the 1930s, White enjoyed support and a gradually rising reputation among a small group of writers, particularly those collected by Peggy Guggenheim at Hayford Hall, a well-patronized retreat for artists. White first met her close friends Emily Coleman and Djuna Barnes at this time. *Frost in May* was released in 1933, and White published a handful of short stories while also working as a journalist and theater critic.

As her daughters grew up largely without her and she continued to struggle with her mental health, White was always energized by volatile intellectual company. The decades of her steady but difficult productivity are marked by the influence of a wide range of artists and philosophers, including modernists, members of Bloomsbury, and surrealists. Dylan Thomas, Henry Miller, and Anaïs Nin were among the many contemporary artists with whom White talked about mental illness, sexuality, writing, and religion.

The critical and popular success of *Frost in May* had an unlikely result. In 1940, Peter Thorp wrote White a letter about the novel, opening a year-long correspondence that focused primarily on questions of faith and doubt. Wartime postal delays and paper conservation did not impede this intimate relationship, which, along with other forces "natural and supernatural," urged White's reconversion to Catholicism in 1940 (*The Hound and the Falcon*, 1983, xviii). The same year, White survived a bombing of the BBC offices in evacuated London, where she worked. In 1965, her letters to Thorp were published as *The Hound and the Falcon*, which was an astounding success and prompted hundreds of letters like Peter's first one to Antonia.

In the 1950s, White began her very successful career as a translator of French works. At the same time, she was able to produce the Clara Batchelor trilogy, which received varied critical opinion but were financially successful. White continued her work as a translator for nearly thirty more years, until 1976.

During a period of medical problems and grief for dying friends, White met Carmen Callil, the "reviving angel" who created the resurgence of critical success for *Frost in May* (Dunn 1998, 417). Callil, editor of the feminist publishing house Virago Press, reissued *Frost in May* in 1978 as the inaugural work in the Virago Modern Classics series. The Clara Batchelor series quickly followed; all three books were released at the same time. White gave interviews, and Callil negotiated television and radio contracts. Public response to the novels was outstanding. White, at age seventy-nine, received numerous letters from readers. According to Dunn, Carmen Callil was also Antonia's last great friend (418).

Never entirely free from mental depression, White struggled with her work and her image of herself as a daughter, wife, and mother for the rest of her life. She had genial reunions with a few of her friends and ex-husbands in the years before her death, and she felt reconciled with her daughters. Antonia White died of cancer on April 16, 1980. In the preface to *The Hound and the Falcon*, she comments on her problems with faith: "I went on wrestling with them like a bad swimmer in a rough sea, now coming to the surface, now being helplessly submerged again before finding some spar to hold onto" (xviii). This description also aptly represents the self-doubting but successful writer's feelings about her family, her friendships, and her art.

PLOT SUMMARY

Arriving at the Convent of the Five Wounds in Lippington, England, nine-year-old Catholic convert Fernanda Grey is offered a strange blessing. As Nanda and her father get off the bus, an Irish woman who is pleased to meet the new Catholics prays that Nanda will give her life to God in return for the grace that prompted her father's conversion.

The convent at Lippington is formidable, busy, cold, and regimented. Nanda is an intelligent, middle-class English child who learns obedience and catechism among aristocratic, European classmates. Although she is a passionate new Catholic, the culture is alien to her. The convent, and by implication the Church itself, is a different world: rooms have saints' names, fellow students are the daughters of British gentry or Continental diplomats. The school's rules and even language are distinct from the outside order. The children's parents are replaced with "Mothers" of Discipline and of Recreation. Disliked foods must be eaten for self-mortification; intimate friendships are forbidden; hair must be controlled; some words like "exemption" have strange meanings; even a child's sleeping position is altered as she must be readied for death at every moment. One of the most painful changes for the classically educated, imaginative Nanda is being forced to read stories of saints and martyrs instead of her beloved poetry and fairy tales.

Nanda finds that her new faith takes root and her spirituality deepens even amidst this harsh regimen with its denial of human intimacy. She adjusts to the junior school quickly by adhering fully to the rules. Like the other girls, she learns the practices of mortification and denial, but she also must learn to suppress her envy of the wealthier girls who have "country houses and . . . ponies of their very own" (*Frost in May*, 27). She never feels truly Catholic, however, and is not allowed to forget that she is a convert.

The plot of the novel follows the microcosm of a day at Lippington within the macrocosmic calendar of holy day celebrations that fall during the school year. Scenes depict the rising bell, morning devotions, the three Angelus prayers throughout the day, prayers before and after class, rosaries, novenas, and prayers in chapel. Examination of conscience is followed by confession on Saturday, after which exemptions—rewards for good behavior—are given out. Sundays bring Mass, a sermon, and Benediction. Interruptions to this routine are welcome and festive, whether they are caused by Easter, the death of a nun, or by a convent-wide illness that allows the rules to be briefly loosened.

Nanda's progress through four years in first the junior and then the senior school is fairly smooth, and she earns her pink ribbon, much to her father's pleasure. She exceeds her friends—even lifelong Catholics—in her knowledge of doctrines such as transubstantiation and the Immaculate Conception. More impressive is her private development of a fuller, philosophical involvement in matters of the spirit. Her conflicts with the nuns are infrequent but telling. More than once she is chastised for reading forbidden writers, even the Catholic poet Francis Thompson. She is reprimanded for repeated incidents that suggest she holds dear a "particular friendship" or best friend.

Pious and creative, Nanda begins to write a conversion novel of her own, peopled by wicked characters whom she plans to convert in a triumphant ending. But the unfinished novel, with its "languid ecstasies" and "kiss of burning passion," is discovered by the Mother Superior (202). Nanda's father takes this adolescent scrabble as evidence of a "a sink of filth and impurity" hidden within his daughter, and he rejects her (216). Thus, Nanda begins as a convert and ends essentially as an orphan. She is removed from the school on the same day that her Protestant friend Clare Rockingham converts to the Catholic Church. The Mother Superior explains that Nanda has learned humility through sacrifice and that God will be generous to her. For Nanda, however, "nothing . . . would ever be the same again" (221).

MAJOR THEMES

The central theme of *Frost in May* is conversion, the transformation of the self. The novel begins with Fernanda Grey's arrival at an English convent school and ends with her expulsion from it four years later. The complexity and realism of the novel arise from White's depiction of two processes occurring at the same time: the coming of age of a young girl and the coming into faith of a young convert. The concurrence of these processes makes the novel a *bildungsroman* and a spiritual progress. Both types of plot present the quest of a youthful hero for an identity, secular or spiritual. As a school novel, *Frost in May* depicts Nanda's coming of age, structured as a series of rites of passage that involve initiation, oppression, rebellion, and passion. But as a religious novel, *Frost in May* also portrays the growth of a soul's love and fear of God and the Church. In spare but sparkling prose, White charts the progression and suppression of nine-year-old Nanda in the Convent of the Five Wounds, where the child grows into deep emotional attachment to the Church but where she also finds her childhood self growing a hardened core of rebelliousness in response to the spiritual and disciplinary methods of the convent.

This short novel, written in a detached, third-person point of view, depicts a critical crux of the Catholic faith with an accuracy so crystalline and intimate that its ironies are painful to realize. The crux is this: a person born into the legacy of Jesus' sacrifice for humankind must, like him, relinquish the human self to save the spiritual self. White examines this paradox for one young woman using two primary tropes, conversion and sacrifice. The methods of the Lippington convent—primarily the mortification of the body and a program of sanctified suffering—reflect, in part, traditions of the Church, but they also rely on intense psychological punishment and the ultimate goal of crushing the individual will.

In the sense that, with conversion, one gives up the old life for the new, conversion is amplified in the novel because it is applied not only to the sacred but also to the mundane; not just to the spirit but also to the body and the entire self. This profound feeling of transformation is the prevailing mood of *Frost in May*'s early chapters. Nanda has converted before she arrives at the school, but the most lasting changes occur while she is a student there. Entering Lippington, White's narrator suggests, is like being orphaned; Nanda is removed briskly and professionally from her parents and taken into the home of her new "mothers": Mother Radcliffe, the Mistress of Discipline; Mother Frances, head of the junior school; and *Mater Admirabilis*, the Blessed Mother. "Home for a Catholic is wherever our Lord is," says Mother Radcliffe, walking Nanda through the doors, but the child has already marked herself as "a very raw convert" with her nervous left-handed sign of the cross (19).

After just five days as a convent child, Nanda does not know whether her parents will recognize her as she feels "so much unpicked and resewn and made over to a different pattern" (36). Every element of daily life has changed for Nanda and creates change in her. She adapts to dressing in uniform, plaiting her hair, obeying bells, eating burnt cabbage, and reciting prayers, but the Catholic world remains foreign. Nanda must contend constantly with the cradle Catholic girls' accusations and her own feeling that she is not a "true" Catholic, that she will never really understand the *sine qua non* of Catholicism.

A good part of Nanda's difference from the other girls arises from her social class. While Nanda feels awkwardly middle class among aristocratic girls who describe royal ceremonies and grieve over the pet horses they left at home, White does not allow her protagonist to see the full influence of class in the convent. The third-person narrator—speaking descriptively, not sympathetically—invites the reader to judge the sisters who give the poorest children the oldest books and the most arduous chores. Readers see, although Nanda only glimpses, that the upper-class European girls are never as forcibly molded into shape or as closely surveilled. The sleepy looks and disobedient curls of a Spanish diplomat's daughter are largely ignored by the nuns, as is Leonie de Wesseldorf's odd boy's hat and dingy but expensive coat.

Nanda is different not only from the Catholic girls but also from the unconverted. Protestant Clare Rockingham, forbidden by her parents to become a Catholic, is one of Nanda's beloved friends in the senior school. Clare sees the excessive legalism in the Church's teachings more clearly than Nanda does, but she desires to be a Catholic nonetheless. The girls lend her their rosaries and pray for her conversion. When Nanda offers up her retreat for Clare's conversion, anxiety flashes over her: "Suppose that, in return for the conversion of Clare Rockingham, God should demand the dedication of her own life? Would she be equal to so heroic a sacrifice?" (127).

This second trope, that of sacrifice, is interwoven with conversion from the beginning of the novel. Two elements that White repeats throughout *Frost in May* are Nanda's fear of vocation and the narrative's allusions to pagan and Christian sacrifice. The novel's opening Benediction is ironic. Irish Bridget Mulligan suggests that Nanda thank God and pay him back for her father's conversion with her own vocation. The great grace of a daughter sacrificing herself for her father can be read another way: Mr. Grey is a classics master delivering his daughter to the Church, and readers often see the novel's opening as an oblique allusion to Agamemnon's sacrifice of Iphigenia to the gods. Nanda's expulsion from the convent occurs on Good Friday, and it is followed by Clare's conversion, for which Nanda has prayed. The sacrifice of Nanda can be seen as parallel to the suffering and self-sacrifice of Christ. But the classical allusion remains; the final sacrifice of Nanda is not just made for the gods, so to speak. It is made for and by the father, who is both appalled by his daughter's unfinished novel and relieved that he will not have to pay her tuition anymore. Sacrifice in battle is also called for by Mother Radcliffe, who asserts the convent's goal: "We work today to turn out, not accomplished young women, nor agreeable wives, but soldiers of Christ, accustomed to hardship and ridicule and ingratitude" (118).

The novel also presents conversion and sacrifice in the form of religious vocation. Nanda fears the call, the "heroic sacrifice" she believes she is inadequate to make. But her emotions and aesthetic eye are taken in by the beautiful ceremony of conventual vows. In two separate scenes, Lady Moira Palliser and Hilary O'Byrne are accepted as postulants, robed, and shorn of their hair as they make their first vows. Nanda notes the joy on a novice's face, and she knows that a vocation is "the supreme good" while the secular life is but a "wretched crust" (54). For fear of being called to such a vocation, Nanda is afraid to listen to God. For fear of failing or being insufficient, she cannot reach a full spiritual satisfaction. Her constant worry that she cannot sacrifice "enough" and that she is not Catholic "enough" causes Nanda occasional spiritual dryness and tightens the fist of her will.

Through junior and senior school, this problem of her Catholic identity erodes not Nanda's faith or her first "secret, delicious joy" in "thinking about religion" (19) but her sense of self-identity. Her knowledge of complex doctrine does not seem to make her a "real" Catholic, nor does her desire to please God, nor even her obedience. Branded a convert from the beginning, Nanda always suspects that she is not experiencing her faith in the way that others do. Although she is on the "inside" of the Church, she is always an outsider. When the children are represented as animal figures in a Christmas manger tableau, Nanda is placed close to the Lord, "in the very door of the stable," but she is assigned the role of an "obstinate little pig" because she does not know how to change the hard core of self that chafes at abnegation (65).

The Convent of the Five Wounds teaches humility, obedience, and rejection of the world primarily through sacrifices of the body, mortification of the senses and their pleasures. The girls learn immediately "to do things [they] don't like" (27). Quickly, too, they learn the spiritual value of giving up things they do like, like eating puddings or reading poetry. The practice of mortification is based, at Lippington, on the logic of the slippery slope. The older girls explain: "If you give way to yourself in little things, you'll give way to yourself in big ones later on. Perhaps one day when you are grown up, you'll be faced with a really grave temptation . . . to mortal sin. If you've learnt to control yourself in small ways, you'll have got the habit of saying 'no' to the devil at once" (27). Nanda enters into these sacrifices without complaint. She gives up pleasures like smelling a flower, and she chokes down the horrid cabbage, willing to perform these small privations and penances. At first, she is pained only by the sacrifice of poetry and imaginative literature, which she is forbidden to read. In the senior school, however, the mortification is more weighty and defiance is more tempting. The girls grow to love each other, yet they are forbidden "particular friendships" (144). They are also asked to reject vanity by retreating from their talents. When Leonie becomes a glorious Beatrice in the class's rendition of Dante's *Paradiso*, she is pulled from the play because she shows pleasure and skill in her role. Prevented from fulfilling their abilities and denied the intimacy of friendships, the girls cannot come of age. They are fully innocent, but they are restrained from the natural movement to experience their own gifts. They learn the hardships of being "soldiers of Christ" on a secular and spiritual level without being allowed the counterbalance of secular joys.

For Nanda, who does glory in the presence of Christ and the companionship of his Mother, spiritual joy alone cannot completely fill this void. Her First communion is depicted like a nightmare, shown entirely through Nanda's point of view. The longed-for fulfillment of the desire for Christ's body fails to occur when "at the supreme moment, she had not caught fire": "With all her efforts, all her devotion, there was something wrong with her" (85). Yet after the ceremony, when she reads her forbidden Francis Thompson poems, she feels "something . . . happening to her . . . that had not happened when she made her First Communion" (103). Although the poems are religious, Nanda knows that the ecstasies she feels in reading them have nothing to do with God.

Throughout the novel, the convent girls are forced to sacrifice the joy of experiencing art. Their plays are edited; their books are confiscated; their writings are read and censored. The child who draws dogs with nuns' faces is expelled. Even the ability to interpret art is gently lifted from the girls and given to God. The girls' favorite painting is a *Mater Admirabilis*, the Blessed Mother as a young girl dressed in pink. Mary's heavenly expression—the story goes—was not created by the young student who painted her. Unable to get the face just right, the girl had given up, but the curtain was then pulled back to reveal the Virgin perfected, completed by a supernatural brush.

In the convent school, writing is the most suspect form of art for it involves communication and, of course, the individual will. Even the girls' letters home are opened and read by the nuns. The confiscation of the book *Dream Days*, which occurred when Nanda was in junior school, reminds Nanda to hide her Francis Thompson and, even more, the unfinished draft of the novel she is writing. But the convent approves of other types of narrative: saints' lives, accounts of martyrdom, and the sensational tales related by the nuns, particularly by Mother Poitier, the convent's resident Scheherezade. Girls may read of the horrifying death of the English martyr Margaret Clitheroe, but they must avoid all vulgar, silly stories, especially those by non-Catholic writers. Mother Poitier's stories might be called "Catholic gothic": they captivate an imagination-starved audience with ghosts and horrible punishments, but they also act as moral lessons on such issues as avoiding lies, remembering prayers, and the sanctity of suffering. The girls are told approvingly of a fellow first communicant, a poor child who suffered the whole ceremony with her veil pinned to her ear because she thought the pain was part of the sacrament.

One secular interpretation of conversion, argues Jeanne Flood in an essay on *Frost in May*, is "the more sinister one of changing the person into . . . someone more acceptable to him who forces the change" (1983, 133). What seems sinister in *Frost in May* is the nuns' power and authority over this change and their designation of the individual will as an enemy to faith. If we accept Flood's terms, we must ask who is forcing the change. Is the child being remade in order to be acceptable to God or to the nuns? Named for Christ's five wounds, the convent requires the renunciation of the self. Mother Radcliffe describes the system several times in the novel, always in the same language: "No character is any good in this world unless that will has been broken completely. Broken and re-set in God's own way" (145). Comforting Nanda after her father's rejection, Mother Radcliffe speaks for God, saying that he asks for sacrifice, especially of the things closest to us. But the nun also remarks about her own role in the process: "I had to break your will before your whole nature was deformed" (219). Self-will sickens and alters the nature given by God. Mother Radcliffe likens Nanda's will to a diseased tooth that must be pulled out; Nanda is like a "germ-carrier" (220).

The novel's most complex religious questions arise in its disturbing resolution. In this coming-of-age story, Nanda's forced departure from the convent is an expulsion from a paradise of friendship, youth, and frequent spiritual joy, but it also frees her from restriction and repression. Nanda leaves the convent broken, most especially by her father's wish that he "never had a daughter" (216). She is orphaned and cast out, but her great sacrifice may be sanctifying in itself. Her suffering, in a Christian context, does not need to be deserved by her or followed by earthly reward. Her submission to this suffering may be seen as an acceptance of God's will. In *Frost in May* these questions remain, but they are answered in part in the novels to follow, *The Lost Traveller*, *The Sugar House*, and *Beyond the Glass*. In a second version of the expulsion, Clara Batchelor (the now-renamed protagonist) discovers that her removal was the will of her father, not a demand of the sisters. Only if Mr. Grey/Claude Batchelor is an instrument of God can the rejection be seen as God's will. Even more important is the condition of Nanda's will. It has been broken, and Nanda dutifully obeys her father and the Mother Superior. Earlier in *Frost in May*, at Moira Palliser's clothing ceremony, the priest had bid the young girls to "go mad for the love of God"—to renounce the world and even apparent reason, to be crazy for God (53). Nanda's reincarnation, Clara Batchelor, takes on this charge in a different way. In a later novel, she goes to a madhouse, where she is often silent, alone, and restricted. In *Frost in May*, Nanda Grey, fearful of vocation and weakness, kneels before the Blessed Sacrament at the novel's end. There is no glimpse of her future. She had once thought of the Church as "like Fuji Yama ... massive, terrifying, beautiful and unescapable; the fortress of God, the house on the rock" (137). At the end, she has escaped the terrifying fortress, cast out of her Father's house on the rock.

CRITICAL RECEPTION

The revival of Antonia White's fiction by Carmen Callil at Virago occurred at a fortunate time. Had the novels never returned to print as they did in 1978 and 1979, they almost surely would not have received critical attention from contemporary scholars who read *Frost in May* primarily in terms of feminist, psychoanalytical, and autobiographical theory. Because Callil felt so strongly about the novels—giving *Frost in May* the honor of being the first Virago Modern Classic, writing the introductions, and following *Frost* with the reissue of the Clara trilogy a year later—the early 1980s saw several important critical treatments of the fiction, all of which discuss the crisp clarity of White's prose, the novels' multiple modes of discourse, and the close correspondence between the life of White's central character (Nanda Grey/Clara Batchelor) and her own.

Among the most important of these critical evaluations are several introductions to White's work. In 1948, Elizabeth Bowen provided an introduction to *Frost in May* that was then reprinted in the Virago edition. Bowen called *Frost in May* the only coming-of-age school story "that is a work of art" ([1948] 1978, v). She points to White's mastery of point of view, atmosphere, and timing as the source of the novel's profound effect. She writes, "In the biting crystal air of the book the children and the nuns stand out like early morning mountains" (ix). More recently, in *The Gender of Modernism*, Jane Marcus introduced an Antonia White story with an analysis of narrative that gives most of its space to *Frost in May*. Marcus claims that White's four novels "constitute a whole discourse on the writing woman's life in the twentieth century" (1990, 597), but she calls White's "contribution to modernism ... a major redefinition of female autobiographical forms" (598). Marcus identifies the novel's detached, distant third-person voice—the voice of the authoritative narrator—as the source of its artistic success and notes its radical alteration of the usual personal, sympathetic, confessional voice of female life-writing. Indeed, in the quality of its voice, *Frost in May* is most often compared not to another woman's autobiographical work but rather to James Joyce's *Portrait of the Artist as a Young Man*.

The close correspondence between the content of the novels and the events of White's life has prompted most of the scholarship on *Frost in May*. Certainly, the novel is most often discussed as a form of autobiography or women's writing. Several critics call *Frost in May* an exemplar of the life-writing form, while they note that White also experiments with and subverts the conventions of autobiographical fiction. *Frost in May* does contain several episodes that correspond to events in White's life: the left-handed sign of the cross, the influence of Francis Thompson's poetry, the writing of a sensational novel, the fear of a religious vocation, the lurid stories told by the nuns, the bathing in tents, and the influence of a "particular" friend, Charlotte d'Erlanger. The novel's climax and painful ending are also based on White's similar experience, in which she was seemingly expelled from the convent for writing a novel. She did not find out until years later that the removal was authored by her father, who saw it as an opportunity to save tuition money, and not by the nuns, who had offered to send her to another convent school in Newcastle.

These parallels and White's feelings about her time in Catholic school are described in several places, most particularly in Jane Dunn's biography, *Antonia White: A Life* (1998), and in two memoirs by White's daughters, Lyndall Passerini Hopkinson's *Nothing to Forgive* (1988) and Susan Chitty's *Now to My Mother* (1985). Susan Chitty also wrote the introduction to *As Once in May* (1983), which includes the unfinished piece "A Child of the Five Wounds," early material that was later incorporated into *Frost in May*.

Jeanne Flood explores the autobiographical center of *Frost in May* and the Clara novels, in which White reveals the "authorial struggle against silence" (1983, 132). In *Frost in May*, Nanda's writing is a creative act, but it also reveals a self that is repugnant to her father. Ironically, Flood points out, Nanda intends her novel to resolve as a fulfillment of the Catholic values she has assimilated: remorse for sin, reward and punishment, and conversion of the self. Ellen Cronan Rose, Mary Lynn Broe, and Mary Therese Strauss-Noll also examine *Frost in May* as an expression of White's troubled relationship with her father, Cecil Botting. Rose discusses James Joyce's success and White's relative failure to "achieve artistic maturity and authority" in terms of their relationships with their fathers (1991, 239). Strauss-Noll joins this critical discussion of White's "contradictory relation" with her father, emphasizing that the complex male-female relationship between them, while oppressive and psychologically painful for White, was also the source of her greatest fiction (2000, 129). Broe's essay links the disturbances in the "sexual order" of White's relationship with her father to difficulties in the "textual order" of her writing (1989, 42). The modernist writers community at Hayford Hall, says Broe, provided White and other women writers with an alternative to the "exile" and "silence" (45, 49) they had experienced in trying to write their "daughter's texts" (75).

Another "alternate female sexual economy" is the subject of Paulina Palmer's essay, which defines *Frost in May* as one type of lesbian novel (1991, 91). Female friendships are restricted and repressed, Palmer says, but there is a hidden culture in which acts such as hair-brushing, singing, and, of course, writing become subversive and erotic.

Substantive articles on *Frost in May* have appeared in the interdisciplinary journals *Cithara: Essays in the Judeo-Christian Tradition* and the *Journal of Literature and Theology*. Philip O'Mara emphasizes the sacrificial qualities of Nanda's (and Clara's) suffering, pointing out that this young woman's adherence to her faith—despite the oppressiveness of its methods—is a submission to the "obscurity of Providence and the consequent necessity of faith" (1988, 34). Although Nanda/Clara deeply fears a vocation, she undergoes her own suffering as a "parallel vocation," as is shown when her prayers for others—particularly the conversion of Clare Rockingham—are answered just after Nanda's own expulsion by school and father (35). Julietta Benson argues that White's novel engages in critical questioning about the "semantics of Catholic belief" rather than merely satirizing or condemning the Church's methods. White depicts the deep conflicts of a reasoning, questioning human being when faced with the demands and dilemmas of the Catholic faith. The novel's rhetorical complexity, claims Benson, arises from the conflict of religious values of community and obedience with the contemporary secular values of individualism and autonomy. This conflict and others that repeat it create an "interplay between belief and 'dis-belief'" that energizes the novel (1993, 301).

Several of these analyses bring together the politics of religion and feminism, often linking these to White's personal experiences. The most comprehensive scholarship uses these issues to discuss the artistic effect of Antonia White's novels as well as her place as a modernist writer.

NOTE

Antonia White, *Frost in May* (New York: Dial, 1980). All references are to this edition.

WORKS CITED

Benson, Julietta. 1993. "'Varieties of Dis-Belief': Antonia White and the Discourses of Faith and Skepticism." *Journal of Literature and Theology* 7: 284–301.

Bowen, Elizabeth. [1948] 1978. Introduction to *Frost in May*, by Antonia White, v–x. New York: Dial. Reprint, London: Virago.

Broe, Mary Lynn. 1989. "My Art Belongs to Daddy: Incest as Exile, the Textual Economics of Hayford Hall." In *Women's Writing in Exile*, ed. Mary Lynn Broe and Angela Ingram, 41–87. Chapel Hill: University of North Carolina Press.

Chitty, Susan. 1985. *Now to My Mother: A Very Personal Memoir of Antonia White*. London: Weidenfeld and Nicolson.

Dunn, Jane. 1998. *Antonia White: A Life*. London: Jonathan Cape.

Flood, Jeanne. 1983. "The Autobiographical Novels of Antonia White." *Critique: Studies in Contemporary Fiction* 24: 131–49.

Hopkinson, Lyndall Passerini. 1988. *Nothing to Forgive: A Daughter's Story of Antonia White*. London: Chatto and Windus.

Marcus, Jane. 1990. "Antonia White (1899–1980)." In *The Gender of Modernism: A Critical Anthology*, ed. Bonnie Kime Scott, 597–603. Bloomington: Indiana University Press.

O'Mara, Philip R. 1988. "Trust Amid Sore Affliction: Antonia White's Novels." *Cithara: Essays in the Judaeo-Christian Tradition* 28, no. 1: 33–43.

Palmer, Paulina. 1991. "Antonia White's *Frost in May*: A Lesbian Feminist Reading." In *Feminist Criticism: Theory and Practice*, ed. Susan Sellers, 89–108. Buffalo, NY: University of Toronto Press.

Rose, Ellen Cronan. 1991. "Antonia White: Portrait of the Artist as a Dutiful Daughter." *LIT* 2: 239–48.

Strauss-Noll, Mary Therese. 2000. "A Passionate and Troubled History: Antonia White and Her Father." *Pennsylvania English* 22, no. 1–2: 129–42.

White, Antonia. 1983. *As Once in May: The Early Autobiography of Antonia White and Other Writings*, ed. and intro. Susan Chitty. London: Virago.

———. 1983. *The Hound and the Falcon*. London: Virago.

— **Meoghan Byrne Cronin**

Larry Woiwode [1941–]

Beyond the Bedroom Wall

BIOGRAPHY

Larry Woiwode was born on October 30, 1941, in Carrington, North Dakota, and lived in nearby Sykeston until he was eight years old. Although he has resided in various places around the country, he and his wife Carole have lived in North Dakota for many years, and Woiwode has said, "I'm not sure I was ever an Easterner" (Watson 1996, 156). As Woiwode relates in his memoir, *What I Think I Did*, his great-grandfather "filed a homestead claim in Dakota Territory in 1881... in the Red River Valley, three hundred miles from [the Woiwodes'] present farm" (2000, 22). "My great-grandfather Charles was smuggled out of Upper Silesia in 1867 by his father, John," Woiwode writes, "because he was at the legal age for military conscription in Germany, ten. John wrapped him in a feather bed and carried him over his shoulder onto a ship bound for America, where Charles said he was sat upon and shoved around during the journey, but kept silent.... That silence and sense of exile he passed on" (21). In a helpful biographical sketch, Michael Connaughton suggests that "The harsh climate, stark beauty, and pervasive loneliness of this remote corner of rural America and its dignified, somewhat fatalistic Northern European populace provide the inspiration and much of the material for his fiction and poetry" (1980, 387). In his memoir, Woiwode also discusses the vital importance of his North Dakota upbringing to his development as a writer and a faithful Christian. Now a member of a Reformed Presbyterian congregation, Woiwode was raised a Catholic, and he describes in his memoir how he grew up hearing Scripture recited each day at parochial school and recalls "the melt of a communion host on my tongue, its sticky flat hole opening to my toes. How, after that, I'm new" (75). Woiwode's literary imagination has been formed by his North Dakotan upbringing and is both Scriptural and sacramental.

In *What I Think I Did*, Woiwode refers to a trunk of childhood memories that he opened as he began to write *Beyond the Bedroom Wall*. His parents, Everett and Audrey, are the models for the novel's saintly hero and heroine, Martin and Alpha Neumiller. Like Charles Neumiller in the novel, Larry Woiwode has an older brother, a younger brother, and two younger sisters. Their parents provided "an ordered spirit" (2000, 49) to their Sykeston home. This order was ruptured, however, with the death of Audrey on January 30, 1951, soon after the family's move to Manito, Illinois.

At the University of Illinois at Urbana-Champaign, Woiwode was influenced by a series of important writing teachers; his drama teacher, Charles Shattuck, was especially encouraging and introduced him to his friend, William Maxwell, the great writer and *New Yorker* editor. Woiwode moved to New York in 1964 and, under Maxwell's loving mentorship, published his first story in the *New Yorker* in 1965 and would continue to publish there over the next ten years. Many of these, revised, would constitute much of *Beyond the Bedroom Wall*.

On May 21, 1965, Woiwode married Carole Ann Peterson. The couple has four children—Newlyn, Joseph, Ruth, and Laurel—and a number of grandchildren. Woiwode's first novel, *What I'm Going to Do I Think*, was published in 1969. It portrays the early days of a just-married couple, Chris and Eileen. The novel won the PEN/Faulkner Award for first fiction, and Woiwode continued publishing stories about the Neumiller family. In 1975, the long-awaited *Beyond the Bedroom Wall: A Family Album* was published and received with great praise. On the front page of the *New York Times Book Review*, John Gardner testified that "nothing more beautiful or more moving has been written in years" (1975, 1). The novel was nominated for the National Book Critics' Circle Award and the National Book Award.

In the wake of literary success, however, Woiwode experienced familial stresses and strains—along with a renewal of faith. He vividly describes this passage in his life in a 1979 interview for *Christianity and Literature*:

With *Beyond the Bedroom Wall*, things that I wrote about began to happen in my life as I'd write them, or seem to, or I'd see shades of them in the newspapers. At other times it felt I was holding parts of the world in place, or affecting it in ways not necessarily healthy. Then, about four months after publication of the book, my father died. All through the book I'd been fighting belief, because I was dealing with generations whose lives were built around the Bible and Christ, and I'd come to the moment of saying, Yes, I believe, but then, as for me, well, let me do what I want. And proceeded to do it. My father had always been an example to me of what Christianity could be, and when he died it was not only as though my past had been severed, but there was no one to talk to whose motives I could wholly trust about what had been happening around the writing of the book; the fighting belief, the sensations I've mentioned. *Bedroom Wall* was written specifically for him. Fortunately, he'd lived long enough to go through the galleys of it with me. We passed them back and forth, nearly wordlessly, with small questions to one another here and there, across the hallway of a retreat house where he was working as a janitor and had got me a room. I lost consciousness once, is the only way I can describe it, and the next thing I knew I had his slippers on and he was walking me up and down the hallway. My state was fragile then, to say the least, and about three months after he died, with guilt and other pressures coming down, I was drinking and taking drugs to sleep, but couldn't do even that, and reached a point where I was at a sink cutting my wrists merely to bring matters to stop. It seemed I could go either all the way into madness or death or total oblivion, it wasn't clear which, and then I felt pulled back. I started looking forward to a pastor to come and read Psalms to me in the hospital. I'd started reading the New Testament before this, after reading most of it through at a stage of working on *Bedroom Wall*, and as I continued reading it, it came clear who it was who'd called me back. (Walhout et al. 1979, 15–16)

Woiwode's wife, Carole, also experienced a conversion at this time, and this shared experience healed a rift that had emerged in their marriage. In 1977, they joined a Reformed Presbyterian church. In a 1991 interview for *Renascence*, Woiwode reflected again on this conversion experience, but this time he accentuated its continuity with his Catholic upbringing:

Now at first, to a neo-evangelical audience, I probably would have been willing to describe this as a moment of conversion, but as I became more astute in my own theology . . . and because of my childhood, when I was catechized clearly in the essential doctrines of the Christian faith, I came to see my whole life as a spiritual movement forward. And I was grateful for every moment of it—including the days when I was rapped on the knuckles by the nuns for not knowing the answer to the catechism. . . . [M]y view has become more and more Augustinian, in that I see the potential, which scripture speaks of, of being chosen in Him from before the foundation of the world, so that, in response, we should be holy and without blame before Him in love. (Block 1991, 22)

In 1981, Woiwode published *Poppa John*, a short novel about an aging television actor who is "broken down" by grace over the course of an eventful Christmas weekend in New York City (197). In 1983, he began teaching at the State University of New York at Binghamton and helped sustain the creative writing program that John Gardner had invigorated until his tragic death in a motorcycle accident in 1982. In 1988, Woiwode left that position and he and his family settled permanently in North Dakota, where his children continued their home-schooling. That year, he published *Born Brothers*, which is written from the perspective of Charles Neumiller and emphasizes his relationship with his brother, Jerome. In 1989, *The Neumiller Stories* appeared, a collection of thirteen stories, ten of which had been revised and published as part of *Beyond the Bedroom Wall* and three of which, from the 1980s, had not previously been collected.

The novel *Indian Affairs* (1992) continues the story of Chris and Ellen. A collection of short stories, *Silent Passengers*, was published in 1993. Woiwode has also written numerous works of nonfiction: a collection of poems, *Even Tide* (1977), the title of which evokes "the way the two in marriage are evenly tied, or not, and the time of day when healing happened in Jesus' life" (*What I Think I Did*, 2000, 26); a book of reflections on the Acts of the Apostles (*Acts*, 1993); *The Aristocrat of the West: Biography of Harold Schafer* (2000); and the first volume in a planned autobiographical trilogy, *What I Think I Did* (2000), much of which describes his family's struggle to survive the 1996 North Dakota winter, the fiercest in the history of that state. In 1995, Woiwode was named North Dakota's poet laureate. Much as William F. Lynch describes the task of the Christian imagination in *Christ and Apollo* (1975), Woiwode believes that his task as a writer is to plunge into the particularities of place and person in order to emerge with universal truths, as he explained in the *Renascence* interview: "The deeper a writer penetrates into *region* the more the writer enters it. . . . [T]he more specific a simple sentence is about a place in North Dakota . . . the more someone from outside that region seems to read universality into it" (Block 1991, 18).

PLOT SUMMARY

Beyond the Bedroom Wall is a three-generation family saga that centers on Martin and Alpha Neumiller and their five children—Jerome, Charles, Tim, Marie, and Susan—a Catholic family with roots in North Dakota. Its "Prelude" begins with excerpts from the journals of Alexander Henry, "one of the first English-speaking explorers to enter North Dakota" (*Beyond the Bedroom Wall*, 3), in 1800 and 1801; the "Prelude" continues with "The Street," in which Tim, liminally poised between waking and sleeping, remembers the street in Hyatt, North Dakota, where he and his family lived for the first six years of his life.

In his review of the novel, Jonathan Yardley observed that "So much occurs in [Martin Neumiller's] life, and the lives interwoven with it, that summary is impossible" (1975, 21). However, one can highlight events that occur in each of the novel's five long parts, especially those that accentuate the novel's Catholic milieu.

Part one focuses on the courtship and marriage of Martin and Alpha. In 1935, Martin's father Charles, a devout Catholic, buries his father Otto in their unconsecrated farmland. Unexpectedly, the community of Mahomet arrives for the burial. Around this time, Martin courts Alpha, and he proposes to her while snow-bound at her family's home. Unexpectedly, Alpha's Lutheran (and anti-Catholic) parents awaken Martin in time for Mass on January 1, a Holy Day of Obligation. Anticipating and wishing to forestall prejudice, Martin seeks work as a teacher and states bluntly in his resume, "I am a Catholic, but have lived all my life in a Protestant community, so that I can be at ease among Protestants as well as Catholics" (*Beyond the Bedroom Wall*, 98). Alpha keeps a journal every day for five years, between 1936 and 1940. The journal records in intimate detail her anticipation of marriage to Martin and their early days as a couple. One entry, for example, reads, "Went to Church this a.m. with Elaine—the first time I'd been to a Catholic Mass. I couldn't understand the Dope's Lingo, as Daddy calls it, or why they were sitting and standing and sitting and kneeling all the time, so I just sat. They didn't sing any hymns" (107). But she agrees to take catechism lessons with Father Krull, a Neumiller family relation. Father Krull appreciates Alpha's intellect and passion, and the two become friends. In time, Alpha embraces the Catholic faith wholeheartedly.

Part two focuses on the Neumiller's family life in Hyatt, North Dakota. Father Schimmelpfennig—a German priest who had resisted the Third Reich—allows the growing family to purchase inexpensively a spacious new home that another large Catholic family, the Russells, "nearly monastic in their devotion to the faith" (148), had vacated. One day, young Father James Russell, on his way to a conference on sacramentals, stops to look at his old house, quizzes the children in their catechism, and blesses them. Tim, the youngest boy, often left behind by Jerome and Charles, befriends an older mentally retarded boy. Alpha observes and allows the friendship and responds to it with prayerful concern. She and

Martin pray with great intensity when six-year-old Charles develops double pneumonia and is near death. Charles recovers and recalls his initiation in second grade into "the club that met in secret in the Black Forest" (210), in which he was interrogated by Kuntz, "The Ruler," about his commitment to the Catholic faith. Privately, Charles wonders if he truly believes in God, then hears the trees whisper, as if in reply, "yessss" (231). Charles—who will become an actor as adult—performs as a cowboy in a talent contest. He earns first prize but also his mother's scorn for losing his cool on stage. Martin, with his growing family, becomes ambitious and restless. He takes on a series of different jobs—farming, selling insurance, plumbing—a precursor to his decision to move the family to Illinois.

Book three is a book of sorrows. The family moves to Illinois with Martin trusting in the verbal promises of a new job and a new home. Both promises are broken; the job offer is retracted because he is a Catholic. The family, which now includes five children, moves into a dank house where Alpha, pregnant with her sixth child, falls very ill. Her daughter is stillborn, and, soon afterward, Alpha dies. The chapters that follow record the grief experienced by Charles, by Ed Jones, Alpha's father, and, most deeply, by Martin, who must now raise and discipline his children alone amidst their roughhousing and sexual curiosity.

Part four portrays the children coming to maturity. Tim develops as a poet. Marie, who was five when Alpha died, relies on photographs to remember her mother. Martin returns to teaching and, within six years of doing so, has become a principal again and remarries. Charles is away at college when he learns of grandfather Charles's death, just as Martin was when his grandfather died. The family reunites for his funeral. Part five portrays the children as adults, dispersed throughout the country, withdrawing from the practices of their family faith but finally reuniting on the occasion of the death of Martin's second wife, Laura.

MAJOR THEMES

The Catholic heart of *Beyond the Bedroom Wall* can be discerned if the reader approaches the saga of the Neumiller family as a depiction of a "domestic church" or "the church in miniature." This depiction has a number of emphases: a sacramental sense of physical reality, the sacerdotal presence of priests, but the most prominent is the saintly life of graced virtue lived by Alpha and Martin, which impresses itself indelibly upon the memories of their children.

Although Alpha's parents are deeply suspicious of Catholics, she finds herself drawn to Catholicism through Martin and her friendship with two priests. "Alpha'd heard [her mother] say that the biggest bane on the entire human race, other than cigarettes and alcohol, was the Roman Catholic Church" (117), but she finds herself "fighting an affection for the Catholic Church," especially as "Martin partly helped change her mother's predisposition against Catholics" (119). Her friendship with Father Krull, from whom she receives catechism lessons before she and Martin marry, deepens her affection. Father Krull respects her fierce intelligence—they argue about theology—and deeply respects her freedom. With great "moral authority," he warns Martin, "Don't you ever, ever, even if your life depends on it, try to persuade that girl to become a Catholic, do you hear?" (125). In her last session with Father Krull, as Alpha relates in her journal, she "wanted to say some kind words to him . . . and then he said, 'Why don't we just spend these last few minutes together in silence?' I listened and heard the Lord in currents of wind through wheat or flax! I'm alive at last or have died" (127). She also befriends and studies with the parish priest in Hyatt, Father Schimmelpfennig, and this relationship culminates in her conversion to Catholicism:

> She'd studied under Father Schimmelpfennig for five years in a dilatory way, and was brilliant, prideful, witty, well read, limited, uncompromising, hyperbolic and extreme, open-minded, too critical both ways, serene, conservative, saintly, down to earth, yet a romantic who could feed on the food of illusion, and Father's fingers began trembling now, in the way they'd trembled only once, when he was ordained, as he took from the gold-lined ciborium a consecrated host and placed it on the curved bridge of Alpha Neumiller's wet, extended, orange-pink tongue. (231)

Later, after the trial of Charles's illness, and just before her own, Alpha recalls this moment and comes to understand why she has embraced Catholicism: "She'd converted because of the feeling of light, a light she'd sensed but couldn't quite see. The more she studied the Bible and the catechism, the stronger the light became. . . . Since her First Communion, the light had stayed" (256). In his funeral homily for Alpha, Father Schimmelpfennig calls Alpha a saint.

So too is Martin. His formative model is his own father, Charles, who is immensely charitable toward each person he meets. He pleads to his wife on behalf of the ever-cursing Ed Jones, arguing, "Anybody who uses God's name as often as Jones has God's praise in his heart, or at least His fear" (68). Martin recalls the day when, as a child, he absently flung a stone at the family's prize cow and struck the Guernsey dead. "I expected a licking to last me the rest of my life," he tells his sons, "but instead Dad lifted me to my feet and said, 'Come home and eat now. You've suffered enough'" (181).

Like Alpha, Martin is very much a person of prayer. When stuck at the Jones's home on the night he proposes to Alpha, he prays the rosary on the buttons of his shirt (64). The next morning, "Martin was kneeling in the furnace-heated warmth of St. Boniface Church in Wimbledon, asking God if Alpha could be his wife" (97). He attends Mass every day (179). The reader receives a brief glimpse of Father Schimmelpfennig's view of Martin: he sees him as "Biblical . . . because of purity and strength of character came out of unclouded ingenuousness. Over the years, Martin had become his best friend and confidant, his confessor, practically, and Martin had three intelligent, promising young sons. You could never tell where priest material might spring from!" (150). Martin experiences deep doubts about God's reality and goodness during his son's, Charles's, illness (203), but in the wake of Alpha's death, nearly exhausted from grief, he hears her voice and a constant "children's choir singing, 'At the cross her station keeping, stood the mournful mother weeping.'" He awakens to the arrival of Father Schimmelpfennig, who has driven twenty-two hours to give Alpha's eulogy at her funeral (311). Perhaps most markedly, and despite the profound suffering he undergoes, Martin is characterized by a sense of wonder: "Where others saw no mystery, he could find it, and kept himself in a constant state of childlike wonder, exuberance, and joy" (152).

The children of Martin and Alpha—especially their three sons, whom the reader comes to know most fully—are formed by the sanctity of their parents.

Jerome, the eldest, remembers the story his father tells of his own father's forgiveness (478); at early Mass, he recalls "his only intimation of heaven—especially on the final hymn, 'Holy God, We Praise Thy Name,' when it became clear that his grandfather's only means of expressing emotion was in song" (492). When he is younger, soon after Alpha's death, Charles's deepest desire is fulfilled on a fishing trip with Father Schimmelpfennig after he catches the biggest fish: "He'd always wanted to be a hero to somebody, and especially Father if he had his choice, and now was, by Father's word, and Father had also called him pure, which was what he'd needed to hear, for some reason, since the night his mother died" (353). Later, as a young married man, he sees himself as a "doomed Catholic" (607), yet he prays to God while touching his wedding ring, hoping that his pregnant wife, Catherine, will give birth to a daughter (600). And, finally, Tim, who becomes a poet, provides the final line of the novel, in the poem that forms the novel's envoi and its final prayer: "And this long hour of last light, Lord, and goodbye" (623).

The long narrative of *Beyond the Bedroom Wall* closes on a note of gratitude. Late at night, on the occasion of the family's gathering to mourn the death of Martin's second wife, Laura, Martin speaks to Charles and compares his life to a book. He declares that now he is ready to "close the book" (618). But, in the last words of the novel, he reconsiders: "his father lifted his hands to apply quotes, and said, 'Tomorrow I'll probably wake and say, "To Be Continued for Life." The birds are already singing now. Listen to how many of them there are out there. Oh, let's both of us get back to our beds and try to sleep for a while. We all need some sleep around here. Sleep well. And thank you for being here with me. Sleep well, sleep well'" (618–19). This closing note is appropriate, for the novel as a whole, despite all the suffering it records, reverberates with a tone of gratitude. A note of thankful wonder in the face of created mystery is struck at the start in the novel's epigraph, by Erik Erikson, "'Reality,' of course, is man's most powerful illusion; but while he attends to this world, it must outbalance the total enigma of being in it at all." Martin, gifted with a sense of wonder, is grateful not only to Charles, who has listened to his stories for years, but—by extension—also to the reader, who has attended to these stories for 620 pages, and to God, who has granted him a life that he sees as a book, as a narrative with an integral wholeness of form.

But Martin can neither write this narrative himself nor close the cover of the book that is his life. Martin reopens his hands, and accepts its continuing openness, its unfinalizability, that which is "to be continued for life." In *After Virtue*, Alasdair MacIntyre (1997) observes the narrative quality that brings a unity to a person's life: lived lives are marked by a sense of teleological closure and yet, at the same time, by openness and unpredictability. Martin—father of five, twice married, twice a widower, teacher, saint—does not know what the next day will hold, how it might be unexpectedly graced. He can intimate its wholeness. But as he says good night to Charles and the reader, he remains receptive, for the final form of that life is uncertain.

Nor can Martin himself bring final form to his life story. In the novel, we learn that he has tried. When they are little boys, his sons discover the beginnings of his manuscript in the desk in the attic, but they find only titles of chapters (158). Martin never finishes his book. He needs another to bring written narrative form to his life. By implication, that other will be his son, Charles.

Larry Woiwode—the middle brother who wrote *Beyond the Bedroom Wall* in pious homage to his own mother and father—is artistically suggesting a wisdom arrived at philosophically by theorist Mikhail Bakhtin, an insight that bears a kinship to Catholicism's pervasively communal emphasis: we cannot, by ourselves, give final form to our own lives. On the horizontal level we need another person, one who can see things we cannot—the quality of the sky, for example, behind our heads. With his or her position of "outsideness," the other person can grace our lives with a sense of form, with what Bakhtin calls "rhythm." Furthermore, as Bakhtin suggests in his later writings, we articulate our sense of our life's meaning, faithful that we are in the presence of a vertical presence, if you will, the silent, attentive presence that Bakhtin calls our "Superaddressee." This is one who can understand us in the way in which we most deeply desire, intend, and hope to be understood.

This, then, is the final way in which the Neumiller family portrayed in *Beyond the Bedroom Wall* emerges as a domestic church and church in miniature: as in the Church, the life story is spoken and entrusted to a community of others, and the other—here, by implication, Charles—will grant the story narrative form, bring it to loving consummation. Martin's story is entrusted to the community in a way analogous to that of Scripture—in which Woiwode immersed himself when he wrote his novel, in order to understand his parents' lives—in a way similar to that in which the Church hands down the lives of the saints. In this novel, the communion of saints extends through space and time, not only in memory but in real presence: at least five times in the novel, characters receive palpable impressions that deceased loved ones are present (52, 129, 231, 433, 616). Charles, sleepily, imperfectly present to his father, is entrusted with and will tell Martin's story.

When *Beyond the Bedroom Wall* was published in 1975, it was highly praised but often criticized for lacking a unified plot. But what seems to be a lack may be part of Woiwode's purpose, for if we are created by a loving Creator, and if we tell our lives with trust into the faithful ears of our Superaddressee, we do not have to provide the plot ourselves. The plot, the "master story"—creation, redemption, sanctification—is given, granted. As Frank Kermode beautifully observes in *The Sense of an Ending* in response to another Catholic writer, such a narrative sense "reflects, however imperfectly, a universal plot, an enchanting order of beginning, middle, and end, concords so apt and unexpected that you laugh or weep when you stumble on them; peripeteias so vast and apparently uncontrolled that nothing in the literature of comedy or tragedy can do more than faintly image them" (1966, 132). *Beyond the Bedroom Wall* images and represents that which is given and then retrieved through remembering. Each of its forty-four chapters finely attends to the particulars of person and place and to the moments of graced epiphany that can and do transpire within families, within communities, and within the Church.

CRITICAL RECEPTION

Almost without exception, the many reviews of *Beyond the Bedroom Wall* were immensely positive. Within the context of these deeply appreciative reviews, one issue frequently recurs: does this long series of detailed family "snapshots," seen from various points of view, hang together as a unified novel? Jonathan Yardley, for example, called it "a beautiful novel" and claimed that "[a]mong contemporary novelists only Updike writes affectingly and knowingly about domestic life," yet he judged it "too long by a third, [with] its last 200 pages carry[ing] only a shadow of the force contained in the first 400" (1975, 21). An anonymous reviewer for the *New Yorker* also observed that "the novel thins considerably toward the end" yet affirmed that Woiwode's sense of the intricacy of family ties "is extraordinary" (1975, 56). Amanda Heller, however, praised the deeply affecting art of the novel and was "surpri[sed] to see [the various previously published short stories] come together with such impressive effect" (1975, 108). Christopher Derrick judged "the quality of the writing [to be] quite remarkable" but also noted its "bulky and chaotic" form, "the kind of thing you spread all over the table for an evening of family nostalgia" (1977, 740). Robert Leiter noted the novel's varied points of view but also its "basically linear progression . . . its smooth, dreamlike flow." The novel's theme of redemptive memory recalls Proust, "[a]nd like Proust's great work, Woiwode's should not be read quickly, but rather in long slow draughts that will not blur its beauty and power" (1975, 39). Paul Gray also praised Woiwode's "fine talent for description, coupled with a Proustian ability to recreate the past" (1975, 80). Peter Prescott lauded Woiwode's capacity to inhabit the varied consciousnesses of his narrators—"he is equally at ease with a young girl rejoicing in her talent and with an old man cursing God"—but wondered whether the book was truly a novel, given Woiwode's dispensing of "the unities of plot and narration" (1975, 85).

A second issue recurs in these reviews: is the novel sentimental in its portrayal of deep emotion? Christopher Lehmann-Haupt concludes that it is indeed "sentimental—sentimental in the very best sense of the word—but sentimental, not tragic or ironic" (1975, 35). In a review insensate to what she labels Woiwode's "homespun warmth," Maureen Howard claimed "Woiwode has one tone—sincerity veering on sentimentality. If he had kept the novel uncluttered it would have attained the simple mimetic appeal of *Our Town*" (1976, 408). Roger Sale's review anticipated this sort of criticism and responded cogently:

> Does [Woiwode's "Family Album"] sound a perfect formula for sentimentality? It is no more so than is "East Coker": "Home is where one starts from. . . . " Like Eliot, Woiwode perceives a time for "the evening with the photograph album" and that "Love is most nearly itself / When here and now cease to matter." But whereas Eliot filtered and displaced his autobiographical sense of home and family, Woiwode succeeds by being personal, by putting his imagination at the service of memory, and by realizing in this way that love really is most nearly itself when the here and now cease to matter. He is remembering the Neumillers in the years before he was born. (1975, 31)

Sale's review hints at the spiritual dimension of Woiwode's novel. So too does Joseph Lovering's appreciation: "Woiwode's emphasis on the spiritual side of man's nature, and his proper yet realistic proportioning of the naturalistic side of that nature, is a fine thing to witness in a modern novel" (1975, 264). Stephen Koch declared the novel "drenched in Roman Catholicism" yet critiqued it for giving "religion no intellectual attention" (1975, 31).

Given Woiwode's later appreciation of the spiritual and artistic achievement of John Gardner's "monumental" (1984, 330) final novel, *Mickelsson's Ghosts*, it is apt that Gardner was perhaps best able to appreciate both the spiritual and artistic achievement of Woiwode's masterpiece:

> From the beginning to the end of this novel, Woiwode's dramatization of the problem of getting a hold on reality—the problem of fully realizing what lies out there at the edge of dreams and memories, "beyond the bedroom wall,"— is simply brilliant. . . . Ultimately, by devices of which some readers will disapprove, the link of love, fragmentary shared experience, and faith links all humanity together in *Beyond the Bedroom Wall.* . . . Partly by the brilliance of his storytelling, partly by the beauty and fundamental good-heartedness of the story he tells, Woiwode nails the dramatic truth summed up abstractly in his epigraph from Erik Erikson: "'Reality,' of course, is man's most powerful illusion; but while he attends to this world, it must outbalance the total enigma of being in it at all." (1975, 2)

NOTE

Larry Woiwode, *Beyond the Bedroom Wall: A Family Album* (New York: Farrar, Straus and Giroux, 1975). All references are to this edition. Copyright © 1975 by Larry Woiwode. Used by permission of Farrar, Straus and Giroux, LLC. Quotations from the interview with Clarence Walhout, John Timmerman, and Edward Ericson used by permission of *Christianity and Literature*. I wish to express my gratitude to Monica Kunecki for her research assistance in this essay.

WORKS CITED

Block, Ed, Jr. 1991. "An Interview with Larry Woiwode." *Renascence* 44, no. 1 (Fall): 17–30.

Connaughton, Michael E. 1980. "Larry Woiwode." In *Dictionary of Literary Biography, Vol. 6: American Novelists Since World War II*, 2nd series, ed. James E. Kibler Jr., 387–91. Detroit: Gale/Bruccoli Clark.

Derrick, Christopher. 1977. Review of *Beyond the Bedroom Wall*, by Larry Woiwode. *Times Literary Supplement* (June 17): 740.

Gardner, John. 1975. Review of *Beyond the Bedroom Wall*, by Larry Woiwode. *New York Times Book Review* (September 28): 1–2.

Gray, Paul. 1975. Review of *Beyond the Bedroom Wall*, by Larry Woiwode. *Time* 106 (September 29): 80.

Heller, Amanda. 1975. Review of *Beyond the Bedroom Wall*, by Larry Woiwode. *Atlantic* 236 (October): 108.

Howard, Maureen. 1976. Review of *Beyond the Bedroom Wall*, by Larry Woiwode. *Yale Review* 65, no. 3 (March): 407–08.

Kermode, Frank. 1966. *The Sense of an Ending: Studies in the Theory of Fiction.* London: Oxford University Press.

Koch, Stephen. 1975. Review of *Beyond the Bedroom Wall*, by Larry Woiwode. *Saturday Review* 2 (September 6): 30–31.

Lehmann-Haupt, Christopher. 1975. Review of *Beyond the Bedroom Wall*, by Larry Woiwode. *New York Times* 125 (October 14): 35.

Leiter, Robert. 1975. Review of *Beyond the Bedroom Wall*, by Larry Woiwode. *New Republic* 173, no. 18 (November): 39.

Lovering, Joseph P. 1975. Review of *Beyond the Bedroom Wall*, by Larry Woiwode. *Best Sellers* 35 (December): 263–64.

Lynch, William F., S. J. 1975. *Christ and Apollo*. Notre Dame, IN: University of Notre Dame Press.

MacIntyre, Alasdair. 1997. *After Virtue: A Study in Moral Theory*. Notre Dame, IN: University of Notre Dame Press.

Prescott, Peter S. 1975. Review of *Beyond the Bedroom Wall*, by Larry Woiwode. *Newsweek* 86 (September 29): 85–86.

Pritchard, William H. 1976. Review of *Beyond the Bedroom Wall*, by Larry Woiwode. *Hudson Review* 29 (Spring): 156.

Review of *Beyond the Bedroom Wall*, by Larry Woiwode. *New Yorker* 51, no. 45 (December 29, 1975): 55–56.

Sale, Roger. 1975. Review of *Beyond the Bedroom Wall*, by Larry Woiwode. *New York Review of Books* 22, no. 18 (November 13): 31–32.

Walhout, Clarence, John Timmerman, and Edward Ericson. 1979. "Interview with Larry Woiwode." *Christianity and Literature* 29, no. 1 (Fall): 11–18.

Watson, Rick. 1996. "Where the Buffalo Roam: An Interview with Larry Woiwode." *North Dakota Quarterly* 63, no. 4 (Fall): 154–66.

Woiwode, Larry. 1983. *Poppa John*. Westchester, IL: Crossway Books.

———. 1984. "*Mickelsson's Ghosts*: Gardner's Memorial in Real Time." *MSS* 4, no. 12 (Fall): 315–30.

———. 1989. *The Neumiller Stories*. New York: Farrar, Straus and Giroux.

———. 2000. *What I Think I Did: A Season of Survival in Two Acts*. New York: Basic Books.

Yardley, Jonathan. 1975. Review of *Beyond the Bedroom Wall*, by Larry Woiwode. *Washington Post Book World* no. 290 (September 21): K21.

— Paul J. Contino

Selected General Bibliography

Allitt, Patrick. *Catholic Converts: British and American Intellectuals Turn to Rome.* Ithaca, NY: Cornell University Press, 1997.

Aveling, J. C. H. *The Handle and the Axe: The Catholic Recusants in England from Reformation to Emancipation.* London: Blond and Briggs, 1976.

Avis, Paul D. L. *God and the Creative Imagination: Metaphor, Symbol, and Myth in Religion and Theology.* New York: Routledge, 1999.

Baker, Joseph Ellis. *The Novel and the Oxford Movement.* New York: Russell and Russell, 1965.

Bausch, William J. *Storytelling: Imagination and Faith.* Mystic, CT: Twenty-Third Publications, 1984.

Beer, Frances. *Women and Mystical Experience in the Middle Ages.* Rochester, NY: Boydell Press, 1992.

Bergonzi, Bernard. "A Conspicuous Absentee: The Decline and Fall of the Catholic Novel." *Encounter* 55 (August–September 1980): 44–56.

Bochen, Christine M. *The Journey to Rome: Conversion Literature by Nineteenth Century American Catholics.* Rev. ed., New York: Garland, 1988.

Bornstein, Daniel, and Robert O. Rusconi, eds. *Women and Religion in Medieval and Renaissance Italy,* trans. Margery J. Schneider. Chicago: University of Chicago Press, 1996.

Bossy, John. *The English Catholic Community, 1570–1850.* London: Darton, Longman, and Todd, 1975.

Breslin, John B. "The Open-Ended Mystery of Matter: Readings of the Catholic Imagination." In *Examining the Catholic Intellectual Tradition,* ed. Anthony J. Cernera and Oliver J. Morgan, 147–78. Fairfield, CT: Sacred Heart University Press, 2000.

Brinkmeyer, Robert H., Jr. *Three Catholic Writers of the Modern South.* Jackson: University Press of Mississippi, 1985.

Brown, Dale W., ed. *Of Fiction and Faith: Twelve American Writers Talk About Their Vision and Work.* Grand Rapids, MI: Eerdmans, 1997.

Brown, Stephen J. M., S. J., and Thomas McDermott. *A Survey of Catholic Literature.* Milwaukee, WI: Bruce Publishing Co., 1945.

Bynum, Caroline Walker. *Jesus as Mother: Studies in the Spirituality of the High Middle Ages.* Berkeley: University of California Press, 1982.

Cadegan, Una Mary. *All Good Books Are Catholic Books: Literature, Censorship, and the Americanization of Catholics, 1920–1960.* Ann Arbor, MI: UMI, 1988.

Calvert, Alexander, S. J. *The Catholic Literary Revival*. Milwaukee, WI: Bruce Publishing Co., 1935.

Carver, George, ed. *The Catholic Tradition in English Literature*. Garden City, NY: Doubleday, Page, 1926.

Church, R. W. *The Oxford Movement, Twelve Years: 1833–1845*. 1891. Reprint, Chicago: University of Chicago Press, 1970.

Coleman, T. W. *English Mystics of the Fourteenth Century*. Westport, CT: Greenwood, 1971.

Comerford, Kathleen M., and Hilmar M. Pabel, eds. *Early Modern Catholicism: Essays in Honor of John W. O'Malley, S. J.* Toronto: University of Toronto Press, 2001.

Cousins, Anthony D. *The Catholic Religious Poets from Southwell to Crashaw: A Critical History*. Chicago: Sheed and Ward, 1992.

Deen, Rosemary. "Poetry of Conversion and the Religious Life." *Commonweal* 71, no. 24 (March 11, 1960): 656–57.

Desmond, John F. "Catholicism in Contemporary American Fiction." *America* 170 (May 4, 1994): 7–11.

Dolan, Jay P. *The American Catholic Experience: A History from Colonial Times to the Present*. Garden City, NY: Doubleday, 1985.

Dronke, Peter. *Women Writers of the Middle Ages: A Critical Study of Texts from Perpetua (d. 203) to Marguerite Porete (d. 1310)*. Cambridge: Cambridge University Press, 1984.

D'Souza, Dinesh. *The Catholic Classics*. Huntington, IN: Our Sunday Visitor, 1986.

Dulles, Avery R. *The Catholicity of the Church*. Oxford: Clarendon Press, 1985.

Elie, Paul. *The Life You Save May Be Your Own: An American Pilgrimage*. New York: Farrar, Straus & Giroux, 2003.

Eliot, T. S. "Religion and Literature." 1932. In *Religion and Modern Literature: Essays in Theory and Criticism*, ed. Edward E. Ericson and G. B. Tennyson, 21–30. Grand Rapids, MI: Eerdmans, 1975.

Fanning, Charles. *The Irish Voice in America: Irish-American Fiction from the 1760s to the 1980s*. Lexington: University Press of Kentucky, 1990.

Fraser, Theodore P. *The Modern Catholic Novel in Europe*. New York: Twayne, 1994.

Gable, Mariella, O. S. B. *The Literature of Spiritual Values and Catholic Fiction*, ed. and intro. Nancy Hynes, O. S. B. Lanham, MD: University Press of America, 1996.

Gandolfo, Anita. "The Demise of Father O'Malley: Reflections on Recent American Catholic Fiction." *U.S. Catholic Historian* 6 (Spring/Summer 1987): 231–40.

———. *Testing the Faith: The New Catholic Fiction in America*. New York: Greenwood, 1992.

Gardner, Helen L. *Religion and Literature*. London: Faber and Faber, 1971.

Gelpi, Albert. "The Catholic Presence in American Culture." *American Literary History* 11, no. 1 (Spring 1999): 196–212.

Gerhart, Mary. "Whatever Happened to the Catholic Novel?" In *Morphologies of Faith: Essays in Religion and Culture in Honor of Nathan A. Scott, Jr.*, ed. Mary Gerhart and Anthony C. Yu., 181–201. Atlanta, GA: Scholars Press, 1990.

Giles, Mary E., ed. *Women in the Inquisition: Spain and the New World*. Baltimore, MD: Johns Hopkins University Press, 1999.

Giles, Paul. *American Catholic Arts and Fictions: Culture, Ideology, Aesthetics*. Cambridge: Cambridge University Press, 1992.

Gordon, Caroline. *How to Read a Novel*. New York: Viking, 1957.

Greeley, Andrew M. *The Catholic Imagination*. Berkeley: University of California Press, 2000.

———. *Religion as Poetry*. New Brunswick, NJ: Transaction Publishers, 1995.

Green, Garrett. *Imagining God: Theology and the Religious Imagination*. New York: HarperCollins, 1989.

Griffiths, Richard. *The Reactionary Revolution: The Catholic Revival in French Literature, 1870–1914*. New York: F. Ungar, 1965.

Halsey, William M. *The Survival of American Innocence: Catholicism in an Era of Disillusionment, 1920–1940*. Notre Dame, IN: University of Notre Dame Press, 1980.

Hannay, Margaret P., ed. *Silent But for the Word: Tudor Women as Patrons, Translators, and Writers of Religious Works*. Kent, OH: Kent State University Press, 1985.

Hansen, Ron. *A Stay Against Confusion: Essays on Faith and Fiction*. New York: HarperCollins, 2001.

Hardon, John A., S. J. *The Catholic Lifetime Reading Plan*. Royal Oaks, MI: Grotto Press, 1998.

Hawley, John C. *Through a Glass Darkly: Essays in the Religious Imagination*. New York: Fordham University Press, 1996.

Hoehn, Matthew, ed. *Catholic Authors: Contemporary Biographical Sketches, 1930–1952*. Newark, NJ: St. Mary's Abbey, 1948–1952.

James, William. *The Varieties of Religious Experiences: A Study in Human Nature*. New York: New American Library, 1958.

Jasper, David. *The Study of Literature and Religion*. Minneapolis, MN: Fortress, 1989.

Keeler, Mary J. *Catholic Literary France*. New York: Irvington Publishers, 1982.

Kellogg, Gene. *The Vital Tradition: The Catholic Novel in a Period of Convergence*. Chicago: Loyola University Press, 1970.

Ker, Ian T. *The Catholic Revival in English Literature, 1845–1961: Newman, Hopkins, Belloc, Chesterton, Greene, Waugh*. Notre Dame, IN: University of Notre Dame Press, 2003.

Knowles, David. *The English Mystical Tradition*. New York: Harper and Brothers, 1961.

Labrie, Ross. *The Catholic Imagination in American Literature*. Columbia: University of Missouri Press, 1997.

Leigh, David. *Circuitous Journeys: Modern Spiritual Autobiography*. New York: Fordham University Press, 2000.

Lynch, William F. *Christ and Apollo: The Dimensions of the Literary Imagination*. Notre Dame, IN: University of Notre Dame Press, 1975.

Luker, Ralph. "To Be Southern, to Be Catholic: An Interpretation of the Thought of Five American Writers." *Southern Studies* 23 (1984): 3–7.

Maison, Margaret M. *The Victorian Vision: Studies in the Religious Novel*. New York: Sheed and Ward, 1961.

Mariani, Paul. *God and the Imagination: On Poets, Poetry, and the Ineffable*. Athens: University of Georgia Press, 2002.

Matter, Ann E., and John Coakley, eds. *Creative Women in Medieval and Early Modern Italy*. Philadelphia: University of Pennsylvania Press, 1994.

McDannell, Colleen. *The Christian Home in Victorian America, 1840–1900*. Bloomington: Indiana University Press, 1986.

McDonnell, Thomas P., ed. *Classic Catholic Poetry*. Huntington, IN: Our Sunday Visitor, 1988.

McInerney, Ralph M., ed. *The Catholic Writer: Papers Presented at a Conference Sponsored by the Wethersfield Institute, New York City, Sept. 29–30, 1989.* San Francisco: Ignatius Press, 1991.

McVeigh, Daniel M. "Real Presence? Some Reflections on Literature and Sacrament." *Christianity and Literature* 41, no. 2 (Winter 1992): 141–57.

Menendez, Albert J. *The Catholic Novel: An Annotated Bibliography*. New York: Garland, 1988.

Messbarger, Paul R. *Fiction with a Parochial Purpose: Social Use of American Catholic Literature, 1884–1900.* Brookline, MA: Boston University Press, 1971.

Morris, Charles R. *American Catholic: The Saints and Sinners Who Built America's Most Powerful Church.* New York: Times Books, 1997.

Murphy, James H. *Catholic Fiction and Social Reality in Ireland, 1873–1922.* Westport, CT: Greenwood, 1997.

Neuhaus, Richard John. *The Catholic Moment: The Paradox of the Church in the Postmodern World.* San Francisco: Harper and Row, 1987.

O'Connor, Flannery. *Mystery and Manners: Occasional Prose*, ed. Sally and Robert Fitzgerald. New York: Farrar, Straus and Giroux, 1961.

Oden, Amy, ed. *In Her Words: Women's Writings in the History of Christian Thought.* Nashville, TN: Abingdon Press, 1994.

O'Donnell, Donat [Conor Cruise O'Brien]. *Maria Cross: Imaginative Patterns in a Group of Catholic Writers.* New York: Oxford University Press, 1952.

Ong, Walter. *American Catholic Crossroads*. 1959. Westport, CT: Greenwood, 1981.

O'Rourke, William. "Catholics Coming of Age: The Literary Consequences." *New Catholic World* 228 (July–August 1985): 148–52.

Pearce, Joseph. *Literary Converts: Spiritual Inspiration in an Age of Unbelief.* San Francisco: Ignatius Press, 1999.

Peters, Thomas. *The Christian Imagination.* San Francisco: Ignatius Press, 2000.

Petroff, Elizabeth A. *Body and Soul: Essays on Medieval Women and Mysticism.* New York: Oxford University Press, 1994.

———. *Medieval Women's Visionary Literature.* New York: Oxford University Press, 1986.

Quillan, Michael, S. J. "Since Blue Died: Catholic Novels Since 1961." *Critic* 34 (Fall 1975): 25–35.

Reichardt, Mary R. *Catholic Women Writers: A Bio-Bibliographical Sourcebook.* Westport, CT: Greenwood, 2001.

———. *Exploring Catholic Literature: A Companion and Resource Guide.* Lanham, MD: Rowman and Littlefield, 2003.

Reynolds, David S. *Faith in Fiction: The Emergence of Religious Literature in America.* Cambridge, MA: Harvard University Press, 1981.

Ricoeur, Paul. *Figuring the Sacred: Religion, Narrative, and Imagination*, trans. David Pellauer. Minneapolis, MN: Fortress, 1995.

Rowell, Geoffrey. *The Vision Glorious: Themes and Personalities of the Catholic Revival in Anglicanism.* Oxford: Oxford University Press, 1983.

Ryken, Leland. *The Christian Imagination: The Practice of Faith in Literature and Writing.* Colorado Springs, CO: Shaw Books, 2002.

Sayers, Valerie. "Being a Writer, Being Catholic." *Commonweal* (May 4, 2001): 12–16.

Schroth, Raymond A. *Books for Believers: 35 Books That Every Catholic Ought to Read*. New York: Paulist Press, 1987.

———. *From Dante to Dead Man Walking: One Reader's Journey Through the Christian Classics*. Chicago: Loyola University Press, 2002.

Schuster, George N. *The Catholic Church and Current Literature*. New York: Macmillan, 1930.

———. *The Catholic Spirit in Modern English Literature*. New York: Macmillan, 1922.

Scott, Malcolm. *The Struggle for the Soul of the French Novel: French Catholic and Realist Novelists, 1850–1970*. Washington, DC: Catholic University of America Press, 1990.

Scott, Nathan A., ed. *The Broken Center: Studies in the Theological Horizon of Modern Literature*. New Haven, CT: Yale University Press, 1966.

Shell, Alison. *Catholicism, Controversy, and the English Literary Imagination, 1558–1660*. Cambridge: Cambridge University Press, 1999.

Smith, Larry. "Catholics, Catholics Everywhere: A Flood of Catholic Novels." *Critic* 37 (December 1978): 1–8.

Sonnenfeld, Albert. *Crossroads: Essays on the Catholic Novelists*. York, SC: French Literature Publications, 1982.

Sparr, Arnold J. "From Self-Congratulation to Self-Criticism: Main Currents in American Catholic Fiction, 1900–1960." *U. S. Catholic Historian* 6 (Spring/Summer 1987): 213–30.

———. *To Promote, Defend, and Redeem: The Catholic Literary Revival and the Cultural Transformation of American Catholicism, 1920–1960*." New York: Greenwood, 1990.

Steiner, George. *Real Presences*. Reprint, Chicago: University of Chicago Press, 1991.

Surtz, Ronald E. *Writing Women in Late Medieval and Early Modern Spain: The Mothers of Saint Teresa of Avila*. Philadelphia: University of Pennsylvania Press, 1995.

Szarmach, Paul E., ed. *An Introduction to the Medieval Mystics of Europe*. Albany: State University of New York Press, 1984.

Taves, Ann. *The Household of Faith: Roman Catholic Devotions in Mid-Nineteenth Century America*. Notre Dame, IN: University of Notre Dame Press, 1986.

TeSelle, Sallie. *Literature and the Christian Life*. New Haven, CT: Yale University Press, 1966.

Thorp, Willard. *Catholic Novelists in Defense of Their Faith, 1829–1865*. New York: Arno, 1978.

Tynan, Daniel J., ed. *Biographical Dictionary of Contemporary Catholic American Writing*. New York: Greenwood, 1989.

Underhill, Evelyn. *The Mystics of the Church*. Greenwood, SC: Attic Press, 1975.

Wheeler, Michael. *The Old Enemies: Catholic and Protestant in Nineteenth-Century English Literature and Culture*. Cambridge: Cambridge University Press, 2004.

White, James A. *The Era of Good Intentions: A Survey of American Catholic Writing, 1880–1915*. 1958. New York: Arno, 1978.

Whitehouse, J. C., ed. *Catholics on Literature*. Dublin: Four Courts Press, 1997.

———. *Vertical Man: The Human Person in the Novels of Graham Greene, Sigrid Undset, and Georges Bernanos*. New York: Garland, 1990. Rev. ed., London: The Saint Austin Press, 1999.

Wiesner-Hanks, Merry, ed. *Convents Confront the Reformation: Catholic and Protestant Nuns in Germany*, trans. Joan Skocir and Merry Wiesner-Hanks. Milwaukee, WI: Marquette University Press, 996.

Wilson, Katharina M., ed. *Medieval Women Writers*. Athens: University of Georgia Press, 1987.

Wolff, Robert Lee. *Gains and Losses: Novels of Faith and Doubt in Victorian England*. New York: Garland, 1977.

Wood, Ralph C. *The Comedy of Redemption: Christian Faith and Comic Vision in Four American Novelists*. Notre Dame, IN: University of Notre Dame Press, 1988.

Woodman, Thomas M. *Faithful Fictions: The Catholic Novel in British Literature*. Philadelphia: Open University Press, 1991.

Zinsser, William, ed. *Spiritual Quests: The Art and Craft of Religious Writing*. Boston: Houghton Mifflin, 1988.

Index

Note: Page numbers in **bold** type indicate main entries.

Stein and, 660–70. *See also* Existentialism; Phenomenology
Physiologus, 191
Piaf, Edith, 711
Pick, John, 345
Piehl, Mel, 156
Piero della Francesca, 656
Pietà (statue), 222
Pigott, Edward, 560
Pilgrim at Tinker Creek (Dillard), 167
Pilgrim in the Ruins (Tolson), 541
Pinamonti, Giovanni Pietro, 366
Pinkerton, John, 220
Pio, Padre, 594
Pius IX, 508
Pius X, 43, 703
Pius XI, 49, 350, 482, 661, 666
Pius XII, 161, 604
Place: Belloc and theology of, 33–34, 37; Eliot and, 223; Everson and, 259; John of the Cross and metaphors of, 354–55; Koch and, 398
Plaskow, Judith, 476
Plato: More's *Utopia* and, 487, 488; on philosophy's role in politics, 485–86, 487
Platt, Michael, xxvii
Plotting Women: Gender and Representation in Mexico (Franco), 377
Pluralism: Cather and, 81
Plutarch, 487
Plutus (Aristophanes), 247
Podles, Mary Elizabeth, 185
Poems of Gerard Manley Hopkins, 340–45
Poems Penyeach (Joyce), 361
Poems, Protest, and a Dream (Peden), 376
Poems (Rossetti), 607
A Poet Before the Cross (Claudel), 127
Poetic Art (Claudel), 130
"Poetry and Peace: Some Broader Dimensions" (Levertov), 432
Poetry: Hopkins and language of, 343–44
Poetry Review, 650
Poets' Corner, Westminster Abbey, 93
Poland, 639–47
Political activism. *See* Social justice
Politics: Böll's liberal, 54–55, 60–61; Brownson versus radical, 71; Catherine of Siena and, 84; Chesterton and, 107; Meynell and, 461, 470; philosophy and, in More's *Utopia*, 485–87
Pope, Alexander, 187, 552–61; *Essay on Man*, 555–61
Popes: Dante on, 153
Poppa John (Woiwode), 786

Porter, Katherine Anne, 279, 522, 563–73; *Ship of Fools*, 564–73
A Portrait of the Artist as a Young Man (Joyce), 360, 361–67, 453, 780
Positivism: Sienkiewicz and, 639–40
Postmodernism: Cather and, 81; Joyce and, 366–67; Lax and, 414, 415, 418, 419; Levertov and, 436–37; Weil and, 770
Poulenc, Francis, 42, 428
Poulson, Edwa, 255
Pound, Ezra, 124, 153, 360
Poverty: Bernanos on, 46–47; Day and the poor, 155–64
Powell, Amanda, 376
Powell, Lawrence Clark, 255
The Power and the Glory (Greene), 299–306, 325, 424
The Power of Confidence (De Meester), 712
Powers, Jessica, 585–95; poems of, 585–95
Powers, J. F., 575–84; *Morte d'Urban*, 575–84; as satirist, xxv
Praeterita (Ruskin), 495
The Praise of Folly (Erasmus), 245–53, 485, 487, 490
Pranger, M. B., 26
Pranzini, Henri, 705
A Prayer for Owen Meany (Irving), 308
Preaching: Dominican Order and, 86, 91; Suso and, 682, 689–90; women and, 90–91, 328–29
Predestination: Chaucer on, 94–95
A Preface to Chaucer (Robertson), 103
Preludes (Meynell), 461
The Prelude (Wordsworth), 21
Pre-Raphaelite Brotherhood, 612–13
Presbyterianism, 191
Prescott, Peter S., 314, 792
Present Position of Catholics in England (Newman), 500
Pressley, Eugene, 564, 569
Price, Martin, 584
Pride: Augustine on, 559; Pope on, 559; Sayers on, 621; Thomas Aquinas on, 559, 621
The Prime of Miss Jean Brodie (Spark), 650
Princeton Dante Project, 152
Prior, Matthew, 196
Private Thoughts upon Religion and Private Thoughts upon a Christian Life (Beveridge), 497
The Professor's House (Cather), 74, 78
Progress: absence of, in Christian world view, 110; Chesterton on, 108–10; Undset on, 729

About the Editor and Contributors

Mary R. Reichardt is a professor of literature and Catholic Studies and the director of the master's program in Catholic Studies at the University of St. Thomas in St. Paul, Minnesota. She received a Ph.D. in English from the University of Wisconsin–Madison in 1987. Her teaching and research interests include Catholic literature, American literature, women's literature, autobiography, and the short story. The author of seven books, her previous works on Catholic literature are *Catholic Women Writers: A Bio-Bibliographical Sourcebook* (Greenwood 2001) and *Exploring Catholic Literature: A Companion and Resource Guide* (Rowman and Littlefield 2003).

C. N. Sue Abromaitis received her Ph.D. from the University of Maryland and has written and lectured on Alexander Pope and J. R. R. Tolkien, among other literary figures. She is a professor in the Department of English at Loyola College, Maryland, where she has taught since 1962. A Lady of the Equestrian Order of the Holy Sepulcher of Jerusalem, she is a member of the boards of the Fellowship of Catholic Scholars, the Maryland Catholic Conference, the Cathedral Foundation, and Mount de Sales Academy.

Ann W. Astell received a doctorate from the University of Wisconsin–Madison in 1987 and is professor of English and director of Medieval Studies at Purdue University. She is the author of five books on medieval and medievalist literature and the recipient of numerous awards, including a John Simon Guggenheim Memorial Fellowship (2001–2002).

Virginia Brackett serves as chair of the English Department at Triton College in River Grove, Illinois, where she is also coordinator for the Scholars Programs and co-editor of the arts journal, *Ariel*. She has published seven books: her biographies for young readers on Virginia Woolf and Sandra Cisneros were published in 2004 by Morgan Reynolds Press.

Kathleen Burk holds an A.B. degree from Spring Hill College and a master's degree and Ph.D. from the University of Dallas. She is an essayist, editor, and a Pushcart Prize–nominated poet. She is currently the director of the Philosophy and Letters Program at the University of Dallas.

Victoria Carlson-Casaregola is a graduate of the Creative Nonfiction Program at the University of Iowa. She is a writer whose work has appeared in a number of national publications, including *The Christian Science Monitor* and *U.S. Catholic*. She teaches at both Saint Louis University and at Cor Jesu Academy in St. Louis, Missouri.

Vincent Casaregola is an associate professor of English at Saint Louis University, where he directs the English Department Writing Program. He has published scholarly articles on a variety of subjects, including rhetorical theory, the history of rhetoric, and a range of literary genres and periods.

Paul J. Contino is an associate professor of Great Books at Pepperdine University. He also serves as associate director of Pepperdine's Center for Faith and Learning, and he is co-editor of the journal *Christianity and Literature*. He has published essays on Dostoevsky, Flannery O'Connor, and Andre Dubus, and he co-edited *Bakhtin and Religion: A Feeling for Faith* (Northwestern University Press 2001).

Mark Cronin is the director of Academic Advisement and the Honors Program at Saint Anselm College, where he also teaches humanities and in the English Department. He has published articles on Dickens, Thackeray, and Kipling. His other academic interests include contemporary American fiction and the subject of adaptation.

Meoghan Byrne Cronin is an associate professor of romantic and Victorian literature at Saint Anselm College in Manchester, New Hampshire, where she is also the coordinator of freshman composition. Her published scholarship has focused on the novels of Thomas Hardy. She is currently at work on a book-length project tentatively called "Faith and the Orphaned Schoolgirl," which defines the British convent-school novel and examines its relationship to the female *bildungsroman*.

Stacey Lee Donohue is an associate professor of English at Central Oregon Community College in Bend, Oregon, and editor of the Community College Humanities Association newsletter, *The Community College Humanist*. She received her Ph.D. in English from the Graduate School and University Center of the City University of New York in 1995 and has presented and published a variety of articles on teaching and literature.

Mary Frances Dorschell, O. S. U., received an M.A. in Spanish and Latin American literature from the Universidad Iberoamericana (Mexico City) and an M.A. and Ph.D. in French literature from the University of Western Ontario. She is an associate professor of French and chair of the Department of Modern Languages at Brescia University College in London, Ontario. Her book, *Georges Bernanos' Debt to Thérèse of Lisieux*, was published by Mellen University Press in 1996, and her most recent publication is "Mentors and Protégés: Spiritual Evolution in Georges Bernanos' *Under Satan's Sun* and *The Diary of a Country Priest*" (*Christianity and Literature*, Autumn 2002).

Deanna Delmar Evans, a professor of English at Bemidji State University in Minnesota, has published articles in several collections and journals, including *Neophilologus*, *Studies in Scottish Literature*, *Medieval Feminist Newsletter*, *Medieval Association of the Midwest Journal*, and *Minnesota English Journal*. She has also written entries for *Dictionary of Medieval Biography*, *Medieval Folklore*, *The Rise of the Medieval World: 500–1300*, and *Catholic Women Writers*, and has other journal articles and encyclopedia items forthcoming. Her most recent publication is an edition of the late medieval poem "The Babees Book" in *Medieval Literature for Children*.

Joseph J. Feeney, S. J., is a professor of English at Saint Joseph's University in Philadelphia and co-editor of the journal *The Hopkins Quarterly* and the book *Hopkins Variations: Standing Round a Waterfall*. He has discovered a Hopkins poem (the comic "'Consule Jones'"), a poetic fragment, four letters, and a short story, all first published in *TLS: The Times Literary Supplement*. He has written over a hundred essays on Hopkins, on British, Irish, and American writers, and on Jesuit education; was a visiting professor at Georgetown, Santa Clara, and Seattle universities; and is writing a book on the playfulness of Hopkins.

Candice Fredrick is an associate professor in the Advanced Studies Department at Azusa Pacific University. She has written two previous books, *Women, Ethics and the Workplace* and *Women Among the Inklings*.

Van C. Gessel is dean of the College of Humanities and a professor of Japanese at Brigham Young University. He received his Ph.D. in Japanese from Columbia University. He is the author of two scholarly books on modern Japanese literature: *The Sting of Life: Three Contemporary Japanese Novelists* (Columbia University Press 1989) and *Three Modern Novelists: Soseki, Tanizaki, Kawabata* (Kodansha International 1993); co-editor of *The Showa Anthology* (Kodansha International 1985); editor of two volumes on modern Japanese novelists for the Dictionary of Literary Biography series; and translator of six literary works by Shusaku Endo, including *The Samurai* and *Deep River*.

Trudis E. Goldsmith-Reber is an associate professor of German Studies at McGill University, Montreal, Quebec. She received her doctorate in theater from the University of Köln and also trained professionally for the theater in Düsseldorf. She has acted in and directed theater performances in Cologne, Bonn, and at Montreal's International Theatre, and has also worked as a programmer for the Cologne-based television station WWF/WDR. She has published on modern German literature, drama, theater, and film.

F. Elizabeth Gray teaches Victorian literature at Massey University, New Zealand, having previously taught at the University of Virginia. She has published articles on nineteenth-century women's verse in *Victorian Poetry* and *Christianity and Literature*, and she created the Alice Meynell website at http://xroads.virginia.edu/~Public/feg/alice/am1.html. Her research interests include the nineteenth-century periodical press and the poetry of Christina Rossetti.

Mary Theresa Hall is an associate professor of English at Thiel College in Greenville, Pennsylvania. Her teaching and research interests range from linguistics and the history of the English language to spiritual autobiography and issues in higher education. She is the author of *Country Parsons, Country Poets: George Herbert and Gerard Manley Hopkins as Spiritual Autobiographers*. Among her recent publications are an essay on Thérèse of Lisieux in *Catholic Women Writers*; "A Collage: A Coda on Peter Elbow," in *Writing with Peter Elbow*; and "On the Margin of Discovery" in *Teacher Commentary on Student Papers*.

John J. Han is an associate professor of English at Missouri Baptist University in St. Louis and editor of *Intégrité: A Faith and Learning Journal*. His publications include articles on the *Ancrene Wisse*, Andrew Marvell, Flannery O'Connor, John Steinbeck, ethnic American literature, and Christian multiculturalism. He is currently working on two book-length projects: Puritan writers and faith-learning integration.

Patrick Hicks currently teaches literature and creative writing at Augustana College in Sioux Falls, South Dakota. He has lived throughout Europe, including long residencies in Northern Ireland, Germany, Spain, and England. His fiction, poetry, and academic work have been featured in a number of national and international publications.

Robert Ellis Hosmer Jr. is senior lecturer in the Department of English Languages and Literature at Smith College, where he has taught courses in fiction, poetry, and recent British writing, as well as advanced seminars on contemporary British women writers, Virginia Woolf, and Muriel Spark, since 1990. His publications include *Contemporary British Women Writers: Narrative Strategies* (Macmillan 1993). His essays, reviews, and interviews have appeared in the *Boston Globe*, the *New York Times*, the *Chicago Tribune*, *America*, *Commonweal*, the *Southern Review*, and the *Paris Review*. Two projects on Muriel Spark are in progress.

Kathleen Jacquette is an assistant professor at the State University of New York at Farmingdale. Her research interests include women writers, Irish writers, and Catholic writers. Her Ph.D. dissertation was titled "Irish, Female, and Catholic—the Vision of Patriarchy in the Fiction of Edna O'Brien."

Maria Keaton is a doctoral student at Marquette University, specializing in British Renaissance and British Victorian literature. Her publications include "The Mother's Tale: The Development of Juno in *Juno and the Paycock*," in *New Hibernia Review* (Winter 1999) and the introductions to the four-volume set of the reprinted works of religious prose by Christina Rossetti, published simultaneously by Thoemmes Press and Edition Synapse in 2003.

Ian Ker has taught both English and theology at universities in the United States and Britain, where he is now a member of the Oxford theology faculty. He is the author and editor of twenty books on Newman, including *John Henry Newman: A Biography* (1988). His most recent book is *The Catholic Revival in English Literature, 1845–1961* (2003).

Anne H. King received her doctorate from Fordham University in 1987. Her research interests include medieval mysticism, spirituality, Trinitarian theology, Celtic spirituality and theology, and other systematic topics. She has published a number of articles and a book on Hildegard of Bingen; has written articles on other female mystics, including Teresa of Avila and Julian of Norwich; and is currently working on a forthcoming publication on comparative Celtic spirituality and kinship structures. An associate professor, she has been a member of the Theology Department at the University of St. Thomas in St. Paul, Minnesota, since 1985.

Ross Labrie, who teaches at the University of British Columbia in Vancouver, is the author of six books on American literature. These include *The Catholic Imagination in American Literature* (1997) and two books on Thomas Merton, *The Art of Thomas*

Merton (1979) and *Thomas Merton and the Inclusive Imagination* (2001). He has also served as an international advisor to the International Thomas Merton Society and is on the advisory board of the *Merton Annual*.

Maria LaMonaca is an assistant professor of English at Columbia College in South Carolina. She is currently working on a book project tentatively titled "Catholicism and the Victorian Woman Writer, 1830–70." Her articles on religious discourse and Victorian women's writing have been published in *Studies in the Novel*, *Victorians Institute Journal*, and *Nineteenth-Century Studies*.

Janine Langan is the founder of the successful Christianity and Culture Program at the University of Toronto. Now in its twenty-fifth year, the program offers students access to the great moments of Christian artistic, social, philosophical, and spiritual tradition. She has published on Hegel and Mallarme, Job, Newman, Pascal, Dostoevsky, Teilhard de Chardin, Simone de Beauvoir, and Pope John Paul II, and she has lectured widely on Christian art, Christian education, and Christian responsibility to culture.

Edyta Laszczewska was born in Poland and attended schools in Poland and Switzerland before moving to Canada to pursue her university studies. She is currently a Ph.D. candidate in the Department of German Studies at McGill University in Montreal, working on the application of Wolfgang Iser's theory of aesthetic response to the interpretation of German medieval texts. Her main area of scholarly interest is the inherent variability of the medieval text.

James A. Levernier is a professor of English at the University of Arkansas at Little Rock, where he specializes in the multicultural literatures of early America. He is the co-editor of *American Writers Before 1800* (three volumes) and of *The Indians and Their Captives*, and he is co-author of *The Indian Captivity Narrative, 1550–1900* and *Structuring Paragraphs and Essays*.

Robert P. Lewis is an associate professor of English at Marist College in Poughkeepsie, New York, where he also serves as coordinator of the Catholic Studies minor. He has degrees from Manhattan College and Columbia University and holds a Ph.D. in Victorian literature from New York University. He has published articles on the religious dimensions of George Eliot's fiction and is currently exploring the theological overtones of contemporary American fiction writers.

Raymond N. MacKenzie is a professor of English at the University of St. Thomas in St. Paul, Minnesota. He has published a number of articles on literature, ethics, and the history of publishing. He is the author of a biography of the novelist Viola Meynell (Edwin Mellen 2002), and he has recently published a translation of François Mauriac's *God and Mammon* and *What Was Lost* (Rowman and Littlefield 2003).

Sam McBride is a senior professor of general education at DeVry University, Pomona. He teaches writing, speech, and literature, including a course in J. R. R. Tolkien's *The Lord of the Rings*. With Candice Fredrick, he authored *Women Among the Inklings: Gender, C. S. Lewis, J. R. R. Tolkien and Charles Williams*.

Kevin T. McEneaney has authored the "Mary Lavin" entry for the *Encyclopedia Americana*, as well as numerous other entries. He is co-editor of the *Irish Literary*

Supplement and the author of *The Enclosed Garden* (1991) and *Longing* (1997). He teaches at Marist College in Poughkeepsie, New York.

Brendan McManus is an associate professor of history at Bemidji State University in northern Minnesota. He received his Ph.D. from Syracuse University, writing his dissertation on a juristic commentary by Laurentius Hispanus (d. 1248). His interests include Roman and canon law in the high and later Middle Ages and political theory.

Jeannine Mizingou is an assistant professor of English at Nyack College in New York City. She earned a B.A. in English at Waynesburg College and an M.A. and Ph.D. in English at Duquesne University. She has published academic articles in *Religion and Literature, Christianity and Literature, Logos: A Journal of Catholic Thought and Culture*, and *The Merton Annual*. Her publications also include a book of poetry and nonfiction essays in magazines with international circulation. She has presented talks on religion and literature at various national conferences.

Molly Morrison is an assistant professor of Italian at Ohio University in Athens, Ohio. She is the advisor for Ohio University's Certificate in Italian Studies. Her primary research interests are medieval and Renaissance Italian literature. She has published articles on various Italian holy women and on Dante.

Jane F. Morrissey, a Sister of St. Joseph, has served since 1963 as a high school and college teacher, director of the congregational Office for Justice and Peace, pastoral minister in an inner city Hispanic parish, and most recently as congregational president. She earned her doctorate at the University of Massachusetts in Amherst. Her publications include essays on medieval poetry, contemplative literature, and teaching justice and peace. She is also co-author of a collection of Guatemalan oral stories on Hermano Pedro Betancur, the first canonized saint of Central America, entitled *Gracias, Matiox, Thanks, Hermano Pedro: A Trilingual Anthology of Guatemalan Oral Tradition.*

Russell Elliott Murphy was educated at the University of Massachusetts. He is a professor of English and chair of the department at the University of Arkansas at Little Rock. The founding director of the annual St. Charles Borromeo Conference on Catholicism in Literature, he has published widely on Gerard Manley Hopkins, William Butler Yeats, and T. S. Eliot. Since 1987 he has been the editor of the *Yeats Eliot Review.*

Ann V. Norton received a doctorate in English literature from Columbia University. She is an associate professor of English at Saint Anselm College in Manchester, New Hampshire, where she teaches nineteenth- and twentieth-century British literature. Her book, *Paradoxical Feminism: The Novels of Rebecca West*, was published in 2000, and she has written on Virginia Woolf, Edna O'Brien, Mary Lavin, Antonia White, and Anita Brookner.

Freda Mary Oben is known internationally as an Edith Stein scholar. Other interests include human rights, particularly the questions of women, race relations, and religious bigotry. She is a convert from Judaism. Her doctorate was earned at Catholic

University of America, and her last teaching posts were at Howard University and Washington Theological Union.

Angela O'Donnell teaches English and American literature at Loyola College in Maryland. She is particularly interested in exploring the relationship between poetry and faith as a reader, as a teacher, and as a poet. Her poems have appeared in a number of journals, including *America, Hawaii Pacific Review, Potomac Review, Runes, Studio: A Journal of Christians Writing, Xavier Review,* and *Windhover.*

Brennan O'Donnell is a professor of English and director of the Honor's Program at Loyola College in Maryland. His scholarly interests include poetry and poetics (especially the poetry of William Wordsworth), the English romantic period, and religion and literature. He recently co-edited a collection of essays on Andre Dubus, published in *Religion and the Arts* (2002). He is currently at work with co-author Paul Contino on a book about contemporary American Catholic writers.

Douglas Lane Patey is Sophia Smith Professor of English at Smith College, where he also directs the college's program in the History of Science and Technology. A specialist in eighteenth-century British literature and philosophy, his publications include *Probability and Literary Form: Philosophic Theory and Literary Practice in the Augustan Age* (Cambridge University Press 1984), *Evelyn Waugh: A Critical Biography* (Blackwell 1998), and most recently, *Of Human Bondage: Historical Perspectives on Addiction* (Smith College Studies in History 2003).

Joseph Pearce is writer-in-residence and associate professor of literature at Ave Maria University in Florida. He is the author of thirteen books, including biographies of Hilaire Belloc, G. K. Chesterton, J. R. R. Tolkien, C. S. Lewis, Alexander Solzhenitsyn, Oscar Wilde, and Roy Campbell. He co-edits the *St. Austin Review (StAR)*, a Catholic cultural journal (www.saintaustinreview.com). He has written for numerous publications in Europe and the United States, both academic and otherwise.

Paul M. Puccio is an assistant professor of English at Bloomfield College in Bloomfield, Pennsylvania. His teaching and research interests include Victorian literature, British school and college fiction, contemplative writing and teaching practice, and contemporary theater. He is also engaged in work on the nature of contemporary institutional culture in higher education. He has published in *Writing on the Edge, Dialogue, Modern Language Studies, Dickens Quarterly, Kritikon Litterarum, Family Matters in the British and American Novel,* and *Reading Stephen Sondheim.*

Patrick Reilly was educated at the University of Glasgow and Pembroke College, Oxford, and is emeritus professor and former chair of English literature at the University of Glasgow. His publications include *Jonathan Swift: The Brave Desponder* (University of Manchester 1982); *George Orwell: The Age's Adversary* (Macmillan 1986); *The Literature of Guilt: From Gulliver to Golding* (Macmillan 1988); *"Nineteen Eighty Four": Past, Present, and Future* (Twayne/G. K. Hall 1989); *"Tom Jones": Adventure and Providence* (Twayne/G. K. Hall 1991); *"Lord of the Flies": Fathers and Sons* (Twayne/G. K. Hall 1992); and *The Dark Landscape of Modern Fiction* (Ashgate 2003).

Katherine G. Rodgers received her Ph.D. in Renaissance Studies from Yale in 1992. Her publications include an edition of Thomas More's "Treatise on the Last Things"

(Yale University Press 1997) and "George Herbert on the Last Things" (1998). Her present research looks at rhetorical strategies in the speeches of Elizabeth I. She is currently a lecturer in the composition program at California State University, Sacramento.

Robert Royal received his Ph.D. in comparative literature from the Catholic University of America and has taught at Brown University, Rhode Island College, and The Catholic University of America. He is currently president of the Faith and Reason Institute in Washington, D.C. A columnist for *Crisis* magazine, his articles have appeared in numerous scholarly journals and other publications. His books include *The Virgin and the Dynamo: The Use and Abuse of Religion in the Environment Debate* (Eerdmans 1999), *Dante Alighieri* in the Spiritual Legacy series (Crossroad 1999), and *The Catholic Martyrs of the Twentieth Century: A Comprehensive Global History* (Crossroad 2000).

Gerald J. Russello is a lawyer practicing in New York City. He is the editor of *Christianity and Western Culture: Selections from the Work of Christopher Dawson* (CUA 1998). He has contributed essays to many publications, including *Renascence* and *Logos*.

Josef Schmidt has published extensively on German renaissance and reformation literature. He has also done research on popular religious literature. Another of his interests is Christian mysticism: he has written introductions to the works of John Tauler and Angelus Silesius (for the Paulist Press Classics of Western Spirituality series), as well as a translation from the French (with Marion Moamai) of the autobiography of the French mystic Marie de l'Incarnation (in the Johannes Verlag of Hans Urs von Balthasar).

Karl Schmude is an Australian academic librarian and freelance writer. He formerly served as director of libraries at the University of New England in Armidale, New South Wales, and is now part of an emerging Catholic liberal arts institution, Campion College Australia. His research interests include the history and literature of Christian culture and Catholic writers in Australia, and he has published articles and reviews on these topics in both Australian and international journals.

Gerald Michael Schnabel is an emeritus professor of history at Bemidji State University in Minnesota where he taught from 1967 to 1999. Both his undergraduate and graduate studies were done at the University of Wisconsin–Madison. He has taught courses in and researched American intellectual and religious history, Victorian England, English cultural history, and American colonial and revolutionary history. At Bemidji State University he served as chair of the History Department, as coordinator of the Religious Studies Program, and as a faculty member in the Honors, International Studies, Women's Studies, Peace and Justice Studies, and Space Studies programs.

Adam Schwartz received his Ph.D. from Northwestern University and is an assistant professor of history at Christendom College. He has written over forty articles, essays, and reviews on topics in modern British Christian thought. His study of Catholic convert intellectuals in twentieth-century Britain is forthcoming from Catholic University of America Press.

Debra L. Stoudt is a professor of German in the Department of Foreign Languages at the University of Toledo where she has taught since 1987. She is the co-editor of *Medieval Sermons and Society: Cloister, City, University* (FIDEM 1998) and has published articles on the letters and sermons of the medieval German mystics and on the medical and alchemical manuscripts of sixteenth-century Heidelberg.

Elizabeth Bachrach Tan is an independent scholar and director of education at Maple Ridge Church in Amherst, Massachusetts. She is co-editor of *The Academy and the Possibility of Belief: Essays on Intellectual and Spiritual Life* (2000) and wrote about American spiritual autobiographies in her dissertation "Standing on Holy Ground: The Sacred Landscapes of Annie Dillard, Kathleen Norris, and Frederick Buechner." Her research interests include spiritual autobiography, contemporary religious discourse, discourses of space, and religious education. She also works as a freelance editor and writer.

Michael R. Tobin received a Ph.D. from the University of Western Ontario in London, Ontario, in 1985. He is currently an associate professor of French at St. Thomas More College in the University of Saskatchewan, Canada. He has published extensively on Bernanos in scholarly journals in the United States and Canada and has recently completed a book on the theological source of Bernanos's creative imagination.

Patricia Mary Vinje received her doctorate in historical theology and spirituality from Marquette University in Milwaukee, Wisconsin, before teaching at universities in Dallas, Baltimore, and Chicago. Her writings include books on Catherine of Siena and Julian of Norwich and numerous articles on Scripture, the sacraments, and prayer. At present she lives as a consecrated solitary in central Wisconsin.

Mary Warner is a School Sister of Notre Dame and an associate professor of English and director of English education at Western Carolina University, where she has worked since 1996. She has published a number of essays on Jessica Powers, including "Who Speaks for Winter? Jessica Powers: Poet and Mystic" in *Renascence* (Summer 2002). She also wrote the chapter "Faith Born of Anguish: Sarah Miles as Profligate and Apostle" for *Graham Greene and Perspective of Religious Faith*, edited by William Thomas Hill. Her current research and forthcoming book are on adolescents in their search for meaning and on guiding teens to sacred texts.

Wendy A. Weaver is pursuing a Ph.D. in English and is a teaching assistant at Marquette University, Milwaukee, Wisconsin. She has previously worked as the editorial assistant for *Renascence: Essays on Values in Literature*, published by Marquette. She was awarded a graduate fellowship for Collegium's 2003 colloquy, and she has published an article in *Logos: A Journal of Catholic Thought and Culture*. Her areas of interest include autobiography, poetry, and spirituality in literature.

Thomas Werge is a professor of English at the University of Notre Dame and co-editor of the scholarly journal *Religion and Literature*. He has written on the religious dimensions of early and nineteenth-century American literature and on such figures as Dante, Dostoevsky, and Simone Weil.

J. C. Whitehouse studied at the universities of Sheffield, Besançon, Paris, and Bradford. He has translated three of Georges Bernanos's novels, and his published work on

Catholic literature includes the books *Vertical Man, A Study of the Human Person in the Novels of Graham Greene, Sigrid Undset, and Georges Bernanos*, and *Catholics on Literature*, a collection of reflections by Catholic authors. He has also published many articles on Bernanos, Undset, Greene, and Brian Moore, and on Catholic writing in journals in Britain, France, America, Germany, and Brazil. Formerly reader in comparative literature at the University of Bradford, England, he is currently enjoying an active retirement.

Brian Wilkie served as a professor of English and a member of the comparative literature faculty at the University of Arkansas from 1985 to 2003. Before coming to Arkansas, he also taught at the University of Wisconsin, Dartmouth College, and the University of Illinois. He published scholarly books and articles on the major English romantic poets, especially William Blake, and on Jane Austen, Virgil, the epic tradition, general literary topics, and American literature. He also co-edited a major anthology, *Literature of the Western World*, which is now in its fifth printing. Professor Wilkie passed away in December 2003.

David Williams is a professor of English and Kennedy Smith Professor of Catholic Studies at McGill University, Montreal, Canada. He is the author of *Deformed Discourse: The Function of the Monster in Mediaeval Thought and Literature*, which received the Raymond Klibansky Prize for Most Outstanding Book in the Humanities (1997–1998). He is the author of several other books and articles on Chaucer, Alexander the Great, medieval language theory, and related subjects. He teaches various courses including Chaucer, the Bible and Literature, Saints' Lives, and the Culture of Death.

Ralph C. Wood received his Ph.D. from the University of Chicago and is university professor of theology and literature at Baylor University in Waco, Texas. His major book, still in print, is entitled *The Comedy of Redemption: Christian Faith and Comic Vision in Four American Novelists* (Notre Dame 1988). He is also the author of *Contending for the Faith: The Church's Engagement with Culture* (Baylor 2003) and *The Gospel According to Tolkien: Visions of the Kingdom in Middle-earth* (2003). *Flannery O'Connor's Christ-Haunted South: Her Region and Religion* was published by Eerdmans in 2004.

Thomas D. Zlatic holds a Ph.D. in American literature from St. Louis University. His primary research interests currently are Herman Melville, Mark Twain, and Walter J. Ong. His published works include articles in *American Literature, Nineteenth-Century Literature, Clio*, and *Papers on Literature and Language*.